AMERICAN HORIZONS

AMERICAN HORIZONS

U.S. HISTORY IN A GLOBAL CONTEXT

Third Edition

Volume II

Michael Schaller
University of Arizona

Janette Thomas Greenwood
Clark University

Andrew Kirk
University of Nevada, Las Vegas

Sarah J. Purcell
Grinnell College

Aaron Sheehan-Dean
Louisiana State University

Christina Snyder
The Pennsylvania State University

with contributions by:
Robert Schulzinger
University of Colorado, Boulder

John Bezís-Selfa
Wheaton College

New York Oxford
OXFORD UNIVERSITY PRESS

Oxford University Press is a department of the University of Oxford. It furthers the
University's objective of excellence in research, scholarship, and education by publishing worldwide.
Oxford is a registered trade mark of Oxford University Press in the UK and certain other countries.

Published in the United States of America by Oxford University Press
198 Madison Avenue, New York, NY 10016, United States of America.

For titles covered by Section 112 of the US Higher Education
Opportunity Act, please visit www.oup.com/us/he for the latest
information about pricing and alternate formats.

Library of Congress Cataloging-in-Publication Data

CIP data on file with Library of Congress
ISBN: 9780190659493

9 8 7 6 5 4 3 2 1
Printed by LSC Communications Inc.
Printed in the United States of America

DEDICATION

To all our students.
The individual authors would also like to dedicate this book to the following people.
Michael Schaller: *to GS, N, G, & D*
Janette Thomas Greenwood: *to M, E, & S*
Andrew Kirk: *to L, H, & Q*
Sarah J. Purcell: *to H, E, & M*
Aaron Sheehan-Dean: *to M, L, & A*
Christina Snyder: *to JFL*

⊘BRIEF CONTENTS

CONTENTS

CHAPTER 17

A New Industrial and Labor Order, 1877–1900 · 577

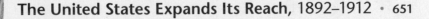

CHAPTER 20

An Age of Progressive Reform, 1890–1920 • 683

CHAPTER 23

A New Deal for Americans, 1931–1939 · 789

Arsenal of Democracy: The World at War, 1931–1945 · 825

Prosperity and Liberty Under the Shadow of the Bomb, 1945–1952 · 863

CHAPTER 26

The Dynamic 1950s, 1950–1959 · 897

CHAPTER 27

The Optimism and the Anguish of the 1960s, 1960–1969 · 937

CHAPTER 28

The Vietnam Era, 1961–1975 · 973

CHAPTER 29

Conservatism Resurgent, 1973–1988 · 1007

MAPS

PREFACE

A *merican Horizons* offers students in American history courses the opportunity to put that story in a global context.

For more than 500 years, North America has been part of a global network centered on the exchange of peoples, goods, and ideas. Human migrations—sometimes freely, sometimes forced—have continued over the centuries, along with the evolution of commerce in commodities as varied as tobacco, sugar, and computer chips. Europeans and Africans came or were brought to the continent, where they met, traded with, fought among, and intermarried with Native peoples. Some of these migrants stayed, whereas others returned to their home countries. Still others came and went periodically. This initial circulation of people across the oceans foreshadowed the continuous movement of people, goods, and ideas that made the United States. Such forces have shaped American history, both dividing and unifying the nation. American "horizons" truly stretch beyond our nation's borders, embracing the trading networks established during and after the colonial era as well as the digital social networks connecting people globally today.

American Horizons tells the story of the United States by exploring this exchange on a global scale and placing it at the center of that story. By doing so, we provide a different perspective on the history of the United States, one that we hope broadens the horizons of those who read our work and are ever mindful of the global forces that increasingly and profoundly shape our lives. At the same time, *American Horizons* considers those ways in which U.S. influence reshaped the lives and experiences of people of other nations.

U.S. history is increasingly perceived, interpreted, and taught as part of a global historical experience. The mutual influence of change—of global forces entering the United States and of American ideas, goods, and people moving out through the world—has been a consistent feature since the 16th century. Although most Americans today are aware that their influence is felt abroad and are increasingly aware of the influence of events abroad on their own lives, they tend to think of these as recent developments. In fact, those earliest exchanges of beliefs and products some 500 years ago established a pattern of interaction that continues today.

We have written a narrative that encourages readers to consider the variety of pressures that spurred historical change. Some of these pressures arose within America, and some came from outside. In the 1820s, the global market for whale oil shaped labor conditions throughout New England. At the same time, the American political system was transformed by the unique inheritance of the American Revolution and the relative abundance of land in North America. In the 1940s and 1950s, the federal government designed a unique set of policies to help World War II veterans readjust to civilian life, whereas the civil rights movement unfolded within a global context of decolonization in Africa and Asia. Topics such as these help readers consider the relationship between local and global forces that shaped American history.

American Horizons presents an opportunity to view the nation's history as more than a mere sequence of events for students to memorize. Although adhering to the familiar chronological organization of this course, our narrative style and structure provide the flexibility of shifting emphasis from time to time to the global aspects of American history. Although the story of the United States is always at the center, that story is told through the movement of people, goods, and ideas into, within, or out of the United States.

How did the United States emerge from a diverse set of colonies? How did colonists interact with Native American nations? How did the United States become a major player on the world stage of nations? What qualities make the United States unique? What does the United States share with other nations and empires? History includes many story lines that contribute to this narrative. *American Horizons* is the story of where this nation came from and how its people have been shaped by their own values as well as their interactions with the rest of the world. It recognizes that many of the significant events in American history had causes and consequences connected to developments elsewhere and presents those events accordingly. *American Horizons* depicts this intersection of storylines from many nations that influenced, and were influenced by, the United States of America.

As readers engage with the text, we encourage them to think explicitly about what makes history. What matters? What forces or events shaped how people lived their lives?

The Development Story

The six coauthors of this book specialize in a variety of time periods and methodologies. Based on our research and teaching, we all share the idea that the nation's history can best be understood by examining how, from the precolonial era forward, the American experience reflected the interaction of many nations, peoples, and events. We present this idea in a format that integrates traditional narrative history with the enhanced perspective of five centuries of global interaction.

About the Third Edition

This new edition of *American Horizons* is comprehensive yet concise enough for instructors who prefer a more economical option for their students without forgoing the primary advantages of a traditional, longer text. This has been achieved without sacrificing the kinds of features, images, tables, maps, and figures expected in this course.

HALLMARK FEATURES

- Each chapter begins with a compelling story at the core of the chapter theme.
- **Global Passages** boxes feature a unique story illustrating America's connection to the world.
- A rich graphics program of maps and figures helps students explore essential chapter themes.
- Timelines highlighting significant happenings in North America *and* the rest of the world, presented in parallel, provide students with a global context for American events.
- America in the World maps at the end of each chapter visually summarize the key themes of exchange (of peoples, goods, and ideas between America and other nations) discussed in each chapter.
- Key Terms and People: list at the end of each chapter help students recall the important people and events of that chapter.

- Throughout the chapters, Study Questions test students' memory and understanding of the chapter content. Chapter-ending **Review Questions** ask students to think critically and analyze what they have learned.

New to the Third Edition

NEW COAUTHOR

The *American Horizons* team welcomes new coauthor Christina Snyder, Professor of
History at The Pennsylvania State University, to the third edition. Christina was responsible for revising Chapters 1–5 and brings her knowledge of colonialism, race, slavery, and Native North America to this edition.

NEW GLOBAL PASSAGES BOXES

For the third edition, the following Global Passages boxes have been refreshed with new
examples of key global connections.

- Chapter 17: A Revolution in Food
- Chapter 22: Hollywood Sells America to the World
- Chapter 24: A Battle of Books and Ideas
- Chapter 26: The International Geophysical Year
- Chapter 29: Bombs Away: The B-52 and America's Global Military Footprint
- Chapter 30: The 1965 Immigration Act and Its Consequences
- Chapter 31: Reefer Madness: Cycles of Repression and Reform in the Long War
on Drugs

NEW AND REVISED CHAPTER CONTENT

Chapter 15

- Expanded discussion of the pursuit of women's suffrage in the 1870s.

Chapter 16

- New chapter opener about the Arizona copper mining industry.
- Expanded discussion of the role of women in the West and intermarriage.

Chapter 17

- Additional content about African American labor under the convict lease
system.

Chapter 18

- Expanded discussion of discrimination toward Chinese immigrants.
- Revised discussion of charity organizations and the efforts of social reformers
to combat urban vice.

Chapter 20

- Expanded coverage of the influence of socialism and the global workers'
movement.

Chapter 22

- Expanded discussion of sexual conventions to account for the development of
gay culture and communities in urban areas.

Chapter 23

- New chapter opener about the Bonus Expeditionary Force and the Hoover administration's response to it, which inspired FDR's pledge to deliver a "new deal" to the "forgotten man."

Chapter 26

- New chapter opener discussion of the film *High Noon*'s impact as a metaphor for the Red scare and its influence on the Polish Solidarity movement.

Chapter 29

- New chapter opener on the Iran-Contra affair.

Chapter 31

- Revised and expanded discussion of the history of health care in the United States, including the implementation of the Affordable Care Act.
- New section addressing gun violence and gun safety legislation in the United States.
- Addendum on the election of President Donald J. Trump.

Additional Learning Resources

Oxford University Press offers a complete and authoritative package of learning resources for students and instructors.

Reading American Horizons, Third Edition: This two-volume primary source collection (ISBN for volume I: 9780190698034; ISBN for volume II: 9780190698041), expertly edited by the authors of *American Horizons*, provides a diverse set of documents (both textual and visual) that situate U.S. history in a global context. The more than 200 documents—25 of which are new to this edition—cover political, social, and cultural history. Each document includes a headnote and discussion questions. A significant discount are provided when *Reading American Horizons* is packaged with *American Horizons*. Contact your Oxford University Press sales representative for details.

Dashboard (www.oup.com/us/dashboard): Simple, informative, and mobile, Dashboard is an online learning and assessment platform tailored to your textbook that delivers a simple, informative, and mobile experience for professors and students. It offers quality content and tools to track student progress in an intuitive, web-based learning environment; features a streamlined interface that connects students and instructors with the most important course functions; and simplifies the learning experience to save time and put student progress first.

Dashboard for *American Horizons*, third edition, includes:

- An embedded e-book that integrates multimedia content, providing a dynamic learning space for both students and instructors

Each chapter includes:

image analysis

map analysis, interactive timelines, and quizzes

◁)) audio flashcards

▤ document analysis

Many chapters also include ▷ video analysis

- The complete set of questions from the test bank that provide, for each chapter, multiple-choice, short-answer, true-or-false, and fill-in-the-blank and essay questions

Ancillary Resource Center (ARC): This online resource center (https://arc2.oup-arc.com/), available to adopters of *American Horizons*, includes:

- **Oxford University Press's Video and Image Library:** Designed to engage students and stimulate class discussion, the video library consists of 40 videos. Each video was custom-produced by Oxford University Press and runs between two to three minutes, with topics that range from "The Life and Death of John Brown" to "The Disco Wars." The Image Library includes over 2,000 images, organized by period, topic, and region. To see a demo video and sample PowerPoint module, contact your Oxford University Press sales representative or go to https://arc2.oup-arc.com/access/us-history-image-and-video-library.
- **Instructor's Resource Manual:** Includes, for each chapter, a detailed chapter outline, suggested lecture topics, learning objectives, quizzes, tests, sample syllabi, in-class discussion questions, and suggested Web resources.
- **PowerPoints and Computerized Test Bank:** Includes PowerPoint slides and JPEG and PDF files for all the maps and photos in the text. The computerized test bank includes:
  - **Quizzes** (two per chapter, 25 multiple-choice questions each)
  - **Tests** (two per chapter, offering 10 identification/matching, 10 multiple-choice, 5 short-answer, and 2 essay questions)

Course Cartridges: Complete Course Management cartridges are also available to qualified adopters.

Student Companion Website: The open-access companion website for *American Horizons* (www.oup.com/us/schaller) helps students review what they have learned from the textbook as well as explore other resources online. Resources include the following:

- **Note-taking guides** help students focus their attention in class.
- **Multiple-choice and identification quizzes** *different* from those found in the Instructor's Manual/Test Bank) allow students to assess their knowledge of a topic before a test.
- **Interactive flashcards** using key terms and people listed at the end of each chapter help students remember who's who and what's what.
- **Weblinks** encourage students to explore topics of interest.
- **Author videos** allow students to listen to the authors discuss the content of each chapter.

Other Oxford Titles of Interest for the U.S. History Classroom

Oxford University Press publishes a vast array of titles in American history. The following is just a small selection of books that pair particularly well with *American Horizons*. Any of the books in these series can be packaged with *American Horizons* at a significant discount to students. Please contact your Oxford University Press sales representative for specific pricing information or for additional packaging suggestions. Please visit www.oup.com/us for a full listing of Oxford titles.

New Narratives in American History

At Oxford University Press, we believe that good history begins with a good story. Each volume in this series features a compelling tale that draws on a sustained narrative to illuminate a greater historical theme or controversy. Then, in a thoughtful afterword, the authors place their narratives within larger historical contexts, discuss their sources and narrative strategies, and describe their personal involvement with the work. Intensely personal and highly relevant, these succinct texts are innovative teaching tools that provide a springboard for incisive class discussion as they immerse students in a particular historical moment.

- *Escaping Salem: The Other Witch Hunt of 1692*, by Richard Godbeer
- *Sleuthing the Alamo: Davy Crockett's Last Stand and Other Mysteries of the Texas Revolution*, by James E. Crisp
- *In Search of the Promised Land: A Slave Family in the Old South*, by John Hope Franklin and Loren Schweninger
- *The Making of a Confederate: Walter Lenoir's Civil War*, by William L. Barney
- *"They Say": Ida B. Wells and the Reconstruction of Race*, by James West Davidson
- *Wild Men: Ishi and Kroeber in the Wilderness of Modern America*, by Douglas Cazaux Sackman
- *The Gentle Subversive: Rachel Carson, Silent Spring, and the Rise of the Environmental Movement*, by Mark Hamilton Lytle
- *"To Everything There Is a Season": Pete Seeger and the Power of Song*, by Allan Winkler
- *Tales from a Revolution: Bacon's Rebellion and the Transformation of Colonial America*, by James D. Rice

Critical Historical Encounters

The volumes in this Oxford University Press book series focus on major critical encounters in the American experience. The word "critical" refers to formative, vital, transforming events and actions that have had a major impact in shaping the ever-changing contours of life in the United States. "Encounter" indicates a confrontation or clash, oftentimes but not always contentious in character, but always full of profound historical meaning and consequence. The Critical Historical Encounters series emphasizes formative episodes in America's contested history. Each volume contains two fundamental ingredients: a carefully written narrative of the encounter and the consequences, both immediate and long-term, of that moment of conflict in America's contested history.

- *For Ourselves and Our Posterity: The Preamble to the Federal Constitution in American History, by* Peter Charles Hoffer

- *Marching Across the Color Line: A. Philip Randolph and Civil Rights in the World War II Era, by* David Welky
- *Pennsylvania Hall: A "Legal Lynching" in the Shadow of the Liberty Bell,* Beverly Tomek
- *The Battle of Ole Miss: Civil Rights v. States' Rights, by* Frank Lambert
- *The Making of a Patriot: Benjamin Franklin at the Cockpit,* by Sheila L. Skemp
- *The Jerry Rescue* (Angela F. Murphy)

Acknowledgments

A book as detailed as this draws on the talents and support of many individuals. Our first thanks must certainly go to our families for their support and patience during the development of this textbook. We would also like to acknowledge the team at Oxford University Press for their support in making this book a reality. Thanks go first to our editor, Charles Cavaliere, who encouraged and challenged us at every step of the process. Publisher John Challice supported the project at an early stage and spurred us to think broadly about how we envisioned it. We appreciate the able assistance of development manager Thom Holmes and development editor Maegan Sherlock. Editorial assistant Rowan Wixted was especially helpful in wrangling the art program for the book. We thank the Oxford production team, led by manager Lisa Grzan, and production editor Micheline Frederick, for their encouragement and help in generating this book and shaping its final form. The interior and cover design were created by art director Michele Laseau. The innovative map program was created by International Mapping.

Manuscript Reviewers

We have greatly benefited from the perceptive comments and suggestions of the many talented scholars and instructors who reviewed *American Horizons.* Their insight and suggestions contributed immensely to the published work.

Reviewers of the Third Edition

Nicole Anslover
Indiana University Northwest

Joseph Bagley
Georgia Perimeter College

Robert Caputi
Erie Community College

Donald C. Elder III
Eastern New Mexico University

A. James Fuller
University of Indianapolis

R. Scott Huffard, Jr.
Lees-McRae College

Richard Hughes
Illinois State University

Hannah Kim
University of Delaware

Mark A. Mengerink
Lamar University

Deirdre P. O'Shea
University of Central Florida

Matthew Pehl
Augustana College

Steven D. Reschly
Truman State University

Beth Slutsky
California State University, Sacramento

Brandon Wolfe-Hunnicutt
California State University, Stanislaus

Reviewers of the Second Edition

Ian J. Aebel
Virginia State University

Cynthia Counsil
Florida State College at Jacksonville

Brittany Fremion
Central Michigan University

Larry Grubbs
Georgia State University

Thomas Humphrey
Cleveland State University

Christopher Jones
College of William and Mary

Bill Mauzey
Metropolitan Community College

Karen Miller
Oakland University

Jeremy Neely
Missouri State University

Chad Parke
University of Louisiana Lafayette

Mary Ellen Rowe
University of Central Missouri

Diane C. Vecchio
Furman University

Felicia Viator
San Francisco State University

Reviewers of the First Edition

Stanley Arnold
Northern Illinois University

Shelby M. Balik
Metropolitan State College of Denver
University of Colorado

Eirlys M. Barker
Thomas Nelson Community College

Toby Bates
University of Mississippi

Carol Bender
Saddleback College

Wendy Benningfield
Campbellsville University

Katherine Benton-Cohen
Georgetown University

Angela Boswell
Henderson State University

Robert Bouwman
North Georgia College & State University

Jessica Brannon-Wranosky
Texas A&M University–Commerce

Blanche Brick
Blinn College

Howard Brick
University of Michigan

Margaret M. Caffrey
University of Memphis

Jacqueline B. Carr
University of Vermont

Dominic Carrillo
Grossmont College

Brian Casserly
Bellevue College

Cheryll Ann Cody
Houston Community College–
Southwest College

Elizabeth Collins
Triton College

Edward M. Cook, Jr.
University of Chicago

Cynthia Gardner Counsil
Florida State College–Jacksonville

C. David Dalton
College of the Ozarks

David Dzurec
University of Scranton

Brian J. Els
University of Portland

Kevin Eoff
Palo Verde College

Richard M. Filipink
Western Illinois University

Joshua Fulton
Moraine Valley Community College

David Garvin
Highland Community College

Glen Gendzel
San José State University

Tiffany Gill
University of Texas–Austin

Aram Goudsouzian
University of Memphis

Larry Gragg
Missouri University of Science and Technology

Jean W. Griffith
Fort Scott Community College;
Labette Community College

Mark Grimsley
Ohio State University

Elisa M. Guernsey
Monroe Community College

Aaron Gulyas
Mott Community College

Michael R. Hall
Armstrong Atlantic State University

David E. Hamilton
University of Kentucky

Peggy J. Hardman
Eastern New Mexico University

Kristin Hargrove
Grossmont College

Claudrena N. Harold
University of Virginia

Edward Hashima
American River College

Robin Henry
Wichita State University

John Herron
University of Missouri–Kansas City

L. Edward Hicks
Faulkner University

Matt Hinckley
Richland College

D. Sandy Hoover
East Texas Baptist University

Jerry Hopkins
East Texas Baptist University

Kelly Hopkins
University of Houston

Kenneth W. Howell
Prairie View A&M University

Raymond Pierre Hylton
Virginia Union University

Bryan M. Jack
Winston-Salem State University

Brenda Jackson-Abernathy
Belmont University

Volker Janssen
California State University–Fullerton

Lawrence W. Kennedy
University of Scranton

William Kerrigan
Muskingum University

Andrew E. Kersten
University of Wisconsin

Todd Kerstetter
Texas Christian University

Patricia Knol
Triton College

Jeffrey Kosiorek
Hendrix College

Peter Kuryla
Belmont University

Peggy Lambert
Lone Star College–Kingwood

Alan Lehmann
Blinn College

Carolyn Herbst Lewis
Louisiana State University

Christopher J. Mauceri
Farmingdale State College of New York

Derrick McKisick
Fairfield University

Marian Mollin
Virginia Tech

Linda Mollno
Cal Poly Pomona

Michelle Morgan
Missouri State University

Susan Rhoades Neel
Utah State University

Caryn E. Neumann
Miami University

Jeffrey Nichols
Westminster College

Christopher H. Owen
Northeastern State University

Jeffrey Pilz
North Iowa Area Community College

Amy M. Porter
*Georgia Southwestern
State University*

William E. Price
Kennesaw State University

Emily Rader
El Camino College

Matthew Redinger
Montana State University–Billings

Yolanda Romero
North Lake College

Jessica Roney
Ohio University

Walter L. Sargent
University of Maine–Farmington

Robert Francis Saxe
Rhodes College

Jerry G. Sheppard
Mount Olive College

Robert Sherwood
Georgia Military College

Terry L. Shoptaugh
Minnesota State University–Moorhead

Jason H. Silverman
Winthrop University

Nico Slate
Carnegie Mellon University

Jodie Steeley
Merced Community College

Jennifer A. Stollman
Fort Lewis College

James S. Taw
Valdosta State University

Connie Brown Thomason
Louisiana Delta Community College

Kurt Troutman
Muskegon Community College

Stanley J. Underdal
San José State University

David Voelker
University of Wisconsin–Green Bay

Charles Waite
University of Texas–Pan American

R. Stuart Wallace
*NHTI-Concord's Community College;
University of New Hampshire–Manchester*

Pamela West
Jefferson State Community College

William Benton Whisenhunt
College of DuPage

Louis Williams
St. Louis Community College Forest Park

Scott M. Williams
Weatherford College

Mary Montgomery Wolf
University of Georgia

Bill Wood
*University of Arkansas Community
College–Batesville*

Melyssa Wrisley
Broome Community College

Charles Young
Umpqua Community College

Nancy L. Zens
Central Oregon Community College

ABOUT THE AUTHORS

Michael Schaller (Ph.D., University of Michigan, 1974) is Regents Professor of History at the University of Arizona, where he has taught since 1974. His areas of specialization include U.S. international and East Asian relations and the resurgence of conservatism in late 20th-century America. Among his publications are *Altered States: The United States and Japan Since the Occupation* (Oxford University Press, 1997), *The U.S. and China into the 21st Century* (Oxford University Press, 2002), *Right Turn: American Life in the Reagan-Bush Era* (Oxford University Press, 2007), and *Ronald Reagan* (Oxford University Press, 2011).

Janette Thomas Greenwood is Professor of History at Clark University (Ph.D., University of Virginia); and specializes in African American history and history of the U.S. South. Books include *The Gilded Age: A History in Documents* (Oxford University Press, 2000), *Bittersweet Legacy: The Black and White "Better Classes" in Charlotte, 1850–1910* (University of North Carolina Press, 1994), and *First Fruits of Freedom: The Migration of Former Slaves and Their Search for Equality in Worcester, Massachusetts, 1862–1900* (University of North Carolina Press, 2010).

Andrew Kirk is Professor and Chair of History at University of Nevada, Las Vegas (Ph.D., University of New Mexico) and specializes in the history of the U.S. West and environmental history. Books include *Collecting Nature: The American Environmental Movement and the Conservation Library* (University Press of Kansas, 2001), *Counterculture Green: The Whole Earth Catalog and American Environmentalism* (University Press of Kansas, 2007), and *Doom Towns: The People and Landscapes of Atomic Testing* (Oxford University Press, 2017).

Sarah J. Purcell is L. F. Parker Professor of History at Grinnell College (Ph.D., Brown University); and specializes in the early national period, antebellum United States, popular culture, politics, gender, and military history. Books include *Sealed with Blood: War, Sacrifice, and Memory in Revolutionary America* (University of Pennsylvania Press, 2002), *The Early National Period* (Facts on File, 2004), and *The Encyclopedia of Battles in North America, 1517–1916* (Facts on File, 2000).

Aaron Sheehan-Dean is the Fred C. Frey Professor at Louisiana State University (Ph.D., University of Virginia); and specializes in antebellum United States and the U.S. Civil War. Books include *Why Confederates Fought: Family and Nation in Civil War Virginia* (University of North Carolina Press, 2007), *The View from the Ground: Experiences of Civil War Soldiers* (University Press of Kentucky, 2006), and *Concise Historical Atlas of the U.S. Civil War* (Oxford University Press, 2008).

Christina Snyder is the McCabe Greer Professor of History, The Pennsylvania State University. She researches colonialism, race, and slavery, with a focus on Native North America from the pre-contact era through the 19th century. Snyder is the author of the award-winning book *Slavery in Indian Country: The Changing Face of Captivity in Early America* (Harvard University Press, 2010). Her most recent book is *Great Crossings: Indians, Settlers, and Slaves in the Age of Jackson* (Oxford University Press, 2017). At Indiana University, Snyder offers courses in Native American studies and U.S. history.

AMERICAN HORIZONS

East shakes hands with West at the laying of the last rail that joined the Central Pacific and Union Pacific Railroads on May 10, 1869.

CHAPTER 15

Reconstructing America

C ato, Stepney, Jane, Porter, Patience, and Peggy were among many enslaved black Southerners who lived on plantations in Liberty County, Georgia. In early 1865, they watched as the first wave of deserters from Sherman's Union army came through the county. The Union "bummers" raided plantation houses and slave cabins alike, taking everything edible (and much that was not) and shooting animals they could not carry away. One Confederate described the raiders as "lost in the world of eternal woe. Their throats were open sepulchers, their mouths filled with cursing and bitterness and lies." Despite the hardship they suffered, enslaved people living in the region did nothing to obstruct the Union army. Cato and Stepney, who both organized and managed slave labor under the eye of a white overseer, effectively supported the Union by their inaction. Their stature in the community surely influenced others. They behaved, in the bitter but accurate words of a local slaveholder, as though they "now believe themselves perfectly free." In Liberty County, and throughout the rural South, whites and blacks shared a world based in the hierarchy of slavery and racial dominance and organized around the production schedules of staple crops. As Cato and the others observed the Yankee conquest of Georgia, they saw the dawning of a new era and began to work out what freedom meant. A wide range of choices, opportunities, and perils awaited black Southerners across the region.

Cato and his wife Jane, who lived on a nearby plantation, bided their time through the collapse of the Confederacy. Cato's long experience working the land and managing workers led him to reject the authority of a new overseer hired in late summer 1865. Cato's former owner denounced him as "a most insolent, indolent, and dishonest man." In response, Cato and his wife exercised their freedom in the most fundamental sense—they left Liberty County altogether, moving to nearby Savannah. No longer able to control her former slaves, Cato's ex-owner lashed out by asserting that black people would not last: "With their emancipation must come their extermination."

Despite the rising anger among whites, many freedmen and freedwomen remained in Liberty and set about making contracts for their work. Porter and Patience stayed in the area, and in spite of the fluctuating labor agreements with area planters, they managed to buy their own farm outright. Patience's brother Stepney resided on Arcadia, a coastal plantation that supported two lucrative crops: rice and Sea Island cotton. He began to manage much of the former plantation land at Arcadia and helped coordinate the rental and purchase of land by freed people. The close family networks established among the Gullah people, as the black Southerners in this region were known, undoubtedly aided many in their transition to freedom.

Unfortunately, few freed people experienced the success they did. Peggy, who had lived on the same plantation as Cato, moved to Savannah but contracted smallpox and died. Some freed people began to labor for wages on the plantations that they had once farmed as slaves, but this rarely brought them the financial independence they desired. Others rented land or farmed on shares, splitting the proceeds from the yearly crop with the landlord. The sharecropper system, adopted widely across the South, trapped tenant farmers in cycles of debt and prevented the Southern agricultural sector from diversifying as the world cotton market collapsed. In Liberty County, as elsewhere in the South, the reintegration of the Southern economy into the larger global market reflected the efforts Southerners and Northerners made to reconstruct the nation. But Southerners' failure to build a sustainable and humane economy or a just social and political system represented one of the worst legacies of Reconstruction.

⊘ THE YEAR OF JUBILEE, 1865

The dramatic changes underway in the South and the nation produced surprising outcomes. At the end of the Civil War, white Southerners were defeated and resentful, whereas black Southerners celebrated **Jubilee**, their deliverance from bondage. Northerners likewise celebrated because they had preserved the Union and extinguished slavery in the United States. But great questions remained: What role would recently freed slaves play in American life? What rights would they possess? What obligations did the federal government have to ensure a meaningful freedom? For Washington, the first order of business was re-establishing loyal governments in the South and bringing the region back into a normal relationship with the nation. No precedents guided this process, and grand constitutional questions about the nature of the Union and the meaning of republican government acquired real political weight. Republicans and Democrats, Northerners and Southerners, and blacks and whites divided over the answers to these questions. The wartime task of reunion gave way to the postwar task of Reconstruction, which entailed reorganizing the Southern political system and rebuilding shattered public and private institutions.

African American Families

Of the nearly four million enslaved people in the South before the Civil War, approximately 500,000 fled to freedom during the war and the rest claimed their freedom at the war's conclusion. The most important task confronting freed people was re-establishing families broken by slavery. White Southerners wanted to restore what they considered normal labor relations, but for black Southerners the desire to reunite displaced family members outweighed even the desire for a steady wage. Sales had often dispersed family members across states or even abroad, but in many cases, parents or siblings retained enough information to track down relatives. Through the late spring and summer of 1865, as white Southern soldiers headed home in defeat, black Southerners took to the road, following letters, reports, and rumors to track the exodus of children, parents, siblings, and loved ones as a result of slave sales. Black Union soldiers had a harder time than most freedmen because they were kept in the service occupying Southern towns into 1866, thus prolonging their reunions with

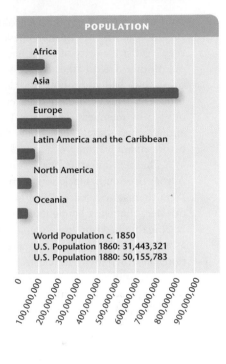

POPULATION

Africa

Asia

Europe

Latin America and the Caribbean

North America

Oceania

World Population c. 1850
U.S. Population 1860: 31,443,321
U.S. Population 1880: 50,155,783

0
100,000,000
200,000,000
300,000,000
400,000,000
500,000,000
600,000,000
700,000,000
800,000,000
900,000,000

VICTORY FOR THE NORTH
After four long years, Northerners celebrated Union victory in the Civil War and the end of slavery. But the war's conclusion only began the struggle to define what freedom would mean in practice.

family members. As a South Carolina unit wrote to Union general Daniel Sickles, "The Biggest Majority of our mens never had a Home Science this late War Commence . . . the Greatist majority of them had Runaway from Rebels master & leave they wives & old mother & old Father & all they parent. . . . But General now to see that the war is over . . . we hadent nothing atall & our wifes & mother most all of them is aperishing. [sic]" The army eventually released these soldiers from service, and they quickly sought out family members. This movement added to the uncertainty of the postwar period and alarmed whites who expected blacks to stay and continue the work they had done before emancipation.

The next question that confronted freed people was what work they would do. Across the South, black Southerners faced several choices: wage labor, renting land to farm themselves, sharecropping, or some combination of the three. But the question of where that work happened often took precedence. "If I stay here, I'll never know I'm free," explained one freedwoman as she left the plantation on which she had labored as a slave. Many thousands made the same choice, leaving behind farms and plantations on which they had been raised in favor of a new, if uncertain, life somewhere else. Often, they moved to cities, most overcrowded from the influx of refugees during the war (Map 15.1). Memphis and Nashville both grew by more than a third between 1860 and 1870, while Atlanta's population more than doubled. The movement of freed people into Southern cities created a labor glut, and the problem of unemployment exacerbated white fears of black criminality.

In rural areas, labor contracts and work were the most pressing priorities. Because they did not own land, most freed people had to work for wages. The main challenge

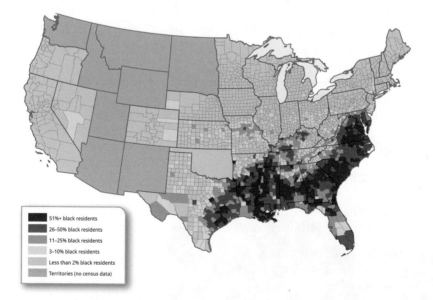

■	51%+ black residents
■	26–50% black residents
■	11–25% black residents
■	3–10% black residents
■	Less than 2% black residents
■	Territories (no census data)

map analysis

MAP 15.1 Black Population of the United States, 1880 Despite the opportunities for movement created by emancipation, few former slaves had the resources to make a full relocation out of the region. As a result, black Americans continued to live predominantly in the South until the second and third decades of the 20th century.

was working out fair and enforceable contracts with former masters or other whites. The Bureau of Refugees, Freedmen, and Abandoned Land (usually called the **Freedmen's Bureau**), established within the U.S. Army in early 1865, helped adjudicate labor disputes in the summer and fall of 1865. Led by former Union general Oliver Otis Howard, the bureau also distributed food rations to blacks and whites during the hard winter that followed and initiated the building of schools, hospitals, and other communal institutions. Despite this important work, elite Southerners resented the intrusion of the federal government and joined with Northern Democrats to denounce the bureau as an unnecessary federal imposition on states' rights. Even moderate Northerners expressed concerns about the freed people's work ethic. Because slaves had labored without incentive, whites did not expect them to understand paid work. In fact, most African Americans adjusted quickly, even when they could not rely on landowners to fairly fulfill the terms of labor contracts. One man, who had relocated to Ohio at the war's end, responded to a request from his former master to return to Tennessee with a request of his own: "We . . . [are] asking you to send us our wages for the time we served you. . . . Here I draw my wages every Saturday night," wrote Jourdan Anderson, "but in Tennessee there was never any pay day for the negroes any more than for the horses and the cows. Surely there will be a day of reckoning for those who defraud the laborer of his hire."

Advice from a Freedmen's Bureau officer to recently freed slaves (1866)

Southern Whites and the Problem of Defeat

The spring and summer of 1865 exhilarated and bewildered Americans throughout the country. The most shocking event was the assassination of Abraham Lincoln. After celebrating the official surrender of Lee's Army of Northern Virginia on April 12, 1865, Lincoln attended a play on the evening of the 14th, Good Friday. John Wilkes Booth, a member of America's most famous acting family, organized a conspiracy to kill Lincoln and several cabinet members. Booth shot Lincoln in his box at Ford's Theater while a conspirator attacked Secretary of State William Seward in his home. Lincoln, unconscious but still alive, was taken to a house across the street from the theater, where doctors tried to save him. Cabinet members, generals, and other officials visited the room where he lay. Lincoln died just after dawn. Secretary of War Edwin Stanton summarized the grim morning and its effect on America's memory of Lincoln: "Now he belongs to the ages." Booth escaped into Maryland before being killed by U.S. troops. Grief and anger flooded across the North, with many citizens blaming the conspiracy on Jefferson Davis, who fled south after evacuating Richmond in early April. Despite the controversies he stoked as president, Lincoln earned the deep appreciation of Northerners by steering the country through the crisis of disunion. Walt Whitman, who had seen Lincoln on his melancholy early morning walks around Washington, spoke for many when he lamented:

Abraham Lincoln, the Martyr, Victorious by John Sartain (1866)

> O the bleeding drops of red,
> Where on the deck my Captain lies,
> Fallen cold and dead.

Some Southerners, Robert E. Lee among them, recognized Lincoln's generosity late in the war and regarded his murder as damaging to their interest. Others, however, could not help but exalt this final turn of events. "Hurrah! Old Abe Lincoln has been assassinated!" a South Carolina woman wrote in her diary. "Our hated enemy has met the just reward of his life." Northerners could not comprehend such an attitude. For them, the restoration of the Union brought relief and confirmation of God's favor over their society. Even as Southerners struggled to reconcile their religious understanding of defeat—many believed it was another test offered by God for his chosen people—they resisted the political consequences of Union victory. Some refused to accept the outcome and abandoned the United States rather than live under what they considered an enemy government. A number of high-ranking Confederate military officers fled to South America, fearful of punishment they might receive from the Union government. Edward Porter Alexander, Lee's chief of artillery, laid his plans on the retreat to Appomattox: "I had made up my mind that if ever a white flag was raised I would take to the bushes. And, somehow, I would manage to get out of the country & go to Brazil. Brazil was just going to war with Paraguay & I could doubtless get a place in their artillery. . . . [T]hen for once I would be on the winning side." Several thousand white Southerners relocated to Brazil (although not Alexander), where they created an expatriate community in one of the last two major slave societies remaining in the Western Hemisphere. More than 10,000 Confederates exiled themselves after the war. This exodus carried men, and sometimes their families, around the world. Many ended up serving as military advisors to foreign governments—including Britain, France, and Germany—and several were employed by the Khedive of Egypt.

Even as white Southerners lamented the war's outcome, they sought the easiest path toward readmission to the Union in hopes of restoring some measure of normality in the South and because it might allow them to retain authority over the freed people. So, despite their vigorous pursuit of independence and their wartime insistence that the Confederacy was a separate nation, many Southerners assumed that they could quickly and easily resume their old position within the United States. Northern Democrats largely agreed. They had long believed that Southerners could not leave the Union, so restoration of rights, especially property rights for Southern whites, would be a simple matter of affirming their future loyalty. Republicans resisted these easy terms but fought among themselves about the proper way to rebuild the nation's political system.

White Southerners also grappled with restoring order in their communities and explaining defeat to themselves. This proved particularly challenging for Southern men. In the prewar era, white men had claimed authority by promising to protect and care for members of Southern society they viewed as inferior to them, including women, children, and black people. Confederate defeat revealed the failure of paternalism. Southern women, in particular, had been forced to assume new burdens and responsibilities during the war. Some had worked in male occupations, including industrial enterprises, and others had managed plantations and household budgets. Would these wartime changes carry over to a new social order in the postwar period? On Virginia plantations, for instance, the economic consequences of defeat and emancipation forced men and women to share tasks and roles that had been distinct before the war. The ethic of mutuality that developed in some rural communities around the South came more from necessity than ideology, but it still challenged one of the core aspects of prewar gender relations. In other places, the effects of the war compelled some women to reaffirm hierarchy rather than press forward with changes. To do this, white women relinquished their wartime responsibilities and advocated traditional gender relationships. As one editorial in a Georgia newspaper noted, "A married man falling into misfortunes is more

"The Conquered Banner" by Fr. Abram Joseph Ryan (1865)

apt to retrieve his situation in the world than a single one, chiefly because . . . although abroad may be darkness and humiliation, yet there is still a little world of love at home of which he is monarch."

Emancipation in Comparative Perspective

Americans followed neither an inevitable nor an entirely distinct path after emancipation. Both Jamaica and South Africa experienced similarly sudden and disruptive emancipation moments in the mid-19th century. Although both places functioned as British colonies when they freed their slaves, in all three societies, whites responded to emancipation by championing racial supremacy. This pursuit took different forms. In Jamaica, white elites used the emerging scientific consensus behind racial hierarchy to abdicate local control to London. As a consequence, white property holders on the island were protected at the expense of black workers. In South Africa, local whites achieved greater autonomy from the colonial office, and although they allowed black voting, whites retained economic and social power. Unlike Jamaica, which had a society sharply divided between a small number of white elites and a high number of landless blacks, South Africa possessed a sizeable rural white population. Like its Southern counterpart in the United States, rural whites joined with elites to resist emancipation and, when resistance proved futile, worked to establish white supremacy.

A pivotal moment in Jamaican emancipation came 30 years after the start of the process. In the fall of 1865, as Americans struggled to devise the rules and goals of their own post-emancipation Reconstruction, word spread through the hemisphere of a rebellion of black farmworkers in Jamaica. The Morant Bay Rebellion stemmed from inequities in post-emancipation Jamaica. The black laboring class continued to be denied access to land and political power, a consequence of policies designed by white leaders that restricted blacks to working as agricultural laborers. The rebellion consumed the eastern half of the island and left hundreds of black laborers dead and hundreds more beaten by state militia forces. American newspapers tracked the event and filtered it through the perspectives of the ongoing struggle over the role of the freedmen in American life. A Southern newspaper described "terrible massacres of the whites" by bands of deranged blacks. They "shuddered to think of what would be the effect of these incendiary teachings in the lately populous slave regions of the South." In contrast, American abolitionists used the event as an object lesson in why full equality and political rights were necessary for all Southerners. According to Senator Charles Sumner, the freedmen of the South "were not unlike the freedmen of San Domingo or Jamaica . . . and have the same sense of wrong."

Excerpt from speech by Senator Charles Sumner (February 1866)

The United States avoided a Morant Bay Rebellion, although it did not grant freed people the degree of freedom Sumner recommended. A key distinction between the three experiments in Reconstruction proved to be the nature of political change in each society. In Jamaica, a mulatto elite, composed mostly of the descendents of slaveholders and their slaves, entered into the political system, but they mostly sided with the white elite. When legislators granted blacks the right to vote in South Africa, they also enacted a property restriction that ensured white domination. In contrast, black Southern men received the vote without restriction. This helped make American Reconstruction the most radical of those slave societies that experienced emancipation in the 19th century.

quiz

STUDY QUESTIONS FOR THE YEAR OF JUBILEE, 1865

1. How did white and black Southerners respond to the end of the Civil War?

2. What did each group want for the postwar world?

⊘ SHAPING RECONSTRUCTION, 1865–1868

In 1865, a small group of Republican congressmen and senators had high hopes for a vigorous Reconstruction plan. These men—and a substantially more diverse body of black and white male and female reformers who urged them on—foresaw not just the expansion of free labor but a redistribution of Southern wealth and an egalitarian political order that included black male suffrage. Between 1865 and 1866, this group—known as the "radical Republicans"—went from the margins to the center of the political debate, and they did so largely because Northerners perceived President Andrew Johnson as currying favor with an unrepentant South. The fight that erupted between Johnson and his own party in Congress opened strange new rifts in American politics and propelled Republicans toward a surprising and dramatic shift in Reconstruction. In a series of clashes with Johnson, congressional Republicans adopted increasingly radical measures meant to secure the fruits of Union victory in the war and protect the rights of the freed people.

Andrew Johnson's Reconstruction

As the uncertainty of spring gave way to summer, Southern whites confidently assumed they would be allowed to continue with "self-reconstruction." Under this theory, white Southerners reaffirmed their loyalty to the United States through existing political systems. With Congress out of session, Andrew Johnson, the Tennessee Unionist who had become president after Lincoln's assassination, set the terms. Despite radicals' hopes that Johnson would impose strict conditions on the reentry of Southern states, he set the bar low. He required Southerners only to repudiate secession and state debts incurred during the war and confirm emancipation by ratifying the **Thirteenth Amendment**, which outlawed slavery in the United States. Johnson also extended amnesty to most of the high-ranking military and civilian officials of the Confederacy. Over the summer of 1865, Johnson restored voting and property rights to thousands of these men. In some cases, this process divested black families of land they had been given by the U.S. Army during the war. Before the war, Johnson had been a bitter enemy of the plantation elite, championing the cause of the white artisans and nonslaveholding farmers of East Tennessee. But in his efforts to keep pace with the shifting political alignments of the postwar era, Johnson became a staunch defender of white supremacy and recast himself as the defender of embattled white elites.

In fall 1865, Southern states held new state elections. In the upper South, a significant number of former Whigs and Unionists won, but voters in the lower South largely reelected Democratic Party elites who had led the region during the war. Alexander Stephens, the former vice president of the Confederacy, was elected U.S. senator from

Georgia. Most Northerners, and even some Democrats, reacted with shock and anger. Did Southerners really imagine they could send the very men who had led a bloody rebellion against the United States to serve in Congress? Andrew Johnson accepted the results as a product of the democratic process, and radical Republicans grew increasingly uneasy with Johnson's leniency.

Forced to accept emancipation, reconstituted state governments across the region adopted a series of laws known collectively as the "**black codes**" in the fall of 1865, which proscribed both the extent and the limits of freedom for black residents in the region. The rights granted to freed people included the right to marry, to own property, and to participate in the judicial process through suing and being sued and giving testimony in court cases, but the legislators paid much more attention to restrictions on black freedom. The most nefarious of these were the "apprenticeship" laws, which gave county courts the authority to take children away from parents if local judges decided those parents were not capable of providing for them. Children would be assigned a place to work by the court, with the "former master" having priority. Black Southerners and many Northerners perceived this as a blatant attempt to reimpose slavery. The codes also focused not just on ex-slaves but on "all freedpeople, free negroes, and mulattoes," effectively creating a new legal designation in Southern law that singled out black people, whereas previously status (free or slave) had been the key distinction among residents.

Selected statutes from the Mississippi Black Code (1865)

For Northerners, the second half of 1865 proved nearly as disorienting as the first half. Just as they experienced the elation of victory and anguish over Lincoln's assassination, Northerners moved from supporting Johnson's initial measures to reconstruct the South quickly to anger at Johnson's capitulation to Southern arrogance. Carl Schurz, a prominent Civil War general and radical Republican, had been sent on a tour of the South by Johnson in late 1865 to assess the situation, but his findings undercut support for Johnson's policies. White Southerners did not think of themselves as Americans and did not trust black Southerners to work in a new free labor economy. Schurz concluded, "It is not only the political machinery of the States and their constitutional relations to the general government, but the whole organism of southern society that must be reconstructed, or rather constructed anew, so as to bring it into harmony with the rest of American society." As Congress reconvened in December 1865, its members weighed the merits and methods of reconstructing the South. After much debate, Congress slowed down the process of Reconstruction by refusing to seat the delegations recently elected from Southern states. As one constituent wrote to his congressmen, "Let these rebellious states know and feel that there is a power left that can reach and punish treason."

Excerpt from Carl Schurz, *Report on the Condition of the South* (1865)

The Fight over Reconstruction

The desire to punish the South for its refusal to accept the verdict of war manifested itself in the first session of the 39th Congress. These were the men elected in fall 1864, at the moment of the Union's triumph at Atlanta, Mobile Bay, and the Shenandoah valley. They came into office on Lincoln's coattails, and they were overwhelmingly Republican. They held more than a 2:1 advantage in the House of Representatives and a 3:1 advantage in the Senate. Further, as Johnson alienated himself from moderate Republicans, the balance of power in the party shifted toward the radicals. So it was with relative ease that Republicans overcame Democratic objections and refused to seat the congressional delegations sent to Washington by the former Confederate states. Doing so amounted to a public challenge to Johnson's leadership and slowed down Reconstruction. Although Republicans would never have a free hand from their constituents, who worried about Reconstruction's costs and duration, a majority of Northerners and many Southern unionists wanted to reevaluate the purpose and direction of Reconstruction policy in late 1865 and early 1866.

Republican congressmen worried about the economic state of the former Confederacy. In the spring and summer, many freed people signed work contracts with former masters and others. Some of these promised weekly paydays, others by the month, and still others only once a year after harvest. Even if the contracts had been fairly conceived, conflict would have been likely. Union and Confederate forces alike had destroyed huge swathes of the Southern landscape, tearing down fence rails for firewood and tearing up railroads to weaken the Confederates' ability to fight. Most economically damaging of all was emancipation, which represented a capital loss of at least $3 billion for white Southerners. By one estimate, slave property comprised 60 percent of the wealth of the Deep South cotton states. The results of the Civil War in per capita terms were striking: the average total wealth of all Southern farm operators dropped from $22,819 in 1860 to $3,168 a decade later. Freed people thus entered the labor market during a period of severe economic contraction, with most farmers possessing little cash with which to pay workers.

Photographs of destruction in the South

Because of the immediate necessity for freed people to sign a contract of some sort and begin earning money, they were in a poor position to negotiate with landowners. Agents of the Freedmen's Bureau served as the only check on exploitative labor agreements. Freedmen's Bureau agents settled labor disputes when they arose, but the bureau fielded only 900 agents in the whole South, which rarely amounted to more than 1 per county. Despite the importance of their work, Johnson and congressional Democrats denounced the Freedmen's Bureau as an unwarranted extension of federal power. A typical political cartoon condemned the bureau as "an agency to keep the negro in idleness at the expense of the white man." White Southerners were much less subtle in their critique. Josiah Nott, an Alabamian and prominent prewar doctor, fumed against the reorganization of Mobile's public space to accommodate African Americans. "See how the damd Military, the nigger troops, the Freemen's Bureau spit upon us and rub it in." Republicans remained committed to a limited government, and many were concerned about the constitutional issues raised by the Freedmen's Bureau, but most regarded the work as too important to abandon. In 1866, Congress approved a one-year renewal of the bureau. Johnson vetoed the bill and, in a sign of growing Republican solidarity, Congress overrode his veto.

Partisan politics played a large role in shaping the nature of Reconstruction. The Republican Party was only a decade old and had yet to establish any presence in the Southern United States, which it needed if it was to remain a viable entity. Democrats had alienated Northern voters by their opposition to Lincoln's policies during the war. Reconstruction occurred in this moment of partisan fluidity. Republicans sought to build a coalition of "loyal" voters—drawing on former Unionists in the South and African Americans if they were enfranchised, along with their core base in the North. A key component of their rhetoric in the period focused on the "bloody shirt," a patriotic appeal to reward Republicans for steering the country through the Civil War.

They condemned Democrats as traitors who had abetted the Confederacy. Republicans benefited from the rise of the veteran as an American icon during this period. In previous wars, veterans had been honored, but only after the Civil War was military service promoted as the purest expression of civic pride. Veterans themselves played a key role in promulgating this idea. As the head of the Grand Army of the Republic, the Union veteran's association, Major General John Logan advocated this idea most forcefully. According to Logan, "It is wholly safe to say that in his [the veteran's] character of defender of right and justice, with no features of the despoiler and oppressor, and in his attributes of lofty patriotism, of unselfish, inflexible, and enduring courage, of patience under suffering, and of moderation under victory, . . . he has no faithful counterpart in any age of the world."

Memorabilia of the Grand Army of the Republic

Fresh from his defeat over the renewal of the Freedmen's Bureau, Johnson picked another fight with Congress, this time over the 1866 Civil Rights Act. The first instance of federal law designed expressly to protect the rights of citizens, rather than prohibiting the actions of government, the bill was authored by moderate Republican Lyman Trumbull of Illinois and was intended as a middle ground between radicals who wanted strong intervention in Southern states and conservatives who feared the centralizing nature of such action. The bill established a common national citizenship for all people born in the United States and promised the "full and equal benefit of all laws and proceedings for the security of person and property." It also empowered federal courts to hear violations of rights, but the bill principally protected people against state rather than private action. Johnson refused to accept even this moderate measure and vetoed the bill. Johnson's explanation, as with his earlier veto of the Freedmen's Bureau, conveyed his refusal to accept the "centralization" of power initiated by the bill. Johnson also made white supremacy an important part of his veto, arguing that by granting black Americans equal access to the law, it denied rights to whites. To Johnson's horror, the bill seemed to grant "a perfect equality of the white and colored races." Congress again overrode Johnson and passed the legislation. Johnson's opposition to these two central measures and his intemperate veto messages isolated him politically and pushed the sizeable body of moderate Republicans closer to the radicals.

The Civil War Amendments and American Citizenship

After the Civil Rights Act passed, Republicans began debating what would become the **Fourteenth Amendment**. Again, Republicans quarreled among themselves about the propriety of creating federal safeguards for individual rights. And again, moderates won the day, this time crafting a broad guarantee of national citizenship and equality before the law but offering no specific protection of freed people's political rights. The second section of the amendment punished states that denied the vote to black men by reducing their representation in Congress. Under the prewar constitution, enslaved people counted as three-fifths of a free person for the purposes of apportionment; under the Fourteenth Amendment, if not enfranchised, they would effectively count as zero-fifths. This feature might compel Southern states to enfranchise black men, but it put little pressure on Northern states to do the same because ignoring their small black populations did not substantially reduce Northern representation in Congress. The amendment also repudiated the debt accumulated by the Confederate and Southern state governments, leaving the millions of dollars issued during the war in bonds and currency worthless.

EMANCIPATION DAY   African Americans held Emancipation Day ceremonies, like the one pictured at the center of this image, to commemorate Union victory and their deliverance from bondage. Despite the opposition of Southern whites, Southern blacks continued to celebrate Emancipation Day and the Fourth of July well into the 20th century.

Lord Glenelg on emancipation and social transformation in the British colonies (1837)

A comparative framework is again useful. In post-emancipation Jamaica, the British had pursued a similarly bold plan for full civil equality, although imposed through the policies of the colonial secretary, Lord Glenelg, rather than through a constitution. In 1837, Glenelg explained that the "great cardinal principle of the law for the abolition of slavery is, that the apprenticeship of the emancipated slaves is to be immediately succeeded by personal freedom, in the full and unlimited sense of the term in which it is used in reference to the other subjects of the British Crown." Glenelg's policies held for a decade, but by the late 1840s, the government had imposed restrictions on the right to vote and eventually suspended Jamaican self-government entirely. In Jamaica and the United States, the central governments issued broad grants of civil equality to recently freed slaves only to back away from these to give landholders more control over their labor force and to prevent black people from entering the political system.

The issue of black voting lurked just beneath the surface of the disputes among Southerners, Johnson, and congressional Republicans. Radicals and even some moderates had long believed in the wisdom and justice of the measure. In 1864, as loyal representatives of Louisiana considered a new state constitution, Abraham Lincoln had suggested voting privileges for the men of color, "especially the intelligent and former soldiers." A partisan imperative was at work as well. Republicans knew that the end of slavery also meant the end of the three-fifths principle in the Constitution, where five enslaved people were counted as three free people for the purposes of enumeration. If unmodified, emancipation would increase the South's representation in the House of Representatives and the electoral college. Enfranchising black men would give Republicans the means to defend themselves and also ensure that the party could build a base of support in the South. Participants in the struggle to adapt political and civil frameworks in a post-emancipation world understood their effort in a global context. Henry Turner, a leading black minister, equated emancipation and the postwar amendments with "the almost instantaneous liberation of the Russian serfs, and their immediate investiture with citizens' immunities." Even as the amendment expanded rights for some, it contracted rights for others. Article I of the constitution refers only to "people" in sections on voting, but the Fourteenth Amendment set the minimum requirements as "male inhabitants" at least 21 years of age.

Shortly after passage of the Fourteenth Amendment, Republicans began work on the **Fifteenth Amendment**. Ratified in 1870, the amendment issued a blanket prohibition against denying the right to vote on the basis of race. The amendment's failure to enfranchise women incensed women's suffrage advocates, who had been working since the 1830s to win women the right to vote. Leading suffrage activists, such as Susan B. Anthony and Elizabeth Cady Stanton, had essentially paused their work on this project during the war to help further emancipation. Congress's failure to consider women's suffrage created deep bitterness and led to tensions within the movement along racial lines. Elizabeth Cady Stanton railed, "Think of Patrick and Sambo and Hans and Ung Tung who do not know the difference between a Monarchy and a Republic, who never read the Declaration of Independence . . . making laws for Lydia Maria Child, Lucretia Mott, or Fanny Kemble." Stanton's angry comparison of immigrants with the leaders of the women's rights movement underscored how personally she resented the missed opportunity in constitutional reform. Despite the setback, women's suffrage activists pressed their efforts at the state level, where 14 state constitutional conventions considered women's suffrage between 1867 and 1879.

Excerpts from the Fourteenth and Fifteenth Amendments (1868, 1870)

The Fifteenth Amendment also completed a fundamental shift in the language of the Constitution and American conceptions of freedom. The first 10 amendments to the Constitution all deny the ability of Congress to legislate on certain topics—they provide a "negative liberty" by protecting the people from government action. The Thirteenth, Fourteenth, and Fifteenth Amendments all conclude with the language "Congress shall have the power to enforce this provision." The postwar amendments rely on the idea of "positive liberty"—grants of power to Congress for it to protect the freedom of certain aspects of Americans' lives.

The fighting between the radicals and the president had long-term significance. It empowered Congress to act decisively when the president would not. Georges Clemenceau, the future prime minister of France, came to the United States in 1865 as a journalist. Clemenceau, an ardent liberal who had come to the United States to study democracy after the war, approved. "Congress may, when it pleases, take the President by the car and lead him down from his high seat, and he can do nothing about it except to struggle and shout. . . . At each session they add a shackle to his bonds, tighten the bit in a different place, file a claw or tooth, and then when he is well bound up, fastened, and caught in an inextricable net of laws and decrees, more or less contradicting each other, they tie him to the stake of the Constitution and take a good look at him."

Irish Americans and the Fenian Struggle

M any of the Irish Americans who participated in the Civil War believed it was part of a broader liberal movement toward self-determination and democracy for all the world's people. In particular, they supported the Fenians, who aimed to end British control of Ireland. Not long after the South fell to defeat, the Fenians attacked the empire. In May 1866, an army of 800 men invaded Canada and captured Fort Erie. "We have taken up the sword to strike down the oppressor's rod," declared the army's leader, General John O'Neil, "to deliver Ireland from the tyrant, the despoiler, the robber." Although O'Neil's invasion soon faltered and casualties were few (less than a dozen), the attempt revealed Irish Americans as earnest foes of Britain, complicating the already strained diplomatic relations between the United Kingdom and the United States and demonstrating the revolutionary energy generated by the Civil War.

Within a few years of Appomattox, Fenians had organized hundreds of groups in 18 states and 3 territories, comprising perhaps 45,000 members. These men drew on their military training in the Civil War to design plans for emancipating Ireland. They were also emboldened by a change in American immigration law. During the debate over the Fourteenth Amendment, Maine senator William Pitt Fessenden inserted two words into the first section. His change, adopted without a vote, granted citizenship to "naturalized" residents. This provision promised a conflict with Britain, which adhered to the idea of "perpetual allegiance," in which people owed loyalty to the sovereign under whom they were born for their entire life.

Congressional Reconstruction

Thaddeus Stevens, a Pennsylvania Republican, played a key role in the conflict with Johnson and the creation of federal protections for individual rights. Stevens helped lead the radical Republicans in Congress and served as perhaps the ablest and most dedicated white proponent of meaningful freedom for African Americans. Stevens owned a forge in Pennsylvania where he employed and paid equally both black and white workers. In Congress, Stevens used logic, rhetoric, and strong-arm parliamentary tactics to advance his agenda. Like other radicals, Stevens regarded the Southern states as having actually left the Union. He believed that Southern states could now be subjected to specific terms before they were granted reentry into the Union. For Stevens, the most important change—one compelled by humanity and justice as well as political necessity—was to diminish the clout of the white elites in Southern life and elevate the freed people. Stevens believed that this could be accomplished only if the government broke up the great landholdings of the prewar era and distributed the land to former slaves, but President Johnson killed a brief experiment with resettlement undertaken by General William T. Sherman in early 1865. Despite Stevens's urging, Republicans could not bring themselves to advocate the redistribution of property.

Thaddeus Stevens on racial equality and suffrage (1867)

In early 1867, the British arrested 28 Fenians in Ireland, including two former Union army officers. Secretary of State Seward reminded the American ambassador, Charles Francis Adams, that "faithful service in the armies or navy of the United States during the rebellion constituted an enhanced claim of persons so serving to the consideration of the Government which they have helped to perpetuate." Irish Americans in the United States inflamed the situation with massive rallies that called on Congress and the president to defend its naturalized citizens abroad. Seward pushed Adams more, noting that Britain's claim to perpetual allegiance "awakened a general feeling of resentment and deeply wounded our pride of sovereignty." As the two nations neared war over the matter, Congress passed a law (along with the Fourteenth Amendment) guaranteeing the right of immigrants to naturalize and of the government to protect them as it would native-born citizens. The veterans and a host of Fenians were eventually released from jails in England, Ireland, and Canada in 1870 when Parliament passed a law allowing British citizens to renounce their native citizenship and naturalize abroad. The liberalization in American and British law stemmed from a most unlikely constituency— nativists in the United States had targeted Irish immigrants in the 1850s as unworthy of citizenship, but the Civil War and Reconstruction spurred a profound rethinking of the meaning and weight of citizenship.

- Why did the U.S. government protect American Fenians even when they took up arms against the British Empire?
- How did the naturalization of Irish immigrants as Americans relate to making freed people citizens at the same time?

For Stevens, the Southern reaction to the Fourteenth Amendment proved the necessity of radically reordering Southern politics. After quick passage by Congress, white Southerners overwhelmingly rejected the measure. The boldness of the Southern refusal to consider the Fourteenth Amendment and the increasingly violent racial politics of the region—whites killed dozens of African Americans in Memphis and New Orleans during riots in the summer of 1866—pushed Congress to seize control of Reconstruction completely. In March 1867, Congress passed the first of a series of Reconstruction Acts. Dramatic in their scope, the legislation consolidated the ex-Confederate states into five military districts, with former Union generals acting as military governors (Map 15.2). To return to the Union, Congress required states to ratify the Fourteenth Amendment and revise their constitutions to provide for black male voting.

The legislative changes of 1867 signaled the decisive shift of power within Washington to Capitol Hill. Angry Republicans hamstrung Johnson with laws of bewildering intricacy in the hopes of creating a pretext for impeaching him. After clashing with Congress over the constitutionality of these laws in mid-1867, the House of Representatives impeached Johnson. The first U.S. president to ever be impeached, Johnson remained in office because the Senate failed to convict him by one vote. However,

ANDREW JOHNSON'S SENATE TRIAL
The impeachment of Andrew Johnson and his subsequent trial in the Senate (pictured here) established the clear dominance of Congress over the process and politics of Reconstruction.

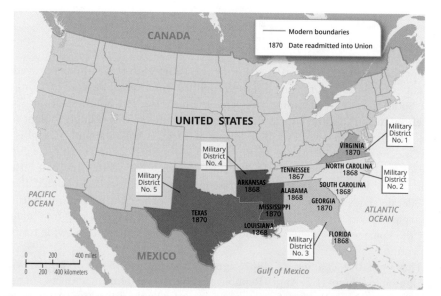

MAP 15.2 Military Districts Established by the Reconstruction Acts, 1867 One of the most radical pieces of legislation passed by the Reconstruction Congresses, these acts divided the South into five districts commanded by a military governor (usually a former Union army general). States had to revise their own constitutions to provide for universal manhood suffrage and ratify the Fourteenth Amendment before being returned to state status.

politically he was powerless. By the end of the year, Republicans turned with relief to selecting Johnson's successor, choosing the enormously popular Union general Ulysses S. Grant. Grant won the election easily in 1868, running on a platform of sectional reconciliation under the slogan "Let Us Have Peace." Despite his optimism, little sectional peace prevailed during Grant's presidency. White Southerners resented the changes forced on them through the Reconstruction Acts, but with no voice in Congress besides a few ideologically sympathetic Northern Democrats, they had little choice but to submit.

The first charge to the military governors now administering the Southern states was to hold elections to select delegates for state constitutional conventions. Black men participated in the election and helped produce a strong Republican victory, including the election of a majority of black delegates in South Carolina and Louisiana. In other Southern states, black delegates comprised only a small percent of the delegates, but even that small number invalidated the entire process for most white Southerners. The victories in the South confirmed that the Republican Party would stay competitive in the region as long as it could maintain the support of African American voters.

STUDY QUESTIONS FOR SHAPING RECONSTRUCTION, 1865–1868

1. Why did Republicans endorse a more radical Reconstruction policy than Andrew Johnson?
2. How did the changes made by Congress reshape the relationship between state and federal power?

quiz

RECONSTRUCTION IN THE SOUTH, 1866–1876

Even as Congress and the president fashioned and refashioned Reconstruction in Washington, black and white Southerners shaped the postwar world on the ground. They disputed the terms of work, housing, property, politics, and social relationships. For black Southerners, the first order of business was to create autonomous lives. True emancipation required not just free individuals but communities dedicated to uplifting and supporting their members. Politically, Reconstruction entailed creating Republican governments that would implement the policies articulated by Congress. Politics monopolized the public's attention, but the success of Reconstruction, and the ability of African Americans to make their freedom real, hinged on rebuilding the Southern economy.

African American Life in the Postwar South

The efforts that black Southerners made to reconstitute their families in the wake of emancipation laid the foundation for their postwar communities. The neighborhoods that defined the life of enslaved men and women in the plantation districts became the basis for new free communities. Churches occupied the heart of these new communities. In some cases, they were new congregations; in others, they were biracial parishes

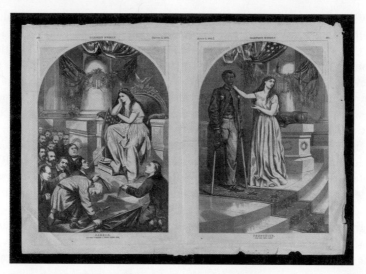

"SHALL I TRUST THESE MEN, AND NOT THIS MAN?" Republicans hoped to leverage public sympathy for black veterans, who had sacrificed for the Union, into support for black male suffrage. In this illustration featured in *Harper's Weekly*, Columbia, personifying the United States, debates pardoning Confederate soldiers (left) when the African American Union soldier (right) is still denied suffrage.

from before the war that split into separate white and black churches after the war. By 1866, 62 percent of black Methodists had left their prewar churches. But more people came to the independent black churches after the war, and those who did joined a community that played a key role in reconstructing the South. As one Freedmen's Bureau agent noted in his survey of influential black leaders in his area, "Gibbons, a mulatto, is a farmer, and was formerly a slave. He, too, is a Baptist preacher. . . . As a preacher he is very popular, and has a large influence."

Another key change came with the Freedmen's Bureau and its drive to build schools. Before the Civil War, no Southern state maintained a public education system. Northerners viewed education as essential to both political and economic progress. Many Northerners believed that nonslaveholding whites supported secession because they could not see through the misleading rhetoric of slaveholding elites. African Americans, in particular, viewed education as essential. Beginning in contraband camps during the war, freed people sought out literacy. Denied to them as slaves, literacy and higher education promised a life beyond the fields and satisfied many people's desire to read the Bible themselves. People of all ages lined up at churches and schools where instruction was available throughout the day and usually well into the evening. Despite complaints from white Southerners about the cost, public education proved one of the lasting accomplishments of Reconstruction-era governments.

Excerpt from Frances Ellen Watkins Harper, "Coloured Women of America" (1878)

The eagerness with which black Americans embraced their new lives as full citizens of the United States manifested itself in public celebrations of Emancipation Day and the Fourth of July. The first of these events began during the war itself, in Union-occupied territory on the Sea Islands of South Carolina where Union general Thomas Wentworth Higginson listened to a crowd of freed people spontaneously burst into the national anthem when the flag was raised. "I never saw anything so electric; it made all other words cheap; it seemed the choked voice of a race at last unloosed." Higginson captured the people's awareness of their fuller lives as free men and women. "Just think of it; the first day they had ever had a country, the first flag they had ever seen which promised anything to their people." Such celebrations formed the bedrock of an emerging black culture. The most enduring of these events, "Juneteenth," began in Texas as a commemoration of the war's end and evolved into a celebration of African American freedom that continues today.

The parades and festivals that accompanied these events provided an opportunity for community leaders—teachers, ministers, and politicians—to speak on themes both historical and contemporary. The messages they broadcast varied by place, gender, class position, and political ideology. Some emphasized cooperation with whites, whereas others preached self-help. **Martin Delany**, the highest-ranking black officer during the Civil War, told a South Carolina audience in 1865, "I tell you slavery is over, and shall never return again. We have now 200,000 of our men well drilled in arms and used to War fare and I tell you it is with you and them that slavery shall not come back again." Some spoke through the language of religion and salvation, whereas others used the secular language of rights and law. Regardless of their differences, all of the speakers emphasized that black people would remain a permanent and progressive force for change and democracy within America. Rather than distancing themselves from the past, Southern African Americans proudly remembered the perseverance of their ancestors through generations of slavery. Later, anthropologists such as Zora Neale Hurston collected the stories that emerged in this era, a blending of old African motifs and legends in New World settings. The rabbit trickster so central to West African stories played a key role in the legends of the antebellum and postbellum South as "Brer Rabbit" before being incorporated into American culture as Bugs Bunny in the 20th century.

Photographs of former slaves, early 20th century

The festivals through which black Americans celebrated emancipation and Union victory also provided an opportunity for political organization. The Union League emerged as the most important institutional support for black politics. Started during the war by the Republican Party, Union League clubs became social and political centers in many of the North's largest cities. After the war, the Leagues transformed into a grassroots movement that helped black Southerners organize themselves politically. Albion Tourgée, a Northern lawyer who lived in North Carolina during Reconstruction, wrote a famous novel, *A Fool's Errand*, that chronicled his experiences with Reconstruction. He described the Union Leagues as organizations that cultivated "an unbounded devotion for the flag in the hearts of the embryonic citizens, and kept alive the fire of patriotism in the hearts of the old Union element." The "fool" of the novel's title fails to appreciate the depth of hostility manifested by white Southerners against both their black neighbors and Northerners who come south. As Tourgée noted, a more farsighted man might have seen the organization of black citizens and voters as a "grim portent" of the conflict to come.

Even though the Civil War ended the split in the U.S. economy between free and slave labor, it did not equalize wages between the two sections or between the races. The South replaced slavery with a low-wage, free labor system; within that, African Americans consistently received lower pay for equivalent work done by white workers. Most black Southerners remained agricultural workers, but very few worked their own land. Instead, Southerners expanded a prewar practice called sharecropping in which landless workers signed contracts to take up residence and farm plots of land, often

A share-cropping contract (1886)

on property belonging to former slaveholders. In exchange for leasing land, property owners claimed 50 percent or more of the profits at harvest time. When sharecropping first came into use, it met the needs of property owners who required labor to farm the land but had no money with which to pay wages and workers who wanted more autonomy. **Sharecroppers** set their own schedules and supervised themselves in the field, but crucially it was usually landowners who chose the crop.

All across the Deep South and much of Arkansas, Tennessee, and North Carolina, that choice was cotton. Merchants, among the few actors in the postwar Southern economic system with access to credit, insisted on receiving cotton. The changes in the global cotton market, however, produced price fluctuations and great uncertainty for growers. Adding to the structural problems, white landowners exploited their laborers and merchants squeezed them on prices for goods and supplies. Egypt and India entered the global cotton market during the Civil War, adding competition and uncertainty for U.S. producers. As a result, sharecropping quickly trapped farmers in cycles of debt. Most signed the contracts hoping to produce enough to clear a surplus and over time accumulate the money to buy their own land. This rarely happened, and tenant farming dominated the South for the next 50 years. The results ensured overuse and poor treatment of Southern lands, a stunted regional economy, and little progress for African American farmers. As Georges Clemenceau, who toured the country in the late 1860s, observed, "The real misfortune of the negro race is in owning no land of its own. There cannot be real emancipation for men who do not possess at least a small portion of the soil."

RECONSTRUCTION OPPORTUNITIES The political opportunities African Americans experienced during Reconstruction were not matched by economic opportunities. Across much of the Deep South, the only work available to black men and women continued to be agricultural labor in cotton fields.

Republican Governments in the Postwar South

The Republican state governments established after the constitutional conventions in 1867–1868 were fragile and awkward alliances between groups with widely divergent interests. Black Southerners represented by far the largest component of the party. They wanted to receive a genuinely fair opportunity to perform work, buy land, gain an education, and live independent lives. White Northern Republicans, labeled "**carpetbaggers**" by conservatives because they assumed Northerners were coming South only to make quick money, focused on economic development. As the national party shifted to support black voting, its Southern wing did so as well, although this was never a priority for the leaders who represented the region in Congress and statehouses. Native white Southerners proved the most troublesome part of the coalition. They had to brave the scorn of fellow whites when they joined the party. Usually prewar Whigs or wartime Unionists, white Southerners rarely came to the party with any interest in black voting or civil rights. Instead, they rejected the Democrats as the party that had led the region into secession and war and hoped that a Republican commitment to free labor would create a firm foundation for the new South. Democrats eagerly exploited the tensions within the Republican Party.

In those states with well-established free black communities before the Civil War, black voters demonstrated a diversity of political opinion. Charleston, Savannah, and New Orleans all included independent, educated, and prosperous communities of free people of color, many of whom carried into the postwar world conservative values on economics and community leadership. The split within black communities can be seen clearly in the case of Mobile, Alabama. After the Union navy captured the port city in August 1864, enslaved people flooded into it seeking freedom. Following the initial flush of enthusiasm in the late 1860s, a deep division opened within the black community. On one hand, well-educated, middle-class blacks pursued a moderate politics focused mostly on economic recovery and the protection of property. To achieve these goals, they advocated cooperation with white Southerners who worked with the Republicans. A larger group, mostly freed people, pushed more aggressively for the protection of civil rights and education, and they did so without white allies. At a volatile moment in summer 1866, a group of black leaders of "the better class," according to the city's conservative paper, approached the mayor to "place themselves on record as good law abiding citizens" and commit themselves to helping suppress any disturbances caused by "either Yankee agitators or New Orleans negroes."

In many places, white conservatives initially boycotted elections that resulted from the constitutional conventions of 1867–1868. Hoping to undermine the legitimacy of these new governments, they succeeded only in hastening Republican dominance. In other states, some conservatives made alliances with Republicans to create coalition governments. But the 1872 national elections, in which Ulysses S. Grant was reelected despite substantial opposition within his own party, revealed a weakness that Democrats longed to exploit. Beginning in 1873, white conservatives returned to the political system and used charges of corruption and profligacy to defeat the Republicans. Both charges contained some merit—Republican legislators in the South, like those of both parties in state governments all across the country, were susceptible to the bribes and favors of the rich and well connected. The wide scale of corruption within Grant's administration had even threatened his reelection. Also, the policies that Republicans implemented—especially public education—required new taxes. Before the war, slaveholders and large property owners had shouldered most of the tax burden, but with no slave property to tax, postwar state governments imposed property taxes on a much broader range of people. Even though the children of white property owners benefited from public education, they condemned the taxes required to pay for them. Democrats capitalized on these policy disputes and campaigned vigorously on the platform of white supremacy to retake state governments. In Virginia, the leaders of the "straight-out" ticket, which refused to compromise with moderate Republicans, explained that "to save the state, we must make the issue *White and Black* race against race and canvass red hot—the position must be made so odious that no decent white man can support the radical ticket and look a gentleman in the face." In Louisiana, Alabama, and other Southern states, this approach yielded electoral victories for Democrats in 1874, 1875, and 1876.

Cotton, Merchants, and the Lien

In 1865, the Southern United States was part of a region, extending south through Central America and the Caribbean and into northeastern Brazil, where plantation agriculture predominated. In the United States, cotton predominated; in the Caribbean, sugar; and in Brazil, coffee (Figure 15.1). Staple crop agriculture required huge plots of land, a large labor force, and high volumes of capital and credit. The plantation system changed but did not disappear after the Civil War. The major change entailed the use of tenant labor or sharecropping in place of the gang labor used under slavery, but land continued to be owned in large allotments and management functioned as it had before the war. Even though many sharecroppers worked with some autonomy, landowners determined crop choices, fertilizer use, and harvest dates.

COTTON PRODUCTION PROSPERED   Despite the numerous obstacles to cotton production, Southern river and ocean ports looked much as they had before the Civil War, with bales of cotton stacked and ready for transport, only now into an increasingly competitive global market.

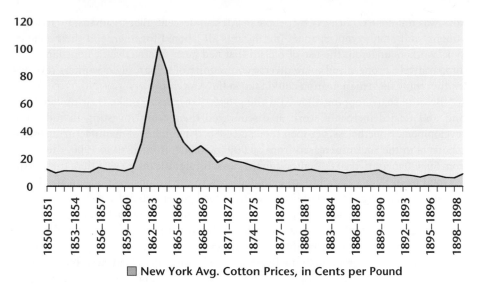

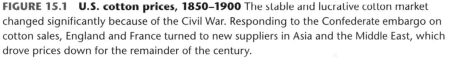

☐ **New York Avg. Cotton Prices, in Cents per Pound**

FIGURE 15.1 U.S. cotton prices, 1850–1900 The stable and lucrative cotton market changed significantly because of the Civil War. Responding to the Confederate embargo on cotton sales, England and France turned to new suppliers in Asia and the Middle East, which drove prices down for the remainder of the century.

Even with the scattered residential pattern typical of the postwar era and the substantial effort made by sharecroppers to claim ownership of the crop, landowning planters continued to dominate Southern agriculture. They did so partly through the effective control of the **crop lien**, which represented farmworkers' claim to ownership of the crops they raised. In Georgia, North Carolina, and Tennessee, the state supreme courts all ruled that the portion of crops given to a sharecropper constituted a wage. This removed from the sharecroppers any legal claim over the crops that they planted, raised, and harvested.

One of the few groups of workers to exercise some control over labor conditions and wages were sugar workers. Sugar's value had spurred Europeans' initial effort to import millions of Africans to the New World. Sugar growing and especially the process of harvesting earned an infamous reputation as the most deadly agricultural work in the Americas. It also required significant skill. Because the sugar cane had to be harvested at exactly the right moment and quickly processed, those workers with knowledge of the crop possessed more leverage to negotiate better terms with their employers. In the decade after emancipation, sugar workers—mostly in Louisiana's southern parishes— used politics and collective action to halt wage cuts and pursued the right to produce garden plots. Even after the Democrats regained power in the states, black sugar workers stayed their ground. Several large strikes in the early 1880s, some with white and black workers cooperating, laid the ground for the broader organization of workers under the **Knights of Labor** at the end of the decade. A white supremacist regime gained power in the state in the 1880s and used violence to crush black resistance. In the other major sugar-producing country in the hemisphere—Cuba—the post-emancipation story evolved differently. By the 1880s, when Cuba's emancipation took full effect, sugar work was not done exclusively by people of African descent. Black Cubans, mixed-race Cubans, and more recent Spanish immigrants all labored together, and their solidarity as workers undercut the use of racism that had been so effective in Louisiana. The comparatively stronger and more diverse community of Cuban sugar workers revealed another route that emancipation could take in the Americas.

Because sharecropping allowed white property owners to make their money from land and related merchant work, it discouraged them from investing in industrial development. Nonetheless, between 1860 and 1880, the number of manufacturing establishments in the South increased from 30,000 to 50,000; from 1880 to 1900, they grew from 50,000 to nearly 120,000, although this was still significantly lower than the Northern total from 1860. The failure to build factories in the Reconstruction-era South was not for lack of trying. The Republicans who assumed power in Southern states in the late 1860s and 1870s set economic development as their number one goal. The most important vital element of this plan was the railroad. Northern Republicans especially had a mystical faith in the railroad's ability to spur development of all sorts. As a Tennessee Republican asserted, "A free and living Republic [will] spring up in the track of the railroad as inevitably, as surely as grass and flowers follow in the spring." Unfortunately, Southern states and Southern investors could not meet the capital demands of new railroad construction. Northern and foreign investors found more lucrative and less risky places to put their money, and despite significant public attention, few new lines were built. What the fever for railroad construction did spur was corruption in state governments. Having perfected their skills on Northern legislatures in the prewar and wartime era—an old saying noted that the Pennsylvania Railroad could do anything with that state's legislature that it wanted except refine it—the lobbyists and agents who came south gained support among legislators by distributing discounted company stock. Frequent charges of corruption weakened Republicans at the polls. Other Republican policies did more to earn the support of their constituents, most importantly Republican efforts to give sharecroppers and tenant farmers control over crop liens.

STUDY QUESTIONS FOR RECONSTRUCTION IN THE SOUTH, 1866–1876

quiz

1. What was the experience of Reconstruction like for freed people in the South?
2. How did freed people in the South protect their interests? How did whites seek to subvert those interests?

THE END OF RECONSTRUCTION, 1877

For most of the 100 years following the end of Reconstruction, historians described the period as its contemporary white critics did—as the unconscionable elevation of blacks to positions of power from which they deprived whites of their rights. Sympathetic to Southern whites and grounded in openly racist assumptions about the moral and intellectual inferiority of black people, these historians promoted a factually inaccurate and deeply compromised view of the era as one that attempted too much and failed. Thanks to a fundamentally different attitude about the meaning of race and a generation of research, historians today hold a nearly opposite view. They regard congressional Reconstruction as well intentioned and appropriate to the situation. In their view, Reconstruction failed because the federal government did not persevere against Southern white resistance. The demise of Reconstruction—defined as the end of Republican governments in the region—came because of forces both internal and external to the South. The changes in how historians have accounted for that end and the meanings they have attached to it reveal how long it took America to outgrow the racial and political values of the era.

The Ku Klux Klan and Reconstruction Violence

The bitterest and most violent opponents of Reconstruction, and black freedom more generally, emerged at the very start of the era. In late 1865, a small group of men gathered in Pulaski, Tennessee, and organized the **Ku Klux Klan (KKK)**. Membership in the group spread by word of mouth across the state and soon through the region. Klan members sought to deny African Americans any legitimate role in the public sphere. As a white newspaper enthusiastically reported about the Memphis chapter in 1868, "It is rapidly organizing wherever the insolent negro, the malignant white traitor to his race and the infamous squatter are plotting to make the South utterly unfit for the residence of the decent white man. . . . It is purely defensive, and for the protection of the white race. . . . It will arrest the progress of that secret negro conspiracy which has for its object the establishment of negro domination." They also targeted white Republicans—especially native white Southerners who cooperated with the party—for their efforts to build an interracial democracy in the South. Klan members whipped, beat, burned, and

Affidavit from a black woman regarding Klan violence in Georgia (September 1866)

KU KLUX KLAN The Ku Klux Klan, a terrorist group bent on re-establishing white supremacy after the end of slavery, came to dominate many regions of the South. Klansmen pursued black leaders of all stripes—politicians, ministers, businessmen, and teachers—and their white allies with brutal violence.

killed all manner of community leaders through the South. They targeted ministers, teachers, political leaders, and successful businessmen and farmers. The high point of Klan-related violence came in response to the Reconstruction Acts and to the prominent role played by Africans Americans in the reorganization of Southern life between 1868 and 1871.

Excerpt from the testimony of a black voter about Klan violence in South Carolina (1871)

Klan violence grew so public and so extreme that Congress finally took action. In 1870–1871, Republicans passed a series of laws, collectively known as the Force Acts, designed to impede the operation of the Ku Klux Klan. They did this by punishing as a federal crime any attempt to obstruct a person in the practice of a designated civil right. One of the Klan's most effective weapons was intimidation of black voters. The Enforcement Acts targeted this practice directly by designating as conspiracies any attempts to coerce black men at the polls or deny them access to the vote. Congress created the Department of Justice and tasked it with bringing cases against those men who used violence to enforce white supremacy. Finally, in 1871, Congress held hearings at which both victims and alleged members of the Klan told their stories to a national audience. Although the Justice Department was underfunded and less energetic in its prosecutions than Southern Republicans wished, it initiated thousands of prosecutions and secured hundreds of convictions across the South, driving the Klan underground.

Even with their success against the Klan, Northerners did not eradicate violence in Southern life. Klan members became, in effect, an arm of the Democratic Party. In Louisiana, the Knights of the White Camellia and the White League superseded the Klan. Mississippi saw the creation of "rifle clubs." Regardless of the terminology, after 1871, Southern whites reorganized their attack on Republican governments in the states. Louisiana saw a particularly bitter struggle. White conservatives in the state opposed the election as governor of Henry Warmoth, a Northern lawyer and Civil War officer who operated mostly as a party of one, appointing men loyal to him alone and throwing the state into chaos. He was succeeded by William Kellogg, a radical Republican even more noxious to Louisiana Democrats. Kellogg was aided by a sizeable body of white Southerners, including James Longstreet, Lee's beloved corps commander and the most famous ex-Confederate Republican. Louisiana Democrats contested the election of Kellogg in 1872, setting up a rival government, and when the federal government recognized Kellogg as the duly elected state leader, they turned to violence as the means to unseat him.

All across Louisiana in 1873, conservatives began organizing themselves and forcing Republicans out of office. Sometimes they simply intimidated the local sheriffs, judges, and tax assessors who comprised the body of local government in the state. Other times they committed violence against officeholders or their families. The most notorious episode involved an attack on the northern parish town of Colfax. Residents of the town learned of the plan in advance, and perhaps 200 black men from the area converged on the courthouse on the morning of Easter Sunday, 1873. Armed with a variety of weapons, they came to protect the men they had elected. A white militia composed of several hundred men organized nearby, rode into town, and drove the defenders back into the courthouse, which they set afire. The attackers shot men as they escaped and captured more, executing 37 that evening. By nightfall, they had killed probably 150 people in the worst racial massacre in U.S. history. The lesson to Republicans around the state was clear—white Democrats would stop at nothing to

MAY 10, 1873.]   HARPER'S WEEKLY.

THE LOUISIANA MURDERS—GATHERING THE DEAD AND WOUNDED.—[SEE PAGE 396.]

COLFAX MASSACRE   The Colfax Massacre embodied the ultimately successful strategy used in Louisiana, Mississippi, and South Carolina to drive the last Republicans from the region. The failure of local, state, and federal authorities to find any justice for the victims stands as one of the worst tragedies of Reconstruction.

purge them from office. Although Kellogg hung on until 1876, Republican government around the state slowly gave way in the face of this terrorism. Whites in other Southern states observed the success of Louisiana conservatives, and many adopted the same strategy.

Northern Weariness and Northern Conservatism

Governor Kellogg's metropolitan police force helped keep order in New Orleans, but without the support of the federal government, he could do little to protect fellow Republicans in outlying parishes. In a few isolated instances, President Grant sent U.S. troops back into the South to help quell disorder. Interventions such as these exposed Grant to the charge that his administration had failed to secure the peace he had promised in 1868. It opened Republicans to criticism from fiscal conservatives about the continuing expense of Reconstruction and, more cynically, from those who felt that black Southerners needed to defend themselves from whites or suffer the consequences. White Southerners also mastered the art of spreading misinformation;

they convinced many Northerners that black people could not be trusted to participate in democratic governance. The violence in Mississippi in 1875 drove the governor, a young white Northerner named Adelbert Ames, to request federal troops. Grant had responded positively in 1874, sending a small contingent of troops to Vicksburg. The situation deteriorated even more the following year. Ames's telegram to the White House explained the dire situation: "I am in great danger of losing my life. Not only that, all the leading Republicans, who have not run away, in danger. . . . The [White] league here have adopted a new policy, which is to kill the leaders and spare the colored people, unless they 'rise.'" This time Grant worried more about weakening Republicans at the polls in the North than about defending Republicans in the South. "The whole public are tired out with these annual autumnal outbreaks in the South . . . [and] are ready now to condemn any interference on the part of the Government," he told his attorney general. Grant, who had conquered Vicksburg for the Union in 1863, sent no troops this time.

Federal courts likewise reflected Northern impatience with the duration and expense of Reconstruction in their increasing reluctance to support black or Republican plaintiffs. The most important of these cases revolved around the defendants arrested for leading the Colfax Massacre. Unable to secure justice in local courts, federal prosecutors sought a conviction on charges of violating the civil rights of the murdered officeholders. In *United States v. Cruikshank*, the Supreme Court ruled that the Fourteenth Amendment protected citizens against only official state actions and not private violence. Because the massacre's ringleader, William Cruikshank, had operated without state sanction, the amendment offered no protection. Cruikshank went free, and in the process, the court dramatically narrowed the scope of protection offered by the Fourteenth Amendment. The *Cruikshank* case was decided in 1876, the same year that a new Republican won the presidency. Rutherford B. Hayes, a Union general like his predecessor Ulysses S. Grant, entered office under a storm of controversy. He secured the office after the contested election of 1876, when Republicans and Democrats clashed over the returns from Louisiana, Florida, and South Carolina (Map 15.3). Both sides agreed to count the presidential ballots for Hayes but gave Democrats control at the state level. This ended the last three Republican state governments in the South and initiated an era of Democratic dominance that lasted for most of the next century. Shortly after his inauguration, Hayes recalled the last few thousand U.S. troops out of the South, officially ending the period of Reconstruction.

Northerners' fatigue with Reconstruction also resulted from their preoccupation with the rapid changes happening in other parts of the country. The wave of city building in the 1840s and 1850s that had developed during the technological boom of that era increased after the war. Immigrants continued to pour into Northern cities, where their rapid incorporation changed the political contours of the region. Legislation passed by the dynamic wartime Congress also began to bear fruit. The most important of these was the **Homestead Act**, which allowed families to claim 160 acres of land if they improved it over five years of residence. The bill opened the western United States—mostly land gained in the Mexican War or through the Louisiana Purchase—to white settlement. Accompanying settlers in the movement west was the nation's first Transcontinental Railroad, which had also been authorized by the 37th Congress. Congressmen, land developers, and businessmen regarded the railroad line, which reduced

Excerpts from majority opinion in *United States v. Cruikshank*

MAP 15.3 1876 Presidential Election, by State Although the Republican presidential candidate, Rutherford B. Hayes, was credited with the electoral votes of Louisiana, South Carolina, and Florida, these states all elected Democratic governors and legislatures. This ended the presence of statewide Republican rule in the South and marked the end of political Reconstruction.

travel time between the Atlantic and Pacific coasts from months to days, as the nation's most important economic development measure.

As the Union Pacific laid track, Indian communities of the West resisted. During the Civil War, Indians had exploited the opportunity of a distracted United States and

WESTERN MIGRATION By settling the long-standing political conflicts over the future of slavery, the Civil War set in motion massive white migration into the western states and territories. This process brought white Americans into more intimate contact, both benign and malignant, with Native peoples all across the western landscape.

interactive timeline

TIMELINE 1865–1888

AMERICA	YEAR	THE WORLD
Jan Congress proposes Thirteenth Amendment **Mar** Congress establishes Bureau of Refugees, Freedmen, and Abandoned Lands **Apr** Robert E. Lee's army surrenders to Ulysses S. Grant at Appomattox, Virginia **Apr** Abraham Lincoln assassinated by John Wilkes Booth **Apr** Joseph Johnston's army surrenders to William T. Sherman at Durham, North Carolina **Oct** Morant Bay Rebellion in Jamaica **Dec** Ratification of Thirteenth Amendment abolishes slavery in United States Southern state legislatures pass "black codes" Ku Klux Klan organized in Pulaski, Tennessee	**1865**	
Feb President Andrew Johnson vetoes Freedmen's Bureau reauthorization bill **Mar** President Andrew Johnson vetoes 1866 Civil Rights Act **May** Memphis race riot **Jun** Congress proposes Fourteenth Amendment **Jul** Congress overrides Johnson's veto of Freedmen's Bureau Act and Civil Rights Act **Jul** New Orleans race riot	**1866**	Austro–Prussian War
Mar Congress passes Reconstruction Acts Southern state constitutional conventions begin across the South with mixed-race delegates	**1867**	Karl Marx publishes *Das Kapital* Russia sells Alaska to United States Dominion of Canada established
Feb House of Representatives votes to impeach Andrew Johnson **Apr** Senate votes not to convict Andrew Johnson **Jun** Ratification of Fourteenth Amendment establishes rights and due process for citizens **Nov** Republican Ulysses S. Grant elected president	**1868**	Meiji Restoration in Japan begins rapid modernization
Feb Congress proposes Fifteenth Amendment **May** Transcontinental Railroad completed	**1869**	Suez Canal, built by French, opens in Egypt
Feb Ratification of Fifteenth Amendment prohibits discrimination in voting on the basis of race or previous condition of servitude **May** U.S. Congress passes "Force Act" giving it power to crack down on the Ku Klux Klan (followed by complementary legislation later in 1870 and 1871)	**1870**	Franco–Prussian War begins War of the Triple Alliance ends with at least 60 percent of Paraguayan population dead

undermanned forts to re-establish a position of strength. With the coming of peace in 1865, a newly expanded, trained, and disciplined U.S. Army moved west. The Sioux, in particular, had challenged U.S. authority during the war, culminating in a wide-scale uprising in Minnesota that was violently suppressed by the army. Military tribunals had originally sentenced 303 men to death for crimes against settlers during the Minnesota conflicts, but Lincoln commuted the death sentences for 264 prisoners and allowed the execution of 39 others. After the war, western Indians faced an emboldened army without the aid of a sympathetic executive. The shift away from Indians' hunting and low-impact farming practices to the more intensive style of American agriculture caused significant change throughout the Great Plains and the West, and within a few decades spurred a preservation movement aimed at balancing the development of the region and conserving its natural beauty.

AMERICA	YEAR	THE WORLD
Congress holds Ku Klux Klan hearings to assess and publicize violence against freed people and their white allies in the South	1871	Brazil passes gradual emancipation law Rome declared capital of unified Italy Franco–Prussian War ends, Napoleon III overthrown, and Third Republic of France established Rising of the Paris Commune Germany victory in Franco–Prussian War yields unified Germany
Nov Republican Ulysses S. Grant reelected president First national park created at Yellowstone in Wyoming territory	1872	
Apr Colfax Massacre in northern Louisiana kills approximately 150 people	1873	
Nov Democrats gain control of U.S. House of Representatives	1874	
Mar Congress passes 1875 Civil Rights Act	1875	
Mar Supreme Court issues *United States v. Cruikshank* verdict, which restricts meaning of Fourteenth Amendment to protection against actions taken by state actors George Armstrong Custer and his forces are defeated at Battle of Little Bighorn	1876	
Mar Rutherford B. Hayes inaugurated president; recalls last U.S. troops from the South Democrats seize control of last three Southern states (Florida, South Carolina, and Louisiana)	1877	
Albion Tourgée publishes *A Fool's Errand*	1879	
	1886	Cuba abolishes slavery
	1888	Brazil abolishes slavery

Legacies of Reconstruction

Before John Muir, one of the most important environmental activists of the era, gained fame as a protector and champion of the American West, he toured the South during Reconstruction. Leaving his home in Indianapolis in early 1867, Muir walked south to Florida, observing flora, fauna, and the human wildlife along the way. In addition to wry observations about the "long-haired ex-guerillas" of the Tennessee and North Carolina mountains, Muir chronicled the attitudes of the white and black citizens with whom he interacted on his trip. In Georgia, he observed, "The traces of war are not only apparent on the broken fields, burnt fences, mills, and woods ruthlessly slaughtered, but also on the countenances of the people. A few years after a forest has been burned, another generation of bright and happy trees arises.... So with the people of this war-field. Happy, unscarred, and unclouded youth is growing up around the aged, half-consumed, and fallen parents, who bear in sad measure the ineffaceable marks of the farthest-reaching and most infernal of all civilized calamities." The sadness that Muir observed in 1867 had changed to anger a decade later. Southern whites ended Reconstruction embittered against African Americans for the efforts they had made to claim civil rights; contemptuous of the federal government for assistance—however meager—they had given that effort; and deeply suspicious of the open, bipartisan politics that had flourished briefly in the 1870s. All three of these attitudes weakened the South over time and encouraged whites to regard the most important political and social goal for their communities as the violent protection of white supremacy.

The unwillingness of federal authorities to enforce the civil rights laws and especially the Fourteenth and Fifteenth Amendments left Southern African Americans isolated, but blacks were never solely victims. From the earliest days of North American slavery, they had resisted the institution, and their actions during and after Reconstruction reveal a similar refusal to be defined by white actions. In early 1866, a group of "colored citizens" in Florida complained to then Secretary of War Grant that "the Civil authoritys here are taking from the Colord People all the fire arms that they find in their Persesion, including Dubble barrel Shot Guns, Pistols of any kind." Without the means of self-defense, they would be reliant on the government for their protection. Years before, Frederick Douglass had observed of black Americans, "It is enough to say, that if a knowledge of the use of arms is desirable in any people, it is desirable in us." As the Florida men who petitioned Ulysses Grant made clear, it remained desirable and, sadly, imperative after the war as well. Perhaps anticipating the day when Northerners would abandon the effort, they closed by noting, "If Congress Do not Stand Squarely up for us, and Make Laws that Will Protect us, over the heads of the States, We are Nothing More than Searfs." Congress did not stand up "squarely," but Southern African Americans forged ahead on their own. They pursued an egalitarian politics through the Republican Party, and many protected and used that vote until the end of the century. They also built communities, churches, schools, and businesses. These institutions and the networks of support and self-improvement that developed among them sustained black Southerners until another struggle against Southern violence produced America's Second Reconstruction—the civil rights movement of the 1950s and 1960s—and the nation finally stood square.

STUDY QUESTIONS **FOR THE END OF RECONSTRUCTION, 1877**

quiz

1. Why did Reconstruction end in 1877?

2. What explains the Northern willingness to abandon the policies they initiated in 1867?

Summary

- In common with Brazil and Cuba, the two other major slave societies in the hemisphere, the American South struggled to reorganize its labor and landholding systems in the wake of emancipation.
- Unlike in those two nations, in America, blacks gained the vote and helped build new systems of public education over the opposition of Southern whites.
- Southerners needed money to rebuild and modernize the region's infrastructure, but stripped of capital by war and relying primarily on agricultural enterprises, they had little success attracting American or European funds.
- Conservative Southern whites used both voting and violence, the latter formalized in the Ku Klux Klan and white militias, to defeat the Republican governments that represented such a sharp break with the region's past and end Reconstruction.
- Northerners, eager to develop the West and extend American influence within the Caribbean and across the oceans and weary of the expense and trouble of the South, consented to a return to Democratic rule, but the community building and education already enacted by African Americans created the networks that sustained them through the years of Jim Crow.

Key Terms and People

black codes 513	Homestead Act 532
carpetbaggers 525	Jubilee 506
crop lien 527	Knights of Labor 527
Delany, Martin 523	Ku Klux Klan (KKK) 529
Fifteenth Amendment 517	sharecroppers 524
Fourteenth Amendment 515	Stevens, Thaddeus 518
Freedmen's Bureau 509	Thirteenth Amendment 512

◁))

audio
flashcards

Reviewing Chapter 15

1. How did the United States' experience of emancipation and nation building compare to that of other countries in the mid-19th century?
2. Was the Civil War and Reconstruction a "watershed" in American life? Explain what changed and what remained consistent.

Further Reading

Blight, David W. *Race and Reunion: The Civil War in American Memory*. Cambridge, MA: Belknap Press, 2001. The fullest account of changes in the memory of the Civil War, especially the willingness of white Northerners to marginalize the history of slavery and emancipation in the conflict.

Foner, Eric. *Reconstruction: America's Unfinished Revolution, 1863–1877*. New York: Harper and Row, 1988. A comprehensive history of Reconstruction with particular attention to labor and emancipation in the South.

Litwack, Leon F. *Been in the Storm So Long: The Aftermath of Slavery*. New York: Vintage, 1980. A vivid chronicle of the experience of emancipation for black Southerners.

Perman, Michel. *The Road to Redemption: Southern Politics, 1869–1879*. Chapel Hill: University of North Carolina Press, 1984. The clearest analysis of the national- and state-level politics that produced the end of Reconstruction.

Ransom, Roger L. and Richard Sutch. *One Kind of Freedom: The Economic Consequences of Emancipation*. Cambridge, UK: Cambridge University Press, 1977. A comprehensive economic analysis of the effects of the Civil War on the South.

Silber, Nina. *The Romance of Reunion: Northerners and the South, 1865–1900*. Chapel Hill: University of North Carolina Press, 1993. An elegant study that emphasizes the cultural dimensions of the Northern shift toward reconciliation after the Civil War.

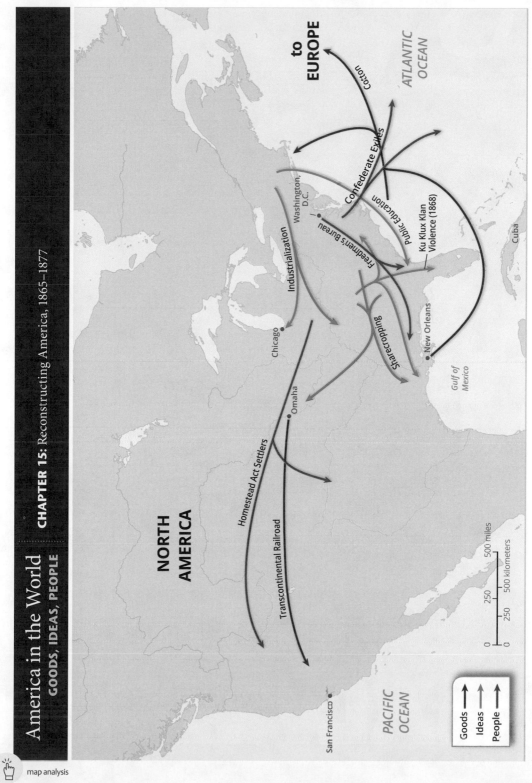

America in the World
GOODS, IDEAS, PEOPLE

CHAPTER 15: Reconstructing America, 1865–1877

to
EUROPE

ATLANTIC
OCEAN

Cotton

Confederate Exiles

Public Education

Washington,
D.C.

Industrialization

Freedmen's Bureau

Ku Klux Klan
Violence (1868)

Cuba

Chicago

Sharecropping

New Orleans

Gulf of
Mexico

Omaha

NORTH
AMERICA

Homestead Act Settlers

Transcontinental Railroad

PACIFIC
OCEAN

San Francisco

→	Goods
→	Ideas
→	People

0   250   500 miles

0   250   500 kilometers

map analysis

Hamburg-Antwerp to Galveston passenger line poster.

Forging a Transcontinental Nation

1877–1900

T he gold rush of 1849 brought fortune seekers from around the globe to California. Ten years later, Colorado discoveries of gold and silver brought another wave of migration to the Rocky Mountains. Gold also brought prospectors and investors to the Arizona territories in the 1860s, but the discovery of rich copper deposits 75 miles north of the Mexican border ultimately transformed the economy of the region. American brothers Jim and Robert Metcalfe found copper in 1870 while traveling as army scouts searching for Apache resistance leaders Victorio and Geronimo.

News of the Arizona discoveries brought entrepreneur Henry Lesinsky, an eastern European Jew who exemplified the remarkable mobility of the region and the age. As a boy, he immigrated to England; later, he left to prospect for gold in Australia and then traveled to mines in California, Nevada, New Mexico, and finally the Arizona territory. Lesinsky made little from gold or silver but made a fortune selling supplies to U.S. troops fighting Indians. He used the funds to buy out the Metcalfes' copper claims and founded the Longfellow Copper Mining Company in 1873. Using a combination of Australian mining techniques, Detroit financing, Baltimore smelting, and Mexican labor, Lesinsky created the transnational model for the **"copper borderlands"** (see Map 16.2 later in the chapter).

By the 1890s, most Arizona copper was controlled by the powerful Phelps Dodge Company, centered in Bisbee. American companies such as Phelps Dodge and William Cornell Greene's Cananea, Mexico, copper mining empire linked the United States and Mexico through the exchange of metal, labor, and capital. As the United States expanded its communication system with millions of feet of copper wire, the mineral networks gained importance. American and Mexican

businessmen negotiated mutually beneficial transbor-
der relations ahead of official diplomacy and national
policy.

Mexican laborers did the bulk of the low-paying
work in the copper mines of the Southwest early on but
faced stiff competition from Chinese workers who came
to the region with the railroads. Anti-Chinese sentiment
quickly sparked violence and regulations, with Anglo
residents, Mexican laborers, and Chinese workers all
vying for jobs in territory that was still claimed by several Indian nations and not under
the full control of the U.S. government. Entrepreneurs like Lesinsky and the Goldwater
family took advantage of these fluid labor markets and chaotic border opportunities
in the 1880s, making fortunes provisioning the U.S. Army, which had been sent to the
region to bring order to a swirling mix of peoples and claims and knit the West to the
rest of the nation.

MEETING GROUND OF MANY PEOPLES

Born on March 31, 1878, on the sandy barrier island town of Galveston, Texas, Jack
Johnson, nicknamed the "Galveston Giant," became the first black heavyweight champion of the world and one of the most famous men of his time. Raised in one of Galveston's toughest neighborhoods, Johnson was witness to and a product of the whirlwind
of cultural change and racial conflict of his age.

The story of Johnson and his hometown of Galveston, like that of the copper borderlands, captures many critical issues involved in forging a transcontinental nation
between the end of Reconstruction and the turn of the 19th century. Powered by the
globalization of markets, international political and ethnic tensions, emerging economic opportunities, and advertisement by government and industry, Galveston was a
gateway for the world's people, goods, and ideas streaming in and out of the American
West. Strategically positioned on the edges of the Mexican north, the West, the South,
and the Gulf of Mexico, Galveston was seen by many as the entry point to a new era in
American history. However, Galveston was also a contested region of the nation in the
aftermath of Reconstruction.

Racial prejudice governed the social structure of Johnson's birthplace, but Galveston's vibrant African American community wielded influence through the Negro
Longshoremen's Association. Its members interacted with Jews from Poland, German
Lutherans, Catholic Italians, and the thousands of other immigrants from around the
world who flowed through the island. Accustomed to multicultural life, Johnson flouted
racial conventions with open relationships with white women and triggered national
race riots when he won the "fight of the century" in 1908 against the white heavyweight
champion of the world, Tommy Burns.

Johnson's tumultuous career mirrored the contest of old racial ideals, new multicultural opportunities, and lingering prejudice that characterized the American West
between 1877 and 1900. Prewar racial hierarchies of black and white grew complicated

during the settling of the West. Foreshadowing America's multicultural future, Indians, Europeans, Hispanics, Asians, Mormons, and African Americans in the West competed and cooperated with one another.

Changing Patterns of Migration

According to historian Frederick Jackson Turner, the 1890 census indicated the western frontier had "closed." Census data analyzed by Turner showed that all of the land west of the Mississippi was "settled" by virtue of having people listed as residents in most counties. For Turner, this census demonstrated the end period of centuries of conquest. Turner used this information as the basis for his influential thesis that described the settlement of the West as a "frontier process" in which immigrants became Americans by confronting and conquering a "virgin land." For those like future president Theodore Roosevelt, who viewed the process of western settlement as the experience that made America exceptional and superior to other nations, the notion of a closed frontier caused great anxiety. Where next, Roosevelt and others wondered, would Americans recreate themselves through the conquest of new lands if there was no frontier?

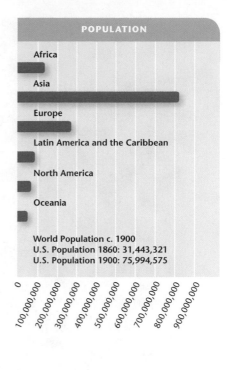

Despite the census evidence, people could still find plenty of open western spaces in the post–Civil War decades. Significant sections of the West remained virtually empty well into the 20th century. Between 1877 and 1900, millions of people from all points of the globe and every region of the United States moved into the West. Within the West, internal migrations reshaped the region's character, depopulating some areas and resettling others. But many of those who sought frontier opportunity in the West ended up in cities regardless.

By 1890 the vast majority of western migrants had settled in cities such as Denver (133,000), San Francisco (380,000), Los Angeles (124,000), Salt Lake City (53,000), and hundreds of towns scattered like islands in an ocean of sparsely inhabited land. Contrary to popular perception, the West was the most urban region in America and remains so today. The lure of open land, farming, and remote mines scattered people throughout the West, but environmental and economic forces drew them together again in cities. Denver and San Francisco were **instant cities** that grew from tiny outposts to booming metropolitan areas in less than a decade and boasted all the luxuries of eastern society. These cities grew so quickly because of changing post–Civil War migration patterns.

After the Civil War, migration patterns changed for several reasons. Railroads made foreign and internal immigration far easier (Map 16.1). Likewise, internal migration increased with rapidly expanding regional railway networks. Economic downturns, environmental disasters, and an influx of new immigrants, who lowered wages

image
analysis

THE IDEALIZED WEST "The Heart of the Continent," 1882, booster brochure of the idealized West captures the utopian vision that drew millions to the region. Look closely and you will notice all the icons of settlement. The book told potential settlers they would find "an empire grander in its resources than any emperor or czar . . . ever swayed over."

and often raised prejudices in other regions, pushed internal and foreign migrants to the West. In 1877, tens of thousands of African American "**Exodusters**" fleeing rising racial violence at the end of military Reconstruction migrated from the South to the West, founding new towns and joining other workers and entrepreneurs hoping for a new start. All were pulled by the lure of new opportunities and moved frequently to take advantage of emerging markets and employment.

Women moved with their families and on their own and contributed a disproportionate amount of the daily labor required to establish businesses, homes, towns, and communities across the West. Women's diaries of migrations reveal much of what historians know of daily life and the history of settlement. European and Euro-American women responsible for inhabiting a little-understood region faced environmental challenges that Indian women had known for thousands of years. Stories of generations of intermarriage revealed by women's diaries and family histories show the deep intertwining of culture, race, and ethnicity characteristic of the region and going all the way back to the earliest interactions between Indigenous peoples and Spanish colonizers. European racial and ethnic identities were privileged in the West, so it was not uncommon for people of mixed heritage to choose to emphasize one aspect of their genetics while hiding another. The more intimate historic sources left by western women and the oral traditions of Indigenous women

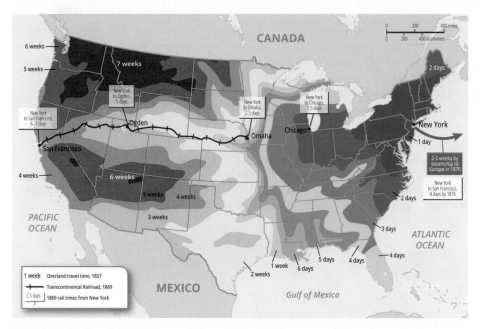

MAP 16.1 Technology, Time, and Space This map shows travel times between the 1850s and 1870s. Before the 1840s, sailing ships took an average of five to six weeks to cross the Atlantic. An overland trip or a voyage around Cape Horn could take months or even years. By the 1870s, the same distances could be covered in a week.

often reveal the deep entanglements of race, class, ethnicity, and culture hidden by official documents.

Women of all backgrounds moved extensively throughout the West, but their mobility was often constrained more than men's because they needed to maintain homes, businesses, ranches, and farms, while men moved in search of gold and jobs. Immigrant women suffered the hardscrabble realities of making a home in the West but also gained greater autonomy and power than their counterparts in more settled regions of the United States. This access and independence was reflected in western states' early voting rights acts for women and the prominence of women in western businesses and industries. The concept of the "frontier" was different for immigrant women just as it was different for men depending on their race and ethnic background.

Photographs of women in the American West

Mobility was a key characteristic of the global economy in the 19th century. The American frontier experience was not unique. So-called **settler societies** in South America, Australia, and Canada also depended on significant internal and external migrations to solidify control of vast territories and negotiate with or displace indigenous peoples ahead of state-sponsored efforts. No destination, however, could compare with the United States in the astounding diversity of immigrants pouring into a region already remarkably multicultural. There were many melting pots around the globe, but they melted two or three predominant immigrant groups. In the United States and in the West in particular, immigrants from virtually everywhere lived together with thousands of Native Americans, freed slaves, Hispanics of many origins, Asians, and Euro-Americans of all types.

Mexican Borders

Much of what Americans think of as the "West" was long the Spanish and then the Mexican north. This "Far North" was a vast region only loosely controlled by distant Mexico City. Violent wars with powerful Indian tribes strained Spain's and then Mexico's control of northern provinces and paved the way for U.S. seizure of vast Mexican territories after the U.S.–Mexican War (1846–1848). Politics, economics, and an unstoppable tide of migrants conspired against Hispanic control in much of what became the American West. The U.S. Southwest and the Mexican north were seamlessly linked by nature and divided only by politics. These regions shared a contiguous desert ecosystem that stretched through what are now Arizona and California and north into Utah and Nevada. Spaniards, Indians, and Anglos in search of mineral wealth and rangelands moved throughout the region and fought for control of its resources for centuries (Map 16.2).

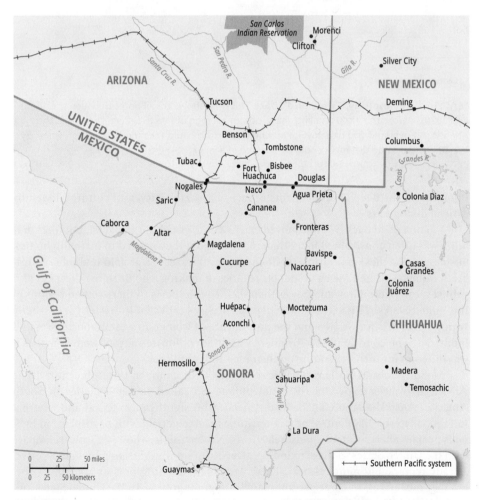

MAP 16.2 Borderlands This map of the "copper borderlands" shows how economy and ecology were sometimes more important than national borders in developing regions. The remarkable movement of people, goods, and ideas throughout this contested zone shaped the national histories that followed.

Whereas groups such as the Texas Rangers systematically terrorized Mexicans after the Mexican War, U.S. and Mexican entrepreneurs shared a desire to capitalize on the movement of labor, capital, and commodities across political borders.

On the fuzzy U.S. Mexican borderlands of the late 19th century, Mexicans moved back and forth across *La Linea* with relative freedom. Migrant laborers moved north to the "West" along centuries-old migration corridors. The El Camino Real corridor running south to north linked Mexico City to Zacatecas, Durango, Chihuahua, El Paso, Albuquerque, and Santa Fe. The web of trails that comprised the Sonoran corridor funneled workers throughout the copper and cotton corridors and linked copper labor routes to the seasonal cotton fields stretching from Yuma, Arizona, to California's San Joaquin valley near Los Angeles. By 1900, Mexicans made up 60 percent of all copper and seasonal farmworkers. Mexicans who worked in the United States received less pay than Anglo workers, were barred from union participation, faced prejudice and segregation, and were "sent packing"—sometimes at the point of a gun—during economic downturns. Despite these hardships, Mexican laborers in the late 19th century fared better than Chinese.

Towns of the "copper borderlands," late 19th and early 20th century

Chinese Exclusion

Although the Chinese are remembered in American history primarily for their role in building the Transcontinental Railroad, their importance in the West extended far beyond that single event. Chinese immigrants who came to work on the railroads, mines, and fields were part of a global Chinese diaspora and the "coolie trade" that sold contract Chinese laborers and Chinese women as indentured laborers and sex workers who lived little better than slaves. From the 1840s to the 1870s, Chinese immigrants, free and contracted, moved to Australia, Southeast Asia, Peru, Cuba, and California. Those who migrated left sparse opportunities, a rigid class system, and grinding poverty in 19th-century south China. No immigrant group faced more persistent racism and violence than the Chinese. Businesses sought out Chinese workers for their cheap and exploitable labor with the assumption that they would eventually return to China. The Chinese usually migrated as individuals and were overwhelmingly male in the first waves but were later joined by women and entire families, and during all phases of immigration they quickly developed community-building strategies to fight against racism and segregation. The Chinese managed to build successful enclaves wherever they went. Anchored by temples such as the Bok Kai Temple of Marysville, California, or woven into instant cities such as Denver and San Francisco, "China towns" became a lasting characteristic of the western urban landscape.

Photo of enslaved Chinese coolie in in Peru

Legendary hard workers, the Chinese laborers were also "stickers": "If you can get them this year you can get them next year," wrote one observer. "They become attached to your place and they stay with you." The Chinese proved indispensable to western development. In California, they comprised half of all agricultural workers. In urban areas and on ranches, Chinese men occupied up to 90 percent of service industry jobs such as laundry and food preparation positions. During the heyday of western expansion, the Chinese were tolerated and sometimes given grudging respect.

Starting in 1870, however, anti-Chinese sentiments increased as the western economy gained importance. In a pattern that repeated throughout the 20th century, communities and industries built by the cheapest foreign labor turned against these workers once they achieved economic stability. The Australians blazed the racist path that Americans followed by enacting Chinese exclusion acts as early as the 1850s. Urged by white labor organizers, anti-Chinese leagues, and community leaders, western states passed laws limiting Chinese opportunities and rights through the 1870s. State laws and political enthusiasm prompted the U.S. Congress to pass the **Chinese Exclusion Act** in 1882. The act, which nominally suspended immigration, was renewed and tightened over the years until harsh immigration restrictions enacted in the early 1920s ended virtually all Asian immigration to the United States. In addition, several western states passed laws restricting Chinese and later Japanese landownership and barred them from several professions. As a consequence of these restrictions, immigration from Mexico rose to meet the need for cheap labor in the California fields. Greeks, Poles, Russians, Japanese, and representatives of virtually every nation diversified the region during the critical period of western settlement.

STUDY QUESTIONS FOR MEETING GROUND OF MANY PEOPLES

quiz

1. What did the word "frontier" mean to Americans in the 1800s?

2. For what reasons did white westerners and white Americans exclude and discriminate against Chinese immigrants?

◉ MAPPING THE WEST

The vast arid region between the Front Range of the Rocky Mountains in Colorado and the Sierra Nevada in California was the last portion of the contiguous United States to be explored and resettled (Map 16.3). This immense landscape became the focus of federal attention in 1853–1854 when teams of surveyors were dispatched throughout the region in search of routes for the Transcontinental Railroad.

Prior to 1865, the U.S. Army conducted most expeditions, and private investors funded geologic investigations in hopes of discovering mineral wealth. Other explorers, such as John C. Frémont, guided pioneers along the Oregon Trail and crossed the Rockies and the expanse of the Great Basin to the Sierra Nevada several times; however, like the army before them, they gave little attention to formal surveying or mapping. Starting in 1869, one-armed Civil War veteran and geology professor **John Wesley Powell** led a series of critically important surveys of the Colorado River system. Powell's expedition was self-funded, with only a few instruments and permission to borrow food from military posts along the way. Setting out at Green River, Wyoming, in four wooden boats, Powell followed the Colorado River through the Flaming Gorge, Desolation, Marble, and Grand canyons. In a second expedition in 1872, Powell explored the expansive Colorado Plateau.

John Wesley Powell, excerpt from *The Exploration of the Colorado River* (1875)

Powell was the first scientist to understand the critical importance of the Colorado River for the arid Southwest. His popular 1875 account of his one-armed adventures, *The Exploration of the Colorado River*, and extensive coverage of his travels by the press in the East established the scientist-explorer as a popular hero. He followed these works with the insightful 1878 *Report on the Lands of the Arid Region*, which advocated the

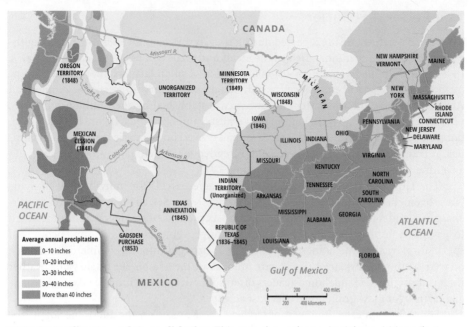

MAP 16.3 Climate and Consolidation This map shows the territorial acquisitions that established the modern U.S. West and set the borders for the nation as we now know it. The majority of this rugged terrain beyond the 100th meridian was arid and inhabited by Indian and Hispanic residents, complicating perceptions of the area as "free" and forcing new inhabitants to learn how to modify their environmental expectations.

necessity of settlement based on his scientific findings about regional environments. Powell, warning that traditional settlement and agricultural practices would fail in the arid West, recommended a realistic approach in evaluating the potential of the region.

In 1879, the U.S. Congress consolidated various survey programs and established the United States Geological Survey (USGS). Under Powell's leadership, the USGS continued surveying and mapping with a new emphasis on careful environmental observation. What had been unknown or characterized by rumor and legend became charted, scientifically categorized, photographed, named, and overlaid with grid lines. More scientific and accurate, the USGS maps nonetheless continued a long tradition of using cartography to obliterate or obscure Indian territorial claims. Misrepresentation of Indian territory contributed to tension and conflict between new migrants and Indians across the region. Government cartographers relied on Anglo conceptions of "improvement" and settlement to determine occupation, leading to frequent diminishment or outright obliteration of Indian peoples from maps.

The surveys established the rough boundaries of the West and created the maps and marked the trails that millions of settlers used to travel to the region. They did not, however, convey the complex cultural landscape or environmental challenges these newcomers faced. A series of foundational federal land acts pulled often-unprepared migrants into the West, where the rush for riches dimmed cautious voices such as that of John Wesley Powell.

The Federal Frontier

The **Homestead Act of 1862**, passed during the Civil War by a Congress free of Southern slaveholder opposition, reflected the ideals and goals of a Republican United States. In keeping with the Jeffersonian vision of a nation of small farmers, the federal government sought to extend the system of individual landownership west. The Homestead Act, expanding the basic system of settlement established by the Ordinance of 1785, provided a means for privatizing expansive western public lands. Before the Civil War, homesteading west of the Mississippi River had proved problematic for individual families, as transactions involving cheap lands intended for individuals quickly evolved into a commercialized system of land speculation.

The Homestead Act provided title to 160-acre parcels for individuals who made "improvements" to the land over a period of five years. Settlers had the option to purchase the land for $1.25 per acre after the first six months of residency, and some opted to pay up front to secure mortgages to fund improvements. This option encouraged speculation by allowing homesteaded land to be brought into the commercial market a quarter section (one quarter of a square mile) at a time at a higher resale value. Rather than improving the land, homesteaders often sold out to other individuals or commercial farms that grew grain crops over vast acreages.

Photographs of homesteaders and frontier towns

For those homesteading west of Dodge City, Kansas, on the 100th meridian (the geographic line of aridity where annual rainfalls drop below 8 inches per year), 160 acres required expensive irrigation works for farming or other dry-land farming techniques. These parcels were also far too small for ranching. In addition, five years was too long to develop the land without the benefit of ownership and access to loans. Congress addressed these problems in 1877 with the **Desert Land Act**. The act, applicable in 11 western states, allowed for homesteading on 640-acre parcels of arid land at 25 cents per acre and provided title within three years for a dollar an acre for settled, irrigated land. However, there was no official definition of how much land and water constituted irrigated cultivation. For much of the desert West, agriculture required massive federal support that came with the creation of the Reclamation Service in 1902. The renamed Bureau of Reclamation (BOR) eventually funded extensive irrigation projects in 16 western states. The simple act of providing land and water to farmers and ranchers enormously expanded the growth and reach of the federal government.

Despite an emphasis on individual landownership, the landscape and environment of the American West resisted familiar patterns of development. As a result, vast sections of public land, especially in the Great Basin, stayed in the hands of the federal government until the 1930s. For migrants converging on the West from all directions, federal land and mineral acts provided a semblance of structure to the spasmodic rushes that characterized settlement prior to the Civil War. Where the gold and silver rushes of the 1840s and 1850s left concentrated populations in the mountain West, the surveys and land acts opened the floodgates for massive migration into the Great Plains region beyond the Missouri River. Perception and myth—as much as fact—powered "land fevers" that drew millions from the farthest reaches of the globe into one of the world's harshest environments.

Promotion and Memory

It is hard to overestimate the power of perception in the creation of the West as both a geographical region and an ideal with lasting global appeal. In 1895, future president

Woodrow Wilson wrote, "The West has been the great word of our history. The westerner has been the type and master of our American life." The "great word" was always more myth than truth, not entirely false but a powerful idea with enough fact to motivate millions to move great distances and suffer enormous hardship. The mythic version of the western story is still celebrated in literature, on film, and on TV. But the myth had a dark side. It justified the mistreatment of Indians and their ancestral environment and contributed to class and racial conflict that characterized the post–Civil War West.

While boosters and promoters made wild claims about the West, early settlers generated widely circulated literature of reminiscences, memoirs, and fictionalized accounts of the frontier process. As individuals or collectively through "pioneer societies," settlers lamented the passing of a grand age even as they exaggerated the savagery of the land and peoples they thought they had conquered. Settlers, together with an influential group of "artists, authors, dreamers, and deceivers," created such a powerful, persuasive mythology that even savvy observers had trouble discerning truth from fiction.

No single person blended history and myth better than **William "Buffalo Bill" Cody**. He was literally a legend in his own time, a man simultaneously a real person and a fictional character of international fame. Cody's heavily embellished life story of migration as a youth from LeClaire, Iowa, to the west, over the Plains and through the Rockies, encompassed all of the experiences global audiences recognized as part of western frontier life: buffalo hunting, Indian fighting, bronco busting, gunslinging, and military scouting. In the 1880s, Cody's "Wild West" shows featured real-life westerners recreating idealized versions of the actual history unfolding in the region at the same time. Cody traveled the world introducing Indian resistance leaders such as Sitting Bull to queens and the young German Kaiser Wilhelm, along with hordes of commoners from Paris to Poland. Annie Oakley shot the tip of a cigarette out of Wilhelm's mouth, and she offered "to do it again" during World War I.

Photos, postcards, and prints of Buffalo Bill

![Buffalo Bill's Wild West Company photograph]

BUFFALO BILL'S WILD WEST COMPANY'S PRESENTATION TO THEIR CHIEF ON HIS BIRTHDAY AT OLYMPIA, LONDON, FEBRUARY 26, 1903   Cody and his troop traveled the world introducing Indian resistance leaders such as Sitting Bull to queens and kaisers, along with hordes of commoners from Paris to Poland. Global perceptions of the United States and the U.S. West were shaped as much by these cultural ambassadors as any other source.

Such globetrotting shows provided one of many powerful nodes of transnational cultural exchange linking the frontier West to the world. Even as millions of immigrants crossed oceans from all directions to reach an actual place they knew as the "West," Cody and other Americans—taking the mythic West out to the world—left an indelible impression of a particular facet of American identity that celebrated individual violence and heroic conquest. The reality of violence and valor in the region, however, was far more complex.

The Culture of Collective Violence

Dime novels, Wild West shows, and the 20th-century movies yet to come told stories of righteous individual violence. The "western" genre in all its forms had two basic narratives: the gunfight in the street between a good man and an outlaw, and brave pioneers versus murderous Indians. Foreign authors such as German Karl May, who never traveled to the West, sold millions of stories of individual violence that circled the globe. Buffalo Bill raised the appetite for them by reenacting an idealized version of regional violence. Figures like the violent young criminal Billy the Kid gained international fame for exploits that bore little resemblance to their decidedly unromantic lives. Thousands died bloody deaths in the violent West, but rarely were they lone figures dueling heroically in the streets. Individual violence was most often criminal or reckless, with cheap alcohol as the fuel.

Collective violence was disturbingly premeditated and often carried out by otherwise upstanding community members or soldiers. The myth of individual violence conceals a more disturbing reality of group violence involving regular citizens and whole communities. Horrific organized violence against Indians, such as the profoundly disturbing Sand Creek and Wounded Knee massacres, was much more brutal and common than were gunfights. The idea that military action or group vigilantism provided a necessary corrective to the disorder of the frontier justified much of the violence in the West well into the 20th century. Prominent community and religious leaders joined "vigilance leagues" in San Francisco and Denver. Western papers wrote favorably about vigilante lynching mobs that "saved county money" and time by executing criminals without delay or due process. Western corporations hired thugs to break strikes, remove unwanted workers, or impose order by threatening violence in company camps and towns. Corporate, state, or community driven, the culture of violence in the West established in the 19th century enabled force and extralegal coercion to become normal practices in the next century.

Racial and ethnic violence were common in the 19th-century United States. Few non-Indian groups, however, suffered like the Chinese in the West. Throughout the 1870s and 1880s, Chinese immigrants were beaten and murdered with shocking regularity and with little consequence for the perpetrators. Like blacks in the South, individuals and small groups of Chinese workers faced violence and lynching from rival white workers and ethnic groups. In 1880, violence reached a new level when an enraged mob of 3,000, yelling, "Stamp out the yellow plague," stormed into Denver's "Hop Alley," a Chinese enclave. The mob lynched one man in the street, injured hundreds, and burned or dismantled Chinese businesses and homes. Five years later, race riots left 51 Chinese miners dead in Rock Springs, Wyoming. Viewing the survivors of the riots, Chinese consul Huang Sih Chuen lamented, "Words fail to give an idea of their sufferings, and their appearance is a sad one to human eyes to witness."

Anti-Chinese mob violence in Denver, 1880

WOUNDED KNEE AFTERMATH This disturbing image by G. Trager of a mass grave filled with 146 frozen bodies at Wounded Knee captures the shocking banality of violence in 19th-century America. The men in the grave and lining the pit don't appear celebratory or remorseful as they look at the Indians they killed. Photographs of the aftermath of battle challenged popular perceptions of the romantic character of violence in the contested West.

STUDY QUESTIONS FOR MAPPING THE WEST

1. Why did government-sponsored surveys and land acts encourage migration to the West?
2. How does the history of collective western violence differ from the myth of the gunfight in the street?

quiz

⊘ EXTRACTIVE ECONOMIES AND GLOBAL COMMODITIES

Out of the jostling coach window the arid landscape speeds by. Dusty frontier passengers listen for the crack of the driver's whip as he struggles to escape from the outlaws close behind. As the coach rounds a corner, startled kangaroos scurry away. The early 1960s Australian TV show *Whiplash* popularized the story of American businessman and stage travel pioneer Freeman Cobb. Cobb was one of thousands of Americans who moved through the frontiers of the West and on to other developing regions as part of a global exchange of expertise and experience. Most of these multinational business pioneers worked in the extractive economy. Converting natural resources into commodities was the primary economic engine of the American West. Individuals led the way, but by the 1890s, corporations had consolidated many of the industries across the region. The incorporation of the extractive economy of the West created economies and workscapes in stark contrast to the popular individualistic stories of the region circulating throughout the world.

Between 1877 and 1900, the dramatic expansion of railroad, communication, and financial networks throughout the American West enabled phenomenal growth in industrial ranching, farming, mining, and timber production. Eastern and European industrialization created huge demand for western commodities. The Great Plains became the "bread basket of the world," the great forests of the Rockies and the Pacific Northwest yielded tremendous quantities of lumber, and mines blasted deep into the Sierras and Rockies produced hundreds of tons of precious metals. The cattle ranches of the West became massive after the invention of the refrigerated railcar made it possible to turn Texas cows into New York steaks. The promise of quick wealth drew eastern U.S. and foreign investors. With the support of several administrations of the federal government that encouraged and funded this economic explosion, the once peripheral West became an important hub of American and global economic activity.

Mining and Labor

The mineral rushes of the mid-1800s pulled migrants to the West from all parts of the United States and the globe and generated staggering wealth. The Comstock Lode in Nevada alone produced $96 million in silver—more than the combined total from all previous recorded American mining.

Legends spread around the world of instant riches from gold found lying on the ground. A handful of early arriving individuals in California did get rich with little effort. But western mining quickly became a game for serious international capitalists and a new class of engineers working in a complicated web of global exchange, although not before mining created the most diverse collection of nationalities in modern history. In western mining camps, conversations could be heard in English, Chinese, French, Spanish, German, Italian, Hawaiian, and many American Indian dialects. Following the Civil War, industrialized mining turned individualistic prospectors and others into laborers who formed powerful unions such as the Western Federation of Miners (WFM; 1893) and later the Industrial Workers of the World (IWW), or "Wobblies." Still, the get-rich-quick myth persisted long after industrialization and fueled migration into the 20th century.

After the 1870s, the struggle for gold, silver, coal, and copper transformed into a fight between labor and capital complicated by racial and ethnic strife. Industrial mining was terribly dangerous. Mines such as the Comstock in Virginia City, Nevada, dug to unprecedented depths, made collapses and other forms of industrial accidents commonplace. Coal miners in Colorado faced these dangers along with deadly coal dust that killed slowly through disease or swiftly through explosion. Miners were crushed, suffocated, dismembered, and infected daily, providing vivid reasons to act collectively. But ethnic tensions often stifled western labor organization. The universal appeal of mineral wealth was not matched by a uniformity of interests among competing ethnic groups in mining towns. The cemetery of tiny Ely, Nevada, tells the tale of enclaves and

BELCHER MINE   The underground working world of the Comstock Lode in Gold Hill, Nevada, shown in the "Sectional Views of the Belcher Mine." Illustrations like this were designed to show the success of the companies that controlled the mines at conquering nature and engineering challenges. If you look closely, they also reveal something of the working conditions of the miners.

segregation that often characterized western mining camps. Ely's graveyard was neatly divided into a grid of ethnicity and race, with Anglos placed in the choicest ground near the street; followed by Cornish and Irish; Poles and Russians; Mexicans; and, finally, the Chinese in the barren backwash.

When miners did successfully organize, owners often responded with violence. The gunning down of seven strikers in Coeur d'Alene, Idaho, led to the founding of the WFM. An angry young silver miner, **"Big" Bill Haywood**, joined in response and went on to a storied career as an IWW leader loved by workingmen and hated by the corporations. He battled the federal government, was imprisoned during World War I, and would later die in exile. He was buried in the Kremlin.

Known as the land of individualism, the West was in fact the site of many of the most important battles between collectively organized labor, consolidating corporate capital, and an expanded federal state.

Business Travelers

Mine owners imported labor and investment for their enterprises as they exported minerals and wealth to investors. Woven into this dynamic economic transfer was a transnational exchange of culture and expertise. The mineral rushes created powerful and easily transferable business models. American businessmen Freeman Cobb, for example, used his experience with Wells Fargo to create successful stagecoach companies in Australia and South Africa.

Businessmen trained in the boom and bust economies of the West excelled at grand schemes in extractive industries, complex irrigation systems, and transportation networks. Americans like Cobb, who had traveled across America from Maine to California, kept moving west to the Australian gold fields or south to Peru, where they helped build vast railroad networks over difficult terrain. Or, like young future president **Herbert Hoover**, who combined talents in engineering with business, they became ambassadors of American culture who blended frontier knowledge with technical prowess. Although never as numerous as their British counterparts, American businessmen abroad nonetheless built connections that created significant global networks that sometimes ran ahead of federal foreign policy. American business and engineering skills combined with the globally appealing mythology and iconography of the West created a potent brew of reciprocal relationships and cultural exchange.

Railroads, Time, and Space

By 1900, 40 percent of westerners lived in urban centers linked to the world through vast transportation and communication networks of railroads, steamships, undersea telegraph cables, and overland telephone lines. Between 1877 and 1900, the United States had become dependent on new technologies that linked remote urban outposts to the rest of the nation and the world. The web of steel rails and copper wires that spread across the continental United States by the turn of the century made possible the phenomenal growth of the West and permanently bound the region to the national and the world economy.

Generous federal land grants and subsidies pushed the completion of the Transcontinental Railroad. There were efforts to construct transcontinentals in Mexico, Russia, India, and Canada, each built by different versions of publicly subsidized corporate enterprises plagued by graft and scandal. When the U.S. transcontinental was finished, it opened the Great Plains and connected the Pacific to Atlantic and Gulf ports, spurring rapid global exchange, but not always in the ways its builders hoped. In 1869, the driving of the golden spike linking the last rail from east to west ended the first phase of western railroad development. Between 1869 and 1900, regional railroad entrepreneurs such as "empire builder" James J. Hill stepped in when the "robber barons" of the transcontinental epoch moved on to greener pastures. A Canadian, Hill migrated to St. Paul, Minnesota, and saw opportunity for transportation development across the northern borderlands. Hill first linked the expansive Canadian prairie with the Great Plains and distant markets with lines between St. Paul and Winnipeg, Canada. Throughout the 1880s, Hill connected his Great Northern Railway lines east to Chicago and finally in 1893 west to Seattle and the Pacific.

Railroad map of the United States, 1883

Regional rail development in the 1880s and 1890s used 25 percent of U.S. annual timber production and spawned the massive or "bonanza" wheat farms of the Dakotas and the fruit and vegetable economies of Arizona and California. Western coal mining grew from regional rail demands for cheaper energy. A combination of federal land grants and savvy land deals with boosters and politicians gave the railroads massive checkerboard tracts of land to sell to cash-poor migrants.

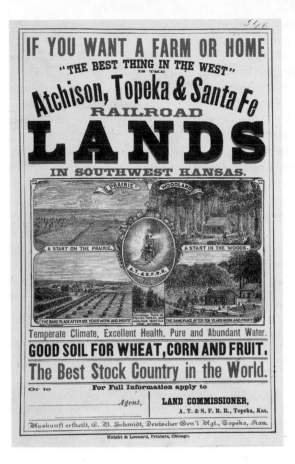

ATCHISON, TOPEKA & SANTA FE (ATSF) RAILROAD HANDBILL ADVERTISING CLIMATE, HEALTH, AND WATER IN LAND IN THE WEST Handbills like this were widely distributed throughout Europe. Even for those who could not read English, the message was clear.

Although land was cheap, transportation costs were not. Farmers and ranchers who bought land from the railroads or acquired homesteads depended on the railroad for access to the world markets that dictated the values of their crops and animals. The railroads even set the farmers' clocks when they established "time zones" in the 1880s. The large distances traversed by U.S. and Canadian railroads especially necessitated a closely regulated system of time to replace the confusion of the solar time that had shaped the lives of humans for millennia. Railroad land grants continue to this day to shape life and economies in the West, where companies such as the Southern Pacific maintain large landholdings and control critical transportation corridors.

Farmers suffered more than any other group from the unpredictability of international commodities markets. Migrant families who rode Jefferson's yeoman dream of self-sufficiency and independence into the heartlands opened by the rails often found themselves at the mercy of powerful distant forces. Many migrants were Russian-Germans driven across the globe by new immigration restrictions imposed by Czar Alexander II that forced them out of Russia. Railroad owners sent American agents loaded with German-language brochures to the steppes of Russia to sell the promise of Kansas and Nebraska to the persecuted Germans. Whole German villages arrived in Galveston bound for Oklahoma and the Plains.

During the 1880s, when unusually high rainfalls produced bumper crops across the Plains, the populations of Kansas and Nebraska increased by 43 percent and 134 percent, respectively. The Dakotas increased their population by 278 percent. These population increases and development helped seven territories become states in the 1880s and 1890s. The possibilities seemed limitless: for a time, production soared and consistent rain seemed to confirm booster claims. Dry years and wildly fluctuating international commodities markets in the late 1880s and throughout the 1890s, however, demonstrated the elusiveness of long-term success. Time revealed that devastating bust cycles were a normal part of western agriculture—if not the economy in general. Droughts in the 1890s baked crops year after year and sparked a long series of agricultural depressions that fueled political unrest.

The Populist movement rose out of the ashes of the arid conditions of the 1890s when farm economies collapsed. Geographically dispersed farmers seeking collective organization faced significant challenges. Farmers united first through social organizations such as the Grange and then political alliances that linked South and West. Encouraged by fiery leaders such as **Mary Elizabeth Lease** to "raise less corn and more hell," farmers formalized their Populist Party at an 1892 convention in Omaha, Nebraska. Lease was representative of the Populists. Born to Irish immigrant parents in Pennsylvania, she moved to Kansas in 1870 to teach, met her husband, and started a family. The couple lost everything in the crash of 1873. They moved to Texas, where Lease joined prohibition and women's suffrage groups, followed by a move back to Kansas, where she gave her energy and powerful voice to the growing Populist Party. Lease became one of the movement's most effective speakers. Critic **William Allen White** thought a woman's place was in the home and labeled her a "harpie" in his famous essay "What's the Matter with Kansas?" Undeterred, "Yellin' Mary Ellen" became a legendary stump speaker before moving to New York to work as a lawyer and lecturer.

The Populist Party "Omaha Platform" advocated socialization of the nation's railroads and other reforms aimed at empowering family farmers in the industrial age. In the long run, agribusiness, industrial ranching, and federal subsidies provided the only consistently successful method for reaping the riches of the Plains.

Mary Elizabeth Lease, " Wall Street Owns the Country" (1890); William Allen White, "What's the Matter with Kansas?" (1896)

Industrial Ranching

U.S. ranching practices evolved from global traditions. From the Iberian Peninsula by way of Mexico came ranching, which incorporated horse culture, open-range grazing, a tradition of competitive contests between workers, and much of the original cattle stock. From the British Isles by way of the Ohio River valley came ranching practices that valued beef and milk over hide and tallow, relying on haymaking to feed cattle in different seasons and highly trained dogs to move herds overland. In Texas and California, these two distinct traditions fused in unique ways, blending different aspects of Hispanic and Anglo practices and adapting innovative strategies to cope with the arid environment of the region. While the Texas ranching industry birthed the iconic figure of the cowboy and the accoutrements of western horse culture, the California beef industry evolved into the corporate agribusiness model of the 20th century.

It was the Spanish who brought cattle to the New World. As early as 1500, Spanish *vaqueros* (cowboys) tended large herds in the Caribbean with the help of African slaves, who contributed knowledge and lasting terminology to the bovine industry. The word *dogie,* cowboy slang for a motherless calf, derives from the Bambara language brought to North America by West African slaves. As Spain's empire spread across the Caribbean and into North and South America, cattle played a central economic role. Some Indian tribes, such as Seminole and Choctaw of the Southeast, adopted cattle raising, and the "Five Civilized Tribes" brought their herds on the Trail of Tears from the Southeast to the Oklahoma territory. In Texas, black and Hispanic cowboys shared their expertise from Africa, South America, and the Caribbean with white cattle workers and European immigrants who took that knowledge into the expanding markets of the West.

Between 1866 and 1884, ranchers shipped over five million Texas cattle north to slaughterhouses. This style of ranching influenced the industry's development in the Southwest and throughout the northern Great Plains into Canada. As the industry expanded, eastern and foreign speculators in land and livestock invested millions of dollars in creating a system of absentee ownership that birthed the "beef bonanza" of the 1880s. But, like bonanza farmers, ranchers went bust at the height of production during a cycle of drought and extreme winters. Ecological devastation caused by overgrazing, brutal winters, and encroachment of farms and the barbed wire fencing invented in 1868 ended the "open-range era."

Corporate Cowboys

Not everyone went bust, however. In 1858, San Francisco businessmen Henry Miller and Charles Lux, immigrants from southwestern Germany, formed Miller & Lux, a corporation that pioneered vertical integration—overseeing the cattle from birth to butcher shop—to the industry. Born into a family of butchers, both men had immigrated to the United States in the 1840s and eventually arrived in San Francisco in the early 1850s following the gold rush. Similar to other industrial firms of the late 19th century, the Miller & Lux corporation reduced investment risks, developed a segmented system of labor, and integrated all aspects of production into a tightly controlled business model. They employed a vast pool of low-wage immigrant workers divided by trade and race. Given their unique understanding of the California landscape and superior equestrian skills, Mexican vaqueros formed the backbone of the skilled labor force as they conducted roundups, brandings, pasturing, and culling of cattle herds. Chinese workers provided domestic labor services, especially as cooks, and southeastern Europeans provided field labor, constructing irrigation works and haying. The company contracted with the Southern Pacific Railroad to provide transportation at a low rate and in exchange gave the railroad a transportation monopoly on its product. This corporate model of ranching allowed control over every aspect of beef production, manipulated the environment to increase production, and formed the model for modern agribusiness in California's Central Valley.

The best-known character of the western story, the cowboy, was on the stage for only a short time and looked little like the image popularized by literature and later movies. A more unlikely hero than the cowboy is hard to imagine. Cowboys were laborers who worked long and hard and earned little. They spent their days and nights in filthy primitive conditions with dangerously unpredictable animals and often died unromantically on the job. Most cowboys were white laborers from Texas or Louisiana, but at least a third were African American, Mexican, or Indian. Cattle drives featured

Frederic Remington, "Arizona cowboy" (1901)

a potent brew of racial prejudice and rivalry that contributed to difficult working conditions and violence. The cowboy period of long summer cattle drives on the open range lasted less than 20 years before the onslaught of migrants, barbed wire, cities, and government regulation and systematic distribution of land ended it.

Frontier hardships were reimagined with the advent of the rodeo. Turn-of-the-century rodeos featured the skill and spectacle of the ranch hand. Real cowboys such as Bill Pickett, an African American ranch hand, entertained thousands with their "bull-dogging" feats. Hispanic vaqueros competed in the *charreada*, a highly costumed and stylized performance, whereas Indians developed their own version of the rodeo on reservations, incorporating their own spiritual beliefs. The struggles of the cattle business and its workers became part of the mythology of the West while the complicated history faded.

STUDY QUESTIONS FOR EXTRACTIVE ECONOMIES AND GLOBAL COMMODITIES

1. What global trends shaped the development of the extractive economy of the West?

2. How did the myth of the cowboy contrast with the life of cattle workers?

quiz

⊘ CLEARING THE LAND AND CLEANSING THE WILDERNESS

After a five-day fight, the exhausted Indians agreed to surrender. There were only 430 left after a remarkable 1,500-mile running battle throughout Montana. The leader of the remaining Nez Perce, Chief Joseph, captured the tragic spirit of the moment. "I am tired of fighting," he told his captors. "It is cold and we have no blankets. The little children are freezing to death. I want to have time to look for my children. . . . Maybe I shall find them among the dead. I will fight no more forever."

Continental empire building in the West between 1877 and 1900 was more than the adventure of imagined cowboy heroes or a convenient final act for Wild West shows. Dreams of material wealth and the lure of "free" land pulled millions of immigrants from across the globe to the region. Environmental challenges demonstrated the perils of hasty government policies and dashed many settlers' dreams. In the years to come the shocking environmental consequences of the extractive economy spurred a conservation movement and led to the creation of the world's first national park. During the same period, new efforts to refashion Indian policy resulted in the greatest injustices of the age.

The land in the West was not "virgin"; nor was it empty. It was not the *tabula rasa* that promoters led migrants to believe. Early explorers, trappers, and gold seekers traveled through extensive regions of Indian lands stretching from the Canadian border in the North to Mexico in the South. Set aside for hundreds of different Indian tribes removed from their ancestral lands in the East and South, this swath of territory stood squarely in the path of national, corporate, and individual goals after the

Civil War. By 1877, pioneer trails, settlements, and the Transcontinental Railroad had penetrated fragile tribal borders. New migrants encountered a cultural and environmental landscape created by cycles of violence and shifting alliances that challenged the simple borderlines on their maps.

Transportation corridors tightly linked the West to the industrializing world. Changing perceptions of the "Great American Desert" of the Plains and Southwest combined with the Homestead and Desert Land acts and discoveries of gold to make Indian lands, once thought worthless, appealing. For Indians, dire consequences followed the ever-rising tide of people flowing into and through their lands.

The "Indian Wars," well underway by the close of Reconstruction, expanded as the military moved out of the South and reinforcements moved quickly into the West. The military in the West was small and ethnically diverse—in essence, a police force enforcing ethnic apartheid in the region. These wars rarely involved large battles but featured protracted guerrilla warfare as Indians fought with and against U.S. troops and rival tribes. In June 1876, the Battle of Little Big Horn, where Custer and the 7th Cavalry fell to Oglala Sioux leader Crazy Horse and Sitting Bull of the Hunkpapa Sioux, was a rare victory for Indians pressured by accelerating U.S. expansion. In the decisive year of 1877 following Custer's instantly mythologized "last stand," Crazy Horse surrendered and was executed at Fort Robinson, Nebraska. Later that same year, after an epic 1,500-mile journey, Nez Perce resistance leader Chief Joseph surrendered to General Oliver Howard. Finally, Congress, repealing the Fort Laramie Treaty, took the Black Hills from the Lakota and opened the region for gold seekers and land speculators. This quick series of military actions set the stage for a civilian invasion of Indian lands and a century-long reconsideration of the best use of this newly secured territory.

Final words of Crazy Horse (1877); the surrender of Chief Joseph as reported by *Harper's Weekly*

Conflict and Resistance

In the 1880s and 1890s, military action and federal legislation in tandem with cultural and economic forces erased established Indian territorial lines drawn under the Fort Laramie Treaty and thus drastically reduced the amount of Indian-controlled land and isolated Indians against their will on small scattered reservations.

The visible boundaries of Indian lands could still be mapped in the late 1870s, but they remained contested regions. The lines on maps provided only an illusion of geographic organization during a time of shifting borders, tribal movements and alliances, and disastrous government policies. In 1869, newly elected president Ulysses S. Grant, concerned by public criticism of the corrupt Department of Indian Affairs, met with a coalition of Christian leaders who urged him to adopt a peaceful Indian policy based on Christianity. Weary of war, the president replied, "Gentlemen, your advice is good. Let us have peace."

The landmark Indian Appropriations Act of April 10, 1869, authorized the president to appoint a commission to "exercise joint control with the Secretary of the Interior" over Indian appropriations. Grant chose a personal friend, General Ely Samuel Parker, a Tonowanda-Seneca member, as the first chair of the Board of Indian Commissioners. Under Parker's leadership, the board initiated what became known as the "**Peace Policy**." Between 1869 and 1876, however, competing goals made peace impossible to achieve. The Indian commissioners and leaders of various Christian denominations provided Indians with food and clothing in exchange for promises to abandon cultural traditions and to assimilate into American society. Simultaneously, Indians were pushed, often under direct military threat, to move to increasingly smaller reservations on land considered unsuitable for migrant settlement or industry. By the 1880s, the U.S. government acknowledged that the only Indian territory left was that on rapidly shrinking reservations. At the same time, and with strong public support, the U.S. military waged constant war with the same people that Indian commissioners and the U.S. Department of the Interior were working to assimilate (Map 16.4). General Philip Sheridan infamously captured the contradictions of the Peace Policy when he remarked, after an introduction to a Comanche chief, "The only good Indians I ever saw were dead." More insightfully he also said, "A reservation is a piece of land occupied by Indians and surrounded by thieves."

Born out of concern with fraud and abuse by Indian agents, the Peace Policy neither promoted peace nor stemmed the "rot of corruption" that tainted the Grant administration. The mission to Christianize the Indians, however, continued to play a central role in U.S. Indian policy through the early 1930s, when an "Indian New Deal" inaugurated a new era of reform.

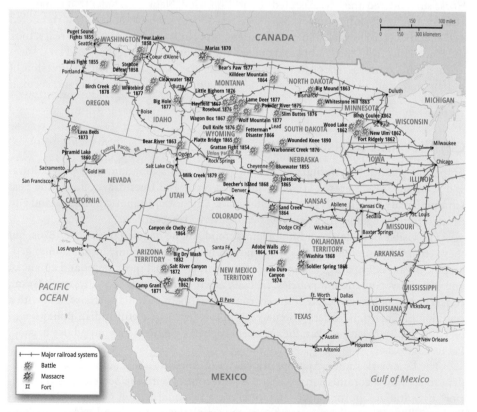

map
analysis

MAP 16.4 Indian Battles and Railroad Lines Conflict between Indians and immigrants preceded the advance of the railroads, but this new technology accelerated conflict, facilitated military and commodity transport, and helped hasten the near extinction of the buffalo.

Education for Assimilation

Of the disputes that defined the Peace Policy era, none was—and remains—more controversial than Indian education. The idea was simple. Take children away from their "ignorant" parents and "backward" communities and train them to be Americans who cherish individualism and republicanism over tribal life. Reformers, convinced that "the time for fighting was passed," called for an "army of Christian school teachers" to lead Indian children from "barbarism" toward civilization and salvation.

In 1870, Congress supported assimilation with a $100,000 appropriation to establish federal industrial schools mainly on existing reservations. These early efforts often failed because Indian parents resented efforts to dismantle their cultures through their children and because students simply ran away. Administrators, replacing reservation-based day schools with remote boarding schools, separated children from their parents. Industrial education for Indians drew support from the notions of **social Darwinism** and from the efforts of pragmatic reformers in the American South such as Samuel Armstrong, founder of the Hampton Institute in Virginia. Armstrong had advocated the development of trade skills as a mechanism for gradual assimilation of freed slaves. In 1879, 84 Lakota children became the first students at the Carlisle, Pennsylvania, Indian Training School. Their education there marked the beginning of a generation-long effort to assimilate Indian children coercively in 81 schools from Carlisle to Riverside, California. Carlisle School founder **Richard Henry Pratt** studied the Hampton model as he developed his ideas for an Indian school system.

The story of Indian education is complicated. Students sometimes went willingly to the boarding schools for personal reasons or as an escape from the humiliation and privation of the reservation. Other students were lured with vague promises of exciting trips. Some parents willingly signed over their children hoping that education promised them a better life. Others signed without realizing their children would be sent far away for extended periods. The Indian children bore the most painful burden as they left their families for the military-like routines of boarding school. Many years later, **Plenty Kill**, a Lakota Sioux, remembered a "sad scene" as Indian children said goodbye to their parents. Separation from their parents was the first step in a process that isolated Indian children from their culture and traditions. At the schools, teachers gave children new names and clothes: uniforms for boys and long dresses for girls. The setting, lifestyle, and curriculum were designed to teach Indian children to conform to the ways of the white world. At Carlisle, Pratt told arriving students and visitors that he would "kill the Indian to save the man."

 Gertrude Simmons Bonnin/ Zitkala-Sa, excerpt from " School Days of an Indian Girl" (1900)

By 1900, the U.S. government had spent $2,936,080 on Indian boarding schools. Between 1877 and 1900, enrollment increased from 3,598 to 21,568 students, or 50 percent of school-age Indian children. Despite these numbers, the assimilation-through-education experiment failed to destroy Indian culture. Indian schools created a generation of students who returned home as agents of cultural change with valuable knowledge of the workings of the white world and a new awareness of collective Indian identity that fostered a more united Indian civil rights front. Others, "too white to be red, too red to be white," left the schools with no real cultural identity and little chance for success in either world.

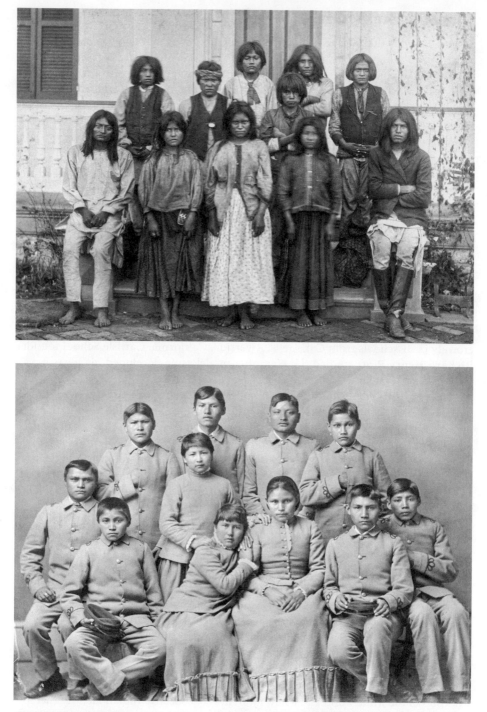

CHIRICAHUA APACHES Both of these photographs of Chiricahua Apaches—on arrival at the Carlisle Indian School and after "training," captured in 1886—are obviously carefully composed images. What is the message they are meant to convey?

The Destruction of the Buffalo

In the United States, the destruction of the buffalo changed ecologies and economies. Alongside government policies for war or peace, and education or removal, a contest over animals and land use greatly influenced changes in traditional tribal life for the Plains Indians. Economic and environmental forces, linked with changing perceptions of the natural world, undermined the ability of Indians to use natural resources that had supported them abundantly for thousands of years.

On the plains of the 1870s open-range cattle drives, an expanding web of rail lines, hunting, environmental factors, and politics contributed to a rapid decline of the once vast herds of American buffalo. For the Plains Indians, buffalo provided food and shelter, dictated tribal migration patterns, was a vital trade commodity, shaped diplomatic relations between tribes, and played a central role in culture and religion. For millennia more than 24 million buffalo had migrated seasonally throughout the plains and valleys west of the Missouri River. In the 1840s, the ability to use horses and steel to harvest the buffalo helped the Comanche forge an unprecedented empire covering six U.S. states and several Mexican *estados* in the 1840s. Between the 1830s and 1870s, however, the herds that had moved "over the land like the shadows of scudding clouds" began a dramatic decline toward near extinction.

The decline of buffalo began before the Civil War when Indians and whites observed significant declines in numbers, especially on the northern Plains. Observers also noted starvation and new migration patterns among Indian peoples of the upper

MOUNTAIN OF BUFFALO SKULLS, 1880 This iconic image of slaughter helps convey some sense of the scale of the buffalo hunts that nearly wiped out the species.

Settler Societies and Indigenous Peoples

The experience of Indians in the United States was not an isolated phenomenon in the treatment of Native peoples. Canadians used similar education programs to assimilate their "First Nations," and Australian officials attempted assimilation through education before resorting to more violent measures. In geographically isolated Australia, for example, expansion into lands occupied by Indigenous peoples shared key characteristics with the American experience. Occupation by newcomers required conquest. Similar to the American West, in Australia there was an explicit desire by state authorities to dominate Aboriginal peoples and redistribute their lands to leading-edge entrepreneurs, capitalists, and migrating settlers. In both places, virgin soil epidemics—before the onslaught of significant waves of settlers—did much of the early damage to lives of the Indigenous peoples as they disrupted cultural patterns and caused strife among the tribes. And, in Australia under British rule and in the West during the 19th century, distant governments and their local representatives used questionable diplomacy or outright military force to undermine Indian and Aboriginal peoples' ability to survive. American Indian policy was brutally pragmatic but always hotly debated, with significant voices of dissent. The British in Australia were even less idealistic than Americans in their dealings with Indigenous tribes. After limited efforts to negotiate with the widely dispersed Aboriginal tribes, the British simply gave up and declared the area *terra nullius*, or empty land.

Both of these regions featured strikingly similar arid ecosystems that offered few real opportunities for unsupported individuals to thrive with or without Indigenous peoples. Successful ranches in both regions operated on corporate models supported by elaborate government-funded irrigation and transportation projects along with direct subsidies. Even large industrial endeavors such as mining required state military support to open and secure lands occupied by Indians or Aboriginals. The transfer and destruction of species also played a central role in the settler societies of the West and Australia. Species removal and addition undermined the ability of the Indigenous peoples to live in traditional ways. Cattle and sheep in Australia and New Zealand transformed

Plains. Lakota, Cheyenne, Kiowa, and Arapahoe suffered greatly from declining buffalo populations in the 1840s and 1850s. The demise of the buffalo herds in the decades before the Civil War was universally attributed to the activities of migrants who hunted the animals for food and sport and forced buffalo from the grazing grounds of their cattle. General William Tecumseh Sherman echoed common perceptions that in the contest for grass, cattle beat buffalo and cowboys beat Indians. For him, replacing "the wild buffaloes by more numerous herds of tame cattle, and . . . substituting for the useless Indians the intelligent owners of productive farms and cattle ranches" was a logical and desirable frontier process. Cattle drives and ranching, overland migration, and depletion of resources contributed to the decline of the buffalo, but hunting and a short-lived but expansive market for buffalo hides was even more significant.

environments and economies just as replacement of the buffalo with cattle altered the American West. In Australia, devastation of entire regions by plagues of European wild rabbits and exotic species undermined thousands of years of careful land practices by the Aboriginal people.

Settlers and Aboriginals in South Australia, ca. 1850

Dislocation of one group of Indigenous people was sometimes spurred by the migration of other groups that had been pushed out of traditional homelands by circumstance or force. Poland offers one interesting example. During the years between the end of the Civil War and the start of World War I, a multitude of immigrants made their way from Poland to the United States. In the 19th century, Poland was a country defined by contested internal and external borderland regions, transnational cultural exchange, and rapidly shifting patterns of migration. As in the West, internal ethnic struggles tied to national politics and external economic and political pressures drove the movement of people.

Situated in the "heart of Europe," Poland weathered many centuries of territorial struggles, international tensions over conflicting claims of regional control, and profound conflict over the rights of Jews in particular. Polish Jews maintained their own language and culture within the shifting Polish state. Like Indians and Aboriginals, they negotiated a tenuous autonomy with governments divided over their place in Poland's future and with a Christian population that mostly feared and hated them. Between the 1850s and 1914, the Polish state worked to assimilate Jews with the hope that they might abandon the cultural and linguistic traditions that made them distinct and placed them in the way of evolving notions of Polish national *spoleczenstwo* (society) and progress. These pressures caused Polish Jews to struggle to maintain their identity in their traditional homeland and forced many to choose migration across the Atlantic to new frontiers like the American West.

- How does the Aboriginal experience with the British enrich our understanding of American Indian history?
- Given the similarities between global settler societies and Indigenous experiences, does the American frontier process seem exceptional?

The decimation of the great buffalo herds began with Indians caught in a convergence of ecological, political, and economic change. In the decades before the Civil War, some Plains tribes resolved old tensions and forged new alliances to cope with migrant encroachment on tribal lands. Indians were simply not caught up in global changes in land use facilitated by the Industrial Revolution; they were also, as they had always been, agents of environmental change. Between 1840 and 1870, facing increasing waves of migration and infiltration of their hunting grounds, Indians participated in the growing hide trade while maintaining traditional hunting practices. The interplay of migrant intrusion, tempting market forces, U.S. Army aggression, and new Indian alliances that freed time and resources for hunting contributed to the buffalo's decline.

For buffalo-hunting Indians, the true crisis came in the 1860s and 1870s when the Transcontinental Railroad enabled mass hunting and an international hide trade. Mechanizing industries used leather hides for machine belts. High demand caused shortages. Factory owners imported tanned hides from South America but longed for a cheaper substitute. Entrepreneurs, developing new methods for tanning buffalo hides, created a better product at less cost. Buffalo hunters then followed the rails, and new train lines carried the hides to the factories of the East.

Buffalo hide yard, Dodge City, Kansas (1878)

Legendary hunters such as Buffalo Bill were credited with killing a thousand animals a day. Though the numbers were often exaggerated, between 1865 and 1883, hide hunters did kill vast numbers of buffalo and pushed the already declining buffalo population to the edge of extinction. Hunters, killing from slowly moving trains with high-powered rifles, skinned the animals and left their huge bodies to rot. Military leaders, understanding that the destruction of the buffalo crippled Indians who depended on them, encouraged the slaughter. "If I could learn that every Buffalo in the northern herd were killed," General Sheridan proclaimed in 1881, "I would be glad." Sheridan almost got his wish. Migrants passing over trails in the 1880s remarked on the vast fields of bleached bones, piles of skulls, and displays of heads and hides—grisly evidence of the systematic slaughter of a species. Congress belatedly commemorated the iconic herds by coining a "buffalo nickel" in 1913, with an image of an American Indian on the reverse. Millions of these tiny tributes changed hands until the 1960s.

The Dawes Act and Survival

In 1887, Congress passed the **Dawes Act**, or **General Allotment Act**, yet another new phase in federal Indian policy. The Dawes Act, dividing reservation land into individual parcels, turned tribal land into individual pieces of property. Reformers hoped that the act would protect Indians against fraud and land grabbers better than the reservation system had and would enable Indians, too, to enjoy the Jeffersonian yeoman dream that drew so many migrants to the West. For supporters like Teddy Roosevelt, the Dawes Act served as a "mighty pulverizing engine to break up the tribal mass," to the benefit of the individual Indian. The act also granted Indians U.S. citizenship and offered Indians greater protections from U.S. courts.

Like all of the Indian policies of the 19th century, allotment was the product of reformers' hopes and Indian haters' prejudice. Regardless of motive, the results for Indians were disastrous. Like Indian education, allotment sought to assimilate Indians into broader society through direct intervention in daily tribal life and culture. The reservation system was hated by most Indians, but allotment proved much more insidious. Between the passage of the act in 1887 and its repeal in 1934, American Indians lost two-thirds of their remaining lands, or more than 90 million acres. The division of the reservations into thousands of individual holdings made large-scale fraud and legal sales of tribal lands not harder, but easier, and the solid blocks of reservation became a mind-boggling checkerboard of vulnerable dispersed lands. Allotment created a complicated map that has vexed courts and putative Indian landowners to the present. Contrary to the optimistic hopes of reformers, sustainable Indian farming and self-sufficiency declined after 1887. Indian farmers and ranchers faced the same unforgiving environmental challenges as did all residents of the region.

Disillusioned by the confluence of failed government policies, ecological catastrophe, cultural collapse, and the erosion of tribal sovereignty, some Indians turned to the **Ghost Dance** religion led by Paiute prophet Wovoka. The divestment of Indian lands through allotment fueled the movement. Ghost dancers wore distinctive white costumes, and the mystery surrounding the religion and the dancers' beliefs about achieving a deathlike state of grace gave the movement its popular name. Although Wovoka envisioned a peaceful coexistence of Indians and whites, Lakota Ghost Dance followers, such as Sitting Bull and Kicking Bear, rejected that vision and insisted instead that violence remained the only option for Indians. Some Sioux Ghost Dancers believed that if they united in violent uprising, they would spark an apocalypse that would raise the dead and restore the land and animals. The number of Ghost Dancers was small, but enough participated to raise concern with the Office of Indian Affairs, which outlawed the religion in 1890, and with the military, which strengthened positions on the northern Plains.

On December 15, 1890, soldiers killed Sitting Bull during a raid on his Standing Rock cabin. Troops with the U.S. 7th Cavalry then followed Minneconjou Ghost Dancers and their leader Big Foot to Wounded Knee, South Dakota, where they met up with Chiefs Short Bull and Kicking Bear. On the morning of December 28, soldiers surrounded the dancers. After a brief confrontation with a medicine man named Yellow Bird, a shot rang out and the soldiers—opening fire with light artillery—killed between 150 and 300 Indian men, women, and children.

In 1893, only two years after the killing of Lakota Ghost Dancers and their families, the U.S. government attempted to rewrite the tragic history of government treatment of Indians into a story of success. At the World Columbian Exposition in Chicago, commemorating the 400th anniversary of Columbus's arrival in the Western Hemisphere, the fair celebrated "A Century of Progress." Half of the U.S. government buildings featured American Indian exhibits with a special emphasis on federal Indian education and assimilation programs. Near the government pavilion a Smithsonian Institution exhibit presented careful reconstructions of traditional Indian cultures. Representatives of Pueblo, Navajo, Sioux, Apache, and Nez Perce traveled to Chicago to participate in the Smithsonian exhibits. Chicago fairgoers saw in these exhibits the ambivalence toward Indians that had characterized the period. Indians were feared and revered; their passing to a new stage of history was hailed and lamented. Indians displayed themselves as culturally viable members of tribes with a past and future next to exhibits that portrayed them as something akin to natural artifacts.

Tourism, Parks, and Forests

The perceived closing of the frontier and unprecedented conquest of the environment between 1877 and 1900 caused anxiety about the depletion of resources and destruction of natural wonders. As Americans saw their manifest destiny of a transcontinental empire achieved, frontier nostalgia shaped culture and policy. The need to protect remnants of the frontier gained national attention as early as the 1870s. Eastern and European travelers, lured to the exotic Wild West by writers such as Mark Twain and artists such as Thomas Moran and Albert Bierstadt, found natural wonders but also graphic evidence of human impact. Even from train windows, tourists viewed mountains of buffalo skeletons; denuded forests; toxic mining waste and blasted landscapes; and trails of discarded possessions, tin cans, and trash.

interactive timeline

TIMELINE 1868–1900

AMERICA	YEAR	THE WORLD
Apr Treaty of Fort Laramie creates Great Sioux Reservation in Black Hills	**1864–1868**	Chinese floods, famine, and Opium Wars push millions to seek opportunity in North America Canadian Pacific Railroad cuts across vast swaths of First Nations territory
May Transcontinental Railroad Central Pacific and Union Pacific lines meet in Utah **Apr** Indian Appropriations Act signed; "Peace Policy" begins **May** John Wesley Powell launches a series of surveys of the Colorado River	**1869**	
	1870	Ninety-four British companies register to invest and mine ore in the American West
Mar Yellowstone is designated America's first national park	**1872**	
Aug Custer Expedition discovers gold in Black Hills of Dakota	**1874**	
J. W. Powell publishes *The Exploration of the Colorado River*	**1875**	
Jun Battle of Little Big Horn	**1876**	U.S. railroads send agents throughout Europe promising "free land" to immigrants
Feb Congress repeals Fort Laramie Treaty taking the Black Hills from the Lakota **Mar** Congress passes Desert Land Act allowing for purchases of up to 640 acres in arid regions **Sep** Crazy Horse killed after surrendering at Fort Robinson, Nebraska **Oct** Nez Perce resistance leader Chief Joseph surrenders	**1877**	
Mar Jack Johnson, boxer, born to two former slaves in Galveston, Texas J. W. Powell's *Report on the Lands of the Arid Region* published 40,000 Exodusters migrate to Kansas	**1878**	
Mar Congress creates United States Geological Survey **Oct** 84 Lakota children enrolled at the Carlisle, Pennsylvania, Indian Training School	**1879**	
Oct "Hop Alley" violence against Chinese	**1880**	**Nov** Chinese Exclusion Treaty restricts Chinese immigration and citizenship Ferrocarril Nacional Mexicano, the Mexican National Railroad, incorporated in Colorado with agreement with Rio Grande Company

In the mid-19th century, publicity about the "discovery" of the Yosemite valley and several nearby groves of giant Sequoia trees prompted the first western tourist rush. Early entrepreneurs, spurring demand for private enterprises to transport, house, and guide tourists through the area for profit, promoted Yosemite. Recognizing the area's unique scenery and tourism potential, Congress reserved the land for public use. Yellowstone in the northwest corner of the Wyoming territory became America's first official "national park" on March 1, 1872, when President Ulysses S. Grant signed an act designating over 2.2 million acres of geological wonders as a "pleasuring ground for the benefit and enjoyment of the people."

AMERICA	YEAR	THE WORLD
	1882	**May** Chinese Exclusion Act halts Chinese immigration
Summer American buffalo near extinction after last mass hunt on northern Plains Buffalo Bill stages his first Wild West Show	**1883**	
Feb Roosevelt moves to his Dakota cattle ranch	**1884**	
Sep 51 Chinese miners killed during race riots in Rock Springs, Wyoming Buffalo Bill invited to tour England, perform for Queen Victoria and world leaders across Europe	**1885–1886**	Gold discoveries lead to Witwatersrand global rush in South Africa
Feb Dawes/General Allotment Act breaks up Indian reservations	**1887**	**Jun** Buffalo Bill's Wild West Show plays to Queen Victoria in London
Mar Blizzards and cold decimate cattle herds across the Great Plains	**1888**	
Jun Frederick Jackson Turner argues frontier is "closed" **Dec** Sitting Bull killed **Dec** Lakota Ghost Dancers murdered at Wounded Knee, South Dakota	**1890**	
Mar Forest Reserve Act enacted, giving the president authority to remove forested lands from public domain and protect them from exploitation	**1891**	
May Sierra Club founded with John Muir as first president	**1892**	
May Western Federation of Miners (WFM) founded **May** World Columbian Exposition opens in Chicago	**1893**	
	1897	London company sends American engineer and future president Herbert Hoover to Australia gold fields
Sep Storm destroys Galveston, Texas, killing 8,000	**1900**	

The presence of Indians in both parks complicated the global image of Yellowstone and Yosemite as virgin examples of western wilderness. Nez Perce and other northern tribes had moved through, lived in, and modified the Yellowstone region for centuries. In the 1870s, battles between Nez Perce Chief Joseph and General Sherman brought attention to the region. Following the well-publicized battles, park administrators launched a campaign to control and then systematically remove Indians from Yellowstone. Beyond military concerns, officials worried that fears of Indian attack might affect the growing tourist trade. Moreover, the perception of Yellowstone as pristine wilderness left no place for Indians. By 1900, the government had removed Indians

THE GRAND CANYON OF THE YELLOWSTONE (1872, OIL ON CANVAS)   Thomas Moran's painting so inspired viewers that it helped encourage the creation of the first national park. Moran said that he "did not wish to realize the scene literally but to preserve and convey its true impression." The 19th-century viewers were impressed with the romance of an imagined pristine wilderness.

not only from the park but also from the history of the place. Advocates for preservation also failed to recognize the importance of these places for local economies. Generations of working-class ranchers, timbermen, farmers, and miners asked tough questions about who should decide the best use of natural places.

Fitz Hugh Ludlow's impressions of Yosemite (1864)

In the spectacular Yosemite valley of California's Sierras, the Ahwahneechee tribe lived for centuries before the first expeditions "found" this icon of exceptional American nature. The first white visitors closely linked the Ahwahneechee and their village culture with the astounding geological wonders of the "Incomparable Valley." With no significant military conflict with the Indians of the Sierra, military leaders and later the National Park Service "naturalized" the Indians and incorporated them into the park. Brochures described the Ahwahneechee to tourists as quaint natural features to be admired along with bears and waterfalls. As the national parks evolved in the 20th century, Indians were removed or displayed according to the demands of the western tourist industry.

While the government worked out environmental policies in the parks and forests, a wave of grassroots environmental concern ignited a popular preservation movement. Naturalist **John Muir** formalized the movement with the founding of the Sierra Club in 1892. The Sierra Club was an example of growing national concern for the intrinsic value of nature. Inspired by transcendentalist authors such as Walt Whitman and Henry David Thoreau, preservationists advocated the permanent protection of wilderness for its own sake. Their efforts bolstered the utilitarian arguments for conservation expressed by concerned observers such as Theodore Roosevelt and scientists such as **Gifford Pinchot**. Roosevelt and other conservationists worried about the wanton waste of resources and especially forests intentionally burned to destroy Indian refuges or to further the charcoal trade and construction of mines. Industrial timber harvesting, which was reducing American forests at astounding rates, created support for government regulation of this vital national resource. The Forest Reserve Act of 1891 gave the U.S. president authority to remove forested lands from the public domain and protect them from exploitation. This law brought millions of acres under federal protection during the 1890s and early 20th century.

Gifford Pinchot traveled to France and Germany to learn the techniques of scientific forestry. He returned with a vision for the "wise use" of natural resources for "the greatest good to the greatest number for the longest time." America's first professionally trained forester, Pinchot enforced the Appropriations Act first as a member of the National Forest Commission and then as head of the U.S. Division of Forestry. In the early 1900s, he worked with Theodore Roosevelt to dramatically expand the land management role of the federal government. In the space of only three decades, the West had developed to the extent that many believed government protection was the only way to avoid wholesale destruction of the region. The collective realization that the seemingly unlimited resources of the West were finite marked a critical juncture in American history.

STUDY QUESTIONS FOR CLEARING THE LAND AND CLEANSING THE WILDERNESS

1. How did environmental factors contribute to U.S. Indian policy?
2. What did Indian reformers intend to accomplish through their policies? To what degree did they succeed? How did Indians respond?

quiz

Summary

- With the end of the Civil War and completion of the Transcontinental Railroad, American attention turned to the West.
- The federal government created new agencies and sponsored surveys that completed the map of the West and highlighted new opportunities but raised new concerns.
- The Homestead Act and land granted to railroads sparked a new wave of migration.
- Ideas of American exceptionalism shaped government policies and created a powerful myth of the American West throughout the world.
- Indians struggled to retain tribal lands and cultural autonomy in the face of immigrant onslaught, military action, and misguided U.S. reform policies.
- The near extinction of the American buffalo undermined Indian economies and demonstrated the extent of the environmental impact of settlement.
- New technologies collapsed time and space to enable the industrialization of the western extractive economy.
- A highly mobile multicultural workforce labored in a rapidly changing regional economy and was linked to the ups and downs of world markets.
- Ethnic and class tensions fueled a culture of violence.
- The speed and extent of land use in the West inspired grassroots and federal environmental preservation efforts.

Key Terms and People

Chinese Exclusion Act 548

Cody, William "Buffalo Bill" 551

copper borderlands 541

Dawes Act (General Allotment Act) 568

Desert Land Act 550

Exodusters 544

Ghost dance 569

Haywood, "Big" Bill 555

Homestead Act 550

Hoover, Herbert 556

instant cities 543

Johnson, Jack 542

Lease, Mary Elizabeth 558

Muir, John 572

Peace Policy 561

Pinchot, Gifford 572

Plenty Kill 563

Powell, John Wesley 548

Pratt, Richard Henry 563

settler societies 545

social Darwinism 563

White, William Allen 558

Reviewing Chapter 16

1. Where was the West? West of where? When was the West? Did this region have a beginning and an end in time and space?

2. What role did misperceptions about regional environment and culture play in the conflicts that characterized the history of the nation as it moved to consolidate modern borders?

3. What role did the federal government play in the consolidation of the American West?

Further Reading

DeLay, Brian. *War of a Thousand Deserts: Indian Raids and the U.S.-Mexican War.* New Haven, CT: Yale University Press, 2008. Remarkable new perspective on the role of Indian nations and the Mexican War and the creation of the transnational borderlands.

Fixico, Donald L. *Indian Resilience and Rebuilding: Indigenous Nations in the Modern American West.* Tucson: University of Arizona Press, 2013. Excellent study of Indians in the modern West.

Hine, Robert, and John Mack Faragher. *The American West: A New Interpretive History.* New Haven, CT: Yale University Press, 2000. This volume explores in depth and detail a range of issues covered in this chapter.

Hyde, Anne F. *Empires, Nations, and Families: A New History of the North American West, 1800–1860.* Lincoln: University of Nebraska Press, 2012. Remarkably detailed perspective of the people and processes of early western settlement.

Igler, David. *Industrial Cowboys: Miller & Lux and the Transformation of the Far West, 1850–1920.* Berkeley: University of California Press, 2001. Insightful analysis of western industry.

Isenberg, Andrew C. *The Destruction of the Bison: An Environmental History, 1750–1920.* Cambridge, UK: Cambridge University Press, 2000. A riveting account of the near extinction of the bellwether species of the American West.

Truett, Samuel. *Fugitive Landscapes: The Forgotten History of the U.S.-Mexico Borderlands.* New Haven, CT: Yale University Press, 2006. Fascinating account of the complicated environmental, cultural, and economic relations of the transnational borderlands.

Warren, Louis S. *Buffalo Bill's America: William Cody and the Wild West Show.* New York: Vintage, 2005. The embodiment of the myth of the West placed in context and captured in great detail.

White, Richard. *Railroaded: The Transcontinentals and the Making of Modern America.* New York: W. W. Norton, 2011. A darkly insightful new analysis of an often mythologized critical moment in American history.

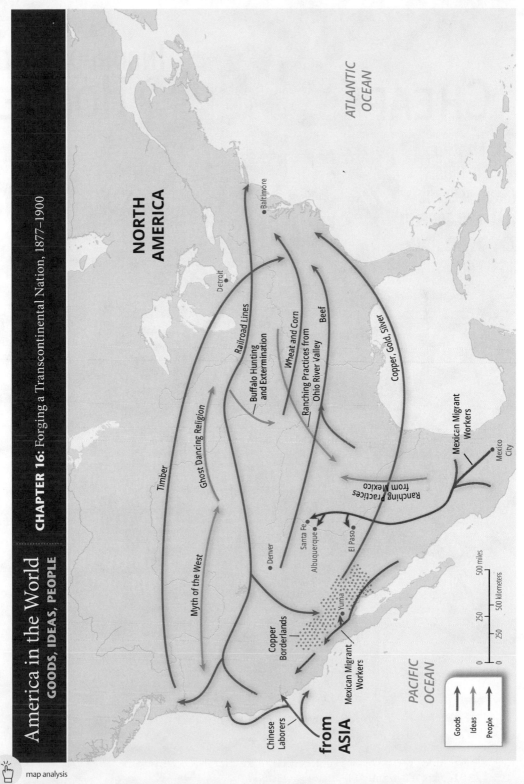

America in the World
GOODS, IDEAS, PEOPLE

CHAPTER 16: Forging a Transcontinental Nation, 1877–1900

NORTH
AMERICA

ATLANTIC
OCEAN

• Baltimore

• Detroit

Railroad Lines

Buffalo Hunting
and Extermination

Wheat and Corn

Beef

Copper, Gold, Silver

Ghost Dancing Religion

Timber

Myth of the West

Ranching Practices from
Ohio River Valley

Ranching Practices
from Mexico

Mexican Migrant
Workers

• Mexico
  City

• Denver

Santa Fe •
Albuquerque •

El Paso •

Copper
Borderlands

Yuma •

Mexican Migrant
Workers

PACIFIC
OCEAN

Chinese
Laborers

**from
ASIA**

0   250   500 miles

0   250   500 kilometers

Goods
Ideas
People

map analysis

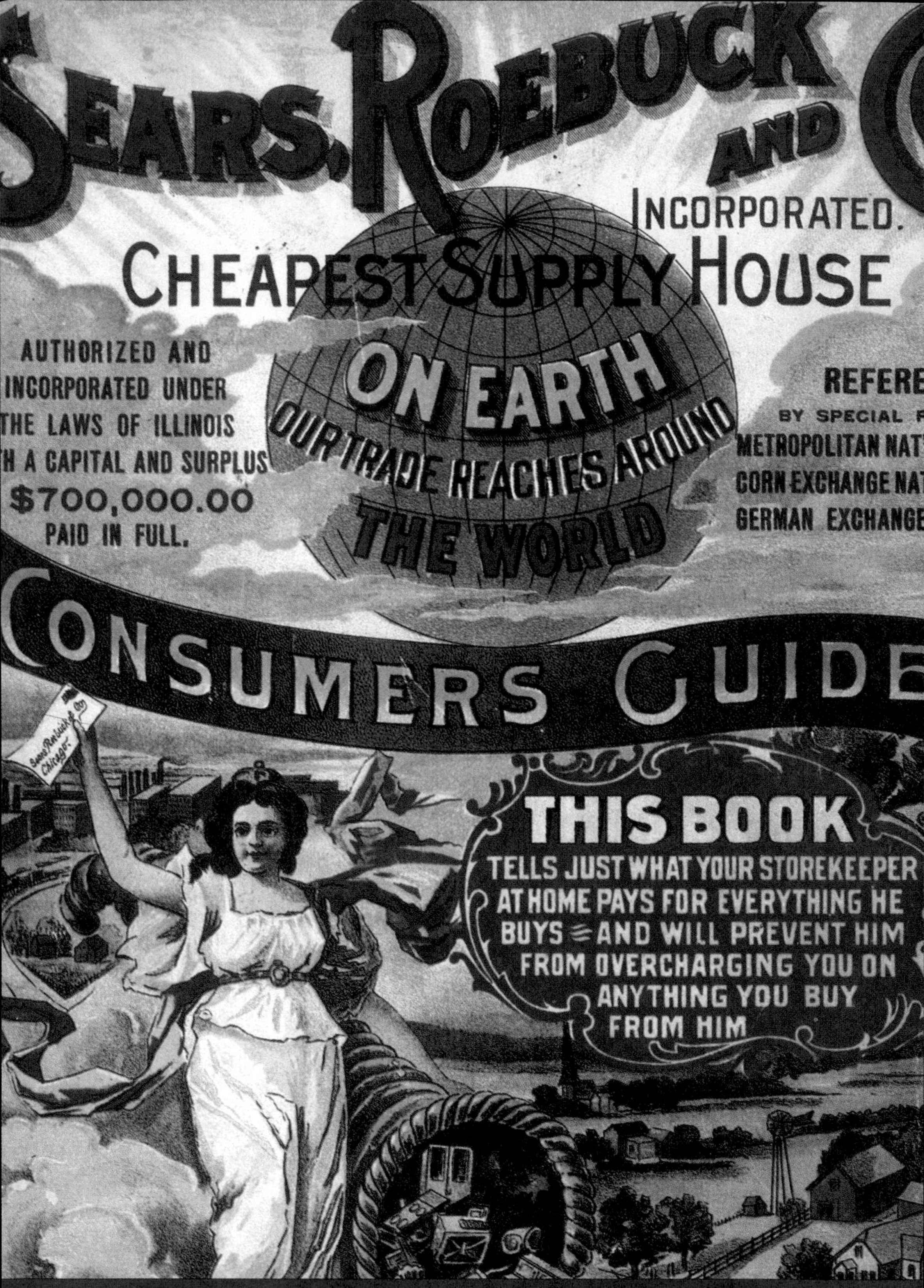

Sears catalogue cover, 1899.

A New Industrial and Labor Order

1877–1900

I n 1903, Englishman Arthur Shadwell traveled to Pittsburgh, the steel manufacturing center of the United States. Although familiar with Europe's industrialization, Shadwell was shocked by what he encountered. "Grime and squalor unspeakable, unlimited hours of work, ferocious contests between labour and capital, the fiercest commercial scrambling for the money literally sweated out of the people." All of these traits, Shadwell noted, had once defined Great Britain as it spearheaded industrialization. Now the United States found itself "Europeanized" to the extreme. Pittsburgh, he believed, was worse than any of its European counterparts.

Homestead, located outside of Pittsburgh, was especially horrific. "If Pittsburgh is hell with the lid off," Shadwell exclaimed, "Homestead is hell with the hatches on." The site of magnate **Andrew Carnegie**'s massive steel works, Homestead "is nothing but unrelieved gloom and grind," where "men sweat out the furnaces and rolling mills twelve hours a day for seven days a week" and live in "rows of wretched hovels where they eat and sleep, having neither time nor energy for anything else." Attempts by workers to unionize to better their condition had "been put down with an iron hand dipped in blood."

To Shadwell, the Pittsburgh-area steel mills signified the ruthless drive of America's industrialists, their "unswerving devotion to money making relentlessly pursued." Accumulating unprecedented riches, they had "fattened on other men's brains and sweat." Carnegie's multimillion-dollar fortune, he asserted, "carries a taint to it."

As Shadwell observed, the United States changed dramatically in the last quarter of the 19th century. Between 1870 and 1905 the nation's economy quadrupled in size. Living standards doubled as wages increased and Americans had access to more and cheaper goods than at any time in human history. Philosopher John Dewey exclaimed at the turn of the 20th century that it was doubtful that "there has been a revolution in all history so rapid, so extensive, so complete." The growth of industrial capitalism transformed the landscape, changed business organization, altered work and the workplace, and spurred migration and immigration worldwide while producing a flood of cheap, mass-produced consumer goods. It also generated both unprecedented wealth and poverty. Since 1873, when writers Mark Twain and Charles Dudley Warner dubbed this era the **Gilded Age**, the name has stuck because it is especially fitting. The United States seemed to be gilded, covered with the gold generated for millionaire industrialists. But that gold covering often proved to be a thin veneer, masking a world of greed, exploitation, and poverty.

The new economic order generated both hope and fear. Troubling questions remained. Had the United States, as Shadwell argued, become Europe, with democracy and opportunity in decline, with a powerful industrial aristocracy ruling over a permanent, exploited working class?

GLOBAL WEBS OF INDUSTRIAL CAPITALISM

With its origins in England in the early 19th century, industrial capitalism transformed the economies of northern Europe and then the United States, tightly knitting together a North Atlantic and then a global economy. Profits derived from commercial capitalism earlier in the century provided the basis for industrial capitalism. Industrial capitalism—the private investment of massive amounts of money in machinery, technology, and enormous, complex factories and processing plants—represented a striking new phase of economic development. The United States entered this new phase of economic development later than many European nations. But by 1900, the nation had emerged as the world's industrial leader. The new industrial order spun webs across the continent, across the Atlantic, and around the world, over which money, technology, people, and goods flowed. American products became well known around the world.

"Big business," as Americans referred to these new enterprises, generated unprecedented wealth for those who emerged victorious in the fierce competition that marked the era. In addition, industry produced more and cheaper consumer goods available to more people in more places than ever before. At the same time, "big business" spawned fears among many Americans. The unchecked power of industrialists, largely unfettered by regulatory laws, raised anxieties as they ruthlessly crushed competition, created monopolies, and wielded excessive influence over government. Moreover, extreme concentrations of wealth in the hands of a few seemed to create an aristocracy in the democratic United States. Was "big business," as industrialists argued, the natural evolution of the economic order that benefited all, or was it instead a new form of tyranny that undermined American ideals?

The New Industrial Order

Industrialization was not new in the United States in the late 19th century. What was new was the size, scale, nature, and function of this second Industrial Revolution. In the first Industrial Revolution, earlier in the century, manufacturing tended to be small in scale, owned by one or two people or a few partners who pooled their capital to start their enterprise. Early industries maintained a personal tone; owners knew their workers and oversaw shop floors. In addition, early shops and mills tended to be limited to areas that had access to wood or water power to drive machines. Although manufactured goods flowed across the Atlantic earlier in the century, many products tended to be distributed locally or regionally, limited by rudimentary transportation networks.

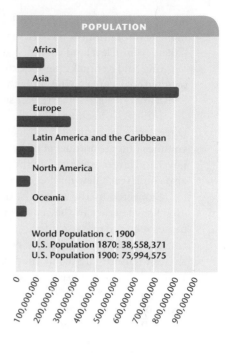

Technological innovations, powered by fossil fuels, made industrial capitalism possible in both the United States and northern Europe. Coal fueled steam engines and machines that were both bigger and faster than those in the first Industrial Revolution. It energized electricity grids that powered manufacturing as well as the railroads that carried these products to new markets. Coal also provided a crucial ingredient for one of the most important new products of this era: steel. Nearly all of the manufacturing regions of the United States and northern Europe sat atop or near rich coal deposits.

With its extensive coalfields, Pennsylvania emerged as the nation's leading manufacturing state. Pennsylvania coal also provided the power for newly emergent industries

THE HOMESTEAD WORKS Carnegie Steel's Homestead Works, located outside of Pittsburgh along the Monongahela River, was the site of both technological innovation and labor strife. The Homestead Works produced 200 million tons of steel in its 105-year history and helped make Pennsylvania the steel capital of the world.

on the East Coast, with New York and Philadelphia leading the nation in manufacturing. Coal from Illinois fueled a second major band of industrialization along the Great Lakes, from Cleveland to Chicago and Milwaukee. The coalfields of West Virginia, Virginia, and Kentucky helped expand the South's textile industry. Western mines contributed coal, copper, zinc, and other minerals crucial to industrialization, and both the South and the Pacific Northwest supplied lumber for the expanding economy.

Innovative technologies spawned new manufacturing processes and products. Huge factories running around the clock allowed manufacturers to produce larger volumes of their product at a lower cost, known as economies of scale. Not only could novel and larger amounts of products be manufactured in more places, but these goods also could reach new markets due to the network of railroads that laced the nation.

Bessemer steelworks, Pittsburgh, Pennsylvania (1886)

Pioneered by the railroads, the **modern corporation** differed from corporations established earlier in the century in size, scale, and organization. First, modern businesses required massive infusions of money, more than one investor or several partners could provide. To finance the cost of building a railroad, railroad corporations sold shares to investors. Second, modern corporations required new forms of management. Railroads found themselves faced with the vast challenge of administering and coordinating a complex enterprise involving the movement of cars over hundreds of miles. A board of directors, representing stockholders, provided general control of the company. A layer of managers, with specialized skills—in engineering, scheduling, and finance, to name a few—oversaw daily operations, with clear lines of authority and communication part of an elaborate bureaucracy.

Modern corporations replicated the railroads' model. Businesses such as oil, steel, and chemical processing also required vast amounts of money to build factories and plants, purchase expensive machinery, and set up warehouses, offices, and distribution centers. Unlike pre–Civil War business and industry, modern business enterprises separated ownership from management. Businesses needed to operate steadily and efficiently to make a profit and required elaborate, carefully coordinated administrative networks made up of departments headed by specialists with specific functions.

The money invested in Gilded Age corporations far surpassed that ventured in antebellum businesses. Before the Civil War, cotton textile mills were the nation's largest industry. Only a few, however, represented over $1 million of capital and employed more than 500 workers; not a single American company was worth more than $10 million. By 1904, over 300 companies in the United States were valued at $10 million. In 1900, Standard Oil was capitalized at $100 million, and in 1901, U.S. Steel became the world's first billion-dollar company, employing over 100,000 workers. Between 1870 and 1900, some American firms ballooned by over 1,000 times.

Industrial capitalism—or big business—was massive and impersonal in its scale, reach, and impact. But even as ownership in large business enterprises multiplied through stockholding and the new economic order grew impersonal, the public still identified individual businessmen with the specific big businesses they helped establish. Andrew Carnegie epitomized big steel; **John D. Rockefeller**, big oil; and **Cornelius Vanderbilt**, railroads.

Big business generated wealth on an unprecedented scale. In 1860, approximately 300 Americans were millionaires. Roughly 40 years later, that number had risen to around 4,500, with many multimillionaires. In the 1870s, the richest Americans were railroad men, such as Cornelius Vanderbilt, who topped the list with an estimated wealth of $100 million. By 1896, oil man Rockefeller and steel king Carnegie were the richest Americans, amassing fortunes of $200–$300 million. Measuring wealth as a percentage of the economy, John D. Rockefeller remains to this day the richest individual in American history, outstripping even contemporary business entrepreneurs such as Microsoft's Bill Gates.

U.S. Industrial Growth in Global Context

The new industrial order was well underway in Europe by the time the American economy began its transition during the Civil War. In 1870, Great Britain was the world's premier industrial power, followed by Germany. But by 1900, the United States had emerged as the globe's leading industrial nation. By that point, the nation produced over 30 percent of the world's manufacturing output (Figure 17.1).

A number of factors account for this remarkable growth. The United States was blessed with an abundance of natural resources. Cotton from southern states, coal

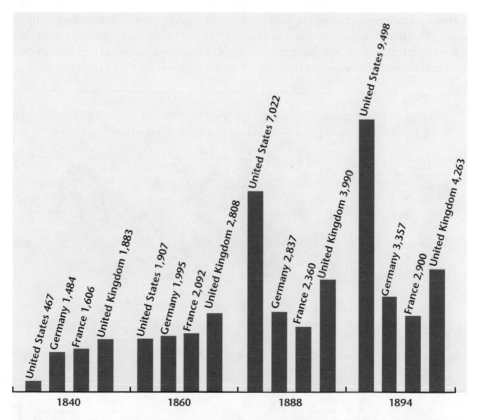

FIGURE 17.1 Manufacturing values, Europe and the United States, 1840–1894 (in millions of dollars) Manufacturing exploded in the United States in the last half of the 19th century. Innovations in industrial organization, technology, and transportation, as well as an abundance of raw materials and cheap labor, all propelled the United States past European rivals.

A panoramic view of the Shenango iron mine in the Mesabi Range, Minnesota (1910)

from Pennsylvania, and iron ore from Minnesota's Mesabi Range provided the raw materials necessary for rapid industrial growth (Map 17.1). The United States also greatly benefited from Great Britain's industrial head start. British investors poured their surplus wealth into the United States, providing a large percentage of the money needed to help capitalize large-scale industry, particularly railroads. In addition, U.S. industrialists, such as Carnegie, capitalized and improved on technological advances in British industry. Carnegie adopted the Bessemer process, invented in England, that transformed brittle pig iron into durable steel. By 1900, Carnegie's company alone manufactured more steel than all of Great Britain. Moreover, the nation's dramatic population growth, through both natural increase and immigration, greatly aided industrial development. As the nation exploded from 31 million people in 1860 to 76 million in 1900, this population supplied labor for rapidly expanding industries as well as a healthy market of consumers to purchase the many goods mass produced by U.S. industry.

Fierce competition characterized the new industrial order. Businesses failed at an alarming rate in the late 19th century; some observers estimated that 95 percent of businesses failed in the 1870s and 1880s. Cheap production, businessmen soon learned, depended on a company's ability to control every aspect of manufacturing as well as the distribution of goods, and they crafted new organizational structures that would be hallmarks of "big business." **Vertical integration** cut costs and guaranteed a regular flow of raw materials for production. Carnegie Steel, for example, owned, in

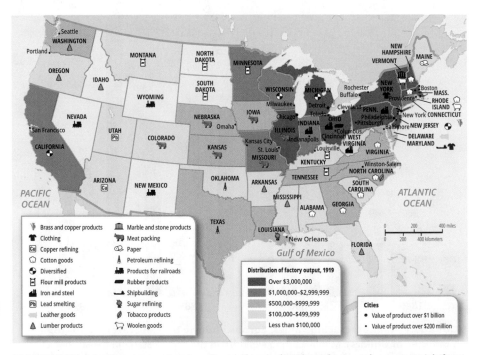

map analysis

MAP 17.1 Rich in Resources An abundance of agricultural products and raw materials from the South and West, manufactured largely in the Northeast and upper Midwest, helped make the United States the world's leading industrial power by 1900.

addition to its massive steel mills, the mines that produced the raw materials needed for steel production—coal, coke, and iron ore—as well as the railroads and steamships to transport raw materials to steel mills. Carnegie also set up sales offices to distribute steel efficiently and thus controlled both the production and distribution processes.

Horizontal integration aimed to tame the destructive elements of vigorous competition. The early oil industry, for example, was especially competitive and unstable. John D. Rockefeller and Standard Oil were notorious for eliminating competitors through secret deals with railroads that penalized rival oil companies and outright intimidation. To guarantee profits, oilmen first created cartels in which they agreed informally to fix prices, set quotas for production, and share enormous profits. But these informal agreements often broke down, and the American public vigorously protested price-fixing.

Seeking a way to centralize control through consolidation, Rockefeller devised the trust. Stockholders in individual oil corporations turned their stock over to a small group of trustees, including Rockefeller himself, who ran the various parts of Standard Oil as one company. In return, the stockholders received profits from the combination but had no direct control over the decisions of the trustees. Standard Oil soon had a monopoly of the oil industry and controlled more than 90 percent of oil refining in the United States by the 1880s. By 1904, its profits reached a whopping $57 million. This first and most notorious trust served as a model: trusts in beef, tobacco, and sugar soon followed.

Although the trust was a specific type of business organization, to the American public the term "trust" became synonymous with any large business combination. To men like Rockefeller, the trust represented the pinnacle of modern business enterprise. But to average Americans it meant the demise of small, independent businesses that could no longer compete as well as higher prices for the consumer. In addition, many feared that trusts placed far too much power in the hands of a few individuals who would inevitably abuse their power.

Combinations and Concentrations of Wealth

Concentrations of wealth in the Gilded Age reflected the growth of combinations, trusts, and monopolies. A study in 1890 concluded that more than half of the nation's wealth was in the hands of just 17 percent of America's families, down from 29 percent in 1860. In the late 1880s, an American economist estimated that the United States suffered greater inequality than England and had developed its own aristocracy.

Public outcry over concentrations of wealth, combinations, and monopolies forced Congress to pass the **Sherman Antitrust Act** in 1890. **Henry Demarest Lloyd's** 1881 investigation of Rockefeller's Standard Oil, "The Story of a Great Monopoly," spawned subsequent articles in the popular press that fanned the flames of public outrage. Lloyd's description of Standard Oil's methods—which included fraud, intimidation, and the purchase of political influence, all at the expense of the consumer—supported his bold claim that "America has the proud satisfaction of having furnished the world with the greatest, wisest, and meanest monopoly known to history." Lloyd famously noted that Standard not only controlled two U.S. senators, but the company had also "done everything with the Pennsylvania legislature except to refine it."

Excerpts from the Sherman Antitrust Act (1890)

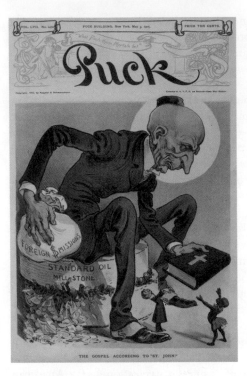

THE GOSPEL ACCORDING TO "ST. JOHN"
This 1905 cartoon criticizes John D. Rockefeller's philanthropy to foreign Christian missions and his fortune gained, according to the cartoonist, through Standard Oil's exploitative methods.

The Sherman Antitrust Act aimed at dismantling "combination in the form of trust or otherwise" that restrained trade. But Congress drafted the law broadly and left many key concepts undefined, such as "fair competition" and "monopoly," leaving it up to the courts to interpret the law's meaning. In 1895, the Supreme Court decided the case of *United States v. E. C. Knight Co.* that centered on the American Sugar Refining Company, which controlled 98 percent of sugar refining in the United States. In an 8–1 decision, the court declared that the federal government could regulate only monopolies involved in interstate commerce. Because the company's refining took place in only one state, the federal government had no right to break up the company. As a result of the decision, Standard Oil, the chief target of antitrust legislation, remained intact until 1911.

The Sherman Antitrust Act also caused unintended consequences. Rather than dismantling unfair combinations, business interests used the legislation to attack unions. Between 1890 and 1897, labor unions were the victims of 12 of the first 13 convictions under the law, as courts agreed with business that unions constituted a monopoly when strikes halted interstate trade. In addition, the courts ruled that although collusion was illegal, business combinations were not. The years 1895 to 1904 saw the largest number of business mergers in U.S. history. Approximately 1,800 major industrial firms vanished in 157 mergers, as tire companies such as Goodyear, oil companies such as Texaco, and food companies such as United Fruit all absorbed smaller competitors.

Federal and state government provided little regulation for the burgeoning economic order. **Laissez-faire** (hands-off) **economics** was gospel to businessmen and the politicians they supported. This economic doctrine insisted that government not interfere with business or the market. Businesses should compete "naturally," unimpeded by government regulation; as a result, society as a whole would benefit. Men like Carnegie and Rockefeller believed that trusts and large, consolidated enterprises represented the natural evolution of business. In addition, their success as "captains of industry," they argued, came as a result of their "fitness"—their ability to adapt to the new economic order. As men who had risen from humble origins, they made no apologies for the massive fortunes they accumulated. Carnegie, for example, had immigrated to the United States from Scotland at the age of 13 and worked in a textile factory before climbing up the corporate ladder to become one of the world's richest men. Many business leaders of the era subscribed to the theory of **social Darwinism**, popularized by British social theorist **Herbert Spencer**. Spencer posited that Charles Darwin's theory of evolution could be applied to human society. Society evolved—and inevitably improved—through competition, with "survival of the fittest." This theory also supported laissez-faire economics.

Despite their devotion to theories about nonregulation and the "self-made" man, American businessmen greatly benefited from governmental aid. Federal support for railroads, protective tariff legislation, a favorable legal climate, and the intervention of state and federal authorities to crush labor movements all fostered the nation's exceptional economic growth and unprecedented profits.

Markets and Consumerism

Cheap, reliable transportation, swift communication systems, and technological advances made national and international markets possible, fueling the industrial growth of the United States. With the nation's extensive railway system, manufactured goods could now be shipped to previously isolated parts of the country. The telegraph, and later the telephone, made it possible to coordinate shipments through instant communication. Inventions such as the refrigerated railroad car, pioneered by Gustavus Swift, made it possible to ship dressed beef from Chicago's stockyards to eastern cities and across the Atlantic.

Mass production spawned a revolution in consumer items. The American public and the world had access to a flood of cheap, affordable items that were unthinkable just years before. Andrew Carnegie cited "the cheapening of articles" as one of the greatest advances in human history. Even "the poor enjoy what the rich could not before afford." Mass production, technological advances, and mass transportation also spurred a revolution in food, making it both cheaper and more accessible. American companies for the first time also mass-produced processed foods that they distributed nationally and globally.

Mail-order catalogues provide one indication of the consumer items available to average Americans in this era. In 1872, **Aaron Montgomery Ward** founded the nation's first mail-order house, as railroads opened up new markets in rural America for cheap goods now being produced in massive quantities. His catalogues featured tens of thousands of items, including farm equipment, Singer sewing machines, straight-edged razors, and gospel hymnbooks. Sears, Roebuck, and Company soon competed with Ward for the rural market. By 1900, Sears processed 10,000 orders a day in its Chicago headquarters. While offering a universe of goods to rural and small-town Americans, the mail-order firms deeply damaged the sales of local merchants, who fought back against these big businesses by sponsoring bonfires of mail-order catalogues. To country merchants, Ward and Sears represented the evils of big business. But to their customers, the mail-order houses offered a huge assortment of affordable goods previously unavailable to them.

After successfully integrating and exploiting the national market, American firms marketed their goods abroad. Long before creating a political empire, Americans built a global commercial empire. Aided by technological innovations such as advances in steamship design and refrigeration and by a decline in transportation costs, American businesses first established international markets in Canada and Europe. They then

Russian advertisement for Singer sewing machines (1914)

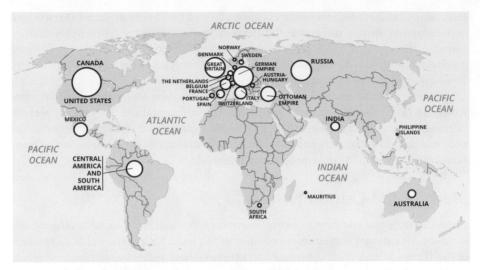

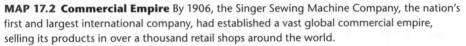

MAP 17.2 Commercial Empire By 1906, the Singer Sewing Machine Company, the nation's first and largest international company, had established a vast global commercial empire, selling its products in over a thousand retail shops around the world.

extended webs of trade into Mexico, South America, and Asia, particularly India, Japan, and China. American businesses competed successfully with their chief industrial rival, Great Britain. A plethora of products—from Singer sewing machines to Heinz pickles— became household names all over the globe.

American companies followed the pattern established by Singer: first selling their products abroad through international sales and distribution systems and then establishing factories abroad, from Europe to Asia, where they could take advantage of raw materials and cheap labor (Map 17.2). By the late 19th century, many American companies had developed into full-fledged multinational corporations. They often presented international marketing not as a means to profit but as a benevolent, noble act, as they provided the "gifts" of their "superior" culture to an "uncivilized" world.

STUDY QUESTIONS FOR GLOBAL WEBS OF INDUSTRIAL CAPITALISM

1. What was new about the new industrial order of the Gilded Age?

2. What were the key factors that made the new industrial order possible?

3. What steps did American businesses take to create global markets?

quiz

⊘ WORK AND THE WORKPLACE

The nation's startling industrial growth came about as the result of people laboring longer and harder than ever before, often in dangerous conditions. Although laborers worked in lethal environments everywhere in the industrial world, in the United States, as Europeans often remarked, work seemed especially ruthless. A Finnish laborer, writing home from Michigan, summarized the plight of the American worker: "Everyone works like hell."

Industrial capitalism transformed the nature of work and the workplace. As early as 1870, for the first time in history, a majority of U.S. laborers worked for someone else, marking the end of the era of the independent, self-employed American. Millions of Americans, like their counterparts in Europe, left the countryside to work in flourishing industries. Industrial laborers worked long and grueling hours in dangerous mills and factories at increasingly subdivided and mechanized tasks, making it possible for even small children to work repetitive, unskilled jobs.

Even before the Civil War, some workers labeled wage work "wage slavery," and condemnations continued as wage labor expanded in the new industrial order. As a critic wrote in 1871, "To put a man to wages, is to put him in the position of a dependent." Once viewed as a step on the ladder to independent landownership, a growing number of Americans found themselves trapped in wage labor positions, a frightening prospect for many. A labor newspaper in 1876 exclaimed, "There was a time when the United States was once the land of promise for the workingman," but now, "We are in an *old country*." Was individual independence, one of the nation's most valued ideals, a thing of the past? Had the new economic order "Europeanized" the United States, as Arthur Shadwell and others argued?

Global Migrations

A large pool of cheap, mobile labor made the new industrial order possible. Tens of millions of men, women, and children left the countryside to work in industrializing regions on both sides of the Atlantic. Migration reached unprecedented levels in the late 19th century. As railroads and steamships provided cheap transportation, European migrants—facing overpopulation, a scarcity of land, political unrest, and stiff competition from mechanized American agriculture—extended traditional seasonal sojourns to European industrial jobs by crossing the ocean to work for higher wages in American industry. Similarly, rural Chinese and Japanese workers crossed the Pacific to labor in mining and railroad construction on the West Coast and later in other industries such as salmon canneries. To the north, French Canadians boarded railroad cars in Quebec and headed south to toil in New England's textile mills. And from the south, Mexicans crossed the border to help construct and maintain railroads in the Southwest.

Rural Americans were also part of the global migration from farm to factory. The southern textile industry, promoted by advocates such as Henry Grady, who sought to create a prosperous post–Civil War "New South" through industrial development, concentrated largely in the Piedmont region of Virginia, North and South Carolina, and Georgia. These mills drew their labor force from white farm families, forced from the countryside by overpopulation, declining cotton prices, and the crop lien system.

Southern textiles, like many other businesses and industries in Gilded Age America, enforced a color bar, hiring only whites. Most African American families remained tied to the land in the South, although some black men did find work in southern coal mines and the lumber industry. But thousands of African Americans who labored in southern industry did so against their will, in a system of forced labor known as the convict lease system. When freed black Americans were arrested under trumped-up charges, such as

Henry Grady on the New South (1886)

A Revolution in Food

Innovations in transportation and technology that fueled industrial capitalism created another revolution, evident to this day in kitchens around the world: a revolution in food. Before the Gilded Age, most people ate "locally"—the food grown on nearby farms. But advances in transportation, technology, and mechanization replaced local foods with food grown and processed in distant places.

Even though the number of American farmers declined by half between 1850 and 1900 as many left the countryside for industrial jobs, wheat production increased approximately eight times as technological advances drastically increased the food supply. In the Midwest and West, farmers cultivated millions of additional acres and mechanized farming with threshers, harvesters, and reapers. Railroads carried the agricultural bounty east to the nation's booming cities and industrial centers with regularity and relative ease. The development of the refrigerated railroad car in 1878 made it possible to transfer fresh meat from midwestern stockyards. Steamships filled their hulls with cheap American grain and saturated European markets. The United States also shipped beef to Europe, outpacing competitor Australia, and soon dominated the market there. In addition, railroads and steamships carried tropical fruits to tables around the world. The United Fruit Company helped make the once-exotic banana, harvested in Central America, a common food item.

The mass production, mass marketing, and standardization of food also began in the Gilded Age. Just as manufacturers processed chemicals and steel, they processed and packaged food: everything from meat to pickles to breakfast cereal. Advances in food preservation as well as assembly line processing diversified diets. By 1868, machine-cut

Meat
packing
plant,
Chicago
(1900)

---

vagrancy, and unable to pay fines and court fees, state and local authorities sold them to mining companies, lumber camps, and plantations that agreed to pay their fines and fees in return for their labor. Enslaved in every sense but in name, convict laborers were bought and sold, worked without compensation, were whipped and brutalized, and labored under inhumane conditions. Some roasted and suffocated to death in mines, and scores died of disease. Their uncompensated labor for companies such as the Tennessee Coal, Iron, and Railroad Company, a subsidiary of U.S. Steel, played a major role in the expansion of southern industry in the Gilded Age and came at a terrible cost.

Likewise, many Chinese and Japanese workers in the West and Mexican workers in the Southwest found themselves largely relegated to agricultural labor.

Blue-Collar and White-Collar Workers

The new economic order divided labor into those who worked with their hands and those who worked with their heads. Manual wageworkers, later known as "blue-collar" workers for the blue work shirts they wore, provided the economy's foundation. Between 1870 and 1910, their numbers increased by over 300 percent as the overall population grew by 130 percent. With production mechanized, factories required mostly unskilled cans, made of thinner steel and manufactured cheaply on assembly lines, had replaced heavy, hard-to-open handmade cans. While not especially tasty by contemporary standards, canned vegetables and fruits proved to be a welcome addition to the family table, especially for workers whose diets previously consisted largely of bread, potatoes, and an occasional piece of meat.

The products of American food companies, such as the H. J. Heinz Company, Campbell's Soup, and the Dole Hawaiian Pineapple Company, soon became available globally, their brands recognized around the world. Heinz, purveyor of baked beans, pickles, and numerous other food products, pioneered global food distribution, first selling its goods in England in the late 1880s. By 1900, Heinz had established distribution centers in Central and South America and Asia. The company bragged that its products "have found their way, literally, to the ends of the earth" and that "the name 'Heinz' has become known in every country and every nation in the world."

Consumers liked processed food for its consistency, accessibility, and low cost. Advertisements helped imprint brand names in the minds of consumers and stressed the quality of their products. But in appealing to the general population, food flavors became increasingly bland. Moreover, without regulations, processed food was anything but hygienic. Food manufacturers freely adulterated their products, with, among other things, lead, dust, dyes, and chalk. Manufacturers were not even required to reveal their product's ingredients. Unhappy consumers, often women, organized protests against the impurity of food products. It was not until 1906 that the federal government strengthened regulation with the Pure Food and Drug Act.

Advertisement for Heinz baked beans, ca. 1890

- What developments made a revolution in food possible in the late 19th century?
- How did the food revolution reflect larger patterns of globalization?

workers. To maximize production and efficiency, workers became, in the words of one late 19th-century commentator, "mechanicalized," as they tended machines or executed simple, mind-numbing, repetitive tasks. A clergyman, testifying before Congress, noted that the typical worker "makes nothing. He sees no complete product of his skill growing into finished shape in his hands." For example, divisions of labor in the ready-made clothing industry eliminated traditional tailoring skills. Sewing machine operators did not fabricate an entire garment but focused only on stitching one part of a garment, such as sleeves, buttonholes, lapels, or pockets.

Some saw mechanization as a "civilizing force" that would lead to "better morals" and even better wages. Others disagreed. Critic Henry George insisted that increasing specialization resulted in "degrading men into the position of mere feeders of machines." Such labor only made the worker "more dependent" while "lessening his control over his own condition." In addition, mechanization resulted in "cramping his mind, and in some cases distorting and enervating his body."

Although skilled workers did not disappear entirely, they were significantly reduced in number and removed from the production process. Most shop floors needed only a few skilled workers to fix machinery or make tools for machines operated by unskilled workers. As work increasingly became "deskilled," these workers lost the most

RUSSIAN STEELWORKERS, HOMESTEAD, PENNSYLVANIA, 1908   Roughly two-thirds of steelworkers were foreign born. The 12-hour shift contributed to an exceedingly large number of deaths and injuries among them. As one investigator wrote, "It is a rare man who can keep his mental faculties keenly alert and centered on one object for twelve consecutive hours."

ground. Their fight to maintain their positions would lead to some of the bitterest labor struggles of the era.

Whereas skilled workers saw opportunities decline, "white-collar" work expanded, as large business enterprises required specialized experts. White-collar workers—dubbed as such for the formal white shirts they wore—were also known as "brainworkers." Finance experts, accountants, advertising agents, and managers, as well as engineers and attorneys, filled the ranks of white-collar jobs. Marketing also required salesmen who traveled on the nation's railway system, selling their goods in small towns and country stores. Unlike blue-collar workers, who labored for hourly wages or were paid by the piece, most white-collar workers worked as salaried specialists. They provided the core of a growing middle class. Although they did not own the businesses that they managed, white-collar workers usually identified with those who employed them, not with the workers whom they managed. This identification had long-term consequences, as white-collar workers provided popular support for antiunion efforts.

Although white-collar workers were almost exclusively white males, the development of the modern office provided new opportunities for women as typists, stenographers, filing clerks, and switchboard operators. By 1900, more than 250,000 women labored in these jobs. The number of female stenographers and

MODERN WORK ENVIRONMENT   The modern office reflected the rise of modern business enterprises and the need for specialized white-collar workers to manage them. In 1870, there were approximately 80,000 clerical workers; by 1920, there were three million.

typists jumped from 4.5 percent of the total to 77 percent by 1900. In the same time period, female telephone and telegraph operators increased from 4 percent to 30 percent. Women office workers especially appealed to employers because they could be paid less than men for the same work. And office work attracted women, as it was cleaner and less taxing than factory labor. They still worked long hours, had to spend much of their income for proper office apparel, and frequently had to deal with harassment from male coworkers. Moreover, whereas male "clerks" used office work as a way to learn the business and as a first step up the corporate ladder, no such opportunities existed for female "secretaries," who, according to prevailing belief, did not have the natural abilities to compete in the cutthroat world of business.

The division between blue-collar and white-collar workers in the United States, compared to Europe, seemed especially extreme. In Europe, smaller-scale, family-owned businesses, with a more familial concern for employees, persisted longer than in the United States. In the hierarchical, corporate structure of American industry, managers grew detached from workers. Constant oversight and severe discipline from managers bent on maximizing production created tension between managers and workers.

Regimentation and Scientific Management

Managers enforced firm rules and regulations on the shop floor. They locked factory gates to keep workers on site and fined workers for tardiness, flawed work, and even talking on the job. Seeking an uninterrupted flow of production and maximum efficiency, managers instituted time studies. **Frederick Winslow Taylor** pioneered "scientific management," or "Taylorism." Armed with stopwatches, and later moving-picture cameras, Taylor and his disciples studied every movement of a worker's task to

Excerpt from Frederick Winslow Taylor, 'Principles of Scientific Management" (1911)

eliminate "false moves" and to "drive the worker into a stride that would be as mechanical as the machine he tends." No job was too lowly for Taylor's efficiency experts. Taylor bragged that he had tripled Bethlehem Steel's coal yard production by determining the most efficient shovel design, the best way for each laborer to brandish his shovel, the optimal shovel load, the perfect number of rest breaks, and a pay formula based on the number of shovel loads dispensed. A well-run factory, Taylor insisted, required every worker "to become one of a train of gear wheels."

Carnegie's steel works also stressed maximum efficiency by running mills 24 hours a day, cutting costs, and increasing volume. He set quotas for production, pitted furnaces against each other in competitions for the most output, and fired managers and work crews who failed to keep pace.

Piecework also contributed to the pressured, regimented atmosphere of the American workplace. Employers believed they could get more out of workers by paying them by the completed "piece" of a product rather than an hourly wage. Numerous mills and factories instituted piecework, as did sweatshops, housed in crowded tenements and apartments, where entire families could be found completing products such as garments or artificial flowers. An investigator in 1913 described a scene in a New York City tenement where a grandmother, mother, and two tiny children labored making artificial flowers for 10 cents a gross (144 flowers), "and if they work steadily, from eight or nine in the morning to seven or eight at night, they may make twelve gross, $1.20." A three-year-old "picks apart the petals," while her four-year old sister "separates stems," and the mother and grandmother finish the flower, repeating the process for hours with mind-numbing regularity.

Not surprisingly, laborers resented pressure to increase production, the intrusion of efficiency experts, and the discipline of ever-watchful managers. Workers at the Watertown Arsenal in Massachusetts, for example, walked out in support of a molder who refused to work under a manager's stopwatch. Women carpet workers in Yonkers, New York, compared their surveillance by managers to incarceration in nearby Sing Sing prison. Workers often simply left jobs they did not like. Turnover was extremely high, especially in textile factories, steel mills, and clothing and machine shops, where most workers changed jobs every three years.

European visitors marveled at the regimentation of the American workplace. A French traveler to the United States noted, "Work in the American shops is altogether different from what it is in France. Nobody talks, nobody sings, the most rigorous silence reigns."

Yet laborers found ways to endure life on the shop floor. Many immigrant workers continued to take the days off for traditional religious holidays not in the American calendar. Others gave themselves a two-day weekend by skipping work on Mondays, observing what came to be known as "Blue Mondays." Cigar makers broke the monotony of the shop floor by appointing one person to read aloud to fellow workers.

Cigar workers, Ybor City, Florida (1920s

Workers also found relief outside the shop walls, creating a vibrant culture of mutual support that helped sustain them in the grueling industrial world. For workingmen, social life centered on the saloon. In addition to being a place to fraternize and drink with fellow workers, saloons provided cheap food and entertainment, such as sing-alongs and boxing matches. While men gathered in saloons, women workers socialized in their homes and neighborhoods as they attended to housekeeping and children, often sharing what little they had. Churches and ethnic organizations provided additional opportunities to socialize and leave the rigors of work behind, with weddings and festivals offering a welcome reprieve.

Working Conditions and Wages

Long hours and a demanding pace took its toll on American workers. With little interference from state and federal government, employers worked their laborers relentlessly. The industry standard was a 10-hour day for six days a week, although workers in some industries, such as steel, regularly worked 12-hour shifts, 7 days a week, with one holiday: the Fourth of July. A Pennsylvania steelworker summarized the unyielding repetition of his life: "A man works, comes home, eats, and goes to bed, gets up, eats, and goes to work."

Without safety regulations enforced by state or federal government, American industry was a cauldron of fatigue, illness, injury, and death. A mule spinner in a Massachusetts textile mill estimated that he walked as many as 30 miles a day to tend his machines. Exhausted and working among dangerous machines, textile workers regularly lost fingers. Those who did not suffer injury died years later from "brown lung," which developed from inhaling fibers in the factory air. Similarly, coal miners expired from "black lung" after years of breathing in coal dust. American railroaders and coal miners died at three times the rate of their European counterparts, who enjoyed some government safety regulations of the workplace. The steel industry was notoriously dangerous with blast furnaces and exposed molten steel in the open hearth; new technologies, adapted by Carnegie for a competitive edge in steelmaking, proved to be especially dangerous. By one estimate, 25 percent of immigrant men working the Pennsylvania steel industry's most dangerous jobs were seriously disabled or killed. Injury or death spelled disaster for working families. With no "safety net"—unemployment, workmen's compensation, or health benefits—and with little legal recourse against powerful corporations, working families regularly found themselves homeless and hungry overnight.

Photographs of coal miners, ca. 1900

Economic Convulsions and Hard Times

In addition to the ever-present threat of injury or death, working families were especially vulnerable to economic cycles of boom and bust. Although the economy grew enormously overall in the last quarter of the 19th century, it did so by fits and starts. Work hours fluctuated from feast to famine, from overtime hours to sudden unemployment. Two severe and prolonged economic depressions, only 20 years apart, from 1873 to 1878 and from 1893 to 1897, affected the United States and all industrialized nations worldwide. Unregulated markets and rampant speculation in complicated, incomprehensible financial instruments led to these upheavals, leaving millions without work. Those who managed to keep their jobs faced both shortened hours and wage cuts.

The Wall Street crash of 1873, precipitated by the failure of Jay Cooke and Company, the nation's largest investment bank, resulted in tens of thousands of business failures—6,000 alone in 1874 and as many as 900 per month in 1878. An article in *Harper's Weekly* in the winter of 1873 reported hundreds of deaths by starvation and 3,000 babies abandoned on doorsteps. In 1893, another Wall Street panic helped trigger a second lengthy worldwide depression even more severe than the depression of the 1870s. The winter of 1893–1894 was especially harsh, with widespread suffering from lack of food, fuel, and housing. In February 1894, for example, *The New York Times* reported the story of 12 Italian families in the city, 50 people "in a starving condition" ready to be evicted from their home where they lived without any food or heat. Families wandered about seeking food and shelter, while men "tramped" across the country, desperately seeking work.

Even in the best of times, a factory worker's wages purchased a living that straddled the poverty line. Although real wages—that is, wages adjusted for inflation—increased between 1860 and 1900 and were high compared to those of Europe, many families could not rely on one income alone and had to supplement the family income through the wages of mothers and children. In 1890, the median household income in the United States was $540. Carroll D. Wright, chief of the Bureau of Labor Statistics in Massachusetts, noted in 1882, "A family of workers can live well, but the man with a family to support, unless his wife works also, has a small chance of living properly."

Women and Children in the Workplace

The number of women in the workplace exploded between 1870 and 1910. In 1870, 1.5 million women worked for wages, the majority in domestic service jobs. By 1910, their numbers had more than quadrupled, and fewer than 40 percent were in domestic service. Women employed in industry concentrated in textile and garment production. Young, single women made up the bulk of the female labor force in the garment trades. Married women often took piecework into their homes.

Although the new economic order provided new opportunities for women, employers also paid women much less—half or less—than men for the same work. In addition, black and Latina women found themselves barred from many jobs open to white women, such as the southern textile industry and secretarial jobs, and instead toiled as domestic servants and laundresses.

Child labor also fueled the new economic order. In 1870, 750,000 children under the age of 15 worked in nonfarm and nonfamily businesses. Twenty years later, that figure had doubled, to 1.5 million, with 18 percent of children between the ages of 10 and 15 employed in nonagricultural work. In depression years, the number of children working in mining and manufacturing spiked. Few child labor laws existed, and when they did, they were seldom strictly enforced. Moreover, the parents of working children, who depended on their income, often opposed such laws; children had long labored on family farms, so labor in a factory or mill did not necessarily seem cruel or unusual. Miner John Brophy, for example, who entered the Pennsylvania coalfields at the age of 12, said, "I was . . . pleased that I could do something to help my family."

But industrial labor involved dangers nonexistent on the farm. Children were especially vulnerable to exploitation and injury, as they worked long hours in hazardous conditions. Employers in some industries, such as textiles, sought out child laborers, because they could pay them less and could more easily control them. Even children could run dangerous machines or engage in a simple, repetitive task on an assembly line. Small children, for example, labored in southern textile mills, their small hands

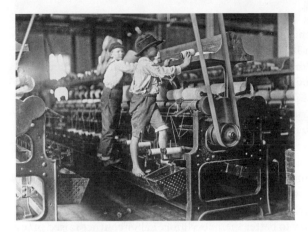

CHILD LABORERS Investigative photographer Lewis Hine took this photo of child laborers at a cotton mill in Macon, Georgia, in 1908. His caption read, "Some boys and girls were so small they had to climb up on to the spinning frame to mend broken threads and to put back the empty bobbins."

especially adept at changing bobbins on weaving machines. Superintendents threw cold water in the faces of sleepy children to keep them awake, but exhausted, inattentive children regularly lost fingers and limbs in machines. Even the tiniest children could be found adding to the family coffers, aiding their mothers with piecework brought into their homes. Reformer Jane Addams reported observing a four-year-old girl "who pulled out basting threads, hour by hour," as she sat at the feet of her immigrant mother, "a little bunch of human misery."

British writer **H. G. Wells** was horrified by child labor in the United States. Traveling in late 19th-century New York, he observed children selling newspapers and blacking boots who later collapsed on the subway from exhaustion. He learned of children as young as five working all night in southern textile mills. Wells noted that England's industrial history was "black with the blood of tortured and murdered children," yet England was far ahead of the United States in factory legislation, having passed protective laws for women and children in the 1840s. Wells blamed the American emphasis on "liberty of property and the subordination of the state to business." Although some Gilded Age reformers protested child labor, few major improvements occurred until the 1910s, when nearly every state passed minimum age and maximum hour legislation.

STUDY QUESTIONS FOR WORK AND THE WORKPLACE

1. How did work and the workplace change in the late 19th century?
2. What role did women and children play in the explosive economic growth of the United States in the late 19th century?

quiz

⌄ WORKERS FIGHT BACK

With worsening working conditions, along with the severe economic convulsions of the Gilded Age and the hardships they left in their wake, workers began to organize collectively into labor unions to fight for a living wage, shorter hours, and better conditions and to offset the power of employers. They framed their battle as a fight for American values against what they viewed as the encroaching Europeanization of their country. "America," explained a union newspaper in 1874, was once "the star" on which the world's workers "gazed" and dreamed of being "their own rulers." But "these dreams have not been realized," and American workers "suddenly find capital as rigid as an absolute monarchy."

Workers crafted a range of strategies for collective action in an attempt to offset the enormous power of industrialists. Whereas some labor unions tried to organize all workers, others attempted to maximize their power by allowing only white, skilled workers to join. Still others insisted that workers would have more clout by organizing along industrial lines, in which strikes would bring entire industries to a standstill.

Conflict between workers and employees exploded. Between 1881 and 1905, 36,000 strikes, involving seven million workers, took place, an average of four strikes per day. Many of these were violent. Even farmers, squeezed by banks, railroads, and "middlemen," organized collectively to try to better their condition. Labor conflict raised many questions and fears among Americans. Did the nation again verge on civil war, this time based on class? What was the best strategy for workers to seek justice and regain the dignity of their labor? Did labor unions threaten the public good or enhance it?

The Great Railroad Strike of 1877

In July 1877, in the midst of economic depression, American workers initiated the first and largest general strike in the nation's history. The **Great Railroad Strike of 1877** set the stage for subsequent conflicts between labor and capital in the late 19th century.

THE GREAT RAILROAD STRIKE OF 1877
Harper's Weekly, a popular newsmagazine, depicts violence in Baltimore during the Great Railroad Strike of 1877. A Maryland National Guard regiment, called out by the governor at the request of the B&O Railroad president to put down the strike, fired on a crowd of pro-strike demonstrators, killing 10.

Reeling from the depression of the 1870s, major railroads, including the Pennsylvania Railroad and the Baltimore & Ohio, cut wages significantly while severely reducing hours of work. Angry brakemen and firemen refused to work. Other railroad workers protested by obstructing the movement of freight trains near Baltimore and West Virginia, but they allowed passenger traffic to pass.

Violent strikes soon broke out in towns along the rails, from Baltimore to Pittsburgh. In addition, sympathetic strikes erupted spontaneously as railroad workers stopped trains as far away as San Francisco; other workers, in solidarity, brought factories, foundries, and building construction to a standstill. In St. Louis, workers inaugurated a general strike that shut down the city for a week, with white and black, native born and immigrant, skilled and unskilled workers united in common cause.

At the request of railroad officials, governors in Maryland, Pennsylvania, and West Virginia sent out their state militias to try to break the strike. In Baltimore, armed militias confronted angry mobs of rock-throwing workers. Even wives and mothers of railroad workers joined in. A Baltimore newspaper described them: "They look famished and wild, and declare for starvation rather than have their people work for reduced wages. Better to starve outright, say they, than to die of slow starvation." Firing into the crowd, the militia killed 10 people, inciting even greater violence. Roughly 14,000 protesters filled the streets of the city, sending a locomotive crashing into freight cars and cutting fire hoses. In Pittsburgh, where local militia sympathized with the striking workers, the governor had to call in troops from Philadelphia. They, too, fired into a crowd, killing 20 people, including women and children. Soon the mob forced the militia to retreat to a roundhouse and then destroyed 39 buildings, 104 engines, 46 passenger cars, and over 1,200 freight cars. More than a hundred people died nationwide.

One newspaper headline labeled the railroad strike "The Lexington of the Labor Conflict." A Massachusetts clergyman called the strikers "the lineal descendents of Samuel Adams, John Hancock, and the Massachusetts yeomen" who revolted against the king a hundred years previously, "only now the kings are money kings." Like the minutemen before them, workers saw the strike as the first shot against tyranny in defense of liberty.

But the strike struck terror in the hearts of many middle-class Americans who saw it as the outbreak of social revolution, foreshadowed in Europe. In 1871, radical workers, and those sympathetic to their cause, declared themselves the governing body of the city of Paris. Ruling the city for two months, the Paris Commune sparked a bloody municipal civil war that left at least 25,000 insurgents and 1,000 troops dead before government authorities suppressed the revolution. The Paris Commune received more newspaper coverage in the United States than any other event that occurred on foreign soil up to that time. Fear that a Communist revolution would spread to the United States gripped many Americans, and the Railroad Strike of 1877 confirmed their suspicions that the movement had migrated successfully to the United States. The press fanned the flames of fear, referring to the "Commune in New York" and the "Commune in St. Louis."

By the end of July, the strike had been broken, largely through the intervention of state and federal authorities on behalf of the railroads. In addition to militia units sent out by governors, President **Rutherford B. Hayes** sent federal troops to break the strike, an important precedent followed by later presidents. Workers found themselves fighting against not only the immense power of large corporations but also state and federal authorities siding with business. Notably, the Great Railroad Strike of 1877 hastened the growth of National Guard (state militia) units. Every state soon followed the lead of northeastern industrialized states to establish National Guards, often housed in massive red-brick armories, a symbol of the state's intent to keep domestic order at nearly any cost. Between 1877 and 1903, the National Guard and federal troops intervened over 500 times to suppress labor disputes.

Fears of communism, socialism, and anarchism placed the judicial system overwhelmingly on the side of employers. In the name of social order and individual rights, courts condemned unions. As one judge explained, strikes were "a serious evil, destructive to property, destructive to individual rights . . . , tending to the disruption of society, and the obliteration of legal and natural rights." Although judges rarely outlawed strikes, they frequently invoked injunctions to restrict strike activity. Even though socialists, anarchists, and Communists made up only a small percentage of the American labor movement, unions would subsequently be branded as "un-American" organizations, bent on fomenting class warfare.

Organizing Strategies and Labor Violence

American workers engaged in a range of strategies to better their lot. These included forming one big union of all workers, creating exclusive craft unions, and building industry-wide unions. Some unions, such as the Knights of Labor, offered an alternative to capitalism, whereas others, such as the American Federation of Labor, embraced the economic order and simply sought "more of the pie."

In the wake of the Railroad Strike of 1877, the **Knights of Labor** emerged as the largest union. Founded in 1869 in Baltimore, the Knights aimed to organize all laboring people into one large, national union. The union offered membership to "the producing masses," regardless of race, gender, or national origin, excluding only "social parasites"—lawyers, bankers, and liquor salesmen. The organization's emphasis on equal rights and equal pay for equal work attracted many women. At the height of its influence, in 1886, the Knights claimed a membership of more than 700,000, with about one-tenth of the membership made up of women.

The Knights of Labor articulated a scathing critique of industrial capitalism, informed by the Declaration of Independence and the Bible, offering an alternative to capitalism. The Knights demanded "to the toilers a proper share of the wealth that they create." They condemned monopolies and concentrations of power in the hands of the few. Declaring that "an injury to one is the concern of all," they also opposed wage labor. They demanded "more of the leisure that rightfully belongs to them," condemned child labor, and emphasized worker education and cooperative institutions. They also insisted on an eight-hour workday. A song that the Knights sang at the end of their meetings summarized this demand: "We want to feel the sunshine; We want to smell the flowers; We are sure God willed it. And we mean to have eight hours."

Preamble to the Constitution of the Knights of Labor (1878)

Both the organization and philosophy of the Knights, however, weakened its effectiveness. The Knights included both skilled and unskilled workers. But unskilled workers were easily replaced and had little leverage in strikes. Although the Knights hoped to achieve their goals within the existing system through collective bargaining with employers, leader **Terrence V. Powderly** discouraged strikes. Even so, the Knights of Labor won several strikes in the mid-1880s. Women textile workers and hatmakers

WOMEN DELEGATES TO THE KNIGHTS OF LABOR'S NATIONAL CONVENTION IN 1886 The Knights welcomed women, who made up about 10 percent of the membership. Several held high positions, including Elizabeth Rodgers, depicted here holding her two-week-old baby. Rodgers was head of the Chicago Knights' assembly and a mother of 12.

engaged in several successful strikes in 1884, leading Powderly to label them "the best men in the Order." The future of the organization seemed bright.

Then, in May 1886, socialist and anarchist leaders organized a meeting in Chicago's Haymarket Square to protest the deaths of four strikers killed at the city's International Harvester plant. When police arrived, someone threw a bomb, the police fired into the crowd, and chaos ensued. When the smoke cleared, 10 people lay dead—6 of them policemen—and 50 people were wounded in the **Haymarket Affair**. Although authorities never established the identity of the bomb thrower, eight anarchist leaders, seven of whom were foreign born, were arrested, tried, and convicted; seven were sentenced to death, despite the lack of evidence linking them to the crime. One of them belonged to the Knights of Labor.

A surge of hysteria against the labor movement, fueled by the perceived infiltration of foreign radicals, swept the country. Union leaders disavowed any connection to the violence at Haymarket, but the incident badly injured the Knights' reputation. Membership dropped drastically. Haymarket convinced many middle-class Americans that the labor movement was bent on destroying the capitalist order.

Even before Haymarket, the Knights of Labor came under attack from fellow workers. Craft unions, made up of skilled workers only, argued that joining forces with unskilled laborers diluted their bargaining power. As hard-to-replace workers, they would have much more clout in negotiations. In 1886, craft unions organized the **American Federation of Labor (AFL)**. Headed by **Samuel Gompers**, the AFL embodied "bread and butter" unionism. Embracing capitalism and rejecting the long-range, utopian goals of the Knights of Labor, the AFL focused narrowly on short term, concrete aims, such as the eight-hour day and better wages. When asked what labor wanted, Gompers simply replied, "More! More today and more tomorrow; and then . . . more and more." Unlike

Samuel Gompers. "What Does the Working Man Want?" (1890)

the Knights, the AFL did not hesitate to strike to achieve its goals. Moreover, unlike the Knights, the AFL excluded women, blacks, and some immigrants—all of whom the AFL viewed as "cheap" competition that lowered wages and the "dignity" of the union.

Under Gompers's leadership, the AFL made considerable gains. By the turn of the century, the AFL boasted about half a million members. Yet because of its exclusive policies, the AFL represented only a fraction of U.S. workers and undercut worker solidarity by driving a wedge between ethnicities. In 1903, for example, the Japanese-Mexican Labor Association (JMLA) conducted a successful strike in California to increase the wages of beet thinners. The JMLA then petitioned the AFL to charter their organization. Gompers refused unless the union kicked out its Chinese and Japanese workers. The JMLA, citing them as "brothers," rejected Gompers's request. Without the support of the AFL, the JMLA collapsed after several years.

One of the most infamous labor conflicts of the era centered on the fight of a craft union at Carnegie's steel mill in Homestead, Pennsylvania. The **Homestead Lockout** pitted one of the nation's premier industrialists, Andrew Carnegie, against one of the country's most successful craft unions, the Amalgamated Association of Iron and Steel Workers. Carnegie viewed the powerful union as an obstacle to maximizing his profits, and with increased mechanization, he no longer relied on skilled ironworkers and steelworkers. Wishing to crush the union once and for all, he and his right-hand man, **Henry Clay Frick**, offered union workers a new contract that would cut their pay by as much as 26 percent. As Carnegie and Frick anticipated, the union rejected the offer outright.

Expecting a violent showdown, Carnegie left the country for his castle in Scotland and put Frick in charge. On June 10, 1892, Frick locked out the steelworkers and placed three miles of barbed wire fencing around the Homestead works. A private army of 300 Pinkerton detectives, hired to defend the steelworks, approached by river barge. Infuriated Homestead workers attacked the barge with cannon shot and a burning raft. Soon both sides exchanged gunfire and seven workers and three Pinkertons lay dead. When the Pinkerton barge landed, a union man, carrying an American flag, forced them to walk through a gauntlet of angry townspeople who punched and kicked them.

At the request of Frick, Pennsylvania's governor sent 8,500 National Guardsmen to restore order and end worker resistance. Even though his carefully constructed image suffered, Carnegie's actions at Homestead proved to be an economic triumph. He crushed the troublesome craft union, reduced his workforce by 25 percent, and replaced workers with machines, increasing profits even during the depression years of the 1890s. He even managed to extend the standard 12-hour shift. Another 40 years would pass before steelworkers again organized successfully.

Other American workers organized along industrial lines. **Eugene V. Debs**, a veteran activist in the craft union the Brotherhood of Locomotive Firemen, believed that railway workers could increase their power by organizing one industry-wide union. In 1893, he founded the **American Railway Union (ARU)**, which waged a successful strike to restore wages cut during the depression.

The next year, in 1894, Pullman Palace Car workers called a strike. In 1881, **George Pullman** built a model factory town outside of Chicago, where his workers manufactured fancy railroad sleeping cars. Pullman hoped that his model town would curb the worst excesses of the new industrial order. But as the depression set in, Pullman cut wages by 28 percent but did not cut rents on the houses where many of his workers lived or the price of groceries in his company store. In May 1894, when Pullman refused to negotiate with his workers, they called a strike. The ARU, at the request of the workers, supported the **Pullman Strike** and refused to move any trains that included Pullman cars. The boycott was so effective, with the union's 150,000 members participating, that train service to Chicago came to a standstill by June, and rail service from the West Coast to the Midwest slowed to a crawl.

Railroad owners soon countered with their own strategy to crush the powerful ARU. They ordered that all Pullman cars be coupled to U.S. mail trains. As the owners knew, interference with the mails justified federal intervention. The attorney general, a former railroad officer, issued an injunction ordering strikers to move the mail trains, and President **Grover Cleveland** sent federal troops to Chicago to enforce the passage of the trains. The strike and boycott soon collapsed, the ARU was demolished, and its members were blacklisted. Using the Sherman Antitrust Act, authorities arrested Debs for conspiring to interfere with interstate commerce and obstructing the mails. Although these charges were eventually dropped, Debs spent six months in jail on contempt charges for ignoring court injunctions aimed at smothering the strike. After Pullman, Debs shifted his focus away from unionism. Convinced that workers would never make any significant progress in the capitalist system, Debs advocated a political solution as a leader and presidential candidate of the Socialist Party of America.

Eugene Debs, "How I Became a Socialist" (1902)

The **United Mine Workers (UMW)**, founded in 1890 as an industrial union like the ARU, opened its membership to all mine workers, skilled or unskilled. Even by Gilded Age standards, working conditions in the mines were especially inhumane and dangerous, with 14-hour days in boom times. Many miners had to live in company housing and received pay in company "scrip" to purchase their food and supplies from company-owned stores.

Unions such as the UMW fought a particularly difficult battle against powerful mine owners and the state governments that supported them. In addition to National Guard units, called out by governors to break strikes, mine owners employed spies to infiltrate labor unions and regularly employed the Pennsylvania Coal and Iron Police, a force established by the state legislature, paid for by mine owners, and known for its strong-arm tactics. Mine owners also regularly blacklisted union members, making it impossible for them to find mining jobs, and evicted union members and their families from company housing.

In addition to the power of the state, miners found it difficult to overcome ethnic divisions, a problem endemic in the nation's labor movement. Recently arrived immigrant miners, desperate for work, generally refused to join the UMW, making it difficult for the UMW to make much headway.

When the depression of the 1890s resulted in wage cuts, two- or three-day workweeks, and a glut of coal on the market, 200,000 miners struck in eight states. But nonunion miners continued to work, ultimately wrecking the strike. In 1897, a UMW organizing campaign in the anthracite fields of Pennsylvania left 24 unarmed miners dead, killed by local deputies. Not until 1903, when a massive coal strike threatened the nation's fuel supply and **Theodore Roosevelt** became the first American president to intervene on the side of labor, would coal miners achieve a major victory.

The Farmers Organize

The nation's industrial workers were not the only laborers who sought relief in collective action. Farmers also found themselves in the grip of global economic forces beyond their control. Even before the deep depression of the 1890s, many of America's farmers faced hard times. Southern farmers, many of whom had struggled with poverty since the Civil War, found themselves entangled in the crop lien system as cotton prices plummeted on the world market beginning in the 1870s and as southern cotton competed with cotton grown in Egypt and India. By 1890, it cost more to grow cotton than the crop could fetch on the market. Western farmers, like their southern counterparts, suffered from declining prices for their crops, particularly wheat and corn. Technological advancements, such as the mechanical reaper and combine and steam-powered thresher, significantly increased production, creating "food factories" in the West, as one observer called them, that drove prices down. By the end of the 1880s, a bushel of wheat had plummeted from $1.19 to 49 cents. Agribusinesses also made it increasingly difficult for small, independent farmers to compete. By the 1880s, one massive wheat farm in the Dakota territory, for example, consisted of 30,000 acres and employed 200 reapers, 30 steam-powered threshers, and 1,000 farmhands to harvest the crop. To make matters worse, as crop prices dropped, railroads, which continued to consolidate and take advantage of their transportation monopoly, sharply increased their freight rates.

Farmers in the South and West found their relentless toil repaid with poverty and the loss of their farms and their independence. As one farmer wrote, "Each year the plunge into debt is deeper; each year the burden is heavier. . . . Cares are many, smiles are few, and the comforts of life are scantier. . . . Humiliation and dependence bow the head of the proud spirit." Frustrated farmers focused their anger on railroads, which charged exorbitant prices; bankers, who charged high interest rates in a tight credit market; and "middlemen," who profited handsomely by selling farmers' products. Like labor activists in America's industries, farmers argued that they alone had the right to the fruits of their labor.

Like industrial laborers, farmers hoped to seize the inordinate power wielded by the few and restore it to "the people" by organizing collectively. Building on the foundations laid by agricultural organizations such as the Grange, the **Farmers' Alliance** spread rapidly from the cotton belt to the western prairies. Started in Texas in the mid-1870s, the Alliance stressed that the only way for farmers to challenge successfully the power of merchants and monopolies was to unite and work together. The Alliance sponsored traveling lecturers, who used powerful evangelical language to condemn economic evildoers and to recruit farmers and their families into their organization.

The Alliance established cooperative stores; cheap transportation clubs; and warehouses for wheat, corn, tobacco, and cotton. Mining a deep seam of bitterness toward the new economic order, the Alliance claimed 1.5 million members by 1890, about one-quarter of them women. They were treated as equals in the organization, even serving as lecturers and officers. As one of them explained, women "are the chief sufferers whenever poverty or misfortune overtakes the family."

African American farmers faced the same problems as their white counterparts, but the Southern Farmers' Alliance barred them from membership. They formed their own parallel organization, the Colored Farmers' Alliance, which spread across the South in the late 1880s. Claiming a million members by 1890, the black organization also stressed education and cooperation. In addition to race, self-interest separated the two organizations. Unlike the white Alliance, made up largely of middling, propertied farmers, many members of the Colored Alliance were tenants and sharecroppers, whose interests were at odds with landowners'.

Technically nonpartisan, the Farmers' Alliance soon realized its political power. In 1890 in the West, some Alliance members created their own independent third party, the People's (Populist) Party. In the South, that same year, the Alliance, although not committing to a third party, helped elect four governors and 19 of 27 congressmen who agreed to endorse the Alliance agenda. Encouraged by their success, and frustrated by the unwillingness of Republicans or Democrats to enact any significant reform, farmers in 1892 created a national People's Party, its agenda summarized by the slogan "Equal rights to all, special privilege to none." Other politicized Alliance members, who remained in the two parties, also became a force to be contended with. As unprecedented economic disaster rocked the nation beginning in 1893, the Populists seemed poised to make an impact nationally, offering an alternative party with a clearly articulated reform agenda.

The Labor Movement in Global Context

American workers did not fight their battle for justice alone. They drew inspiration and ideas from their compatriots in other parts of the world. Moreover, as workers fluidly crossed national borders to seek employment, they carried ideas and experiences about collective action. Although the American labor movement generally was more conservative than that of Europe, some American laborers framed their struggles transnationally, stressing the common plight of workers in all industrial societies, regardless of nationality or ethnicity.

Crossing and recrossing oceans and borders, immigrants carried labor theories, strategies, and experiences with them. Miners from the British Isles, for example, carried strong union traditions to the coalfields of Pennsylvania, where they played a crucial role in founding the United Mine Workers. They even modeled their strikes in the United States on successful strikes abroad. Their 1893 eight-state strike followed the example of British miners several years before. Conversely, immigrants who returned to their home countries from the United States took their experiences as union members back to their home countries. Schooled in the American labor movement, returning immigrants from countries as diverse as Norway, Italy, and Hungary emerged as labor leaders in their home countries. In addition, social and economic theories such as socialism, communism, and anarchism traveled through conduits of immigration.

American labor organizations provided models for unionization in other parts of the world. Workers in Britain, Australia, Belgium, Canada, France, and New Zealand, for example, all replicated the Knights of Labor's organizational structure. As early as the 1860s, some U.S.-based craft unions, including those for printers and cigar makers, were international organizations with a strong presence in Canada. After the Spanish-American War, the American Federation of Labor expanded globally, into Cuba and the nation's new acquisitions—the Philippines and Puerto Rico.

In addition, some labor activists forged bonds with workers in other industrialized nations as they shared common struggles. European and American labor leaders not only carefully studied political developments on both sides of the Atlantic, but also, at times, encouraged worker solidarity across national borders. In the 1880s, when American window glass workers found their jobs threatened by the importation of French, English, and Belgian glass workers, they sent a delegation to those countries and managed to halt further incursions of foreign workers by convincing them of the injury they caused fellow workers in the United States.

Despite the many links among the world's industrial workers, European labor movements fared much better than those in the United States. Comparatively speaking, American labor made relatively few gains and was generally far more conservative. A comparison of U.S. and French workers in this era is especially revealing. Workers in France did not have to deal with the cheap and abundant pool of unskilled labor—largely a result of immigration—that hampered collective action in the United States. Strikes in France tended to be much more successful, as labor could not easily be replaced. As in the United States, the national government regularly intervened in labor disputes in France, but unlike the United States, the French government generally sided with workers over employers. As a result, French workers usually won at least some of their demands.

In the United States, state and federal government, with the support of the public, repressed labor activism and instead emphasized individualism and the defense of property as their revolutionary heritage. By contrast, drawing on the tradition of the French Revolution, the French public pressured government officials to aid workers against the "aristocratic" tyranny of employers. In the United States, middle-class fears of revolutionary worker movements, strengthened by violent incidents such as Haymarket, also placed labor radicals on the fringes. Finally, ethnic divisions, only minimally present in France, drove a wedge in worker solidarity in the United States. Samuel Gompers summarized the trials of American labor and the powerful opposition it faced: "Against us we find arrayed a host guarded by special privilege, buttressed by legalized trusts, fed by streams of legalized monopolies, picketed by gangs of legalized Pinkertons, and having in reserve thousands of embryo employers, who, under the name militia, are organized, uniformed, and armed for the sole purpose of holding the discontented in bondage."

STUDY QUESTIONS FOR WORKERS FIGHT BACK

quiz

1. Compare and contrast the strategies of workers in forming labor unions and the strengths and weaknesses of each approach.

2. What factors accounted for the lack of progress in the American labor movement of the late 1800s?

⊙ THE NEW INDUSTRIAL ORDER: DEFENSE AND DISSENT

The new economic order produced a great deal of anxiety about opportunity and success. Everywhere Americans looked, they saw progress in technological innovations, comforts, and goods unthinkable only a few decades before. But progress also brought misery, violence, and a noticeably tightening and unbalanced social and economic order.

Gilded Age Americans engaged with their counterparts in Europe in passionate discussions about their world. Just as workers shared ideas across national borders, so, too, did businessmen, politicians, and reformers. Some writers dispensed advice about how to succeed in the new harshly competitive economic order, while others debated pressing issues. Could they ameliorate the hostile and often violent labor conflict that threatened to tear the country apart? Were industrial capitalism and its many consequences products of the natural evolution of human progress, or were they unnatural and retrograde, dividing people into warring factions? Might there be more humane alternatives?

Defending the New Order

The new economic order, with its cutthroat competition and its spasmodic growth, spawned a new genre of literature to alleviate the anxieties of middle-class Americans: the success manual. These guidebooks, the forerunners of motivational and self-help literature popular today, were aimed at young men just embarking on their careers. Many of these American manuals drew on the work of Scottish writer Samuel Smiles, who in 1859 published *Self-Help*, a book widely read on both sides of the Atlantic. Acknowledging a loss of faith in the American Dream, success manuals posited a relentlessly upbeat, confident message to encourage readers that success was still possible for those who worked hard. The *Royal Path of Life; or, Aims and Aids to Success and Happiness*, first published in 1877, was the most popular of scores of success manuals published in the late 19th century and sold an extraordinary 800,000 copies. The guide reassured readers that "life is not mean—it is good," and emphasized that young men could still shape their lives; they had a choice to actively steer to the path of success through self-reliance, hard work, honesty, loyalty, frugality, and good character. Traditional values, the manuals insisted, still provided the key to success.

Horatio Alger's popular stories for boys also stressed the importance of individual effort and upright morals for success. But Alger included the crucial element of luck. Alger's main characters, typically plucky, self-reliant newsboys or shoeshine boys, worked in the cutthroat urban jungle of New York. His heroes took control of their lives by saving their money and educating themselves. Their big breaks, however, came through lucky circumstances. Alger's stories promised upward mobility from "rags to respectability" to those who worked hard, yet his emphasis on luck recognized the limits of diligence and character alone. Even so, his books, with titles such as *Strive and Succeed* and *Risen from the Ranks*, reassured middle-class boys and their parents that the American Dream was still alive and well. Alger's books sold millions of copies around the world, providing assurance to generations of boys and men worldwide that they possessed the keys to success in the competitive world of industrial capitalism.

Excerpt from Horatio Alger, *Risen from the Ranks* (1874)

One of the best-known defenses of the new economic order came from the pen of steel magnate Andrew Carnegie. In 1889, Carnegie published a widely disseminated essay entitled "Wealth," positing what became popularly known as **"The Gospel of Wealth."** Carnegie argued that the benefits of industrialization clearly outweighed the problems it created. He acknowledged the "price which society pays for the law of competition" in brutal conflicts between workers and employees and the gap between rich and poor. But "the advantages," he insisted, "are greater still," in the cheap goods and comforts available to all.

Carnegie justified his massive fortune by becoming a public benefactor. "The man who dies rich," he proclaimed, "dies disgraced." Rejecting outright charitable contributions, Carnegie advocated philanthropy to provide "the ladders upon which the aspiring can rise," such as parks, art museums, and libraries—institutions that "help those who help themselves." Practicing what he preached, Carnegie gave away over $350 million by the time of his death in 1919. He funded more than 2,800 free libraries around the world

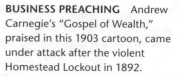

BUSINESS PREACHING Andrew Carnegie's "Gospel of Wealth," praised in this 1903 cartoon, came under attack after the violent Homestead Lockout in 1892.

and made generous financial gifts to colleges and universities, established a pension fund for college professors and steelworkers, and created an institution for international peace. Following in Carnegie's footsteps, John D. Rockefeller gave away even more money than Carnegie, established the University of Chicago, and funded medical research.

The "Gospel of Wealth" sparked debate both nationally and internationally. Carnegie's ideas were discussed broadly in newspapers, journals, and magazines. Carnegie preached his "gospel" in hundreds of speeches on both sides of the Atlantic.

Philanthropy, however, did not convince critics on either side of the Atlantic of the benefits of industrial capitalism. A prominent British minister contended that a truly Christian society would not have millionaires at all, as "millionaires at one end of the scale involve paupers at the other end." Similarly, an American clergyman bluntly stated that the real problem that afflicted society was the distribution—not the redistribution—of wealth and that it was wrong "to make charity do the work of justice."

After the heartless Homestead Lockout in 1892, Carnegie's philanthropy came under especially withering attack. One British newspaper asserted that after Homestead, Carnegie's writings were nothing but "a wholesome piece of satire." Likewise, a St. Louis paper concluded, "Ten thousand 'Carnegie Public Libraries' would not compensate the country for the direct and indirect evils resulting from the Homestead lockout."

Critiquing the New Order

Henry Demarest Lloyd also questioned Carnegie's claims regarding progress and the benefits bestowed by industrial capitalism. Instead, he argued, the new order created a society at war with itself. Lloyd's *Wealth Against Commonwealth* (1894) was a massive exposé of Rockefeller's Standard Oil Company. The book built on his earlier article, "The Story of a Great Monopoly" (1881), which raised support for the Sherman Antitrust Act.

Excerpt from Henry Demarest Lloyd, *Wealth Against Commonwealth* (1894)

Lloyd argued that the new economic order "has killed competition." Even more frightening, "corporations are grown greater than the State." The "winners" sitting atop the economic order now had "the powers of life and death" and "wield them over us by the same 'self-interest' with which they took them from us." Lloyd argued for the importance of the common good over individualism.

Poverty, not wealth, was "the striking feature" of the age. The "cheapness" of goods, so highly touted by Carnegie, resulted in "fortunes for a few, monstrous luxury for them and proportionate deprivation for the people." Lloyd called for a return to the Golden Rule, to "love thy neighbor as thyself." He appealed to workers and farmers to spearhead a spiritual rebirth that would usher in a new, cooperative social order.

As people sought answers in the midst of the depression, Lloyd's book went through four printings in 1894 alone. People around the world debated his ideas. In Great Britain, Lloyd's passionate treatise incited discussion in business, legal, and labor circles and led to condemnation of American trusts; others used Lloyd's analysis to advise British investors to withdraw their investments in the United States. In Canada, Lloyd's tome inspired Canadian oil companies to develop European markets to ward off takeover attempts by Standard Oil. Rockefeller himself commented that he "paid no more attention to all this nonsense than an elephant might be expected to pay to a tiny mosquito." Nevertheless, Lloyd's attack on trusts deeply influenced future Americans, such as **Louis Brandeis**, who would play a part in dismantling some large trusts in the first decades of the 20th century, including Standard Oil in 1911.

Lloyd's writings also launched a new genre of reporting: investigative journalism. Derided by critics as "**muckraking**," his style of journalism inspired a whole generation to investigate nearly every dimension of the new economic order, from child labor to the meatpacking industry. Believing that exposing facts could rouse the American public to demand change, "muckraking" helped bring about major reforms in the late 19th and early 20th centuries.

Published in 1888, **Edward Bellamy**'s *Looking Backward* provided a fictional critique of the new industrial order. Like *Wealth Against Commonwealth,* this utopian novel advocated for a cooperative rather than a competitive society. Bostonian Julian West, put into deep sleep by a hypnotist in 1887, awakens 113 years later, in the year 2000, to a world that he no longer recognizes. Much to his shock, poverty, disease, violent labor struggles, and rampant individualism no longer exist. Instead, a perfect world unfolds before him in which the conflicts and problems of the late 19th century have dissolved before a cooperative, secure society of plenty. Dr. Leete, West's guide in the strange new world, explains that this utopian society evolved naturally and nonviolently. Business consolidations led to one big trust, as the people took it over "in the common interest for common profit." This "nationalism," as Bellamy called it, saw selfishness give way to concern for the common good. All people labored in the national industrial army, and as all jobs contributed to the public good, no job was menial.

Excerpt from Edward Bellamy, *Looking Backward* (1888)

Looking Backward was an instant national and international bestseller, surpassed in the 19th century only by *Uncle Tom's Cabin* in its influence. The book sold half a million copies in the United States alone; both the Knights of Labor and the Farmers' Alliance provided their members with copies. *Looking Backward* was translated into every major

interactive timeline

TIMELINE 1868–1901

AMERICA	YEAR	THE WORLD
May Horatio Alger publishes *Ragged Dick or, Street Life in New York*	1868	Meiji Restoration restores direct imperial rule in Japan and begins modernization process
Dec Knights of Labor founded in Baltimore	1869	Suez Canal opens linking Mediterranean and Red Sea
John D. Rockefeller and partners establish Standard Oil Company	1870	
Mar Paris Commune generates massive newspaper coverage and generates fear of communist revolution in United States	1871	**Mar** Paris Commune takes over French capital for two months until vanquished by government forces
Aug Aaron Montgomery Ward pioneers nation's first mail-order catalogue	1872	
	1873	**Sep** Stock market panic sets off worldwide economic depression that lasts until 1878
	1874	**Apr** Jennie Jerome marries Lord Randolph Churchill, the first of scores of transatlantic Gilded Age marriages of wealthy American heiresses to European aristocrats
Jul Great Railroad Strike sparks violence and nationwide general strike	1877	
Mar Henry Demarest Lloyd publishes "The Story of a Great Monopoly," an exposé of Standard Oil	1881	
May 4 Bombing in Chicago's Haymarket Square **Dec** Craft unions organize American Federation of Labor under the leadership of Samuel Gompers	1886	**Jan** Karl F. Benz, German engineer, patents first commercial automobile

European language as well as Chinese and Hindi. The novel found especially fertile ground in nations buffeted by massive industrialization. In Russia, the novel was tremendously popular in socialist, labor, and student circles. A German commentator remarked that "one could hear nothing else but Bellamy." In Britain, the book sold 100,000 copies by 1890 and sparked widespread debate. Whereas Marxists dismissed the book for its rejection of class-based revolution, members of the middle class found it particularly attractive, as it promised a peaceful transition to a just future, through evolution rather than violence. Bellamy inspired a whole generation of progressive social reformers in the United States and abroad.

STUDY QUESTIONS FOR THE NEW INDUSTRIAL ORDER: DEFENSE AND DISSENT

quiz

1. What do success manuals, Lloyd's "muckraking," and Bellamy's utopian novel suggest about the concerns and anxieties of Americans and their European counterparts regarding the new industrial order?

2. Who do you think makes the most convincing arguments: defenders of the new industrial order or those who criticized it?

AMERICA	YEAR	THE WORLD
Jan Edward Bellamy publishes *Looking Backward: 2000–1887,* an internationally influential utopian novel	**1888**	
Jun Andrew Carnegie publishes "Wealth," which justifies industrial capitalism's benefits for society, partly through philanthropy	**1889**	
Jan United Mine Workers organized as union **Jul** Sherman Antitrust Act aimed at dismantling monopolies inadvertently sets off flurry of corporate mergers	**1890**	
Jun Homestead Lockout begins, resulting in the crushing of Amalgamated Association of Iron and Steel Workers **Jul** The People's (Populist) Party founded in Omaha, Nebraska	**1892**	
Jun Eugene V. Debs organizes American Railway Union, an industrial union	**1893**	**Mar** Wall Street panic precipitates international economic depression that lasts until 1897
May The Pullman Strike, led by the American Railway Union, begins; ends in August with President Cleveland's use of federal troops **Sep** Henry Demarest Lloyd publishes *Wealth Against Commonwealth,* an attack on Standard Oil and unbridled capitalism	**1894**	
Jan *United States v. E. C. Knight Co.* rules that federal government can regulate only monopolies involved in interstate commerce	**1895**	
Feb U.S. Steel becomes world's first billion-dollar industry	**1901**	

Summary

- In the last quarter of the 19th century, a new industrial order linked the United States to a global economy and the creation of networks through which money, technology, labor, goods, and ideas flowed. By 1900, the nation had emerged as the world's industrial leader.
- The new industrial order changed the nature of work and the workplace. Mechanization and specialization greatly reduced the need for skilled labor. White-collar managers and employers emphasized productivity and profits at the expense of blue-collar workers, and workers regularly faced unemployment and underemployment during economic downturns.
- The Gilded Age was a battlefield of industrial warfare, of bloody strikes and lock-outs that pitted worker against employer.
- American workers forged ties and drew inspiration from fellow workers abroad. But in the Gilded Age, American workers made little headway, especially compared to their French counterparts.
- The new industrial order, with both its promise and its problems, sparked international conversations that both defended and attacked it.

Key Terms and People

audio
flashcards

Alger, Horatio 605
American Federation of Labor (AFL) 599
American Railway Union (ARU) 600
Bellamy, Edward 607
Brandeis, Louis 607
Carnegie, Andrew 577
Cleveland, Grover 601
Debs, Eugene V. 600
Farmers' Alliance 602
Frick, Henry Clay 600
Gilded Age 578
Gompers, Samuel 599
"The Gospel of Wealth" 605
Great Railroad Strike of 1877 596
Hayes, Rutherford B. 597
Haymarket Affair 599
Homestead Lockout 600
horizontal integration 583
Knights of Labor 598

laissez-faire economics 584
Lloyd, Henry Demarest 583
modern corporation 580
muckraking 607
Powderly, Terrence V. 598
Pullman, George 600
Pullman Strike 601
Rockefeller, John D. 580
Roosevelt, Theodore 601
Sherman Antitrust Act 583
social Darwinism 585
Spencer, Herbert 585
Taylor, Frederick Winslow 592
United Mine Workers (UMW) 601
United States v. E. C. Knight Co. 584
Vanderbilt, Cornelius 580
vertical integration 582
Ward, Aaron Montgomery 585
Wells, H. G. 595

Reviewing Chapter 17

1. Did the benefits of industrial capitalism, as Andrew Carnegie asserted, outweigh the negative consequences? Use examples from the chapter to support your argument.
2. Discuss ways that the relationship between workers and employers changed in the Gilded Age.

Further Reading

Blackmon, Douglas A. *Slavery by Another Name: The Re-enslavement of Black Americans from the Civil War to World War II.* New York: Anchor, 2009. The shocking story of the re-enslavement of black Americans through the convict labor system and the role of their labor in the industrializing New South.

Domosh, Mona. *American Commodities in an Age of Empire.* New York: Routledge, 2006. Explores the commercial empire established before the political empire in the late 19th century with a focus on the nation's five largest international companies, including Singer Manufacturing and the H. J. Heinz Company.

Kiple, Kenneth F. *A Moveable Feast: Ten Millennia of Food Globalization.* New York: Cambridge University Press, 2007. Examines the history of food globalization over thousands of years with an especially valuable chapter on industrialization and food.

Nasaw, David. *Andrew Carnegie.* New York: Penguin, 2007. A comprehensive look at the life and times of Andrew Carnegie and his rise from impoverished immigrant to one of the world's richest and most powerful men.

Rodgers, Daniel T. *The Work Ethic in Industrial America, 1850–1920.* Chicago: University of Chicago Press, 1978. A classic study of the changing nature of work and the response of laborers to the new industrial order.

Trachtenberg, Alan. *The Incorporation of America: Culture and Society in the Gilded Age.* New York: Hill and Wang, 2007. A comprehensive examination of the impact of industrial capitalism on American culture.

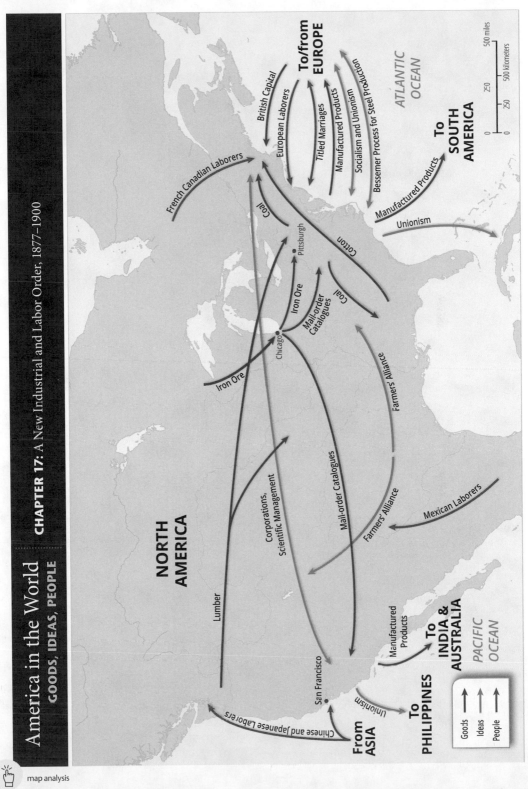

America in the World
GOODS, IDEAS, PEOPLE

CHAPTER 17: A New Industrial and Labor Order, 1877–1900

NORTH AMERICA

ATLANTIC OCEAN

PACIFIC OCEAN

To/from EUROPE

To SOUTH AMERICA

To INDIA & AUSTRALIA

To PHILIPPINES

From ASIA

British Capital
European Laborers
Titled Marriages
Manufactured Products
Socialism and Unionism
Bessemer Process for Steel Production

Manufactured Products

Unionism

French Canadian Laborers

Coal

Cotton

Pittsburgh

Iron Ore

Coal

Mail-order Catalogues

Chicago

Iron Ore

Farmers' Alliance

Farmers' Alliance

Mail-order Catalogues

Mexican Laborers

Corporations, Scientific Management

Lumber

San Francisco

Manufactured Products

Unionism

Chinese and Japanese Laborers

Goods
Ideas
People

0   250   500 miles
0   250   500 kilometers

map analysis

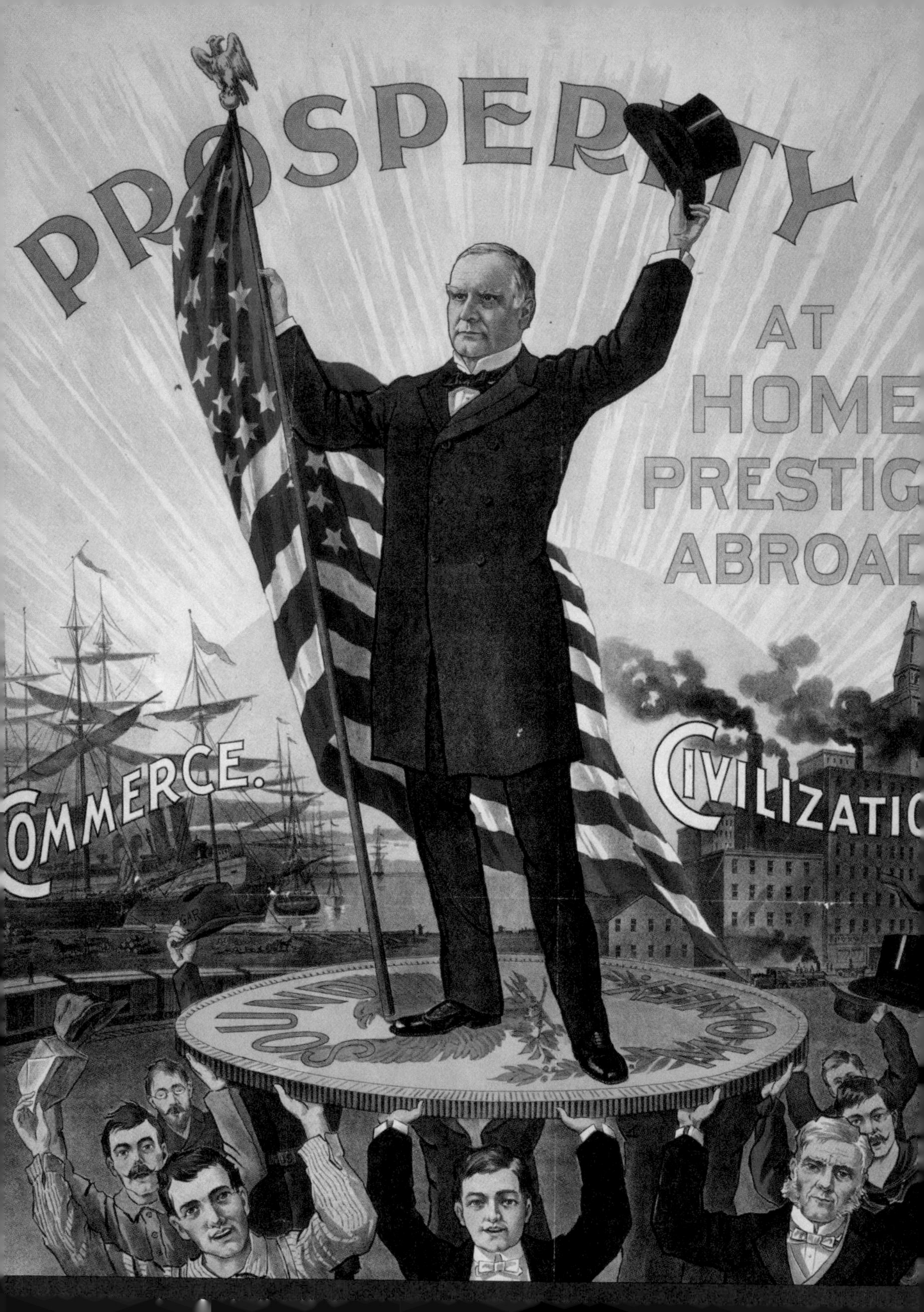
PROSPERITY
AT
HOME
PRESTIG
ABROAD
COMMERCE.
CIVILIZATIO

Cities, Immigrants, Culture, and Politics

1877–1900

I n March 1880, the arrival in New York of Englishman George Scott Railton and seven women associates "created quite a sensation," *The New York Times* reported. The small band, explained the newspaper, constituted "the advance guard of 'The Salvation Army.'" Organized in London 15 years earlier by William Booth, "The Hallelujah Seven" immediately revealed their grand plans for the United States. Marching down the gangplank, holding the Army's flag aloft, they planted their banner in American soil, claimed the nation for God and the Army, and sang a hymn: "With a sorrow of sin, let repentance begin."

Hoping to save the souls of the "unchurched" and eliminate the many "temptations" offered by rapidly expanding Gilded Age cities, the Salvation Army implemented a military approach to bring urbanites under the influence of Protestant Christianity. The Army established "corps" (missions) staffed with "officers" (clergy) assigned military ranks. They wore smart dark blue uniforms trimmed in yellow, their hats encircled with a scarlet ribbon. To publicize their work, they marched through the streets, bearing colorful flags, accompanied by their band featuring brass, drums, and tambourines. "They will preach in the streets to anyone who will listen to them," exclaimed the *Times*. The Army sought souls in barrooms, on street corners, and in brothels and made their first American convert in a saloon hall: a well-known drunk, "Ash-Barrel Jimmy," who earned his nickname after police found him inebriated and frozen—headfirst—in a barrel. The *New York World* labeled the Army "A Peculiar People amid Queer Surroundings."

Although viewed by some as eccentric, the organization spread rapidly to cities around the country, where it is still a presence today. Within a decade of its arrival, the Salvation Army had spread to 43 states. The Army not only fed souls spiritually, but also fed hungry bodies. Thousands of "soldiers"—almost all native-born Protestant men and women—opened soup kitchens and established day nurseries, orphanages, "rescue homes" for prostitutes, and secondhand stores.

The Salvation Army was just one of many approaches to the social problems created by urbanization. London, New York, and other rapidly growing cities faced similar crises and reformers shared ideas and methods for social reform across the Atlantic. Protestant organizations, such as the Salvation Army, especially worried about the lack of moral influence in impersonal cities where temptations like saloons seemed to blossom at every corner. In addition, they hoped to bring immigrants, most of whom embraced Roman Catholic and Jewish faiths, under their influence.

Despite their many good works, the Salvation Army often faced resistance. Street toughs regularly attacked the "Hallelujah Lads and Lasses," pelting them with rotten eggs, rocks, and even dead cats. Roman Catholics especially resented their attempts to convert them to Protestantism. In the end, the Salvation Army made few converts among immigrants.

The story of the Salvation Army reflects the anxieties about urbanization and immigration experienced by many Americans and responses to those concerns. Would the rapid shift from an agrarian to an urban-industrial nation change the character of the United States? Could the nation remain both united and ethnically diverse?

URBANIZATION

Urbanization—a term first coined in the 1880s to describe the unprecedented growth of cities—was a consequence of industrialization and the massive migrations that fueled the new economic order. Urbanization largely defined the United States and other industrializing nations of the world in the late 19th century. As early as 1867, New York journalist Horace Greeley noted, "We cannot all live in cities yet nearly all seem determined to do so." The Gilded Age was the pivotal period for the shift from rural to urban society, a trend that continued into the 20th century. Cities grew both horizontally, sprawling across the landscape, and vertically, as new, taller buildings seemed to pierce the sky. They became increasingly segregated and fragmented by class, race, and ethnicity. The rapid growth of cities transformed the landscape and culture in ways troubling to contemporary observers. Although cities embodied late 19th-century notions of progress and modernity, their growing dominance challenged the traditional Jeffersonian vision of the nation as a land of rooted, rural peoples and raised disturbing questions: Did impersonal, highly diverse cities represent the decline or advance of the republic?

The Growth of Cities

Whereas cities throughout the industrializing world grew during the 1800s, urbanization accelerated rapidly in the last 30 years of the century. At the midpoint of the 19th century, only two cities claimed a population of over a million people—London and Paris. By the turn of the 20th century, New York, Chicago, and Philadelphia in the United States—along with Berlin, Tokyo, St. Petersburg and Moscow, Buenos Aires, and Osaka—had reached, or were fast approaching, that mark. In addition to the growth of massive metropolitan areas around the world, towns and cities of all sizes, from industrial cities to trading centers and county seats, also expanded. But the "great cities," as they were called—those with a population of over 100,000—most often both captured the imagination of the public and stoked its fears.

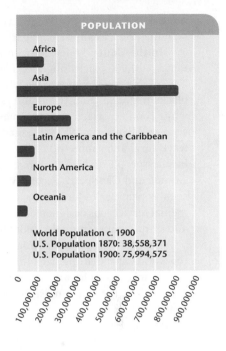

Just as Great Britain pioneered industrial capitalism, it led the way in urbanization. As early as 1800, London claimed a million people; by 1890, three of four people in England lived in an urban area. By contrast, on the eve of the Civil War, only one in five Americans lived in an urban area, defined liberally as a town or city of 2,500 or more. By 1900, 30 million Americans, or two of every five, dwelled in cities. Even though the South and parts of the West remained largely rural, by 1890, the United States was as urbanized as Belgium. By 1880, New York became the first American city to reach a million inhabitants, followed by Chicago and Philadelphia in 1890. The country's "great cities" also jumped significantly, from 14 in 1870 to 38 in 1900.

But as rapidly as urbanization occurred in the United States, cities in other parts of the world matched or outstripped it. Berlin grew roughly as fast as New York and reached a million people by the turn of the century; Sao Paulo, Brazil, and Lodz, in the Russian Empire, outpaced even Chicago's phenomenal development by growing over 800 percent between 1870 and 1900. In all of these cases, migrants from the countryside—internally and internationally—were the key factor in explosive urban growth.

The Peopling of American Cities

Outlook, a popular magazine of the era, pointed out that towns and cities attracted both the rich and poor seeking more opportunity: "The towns are being recruited by those too poor to be able to live in the country, as well as by those too rich to be willing to live there." Overpopulation of the countryside, coupled with agricultural mechanization, in which machines replaced laborers, forced rural peoples to look to cities for work. Worldwide economic depressions also deeply hurt farmers, who lost their farms when they could not pay creditors. For those better off, especially for ambitious young men, towns and cities seemed to offer unlimited business prospects and the chance to enjoy modern technology, such as electricity and telephones, and a whole range of leisure activities, such as amusement parks and vaudeville theater.

In the United States, African Americans continued to flow into cities. Approximately 341,000 blacks migrated from the South to the North between 1870 and 1900, a small migration compared to what would follow in the 20th century. But many more blacks migrated from the countryside to southern towns and cities, where, like their white counterparts, they sought new opportunities. The South's fastest-growing cities, such as Atlanta and Nashville, had larger populations of young blacks who tended to leave rural areas more often than their parents. A small black middle class, made of businesspeople and professionals, developed in these cities as well. Atlanta's Auburn Avenue and Charlotte's Second Ward, for example, featured black-owned businesses, such as pharmacies and banks, and the offices of doctors, dentists, and lawyers. Even menial service jobs designated for blacks in cities, such as domestic labor, waiting tables, and shining shoes, provided more opportunity and freedom than sharecropping.

But more than internal migrants from the countryside, immigrants from around the world expanded the size of towns and cities in the Gilded Age. Most of the 11 million immigrants who arrived in the United States between 1870 and 1900 settled in cities, where they were most likely to find employment. The great majority were Europeans, but Chinese, until their exclusion in 1882, Japanese, French Canadian, and Mexican migrants also came in search of jobs and a better future. Immigrants radically transformed America's cities. By 1900, 60 percent of those who dwelled in the nation's 12 largest urban centers were either foreign born or had parents who had been born abroad. In some cities—such as Chicago, Cleveland, and Detroit—four out of five residents fell into that category.

Types of Cities

The industrial metropolis emerged as the typical city in this period. The three largest American cities in 1900, New York, Chicago, and Philadelphia, all featured diversified industry, business districts, and residential neighborhoods increasingly segregated by class, race, and ethnicity. Chicago, even more than its older East Coast counterparts, epitomized the new metropolis. With a population of roughly 4,000 when it was chartered as a city in 1837, this sleepy, dusty trading town on the shores of Lake Michigan boasted 100,000 residents by 1860. Twenty years later, the city had grown to half a million people, despite a devastating fire in 1871. And in just 10 years, from 1880 to 1890, Chicago doubled its population to a million people, making it the nation's second-largest city (Table 18.1). Ideally situated on the edge of the country's industrial and manufacturing belt to the east and rich farmlands to the west, Chicago emerged as a rail hub and distribution center, and teemed with products from midwestern and western farms and forests that were dispersed throughout the country. Enterprising citizens constructed grain elevators, manufacturing plants, and slaughterhouses, establishing a massive empire of national and international trade. Market and credit networks kept cities such as Chicago inextricably linked to the countryside. Even as urban and rural residents increasingly thought of themselves as different types of Americans—and often as rivals—economic ties established mutual dependency.

Although the industrial metropolis cast a huge shadow, it was not the only type of city that grew at a remarkable rate. Just as railroads powered the growth of the nation's

Table 18.1 Five Largest U.S. Cities: 1860 and 1900

Not only did the nation's five largest cities grow at a phenomenal rate between 1860 and 1900 (New York absorbed Brooklyn in 1898), but they also reflected a geographical shift. In 1860, all five were located on the East Coast; by 1900, Chicago and St. Louis had cracked the list.

RANK	CITY	POPULATION
1860		
1	New York, NY	813,669
2	Philadelphia, PA	565,529
3	Brooklyn, NY	266,661
4	Baltimore, MD	212,418
5	Boston, MA	177,840
1900		
1	New York, NY	3,347,202
2	Chicago, IL	1,698,575
3	Philadelphia, PA	1,293,697
4	St. Louis, MO	575,238
5	Boston, MA	560,892

Source: Eighth and Twelfth Censuses of the United States.

metropolises, they also fueled the expansion of smaller cities. These second tier cities specialized in manufacturing or processing particular products for regional, national, and international markets. Denver specialized in slaughtering and packing western beef. Portland, Oregon, featured the lumber industry, whereas Tampa, Florida, manufactured cigars. One-industry mill towns also mushroomed. Johnstown, Pennsylvania, produced iron and steel; Woonsocket, Rhode Island, manufactured textiles; and Winston-Salem, North Carolina, made cigarettes.

Following patterns of industrialization, urbanization developed unevenly in the United States and occurred most intensely in the Northeast and the manufacturing belt that extended from Pittsburgh to Chicago. By 1910, the Northeast contained 70 percent of the nation's urban population. Despite inspiring images of wide, open prairies, the West also experienced rapid urbanization in the late 19th century, second only to the Northeast and upper Midwest manufacturing belt. The Transcontinental Railroad and its numerous branch and trunk feeders sparked urbanization in the West. In 1900, in the far West, San Francisco remained the region's largest city and the nation's ninth-largest city, with over 350,000; Los Angeles's population just exceeded 100,000. But by 1910, Los Angeles had over 250,000 inhabitants and Seattle, Portland, and Denver had over 200,000. With the growth of these great cities, as well as smaller urban areas, over half of westerners lived in cities by that time.

Only the South remained largely rural, although it, too, experienced urban growth. In 1900, only about 17 percent of southerners lived in a town or city, and the region

Bird's eye views of five American cities, ca. 1880–1900

contained only 11 percent of the nation's urban population. The inland cities of Atlanta, Charlotte, and Nashville emerged as quintessential New South cities, challenging the dominance of Old South coastal cities such as Charleston. Small, modest railroad towns at the time of the Civil War, these new cities exploded in the late 19th and early 20th centuries as trading centers with some industry. They attracted relatively few immigrants but drew many migrants from the countryside. Atlanta, for example, grew by a remarkable 1,521 percent from less than 10,000 people to 155,000 between 1860 and 1900. But New South cities remained relatively small, especially by national standards. New Orleans remained the region's largest city in the Gilded Age, but only the 12th-largest city in the nation.

Cities Transformed and "Sorted Out"

The late 19th-century city differed dramatically from earlier urban centers in its spatial patterns, sprawl, and vertical growth. Earlier in the century, most had been compact "walking cities," as residents lived within walking distance of jobs, stores, and businesses, all located in the city core; city limits extended only as far as people could travel on foot, rarely beyond two miles. Businesses, homes, and factories all shared space in these densely populated areas, and people of all classes, races, and ethnicities lived and worked in close quarters.

Transportation innovations, especially the streetcar, transformed American cities. First implemented in Richmond, Virginia, in 1888, the electric streetcar made it possible to work and shop in the center city while living on its fringes, in suburbs miles from congestion and grime. Electric-powered subways, first introduced in Boston in 1897, provided another source of cheap urban transportation, as did elevated streetcars and cable cars. Gilded Age cities began to sort out by class, race, ethnicity, and land use. Wealthier white residents separated themselves from poorer urban dwellers, especially immigrants and people of color, abandoning the city center, once the most desirable place to live, for quiet and clean residential developments in suburbs.

Subway riders, New York City, 1914

Suburbanization, along with urbanization, was an important characteristic of Gilded Age America. To those well-off enough to afford them, suburbs, with their quiet, tree-lined residential enclaves, offered escape from urban squalor and an easy commute to work by streetcar. Moreover, suburbs offered the privacy of single-family homes, difficult to come by in cities with rising real estate prices and housing demands. In addition, some exclusive suburbs guaranteed that residents would live only among people like themselves, forbidding the sale of property to blacks, Roman Catholics, and Jews.

Cities also grew vertically. The new industrial order required office space to house the armies of white-collar workers needed to run increasingly complex businesses. Congested and densely packed, even with sprawling, horizontal growth, many cities had only one way to go—and that was up. Technological innovations, especially structural steel frameworks, light masonry walls, and plate-glass windows, made skyscrapers—buildings of 10 stories or more—possible for the first time. Chicago boasted the nation's first skyscraper, the 10-story Home Insurance Building, erected in 1885. The electric elevator made even taller buildings practical, and by 1913, New York's Woolworth Building topped 55 stories and remained the tallest building in the world for almost 20 years.

The demand for urban space transformed housing as well. Multifamily housing replaced the single-family home. Apartments for the middle class and well-to-do, common in Europe but new to U.S. cities, shot skyward. Older family homes were sub-divided into cheap and crowded tenement housing for immigrants. In New England mill towns, multifamily triple-deckers dotted the urban landscape.

STUDY QUESTIONS FOR URBANIZATION

1. What factors accounted for rapid urbanization globally in the late 19th century?

2. How did technological innovations transform America's cities?

quiz

GLOBAL MIGRATIONS

No single group contributed to America's urbanization more than immigrants. "Once a person from this area, man or woman, has been seized by this epidemic American fever," reported a Swedish physician in the late 19th century, "there is nothing one can do about it." Between 1870 and 1900, "America fever" swept the globe, as over 11 million immigrants arrived in the United States, more than in the previous 250 years. This tide of immigrants would continue until the outbreak of World War I in 1914; in those 14 years, an additional 13 million immigrants entered the country.

The last quarter of the 19th century and the first years of the 20th witnessed a massive movement of the world's peoples. A consequence of industrial capitalism, this global migration spurred urbanization not only in the United States but also in other industrial nations. Technological advances, especially steamships, made long-distance migration much easier and cheaper. Contrary to popular conceptions, many migrants regularly crossed and recrossed the Atlantic. About one-third of immigrants to the United States returned permanently to their countries of origin.

The United States had always been a nation of immigrants. But the volume and origin of these immigrants, referred to as "new" immigrants—as most originated in south-ern and eastern Europe—created new fears and anxieties. Anti-immigrant sentiment exploded, and Americans debated whether immigration should be restricted. Growing numbers of native-born Americans questioned whether these "new" immigrants could ever be good Americans. Were they, as a congressman argued, "the ignorant, the pauper, and the vicious class . . . utterly unable to discharge the duties of American citizenship"? Or did they have the right, as another congressman contended, to enjoy "'the land of the free' where the outcast of every nation . . . could breathe our free air"?

A Worldwide Migration

Cities around the world attracted a hodgepodge of migrating people. Many were rural peoples unable to sustain themselves in an overpopulated countryside or to compete with mechanized agriculture and cheap, imported grains from the American Midwest. Political unrest, ethnic conflict, and religious persecution persuaded others to look abroad. Uprooted rural people went to where the jobs were, to industrializing cities in Europe and North and South America, Australia, and New Zealand. Whereas the United States attracted the largest numbers of immigrants, Argentina had the largest *proportion* of immigrants (Map 18.1). In 1914, 30 percent of Argentineans were foreign born, as were 70 percent of Buenos Aires residents.

image
analysis

PHYSICAL EXAMINATION AT ELLIS ISLAND   In 1892, the U.S. government opened Ellis Island, the first federal immigration center, in New York Harbor. Upon arrival, all immigrants were examined for physical or mental problems. In this photo, officials examine a woman for an eye disease known as trachoma. Only about 2 percent of immigrants were barred from entering after their physicals and made to return home.

Transoceanic migration extended older trends. European laborers had traditionally migrated to work for seasonal harvests and later migrated to the continent's burgeoning industries. Advances in transportation made migration across the ocean seem like a natural next step. These improvements, as an Irish resident explained, "brought America so near to this country, that it was just around the corner." In the late 19th century, steamships could cross the Atlantic in two weeks or less, compared with sailing ships that took as long as 42 days. Fare wars among steamship lines also drove prices down, making it possible to cross in steerage for as little as $10. The poorest immigrants managed to raise fare money by selling personal possessions or receiving a ticket from someone who had already migrated.

Chinese immigrants in the South

Outmigration did not just flow westward across the Atlantic from Europe. Smaller numbers of migrants from Asia, mostly from China and Japan, streamed eastward, across the Pacific. Before the Civil War, worsening economic conditions drove Chinese, mostly men, to the United States, which they called "Gold Mountain," to work in mines and build railroads on the West Coast. They later dug the irrigation canals, dikes, and ditches that provided the foundation for California's agricultural empire. Some even made their way to the Mississippi delta, where they worked as sharecroppers. Beginning in the mid-1880s, Japanese immigrants also turned eastward, victimized by rising taxes used to fuel industrial and military development. Several hundred thousand Japanese arrived in Hawaii and the United States, where they largely worked as agricultural

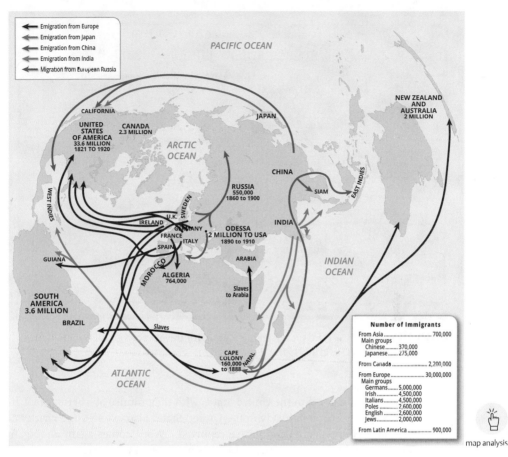

Emigration from Europe
Emigration from Japan
Emigration from China
Emigration from India
Migration from European Russia

PACIFIC OCEAN

CALIFORNIA

JAPAN

NEW ZEALAND
AND
AUSTRALIA
2 MILLION

UNITED
STATES
OF AMERICA
33.6 MILLION
1821 TO 1920

CANADA
2.3 MILLION

ARCTIC
OCEAN

CHINA

WEST INDIES

RUSSIA
550,000
1860 to 1900

SIAM

EAST INDIES

SWEDEN

U.K.

IRELAND

GERMANY
FRANCE
SPAIN
ITALY

ODESSA
2 MILLION TO USA
1890 to 1910

INDIA

GUIANA

ARABIA

INDIAN
OCEAN

MOROCCO

ALGERIA
764,000

Slaves
to Arabia

SOUTH
AMERICA
3.6 MILLION

BRAZIL

Slaves

CAPE
COLONY
160,000
to 1888

NATAL

ATLANTIC
OCEAN

Number of Immigrants	
From Asia	700,000
Main groups	
Chinese	370,000
Japanese	275,000
From Canada	2,200,000
From Europe	30,000,000
Main groups	
Germans	5,000,000
Irish	4,500,000
Italians	4,500,000
Poles	2,600,000
English	2,600,000
Jews	2,000,000
From Latin America	900,000

map analysis

MAP 18.1 Global Migration, 1840–1900 Global migrations accelerated in the late 19th and early 20th centuries with the rise of industrial capitalism. The United States attracted six times more migrants than Argentina, the second-favored destination, and also drew peoples from many more places around the world.

laborers. Mexicans turned to the north, mainly as agricultural workers, lured by higher wages, and regularly crossed the border seasonally. French Canadians from Quebec, faced with an overpopulated countryside and diminishing access to land, headed south, boarding trains for the textile mills of New England.

Economic reasons were not the only motivation for migration. Religious persecution brought eastern Europeans Jews to the United States. Forced to live in the Pale of Settlement in the Russian Empire, under severe restrictions, Jews suffered violent attacks on their villages, known as *pogroms*, with increasing frequency beginning in 1881, when they were wrongly blamed for the assassination of Czar Alexander II.

"America Fever" and the "New" Immigration

"Emigration is spontaneous," an Italian landowner explained to a U.S. immigration commission. "It becomes like a contagious disease. Even the children speak of going to America." Steamship agents promoted "America fever," appearing in even the most

THE "GOLDEN TICKET" Third-class (steerage) ticket for travel aboard a ship from Bremen, Germany, to New York City in 1891. The ticket cost $24.

obscure villages to sell tickets to the United States with the promise of a better life. Letters from friends and relatives already in the United States also extolled the virtues of immigration: as a congressional committee reported, "Word comes again and again that 'work is abundant and wages princely in America.'" Letters also stressed the social equality, religious freedom, and democracy to be enjoyed. At the same time, letters honestly related negative features of American life, particularly the backbreaking labor facing most newcomers, and often insisted that only the toughest should immigrate, warning away those "too weak for America." Employers encouraged immigrant workers to persuade friends and family to migrate to fill the ranks of industry. Responding to the bloody persecution of European Jews, Jewish organizations in the United States aided the immigration of their coreligionists to the United States. Whether through connections with friends, employers, or organizations, most immigrants had well-laid plans by the time they embarked for the United States.

America fever brought immigrants from new parts of Europe, from places previously unrepresented. For the first time, southern and eastern Europeans arrived in large numbers. While northern and western Europeans still dominated from 1870 to 1900, making up roughly two-thirds of immigrants, a flood of southern and eastern Europeans—Italians, Greeks, Poles, Hungarians, Slavs, and Russian Jews—accounted for the other third. Between 1900 and 1914, these immigrants surpassed those from northern and western Europe. Men made up a large majority of immigrants, nearly 70 percent between 1880 and 1910. In some ethnic groups, men dominated even more. At the peak of Italian immigration, in the first decade of the 20th century, men made up 80 percent of that country's immigrant population.

Their origins and massive numbers led Americans to refer to them as "new" immigrants. Native-born Americans tended to use this designation as a negative label, unfavorably contrasting them with "old" immigrants from the British Isles and northern Europe. In comparison, "new" immigrants seemed especially foreign; their cultures, languages, and religions seemed too different for them ever to become "true Americans." Most were Roman Catholic or Jewish, making them especially problematic to native-born, Protestant Americans who believed that they were unfit for self-government. Roman Catholics, they argued, could never be loyal Americans because of their primary allegiance to the pope. Jews seemed especially threatening to Americans who thought of their country as a Christian nation. Asian immigrants, especially the Chinese, seemed even more different and incapable of assimilating into American culture.

Immigrant school-children in Gary, Indiana, ca. 1900

The "Immigrant Problem"

The vast numbers of "new" immigrants and their especially "foreign" origins created a backlash against them. **Nativism**, opposition to immigrants and immigration, spiked in the late 19th century. In union halls, in colleges and universities, on the floor of Congress, and in the popular press, native-born Americans discussed the "immigrant problem." Native-born workers claimed that desperate immigrants worked for very little and drove down their wages. Others drew on social and racial theories to call for an end to immigration. Social Darwinists depicted immigrants, in the words of Francis A. Walker, head of the Bureau of the Census, as "beaten men from beaten races, representing the worst failures in the struggle for existence." Popular racial theories not only asserted the superiority of white-skinned peoples over blacks and Asians but also established a hierarchy of European peoples, with the "Nordic" peoples of northern Europe the "natural" superiors to the darker "Mediterranean" peoples of southern and eastern Europe. Others, drawing on the science of heredity, claimed that the infusion of "inferior racial stock" would "mongrelize" the United States. Still others feared that new cultures, languages, and religions would fragment the nation's fragile unity that it had managed to construct over the course of its history.

In 1887, nativists formed the **American Protective Association** (APA). At its peak in the mid-1890s, the organization boasted half a million members. Advocating strict immigration laws, the APA, like anti-immigrant groups before the Civil War, spread wild conspiracy theories about Roman Catholics. They blamed the economic collapse of the 1890s on the pope and claimed that he sent immigrant laborers as shock troops to overthrow the U.S. government. APA members promised never to employ Roman Catholics if Protestants were available and pledged to keep them from holding any public office.

Other, less conspiratorial groups also argued for immigration restriction. The **Immigration Restriction League**, founded in Boston in 1894, promoted legislation to filter out "inferior" peoples flowing into the country. The depression of the 1890s made many question whether the economy could absorb so many foreigners. During the depression, Congress debated the Immigration Restriction Bill, which would allow only those literate in their own language to immigrate. A Massachusetts congressman condemned the "masses of men who either fester in the slums of our great cities or make predatory incursions into industrial centres, where they work for wages upon which American workingmen cannot live." But others defended immigrants and their invaluable contributions, pointing out that many filled jobs that native-born Americans would not take. Although Congress passed the bill in 1897, President **Grover Cleveland** vetoed it, labeling it "illiberal, narrow, and un-American."

In the 1880s, Chinese immigrants were not as fortunate. Although small in number and once highly prized as railroad workers, the Chinese, more than any other immigrant group in this era, became a target of bigotry and violence. Many native-born Americans viewed the Chinese as people so culturally different that they could never be Americans and placed them in the same inferior racial category as Indians and blacks. Moreover, as many were sojourners planning on returning to China, they maintained their language, dress, and hairstyles; did not outwardly assimilate; and were easily identifiable. A magazine article summed up the stereotypes regarding "John Chinaman": he lived in "squalor and filth," he "gambles incessantly" and "smokes opium," and he was guilty of "degrading white labor to a bestial scale."

Located almost exclusively on the West Coast, the Chinese had suffered economic and legal discrimination for years when the severe economic depression of the 1870s kindled a blaze of anti-Chinese sentiment. White workingmen blamed the Chinese for their unemployment and for driving down wages. With the slogan "The Chinese Must Go," California's Workingman's Party demanded an end to Chinese immigration. Others argued that if Chinese men became naturalized citizens and their numbers continued to grow, they could take over both government and public schools in states like California, overturning the "natural order" of white supremacy. They could then, the journal the *New Englander* warned, threaten Western culture and "teach their own views of science, religion, and morals," even forcing students "to listen to the institutes of Confucius." In 1878, in the case *In re: Ah Yup*, the Ninth U.S. Circuit Court in California denied a citizenship application of a Chinese man. Drawing on contemporary anthropological theories about race, the court ruled that the Chinese petitioner was "Mongolian" and therefore not "white"; only white immigrants—"Caucasians"—could become citizens. By 1882, anti-Chinese sentiment had grown so great that Congress passed the **Chinese Exclusion Act**. The law barred the immigration of Chinese laborers and made it extremely difficult for nonlaborers to enter the country, all but ending Chinese immigration. The first such law in U.S. history, it remained in effect until 1943, with the support of labor organizations such as the American Federation of Labor.

"The Anti-Chinese Wall" (1882)

Prejudice against the Chinese reached far beyond the borders of the United States. Canada, which attracted Chinese laborers to complete the Canadian Pacific Railroad, first limited Chinese immigration in 1885 by requiring a $50 head tax on Chinese entering the country, later increased to $500. Canada also passed a Chinese exclusion act, in effect from 1923 to 1947. From 1901 to 1957, Australia targeted Asian migration, excluding non-Europeans by requiring a test in which immigrants had to write 50 words in a European language.

Another less radical approach to the "immigrant problem" was the attempt to "Americanize" immigrants. A congressman explained in the 1895 debate over immigration restriction: "The newcomers will not change us, but we will change them." Public education served as a key instrument in this process. In 1906, an educator proclaimed the public schools "the sluiceways into Americanism. When the stream of alien children flows through them, it will issue into the reservoirs of national life with the Old World taints filtered out . . . , and the qualities retained that make for loyalty and good citizenship." This definition of "Americanism" had no appreciation for cultural diversity or complex identities; instead, to be an American meant throwing off all of the "inferior" ways of the Old World—language, appearance, culture, and values—for "superior" American ways exclusively. Many public schools, along with night schools established by employers, incorporated lessons in citizenship along with English and history lessons. Americanization efforts could create tensions and misunderstandings in families, as parents often insisted on maintaining their traditional culture and values.

Excerpt from Howard B Grose, *Aliens or Americans?* (1906)

The Round-Trip to America

Despite the rise of nativism, immigrants continued to pour into the United States. With the relative ease of the transatlantic crossing, many immigrants—mostly young men— thought of their sojourn as temporary. They planned to work for the relatively high wages offered in America and then return home. Approximately one-quarter to one-third of immigrants who arrived between 1880 and 1930 did just that. Some ethnic groups had very high rates of return: nearly 9 of 10 Bulgarians, Serbs, and Montenegrins returned to their homelands, whereas 6 of 10 southern Italians remigrated, as did almost half of all Greek immigrants. Some, known as "birds of passage," crossed and recrossed the Atlantic numerous times, including British silk weavers and Italian stonemasons.

Others returned home, not as part of a master plan but because the United States turned out not to be the "golden door" to a better life. Illness or injury sent some home broken and dispirited. Others simply succumbed to homesickness. Still others became disillusioned, especially with the relentless hours of work in dangerous industrial jobs. Some, from Polish Catholics to Swedish Lutherans to observant Jews, cited the nation's "godlessness" and its apparent worship of money instead of a higher power. A Hungarian folk song summed up the feelings of many returnees:

> I boarded the ship on Tuesday morning
> Going back to Hungary.
> God bless America forever,
> Just let me get away.

The transitory nature of this immigration had significant ramifications. Those who planned to return had little interest in joining unions, as strikes and union dues defeated their goal of making as much money as quickly as possible and returning home. Some even worked as strikebreakers to increase their savings. In addition, they also made little effort to assimilate. They did not learn English, attend schools, or become citizens. Temporary immigrants were often criticized, especially by those in labor unions who feared that return migration undercut their efforts and native-born Americans who were insulted that not all immigrants embraced their nation and way of life.

STUDY QUESTIONS FOR GLOBAL MIGRATIONS

1. What factors account for the massive global migrations of the late 19th and early 20th centuries?

2. What explains the rise of nativist sentiment during the Gilded Age? What policies did nativists advocate to restrict immigration?

quiz

Immigrants Who Returned

In 1911, as part of a massive congressional study, investigators traveled to Europe to explore the phenomenon of return migration. Returned immigrants, they found, played major roles as "great promoters" of immigration to the United States. In Italy, investigators found countless examples of successful "Americanos": many had managed to purchase land, even small estates. "Americanos," they found, "live better and have cleaner houses." Many "build a nice cottage" of brick—in an American style, noticeably devoid of "the pigs, donkey, or chickens" that inhabited the houses of Italian peasants. They also "dress well." In addition, as the mayor of a small Italian town pointed out, "those who have been to America do not work as willingly now as before." One villager told the investigators, "The Americans have brought here the paradise."

"Americanos" in Italy, "Amerikanty" in Poland, and "Ok Boys," as they were dubbed in Greece —for their use of that ubiquitous American affirmation—carried money and U.S. culture back to their homelands. Wages earned in mills, mines, and factories made it possible for many to fulfill the dream of landownership. Dramatic increases in landholding occurred in Italy, for example, as a result of return migration. Others purchased businesses or opened shops. American-style houses mushroomed across the European countryside. Their brick or shingle facades, tile roofs, and painted interiors stood in sharp contrast to simple peasant huts. They dressed like Americans, "peacocks," in the view of one Swede, and they incorporated American words into their native languages—"bodi"

◉ STREETS PAVED WITH GOLD?

Evidence of the promise of America—migrants returning with money, glowing letters from friends and relatives—filled immigrants with great expectations. The image of America as a land of "gold" cut across nearly all ethnic groups and nationalities. But many immigrants found the harshness of American life shocking. An Italian immigrant recalled, "We thought the streets were paved with gold. When we got here we saw that they weren't paved at all. Then they told us that we were expected to pave them."

Immigrants filled the ranks of unskilled labor in industrial America. As a minister noted in 1887, "Not every foreigner is a working man but in the cities, at least, it may almost be said that every workingman is a foreigner." Although U.S. wages outstripped those in Europe or Asia, economic cycles of boom and bust, as well as industrial accidents and sickness, made immigrant laborers especially vulnerable. With few safety nets, immigrants devised their own strategies and supportive communities to cope with the uncertainties of American life and the radical changes they faced. Immigrants also faced another perplexing challenge. How much of the Old World should they maintain? How much of the New World should they embrace?

Surviving in "The Land of Bosses and Clocks"

Immigrants provided the foundational labor for the nation's exploding industrial growth. The mechanization of industry made it relatively simple to move into an for buddy in Hungarian, "giobba" for job in Italian. Some also brought back new foods and technology, introducing new farming implements and phonographs to delighted villagers. And they formed their own social clubs, such as the "United States Club" in Denmark and the "George Washington Greek-American Association" in Greece.

But perhaps most importantly, they carried back new ideas. Immersed in American democracy, those who returned seemed far less deferential to authority and social superiors. In addition, some transplanted reform movements to their own countries, becoming temperance advocates, educational reformers, and politicians. Three sojourners even emerged as their nation's leaders: Johan Nygaardsvold, once a construction worker in the United States and active in radical labor politics, became prime minister of Norway in 1935. Oskari Tokoi toiled in mines in the western United States for a decade in the 1890s. When he returned to Finland, he spread the labor union ideas he had learned in the United States and became Finland's prime minister in 1917. Latvia's Karlis Ulmanis labored for eight years in the United States and ultimately served seven times as prime minister.

The bonds between the United States and those who returned remained strong for many years. U.S. troops fighting in Italy in World War II often found themselves greeted affectionately by villagers bearing snapshots and other souvenirs attesting to their time in the United States.

- In what ways did return migrants impact the cultures of their home countries?
- What did they carry back with them from the United States?

unskilled industrial job. Through chain migration, in which immigrants brought family and friends to the United States, specific ethnic groups soon concentrated in particular jobs and industries. Eastern Europeans—Poles, Hungarians, and Slavic peoples—labored in the coal mines and steel mills of Pennsylvania as well as the stockyards of Chicago. Finns predominated in copper mining and smelting in Michigan. Eastern European Jews, many of whom were already skilled in the needle trades, flowed into the expanding ready-made garment industry in New York. Italian men wielded the shovel, dominating municipal work crews in New York, Chicago, and San Francisco, building and paving streets and digging sewer and water lines; several thousand Italians also labored in Louisiana's sugar cane fields, and Italian women toiled in the garment industry.

The labor demands of Gilded Age industry came as a shock. Although some had experience working in European industry, most came from rural backgrounds. To them, the United States seemed like nothing but "the land of bosses and clocks." A Polish immigrant explained in a letter home that in America, one had to "sweat more during the day than during a whole week in Poland." A sweatshop garment worker recalled, "We were like slaves. You couldn't pick your head up. You couldn't talk. We used to go to the bathroom. The forelady used to go after us, we shouldn't stay too long."

Channeled into the most dangerous and demanding jobs, immigrants suffered death and injury at much higher rates than their native-born counterparts. Language barriers contributed to being hurt on the job, as immigrants, working among hazardous machines, did not always understand directions. Overworked and exhausted, they also succumbed to diseases such as tuberculosis and typhoid fever.

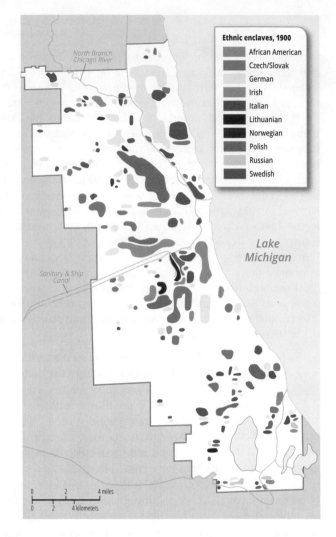

MAP 18.2 Ethnic Enclaves By 1900, Chicago, like most major U.S. cities, was made up of a wide range of ethnic groups. As older immigrant groups, such as the Germans and Irish, moved out of industrial areas on the South Side to neighborhoods with better housing, "new" immigrants, from southern and eastern Europe, moved into areas they abandoned. A small group of southern black migrants also settled on the South Side, forerunners of the massive black migration that would begin with World War I.

Ethnic enclaves, 1900
- African American
- Czech/Slovak
- German
- Irish
- Italian
- Lithuanian
- Norwegian
- Polish
- Russian
- Swedish

North Branch Chicago River

Sanitary & Ship Canal

Lake Michigan

0   2   4 miles
0   2   4 kilometers

Even though real wages earned by American laborers increased significantly in the late 19th century—as much as 50 percent by some estimates—workers, especially immigrants, faced particular challenges maintaining a minimal standard of living. They generally toiled in the lowest-paying jobs, and as the most recently hired, they were often the first fired when the economy slowed. Depressions and economic downturns often resulted in a flurry of return migration.

Those who remained embraced a number of strategies to make ends meet. As most immigrant men did not make enough money to support an entire family, their wives and children pitched in. Before 1900, foreign-born women made up over half of wage-earning women in the U.S. workforce. Earning only one-half to two-thirds of the wages paid to men, they usually left paid employment outside the home after they married or had their first child. But even then they found ways to combine marriage, motherhood, and paid labor. Taking in boarders—cooking, washing, and providing beds for the many single male laborers working in U.S. cities—was an especially common way to supplement the family income. But boarders meant even more backbreaking work for already overburdened women and more crowded living conditions. Some women took in "home work," finishing garments for which they were paid by the piece. Home work allowed women to care for their children while earning money. Children even participated in this work, performing simple tasks such as pulling out basting threads in pieces of clothing.

Sending children to work rather than school had long-term consequences. Italian immigrants, largely unskilled peasants, worked in the lowest-paying jobs. As a result, many found the employment of their children crucial to keeping their families afloat. As one historian has noted, "The peasant shovel was passed from one generation to the next." As late as 1914, 90 percent of Italian girls and 99 percent of Italian boys in New York City left school at the age of 14 to work. By contrast, eastern European Jews, the most literate and skilled of the "new" immigrant groups—and one of the few groups that immigrated as families in this era—generally found employment in higher-paying skilled positions, such as tailoring, in the garment industry. More economically secure, and valuing education, many managed to send their children to school, allowing a relatively large percentage of the next generation to enter managerial and professional occupations.

Creating Community

Immigrants created their own communities in urban and industrial centers that helped cushion their adjustment. (Map 18.2) They clustered not only by ethnicity or nationality but also by region or village. Recently a researcher in Chicago identified 17 separate residential clusters of Italians from distinctive regions of their homeland. Whether forming a "Little Italy," a "Chinatown," "el Barrio," or a "Hunky (Hungarian) Town," immigrants recreated familiar surroundings in a new setting, mixing old and new, tradition and adaptation. Eastern European Jews, for example, constructed a Jewish world on the Lower East Side, complete with newspapers and theater in their own language, Yiddish. Contrasting with the decorum of native-born, middle-class households, which carefully separated private and public life, immigrant family life played out in tenement hallways, stoops, sidewalks, and even the streets where children played and parents socialized. Immigrant enclaves were seldom exclusive, and immigrants rarely remained isolated. Even the largely Jewish Lower East Side included Italians, Poles, and other ethnicities.

In their communities, immigrants created informal networks as well as formal organizations to provide support. Despite their own hardships, immigrant families opened their homes to newly arrived family members and friends, providing them with a foothold in America. Immigrant women shared meager resources and provided each other with food and rent money when unemployment occurred. Self-help organizations also helped immigrants adjust to the United States on their own terms. Mutual aid societies, whose members paid small monthly dues, provided a range of services, including credit and sickness and death benefits. A Pennsylvania anthracite coal town in 1908 boasted societies for Lithuanians, Ruthenians, and Slovaks. Jews organized *landsmanshaftn*, mutual aid societies consisting of people from the same town of origin. Mexican workers in the Southwest, most of whom were barred from unions, formed mutual aid groups. The Alianza Hispano Americana, which started in Tucson, Arizona, in 1894, soon expanded to 275 chapters. Mutual aid societies also organized social events, such as picnics, dances, and concerts.

Immigrant societies often provided the nucleus for churches and synagogues. Although most of the "new" immigrants were Roman Catholic, they resisted joining

Hebrew Immigrant Aid Society poster (1909)

BOILING KETTLE New York's Lower East Side, like many immigrant neighborhoods, was, as social reformer Mary Simkhovitch noted, "not a melting pot but a boiling kettle."

Temple Emmanu-el, San Francisco, (1867)

parishes previously established by Irish and German immigrants. Instead, despite their poverty, they insisted on building and maintaining their own separate ethnic parishes, with their own priests who spoke their language. Ethnic churches often established parochial schools, organized a variety of clubs, and sponsored festivals. Similarly, many religious eastern European Jews rejected the Reformed Judaism pioneered by German Jews earlier in the century, which they viewed as too liberal and American, and instead established Orthodox congregations. Churches and synagogues played an especially important role in providing spiritual, social, and economic sustenance as well as preserving traditional culture.

The immigrant church and synagogue provide valuable insights into the complex ways that religious establishments both aided immigrants in assimilating to American life and maintained tradition. Many offered English classes, taught immigrants about American customs, and encouraged them to seek citizenship. At the same time, religious institutions maintained traditions and ties to the Old World, especially in preserving language.

Ties between the Old and New Worlds helped create transnational identities, especially among those groups with deep migration traditions, such as Italians, Poles, and Jews, who regularly moved across national borders. Rather than embracing a single identity, they maintained complex attachments and loyalties to more than one nation and culture. Moreover, many immigrants also retained translocal ties that connected immigrants from a village or region in one nation with those in another nation.

Becoming American

Not all immigrants wished to retain ties with the Old World. Young people, especially young women, eagerly embraced all things American, throwing off what they viewed as the stifling yoke of Old World ways for modern freedoms. Some young workingwomen rebelled against traditional parental authority and control. They resented the expectation that they turn over their pay packet to their parents. Instead, they asserted their independence, keeping money for themselves to spend on stylish clothing and to socialize with men far from the view of their parents. Candy stores, soda shops, dance halls, amusement parks, and department stores—as well as factory workplaces—drew young people out of their neighborhoods to mingle and become more "American." Many also rejected the tradition of arranged marriages, embracing more American notions of romantic love. Tensions often flared between immigrant parents who wished to maintain Old World ways and children who assimilated American values. Mary Antin, who fled Russia with her family during the pogroms, happily fled "the cage of my provincialism," as she put it. With her sisters, she immediately shed her "hateful European costumes" for "real American machine-made garments" and changed her name from Maryashe to Mary. Antin leapt at the opportunity to take advantage of America's free public school education and pursued a successful career as a teacher and writer.

Excerpt from Mary Antin, *The Promised Land* (1912)

Despite the pressures and tensions faced by immigrants, the United States proved to be a "promised land" for many of them. The streets may not have been paved with gold, but immigrants nonetheless found jobs with wages higher than those in Europe and other opportunities, unthinkable in many parts of the world, such as free public education and political and religious freedom. Free education, as immigrant Mary Antin wrote, was "the one thing" her father was able to promise her in America, "surer, safer than bread or shelter"; education comprised "the chief hope for us children, the essence of American opportunity."

STUDY QUESTIONS FOR STREETS PAVED WITH GOLD?

1. What factors account for the unprecedented volume of immigration to the United States beginning in the Gilded Age?

2. What specific challenges did immigrants face? How did they respond to these challenges?

quiz

⊙ THE PROMISE AND PERIL OF CITY LIFE

Traveling to Chicago at the turn of the 20th century, British writer H. G. Wells marveled at the "creative forces at work." "Men are makers," he contended, "American men, I think, more than most." American cities were full of technological and cultural innovations—electric streetcars, skyscrapers, department stores, and new forms of entertainment. At the same time, Wells noted the "reek" of Chicago's stockyards along with "vast chimneys, huge blackened grain elevators, flame-crowned furnaces and gauntly ugly and filthy factory buildings, monstrous mounds of refuse, desolate, empty lots littered with rusty cans, old iron, indescribable rubbish."

Diversity was another hallmark of the American city. Compared to their European counterparts, cities in the United States attracted a much broader range of people, a mix of humanity described by one observer as "a queer conglomerate mass of heterogeneous elements."

It is little wonder that concerned citizens in both the United States and Europe viewed cities as the primary social problem of the age. Above all, cities were studies in contrasts—beauty and ugliness, wealth and poverty, innovation and decay, promise and peril. Did the city embody the promise of American life, or was it, as minister Josiah Strong argued, a rogue's gallery of "roughs, gamblers, thieves, robbers, lawless and desperate men of all ages"?

A World of Opportunity

Cities teemed with opportunity and energy, offering a universe of activities unimaginable to rural dwellers in the United States or Europe—from new consumer opportunities to novel forms of entertainment. Department stores sprang up in late 19th-century cities. Some, such as Macy's, remain household names even today. Mass production, technological and transportation advances, and exploding urban growth made department stores possible. Designed as "palaces of merchandise," these stores provided the convenience of doing all of one's shopping under one roof. Featuring an abundance of items, goods were organized into "departments"—such as home furnishings, stationery, toys, and clothing—for easy shopping and provided a ready outlet of manufactured goods, shipped by railroad, to the burgeoning city. The development of plate-glass windows allowed merchants to entice passersby with attractive displays of their merchandise, and a new leisure activity—"window shopping"—was born.

An audience watching a ballet performance on a Vitascope (1896)

As working hours decreased and real wages increased, working-class people had both more time and money to enjoy new forms of entertainment. Appealing to both rich and poor, native and immigrant, these entertainments helped bind fragmented cities together, offering common ground and experiences for diverse urbanites. Palatial theaters, which created a fantasy world with grand lobbies and luxurious surroundings, offered vaudeville shows affordable to all. Usually nine-act bills, these variety shows featured comedy routines, music, gymnastics, and animal acts. Sentimental songs, many about the longing for family and friends left behind, provided an emotional outlet for homesick immigrants. Comedy sketches featured stock characters, such as the "hayseed" visitor to the city and ethnic characters that played on contemporary stereotypes—the drunken Irishman; the beer-swilling, jovial German; the conniving Jew. But all were fair game. As audience members laughed with and at each other, humor helped ease ethnic tensions and ultimately created a sense of belonging.

Amusement parks, such as New York's Coney Island, were also a product of the Gilded Age city and sprang up across the country, often at the end of streetcar lines. Fare to Coney Island was a nickel, and those who could not afford to spend more for park rides could still enjoy the festive atmosphere or while away their time at the beach. Amusement parks provided a much-needed outlet for urban dwellers—offering fantasy, thrills, and fun—and were especially attractive to young, single, working people, who relished the freedom and escape from nosy parents and chaperones.

Spectator sports also flourished. While boxing and horseracing enjoyed widespread popularity, professional baseball emerged as the national pastime. The National League

WASHINGTON STREET   The Jordan Marsh department store anchors Boston's main shopping district, Washington Street, in this 1910 postcard depicting the hustle and bustle of "Shopping Hour."

formed in 1876, followed by the American Association in 1882, and then, after its failure, the American League in 1901. Railroad networks enabled teams from around the nation to compete with each other, and the telegraph instantaneously reported scores, published in increasingly prominent sports sections of city newspapers. Professional teams built large ballparks in cities, where crowds became so great that brick and steel facilities soon replaced rickety wooden structures. Baseball helped to create a sense of community in diverse and fragmented cities, as hordes of fanatical followers, rich and poor, native born and immigrant, men and women, cheered on their hometown teams.

Some of the greatest players in the history of the game were born into immigrant families. The national pastime provided them an escape from industrial employment. The Pittsburgh Pirates' **Honus Wagner**, the son of German immigrants, toiled in Pittsburgh-area steel mills before beginning his professional career in 1897. **Napoleon "Nap" Lajoie**, the youngest son of French-Canadian immigrants, labored in the textile mills of Woonsocket, Rhode Island, before signing with the Philadelphia Phillies in 1896. The "national game" was not immune from racial prejudice, however. When some white players, most famously the Chicago White Stockings' "Cap" Anson, refused to compete with blacks, team owners concurred, effecting a "gentleman's agreement" that barred blacks from major league baseball until 1947. During that time, teams were strictly segregated by race. Beginning in the 1880s, African Americans formed their own separate professional leagues, with teams in major cities such as the Cuban Giants (New York) and the St. Louis Black Stockings.

Participatory sports also flourished. Beginning in the 1890s, towns and cities exploded with physical activity. Bicycling became a national craze. Men and women joined hiking and camping clubs. The sports and recreation craze was part of a larger reaction to the regimentation of urban-industrial society. Middle-class Americans especially felt constrained by their dull daily routines and strict notions of respectability. Americans had learned to conform to the discipline of the time clock and to working indoors, whether in an office or factory, but many rebelled, seeking relief outdoors.

Painting by Frederic Remington showing a college football game (1900)

Middle-class men especially worried that city life and white-collar office work had made them "soft" and unmanly and soon vaunted a masculinity that stressed physical prowess and vigorous activity. Among the most forceful evangelists for the "strenuous life" was Theodore Roosevelt, who linked the nation's progress and international prominence to physical prowess. Sickly as a child, Roosevelt took up boxing, wrestling, and horseback riding; spent time on the Dakota frontier; and fashioned himself into a living example of vital manhood as a reform politician, war hero, and president. Men popularized the new and controversial sport of football, created on college campuses, playing in a violent, "manly" style, without helmets or pads. The game, argued one promoter in 1887, "is doing for our college-bred men, in a more peaceful way, what the experiences of war did for their predecessors in 1861–65."

Middle-class women embraced an even more radical ideal: "the **New Woman**." Breaking away from the restrictive ideal of the fragile homebody, the new woman discarded her confining corset and took up bicycling, tennis, and a newly invented game, basketball, first played in 1891 at the YMCA in Springfield, Massachusetts. She regularly participated in vigorous physical activity beside her male counterparts. Outdoor clubs, such as the Sierra Club, attracted large numbers of women who hiked, camped, and climbed mountains. Vigorous physical activity among women drew criticism from numerous physicians who feared that such "unnatural" activity would damage their reproductive organs.

A World of Crises

While cities embodied opportunity and energy, they roiled with crises. Not only were cities disorderly and dirty, they were also dangerous and violent. Most lacked adequate police protection. Scores of sensational books and articles about the traps and terrors of urban life enhanced the city's menacing reputation. Ease of access to saloons, gambling dens, and prostitution, coupled with the anonymity of city life, many feared, led to moral decline. Social bonds seemed to fragment, as men and women left the countryside and close-knit villages to live among strangers.

Cities struggled to house the flood of new arrivals. Indeed, the housing shortage emerged as one of the greatest urban crises. Although tenements mushroomed and could house from 16 to 24 families, and single-family homes were subdivided, there were simply not enough rooms to go around. Population densities in major cities reached alarming proportions, creating health and safety hazards. Landlords did little to maintain property, and inner-city housing deteriorated into slums. Untouched by the technological advances enjoyed by the middle class, the poor crowded in tenements without indoor plumbing, running water, or electric lights.

Overcrowded cities offered few social services to the poor immigrants who desperately needed them. This void was often filled by **political machines**, headed by "bosses" who traded goods and services for votes. Highly disciplined, political machines curried loyal voters by distributing everything from jobs to Christmas turkeys. Journalist **William L. Riordon** explained the role of the "ward boss," in charge of getting out the

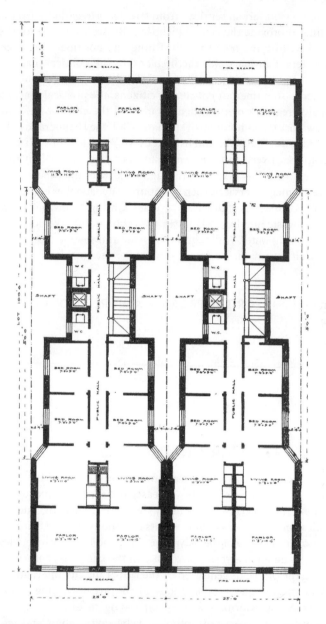

THE RISE OF THE DUMB-BELL TENEMENT Introduced in 1879 as a housing reform, the dumb-bell tenement offered courtyards and more ventilation than tenements built side by side. Dumb-bell tenements sprang up across the urban landscape as cheap, multifamily housing. But occupants still had to endure dark, tiny rooms, and ventilation remained inadequate.

vote for the machine: "Everybody in the district knows him, and nearly everybody goes to him for assistance of one sort or another, especially in the poor tenements."

But political machines often seemed more interested in lining their pockets than improving the lives of those who elected them. As a result, many cities were badly governed. Contracts for urban services, from streetcars to garbage disposal, often went to those willing to provide the largest kickback. Bosses cemented loyalty by dispensing secure and well-paying political jobs, filling city positions with incompetent and corrupt supporters. Patronage was the lifeblood of the political machine and Gilded Age politics. One Chicago alderman bragged that he dispensed 2,000 jobs to loyalists in his ward alone. To numerous concerned citizens, the political machine epitomized a fundamental threat to American democracy and the chief obstacle to creating livable cities. New York City's infamous Tammany Hall, the Democratic political machine established before the Civil War and headed by William M. "Boss" Tweed, epitomized political corruption. Tweed and his cronies stole between $50 million and $200 million dollars from New York City taxpayers through kickbacks and other schemes.

Primitive municipal services, such as impure water supplies and lack of sewage systems, made cities cauldrons of disease. For years, Chicago's sewage system consisted of simply dumping waste into Lake Michigan even though the lake doubled as the source of the city's drinking water. Although both water and sewage treatment facilities improved overall, cities remained polluted, hazardous environments.

STUDY QUESTIONS FOR THE PROMISE AND PERIL OF CITY LIFE

quiz

1. What new entertainments emerged in cities? In what ways did these new pastimes unite diverse urban dwellers? How did they divide city residents?

2. What were the chief problems urban dwellers faced?

◆ TACKLING URBAN PROBLEMS

As cities expanded, concerned citizens around the world shared their ideas about how to attack unprecedented poverty, slums, disease, and social fragmentation. Transatlantic conversations and experiences would, by the turn of the 20th century, gel into progressive politics and social reform movements in both the United States and around the world. As our opening story of the Salvation Army indicates, people, ideas, and strategies flowed back and forth across the Atlantic in the late 19th century as reformers set about attacking the problems generated by the rise of the city internationally.

Reformers struggled to find solutions to the overwhelming problems faced by urban dwellers. Some reformers focused on trying to dilute what they considered the "foreign" influence of Roman Catholicism by saving souls and redeeming cities through Protestant moral instruction. Social purity groups attempted to suppress, often through legal means, what they viewed as the rampant immorality of cities, taking aim at saloons, brothels, and "dangerous" sexuality. Still others sought to build social bonds and bridge the widening chasm between rich and poor, native born and immigrant; still others stressed creating healthy environments. Whatever their approach, all reformers struggled with much larger questions: What was the best way to eliminate poverty and human misery? Could reforms forge a strong, united nation from the diverse, foreign, and impersonal elements of city life?

Saving Souls in Urban America

Minister Josiah Strong articulated a call to arms against the evils of the city in several widely circulated books. He labeled the city "a serious menace to our civilization" and called for Protestant Christians to save the city. Protestant ministers, journalists, and politicians around the nation repeated his rallying cry, which served as the cornerstone of the **Social Gospel** movement. Broad, multidimensional, and international, the Social Gospel insisted that Christian principles be applied to social problems. Reformers dove into the heart of America's cities with the goal of not only alleviating social problems but also saving society's soul.

Excerpt from Josiah Strong, *Our Country: Its Possible Future and Its Present Crisis (1885)*

The Salvation Army was only one of a number of Protestant organizations that attacked "the devil" in U.S. cities and aimed to blunt the influence of Roman Catholicism. Along with city missions, which like those of the Salvation Army featured lively preaching and music to save souls, they established homes to reform prostitutes and shelters for street children, newsboys, and bootblacks. Business interests, fearful of potential revolution among the impoverished, contributed generous financial support. The meatpacking Armour family donated $100,000 to establish the Armour Mission in Chicago after the labor violence at Haymarket in 1886.

Although providing much-needed aid to the impoverished, city missions generally failed to convert immigrants to Protestantism. Neither the Salvation Army nor denominational missions managed to blunt the influence of "Romanism." After several decades of mission work, the American Home Missionary Society reported little progress: "The hostile forces that threaten the future of America" remained "intrenched behind miles of tenement blocks."

Another approach, the organized charity movement, attacked social ills by emphasizing the moral rehabilitation of the poor. Drawing on English examples, Anglican clergyman **S. Humphreys Gurteen** founded the nation's first organized charity in Buffalo in 1877. Horrified by the violence of the Great Railroad Strike, Gurteen transplanted this new approach to the United States. By the 1890s, charity organizations had mushroomed in American cities.

But charity organizations worked under several assumptions that blunted their effectiveness. Disregarding the harsh consequences of industrial capitalism, these groups viewed poverty as moral failure: the poor, they believed, bore responsibility for their condition; character defects, they believed, drove people into poverty. Fearful of creating dependency, charity organizations aided only "the worthy poor." As a result, charity workers, usually middle-class women, regularly investigated families to discern their worthiness and kept close records of their findings. "Friendly visitors," as they called themselves, also met with their charges to uplift them by modeling moral behavior. Not surprisingly, invasions of privacy and condescension did little to build the "neighborly" bonds that visitors hoped to create.

The Social Purity Movement

Rather than converting or persuading individuals to change their ways, some reformers used the law to attack what they viewed as growing indecency that threatened the nation's moral fiber. As urbanites exercised new personal freedoms, social purity reformers tried to curb and suppress their activities. In 1873, Anthony Comstock, a U.S. postal inspector and founder of the New York Society for the Suppression of Vice, helped convince Congress to pass what became known as the **Comstock Act**. This law banned "obscene, lewd, or lascivious material" from the U.S. mail, including anatomy books as well as information regarding birth control and sex education.

Social purity reformers established organizations that targeted urban vice all over the country. Groups such as the Boston Watch and Ward Society, founded in 1878, attacked a wide range of targets, including plays, vaudeville shows, and books that they found risqué. They also attacked sex outside of marriage and worked to criminalize prostitution and same-sex relationships. Many reformers also racialized "dangerous" sexuality, claiming that nonwhites—especially African American and Chinese men—were "oversexed" and potential rapists of white women.

Other social purity reformers targeted the saloon as the source of society's ills. With roots in the antebellum era, the temperance movement aimed to curb and end alcohol consumption. It gained considerable momentum with the increase in immigration and the arrival of large numbers of Roman Catholics. "Rum and Romanism" had long been linked in the minds of American Protestants. In addition, alcohol consumption, high throughout the 19th century, spiked in the Gilded Age. Renewing their crusade against alcohol, temperance advocates argued that alcohol was the root cause of many social problems such as poverty, domestic violence, and crime.

Middle-class women played a leading role in the fight against the saloon, embracing the cause as a defense of the home. They boldly entered saloons—all-male bastions—dropped to their knees, and prayed for the souls of offending drinkers, trying to persuade them to give up "demon rum." But they soon turned from moral suasion to politics to make real change. Unable to vote, these women nevertheless did what they could to influence local elections to ban liquor licenses.

Political involvement in temperance organizations also led many women to fight for the right to vote to extend their moral authority into the political arena. Under the leadership of **Frances Willard**, the **Women's Christian Temperance Union (WCTU)**, formed in 1874 and one of the nation's largest women's organizations, began to advocate for suffrage by 1879. As Willard explained, "the mothers and daughters of America" had a right to voice their opinion on whether "the door of the rum shop is opened or shut beside their homes."

Like many reforms of the era, temperance was an international movement. In 1884, Willard initiated a campaign to ban drinking around the world and dispatched WCTU missionaries, who collected a million names, representing 50 countries, on petitions calling for an end to the saloon. In 1891, the WCTU convened a world conference in Boston with delegates from around the globe.

The Settlement House Movement

A far more sympathetic and innovative approach to urban problems originated in England: the settlement house movement. In 1884, social reformer **Samuel Barnett** established Toynbee Hall amidst the slums of London's East End. The settlement house aimed to create a place where both well-to-do and working classes could live together, with the more fortunate aiding their impoverished neighbors, bridging the gap between rich and poor to connect fragmented social classes into a unified community.

After witnessing the "hideous human suffering" of London's poor on a tour of Europe in the early 1880s, Illinois native **Jane Addams** returned to London and worked at Toynbee Hall. Inspired by her stay, Addams returned to the United States and with her friend **Ellen Starr** purchased a dilapidated mansion in a run-down section of Chicago. There, in 1889, they established Hull House, one of the nation's first settlement houses. By 1900, the number of settlement houses in U.S. cities had reached approximately 100.

Rather than condemn immigrant culture as alien and something to be eliminated, Addams and her fellow workers encouraged pride in traditional culture while smoothing the transition to American life. Hull House offered a range of programs, including sewing and cooking classes, day care and clubs for children, and lectures by university professors. Labor unions also found a welcoming environment there.

Hull House and the settlement house movement represented another dimension of the Social Gospel. To live among the poor and share their lives, Addams asserted, expressed "the spirit of Christ." Moreover, the settlement house provided another antidote to the problem of urban fragmentation as well as a means to instill democracy among the many immigrants who inhabited America's cities. Seeking an "organic" democracy, as she put it, Addams and the settlement house fostered social bonds; as she explained, "the dependence of classes on each other is reciprocal."

Excerpt from Jane Addams, Twenty-Years at Hull House (1910)

The settlement house not only shaped the lives of its neighbors, but also transformed the lives of Addams and the many single, educated, middle-class women who worked with her. A college graduate, Addams had struggled against a feeling of "uselessness" and "futility," as she explained, to find a place in the Gilded Age society and meaningful work. She, and many women like her, found it in the settlement house movement.

HULL HOUSE Jane Addams (1860–1935) summarized the purpose of the settlement house: "To aid in the solution of the social and industrial problems . . . engendered by the modern conditions of life in a great city. It is the attempt to relieve, at the same time, the overaccumulation at one end of society and the destitution at the other."

Creating Healthy Urban Environments

Living among the poor, settlement house workers and other reformers began to see the negative effects of a destructive environment. Rather than blaming the poor for their own problems, they concluded that the environment in which people lived shaped their lives. Poverty and its consequences were not moral failures but social ones.

Excerpt from Jacob Riis, *How the Other Half Lives* (1890)

Journalist **Jacob Riis** played a key role in an environmental approach to social reform. An immigrant himself, Riis arrived in New York from Denmark in 1870 and empathized with the city's poor in ways that few others did. He explored and wrote about the underside of New York City: a world of saloons, gambling dens, brothels, overcrowded and filthy tenements, and swarms of street children. He soon began snapping photographs to document the lives of "the other half," a side of the city rarely glimpsed by the more fortunate, capturing startling images of street urchins and sweatshop workers. In 1890, Riis published his findings in *How the Other Half Lives: Studies Among the Tenements of New York*, which proved to be a powerful weapon for social reform. Through his efforts, some of New York's worst tenements were destroyed and child labor laws more effectively enforced.

STUDY QUESTIONS FOR TACKLING URBAN PROBLEMS

quiz

1. Describe the different approaches reformers took to address urban problems. Where did they agree? Where did they disagree?

2. What were the main obstacles to urban reform?

STREET ARABS IN SLEEPING QUARTERS, c. 1880 This photograph, taken by reformer Jacob Riis and included in *How the Other Half Lives*, shows children sleeping on a steam grate for warmth. Images like these shocked Riis's middle-class audience and proved to be a powerful weapon for social reform.

❤ CHALLENGES TO THE POLITICS OF STALEMATE

Social and economic crises in the late 19th century cried out for political solutions. But after closely observing American politics, British writer Lord James Bryce concluded that neither the Republican nor the Democratic Party "has anything definite to say" on the issues of the day; "neither party has any principles, any distinctive tenets. . . . All has been lost, except office or the hope of it."

Had Bryce queried U.S. voters, they would have violently disagreed with his assessment. They were obsessed with politics. Not only did the two major parties continue to distinguish themselves in terms of economic policy and the role of government, they garnered enough rabid support to foster the highest voter turnout in the nation's history.

Excerpt from James Bryce, *The American Commonwealth* (1900)

At the same time, national politics in the late 19th century, as Bryce suggested, accomplished little of substance. Because the parties were so evenly matched, neither party risked upsetting the precarious balance with innovative legislation, despite the multitude of challenges that the nation faced. Holding on to office, not reform, remained the main focus of politicians.

But by the 1890s, the **People's (Populist) Party**, largely made up of farmers, had formed one of the largest third-party movements in U.S. history and challenged the politics of stalemate. Populists helped set the stage for the decisive presidential election of 1896, which in many ways embodied the conflict between older rural America and the rapidly urbanizing nation. The nation stood at a crossroads: Would it embrace its traditional rural roots or a modern, urban, industrial future?

Key Issues

Tariffs may hardly seem like the subject of passionate politics, but to Gilded Age voters, the tariff was central to national political debate and defined party differences. Republicans supported the protective tariff—a tax on imported goods—to promote American industry and agriculture. Placing a tariff on British steel, for example, increased its cost, making it more likely that builders would purchase American-made steel, helping expand the industry and its labor force. By contrast, Democrats insisted that the protective tariff ultimately raised prices and hurt consumers. Republicans continued to embrace the nationalist vision of the Civil War and advocated using the power of the federal government to promote economic growth, whereas Democrats remained committed to limited government and states' rights.

The currency issue also loomed large. Beginning in 1873, the little-noticed **Coinage Act** made gold the nation's monetary standard. Before this time, both gold and silver had been part of the money supply. But the population exploded in the late 19th century as the money supply remained the same, increasing the value of the dollar and tightening the amount of money available for credit. For those in debt, especially farmers who relied on credit to plant their crops, the monetary situation created a crisis. Some Democrats, and later Populists, saw a massive conspiracy in the Coinage Act, a way that money interests kept credit tight and rates high. Calling the act the "crime of 1873," they began to advocate the coinage of silver to put more money into circulation, make more credit available, and create inflation, which would increase the price that farmers got for their products. Republicans, however, insisted on maintaining "sound money," backed with gold.

A third issue also emerged in the national political arena: civil service reform. Patronage greased the wheels of politics. The party in power secured the loyalty of voters by rewarding them with political jobs on the local, state, and national levels. Although political patronage was nothing new, it reached unprecedented levels of corruption in the late 19th century, adding to the ineffectiveness of government. Reformers in both parties began to call for replacing incompetent party hacks with a professional workforce. After crazed office seeker Charles Guiteau assassinated President **James Garfield** in 1881, Congress finally took action, passing the **Pendleton Civil Service Act** in 1883. The act established the modern civil service and required an examination for a number of federal jobs, including most government departments, customs house jobs, and post office positions. The Pendleton Act eliminated some incompetence and corruption, but it barely made a dent in federal patronage, as more jobs kept being added. In 1900, the federal government still offered the same number of patronage jobs as it had in 1883, the year the law was passed.

Ethnicity, Gender, and Political Culture

The Republican and Democratic parties generally drew their followers from different ethnic and religious backgrounds. Republicans tended to be Protestant and native born, although the party also attracted Protestant German and Scandinavian immigrants. Before disfranchisement in the South, beginning in 1890, African American voters remained loyal Republicans. Advocating the use of government to compel "moral" behavior, Republicans often supported temperance and prohibition. Democrats, on the other hand, rejected the coercive use of government, placing more emphasis on individual freedom. Democrats, through their Irish-dominated city machines, continued to draw Roman Catholic immigrants to their party. In addition, the Democratic Party retained its stronghold in the white South as the party of white supremacy.

Political parties created enthusiasm and loyalty through elaborate rituals and social events, including rallies and parades. Political participation provided a way for men to demonstrate their masculinity and the male ideals of loyalty, courage, and independence. Election campaigns were characterized as "wars" and "battles," with voters as foot soldiers loyally supporting their party's candidate. Above all, party politics remained a male domain, even as some women began to demand the right to vote. Political parties also bonded men of different classes and ethnicities, with political machines especially successful in incorporating immigrant men into the political system. Party loyalty helps to account for massive voter turnout in this era. In 1896, for example, 80 percent of the eligible male electorate voted in the presidential election. Similar high rates occurred in state and local elections.

For most of the late 19th century, voters were almost evenly split between the two parties. Between 1875 and 1897, Republican presidents dominated, but elections were close, with Democratic candidates winning the popular vote in four of five elections. Congress remained almost evenly divided, with Democrats generally controlling the House and Republicans the Senate. With such a precarious balance, party leaders refused to risk alienating any of their voters, and this conservative approach snuffed out the passage of groundbreaking legislation.

The depression of the 1890s ultimately dismantled the politics of stalemate. Soon after President Grover Cleveland, a Democrat, began his second term in 1893, economic panic, fueled by rampant speculation and unregulated markets, plunged the nation into a four-year depression. Although the crisis had deep and complex roots, Cleveland and the Democrats bore the blame. In 1894, the Democrats lost 113 seats in Congress, as the Republicans gained 117, the largest transfer of power in congressional history to this day. Two years later, in 1896, the voters elected **William McKinley** president, ushering in an era of Republican dominance that, with the exception of Woodrow Wilson's two terms (1913–1921), would not be broken until Franklin D. Roosevelt's election in 1932.

The Populist Challenge

To capture the presidency in 1896, McKinley had to fight off one of the largest democratic movements in U.S. history. The presidential election of 1896 saw the zenith of a major third-party movement, the People's (Populist) Party. Many Americans criticized the injustices and corruption of Gilded Age America. But the most thorough program for reform came not from cities but from the countryside, not from labor radicals or middle-class reformers but from farmers, often considered to be among the most conservative Americans.

Once the backbone of the nation, farmers found themselves in the midst of decline, unable to reap the economic abundance enjoyed by many in the Gilded Age. They felt exploited by bankers, who charged them high interest rates on the money they borrowed every year to plant their crops; by railroads, who set exorbitant freight rates to carry their goods to market; and by "middlemen," who reaped large profits from the crops that they marketed. Farmers fell deeper into debt and poverty, with many losing their land in foreclosure. They demanded that federal and state government intervene to ensure "equal rights to all, special privileges to none."

The **Farmers' Alliance**, founded in Texas in the 1870s, provided the foundation for what would become the Populist Party. Quickly attracting an enthusiastic following of farm men and women in the South and West eager to halt their worsening economic condition, the nonpartisan organization soon realized its political clout. By the 1890s, Alliance men dominated eight state legislatures and helped elect four governors and numerous congressmen. "Farmers' legislatures" passed numerous reforms, including legislation aimed at regulating railroads more stringently.

Frustrated with the unresponsiveness of the two major parties, which remained indifferent to their pressing needs, some Alliance members decided to form a third party, the People's (Populist) Party. First appearing in the West in 1890, a national Populist Party burst onto the national political stage two years later. In 1892, the Populists devised a national platform in Omaha and nominated their first presidential candidate, **James B. Weaver** of Iowa.

The party's Omaha Platform provided an eloquent and powerful critique of Gilded Age America. In addition, unlike the two major parties, Populists articulated concrete proposals for a more just nation. "We meet in the midst of a nation brought to the verge of moral, political, and material ruin," the platform's preamble explained, a nation tainted by corruption at every level. The United States had been reduced to "two great classes—tramps and millionaires." The Omaha Platform laid out a series of solutions that included government ownership of railroad, telegraph, and telephone systems and the free and unlimited coinage of silver, which they believed would expand credit and increase the price of their crops. They also proposed subtreasuries to store crops and advance loans to farmers so that they could wait for optimal market conditions to sell

Omaha Platform of the People's (Populist) Party (1892)

interactive timeline

TIMELINE 1873–1901

AMERICA	YEAR	THE WORLD
Feb Congress passes Coinage Act, establishing gold standard for currency **Mar** Comstock Act passed to suppress circulation of literature deemed obscene	**1873**	
Nov Women's Christian Temperance Union (WCTU) founded	**1874**	
Feb Baseball's National League formed, the sport's first "major league"	**1876**	
Dec Clergyman S. Humphreys Gurteen founds nation's first organized charity in Buffalo, New York	**1877**	
Oct Frances Willard elected president of WCTU, leads organization to fight for women's suffrage	**1879**	
New York City becomes first U.S. city to reach a population of one million **Mar** Salvation Army arrives in New York City, establishes city missions throughout the United States	**1880**	
Sep President James A. Garfield dies, shot by frustrated office seeker Charles Guiteau	**1881**	**Mar** Assassination of Russian Czar Alexander II sets off pogroms aimed at Jewish settlements and spurs immigration to the United States
May Congress enacts Chinese Exclusion Act	**1882**	
Jan Congress passes Pendleton Civil Service Act	**1883**	
	1884	Social reformer Samuel Barnett establishes the first settlement house, Toynbee Hall, in slums of London's East End
Fall The nation's first skyscraper built in Chicago **Fall** Congregational minister Josiah Strong publishes *Our Country: Its Possible Future and Its Present Crisis*	**1885**	**Jul** Canada restricts Chinese immigration by requiring a $50 head tax
Mar Anti-immigrant American Protective Association founded	**1887**	

their crops. In addition, Populists endorsed the direct election of senators, a graduated income tax, and protection of labor unions.

Dismissed as "cranks" and wild-eyed crazies by newspapers such as the *New York Times*, Populists often presented a sophisticated explanation of the economic problems of the day. At the same time, the party could speak the language of the common person. The Populist Party was blessed with colorful, passionate, plain-speaking leaders such as Kansan **Mary Elizabeth Lease**, who demanded that farmers "raise less corn and more hell." Despite widespread criticism in the press, dominated by the two major parties, the Populists still garnered a million popular votes and 22 electoral votes for their presidential candidate in 1892. Democrat Grover Cleveland emerged as the victor in the election, defeating incumbent Republican Benjamin Harrison for the presidency.

Between 1893 and 1896, as the nation plunged into economic depression, the People's Party continued to make gains, especially in state legislatures, where they instituted a number of significant reforms, including rewriting state election laws to make

AMERICA	YEAR	THE WORLD
Feb Nation's first electric streetcar introduced in Richmond, Virginia **Oct** National League All-Stars depart on six-month world tour to introduce baseball and expand U.S. influence	1888	
Sep Jane Addams and Ellen Starr open doors of Hull House, nation's first settlement house, in Chicago	1889	
Chicago and Philadelphia reach one million population mark Jacob Riis publishes *How the Other Half Lives: Studies Among the Tenements of New York*	1890	
Dec Basketball, invented by Dr. James Naismith in Springfield, Massachusetts, first played **Nov** WCTU holds international conference in Boston with delegates from around the world	1891	
Jul People's (Populist) Party holds first national convention in Omaha, Nebraska **Nov** Democrat Grover Cleveland defeats Republican incumbent Benjamin Harrison and Populist James B. Weaver for presidency	1892	
May Immigration Restriction League is founded in Boston	1894	
Mar Immigration Restriction Bill is vetoed by President Grover Cleveland **Sep** First subway in United States opens in Boston **Nov** Republican William McKinley defeats Democratic and Populist candidate William Jennings Bryan for presidency	1897	
Jan Professional baseball's American League organized	1901	**Jan** Census shows that population of United Kingdom doubled in 50 years to 38 million **Dec** Australia curbs Asian immigration by requiring European-language literacy test

voting more democratic; setting limits on interest rates; and increasing funding for schools, state institutions, and prisons.

The Election of 1896

Massive unemployment, bank failures, and countless mortgage foreclosures set the stage for the crucial presidential election of 1896. The Populists seemed well positioned to attract the votes of desperate and frustrated Americans. The Democratic Party nominated **William Jennings Bryan** of Nebraska for the presidency. Sympathetic to the plight of farmers, Bryan won the nomination after he electrified the party convention with a speech that became known as "The Cross of Gold Speech." Bryan advocated the free coinage of silver and condemned the gold standard: "You shall not press down upon the brow of labor this crown of thorns, you shall not crucify mankind upon a cross of gold." His speech also stressed the central role of the nation's farmers to the rapidly urbanizing nation. "Burn down your cities and leave our farms," he cried, "and your

Excerpt from William Jennings Bryan's "Cross of Gold" speech (1896)

cities will spring up again as if by magic; but destroy our farms and the grass will grow in the streets of every city in the country." The Populists decided to cast their lot with Democrat Bryan and endorsed his candidacy. At the same time, they nominated their own vice presidential candidate, Tom Watson of Georgia.

The 1896 election, in the words of Kansas journalist William Allen White, "took the form of religious frenzy." The future of the nation seemed to hang in the balance, with Democrat/Populist Bryan representing an older, rural America and McKinley the emerging urban, industrial nation. Bryan crisscrossed the country in the first truly modern presidential campaign, taking his message to the people by logging 18,000 miles by train and giving 600 speeches—sometimes as many as 20 a day—filled with religious imagery and evangelical zeal. By contrast, Republican candidate William McKinley, dubbed by his party as the "Advance Agent of Prosperity," remained rooted to his Canton, Ohio, home, where he conducted a "front porch campaign" in which he spoke with visiting delegations. McKinley promised the American worker "a full dinner pail" through economic prosperity and labeled Bryan's silverite schemes an economic disaster. Backed by big business—banks, businessmen, and industrialists— McKinley and the Republicans spent as much as $7 million on the campaign, with at least $250,000 contributed by **John D. Rockefeller**'s Standard Oil Company.

McKinley handily defeated Bryan in the most decisive presidential election since 1872, a clear sign of the end of political deadlock. Although McKinley polled only half a million votes more than Bryan (7 million to 6.5 million), he swamped Bryan in the electoral college, 271 to 176 (Map 18.3). The Populist Party managed to survive Bryan's crushing defeat but only as a shadow of its former self. Despite its ultimate demise,

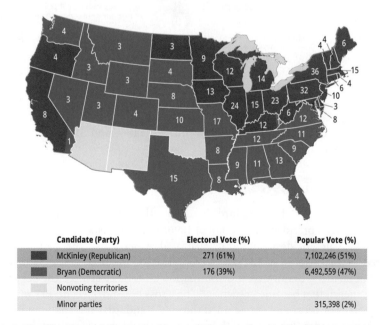

Candidate (Party)	Electoral Vote (%)	Popular Vote (%)
McKinley (Republican)	271 (61%)	7,102,246 (51%)
Bryan (Democratic)	176 (39%)	6,492,559 (47%)
Nonvoting territories		
Minor parties		315,398 (2%)

MAP 18.3 The Election of 1896 The electoral results reflect the general division between industrial/urban America, carried by McKinley, along with several key agricultural states, and rural America, which supported Bryan.

many reforms the party advocated were taken up by progressive reformers in the early 20th century. The basic Populist demand that the federal government intervene on behalf of the people to offset powerful corporate interests would be echoed by progressives within the next 10 years. In addition, other specific reforms, such as the graduated income tax and direct election of senators, would be enacted within the next 20 years. But the defeat and the demise of the farmers' party symbolized the ultimate eclipse of the countryside by urban, industrial America.

STUDY QUESTIONS FOR CHALLENGES TO THE POLITICS OF STALEMATE

1. What were the chief differences between Democrats, Republicans, and Populists?

2. What does the story of the People's Party suggest about the difficulties that third parties face in mounting a challenge to the two-party system?

quiz

Summary

- Urbanization was a hallmark of the late 19th century, in both the United States and other industrializing nations. Cities grew both horizontally and vertically and became increasingly segregated and fragmented by class, race, and ethnicity.
- Immigration, a global phenomenon, greatly contributed to urbanization. Between 1870 and 1900, approximately 11 million immigrants arrived in the United States, and an additional 13 million entered the country between 1900 and 1914. About one-third of immigrants returned permanently to their countries of origin. The "new" immigrants faced severe challenges not only in the reemergence of nativism but also in their adjustment to the harsh demands of the industrial order.
- The nation's cities were studies in contrasts. Rapid urbanization spawned a multitude of crises, which included inadequate housing, primitive municipal services, and corrupt city government. At the same time, cities teemed with opportunity, offering new forms of culture and consumer activities. Social reformers were part of a transatlantic community of reformers who shared a variety of strategies to attack the problems of the city.
- For most of the Gilded Age, national politics was gridlocked, with Democrats and Republicans evenly matched. The parties feared upsetting the precarious balance, so little was accomplished on the national level. The depression of the 1890s helped break the Gilded Age stalemate, and by 1896, the People's (Populist) Party had mounted a major challenge to the two-party system.

Key Terms and People

audio
flashcards

Addams, Jane 638

American Protective Association (APA) 623

Barnett, Samuel 638

Bryan, William Jennings 645

Chinese Exclusion Act 624

Cleveland, Grover 624

Coinage Act 641

Comstock Act 638

Farmers' Alliance 643

Garfield, James 642

Gurteen, S. Humphreys 637

Immigration Restriction League 623

Lajoie, Napoleon "Nap" 633

Reviewing Chapter 18

1. How did immigrants, urban reformers, and Populists address the challenges posed by urbanization and immigration?
2. Which approaches were most successful in your opinion? Why?

Further Reading

Barth, Gunther Paul. *City People: The Rise of Modern City Culture in Nineteenth-Century America.* New York: Oxford University Press, 1980. An exploration of the new culture that emerged in American cities and how urban culture transformed the countryside as well.

Gabaccia, Donna. *Immigration and American Diversity: A Social and Cultural History.* Malden, MA: Blackwell, 2002. A valuable, fresh overview of immigration that explores issues such as individual identities, ethnic group formations, and interactions between immigrants and the native born.

McMath, Robert C., Jr. *American Populism: A Social History, 1877–1898.* New York: Hill and Wang, 1993. An easy-to-read, accessible volume on the often complex story of the Farmers' Alliance and the Populist Party.

Warner, Sam Bass, Jr. *The Urban Wilderness: A History of the American City.* Berkeley: University of California Press, 1995. This classic work places the Gilded Age city within the larger context of urban development.

Wyman, Mark. *Round-Trip to America: The Immigrants Return to Europe, 1880–1930.* Ithaca, NY: Cornell University Press, 1996. Explores the return migration of "new" immigrants and the many consequences of their temporary stay in the United States, including the ideas and goods that they took back with them to Europe.

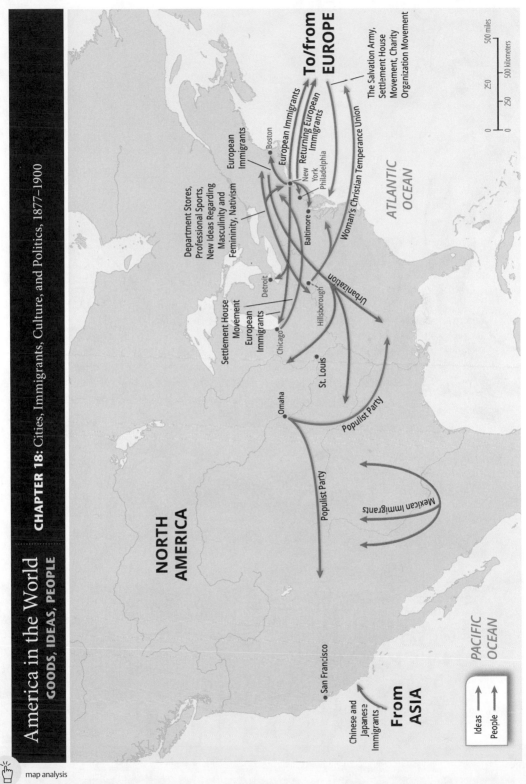

America in the World
GOODS, IDEAS, PEOPLE

CHAPTER 18: Cities, Immigrants, Culture, and Politics, 1877–1900

NORTH
AMERICA

To/from
EUROPE

The Salvation Army,
Settlement House
Movement, Charity
Organization Movement

European
Immigrants

Boston

European Immigrants

New
York
Philadelphia

Returning European
Immigrants

Baltimore

Woman's Christian Temperance Union

Department Stores,
Professional Sports,
New Ideas Regarding
Masculinity and
Femininity, Nativism

Detroit

Urbanization

Hillsborough

Settlement House
Movement

European
Immigrants

Chicago

St. Louis

Omaha

Populist Party

Populist Party

Mexican Immigrants

San Francisco

From
ASIA

Chinese and
Japanese
Immigrants

ATLANTIC
OCEAN

PACIFIC
OCEAN

| Ideas |
| People |

0   250   500 miles

0   250   500 kilometers

map analysis

In this 1901 illustration from the popular magazine *Puck*, Cuba is portrayed as a young boy, and his efforts to build independence prompts a warning from Uncle Sam: "That's right, my boy! Go ahead! But, remember, I'll always keep a Father's eye on you!"

The United States Expands Its Reach

1892–1912

I n 1904, roughly 20 million people visited the St. Louis World's Fair commemorating the centennial of the Louisiana Purchase. Showcasing progress in the United States and abroad, the fair featured the latest technology and carnival rides, and visitors feasted on ice cream cones—first introduced there. But the most popular question asked of fair guides, reported *The New York Times*, was, "Which way to the Philippines?"

The federal government, with the aid of anthropologists, spent $1 million to construct a "Philippines Reservation" at the fair. A living exhibition, the reservation featured 1,200 Filipinos living in native "villages." The United States had taken possession of the Philippines as a result of the Spanish-American War of 1898; after heated debate, U.S. leaders decided to make the islands a colony. Occupation of the Philippines triggered a bloody war for independence, which the United States for the most part had suppressed by the time of the fair. But the brutal war only strengthened criticism of colonization. The exhibition, officials hoped, would offer an excellent opportunity to introduce the Filipino people to the public and help make the case for empire.

Reflecting the racialist thinking of the era, the exhibit showcased a range of Filipinos. Anthropologists arranged them from the most "primitive"—the dark-skinned "Negritos"—to the most "advanced": the Filipino constables who kept order at the exhibit, those "uplifted" by American tutelage. But the "wild savages" attracted the most attention. The Negritos demonstrated their skills with bows and poisoned arrows. The Igorots, another "primitive" group, excited the crowds with "war dances to the beat of the tom-tom." The exhibit asserted that they, like American Indians, could be civilized with education.

The Filipino exhibition did more than entertain and titillate the millions who visited it. (Their lack of clothing created a great deal of controversy.) The federal government hoped it would convince the public that keeping the islands rather than granting them independence was the best choice. The "uncivilized" inhabitants, they posited, offered proof that the Filipinos were simply incapable of self-rule; they needed the United States to educate, guide, and protect them.

The Philippines Reservation reflected the new role of the United States as an imperial power and conflicts over that role. Only a few years earlier the nation had stood at a crossroads. Should the United States take the path to empire, like other world powers? Or should it remain a true republic, unencumbered by colonies? By 1898, driven by the same commercial interests and quests for influence that drove other world powers into a scramble for colonies, the United States had chosen empire. But not all Americans felt comfortable with this new role. The exhibition raised troubling questions about colonization. Could the United States, which had fought for independence as a colony of Great Britain, be a colonial power itself without compromising its ideals? Moreover, had the nation, by stepping out so boldly on the world stage, committed itself to a future of global entanglements and wars from which there would be no turning back?

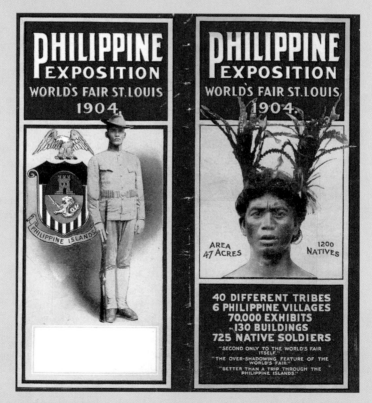

PHILIPPINE EXPOSITION This brochure advertises a "living exhibit" of Filipinos at the 1904 World's Fair in St. Louis, which helped popularize anthropological theories about racial hierarchy and justify imperialism. The images show the range of "civilization" among the Filipino people, from the "advanced" constable to "wild savages."

⊗ THE NEW IMPERIALISM

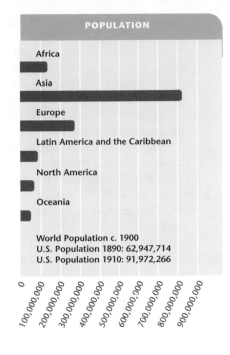

In the last quarter of the 19th century, industrial capitalism spawned a new race for empire. For most of the century, through the 1870s, old European empires, established much earlier in the "New World," declined or disappeared. Revolutions had divested Great Britain, France, Portugal, and Spain of most or all of their colonies in the Americas. But as industrial nations faced severe global economic depressions, first in the 1870s and again in the 1890s, many blamed overproduction for these downturns. Industrial capitalism had produced a glut of goods that simply could not be absorbed in established markets. Finding new consumers in the world's untapped markets, they believed, would solve the problem. Colonies also bestowed prestige on imperial powers as well as access to raw materials. Africa, Asia, and the islands of the Pacific were the most sought-after prizes in the competition for colonies.

Racialist theories, propped up by new allegedly scientific claims of white intellectual and moral superiority over darker-skinned peoples, provided additional justification for colonization. Colonists presented themselves as "uplifting" the uncivilized. Missionaries often laid the groundwork for expansion, and businessmen and political leaders soon followed in their footsteps.

The United States, unlike European powers, did not have a tradition of overseas empire building. After all, the nation had been established by repudiating Great Britain's colonial claims. The political extension of the nation beyond its continental boundaries represented a new departure. But in many ways colonization abroad continued the federal government's policies of westward expansion within the continental United States and its conquest of Indigenous peoples. Even as many Americans remained uneasy about colonization, a combination of crises in the 1890s—economic, social, political, and cultural—thrust the nation into the global competition for empire.

A Global Grab for Colonies

Creating new consumers did not necessarily lead to colonization. The world's strongest industrial powers, Great Britain and the United States, generally preferred "open door" policies. In other words, they asked only for unhindered access to markets where, they confidently believed, they could compete successfully against rivals. But weaker industrial nations preferred the security of colonies. Once nations began to stake colonial claims in less developed parts of the world, international rivalries soon pushed all industrialized nations into a scramble for empire. By 1899, even the United States, which had pursued a commercial empire with great success, had followed its European rivals in creating formal colonies.

The untapped markets of Africa, Asia, and the Pacific, as well as their natural resources, loomed large in the eyes of expansionists. Factories required rubber, vegetable oils, and minerals. Beginning in the 1870s, and accelerating in the 1880s, European powers ruthlessly carved up most of Africa into colonies. In 1884–1885, they met in Berlin—without the presence of a single African nation—to divide much of the continent among themselves. Their actions set off decades of bloody wars on the continent. Although not seeking land, U.S. representatives succeeded in getting a pledge from European powers for an "open door" to market goods in the Belgian Congo.

Imperialists found Asia even more alluring than Africa. European powers partitioned Southeast Asia, as they had Africa in the 1880s, with France acquiring Indochina (present-day Vietnam, Cambodia, and Laos) and Britain annexing Burma (present-day Myanmar). China, a weak nation at the time with 300 million potential consumers, would be the site of numerous conflicts among the rival world powers. European powers and Japan "carved the Chinese melon" into territorial slices of domination as the United States demanded fair access to the China market. In the 1880s and 1890s, many Pacific islands found themselves annexed. Between 1876 and 1915, the world's powers, imposing colonialism around the globe, claimed roughly 25 percent of the world's lands and peoples (Map 19.1).

Illustration from French magazine showing the carving up China (1898)

Race, Empire, Bibles, and Businessmen

As the Philippine Reservation at the St. Louis World's Fair reflected, notions of race justified colonization. Social Darwinism, the theory that applied "survival of the fittest" to both individuals and nations, offered a powerful rationale for empire. The new

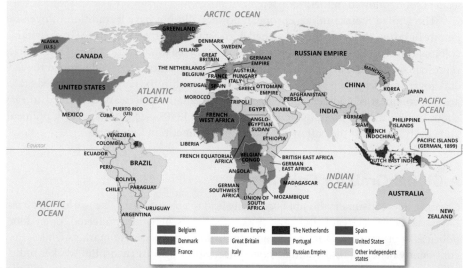

map analysis

MAP 19.1 World Colonial Empires, 1900 A handful of world powers divided much of the globe among themselves. Between 1876 and 1915, Great Britain added four million square miles of land to its empire, Germany more than one million, and Belgium and Italy one million square miles each. The United States added 100,000 square miles, mostly from Spain in 1898.

discipline of anthropology also ranked the world's peoples in a hierarchy, from the un-civilized to the civilized, according to their stage of development.

New scientific theories found support in a growing faith in **Anglo-Saxonism.** As the United States and Great Britain emerged as the world's leading industrial powers in the late 19th century, many began to believe that the English-speaking nations shared common racial characteristics that accounted for their preeminent world standing. Anglo-Saxons, they believed, possessed superior intelligence, were industrious, and had a special talent for spreading freedom and their advanced culture around the world. At the top of the racial hierarchy, Anglo-Saxons bore the responsibility, they believed, to "take up the white man's burden"—as the British poet Rudyard Kipling famously put it—to enlighten those who stood in darkness, to uplift "savage" and "backward" peoples who would gratefully submit to their leadership.

Congregational minister **Josiah Strong** emerged as the leading spokesman for Anglo-Saxonism in the United States and challenged Americans to take the lead in ful-filling their God-ordained mission. His widely read books, such as *Our Country* (1885), called for Americans to Christianize the world and challenged them to "move down upon Mexico, down upon Central and South America, out upon the islands of the sea, over Africa and beyond." Notably, economic benefits were sure to follow: "What is the process of civilizing," asked Strong, "but the creating of more and higher wants? Com-merce follows the missionary."

Josiah
Strong,
excerpt
from *Our
Country*
(1885)

Strong had plenty of proof for that claim. Both European and American mis-sionaries, along with businessmen, served as the advance guard of Western influence throughout the world. They established informal empire by both cultural infiltration and economic control. Intent on converting "heathen" peoples to Christianity in Africa, Asia, and the Middle East, both Protestant and Roman Catholic missions proliferated. Missionaries expected native culture and traditions to yield to their "superior" civilized ways, propagating cultural imperialism as a prelude to political domination. U.S. mis-sionaries zealously worked to create Christian nations wherever they went. In Hawaii, for example, New England missionaries arrived in 1820, following in the wake of whal-ers who frequented the islands for supplies on long voyages across the Pacific. There they established outposts of New England culture and society and worked zealously to stamp out Native culture. With their grasp of local knowledge and Native languages, missionaries proved themselves invaluable to governments seeking influence in far-off lands. Missionaries soon engaged in business and trade. In Hawaii, missionaries quickly evolved into businessmen, purchasing vast tracts of land from Natives and establishing the islands' lucrative sugar industry. By the 1850s, Americans owned 75 percent of busi-nesses on the islands.

Precedent for American Empire

Throughout much of the 19th century, policymakers laid the groundwork for empire abroad, with expansion across the continent and the conquest of Native peoples. Begin-ning with the Louisiana Purchase in 1803, the United States added to its contiguous ter-ritory by peaceful annexation and war. In the modern, progress-filled years of late 19th century, Indians at home and then natives in other lands seemed like the "primitive" losers in the struggle for survival, who "naturally" yielded before a "superior" civiliza-tion. **Theodore Roosevelt**, historian and future president, who would play a key role in establishing the United States as an imperial world power, wrote extensively about westward expansion and viewed the clash between "savagery" and "civilization" as inevitable and necessary.

Treatment of Indians provided important precedents for empire building. Not only did the United States acquire by force lands that had belonged to Indians, but it also rejected the right of Native peoples to rule themselves and imposed direct rule on them. In addition, the Supreme Court ruled in 1884 that Indians born on reservations were not citizens but instead "nationals" who owed allegiance to the United States but had none of the privileges of citizenship—a status that lasted until 1924. These legal concepts were later applied to colonized peoples in both Puerto Rico until 1917 and the Philippines.

The Crises of the 1890s

A combination of crises in the 1890s—economic, social, political, and cultural—thrust the nation into the global contest for empire. Even as the United States extended its global reach into foreign markets after the Civil War, economic convulsions pointed to the need for new markets. In 1865, American exports totaled $281 million; by 1898, they topped $1.2 billion. The depressions of the 1870s and 1890s convinced many Americans that overproduction of goods was the source of economic turmoil. Neither domestic markets nor current foreign markets could longer absorb the immense output of American industry and agriculture. New markets would secure the nation's position as the world's greatest industrial power and guarantee peace domestically. The social turbulence spawned by the depression of 1893–1897—massive unemployment, farm foreclosures, and labor strife—convinced Democrats, Republicans, and Populists alike that new markets would provide the antidote to domestic problems.

In 1893, as the stock market plunged, a young history professor, **Frederick Jackson Turner**, added to the growing anxiety with a highly influential essay titled "The Significance of the Frontier in American History." According to the 1890 census, the frontier had disappeared with the complete settlement of the West. The "closing" of the frontier, he explained, had many serious consequences. Most importantly, because "economic power secures political power," free land in the West had been essential to maintaining freedom and opportunity. The inability of its people to expand into free lands, Turner warned, threatened the very future of the republic.

Support for expansion also came from military experts anxious about international prestige and defense. As European powers and Japan competed for global influence, experts argued that if the United States failed to contend for empire, it would be left behind as a second-rate power in a world where only the strongest survived. Moreover, at the very least, simple self-defense required a vigorous foreign policy. If left unchecked, foreign powers might even dominate in the Western Hemisphere. Although the United States had managed to reduce foreign influence in the Americas with the declaration of the Monroe Doctrine in 1823, Great Britain remained a major player—with its Caribbean possessions, with Canada as part of its commonwealth, and with its domination of South American trade.

To prepare for the nation's new global role, Congress authorized the modernization of the U.S. Navy, a fleet in disrepair since the Civil War. Captain **Alfred Thayer Mahan**, director of the Naval War College, emerged as the leading proponent of a "new navy." In his highly influential series of lectures, published in 1890 as *The Influence* *of Sea Power upon History, 1660–1783,* Mahan contended that history proved that a powerful navy was the key to national greatness and international power. To control the oceans was to control the world. Colonies played a crucial role in Mahan's theory to provide strategic military bases and coaling stations for far-flung global conflicts that were sure to come.

Other Americans in the 1880s and 1890s, like Mahan, advocated for a muscular foreign policy; they viewed war as an antidote to what they deemed the crisis of "overcivilization." According to contemporary observers, middle-class men had grown soft and flabby. They spent too much time working indoors with little physical activity. Whereas their fathers had fought in the Civil War, they slaved away in their offices pursuing money instead of greatness on the battlefield. Many worried that the current generation was not tough enough, their "manly" spirit drained by their soft, white-collar world. In 1894, the *North American Review* feared "idleness and luxury have made men flabby" and suggested that the president "is beginning to ask seriously if a great war might not help them to pull themselves together." Theodore Roosevelt, one of the leading disciples of the strenuous life, challenged the nation to "boldly face the life of strife. . . . Oversentimentality, oversoftness . . ., and mushiness are the great danger of this age and this people." Despite a resurgence in physical activities in the 1890s—especially rough sports such as boxing and football—many young men longed for the ultimate test: to fight in a war to prove their manhood and to reinvigorate the nation.

Excerpt from Theodore Roosevelt, "The Strenuous Life" (1899)

STUDY QUESTIONS FOR THE NEW IMPERIALISM

1. What general factors account for the global grab for empire in the late 19th century?

2. What specific factors pushed the United States into the scramble for colonies?

quiz

THE UNITED STATES FLEXES ITS MUSCLES

The United States had no overarching, long-range plan to create a political empire. Instead, policymakers initially emphasized developing global trade. In the 1880s, Secretary of State **James G. Blaine** explained, "Our great demand is expansion." He noted, however, that this did not mean "annexation of territory" but rather "annexation of trade." But a decade of aggressive foreign policy intent on expanding and protecting the nation's global commercial empire, coupled with the crises of the 1890s, paved the way for political empire.

First asserting dominance in the Western Hemisphere, U.S. policymakers soon defined the nation's strategic interests broadly and forcefully in the Pacific and Asia as well. The three month-long Spanish-American-Philippine War in 1898 paid huge dividends to the United States. Entered into with limited aims—ostensibly to aid Cuban independence and defend American business interests there—the war resulted in control of Cuba, Puerto Rico, Guam, and the Philippines. Although a latecomer, the United States—with its modern navy playing a key role—now joined its European and Japanese rivals as participants in the New Imperialism.

The nation's new and aggressive foreign policy raised many questions that Americans continue to struggle with to this day. What is the role of the United States in the world? What are "American interests"? When, if ever, do American interests justify intervention in foreign countries and wars abroad?

Latin America

The United States had long kept a watchful eye on foreign influence in the Western Hemisphere. The Monroe Doctrine had stood as the foundation of American foreign policy since 1823. Beginning in the 1880s, the United States embarked on a more expansive foreign policy in Latin America to protect markets and U.S. investments there. Secretary of State James G. Blaine, who served under Republican presidents James Garfield (1881) and **Benjamin Harrison** (1889–1893), was the chief architect of this new policy, which would last well into the 20th century. Blaine asserted that the United States must maintain stability in Latin America to guarantee healthy trade and to secure its markets. In 1890, Blaine played a key role in Congress's passage of the first major reciprocal tariff, which allowed certain goods from Latin America, such as sugar and coffee, to enter the country with no tariff as long as Latin American countries allowed the free passage of U.S. goods in turn. Trade with Cuba and Brazil exploded as a result.

Subsequent administrations embraced Blaine's policy. Interference in the internal affairs of Latin American countries soon resulted. In 1893, for example, when Brazilian monarchists, encouraged by the British, threatened to revolt against the recently established pro-American regime, President Grover Cleveland helped quash the revolution at the behest of U.S. business interests.

Venezuela emerged as a trouble spot a few years later, in 1895–1896. A long-disputed border between Venezuela and British Guiana catalyzed U.S. intervention when Great Britain reasserted its claims to territory that included the gateway to trade for much of the continent. Citing the Monroe Doctrine, President Cleveland insisted that the British arbitrate the disputed land claim. When Great Britain ignored his request, an angry Cleveland explained that not only would the United States enforce the Monroe Doctrine in the dispute, but it would also "resist by every means in its power" Britain's Venezuelan claims. Great Britain, caving to U.S. demands, ultimately lost the quarrel, as arbiters sided with Venezuela and the United States reinforced its dominance in the Western Hemisphere.

Hawaii

The United States also engaged in muscular foreign policy beyond the Caribbean. Asserting itself in the Pacific, it protected business interests established earlier by missionaries and traders. In 1875, the American-dominated government of Hawaii had established a reciprocity agreement with the United States that allowed Hawaiian sugar to enter the country duty free; this resulted in the tripling of sugar production in 10 years. But the **McKinley Tariff**, passed by Congress in 1890, ended Hawaii's favored status and threatened the sugar industry there. Immediately, Americans in Hawaii began to pursue annexation to the United States as a solution to their export problems.

As the Hawaiian economy nearly collapsed, **Queen Liliuokalani** threatened U.S. domination when she ascended to the throne in 1891. Four years earlier, Americans in

QUEEN LILIUOKALANI The last monarch to reign over Hawaii, Queen Liliuokalani (1838–1917) was deposed by American planter interests in 1893 and imprisoned for over a year after she was accused of attempting to restore the monarchy in 1895.

Hawaii had implemented a new constitution, referred to by Native Hawaiians as "the bayonet constitution," which stripped the monarchy of most its authority. In 1893, the queen, intent on returning control of the islands to her people —now a powerless minority in their own country—drew up another constitution that restored the monarchy's power and returned political rights to Native Hawaiians. But U.S. missionary-planter interests, headed by **Sanford B. Dole**, organized a coup and overthrew the queen. At their request, supported by the U.S. minister in Hawaii, the U.S. government dispatched marines to prevent the queen and her supporters from fighting back.

Excerpt from Queen Liliuokalani, *Hawaii's Story by Hawaii's Queen* (1898)

American residents established a provisional government and requested annexation to the United States. But after a thorough investigation, President Cleveland rejected their proposal. Hawaii "was taken possession of by the U.S. forces without the consent or wish of the government of the islands." In the meantime, the provisional government established the Republic of Hawaii on July 4, 1894, with coup leader Dole as president. The next year, the new regime arrested the queen, claiming she was involved in a plot to restore the monarchy, and imprisoned her for 13 months. Passing a tariff bill granting the islands favored treatment in selling sugar in the United States, Congress restored prosperity to the sugar planters there.

The Cuban Crisis

The United States had lusted after Cuba for many years. The crown jewel of the Spanish empire in the Caribbean, Cuba is only 90 miles off the coast of Florida. Before the Civil War, pro-slavery advocates discussed annexing the island. And, beginning in the

1830s, American financiers, such as the Atkins family of Boston, invested in the Cuban sugar trade. After the Civil War, these investors became planters themselves. In 1882, E. Atkins & Company of Boston emerged as the largest landowner on the islands.

Cubans, who had long chafed under Spanish rule and had instigated numerous unsuccessful rebellions, launched yet another revolution against Spain in the 1890s. In 1894, U.S. tariff agreements granting Hawaiian sugar favored status plunged Cubans into an economic crisis, as their once-prosperous sugar trade vanished. Economic collapse and unemployment served only to remind Cubans of their lack of political power. In February 1895, Cuban insurgents took advantage of widespread discontent and began to rebel against Spanish authorities. By 1896, under the banner of *Cuba Libre*, revolutionaries took their fight to the countryside. Torching sugar fields, they vowed that there would be no peace, production, or protection of property until Spain granted independence.

Intent on holding on to the last jewel in its once-expansive necklace of colonies, Spain attempted to crush the rebellion with an iron fist. Led by General Valeriano Weyler, Spain increased its army to 200,000 and attempted to quash the rebellion by suffocating the rural, peasant communities providing support to the rebels. In the fall of 1896, Weyler imposed a new policy, *reconcentracíon*, rounding up the rural population and placing its people in camps in fortified towns. Spanish soldiers then destroyed villages, food supplies, peasant fields, and slaughtered animals, any resource that could aid the insurgents. Weyler's policy created hundreds of thousands of refugees, and as many as 400,000 sick and hungry Cubans perished.

Developments in Cuba quickly captured the attention of Americans. The rebellion and the scorched-earth tactics of both sides threatened U.S. investments, estimated at $50 million. Major newspapers, especially those owned by **William Randolph Hearst**

IT 'S GOT TO BE SOONER OR LATER – AND IT LOOKS LIKE "SOONER."

"IT'S GOT TO BE SOONER OR LATER—AND IT LOOKS LIKE 'SOONER. '" Published soon after the United States declared war on Spain, this cartoon portrays a gallant Uncle Sam taking the hand of a female figure, representing independent Cuba, and pointing to a vanquished Spain, represented as a pirate, his sword labeled "400 years of misrule."

and **Joseph Pulitzer**, competed for readers by publishing sensational front-page stories, often fabricated, that described atrocities of "Butcher" Weyler and the Spanish in Cuba. **Yellow journalism** provoked public support for the Cuban rebels, and newspapers cried out for military intervention on behalf of the rebels in their fight for freedom.

Despite calls for war, neither the Democratic Cleveland administration, in its final year when the revolution exploded in 1895–1896, nor the subsequent Republican administration of **William McKinley**, acted hastily. Rather than jump into war, McKinley sought a diplomatic solution to the Cuban crisis. In 1897, he demanded that Spain implement reforms to end the Cuban revolt. Spain complied by removing General Weyler, declaring amnesty for insurgents, and granting Cuba partial independence. But halfway measures only exacerbated the crisis, angering both Spanish loyalists and rebels. When riots by loyalists tore through Havana in late 1897, McKinley ordered the battleship USS *Maine* to Havana Harbor to protect U.S. citizens and property there.

In February 1898, two events pushed the nation to the brink of war with Spain. Early in the month, the *New York Journal* published an intercepted private letter written by Spain's minister in Washington, **Enrique Dupuy de Lôme**. The letter insulted McKinley by calling him a "weak bidder for the admiration of the crowd." As an outraged public cried out for revenge, the drumbeat for war grew steadier and louder. Then, on February 15, the *Maine* blew up in Havana Harbor, killing 260 of 276 American sailors aboard the ship. Most Americans immediately concluded, as did Assistant Secretary of the Navy Theodore Roosevelt, that the explosion was "an act of dirty treachery on the part of the Spanish." A hastily convened Naval Board of Inquiry conducted an investigation and concluded that a detonated mine had destroyed the ship, although no evidence was ever found to implicate Spain. (Most historians today believe a fire in the ship's coal room accidently caused the explosion.) The public clamored even more loudly for war, declaring, "Remember the *Maine!* To hell with Spain!"

On April 11, 1898, after attempting a final diplomatic solution, McKinley asked Congress for a declaration of war against Spain, which it passed unanimously. The Cuban crisis, he explained, "threatened Cuban lives, U.S. property, and tranquility in the U.S. itself." In addition, intervention was a defense of "human rights." To placate those who worried that the United States might try to colonize Cuba—and to protect the beet-sugar industry of his own state from competition with cheap Cuban sugar— Senator Henry Teller of Colorado added an amendment to the war declaration. The **Teller Amendment** stated that the United States would not colonize Cuba.

Newspaper accounts of the destruction of the Maine (1898)

"A Splendid Little War"

The nation embarked on war with Spain in a near-holiday spirit. As men responded enthusiastically to McKinley's call for troops, eagerly embracing the chance to fight, women organized relief organizations to support the war effort. But the nation found itself unprepared for war, and logistical problems plagued the campaign. Many soldiers never received proper equipment or training; they lacked even the most basic necessities, such as tents and mess kits. In addition, they were issued wool uniforms unsuitable for a summer war in a tropical climate.

As soldiers gathered in Tampa, Florida, to embark for Cuba, Commodore **George Dewey** scored the first American victory of the war on the other side of the globe. In February 1898, 10 days after the *Maine* explosion, Assistant Secretary of the Navy

Roosevelt had ordered Dewey to engage the Spanish in their Pacific colony, the Philippines, should war break out. On May 1, Dewey defeated the Spanish fleet in Manila Bay without losing a single man. With the aid of Filipino rebels under the command of **Emilio Aguinaldo**, who were seeking their independence from Spain, Dewey forced the Spanish to surrender the city of Manila. The Philippines had hardly figured into the discussion leading up to the war. But the United States immediately expanded its war against Spain to include the strategically located Philippines. As Captain Mahan noted a few months after Dewey's victory, "the port of Manila is very centrally situated as regards the whole sweep of the eastern coast of Asia." By late June, the first American ground troops had arrived in Manila.

In mid-June, U.S. troops finally left for Cuba, landing in Daiquirí on June 22. Despite numerous logistical problems for the United States, it soon became clear that the Spanish were no match for the U.S. armed forces. The antiquated Spanish navy, with its wooden ships, proved to be an easy foe for the modern steel ships of the U.S. Navy. In Santiago Harbor, just prior to the landing of troops, 12 American ships destroyed the entire Spanish squadron with the loss of one American life. The Spanish also had no war plan for defending against a U.S. invasion, as they were preoccupied with the Cuban insurrection.

ROOSEVELT'S "GREAT DAY" Long seeking military glory, Colonel Theodore Roosevelt called the Battle of San Juan Hill "the great day of my life." Reports of his heroism greatly accelerated his political career, first as governor of New York, then as vice president, and finally as president from 1901 to 1909.

On July 1, 1898, the U.S. Army defeated the Spanish in the war's biggest land battle, at San Juan Hill, as they made their way to Santiago. Colonel Theodore Roosevelt and his First Volunteer Cavalry Regiment, known as the "**Rough Riders**," became national heroes for their daring exploits during the battle. The son of a patrician New York family, Roosevelt resigned his post as assistant secretary of the navy when the United States declared war on Spain and organized his own regiment. The Rough Riders were a motley mix of cowboys, Native Americans, Mexican Americans, several New York City policemen, and Ivy League athletes. The only Rough Rider on horseback, Roosevelt led a risky charge up Kettle Hill, part of the battle for nearby San Juan Hill. With the support of several African American cavalry units, who received little credit, the Rough Riders emerged victorious, their exploits widely reported by the American press. Roosevelt called the battle "the great day of my life."

PUCK.

A TRIFLE EMBARRASSED.

image
analysis

"A TRIFLE EMBARRASSED"   Published at the end of the Spanish-American-Philippine War, in August 1898, this cartoon depicts "Manifest Destiny" presenting Cuba, Hawaii, Puerto Rico, and the Philippines—depicted as racialized babies—to Uncle Sam. They will soon join the previously annexed Texas, California, New Mexico, and Alaska happily playing within the walls of the United States. Uncle Sam exclaims, "Gosh, I wish they wouldn't come quite so many in a bunch; but if I've got to take them, I guess I can do as well by them as I've done by the others!"

On August 12, 1898, the Spanish signed a protocol of peace ending the war after only three months. Within that short time, U.S. war aims had expanded considerably. U.S. forces had not only defeated the Spanish in Cuba and Manila Bay, but also seized Guam and Puerto Rico. In July 1898, just as the war heated up, Congress approved the annexation of Hawaii. On August 14, two days after Spain agreed to end the war—but before word of the war's end reached the Philippines—U.S. troops, with the aid of Filipino rebels, captured the city of Manila. In a matter of weeks the United States had substantially extended its influence and power in the Pacific and Asia.

In Cuba, U.S. objectives shifted from liberation to conquest. Despite its high-toned language regarding Cuban independence, the U.S. war declaration did not recognize the rebels or their provisional government, as the United States remained intent on controlling the war and its aftermath. Refusing to allow the rebels to take an active part in the war, military leaders, as well as journalists, increasingly depicted them in negative racial stereotypes. They seemed surprised that many Cubans were dark skinned and of African descent. One officer described them as "lazy," "cowardly," "dirty," and "child-like," incapable of self-government.

The Spanish-American War

The ease of victory led Secretary of State **John Hay** to refer to the Spanish-American War as "a splendid little war." But it exacted a high toll, much of it unnecessary. In addition to lacking basic equipment and proper tropical uniforms, soldiers suffered from filth and disease. **Clara Barton** and the Red Cross found it nearly impossible to get vital medical supplies and equipment unloaded from ships in Cuba. Soldiers also subsisted on rancid canned beef, full of gristle and maggots, sold to the army by the Chicago meatpacking giant Armour and Company. Many more American soldiers died of food poisoning and disease than Spanish bullets; sickness and disease accounted for approximately 2,500 of 2,900 total deaths.

The Treaty of Paris, signed in December 1898, officially ended the war with Spain, pending Senate ratification. Spain ceded Cuba and Puerto Rico in the Caribbean and Guam and the Philippines, for an additional $20 million, in the Pacific. The war proved to be a stunning debut for the nation as a world power.

STUDY QUESTIONS FOR THE UNITED STATES FLEXES ITS MUSCLES

1. What factors and events led the United States to declare war on Spain in April 1898?

2. How did U.S. war aims change over the course of the Spanish-American War?

quiz

❥ THE COMPLICATIONS OF EMPIRE

The United States generally basked in the glow of victory over Spain. A nation hungry for heroes reveled in Commodore Dewey's exploits in Manila, and the press published numerous stories about the feats of the Rough Riders. Americans also celebrated the evident reconciliation of North and South in the war. The war provided the first opportunity since the Civil War for Northerners and Southerners to fight as a united nation against a common foe. The press highlighted the fact that the first U.S. soldier to die in battle was a Southerner.

But celebration of victory soon gave way to pressing questions. What should the United States do with territories it acquired in the war? The Teller Amendment prohibited the United States from colonizing Cuba, but should the United States maintain control through other means? And what about the other newly procured territories—especially Puerto Rico and the Philippines—where the United States was not bound by any prewar legislation?

The Philippines soon emerged as the focal point for a heated and divisive national debate. The nation seemed poised at a crossroads, with the final choice entailing massive consequences. Should the islands be given their independence? Or should they be colonized in an attempt to secure U.S. interests in the Pacific? Could a republic like the United States be a colonial power without undermining its most cherished values, such as self-determination? Or were colonies an inevitable outgrowth of international greatness?

Choosing the road to empire, the United States soon learned the high cost of that decision, as it fought a protracted, bloody war to subdue a rebellion seeking Philippine independence. Moreover, the nation's presence in Asia guaranteed its involvement in future Pacific wars.

Cuba and Puerto Rico

Just as the United States did not allow Cuban rebels to take part in the war with Spain, they did not allow Cubans to negotiate the peace treaty or determine their postwar fate. Forbidden by the Teller Amendment from annexing Cuba, the United States nevertheless took formal control of the island, rejecting Cuban pleas for independence. Military occupation of Cuba began in January 1899, as General **Leonard Wood** assumed the position of military governor and promised a stable Cuba to guarantee "business confidence." At the same time, the United States did what it could to discredit Cuba's independence movement. According to Major General William R. Shafter, who had commanded U.S. troops in the war, "Why those people are no more fit for self-government than gunpowder is for hell." But the Cuban independence movement remained strong.

Unable to colonize Cuba and soon weary of maintaining military occupation, the United States seized on another form of control through the **Platt Amendment**. Passed by Congress in 1901 as an appendix to a new Cuban constitution, the Platt Amendment gave the United States broad authority to intervene to preserve Cuban independence and forced Cuba to sell or lease land for U.S. naval stations and coaling bases in perpetuity. Outraged delegates to Cuba's constitutional convention opposed the amendment but under intense pressure passed it, 15 to 11. Governor Wood confessed privately, "There is, of course, little or no independence left Cuba under the Platt Amendment." Within five years, in 1906, the United States had sent troops to Cuba to maintain order, and the Platt Amendment served as the basis of U.S.–Cuba relations until 1934.

The Platt Amendment (1901)

Unlike Cuba, Puerto Rico had no protection from annexation. U.S. military forces had invaded the island in July 1898, and for the next 18 months ruled it. In 1900, Congress passed the Foraker Act, defining Puerto Rico as an "unincorporated territory" under congressional control, and a U.S. civilian government replaced military rule. Notably, annexation did not grant citizenship or even civil rights. In a series of cases known as the **Insular Cases**, which would be applied to all of the new territories added to the United States, the Supreme Court ruled that the Constitution did not follow the flag; that is, American rights and liberties did not extend to all lands under U.S. control. Puerto Ricans strongly protested their new status as subjects of the United States. A Puerto Rican newspaper angrily denounced the ambiguous status of Puerto Ricans: "We are and we are not a foreign country. We are and we are not citizens of the United States. . . . The Constitution . . . applies to us and does not apply to us." Although initially limiting the rights of Puerto Ricans, the United States acted swiftly to tie the island to the mainland's economy by passing legislation that facilitated Puerto Rican exports to the mainland. In 1917, the Jones–Shafroth Act granted citizenship—but not full political rights—to Puerto Ricans. To this day, Puerto Ricans cannot vote for the president and have no representation in Congress.

The Philippines

The colonization of the Philippines became one of the most troubling and divisive legacies of the Spanish-American War. After Dewey's victory in May 1898, McKinley seemed interested in controlling only Manila Bay, as a strategic base for commerce and naval operations, rather than all of the Philippine islands. Governing the islands posed numerous difficulties. On the other side of the globe, the Philippines consisted of hundreds of islands extending over 115,000 square miles. Moreover, Filipinos intent on self-government had fought against Spain for independence and had even aided the United States in defeating Spain in hopes of gaining their freedom.

McKinley's intentions soon became clear: the United States would not grant the Philippines independence. Instead, the United States planned to colonize the islands. In December 1898, McKinley articulated a policy of "benevolent assimilation." The Americans came, the president explained, "not as invaders or conquerors but as friends, to protect the natives in their homes, their employments, and in their personal and religious rights." The Philippines would serve as the centerpiece of a new U.S. empire.

McKinley rationalized this choice through a series of considerations. He was convinced that the Filipinos were incapable of self-government. In addition, he feared that if the United States did not control the Philippines, another imperial power would step in and help itself to the islands. The Philippines also seemed especially crucial as a foothold in Asia, to expand America's influence, its naval power, and its global standing.

The Debate over Empire

The colonization of the Philippines sparked bitter debate across the nation. Although a poll found that the overwhelming majority of Americans favored empire, with westerners most supportive, critics swiftly organized. In November 1898, concerned citizens formed the **Anti-Imperial League**, which soon boasted 25,000 members. The league included a wide range of some of the nation's most prominent people, including reformer Jane Addams, former president Cleveland, labor leader Samuel Gompers, African American intellectual **W. E. B. Du Bois**, and steel magnate Andrew Carnegie, who allegedly offered to buy the Philippines for $20 million and grant the Filipinos their independence.

Rudyard Kipling, "The White Man's Burden" (1901); Mark Twain, 'To the Person Sitting in Darkness" (1901)

Anti-imperialists rejected colonization as un-American and inconsistent with the nation's ideals. A republic, they argued, could not be an empire. As Senator **George Frisbie Hoar** of Massachusetts summarized, "The danger is that we are to be transformed from a republic founded on the Declaration of Independence . . . —the hope of the poor, the refuge of the oppressed—into a vulgar, commonplace empire founded upon physical force, controlling subject races and vassal states."

Imperialists denigrated such talk as old fashioned. "America," exclaimed Senator **Albert Beveridge** of Indiana, "is the young man of the nations. We are engaged in our great rivalry with other powers of the world. And this is the destiny of every nation that achieves its manhood." Moreover, he argued, the creation of empire abroad simply continued the march of the flag across "unexplored lands and savage wildernesses." In its triumphal march beyond U.S. borders, the nation continued to fulfill its destiny. The United States must "accept the gift of events," new markets, and trade and the opportunity to provide benevolent rule for people incapable of ruling themselves. If the United States did not act, a foreign foe would surely rule the Philippines.

Anti-imperialists rejected governing the Filipinos without their consent; imperialists countered that the United States had long governed Native Americans without their approval. Antis cited George Washington, the victor over the British Empire, as their symbol; champions of empire claimed Jefferson as "the first Imperialist of the Republic," his Louisiana Purchase precedent for annexation of "savage" and "alien" populations. Anti-imperialists insisted that governing and defending a colony 7,000 miles from California would drain the nation economically; imperialists responded with visions of riches derived from new Asian markets.

THE EMPEROR GETS NEW CLOTHES   This pro-imperialist cartoon depicts a newly enlarged Uncle Sam rejecting antiexpansionist tonic from Carl Schurz, former U.S. senator and vice president of the Anti-Imperialist League, and two fellow anti-imperialists. President McKinley, Uncle Sam's tailor, measures him for a new suit of clothes to fit his new size.

The issue of race figured prominently on both sides of the debate. Some, especially southern senators in the midst of disfranchising black voters, feared the addition of more people of color to the United States. Imperialists assured them that they could be annexed—as Indians had been—without granting them voting rights. At the same time, African Americans criticized the United States for allegedly expanding democracy to the Philippines while denying it to blacks at home. Black leader **Booker T. Washington** endorsed self-governance for the Philippines, remarking, "Until our nation has settled the Negro and Indian problems I do not believe that we have a right to assume more social problems." But imperialists argued that Anglo-Saxons bore a responsibility to govern and ultimately "uplift" their inferiors and to bestow on them the glories of democracy.

After intense debate, the Senate ratified the peace treaty and annexation of the Philippines by a vote of 57 to 27 in February 1899. American voters ratified colonization with the reelection of McKinley in 1900; the Republican Party platform promised Filipinos the "blessings of liberty and civilization." But controversy over these faraway islands was far from over.

The American-Philippine War

Even as the Senate ratified the peace treaty with Spain, the United States found itself entangled in an ugly war of repression against Filipinos demanding their independence.

African Americans and International Affairs

African Americans voiced mixed opinions regarding their country's expanding role in world affairs. Empire building occurred just as they watched their own rights violated with segregation laws, the loss of voting rights, and lynching. As a result, they viewed U.S. imperialism through the lens of their own deteriorating position. Victimized at home, they increasingly identified with people of color around the world who also suffered at the hands of white supremacy. Black Americans, especially soldiers, struggled with the irony of taking up "the white man's burden."

Many African Americans supported U.S. military intervention to liberate Cuba. They identified with the Cuban struggle as the fight of people of color against white European domination. Some even hoped to emigrate to a free Cuba to escape racism in the United States. When Congress declared war on Spain, however, some called it a "white man's war" and questioned whether black men should fight. The black newspaper the *Washington Bee* declared, "The Negro has no reason to fight for Cuba's independence. . . . He is as much in need of independence as Cuba is." Despite this sentiment, more than 10,000 black men volunteered for military service in the Spanish-American War. Many undoubtedly agreed with the Reverend H. H. Proctor of Atlanta, who insisted that "righteous war" provided "splendid opportunities" to remind the nation that "we are a real part of this country."

But black soldiers, serving in segregated units, suffered humiliation and violence. In June 1898, as they waited in Tampa to embark for Cuba, black soldiers rescued a two-year-old black child, the target for a shooting contest: whoever managed to shoot

Led by Emilio Aguinaldo, freedom fighters had aided U.S. troops when they invaded the islands, viewing them as allies against colonialism. When the United States, in turn, colonized the Philippines, Aguinaldo led his warriors against the new imperialists. After fighting a conventional war, in November 1899 Aguinaldo organized a guerrilla campaign against U.S. occupiers. U.S. soldiers could not tell friend from foe, and a bloody, brutal war of attrition ensued. Atrocities abounded as frustrations mounted, yet the United States was unable to subdue the outnumbered, outgunned rebels. In the most notorious incident of the war, Brigadier General Jacob H. Smith, in retaliation for an ambush of American troops in April 1900, ordered his soldiers to make "a howling wilderness" of the island of Samar. He ordered "all persons killed who are capable of bearing arms in actual hostilities against the United States" and insisted that no prisoners be taken. Asked for clarification, Smith replied that any person over the age of 10 "capable of bearing arms" should be killed.

Devolving into a race war, the U.S.-Philippine conflict fueled the brutal treatment of Filipinos—civilians and guerrilla fighters alike. White soldiers regularly referred to Filipinos as "gugus" and "niggers." Moreover, soldiers and officers—along with journalists and politicians—continually compared the Filipinos to Native Americans; in their view, the war against Aguinaldo was just another Indian war. Likening Aguinaldo to Sitting Bull, Filipinos were "savages" who needed to be conquered for their own good.

a bullet through the child's sleeve was declared the winner. Livid black soldiers took to the streets, attacking cafes and saloons that refused to serve them. White civilians also attacked black soldiers, resenting the presence of black men in uniform. In Cuba, black soldiers, despite their contributions, never received the credit they deserved, most notably for their role in the success of the Rough Riders' charge at San Juan Hill; Theodore Roosevelt even questioned their bravery.

The war in Cuba soured many African Americans on empire even before the United States colonized and subdued the Philippines. Many loudly protested imperialism. Several prominent civil rights activists, including W. E. B. Du Bois and Ida B. Wells, joined the Anti-Imperial League; others organized separate black anti-imperialist organizations. Black soldiers serving in the Philippines criticized the treatment of Filipinos, whom some called "our brothers," and wrote letters home that publicized atrocities. Although nearly all did their duty, a few responded to Aguinaldo's pleas to switch sides.

Global imperialism prompted W. E. B. Du Bois in 1903 to pen a powerful essay that began with an eloquent and profound statement: "The problem of the twentieth century is the problem of the color-line,—the relation of the darker to the lighter races of men in Asia and Africa, in America and the islands of the sea." America's race problem, as he pointed out, and his fellow black Americans had come to see, was a slice of a larger global problem.

- What factors account for the identification of African Americans with Cubans and Filipinos?
- What factors inhibited this identification?

FILIPINO PRESIDENT Emilio Aguinaldo (1869–1964) declared Philippine independence from Spain in June 1898; in January 1899, a Filipino constitutional convention declared him provisional president of the Philippines. When the United States refused to recognize Philippine independence, he led a war against the United States and was captured in March 1901.

Indeed, most regular U.S. officers and troops came from the West, with vivid memories of Indian warfare.

After declaring victory several times, the United States finally suppressed the insurgents—for the most part—after three years, in 1902. But rebellion against occupation continued to erupt for many years afterward, and U.S. domination came at a steep price. The United States spent $400 million to stifle the revolt, and more than 126,000 U.S. soldiers fought against the Filipino rebels. Roughly 4,200 Americans and 18,000 Filipinos died in battle; at least 250,000 Filipinos succumbed to gunfire, disease, and starvation. After Aguinaldo's capture in 1901, anti-imperialist Andrew Carnegie wrote a sarcastic note to a friend in McKinley's cabinet: "You seem to have finished your work of civilizing Filipinos; it is thought that about 8000 of them have been completely civilized and sent to Heaven. I hope you like it."

In 1901, **William Howard Taft** became the first governor-general of the Philippines, to aid "our little brown brothers," as he called them, in establishing a civilian government. The United States worked to win the hearts and minds of the Filipino people by investing in a public works program that built roads, bridges, and schools—a program that stressed the same manual training programs offered to Indians and blacks in the United States. At the same time, the United States began transferring some authority to Filipinos who supported their regime.

An Atlantic power before the war, the United States, with the conquest of the Philippines, was now a Pacific power too, with naval bases and coaling stations to extend both its military and its commercial influence. At the same time, however, the acquisition of the Philippines created new vulnerabilities. The islands proved to be difficult and expensive to defend, especially against Japan, the emerging power in Asia. Should the Japanese choose to expand southward, the United States would find itself at war. Less than four decades later, in December 1941, only days after the attack on Pearl Harbor, the Japanese invaded the Philippines and held the islands for most of World War II. The Philippines remained a U.S. colony until 1946.

China

The ratification of the peace treaty with Spain in February 1898 allowed McKinley to address land grabs that threatened to close access to the vast China market. With hundreds of millions of potential consumers for U.S. goods, the China market accounted for $15 million in U.S. exports between 1895 and 1900, quadrupling in those five years. U.S. industries grew increasingly dependent on China, especially textiles, iron and steel, and petroleum. Just recovering from the devastating depression of the 1890s, the United States acted forcefully to blunt any limitations to the lucrative China market.

First Open Door Note by John Hay (1899)

In 1899, Secretary of State John Hay articulated U.S. policy by penning the first "Open Door" notes addressed to the world's powers. The notes requested that they open up areas claimed by each power—its "sphere of interest"—to other nations, such as the United States, to allow them to compete fairly for Chinese trade. He also requested that world powers respect the integrity of China.

Hay's Open Door notes initially prompted only minimal response. Great Britain and Japan affirmed the policy. France, Germany, and Russia evaded a firm commitment to the **Open Door Policy**. Nevertheless, Hay made the claim that the world's powers had consented to the Open Door in China. Confident that the United States could compete successfully on a fair and equal playing ground, Hay had achieved tacit agreement for the United States to market its goods to all of China.

But after years of being invaded and picked apart by foreign powers, the Chinese fought back. In late 1899, a secret organization, "The Righteous and Harmonious Fist"—dubbed the "Boxers" by foreigners for their boxing rituals—began a violent revolt to eradicate "foreign devils" and their influence in China. Their expulsion, they believed, would revitalize their downtrodden nation and usher in a new, glorious age. Encouraged by the **Empress Dowager Cixi**, the Boxers especially targeted Christians— both foreign and Chinese converts—who undermined Chinese traditions. With their rebellion focused largely in Beijing and the surrounding countryside, the Boxers killed suspected Chinese Christians on sight and forced missionaries to flee for protection.

After the Boxers attacked foreign ministries, even killing the German minister and cutting off all communication between Beijing and the outside world, the United States and other powers mobilized quickly and sent an international force to suppress the rebellion. President McKinley ordered 50,000 troops from Manila to China, fearing that the rebellion would be used by other powers to shut the open door and bolster their spheres of interest. By August 1900, the international army had captured Beijing, released besieged foreigners, and smothered the Boxer Rebellion.

Although many praised McKinley as China's savior, anti-imperialists viewed the Boxer Rebellion as another example of wrongheaded foreign policy. In late 1900, Mark Twain pointed out the hypocrisy that the United States invaded China while barring Chinese immigration: "Why should not China be free from the foreigners, who are only making trouble on her soil? . . . We do not allow Chinamen to come here, and I say in all seriousness that it would be a graceful thing to let China decide who shall go there."

STUDY QUESTIONS FOR THE COMPLICATIONS OF EMPIRE

1. In what ways did colonization and America's entry onto the world stage represent a continuation of past policies? In what ways did they represent a break from the past?

2. What were the key arguments made by imperialists and anti-imperialists for and against empire? Which side, in your opinion, made the most convincing case? Why?

quiz

⊘ THE UNITED STATES ON THE WORLD STAGE: ROOSEVELT AND TAFT

Secretary of State John Hay's approach to increasing U.S. power through diplomacy in China set the course for subsequent foreign policy in the 20th century. The United States had joined the imperialist club, but the price had been steep. In the first decades of the 20th century, the United States focused on expanding its commercial empire instead of adding to its territorial empire.

Whether it was Roosevelt's "big stick" or Taft's "dollar diplomacy," presidential power in implementing foreign policy escalated considerably at the expense of Congress. Roosevelt, especially, helped define the modern presidency by often acting quickly and independently in foreign affairs. Although they were a study of contrasts in appearance, personality, and style, neither Roosevelt nor Taft hesitated to commit troops to Latin America in defense of U.S. interests. During their presidencies, from 1901 to 1913, the United States intervened 12 times in Latin America—in Honduras, the Dominican Republic, Cuba, Nicaragua, and Panama.

The United States established itself as the "policeman" of Latin America. This role secured the nation's domination of its neighbors but led to strained relations. With the Philippines as its foothold in Asia, the United States also continued to expand there commercially and to defend any infringement of its trade.

Both Roosevelt and Taft expanded the nation's role and influence on the world stage between 1901 and 1913 and set the course for the leading role the United States would play in world affairs for the rest of the century.

Roosevelt's "Big Stick"

The assassination of William McKinley at the World's Fair in Buffalo, New York, in September 1901, less than a year into his second term, thrust Theodore Roosevelt into the presidency. McKinley had selected the hero of San Juan Hill as his running mate in 1900, and Roosevelt, at the age of 42, became the youngest man ever to hold the office of president. Less than two weeks before McKinley's death, Roosevelt addressed an audience at the Minnesota State Fair. He exclaimed, "There is a homely adage that runs 'speak softly and carry a big stick; you will go far.'" Referring specifically to the enforcement of the Monroe Doctrine, Roosevelt's "homely adage" nevertheless encapsulated his foreign policy. The young president did not hesitate to use a "big stick" to expand American influence and maintain order essential to trade, especially in Latin America. Roosevelt also used the big stick of the presidency to act swiftly and decisively, often without congressional approval. Few presidents—before or since—have relished the role of president as much as Roosevelt, and he stamped his foreign policy with his exuberant and irrepressible personality, boldly leading the United States onto the world stage and guaranteeing its place as a world power.

Political cartoon portraying Roosevelt's "big stick" foreign policy (1904)

The completion of an isthmian canal connecting the Atlantic and Pacific in Central America had been discussed for decades by both the United States and Europeans, and it had been attempted unsuccessfully in the 1880s by France. The colonization of the Philippines and the massive expansion of the China trade made a canal even more crucial so that ships and goods could be moved quickly from the Atlantic to the Pacific. Roosevelt made completion of a canal his highest priority. But the United States remained entangled in the 1850 Clayton–Bulwer Treaty with Great Britain, a pact that neither nation could build a canal without an equal partnership with the other. After providing aid to Britain in the Boer War in South Africa, in which the empire suppressed insurgent settlers of Dutch descent, Secretary of State Hay negotiated an end to the treaty.

The United States considered a number of sites for an isthmian canal. Panama, a province of Colombia, had obvious advantages. Shorter than a Nicaraguan route, the Panama site also featured the partly completed canal constructed by the French, who—overcome by tropical diseases—had halted the project. In June 1902, Congress passed the Spooner Amendment, authorizing the president to pay $40 million to the French company that still owned the construction rights to the canal and to purchase a

PRESIDENT ROOSEVELT GETS TO WORK   To the delight of the public, President Roosevelt traveled to Panama in 1906—the first executive to leave the country while in office—mounted a steam engine, and had himself photographed in "stereoview" digging the canal.

six-mile-wide strip, a canal zone. In return, Colombia would receive a $10 million payment and $250,000 annually for six years.

When Colombia rejected the proposal, an angry Roosevelt labeled the Colombians "banditti" and encouraged the Panamanians to revolt against Colombia. When the province rebelled, the president immediately recognized the new nation of Panama and ordered U.S. warships to prevent Colombian forces from landing in Panama to suppress the revolution. Then, in 1903, the Roosevelt administration signed a treaty with a self-proclaimed representative of Panama—Frenchman Philippe Bunau-Varilla, who had not been in Panama for years but served as a director of the French canal company—granting the United States a 10-mile-wide canal zone, cutting the new nation in half. Panama would receive $10 million initially and $250,000 per year. In addition, the United States promised to guarantee Panama's independence. Panamanians, outraged at being subject to a treaty not signed by a Panamanian, bitterly protested.

Roosevelt's heavy-handed tactics in Panama sparked more criticism than any other act of his presidency. *The New York Times*, for example, labeled his actions "an act of sordid conquest." Mark Twain noted that Roosevelt seemed "ready to kick the Constitution into the back yard whenever it gets in the way." But the public generally supported the president: the United States needed a canal and, with a "big stick," Roosevelt had secured one. He cited it as his greatest achievement as president. Roosevelt later bragged, "I took the Isthmus, started the canal and then left Congress not to debate the canal, but to debate me." The largest construction project in world history, the **Panama Canal** was completed in 1914. The canal reduced the distance from New York to San Francisco from over 13,000 miles to 5,300 miles. But the canal poisoned U.S. relations with Latin America, whose nations viewed the United States as an unscrupulous bully. The canal remained under U.S. control until December 1999, when the Torrijos–Carter Treaty, signed by President Jimmy Carter in 1977, gave control of the canal to Panama.

Roosevelt acted decisively in other ways to ensure U.S. influence in the Western Hemisphere. In December 1904, the president declared an addition to the Monroe Doctrine, known as the **Roosevelt Corollary**: the nation's right to intervene in the internal affairs of Latin American nations to ensure order and to suppress European influence. The "international police power" of the United States, he promised, would be used sparingly, only as a last resort. Not only did the Roosevelt Corollary define the United States as the "policeman" to keep order in Latin America, it also subverted an original intent of the Monroe Doctrine. The doctrine originally aimed at guaranteeing a free marketplace in the Western Hemisphere and supported independence movements in Latin America by forbidding European (and even U.S.) intervention. Now Roosevelt used his expansion of the Monroe Doctrine to ensure not only that the United States would firmly control markets in Latin America but that it would also use its power to quell revolutions, readily defined as "instability." Even though some Latin American governments acted to limit Roosevelt's new doctrine, the United States regularly intervened in the affairs of Latin American nations to ensure "stability."

Roosevelt also worked to maintain the Open Door Policy and access to the vast China market, which both Russia and Japan threatened. In 1904, when Russia claimed Manchuria and Korea, the United States backed Japan's surprise attack on Russia's Pacific fleet at Port Arthur, in China, an action sparking the **Russo-Japanese War**. Japan seemed more sympathetic than Russia to U.S. goals in China. Roosevelt intervened to broker a peace agreement, signed in September 1905. Both nations agreed to maintain the Open Door, recognizing China's national integrity, and each gave up claims to Manchuria. Japan, which had for all intents and purposes defeated Russia in the war, gained some key Chinese ports that had belonged to Russia and, more notably, Korea. As part of a secret deal, Japan promised to refrain from any interference in the Philippines given the United States' recognition of Japan's claims to Korea. Roosevelt's efforts earned him the Nobel Peace Prize in 1906.

The peace treaty reflected Roosevelt's ambitions for Japan. Despite his deep belief in Anglo-Saxon superiority, the president admired the Japanese for their military prowess and industrial might. He hoped that the United States could curb Japan's imperial interests while using it as an ally against the Russians, whom he feared and hated.

U.S.–Japanese relations, however, soon grew tense in 1906 when anti-Japanese hysteria broke out in California. Like the Chinese before them, Japanese immigrants found themselves the targets of anti-Asian discrimination. In 10 years, between 1890 and 1900, the soaring Japanese immigrant population—from 2,000 to 24,000—created a backlash. In addition to segregating schools to keep Japanese children from "contaminating" native-born children, California's legislature threatened to pass an Asian exclusion bill. Anti-Japanese riots also broke out. Outraged Japanese officials demanded that Roosevelt calm the crisis; relations soured so much that war seemed a real possibility. In 1907, the president and Japanese officials reached a "**gentlemen's agreement**": Roosevelt promised an end to anti-Asian hysteria in California, and the Japanese pledged to ban the immigration of adult male laborers to the United States.

The crisis demonstrated Japan's growing strength. In 1907, to make a show of power to the Japanese, Roosevelt dispatched the "Great White Fleet," made up of the navy's 16 battleships, on a world tour with stops in Japan. The Japanese nevertheless continued to act aggressively in Manchuria. They made a secret agreement with the Chinese guaranteeing sole rights to develop a railroad there and subverting a U.S. company's plans.

Puck magazine cover depicting anti-Japanese immigration policy (1907)

In the Root–Takahira Agreement of 1908, Roosevelt recognized Japan's dominance in southern Manchuria, and the Japanese again pledged to uphold the Open Door Policy, already compromised by their control of Manchuria.

Taft's Dollar Diplomacy

By 1908, Theodore Roosevelt had served seven highly eventful years as president, completing McKinley's unfinished term and then being elected in 1904. Although just 50 years old, and still vigorous, Roosevelt chose not to seek reelection. Not only had he made a pledge after his 1904 election not to run again, he also had alienated conservatives in the Republican Party who viewed with alarm his domestic reforms, especially his attempts to limit corporate power, and he feared he might not receive the nomination.

Roosevelt handpicked the rotund William Howard Taft as his successor, and Taft won the presidency in 1908. He hoped to replace Roosevelt's "big stick" with American dollars. "**Dollar diplomacy**" aimed to use the nation's growing wealth, instead of military force, to create order and stability throughout the world. Corporate investment in less developed countries would enrich the United States, Taft believed, while extending and ensuring its influence globally. "Modern diplomacy is commercial," Taft succinctly explained. But Taft's foreign policy, as clumsy as Roosevelt's was deft, led to a number of setbacks.

Taft brought impressive foreign policy experience to the presidency, with special expertise in Asia. He had served as Roosevelt's secretary of war, had experience negotiating with the Japanese, and had served as the first governor-general of the Philippines. But Taft made the mistake of choosing corporate lawyer Philander C. Knox as his secretary of state, who had little foreign policy experience. More concerned with his golf game than global matters, Knox blundered his way through the next four years.

In China, Knox tried to break an agreement recognizing Russia's dominance of northern Manchuria and Japan's dominance of the south. Each had established railroad interests there, but Knox believed that whoever controlled the railroad would control access to the massive China market. In 1910, he proposed that all major powers pool their resources, buy the Russian and Japanese railroads, and then operate them, based on the Open Door Policy. Knox's scheme backfired badly when the former enemies, Japan and Russia, signed a friendship agreement to fend off Knox's plan. Japan also formally annexed Korea and closed the open door in Manchuria, replacing U.S.-made goods with those made in Japan. Knox's attempts to expand trade in other parts of China only worsened U.S. relations with Japan and Russia. A failed railroad scheme, in which a crumbling Chinese government purchased worthless U.S. railroad stock, helped cause the collapse of the regime and bring about a revolution in 1911. An alarmed Theodore Roosevelt, watching his carefully crafted policies unravel in China, condemned Knox's "bumbling."

In Latin America, where the United States dominated, dollar diplomacy achieved more success (Map 19.2). In several Latin American countries, U.S. corporations already controlled the government and economy, making military intervention unnecessary. The Boston-based **United Fruit Company**, for example, had grown dramatically from its origins shipping bananas from Central to North America. United Fruit

interactive timeline

TIMELINE 1890–1914

AMERICA	YEAR	THE WORLD
May Congress authorizes construction of three modern battleships	1890	
Jan Queen Liliuokalani ascends to throne of Hawaiian monarchy	1891	
Jan Sanford B. Dole leads successful coup in Hawaii, deposing Queen Liliuokalani **Dec** Cleveland administration refuses to annex Hawaii	1893	
Jul Republic of Hawaii founded with Sanford Dole as president	1894	**Aug** First Sino-Japanese War begins as China and Japan fight for control over Korea
Jul Crisis erupts between United States and Great Britain over disputed Venezuelan boundary	1895	**Feb** Cuban insurgents revolt against Spanish rule **Apr** Japan wins the first Sino-Japanese War
	1896	**Feb** General Valeriano Weyler implements *reconcentracíon* policy in attempt to crush Cuban revolution
	1897	**Jun** Queen Victoria celebrates 60 years on British throne
Jan USS *Maine* arrives in Havana Harbor **Feb** De Lôme letter published in the *New York Journal* **Feb** USS *Maine* explodes in Havana Harbor, killing 260 U.S. sailors **Apr** Congress declares war on Spain **May** Commodore Dewey defeats Spanish fleet in Manila Bay **Jul** Battle of San Juan Hill **Jul** United States annexes Hawaii **Jul** United States begins military occupation of Puerto Rico **Aug** Spanish-American war ends; peace negotiations begin **Nov** Anti-Imperial League founded in Boston **Dec** Treaty of Paris signed, officially ending Spanish-American War	1898	**Mar** European powers and Japan threaten U.S. "open door" in China
Jan United States establishes military government in Cuba **Feb** Treaty of Paris ratified by U.S. Senate **Sep** Secretary of State John Hay issues first "Open Door" notes **Nov** Aguinaldo implements guerrilla war against United States	1899	**Oct** Second Boer War breaks out over British claims in Transvaal and Orange Free State, lasting nearly three years **Nov** Boxer Rebellion begins in China

controlled not only the banana market but also the railway system, shipping, banking, and the governments of Honduras and Costa Rica. With the tentacles of "The Octopus," as Latin Americans referred to the company, encircling nearly all of the economy and politics in the two countries, the United States did not need to intervene. But in less stable countries such as Haiti, U.S. bank loans helped pull those nations from the brink of domestic turmoil in 1910.

Other parts of Latin America remained more volatile, and Taft did not hesitate to send troops, under the Roosevelt Corollary, to defend U.S. interests. When

AMERICA	YEAR	THE WORLD
Jul Secretary of State Hay issues second set of "Open Door" notes **May** Foraker Act defines Puerto Rico as "unincorporated territory" under congressional control	**1900**	**Aug** International military force, including U.S. troops, arrives in Beijing to crush Boxer Rebellion
Mar Aguinaldo captured by U.S. forces **Feb** Cuba approves constitution ceding much authority to United States **Sep** President McKinley is assassinated; Vice President Roosevelt ascends to presidency	**1901**	
Jun Congress passes Spooner Amendment **Jul** Filipino war for independence ends, although resistance continues for years	**1902**	
Nov Hay–Bunau–Varilla Treaty signed, granting United States rights to build canal in Panama	**1903**	
Nov Theodore Roosevelt wins presidential election **Dec** Roosevelt Corollary announced	**1904**	**Feb** Russo-Japanese War breaks out
	1905	**Jan** Russian Revolution of 1905 begins with mass protests against czarist regime **Sep** Peace treaty negotiated by Roosevelt ends Russo-Japanese War
Mar Roosevelt negotiates immigration agreement with Japan **Dec** Roosevelt dispatches "Great White Fleet" around the world	**1907**	
Nov William Howard Taft elected to presidency	**1908**	
	1910	**Nov** Mexican Revolution begins, ultimately lasting 10 years
	1912	**Jan** Chinese Republic established with overthrow of Manchu Dynasty
Aug Panama Canal opens	**1914**	

rumors spread in 1910 that Nicaragua's dictator planned to make an agreement with Europeans for a second isthmian canal, the United States sent marines to help rebels depose the regime. U.S. investors soon swooped in to purchase Nicaraguan banks and railroads. When in 1912 President Adolfo Diaz offered his country as a U.S. protectorate in exchange for more loans, angry citizens rose up against him. Taft again ordered marines to Nicaragua to protect the pro-American president against his own people. They remained in that country continuously, except for a brief time in 1925, until 1933.

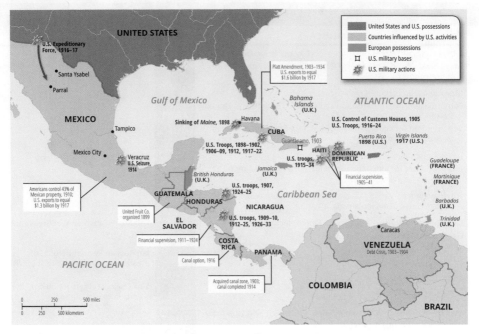

MAP 19.2 The United States in Latin America, 1898–1934 The growth of U.S. economic investment and military presence to defend those interests helped define the United States' relations with Latin America.

STUDY QUESTIONS FOR THE UNITED STATES ON THE WORLD STAGE: ROOSEVELT AND TAFT

quiz

1. Provide examples of the ways in which Roosevelt's foreign policy reflected the phrase, "Speak softly and carry a big stick—and you will go far."

2. Provide examples for Taft's statement, "Modern diplomacy is commercial." Is this statement still true today? Why? Why not?

Summary

- In the last quarter of the 19th century, the world's industrial powers embarked on a scramble for colonies, often called the New Imperialism.
- A combination of crises in the 1890s—economic, social, political, and cultural— thrust the United States into the global scramble for empire.
- Social Darwinism, the new discipline of anthropology, and Anglo-Saxonism all justified the colonization of people deemed racially inferior.
- By 1898, after defeating Spain in a brief war under the leadership of President William McKinley, the United States had acquired Cuba, Puerto Rico, Guam, and the Philippines; annexed Hawaii; and established a global empire.

- Theodore Roosevelt used a "big stick" to expand American influence and maintain order essential to American trade, especially in Latin America.
- William Howard Taft replaced Roosevelt's "big stick" with "dollar diplomacy," emphasizing American investment to establish influence and stability, especially in Latin America.

Key Terms and People

◁))

audio
flashcards

Aguinaldo, Emilio 662
Anglo-saxonism 655
Anti-Imperial League 666
Barton, Clara 663
Beveridge, Albert 666
Blaine, James G. 657
Cixi (Empress Dowager) 671
Dewey, George 661
Dole, Sanford B. 659
dollar diplomacy 675
Du Bois, W. E. B. 666
Dupuy de Lôme, Enrique 661
"gentlemen's agreement" 674
Harrison, Benjamin 658
Hay, John 663
Hearst, William Randolph 660
Hoar, George Frisbie 666
Insular Cases 665
Liliuokalani (Queen) 658
Mahan, Alfred Thayer 656

McKinley Tariff 658
McKinley, William 661
Open Door Policy 670
Panama Canal 673
Platt Amendment 665
Pulitzer, Joseph 661
Roosevelt Corollary 674
Roosevelt, Theodore 655
Rough Riders 662
Russo-Japanese War 674
Strong, Josiah 655
Taft, William Howard 670
Teller Amendment 661
Turner, Frederick Jackson 656
United Fruit Company 675
USS *Maine* 661
Washington, Booker T. 667
Wood, Leonard 665
yellow journalism 661

Reviewing Chapter 19

1. What assumptions did the foreign policies of Presidents McKinley, Roosevelt, and Taft share? Where did their foreign policies diverge? Were their foreign policies more similar than different? Defend your answer.
2. What did the United States gain by expanding its political and commercial empire? What were the costs of empire? Did gains outweigh costs? Explain.

Further Reading

Hoganson, Kristin L. *Fighting for American Manhood: How Gender Politics Provoked the Spanish-American and Philippine-American Wars*. New Haven, CT: Yale University Press, 1998. Examines U.S. foreign policy in the late 19th century through the lens of gender and shows how debates and decisions were shaped by notions of manliness.

Hunt, Michael H. *Ideology and U.S. Foreign Policy*. New Haven, CT: Yale University Press, 1987. An excellent discussion of the influence of racial ideology on foreign policy.

Kramer, Paul A. *The Blood of Government: Race, Empire, the United States, and the Philippines*. Chapel Hill: University of North Carolina Press, 2006. A transnational history of race and empire that explores the connection between race making and war in the Philippine-American War.

⌄

Lafeber, Walter. *The American Age: United States Foreign Policy at Home and Abroad Since 1750*. New York: W. W. Norton, 1989. A sweeping look at American foreign policy with especially helpful chapters on the foundations of American "superpowerdom" and the "turning point" of McKinley's presidency.

Musicant, Ivan. *Empire by Default: The Spanish-American War and the Dawn of the American Century*. New York: Henry Holt and Company, 1998. A thorough overview of the Spanish-American War.

Rydell, Robert W. *All the World's a Fair: Visions of Empire at American International Expositions, 1876–1916*. Chicago: University of Chicago Press, 1987. An engaging look at international expositions in the age of empire, including the 1904 St. Louis World's Fair and the Philippines Reservation.

America in the World
GOODS, IDEAS, PEOPLE

CHAPTER 19: The United States Expands Its Reach, 1892–1912

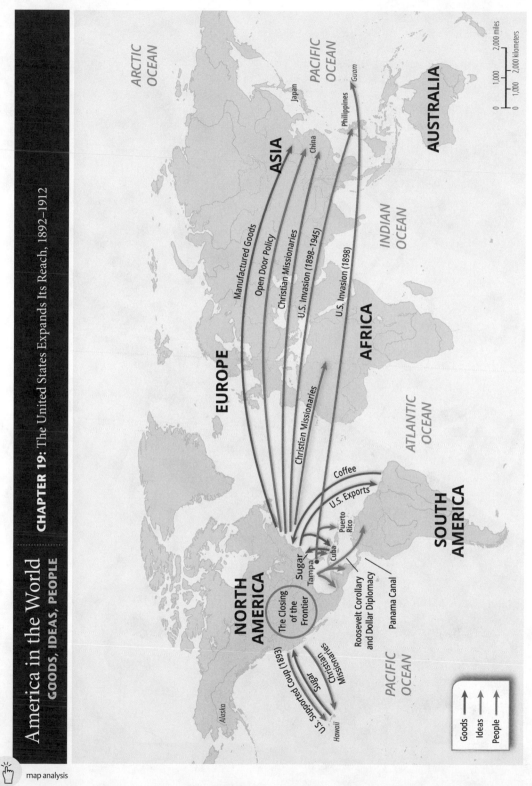

map analysis

Probably taken during the May 1 labor parade in New York City, this 1909 photo shows two girls wearing banners that exhort "ABOLISH CHILD SLAVERY!!" in English and Yiddish.

An Age of Progressive Reform

1890–1920

I n June 1900, social reformer Jane Addams, accompanied by fellow activist Julia Lathrop, crossed the Atlantic to attend the Paris Exposition. Addams had been appointed as a juror for the "Social Economics Exhibit" at the international world's fair. The exhibit especially attracted the two reformers, as it provided a chance to learn how other countries addressed major problems facing the rapidly industrializing and urbanizing world. Addams and Lathrop, both of whom had witnessed firsthand the disastrous 1894 Pullman strike, were, as Addams explained, "enormously interested" in how other nations approached the problem of workers' housing.

Addams and Lathrop also took part in the meeting of the International Council of Women (ICW), one of many international conferences held at the exposition. The conference stressed the special responsibility of women to protect, educate, and elevate society. In addition, they attended the convention of a "dissenting group of radical feminists" that had broken with the more moderate ICW. They witnessed a lively debate among French "militant suffragists," according to Addams, who attacked the sexism of their country's legal system with such explicitness that the shocked U.S. delegation—except for Addams and Lathrop—marched out "in a huff."

The experiences of the two women in Paris point to several key aspects of progressivism, a movement that flowered from the 1890s through World War I. Men and women in industrializing and urbanizing societies around the world, usually from the middle class, attacked a wide range of social and economic problems with the tools of rationality, organization, and science, and they shared their ideas across national boundaries. Women like Addams and Lathrop played an especially important role in progressivism, and their defense of the household and children propelled women into the public arena. Although progressives around the world shared their ideas for a better world, progressivism in the United States contained distinctive features. As reflected in the U.S. response to radical French feminists, progressive reform in the United States tended to be more conservative and more moralistic than its European counterparts, which often limited change.

Progressives and their many reforms prompted questions that Americans still struggle with today: Do state and federal governments have a role in intervening on behalf of the public good? Are there limits to their power? How is the public good defined?

PROGRESSIVISM AS A GLOBAL MOVEMENT

In industrial societies around the world during the late 19th and early 20th centuries, concerned citizens grappled with what they called the "social problem," a term that encompassed all of the plights of the urban-industrial city—labor conflicts, unprecedented poverty, slums, disease, social fragmentation, and ineffective city government. Worldwide economic depressions left millions unemployed and hungry. Industrial warfare raged between workers and employers. Cities around the globe burst at the seams and degenerated into cauldrons of disease and despair. The world seemed to be spinning out of control.

These crises bound together a diverse international group of reformers known as progressives. Mostly educated members of the middle class, they engaged in a broad range of reforms. As progressive William A. White recalled, "We and all the world in those days were deeply stirred. Our sympathies were responding excitedly to a sense of injustice that had become part of the new glittering, gaudy machine age."

Progressive solutions to social problems crossed back and forth across the Atlantic and encompassed Latin America, Japan, China, Australia, and New Zealand as progressives established international networks and organizations. U.S. progressives eagerly embraced ideas from abroad and adapted and modified them to fit the specifics and needs of their own country.

Nodes of Progressivism

Although social reformers had long attempted to deal with the problems of industrializing, urbanizing society, progressives attacked them in new and varied ways. Although never a unified movement, progressive reform coalesced around several common themes. Rejecting unregulated markets and cutthroat individualism, but also fearing an all-powerful state, progressives sought a middle way to conserve capitalism while eliminating its excesses. They sought reform, not revolution. They demanded state intervention to offset the power of corporations and fought against monopolies to protect what they deemed the "public interest." As Theodore Roosevelt, who embodied progressivism, proclaimed in 1912, "This new movement . . . proposes to put at the service of all our people the collective power of the people, through their Government agencies."

Progressives also sought to connect diverse peoples and interests, knitting a fragmented society into an organic whole. Progressives attempted to build bridges between the rich and poor, native born and immigrant, and to foster a sense of common purpose in their increasingly anonymous, segmented world. They were optimistic and energetic, with a deep faith in the malleability of human nature. As one noted, people were "plastic lumps of human dough" to be pressed into form on a "social kneadingboard." Progressives denounced the cult of individualism preferring social connection and cooperation.

Progressives also believed in applying the tools of the modern corporation to social prob-

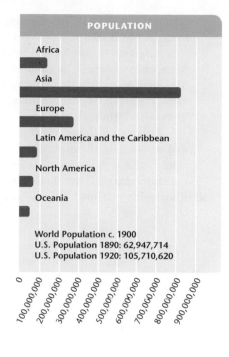

lems. Emphasizing efficiency and specialization, and with great faith in science, they gathered and analyzed information and called on experts to fashion rational solutions. Journalist Walter Lippmann summed up this aggressive, novel approach in 1914: "We can no longer treat life as something that has trickled down to us. We have to deal with it deliberately, devise its social organization, alter its tools, formulate its method, educate and control it."

The Global Exchange of Progressive Ideas

As soldiers in a global war against social ills, progressives shared ideas and practices across national boundaries. U.S. progressives eagerly sought advice from their counterparts around the world, hoping to jump-start reform. Not only did they worry about their own security, fearing social revolution, but they were also troubled that the United States lagged behind the rest of the industrial world in solving its problems.

Progressives around the world connected through a variety of networks. Some, such as muckraker Henry Demarest Lloyd, embarked on a worldwide tour to collect "all the good ideas of Europe and Australasia." Others studied abroad in Europe, where they witnessed governments intervening to provide social services and more livable cities.

Religion provided another link. Advocates of the Social Gospel connected with their European counterparts, especially in England, and shared ideas about implementing social justice. London's Toynbee Hall inspired Jane Addams to establish her Chicago settlement house, Hull House. As she explained, "To share the lives of the poor . . . is as old as Christianity itself." Settlement houses served as incubators for numerous progressive reformers. Roman Catholic social reformers in the United States, Europe, and Latin America drew inspiration from Pope Leo XIII's 1891 encyclical,

Rerum novarum (Of New Things), in which the pope condemned the exploitation of industrial workers and supported state intervention to promote social justice.

Progressives also formed international organizations to address multiple issues, from unemployment to child labor. Journals and magazines such as *Outlook* and *McClure's Magazine*, circulating around the world, provided a valuable forum for new ideas. Progressives even organized study trips abroad, participating in packaged tours to model reform sites.

Although U.S. progressives sought guidance abroad, they adjusted their agenda and strategies to the particular context of their country. They tended to be young and armed with a righteous moralism that easily bled into social control and gave their reforms a unique flavor. Reflecting the crusading spirit of U.S. progressives, Theodore Roosevelt proclaimed, "We stand at Armageddon, and we battle for the Lord."

STUDY QUESTIONS FOR PROGRESSIVISM AS A GLOBAL MOVEMENT

quiz

1. What common concerns and problems did progressives around the world share? How did they share information and possible solutions?
2. Compared to earlier Gilded Age efforts at reform, what was new about the progressive approach?

URBAN REFORM

It is not surprising that urban ills became the first target of progressive reform. As reformer Frederick C. Howe explained, "The challenge of the city has become one of decent human existence." Progressives initially addressed the problems closest to them, those that impacted their daily lives. Every day, middle-class urban dwellers faced a wide range of unavoidable problems. Filth, pollution, unclean water, and lack of sanitary sewage systems spawned disease and misery that knew no neighborhood boundaries. The stench of uncollected garbage wafted from city streets. Even getting to work on the streetcar became a daily challenge, as privately owned companies established monopolies of confusing and highly inefficient systems. Inadequate housing increased the misery of poorer urbanites living in crowded tenements.

Middle-class residents also worried about the moral climate of their cities and were horrified by the proliferation of saloons and prostitution. Progressive women played an especially crucial role as "municipal housekeepers," working to clean up cities— physically and morally—and protecting children and their right to a healthy childhood.

But progressive reform could feel like control to those it aimed to help. White, middle-class progressives often proved blind to the rights of minorities and the working class, and progressives divided by race, region, and gender. In many ways, urban reform embodied fundamental tensions in progressivism: How far could reform in the "public interest" extend before it interfered with individual rights? Did the progressive "public good" benefit everyone or largely the middle class?

The "Good Government" Movement

With many city governments ruled by corrupt political machines unresponsive to urban problems, progressives rallied for "good government"—honest, efficient government that would work for the good of all. Investigative reporters such as **Lincoln Steffens** documented the deep corruption at the core of city governments and confirmed what most city dwellers already knew. In 1904, Steffens published *The Shame of the Cities*, focusing on corruption in six major cities. Steffens insisted that the fault lay not with crooked politicians, "any one class," or the "ignorant foreign immigrant." Instead, he declared, "The misgovernment of the American people is misgovernment by the American people." To get good government, Steffens argued, Americans needed to demand it.

Excerpt from Lincoln Steffens, *The Shame of the Cities* (1904)

Progressives initiated "good government" movements in nearly every city across the country. Spanning both major parties, urban reformers formed national organizations such as the National Municipal League. They organized reform tickets that managed to oust some of the nation's most prominent political machines, including New York's Tammany Hall in 1901. Using the corporation as their model, they established new, efficient, and honest forms of municipal government.

The disastrous Galveston hurricane of 1900 inspired a new model of city governance. To respond quickly and efficiently to the storm's destruction, the city appointed a special commission of expert managers who took charge of various city departments. This system was so effective that it evolved into the city manager system in which nonpartisan experts administered city services, aided by career civil servants. Progressives also revised city charters to eliminate the old ward system of voting whereby each ward elected a representative to city council, a system that perpetuated political machines. They replaced this system with "at large" elections for city offices.

"Good government" also entailed more efficient and effective municipal services. In the late 19th century, political machines awarded contracts for an array of services, such as water, garbage collection, sewage, streetcars, gas, and telephone service. These had become, in the words of one reformer, "private monopolies," "the political masters of the people," charging "unjust rates" and even influencing elections to maintain control. The ownership of streetcar lines became especially contentious in U.S. cities. Impressed by the success of Glasgow, Scotland, in establishing municipal ownership of streetcars, progressives convinced officials in Toledo, Ohio, to purchase the jumble of privately owned transit lines and manage them as a singular efficient system. Following European examples, some cities also took over established municipal water, gas, and electric companies. Although municipal ownership of public services was never as extensive as in Europe, many U.S. urbanites nevertheless benefited from this battle to improve city life.

The Housing Dilemma

Urban housing was another key concern of progressives. Cities sagged under the strain of too many people and not enough adequate housing. Working people, especially, found themselves crowded into unhealthy tenements and subdivided apartment buildings with little fresh air or sanitation. Some sections of U.S. cities were among the most overcrowded in the world. At the turn of the 20th century, New York's Lower East Side had the highest recorded population density in world history. Not only did the squalor of working-class housing create serious public health issues, but progressives also viewed the right to decent housing as a matter of social justice.

To address this issue, **Florence Kelley**, a veteran of Hull House, formed the Committee of Congestion of Population in New York. Drawing on examples from Europe, India, and Japan, the committee organized exhibits that contrasted the horrors of urban housing in the United States with models of publicly built, clean, working-class apartments in Berlin and London. But neither this committee nor other national housing organizations made much progress, especially when compared to their European counterparts. Clinging to traditional notions of property rights and unwilling to invest tax money for public housing, few city governments responded. The hard work of housing reformers resulted in just over a hundred units built in the entire country; by contrast, Great Britain built 24,000 units. Reformers learned the hard lesson that many Americans, and especially the courts, continued to view government intervention for the public good as a conflict with the Constitution's stress on limited government and protection of private property.

Municipal Housekeeping

Viewing the city as a home, progressive women spearheaded a number of urban reform movements. Protecting their homes had spurred women in the late 19th century to enter the political arena and advocate for temperance. Now, progressive women—as "municipal housekeepers" emphasizing "public motherhood"—extended and broadened their concept of the home to urban society and the community at large.

Women's clubs and organizations established schools and libraries, affordable day care, and home economics courses for working mothers. When officials did little to address adulterated, bacteria-ridden milk that sickened children, women's organizations opened distribution centers offering pure milk. Women's clubs proliferated at such a great rate that clubwomen organized a national association, the General Federation of Women's Clubs, in 1890 to coordinate their activities.

African American women created their own parallel organization, the **National Association of Colored Women (NACW)** in 1896. With the motto "Lifting as We Climb," the largely middle-class organization addressed the needs of black neighborhoods, generally ignored by white urban reformers and politicians, by establishing hospitals, orphanages, kindergartens, and day care facilities. Black women's clubs also attacked segregation and **lynching** and defended the respectability of black women, often popularly depicted as women with questionable morals.

Perhaps no reform effort illustrates "public motherhood" more than progressives' efforts to ensure a healthy childhood. Middle-class women were especially appalled by the contrast between the sheltered, nurtured lives of their own children and those of the working class, who labored in perilous conditions to support their families. As new psychological theories stressed the importance of childhood and adolescence in shaping the future adult, reformers, especially women, demanded a "right to childhood" for all. Florence Kelley and other settlement house workers in New York formed a child labor committee; armed with facts and statistics, they pushed for legislation and managed to get child labor laws passed in both New York and Illinois in the first years of the 20th century.

Then, taking their battle to the national level, they formed the National Child Labor Committee in 1904. They hired photographer **Lewis Hine** to document child labor, and his poignant images of children, aged by their toil in treacherous industrial settings, raised public awareness. But stiff resistance on the part of both employers and parents blunted reform. Poor parents often relied on their children's income to sustain their families and resented reformers' intrusion in their lives. Although Congress passed the modest **Keating–Owen Child Labor Act** in 1916, banning interstate commerce in goods produced by child labor, the Supreme Court struck it down two years later as an unconstitutional expansion of government regulation of interstate trade. Once again progressives found their reforms limited by traditional interpretations of the Constitution.

Progressives proved more effective in applying "public motherhood" to the nation's children at the grassroots level. Concerned about the unsupervised play of children in city streets as well as the allure of dance halls for working-class teenagers, reformers tried to create "healthy" and "uplifting" leisure environments. The playground movement, a uniquely American progressive reform led by the Playground Association of America (1906), established over 1,500 playgrounds in over 260 cities in just three years. Boys and Girls Clubs and Boy Scouts and Girl Scouts also offered supervised educational opportunities, teaching middle-class values to working-class children. To counter a dance craze that featured sexually suggestive dances, settlement houses and other organizations offered "respectable" folk dancing.

Scenes of Boy Scouts and Girl Scouts from cigarette trading cards, ca. 1910

But children and teens often rebelled at supervision. An 11-year-old boy in Worcester, Massachusetts, complained, "I can't go to the playgrounds now. They get on me nerves with so many men and women around telling you what to do." Similarly young people rejected the tame dance scene as "slow" or simply refused to abide by the rules. Even when supervised, they continued, noted one observer, "using vile language, smoking cigarettes, and shimmying while dancing." Progressive reforms, especially those aimed at working-class children, young people, and their families, often engendered resentment, as these reforms felt intrusive and controlling.

Public motherhood and municipal housekeeping also led progressives to attack the saloons, cigarettes, and prostitution. Between 1880 and 1900, saloons nearly doubled in number—Americans drank 1.2 billion gallons of beer and malt liquor in 1900, up from 590 million gallons in 1885. Although the saloons were a focal point for working-class and immigrant communities, serving as headquarters for unions, dispensing free or cheap food to hungry workingmen, and providing entertainment, to reformers, the saloon was the devil's workshop. Women reformers especially viewed alcohol as a threat to the sanctity of the home. Men drank up paychecks and abused women and children in drunken rages. Alcohol also sparked crime and led to other vices.

John French Sloan's McSorley's Bar (1912)

Hatchet-brandishing **Carry A. Nation** smashed apart barrooms, which she called "murder mills." National organizations such as the Women's Christian Temperance Union (WCTU), founded in 1874, took a less extreme approach, supporting local elections banning alcohol sales, fighting for state regulations for alcohol control, and sponsoring alcohol education in schools. The Anti-Saloon League, founded in 1895, took the battle to the national level, seeking a nationwide ban on drinking. Between 1906 and 1917, 21 states, mostly in the South and West, passed prohibition laws—despite formidable opposition from liquor interests. In 1919, within the context of resource conservation during World War I, the **Eighteenth Amendment** to the Constitution, barring the manufacture and sale of alcohol in the United States, was ratified. It remained in effect from 1920 to 1933.

Progressive reformers also crusaded against what they deemed immoral sexual behavior, using the state to regulate morality. The explosion of "red light" districts in U.S. cities alarmed many middle-class residents, especially as knowledge of venereal diseases grew. Sensationalist stories in the press of "white slavery" in cities such as Chicago featured unsuspecting young women lured into prostitution rings and held against their will. The white slavery panic also contributed to nativist sentiment. Reformers blamed foreigners for importing women with sexually transmitted diseases, who, through their male clients, infected "innocent wives and children," according to one report, and did "more to ruin homes than any single cause." Congress responded by enacting legislation for the deportation of prostitutes as well as anyone associated with a business, such as a music or dance hall, "frequented by prostitutes or where prostitutes gather." Moreover, Congress passed the **Mann Act** in 1910, making it a federal offense to transport women across state lines "for immoral purposes." By 1920, reformers had eliminated most red-light districts and destroyed commercial prostitution, which had been in existence for about 50 years. In addition, they established social services, such as homes for single urban workingwomen, aimed at keeping them from becoming prostitutes.

Segregation and the Racial Limits of Reform

Although progressives often aimed to strengthen social bonds among society's diverse elements, racial segregation was a product of the progressive era. Some reformers justified segregation as a modern solution to the "race problem," a way to eliminate conflict between the races and to protect blacks from further violence.

Segregation laws, known as **Jim Crow laws**, legally separated people according to race. They originated on southern railroads in the mid-1880s when southern whites grew especially resentful of middle-class blacks who purchased tickets in first-class cars and traveled with them as equals. In addition, when black men sat near unaccompanied white women in the parlor-like cars, white men grew especially anxious regarding the "protection" of their women, as they viewed all black men as potential rapists. As a result, southern states passed legislation separating blacks and whites on railroad cars.

Homer Plessy, with the support of the Citizens' Committee to Test the Constitutionality of the Separate Car Law, challenged Louisiana's 1890 law—which forced blacks to sit in a separate "colored" section—all the way to the U.S. Supreme Court. Plessy's lawyer argued that the Louisiana law denied Plessy equal protection under the law and thus violated the Fourteenth Amendment of the Constitution. In *Plessy v. Ferguson* (1896), the court rejected this claim and upheld segregation, ruling seven to one that the law was "reasonable," as it was consistent with local custom and helped preserve "the public peace and good order." Segregation was constitutional as long as "separate but equal" facilities were provided and the court gave its blessing to state-mandated segregation.

Excerpts from *Plessy v. Ferguson* (1896)

The ruling constituted a massive setback for African Americans. Segregation by both legal statute and unwritten law soon spread to nearly every aspect of southern life. Railroad waiting rooms, streetcars, public parks, movie theaters, and even cemeteries were all segregated. Separate facilities were seldom, if ever, equal, in the South, and segregation provided a daily reminder to African Americans of their inferior status.

Southern progressives often justified segregation as an enlightened solution to the "race problem." Whites attacked blacks with a new ferocity
in the late 19th century—conjuring up frightening images of the "black beast rapist" intent on
ravishing white women—to justify the lynching
of thousands of black men. Lynchings, usually
public affairs in which black victims were often
tortured and then hanged or shot, averaged over
a hundred a year in the 1880s and 1890s, with 241
cases reported in 1892, 180 of them occurring in
the South. Segregation, insisted southern progressives, would protect blacks by reducing interracial contact. Alabama progressive Edgar Gardner
Murphy, an Episcopal clergyman, insisted that the
white South had an "obligation" to "improve" the
black race and could do so only by establishing
a protective wall for blacks. "The segregation of
the race has thrown its members upon their own
powers," he proclaimed; blacks would benefit by
developing "the qualities of resourcefulness."

Northern white progressives did little to
renounce Jim Crow in the South and even supported informal segregation in their own cities.
Although 90 percent of African Americans still
resided in the South in 1900, a black migration to
the North was evident by the 20th century and
accelerated during World War I with new employment opportunities. Even as most northern

**GEORGE MEADOWS, LYNCHED
IN 1889 AT PRATT MINES,
ALABAMA** Antilynching laws were
introduced in Congress in the first half of
the 20th century, and several passed in
the House. But southerners quashed them
in the Senate. In 2005, the U.S. Senate
passed a resolution apologizing for failing
to enact antilynching laws.

schools remained integrated, some organizations, such as the YMCA, rejected black
members. Hotels, restaurants, and department stores regularly refused service to
blacks. Unable to purchase or rent homes in white residential areas, African Americans,
regardless of class, found themselves relegated to segregated neighborhoods.

Even some of the most open-minded progressives, such as Jane Addams, never
managed to bridge the racial divide. Although Hull House opened its arms to European
immigrants, settlement house workers made little effort to reach out to their black neighbors. A Hull House worker noted that when black women attended events, they "were
not always received warmly," as "the settlement seemed unwilling to come to grips with
the 'Negro problem' in its own environs" although "willing to be concerned with the
same 'problem' elsewhere in the city." Like their southern counterparts, many white
northern progressives stressed the development of the black race through "self-help"
organizations.

Segregation, however, did not improve race relations. Anti-black riots exploded in
the nation's cities. In September 1906, a three-day riot erupted in Atlanta when a mob
of armed white men, 10,000 strong and fueled by rumors of a black man's assault of a
white woman, terrorized the city. They targeted black businesses, attacking, killing, and
torturing black men and women in their path and leaving approximately 25 dead and

dozens wounded. The *Atlanta Constitution* reported, "The sidewalks ran red with the blood of dead and dying negroes." Northern cities, including New York and Springfield, Illinois, also experienced anti-black riots.

President Theodore Roosevelt added fuel to the fire by his treatment of black soldiers in Brownsville, Texas. In August 1906, black soldiers were accused of involvement in an incident in which a local white bartender was killed and a police official injured. When questioned by local officials, members of the black 25th Regiment insisted that they had been in their barracks and knew nothing about the affair. Initially, their white commanders supported their claims. But pressured by the local white citizenry, who offered questionable evidence, the officers withdrew their support. When the soldiers continued to deny involvement, the government charged them with a conspiracy of silence. Roosevelt then discharged 167 black soldiers dishonorably—with no trial or due process. The men included Medal of Honor winners and many who had served honorably in Cuba and the Philippines. Although Roosevelt later agreed to allow the discharged soldiers to appeal, only 14 of them were allowed to rejoin the army.

Southern-born **Woodrow Wilson** continued the disheartening display of presidential prejudice after he became president in 1913. Wilson dismissed 15 of 17 black supervisors holding federal positions as well as many working in lower positions. He also refused African Americans ambassadorships to nations where they had traditionally been held, such as Haiti. Moreover, he allowed the segregation of federal offices in Washington. In 1915, Wilson watched D. W. Griffith's film *The Birth of a Nation* in the White House. The film depicted the Ku Klux Klan as the South's saviors after the Civil War and caricatured African Americans as either simpleminded or vicious. By screening the film, Wilson seemed to endorse it.

Excerpt from Booker T. Washington, "The Atlanta Exposition Address" (1904)

Hostility toward blacks elicited a range of responses from black Americans. Some, such as Booker T. Washington, rose to national prominence by advocating a strategy of economic development over political engagement to dampen the fires of race hatred. At the Atlanta Exposition in 1895, Washington delivered an address that would make him famous: he argued that "agitation of questions of social equality is the extremest folly" and urged blacks to prepare themselves for full-fledged citizenship and equality by finding a niche in the southern economy—through industrial education and small business—to earn the respect of white people, who would ultimately reward them with political rights.

Other black leaders, such as W. E. B. Du Bois, criticized what they saw as Washington's accommodation to white supremacy, what Du Bois termed "the Atlanta Compromise." The "burden" for Jim Crow lay not on "the Negro's shoulders," insisted Du Bois, but on "the nation." Blacks needed to fight for the equality they were guaranteed in the aftermath of the Civil War: "The hands of none of us are clean if we bend not our energies to righting these wrongs." To that end, Du Bois helped found the **National Association for the Advancement of Colored People (NAACP)** in 1909. The NAACP investigated and publicized lynching, condemned the segregation of federal offices, and organized protests against the movie *The Birth of a Nation*.

Ida B. Wells, black clubwoman and founding member of the NAACP, spearheaded the attack on lynching. When a mob lynched three black grocers in Memphis in 1892, Wells came to the realization that lynching had nothing to do with the alleged rape of white women. Instead, it was an "excuse to get rid of Negroes who were acquiring wealth and property and thus keep the race terrorized and 'keep the nigger down.'" For

THE NIAGARA MOVEMENT   In July 1905, a group of activists, including W. E. B. Du Bois (pictured at center), met in Buffalo to organize the Niagara movement, which demanded equal rights for African Americans and rejected the accommodationist strategy of Booker T. Washington. The Niagara movement was the forerunner of the NAACP, founded four years later.

EXCLUSIONARY LOCOMOTION
As a young teacher, Ida B. Wells was thrown off a Jim Crow train when she refused to move from a first-class car, for which she had purchased a ticket. Wells initially won damages in court, but a higher court overturned the decision.

revealing this truth in her newspaper, the *Free Speech*, white mobs destroyed her newspaper office and presses. Wells fled the South and settled in Chicago. Threatened with death should she ever return to Memphis, she continued her crusade against lynching by conducting detailed investigations, taking her campaign abroad. She created international alliances with London's Anti-Lynching Committee. Her British lectures forced Memphis city leaders to condemn lynching when they feared that bad publicity might damage their cotton trade with Great Britain. Wells also worked tirelessly for other progressive causes, including woman suffrage.

Excerpt from Ida B. Wells, *Crusade for Justice: The Autobiography of Ida B. Wells*

Despite the heroic efforts of Wells, Du Bois, and countless other black Americans, this period marked a low point in U.S. race relations. In 1908, at one of the meetings of the Niagara movement, a precursor to the NAACP, Du Bois noted this precipitous decline since Reconstruction: "Once we were told: Be worthy and fit and the ways are open. Today the avenues of advancement in the army, navy and civil service, and even in business and professional life, are continually closed to black applicants of proven fitness, simply on the bald excuse of race and color."

STUDY QUESTIONS FOR URBAN REFORM

quiz

1. In what ways did women shape progressivism?
2. How did white progressives justify segregation as a progressive reform?
3. In what ways and on what grounds did black progressives respond?

PROGRESSIVISM AT THE STATE AND NATIONAL LEVELS

Battles against urban ills locally led progressives to harness the power of state governments to intervene on behalf of "the public interest." Just as they aimed to cleanse municipal government, they worked to purify corrupt state legislatures, often in the grip of business interests; elect progressive governors to enact statewide reform agendas; and place politics back in the hands of the people. Successful on the state level, progressives soon seized power nationally, most notably in the three successive progressive presidencies of Republicans Theodore Roosevelt (1901–1909) and William Howard Taft (1909–1913) and Democrat Woodrow Wilson (1913–1921). The election of 1912 saw national progressivism at its height when three progressive candidates vied for the presidency. Incumbent Taft won the Republican nomination. Roosevelt, who chose not to run for a second term in 1908, reentered the presidential fray as the nominee of a new third party. The National Progressive Party, or "Bull Moose" Party, was made up largely of progressive Republicans angry at their party's turn to the right under Taft. With Roosevelt splitting the Republican vote, Wilson, the progressive governor of New Jersey, handily won the election and became the first southern-born president since before the Civil War. Eugene V. Debs, nominee of the American Socialist Party, rounded out the field, garnering nearly a million votes.

Progressive presidents not only broadened the power of the executive, with the aid of progressive Congresses; they, but also used the federal government to regulate big business by breaking up monopolies and demanding consumer protection. Conservation of natural resources emerged as another hallmark of progressivism at the national level.

Progressivism at the state and national levels, like urban reform, was full of tensions and conflicts. "Cleaning up" voting, in the name of democracy, actually reduced the electorate. Limiting working hours, outlawing child labor, and introducing workers' insurance conflicted with individual freedoms, and courts regularly struck down or softened labor reforms. Even progressives who shared a love for nature divided sharply over what actions best supported the public interest.

Excerpt from a campaign speech by Woodrow Wilson at Indianapolis, October 3, 1912 ("The New Freedom')

Electoral Reforms

The state of Wisconsin came to epitomize progressive state politics. Earning the title the "laboratory of democracy," Wisconsin was led by Republican **Robert "Fighting Bob" La Follette**, elected governor in 1900. He instituted a wide range of innovations, known as "the Wisconsin Idea," which were replicated by other states. Reflecting the progressive faith in expertise and rational approaches to problems, La Follette enlisted social scientists from the University of Wisconsin to help draft laws regarding civil service and public utilities and to administer new state commissions on industrial relations, railroads, banking, and natural resources. Wisconsin doubled the taxes on railroads, broke up monopolies, and protected the rights of small farmers. In addition, the state instituted the direct primary, which allowed voters, rather than party bosses, to choose candidates for office.

Wisconsin and many other states also established the **initiative, referendum, and recall**, all proposed by the Populists in the 1890s. The initiative and referendum, adopted originally in Oregon, made it possible for citizens to place legislation directly before voters in general elections; the referendum allowed voters to repeal state legislation that they did not approve of. The recall gave voters the power to remove any public official who did not, in their view, act for the public good.

On the federal level, the **Seventeenth Amendment** to the Constitution was another significant electoral reform. Ratified in 1913, the amendment mandated the direct election of senators by popular vote rather than by state legislators. Muckraker David Graham Phillips's "The Treason of the Senate," published in 1906, helped propel the amendment forward. Describing corporate interests' control of state legislatures and the senators they elected, Phillips wrote, "Treason is a strong word, but not too strong to characterize the situation in which the Senate is the eager, resourceful, and indefatigable agent of interests as hostile to the American people as any invading army could be." Direct election not only brought government closer to the people, an aim of the progressives, but also helped block corporate influence in government.

In addition, progressives worked to refine the electorate, most notably through ballot reform. Previously, parties had controlled the voting process, making it easy to bribe voters with liquor and other gifts. They also printed their own ballots, designated by color, allowing illiterate voters to participate. To reform elections, and to limit the ballot to "qualified" voters, nearly every state adopted the secret, or Australian, ballot along with uniform printing.

When reforming voting, progressives often ignored the role and function of political machines and the corrupt bosses they despised. Their reforms not only smothered the party loyalty and high voter turnout that marked the Gilded Age, but also destroyed services, from Christmas turkeys to jobs, that political machines provided their constituents.

To northern progressives, limiting the vote to the most qualified meant eliminating illiterate, uneducated immigrant voters. In the South, however, white progressives took aim at black voters—educated or not. Although not always springing from the same impulse as northern ballot reform, southern ballot reform coincided with progressive reform. Progressivism provided justification for disfranchisement and a return to unchallenged white supremacy, the aim of white southern Democrats since Reconstruction. Like their counterparts in the North, southern whites claimed that their reforms would reduce fraud and guarantee that the "best" people would vote and win elections. Disfranchisement, southern progressives hoped, would also defuse the threat from Populists, who, in the 1890s, had in some states unseated Democrats and enhanced the power of black Republicans. Disfranchisement would eliminate both the black vote and the vote of "unreliable" whites, cementing the rule of the Democratic Party.

In addition to adopting the secret ballot and the direct primary, every southern state, beginning with Mississippi in 1890 and ending with Georgia in 1908, added a disfranchisement amendment to its state constitution. The amendments effectively eliminated the black vote in the South and ensured white control; whites would never have to contest another election. In the words of a North Carolina newspaper, disfranchisement would "settle this irritating race question" and "remove this ever recurring and festering sore on the body politic" once and for all. Never mentioning race, to avoid outright violation of the Fourteenth and Fifteenth Amendments, southern states set up requirements for voting, including literacy tests, poll taxes, and "understanding clauses," which required the voter to interpret a section of the state's constitution to the satisfaction of the voting registrar.

Although technically "color blind," the new state voting laws included loopholes that allowed illiterate white voters to pass through while blocking even the most highly educated black voters. The **"grandfather clause"** allowed any voter who had voted before 1867, or had a father or grandfather who had voted, to be exempt from the literacy test or other restrictions. Only white voters qualified, because nearly all black voters and their ancestors had been slaves. Moreover, white Democratic legislatures guaranteed that the voting registrar, who determined who was qualified to vote, was always a member of their party and would reject black voters out of hand.

Despite this blatant violation of civil rights, federal courts upheld disfranchisement. Even Republican presidents, whose party in the South consisted almost exclusively of black voters, refused to intervene. In *Williams v. Mississippi* (1898) the Supreme Court ruled that Mississippi's voting requirements did not "on their face discriminate between the races."

Southern disfranchisement of black voters continued, with little change, especially in the Deep South, until the Civil Rights Act of 1964. Congressman **George H. White** of North Carolina, defeated in the 1900 election, was the last of 40 African Americans to serve in the House of Representatives since Reconstruction. In his last speech to Congress in 1901, he predicted that "phoenix-like" African Americans "will rise up some day and come again" to sit in Washington. But it would be another 27 years until Chicagoan Oscar De Priest once again broke into the all-white body and another 64 years until the Voting Rights Act of 1965 dismantled the last vestiges of disfranchisement.

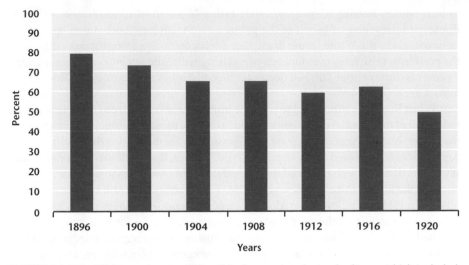

FIGURE 20.1 Declining voter participation Progressive electoral reforms, which included voting restrictions and the demolition of political machines, resulted in declining voter participation and interest.

Attempts by progressives to "improve" the electorate in the North and South managed only to drastically reduce participatory democracy. Whereas progressive-era voting reforms trimmed the electorate in the North, in the South they eliminated large segments of the voting population. They not only excluded the black vote, but also seriously reduced white voting, as poor southern whites refused to pay poll taxes; others simply lost interest in one-party politics. By 1904, overall voter turnout in the South had fallen by 30 percent. Election reform also drastically depressed interest and participation in politics nationwide (Figure 20.1). Turnout in national elections dropped from 80 percent participation to less than 50 percent in 1924. Notably, the progressives' reduction of the electorate sharply contrasted with election reforms taking place simultaneously in Europe, where reformers expanded voting rights to the propertyless and uneducated.

Mediating the Labor Problem

The industrial warfare of the Gilded Age, pitting workers against owners, only increased by the turn of the 20th century. The United States led the world in strikes and lockouts, with more than 1,800 in 1900 and more than 3,000 the next year. Faced with a worsening crisis, progressives demanded federal intervention to try to halt the nation's industrial conflicts.

In the fall of 1902, anthracite coal miners of the United Mine Workers (UMW) organized a massive strike that threatened the nation. The union demanded an eight-hour day, a 20 percent increase in pay, and recognition of the UMW by the mine owners. The owners rejected the demands outright, and miners went on strike as union chief John Mitchell vowed a fight to the finish.

The coal strike precipitated a panic, as the public anticipated a cold, dark winter. Americans depended on coal not only to run factories and fuel railroads but also to heat homes. Fearing what he privately called "a social war," in October President Roosevelt intervened on behalf of the public interest, inviting both union leaders and mine owners to the White House to mediate a settlement. But arrogant owners insulted the president, criticizing him for even negotiating with "the fomenters of this anarchy." By contrast, union head Mitchell deeply impressed Roosevelt, whose sympathies for the miners grew.

When Roosevelt threatened to seize the mines, the owners agreed to arbitration. An independent presidential commission found in favor of most of the miners' demands, and the union won a 10 percent increase in wages and a nine-hour workday. Unlike Gilded Age presidents, who used federal troops to crush unions, Roosevelt used the power of the state to mediate labor conflict and recognized the right of workers to organize.

Despite Roosevelt's example and the UMW's victory, owners still managed to quash unions. In 1914, in Ludlow, Colorado, in the midst of a massive UMW strike, local deputies and state militia, at the request of mine owners, attacked a camp of striking miners who had been evicted from company-owned housing. Drenching the miners' tents with kerosene and setting them on fire, they shot up the encampment with machine guns and killed 14 people, including 11 children. Soon labeled the **Ludlow Massacre**, the gruesome deaths of the victims sparked violent retaliation by the miners. President Wilson reluctantly sent federal troops to restore order, and the strike came to an end.

Whereas some companies simply refused to recognize unions, others created "welfare capitalism" to counter the growing power of unions. They offered new benefits, such as profit sharing, pension plans, baseball teams, and athletic facilities, to enhance worker loyalty and undermine the appeal of unions. The courts continued to defend the property rights of owners at the expense of workers' rights and rejected unions as a threat to the right to contract individually. The right to organize unions would not be guaranteed in law until the New Deal's Wagner Act in 1935. But progressives still managed to diminish the threat of class warfare, as strikes and lockouts declined between 1903 and 1914.

The progressive "middle way"—preserving capitalism through intervention and regulation—faced stiff challenges from a growing number of labor radicals. Labeled the golden age of socialism, the first decade of the 20th century found many young American activists—both native and foreign born—drawn to the global workers' movement. Inspired by the internationalist aspects of socialism and connected with their compatriots through international networks, they were convinced that history was on their side, cheered by the successes of socialism abroad. Whereas some socialists embraced Marxist class analysis and sought to overthrow the system, others downplayed class and hoped to transform capitalism from within. Some stressed the Christian basis of socialism. As Eugene V. Debs proclaimed in 1897, "What is Socialism? Merely Christianity in action." Three hundred socialist newspapers were published in the United States and over a thousand socialists held office, including 56 mayors. Socialist candidate Debs garnered 6 percent of the vote in the presidential election of 1912.

One group that openly sought revolution was the **Industrial Workers of the World** (IWW). The IWW had its origins in the violent labor struggles of western miners. A massive and violent strike organized by the Western Federation of Miners (WFM) in Colorado in 1903 aimed, in the words of their leader, to "overthrow the whole profit-making system." The strike resulted in the illegal arrest and deportation of a number of WFM members. In 1905, members of the WFM organized the IWW, which aimed to create "one big union" of all industrial workers. Headed by charismatic, one-eyed **William D. "Big Bill" Haywood**, the Wobblies, as they were called, rejected the "class collaboration" of the American Federation of Labor and welcomed all workers. The most inclusive labor organization in the nation's history, the IWW welcomed immigrants, women, and all minorities, as well as the unemployed. Moreover, the IWW rejected "go-slow municipal socialism," rejected electoral politics, demanded the overthrow of capitalism, and advocated industrial sabotage. Its main objective was the "emancipation of the working class from the slave bondage of capitalism." While stressing its American roots and declaring the organization "socialism with its working clothes on," the IWW drew on many European influences. By 1912, the IWW claimed 100,000 members. The Wobblies became such a threat that 20 states passed anti-syndicalism laws, aimed at the IWW, making illegal any organization committed to the use of violence, crime, or sabotage.

▷

The Life and Work of Mother Jones

The popularity of socialist and anarchist organizations on the left and the excessive power of corporations on the right compelled progressives to seek a middle ground in seeking justice for workers. Especially influenced by European notions that government was responsible for the welfare of its people, progressives hoped to curb the appeal of socialism by instituting reforms that guaranteed a decent life for all.

Workers' insurance was one such reform. U.S. workers remained the most vulnerable in the industrial world. Victimized by exorbitant industrial accident rates, they had few resources when a family member was injured or died on the job. In Pittsburgh's steel mills, for example, one out of four families of skilled workers received no compensation whatsoever. Few workers had the assets to challenge the deep-pocketed, powerful steel companies in court.

The plight of U.S. workers had become an international embarrassment. President Roosevelt, in his 1908 annual message, found it "humiliating" that at international

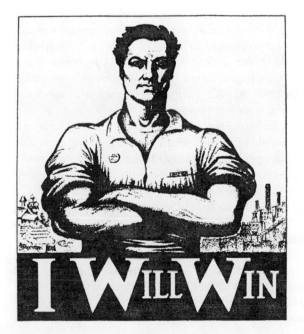

INDUSTRIAL WORKERS OF THE WORLD The founding preamble of the IWW stated, "The working class and the employing class have nothing in common. There can be no peace so long as hunger and want are found among millions of working people and the few, who make up the employing class, have all the good things of life."

conferences, the United States "should be singled out" for its lack of progress regarding employer liability law. Unions, however, originally rejected workers' compensation, fearing they would lose their right to sue. But as courts continued to side with employers, unions supported workers' compensation. Employers, happy to dispense with expensive lawsuits and hoping to undermine the appeal of unions, also supported compensation legislation. In 1910, New York became the first state to enact a workers' compensation law; by 1913, 21 additional states had done so. Notably, Americans modeled their legislation on Great Britain's 1897 law.

Compared with their European counterparts, however, progressives in the United States made little headway with other forms of social insurance. Whereas Germany, France, and Great Britain implemented various types of legislation guaranteeing a pension to the elderly, U.S. progressives found little public support for this idea. Labor unions also opposed any additional programs that would result in deductions from workers' paychecks. Not until the crisis of the Great Depression would Americans implement old-age pensions through the Social Security Act of 1935. In addition, government-sponsored national health insurance also failed in the United States. U.S. progressives, inspired by a 1911 British plan that aided low-income citizens with medical costs, advocated similar legislation. In 1912, Theodore Roosevelt and the Progressive Party made national health insurance a prominent plank in their party platform. But national health insurance—opposed largely by physicians and the pharmaceutical and insurance industries—would not be implemented for another 100 years.

Progressives found more success at the state and national levels in enacting legislation to improve working conditions. Influenced by international organizations and conferences, economists in 1905 established the American Association for Labor Legislation, which lobbied for legislation including workers' compensation and improved working conditions for women and children. The National Consumers' League (NCL), founded in 1898, offered another strategy to improve workers' lives. Modeled on a London organization and replicated across Europe, the NCL used the clout of buying power to effect change. As NCL head Florence Kelley explained, "To live means to buy, to buy means to have power, to have power means to have responsibility." Appalled by the working conditions of store clerks in New York City, who labored long hours for low wages and worked extra hours at no pay, the NCL created lists of stores to be boycotted until they made improvements. By 1904, the NCL claimed 64 leagues in 20 states and expanded their efforts to include child labor and sweatshops.

Reformers regularly faced the intransigence of conservative courts. The courts generally continued to privilege the right of an individual to contract freely regarding the number of hours worked. In 1898, in *Holden v. Hardy*, the Supreme Court upheld a Utah law that limited miners to an eight-hour day, citing the public interest, as miners' work was so dangerous. However, in 1905, in *Lochner v. New York*, the court struck down a New York law limiting the hours of male bakers because, in the court's opinion, the state had no right to regulate their hours and interfere with their right to contract as no health issues, they claimed, were at stake.

Progressives made more headway when they focused on women and children. But even then they saw only limited gains. In 1916, they managed to pass the first federal law regulating child labor, the Keating–Owen Child Labor Act, which banned interstate commerce in goods produced by child labor but was struck down by the Supreme Court as unconstitutional two years later. In 1908, in *Muller v. Oregon*, the Supreme Court upheld an Oregon law limiting the workday of female laundry workers to 10 hours. Defending the law before the Supreme Court, attorney **Louis Brandeis** marshaled a vast array of social scientific data, known as the Brandeis brief. The brief included a large appendix that cited legislation limiting women's labor in Europe. Brandeis argued that long hours of work damaged women's health and, in turn, harmed the future of the nation. The court agreed. In a unanimous decision, the justices concluded that "healthy mothers are essential to healthy offspring."

But, like many progressive reforms, *Muller* produced unintended consequences. Although a victory for workingwomen, it placed them in a separate, unequal, and inferior legal category. Moreover, some employers readily fired their female employees so that they would not be bound by the law.

A horrific tragedy in March 1911 made the plight of workingwomen especially vivid. A raging fire swept through the Triangle Shirtwaist Company in New York's Lower East Side. Employing mostly young Jewish and Italian immigrant women, Triangle was a nonunion shop with atrocious working conditions. Unable to escape the fire—the employers had locked the doors as they feared their workers might steal—workers had access to only one flimsy fire escape that did not even reach street level. As a result, 146 of 500 employees died, either burned alive or killed jumping to the street in desperation. The **Triangle fire** was the worst industrial accident in the nation's history.

William G. Shepherd's eyewitness account of the Triangle Fire (1911)

The tragedy sparked both union organizing and workplace reforms. Blocked from membership by the powerful American Federation of Labor, women workers flocked to their own unions, such as the International Ladies Garment Workers' Union (ILGWU), which had begun organizing even before the fire and grew significantly in its wake. Their efforts were supported by the National Women's Trade Union League, founded by middle-class women reformers. The two groups demanded a state investigation of the fire, collected their own testimonies of fire victims, held rallies publicizing the unsafe conditions in factories, and successfully lobbied the New York state legislature for safer factories. Within two years of the fire, the state passed 30 new laws addressing minimum wages, maximum hours, workplace conditions, and child labor.

Regulating Business: Trust-Busting and Consumer Protection

By 1900, massive corporations dominated nearly every aspect of the U.S. economy. Americans purchased their meat from the "beef trust," sugar from the "sugar trust," and fuel from Standard Oil. Progressives believed that big business was far too powerful and required regulation. But they disagreed on both the means and ends of regulation. Some called for the nationalization of corporations. Others called for various types of governmental regulation to keep capitalism intact. Interventionists also varied by degree. Some, demanding a complete breakup of big business, imagined a return to small, competitive businesses that would compete on a level playing field. Others insisted on only minimal regulation of the worst offenders.

President Theodore Roosevelt made attacks on trusts a hallmark of his presidency. "The executive," he boldly proclaimed, "is the steward of the public welfare." Happily using the "bully pulpit" of the presidency to attack big business, Roosevelt nonetheless did so in a decidedly selective and moderate fashion. He was not opposed to big business in principle and believed that large corporations were not only inevitable—part of the natural evolution of business—but also benefited society through the abundant production of cheap goods and the enhancement of U.S. power globally. There were, he insisted, both good trusts and bad trusts. Only bad trusts—those that engaged in unfair competition and practices—should be broken apart.

Carefully choosing several high-profile trusts to attack, Roosevelt soon gained a reputation as a "trustbuster." In 1902, he took on Northern Securities, a planned railroad monopoly created principally by J. P. Morgan and John D. Rockefeller. The Roosevelt administration successfully dissolved the company by using the Sherman Antitrust Act, charging it with illegal restraint of trade, which led to higher and unfair freight charges for consumers. A few months later, Roosevelt broke up the "beef trust," especially unpopular with the public since the scandal of the "embalmed beef" that poisoned and killed more U.S. soldiers than bullets in the Spanish-American War.

In his second term, Roosevelt continued his selective prosecution of "bad trusts." Promising a "square deal" for the American people, he responded to growing public outrage against Standard Oil. Probably the most hated company in the nation, Standard's reputation, and that of its head, John D. Rockefeller, grew even worse after muckraker **Ida Tarbell** published a massive exposé of the company, beginning in 1902. She depicted Standard as a cutthroat, win-at-all-costs corporation with no concern for the public good and Rockefeller as unscrupulous and "money-mad." Tarbell asserted, "Our national life is on every side distinctly poorer, uglier, meaner, for the kind of influence he exercises."

Excerpt from Ida B. Tarbell, *The History of the Standard Oil Company* (1904)

TRUST HUNTER This 1909 cartoon shows President Roosevelt slaying "bad trusts" while restraining "good trusts."

Tarbell's efforts sparked investigations, and the company soon faced prosecution in eight states. In 1905, a federal investigation revealed a range of illegal practices, such as secret agreements and kickbacks from railroad companies and "monopolistic control" of the oil business. In 1906, the federal government began its prosecution of Standard Oil, and in 1911, the Supreme Court ordered the massive trust dismantled. Roosevelt, learning of the news while on safari in Africa, called the decision "one of the most signal triumphs for decency which has ever been won in our country."

Roosevelt's attack on trusts, however, hardly made a dent in the power of massive corporations. Courts generally remained conservative in their interpretation of the Sherman Antitrust Act and pointed out that only "unreasonable" limits on interstate trade were illegal. Rather than shriveling up, Standard Oil, for example, continued to flourish, with Rockefeller's wealth and power undamaged and even enhanced.

Despite Roosevelt's reputation as a trustbuster, his successor, William Howard Taft, engaged in twice as many antitrust suits as Roosevelt. His administration successfully prosecuted U.S. Steel and the sugar trust. But the corpulent and lumbering president—the antithesis of the charismatic and energetic Roosevelt—never managed to get credit for his accomplishments, as he was unable to maintain the positive relationship with the press and public cultivated by Roosevelt.

Although Taft admired Roosevelt, he was more conservative than his predecessor. During his presidency, he aimed to rein in the expanding federal government. Through a series of missteps, Taft managed to disillusion both the progressive and conservative "Old Guard" wings of the Republican Party. His blunders led to Roosevelt's decision to run as the Progressive (Bull Moose) candidate in 1912, which split the party and guaranteed Taft's defeat by Democrat Woodrow Wilson.

Wilson and Roosevelt laid out two contrasting progressive visions in 1912. Wilson's "**New Freedom**" rejected a distinction between "good" and "bad" trusts and attacked all "bigness," whether in government or business. He hoped to restore small business and fair competition enforced with only minimal government interference. Roosevelt's "**New Nationalism**" advocated expansive government used for the public interest.

As president, however, Wilson did expand the power of the federal government and used it to regulate business. Wilson signed more reform legislation than Roosevelt and Taft combined. In 1913, he signed the Federal Reserve Act, which created a central banking system that provided banking regulation oversight of the nation's monetary policy. The next year, under Wilson's direction, Congress passed the Clayton Antitrust Act, meant to supplement and strengthen the Sherman Act of 1890 by outlawing a number of practices such as holding companies and price discrimination. Moreover, the law outlawed the use of injunctions against labor unions and legalized peaceful strikes, pickets, and boycotts, although subsequent court decisions weakened its effectiveness. The Federal Trade Commission (FTC) was also established in 1914, charged with regulating business activity and halting unfair trade practices.

Another key reform, initiated by the Taft administration and instituted under Wilson's, was the 1913 ratification of the **Sixteenth Amendment**, authorizing a federal income tax on both personal and corporate income. Before this time, the United States had one of the lowest tax rates in the industrial world. Populists, socialists, and progressives had long called for a graduated income tax that would place a heavier tax burden on wealthy individuals and corporations.

Progressives also passed laws to protect consumers. In 1906, 28-year-old writer **Upton Sinclair** shocked the nation with his novel *The Jungle*. A plea for socialism, the novel tells the story of the Lithuanian immigrant Rudkus family and their bitter experiences in Chicago as they are victimized by the heartless industrial and corrupt political order. But, rather than embracing socialism, readers instead focused on the roughly 12 pages out of over 300 that Sinclair devoted to the meatpacking industry. Based on his own investigation, Sinclair turned stomachs with vivid descriptions of rats ground into meat, choleric hogs rendered into lard, and corrupt inspectors passing off tubercular beef to an unsuspecting public.

Meat consumption dropped precipitously. Acting quickly, President Roosevelt called for an independent investigation to verify Sinclair's claims. Not only were they confirmed, but investigators also added new, disgusting stories of their own. In response, the **Meat Inspection Act** and **Pure Food and Drug Act** both passed Congress on the same day in 1906. The Meat Inspection Act required federal inspectors from the U.S. Department of Agriculture to inspect livestock in slaughterhouses and to guarantee sanitary standards. The Pure Food and Drug Act outlawed adulterated or mislabeled food and drugs and gave the federal government the right to seize illegal products and fine and jail those who manufactured and sold them.

image
analysis

Like many progressive reforms, these regulations were modest in scope and aimed at both preserving U.S. business and protecting the public. The meatpacking industry supported regulation to rebuild its reputation and sales. Large meatpackers also hoped that new inspection requirements would eliminate smaller competitors.

GHASTLY GASTRONOMY Hoping that his novel would inspire a socialist revolution, author Upton Sinclair wistfully stated, "I aimed at the public's heart and by accident hit it in the stomach."

Conservation Versus Preservation of Nature

Theodore Roosevelt, an avid outdoorsman, spearheaded another significant Progressive reform at the national level—conservation. By the turn of the 20th century, after decades of wasteful consumption of natural resources, Americans had grown acutely aware of the environmental crisis facing the nation. The country's once vast forests had been seriously depleted, reduced by as much as 80 percent. Mining and oil companies extracted resources with abandon. Much of the nation's farmland had been exhausted. The nation's natural resources, Progressives argued, needed to be managed by experts and used efficiently for the public good.

Naturalist **John Muir** had already convinced many Americans, through his prolific writing, of the value of nature and the tragedy of its loss. Muir's writings generated public support for the establishment of national parks.

In 1892, Muir and his supporters founded the Sierra Club to preserve nature. In 1903, Muir invited the president to visit Yosemite valley in California. Roosevelt and Muir, hiking to the backcountry, shared a campfire and a night under a vivid blanket of stars.

But the two men had different visions regarding the environment. Preservationists such as Muir and the Sierra Club aimed to maintain nature intact, to protect it from development to provide "fountains of life"—in Muir's words—to restore the parched modern soul. Roosevelt, on the other hand, although sharing Muir's love for the wilderness, emphasized the efficient use of natural resources. As a conservationist, he argued that natural resources, carefully managed for future generations, could be used for economic development.

Excerpts from John Muir on Hetch Hetchy (1909)

In 1902, Roosevelt signed the Newlands Reclamation Act, which appropriated proceeds of public land sales in 16 western states to finance irrigation projects in those states. Roosevelt also quickly expanded the U.S. Forest Service and established 150 national forests; he increased fourfold, to 200 million acres, forests under federal control. At the same time, he helped preserve nature by creating five national parks and by declaring the Grand Canyon a national monument in 1908, one of 18 created during his presidency, as well as 51 federal bird reservations and four game preserves (Map 20.1).

The most dramatic conflict between the two arms of environmentalism came to a head over Hetch Hetchy, an unspoiled, strikingly beautiful valley in Yosemite National Park. Conservationists, along with the city of San Francisco, insisted that Hetch Hetchy would best serve the public through the creation of a reservoir to supply San Francisco's

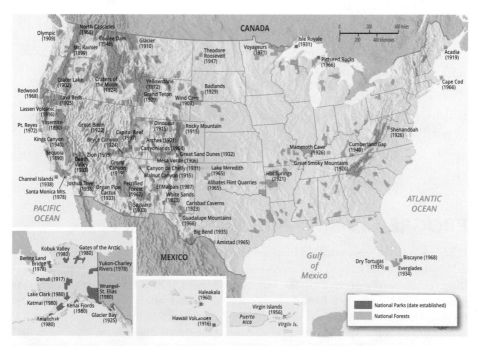

MAP 20.1 Conserving for the Future President Theodore Roosevelt, acting on progressive concerns for conserving and preserving the environment, greatly expanded protected public lands, including five national parks and 150 national forests. An estimated 230 million acres came under federal protection during Roosevelt's presidency.

rapidly growing population. Preservationist John Muir and the Sierra Club demanded that the valley be preserved and made Hetch Hetchy a national story by publicizing their cause through articles, leaflets, and "An Open Letter to the American People" that stressed the value of pristine nature in the lives of modern Americans. The public inundated the federal government with letters pleading for the valley's protection. But in 1913, the conservationists won the battle when Congress approved legislation to dam up the valley, and President Wilson signed the bill into law.

For the defeated preservationists, the outcome at Hetch Hetchy, as Muir put it, was a "dark damn-dam-damnation." But Hetch Hetchy inspired preservationists to expedite the passage of the **National Parks Act of 1916**, which provided a federal preservationist counterweight to the conservationist U.S. Forest Service. The act created the National Park Service to preserve national park lands and "leave them unimpaired for the enjoyment of future generations."

Although progressives succeeded in both preserving and conserving some of the nation's most valuable resources, the establishment of national parks and preserves came at a great cost. Lands placed under federal control, in the West especially, were not empty but home to Indians who, in some cases, had lived there for centuries. In some places, such as Yosemite, Indians remained for awhile on park lands but found themselves under the near total control of the National Park Service. While they served as an attraction to park goers for many years, Indians generally abandoned their traditional ways of life, with many reduced to working as wage laborers in the parks. In other parks, such as Yellowstone, the federal government removed Shoshone and Bannock for the sake of creating a "pristine" wilderness for visitors.

STUDY QUESTIONS FOR PROGRESSIVISM AT THE STATE AND NATIONAL LEVELS

quiz

1. What reforms did progressives enact at the state level?
2. In what ways did state reforms influence the federal government? How did federal reform impact states?

⊘ PROGRESSIVISM AND WORLD WAR I

U.S. progressives responded with mixed sentiments to the outbreak of war in Europe in August 1914 and later to U.S. involvement in 1917. Never united, Progressives found themselves sharply divided by the war. Some viewed it as a tragic setback, whereas others seized the war as a fortuitous moment to expand federal regulatory power and forge a stronger nation and world.

In many ways, World War I proved to be the death knell of progressivism and smothered the socialist surge evident in the first decade of the century. Boldly expanding federal power and the nation's global role, President Wilson and his supporters overreached, sowing seeds for a massive backlash in the postwar years. Conservative opponents used the war to implement their own agenda and to help bring about the demise of progressivism. Socialists and other radicals who opposed the war found themselves targeted as enemies of the nation and suffered arrest and deportation. Although progressives in the United States overall did not have the same success as their European counterparts, they nevertheless initiated reforms that permanently changed the role of government in the lives of the nation's citizens.

A Progressive War?

For some progressives, World War I shattered their faith in human progress and the improvability of human nature. Some progressives had even suggested that humankind had outgrown war. It was unthinkable to them that war and progress could go hand in hand. Both Jane Addams and Wisconsin's "Fighting Bob" La Follette boldly condemned U.S. involvement in the European conflict. Addams predicted that the war would "set back progress for a generation." Braving vicious attacks on her patriotism, she boldly headed an international peace movement that tried to end the war. La Follette was only one of six senators who voted against the war declaration in April 1917, with the popular press depicting him as a German-loving traitor.

Other progressives, however, saw the war as a golden moment, a chance to institute bold changes both at home and abroad. President Wilson, who framed the war as an effort "to make the world safe for democracy," envisioned the United States providing global leadership, molding a progressive world order that would dismantle empires and tyrannical governments and replace them with democratic institutions. He and other progressives also saw the war as an opportunity to broaden public power at home by expanding the scope of the federal government and diminishing the clout of private enterprise. In addition, they hoped to create a sense of common purpose among the people. President Wilson summed up the hopeful sentiments of pro-war progressives in his war address to Congress: "This is our opportunity to demonstrate the efficiency of a great Democracy and we shall not fall short of it."

Uniting and Disuniting the Nation

When Congress declared war against the Central Powers in April 1917, the Wilson administration faced the paramount task of mobilizing the nation on an unprecedented scale. This required a major expansion of federal power and unprecedented intervention in business and labor. New federal agencies, taking charge of regulating nearly every aspect of the economy, advanced the progressive agenda.

The federal government extended its power into a war for the American mind. Fearing disloyalty, especially among "hyphenated Americans," those who had come to the United States as part of the "new" immigration, the Wilson administration embarked on a massive propaganda campaign to ensure the loyalty of all people. German Americans became prime victims of patriotic hatred; labor radicals, especially socialists, also bore the brunt of the federal government's repression. A series of laws, including the Alien Act, the Alien Enemies Act, the **Espionage Act**, the **Sedition Act**, and the Selective Service Act, allowed the federal government to fine, jail, and in some cases even deport anyone who hindered the war effort.

Free speech was an early casualty of the war. Socialist Eugene V. Debs, who had garnered nearly a million votes for president in 1912, was slapped with a 10-year jail sentence for speaking out against the war. The federal government also conducted raids on IWW halls, using the war as a chance to rid the nation of the troublesome Wobblies once and for all. Hundreds of them were jailed, and one was lynched. Although *The New York Times* condemned the murder, the newspaper quickly added that "the IWW agitators are in effect, and perhaps in fact, agents of Germany." Attacks on radical organizations by the federal government continued well after the war, leading to hundreds of arrests and deportations, the fear of subversion amplified by the successful Bolshevik Revolution in Russia in 1917.

The war also heightened racial conflict. When the war halted European immigration, desperate southern blacks seized the opportunity to migrate north and fill the ranks of northern industry. The "Great Migration" changed the face of northern cities, as blacks, leaving the Jim Crow South behind, "voted with their feet." The massive influx of blacks and job competition led to some of the worst race riots in the nation's history. In East St. Louis in July 1917, angry white mobs, incited by a rumor that a black man had killed a white man, raged for a week, leaving at least several hundred blacks dead.

The end of the war in November 1918 did not bring an end to conflict and repression. In 1919, 25 race riots ripped apart U.S. cities. At the same time "100 percent Americanism" soon became channeled into a "Red scare" in which the federal government crushed what remained of radical organizations. Labor unions, intent on keeping the gains they had made during the war while employers aimed to regain their power, called a series of strikes in some of the nation's most important industries, including textiles and steel.

Rather than unite Americans by forging the new, collective nation that many progressives hoped for, the war and its aftermath only divided the country. The war unleashed irrational and often uncontrollable hatred that was the antithesis of the rational and organic progressive vision of society. The public had grown tired of reforming their nation and the world, and many progressives had become disillusioned, their faith in humanity shattered. The U.S. Senate, rejecting the **Treaty of Versailles** that ended World War I and Wilson's Progressive vision to "make the world safe for democracy" in a new world order, reflected the general sentiments of a nation weary of crusades, both domestically and internationally.

Votes for Women

Despite the domestic calamities engendered by the Great War, woman suffrage, fought for by generations of women since the mid-19th century, received a major boost (Map 20.2). In the 1910s, a new generation of suffragists, headed by **Alice Paul**, reinvigorated the movement. In 1907, Paul, a settlement house worker, moved to England to study social work and met suffragists Christabel and Emmeline Pankhurst. Convinced that women would never get the vote with petitions or persuasion, the Pankhursts advocated direct action, which included civil disobedience and hunger strikes. Paul became a disciple of the Pankhursts, participated in numerous protests, and even served jail time for her activities.

Paul returned to the United States in 1910 and immediately joined the **National American Woman Suffrage Association (NAWSA)**, headed by Carrie Chapman Catt. She soon found herself at odds with Catt. Whereas Catt and NAWSA endorsed Wilson for president in 1912 and considered him an ally, Paul borrowed a page from her British mentors and insisted on pressuring Wilson directly, through dramatic protests.

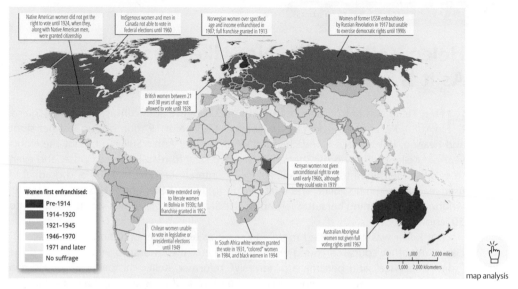

Native American women did not get the right to vote until 1924, when they, along with Native American men, were granted citizenship

Indigenous women and men in Canada not able to vote in federal elections until 1960

Norwegian women over specified age and income enfranchised in 1907; full franchise granted in 1913

Women of former USSR enfranchised by Russian Revolution in 1917 but unable to exercise democratic rights until 1990s

British women between 21 and 30 years of age not allowed to vote until 1928

Kenyan women not given unconditional right to vote until early 1960s, although they could vote in 1919

Women first enfranchised:
- Pre-1914
- 1914–1920
- 1921–1945
- 1946–1970
- 1971 and later
- No suffrage

Vote extended only to literate women in Bolivia in 1930s; full franchise granted in 1952

Chilean women unable to vote in legislative or presidential elections until 1949

In South Africa white women granted the vote in 1931, "colored" women in 1984, and black women in 1994

Australian Aboriginal women not given full voting rights until 1967

0   1,000   2,000 miles
0 1,000 2,000 kilometers

map analysis

MAP 20.2 Woman Suffrage Around the World Women around the world faced resistance to voting rights. In many places, race and education requirements continued to deny many women the right to vote.

SUFFRAGETTE CITY Risking arrest, suffragists bravely protested "Kaiser Wilson" outside of the White House during World War I and implored him to support the vote for women.

KAISER WILSON

HAVE YOU FORGOTTEN YOUR SYMPATHY WITH THE POOR GERMANS BECAUSE THEY WERE NOT SELF-GOVERNED?

20,000,000 AMERICAN WOMEN ARE NOT SELF-GOVERNED.

TAKE THE BEAM OUT OF YOUR OWN EYE.

Helen Keller: "I Do Not Like This World As It Is."

Helen Keller was one of the most famous people of the 20th century. Born in Alabama in 1880, Keller was stricken by an illness at the age of 19 months and lost her sight and hearing. Her isolated world changed when teacher Annie Sullivan taught the eight-year-old Keller to sign words. She rapidly learned how to read Braille, to write, and even to speak. Determined to attend college, Keller entered Radcliffe in 1900 and graduated four years later, the first blind and deaf person to do so. Keller embarked on a successful writing career, penning her autobiography, *The Story of My Life*, which was translated into 50 languages.

But Keller was not satisfied merely to serve as an inspirational figure to the world. Like many other educated young women of the era, she embraced what she called the "spirit of service" and became a progressive reformer. Keller campaigned for woman suffrage, defended radical unions such as the IWW, and criticized capitalism. A diligent student of international affairs, Keller had newspapers, magazines, and the writings of contemporary thinkers from around the world read to her.

In numerous speeches and writings, Keller depicted inattention to injustice as a form of blindness. In 1909, she joined the Socialist Party. In a 1913 speech, she explained, "I do not like this world as it is. I am trying to make it a little more as I would like to have it." Keller proclaimed, "We are all blind and deaf until our eyes are open to our fellow-men." She found poverty and the unequal distribution of wealth especially troubling, declaring herself "the determined foe of the capitalist system." Like many other social reformers, Keller visited slums and sweatshops. She explained, "Of course, I could not see the squalor; but if I could not see it, I could smell it. With my own hands I could feel pinched, dwarfed children tending their younger brother and sisters, while their mothers tended machines in nearby factories." She also called herself "a militant suffragette," advocating civil disobedience and hunger strikes. She fought for the vote, she explained, "because I believe suffrage will lead to Socialism, and to me Socialism is the ideal cause."

Keller also spoke out against the Great War in Europe. Like the IWW, which she supported, Keller depicted the war as a profit-making scheme in which workers "suffer all the miseries of war, while the rulers reap the rewards." She joined the international women's peace movement, led by Jane Addams, aimed at ending the conflict.

Until her death in 1968, Keller continued to battle for social justice and to inspire the world with her personal story. Through her involvement with the American Foundation for the Blind, she fought for the rights of the blind around the world. A truly international

In 1913, Paul organized a massive parade of women down Pennsylvania Avenue that coincided with Wilson's inauguration. The parade turned violent when male opponents assaulted suffragists. In 1916, Paul severed her ties with Catt and NAWSA and with like-minded suffragists formed the **National Woman's Party (NWP)**. Organizing "silent sentinels," the NWP protested outside the White House and boldly continued its actions even after the United States entered World War I. Attacked by angry "patriots" in the heat of figure, Keller met with many of the world's leaders, including Winston Churchill and Golda Meir, and every U.S. president from Grover Cleveland to John F. Kennedy.

- In what ways did Helen Keller embody progressive reform? In what ways did her ideas depart from progressivism?
- In what ways might Keller's disabilities have shaped her response to social injustice?

FIGHTER SINCE BIRTH   Helen Keller in 1914, at the age of 34: socialist, suffragist, and critic of the Great War in Europe.

war, many of the demonstrators were arrested for "obstructing traffic" and sent to prison. There, again following the example of their British sisters, they held hunger strikes. Authorities attempted to force-feed them and even tried to get Paul declared insane. But newspaper reports publicized their plight and garnered sympathy for their cause.

Finally, in September 1918, Wilson linked the war effort and its goals to woman suffrage. The vote for women, he proclaimed, "is vital to the winning of the war." While

interactive timeline

TIMELINE 1885-1920

AMERICA	YEAR	THE WORLD
	1888	**Mar–Apr** International Council of Women founded by women reformers from around the world
	1889	**May** Germany institutes old-age pension and disability insurance following health insurance and accident insurance established several years earlier
Mar General Federation of Women's Clubs established **Nov** Mississippi becomes first southern state to pass disfranchisement amendment to eliminate the black vote	1890	
	1893	**Sep** New Zealand grants women the right to vote, the first country to do so
Dec Anti-Saloon League of America founded	1895	
May *Plessy v. Ferguson* upholds segregation as constitutional **Jul** Black clubwomen form National Association of Colored Women	1896	
Feb U.S. Supreme Court upholds law limiting hours of miners in *Holden v. Hardy* **Apr** In *Williams v. Mississippi*, U.S. Supreme Court rules that Mississippi disfranchisement amendment does not violate Constitution	1898	
Sep Disastrous Galveston hurricane sparks new model of city government	1900	
Feb U.S. Steel is formed, nation's first billion-dollar industry	1901	
Feb Roosevelt administration initiates first "trust-busting" by prosecuting Northern Securities **Oct** President Roosevelt intervenes in anthracite coal miners' strike **Nov** First of Ida Tarbell's 19-part investigative report on Standard Oil published	1902	**Jun** White women in Australia granted right to vote
Mar Lincoln Steffens publishes *The Shame of the Cities*	1904	
Apr U.S. Supreme Court strikes down a law limiting working hours of bakers in *Lochner v. New York* **Jun–Jul** Industrial Workers of the World founded	1905	
Jan Upton Sinclair's *The Jungle* creates public outcry that leads to Meat Inspection Act and Pure Food and Drug Act **Feb** David Graham Phillips publishes "The Treason of the Senate" **Aug** President Roosevelt dishonorably discharges 167 black soldiers after incident in Brownsville, Texas **Sep** Race riot in Atlanta leaves 25 blacks dead and dozens wounded **Nov** Roosevelt administration begins successful prosecution of Standard Oil for "monopolistic control" of oil business	1906	

Alice Paul and her compatriots successfully pressured Wilson, others played a major role in supporting the war effort, a contribution that Wilson could not ignore. Over a million American women labored in war industries at home. Women also served as nurses and telephone operators for the American military and worked as volunteers in France for organizations such as the YMCA. In 1920, the states ratified the **Nineteenth Amendment** to the Constitution.

AMERICA	YEAR	THE WORLD
Jan President Roosevelt designates Grand Canyon a national monument **Feb** In *Muller v. Oregon*, U.S. Supreme Court upholds law limiting hours of female laundry workers **Aug** Anti-black riot erupts in Springfield, Illinois	**1908**	
Feb National Association for the Advancement of Colored People (NAACP) founded	**1909**	**Jan** Old-age pension instituted in Great Britain
June Mann Act, outlawing transport of women across state lines "for immoral purposes," passed by Congress	**1910**	
Mar Fire at New York's Triangle Shirtwaist Company kills 146 employees	**1911**	**Dec** Great Britain's National Insurance Act provides health insurance and unemployment benefits
Nov Three Progressive candidates—Republican Taft, Progressive Roosevelt, and Democrat Wilson—vie for presidency, along with Socialist Debs, with Wilson winning the election	**1912**	**Mar** British suffragette Emmeline Pankhurst arrested and imprisoned for smashing windows, protesting lack of voting rights **Apr** *Titanic* sinks in North Atlantic on maiden voyage, killing over 1,500 passengers
Feb Sixteenth Amendment to U.S. Constitution ratified, authorizing federal income tax **Apr** Seventeenth Amendment to U.S. Constitution ratified, mandating direct election of senators **Dec** Federal Reserve Act passed	**1913**	
Apr The "Ludlow Massacre" in Colorado coalfields leaves 14 dead **Sep** Federal Trade Commission established **Oct** Clayton Antitrust Act enacted	**1914**	
June Suffragist Alice Paul founds National Woman's Party **Aug** Congress creates National Park Service **Sep** Keating–Owen Child Labor Act signed into law	**1916**	**Apr** Women from around the world form International Committee of Women for Permanent Peace (ICWPP)
Apr Congress declares war on Central Powers	**1917**	**Nov** Bolsheviks seize power in Russia
	1918	**Nov** The Great War in Europe ends
Jan Eighteenth Amendment ratified, outlawing manufacture and sale of alcohol	**1919**	
Aug Nineteenth Amendment ratified, granting women the vote	**1920**	

Progressivism in International Context

Compared to their European counterparts, progressives in the United States had only limited success. In housing, social insurance, and factory legislation, progressives found their reforms curtailed by what one European called the "cast-iron constitution": traditional legal concepts that emphasized individual and property rights at the expense of a powerful state intervening for the common good. Moreover, progressives seldom transcended class or race. They too often imposed their own middle-class values on those they aimed to help; white progressives not only remained aloof from the nation's race problems, but also often enhanced them. And, as moderates treading a middle way, they tended to exhibit caution, which limited the impact of reform. Intent on securing their own political power, they diminished the power of those they deemed less worthy, especially immigrants, the working class, and African Americans. Yet they also managed to curb some of industrial capitalism's worst excesses while improving the lives of countless men, women, and children.

Despite the shortcomings of their movement, progressives nevertheless bequeathed a valuable legacy to future generations. Although Americans continue to debate about the primacy of individual rights versus the common good and the proper limits of government, progressives managed to fix permanently in the minds of Americans notions of social justice that insist on the state's responsibility for preserving at least minimal standards of living for its citizens and a rejection of unbridled, unregulated capitalism. In many ways, progressives set the agenda for liberalism in the 20th century, as they deeply influenced Franklin Roosevelt's New Deal and Lyndon Johnson's Great Society. Indeed, their ideas and concerns about the economy, social justice, and democracy remain relevant today.

STUDY QUESTIONS FOR PROGRESSIVISM AND WORLD WAR I

1. Why did the Great War divide progressives so deeply?

2. How did progressive reforms during the war lead to the demise of the movement?

quiz

Summary

- Progressivism was a global movement made up mostly of middle-class reformers. Never a unified movement—divided by nation, region, gender, and race— progressives sought a middle way, conserving capitalism while eliminating its excesses.
- Progressives around the world exchanged ideas across national borders.
- Urban ills became the first target of progressives in the United States and abroad. In the United States, progressives mobilized campaigns for "good government" and more livable cities. Progressive women fashioned themselves as "municipal housekeepers." White progressives justified segregation as a social reform that would eliminate racial conflict. African American progressives fought against segregation as well as lynching and disfranchisement.
- Progressives harnessed the power of state and national governments to institute a series of reforms, including electoral reforms, labor legislation, trust-busting, and consumer protection. Between 1901 and 1920, progressive presidents of both parties sat in the White House.

- Progressives were divided over the nation's involvement in World War I. The Wilson administration used the war to advance a progressive agenda both at home and abroad. But the war engendered divisions at home and prompted a conservative backlash that helped end the progressive era.

Key Terms and People

Brandeis, Louis 701
Eighteenth Amendment 689
Espionage Act 707
grandfather clause 696
Haywood, William D. "Big Bill" 699
Hine, Lewis 689
Holden v. Hardy 700
Industrial Workers of the World (IWW) 698
initiative, referendum, and recall 695
Jim Crow laws 690
Keating–Owen Child Labor Act 689
Keller, Helen 710
Kelley, Florence 688
La Follette, Robert "Fighting Bob" 695
Lochner v. New York 700
Ludlow Massacre 698
lynching 688
Mann Act 690
Meat Inspection Act 704
Muir, John 704
Muller v. Oregon 700
Nation, Carry A. 689
National American Woman Suffrage Association (NAWSA) 708

National Association for the Advancement of Colored People (NAACP) 692
National Association of Colored Women (NACW) 688
National Parks Act of 1916 706
National Woman's Party (NWP) 710
New Freedom 703
New Nationalism 703
Nineteenth Amendment 712
Paul, Alice 708
Plessy v. Ferguson 690
Pure Food and Drug Act 704
Rerum novarum 686
Sedition Act 707
Sinclair, Upton 704
Sixteenth Amendment 703
Seventeenth Amendment 695
Steffens, Lincoln 687
Tarbell, Ida 702
Treaty of Versailles 708
Triangle fire 701
Wells, Ida B. 692
White, George H. 696
Williams v. Mississippi 696
Wilson, Woodrow 692

Reviewing Chapter 20

1. Although progressives disliked much of what they inherited from the Gilded Age, their reforms have often been described as conservative, as an attempt to preserve many aspects of the Gilded Age. Does the evidence presented in this chapter support that interpretation? If so, why? If not, why not?
2. Some people have observed that Americans are living through a second Gilded Age. Are there similarities, in terms of problems and the solutions put forward by progressives, between today and the late 19th and early 20th centuries?

Further Reading

Chambers, John Whiteclay, II. *The Tyranny of Change: America in the Progressive Era, 1890–1920*. New Brunswick, NJ: Rutgers University Press, 2006. A thorough exploration of the progressive era that combines the story of well-known policymakers with the stories of activist workingwomen and -men and the many layers of reform—from grassroots activism to federal policies—they initiated.

McGerr, Michael. *A Fierce Discontent: The Rise and Fall of the Progressive Movement in America.* New York: Oxford University Press, 2003. An engaging overview of the progressive movement in the United States with an emphasis on the impulse of progressives to remake American society in their own image.

Perman, Michael. *Struggle for Mastery: Disfranchisement in the South, 1888–1908.* Chapel Hill: University of North Carolina Press, 2000. An in-depth examination of the disfranchisement of black voters and the reduction of the white electorate that explores the specific circumstances of this development in all 10 southern states.

Righter, Robert W. *The Battle over Hetch Hetchy: America's Most Controversial Dam and the Birth of Modern Environmentalism.* New York: Oxford University Press, 2005. An in-depth examination of the battle over the Hetch Hetchy valley—whether to preserve it or to make it into a reservoir—that helped give birth to the modern environmental movement.

Rodgers, Daniel T. *Atlantic Crossings: Social Politics in a Progressive Age.* Cambridge, MA: Belknap Press of Harvard University Press, 2000. Explores many ways that progressives on both sides of the Atlantic shared ideas and methods to ameliorate social problems in the industrial world.

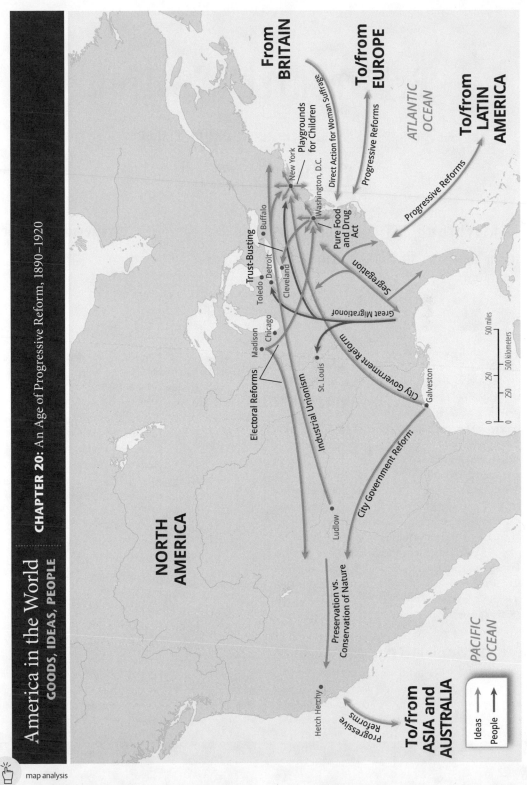

America in the World
GOODS, IDEAS, PEOPLE

CHAPTER 20: An Age of Progressive Reform, 1890–1920

map analysis

From
BRITAIN

To/from
EUROPE

To/from
LATIN
AMERICA

ATLANTIC
OCEAN

Direct Action for Woman Suffrage

Progressive Reforms

Progressive Reforms

Playgrounds
for Children

New York

Washington, D.C.

Pure Food
and Drug
Act

Buffalo

Trust-Busting

Toledo • Detroit •

Cleveland •

Segregation

Great Migration of

Madison • Chicago

Electoral Reforms

St. Louis

City Government Reform

Industrial Unionism

Galveston

City Government Reform

NORTH
AMERICA

Ludlow

Preservation vs.
Conservation of Nature

Hetch Hetchy •

To/from
ASIA and
AUSTRALIA

Progressive
Reforms

PACIFIC
OCEAN

Ideas
People

0   250   500 miles

0   250   500 kilometers

Friedensbotschaft

des

Präsidenten Wilson

am 8. Januar 1918 an den amerikanischen Kongreß gerichtet.

Vollständiger Text.

Anmerkung: Die Stellen, welche in der deutschen Presse nicht wieder-
gegeben wurden, sind unterstrichen.

Meine Herren!

Wieder einmal, wie schon wiederholt vorher, haben die Wortführer der Zentralmächte dem Wunsch Ausdruck gegeben, die Kriegsziele und womöglich eine Grundlage für einen allgemeinen Frieden zu besprechen. In Brest-Litowsk haben Verhandlungen zwischen Vertretern der Zentralmächte und Rußlands stattgefunden, auf welche die Aufmerksamkeit aller kriegführenden gelenkt wurde, um in Erwägung zu ziehen, ob es möglich sei, diese Besprechungen zu einer allgemeinen Friedenskonferenz zu erweitern.

Die Vertreter Rußlands haben nicht allein eine fest-umschriebene Darlegung der Grundsätze, nach denen sie bereit wären, Frieden zu schließen, sondern auch ein ebenso klares Programm für die praktische Anwendung dieser Grundsätze vorgelegt. Die Vertreter der Zentralmächte legten ihrerseits den Entwurf zu einer Vereinbarung vor, der, wenngleich viel weniger klar, einer Auslegung im liberalen Sinne fähig schien, bis erörtert wurde, wie die Einzelpunkte ihres Programms in der Praxis zur Ausführung kommen sollen.

Das Programm der Zentralmächte

trug weder der Souveränität Rußlands noch den Wünschen der Völker, deren Schicksal in Frage stand, Rechnung, sondern erklärte kurzerhand, daß die Zentralmächte beabsichtigen, jeden Fuß breit Landes, das ihre bewaffneten Massen besetzt halten, jede Provinz, jede

Zuwachs ihres Gebiets und ihrer Macht zu behalten.

Die Vermutung ist berechtigt, daß die zuerst vorgeschlagenen allgemeinen Grundsätze eines Übereinkommens von den liberalsten Staatsmännern Deutschlands und Österreichs stammten, von jenen Männern, welche im Begriffe sind, die Macht der Gedanken und der Wünsche ihres eigenen Volkes zu fühlen, während die eigentlichen Bedingungen des wirklichen Abkommens von den militärischen Führern herrührten, die keine anderen Gedanken haben, als zu behalten, was sie erobert haben. Die Verhandlungen wurden abgebrochen. Die russischen Vertreter hatten aufrichtig und im Ernst gesprochen. Sie können solche Eroberungs- und Herrschaftsgelüste nicht unterstützen.

Der ganze Zwischenfall ist bedeutungsvoll, aber auch sehr verwirrend. Mit wem verhandeln eigentlich die Vertreter Rußlands?

In wessen Namen sprechen die Vertreter der Zentralmächte?

Sprechen sie im Namen der Mehrheitsparteien ihrer Parlamente oder im Namen der Minderheitsparteien, etwa im Namen jener militaristischen und imperialistischen Minorität, die bisher nicht nur Deutschlands innere Politik beherrscht hat, sondern auch die Geschäfte der Türkei und der Balkan-

America and the Great War

n January 1918, American forces in France pounded German positions with special artillery shells and aerial bombs. On impact, they disbursed thousands of copies of President Woodrow Wilson's just-announced **Fourteen Points**, a 14-point peace plan. The **Committee on Public Information**, a government agency created in 1917 to "sell the war" at home and abroad, had the document translated into dozens of languages and distributed over 60 million copies worldwide.

Wilson called for replacing secret alliances with "open diplomacy," reducing armaments, expanding world trade, promoting self-rule for eastern Europe's many nationalities, and carrying out an "impartial adjustment of all colonial claims" by taking into account the rights of local people. A democratic Germany, he promised, would be treated fairly. Finally, the president spoke of creating a global "association of nations" to guarantee peace.

Wilson had taken the nation into war in April 1917 with the goal of crushing German militarism and making the world "safe for democracy." By 1918, he had expanded these goals by speaking of "self-determination" for all people as an "imperative principle of action" that must guide the future. These ideas excited not only Poles, Finns, and Slavs who hoped to reconstitute their nations, but also many Indians, Arabs, Chinese, Koreans, Africans, and other subject peoples who hoped American leadership would speed their independence.

At the Paris Peace Conference in 1919, the victors created independent Poland, Czechoslovakia, Yugoslavia, Hungary, and several other eastern European states from the defeated German, Austro-Hungarian, and Russian empires. But none of the many Asians, Africans, and Arabs who descended on Paris won concessions. Great Britain and France not only kept their existing colonies but divided between themselves the former

Ottoman lands in the Middle East and German possessions in Africa. Japan, which had joined the victorious Allies, retained control of Korea and added parts of China seized during the war.

Disillusioned nationalists cried foul. Wilson, they concluded, had never intended the principle of equality and self-rule to apply to Asians, Arabs, Africans, and other people of color. By the summer of 1919, anticolonial demonstrations and uprisings erupted in China, India, Korea, and Egypt. Moderate nationalists who lost faith in democratic promises found inspiration in **Vladimir Lenin**, leader of the new Bolshevik, or Communist, regime taking form in Russia. Only world revolution, Lenin proclaimed, could end colonial oppression.

The "Wilsonian moment" began in 1917 with a burst of global support for American war aims and ended in mid-1919 with the signing of the Versailles Peace Treaty. By then, emerging leaders such as Mao Zedong, Nguyen Tat Than (better known as Ho Chi Minh), and Mohandas Gandhi were determined to seize independence, not wait for it to be granted. The immense destruction caused by global war, along with rising aspirations for freedom partly inspired by the United States, set in motion a revolutionary century whose forces are still at play.

◆ THE SHOCK OF WAR

During the Great War of 1914–1918, combatants harnessed technology and science along with millions of factory workers and peasants to fight on a scale never before seen. Generals launched offensives to kill troops and seize territory and to bleed the enemy into surrendering by crippling the economy and starving civilians. Among the 65 million men mobilized to fight, the war killed between 8 and 10 million soldiers, disabled millions more, and led to the deaths of about 7 million civilians who perished from persecution, disease, or starvation. The war resulted in the overthrow of monarchies in Germany and Austria-Hungary, the dissolution of the Ottoman Empire in the Middle East, and the replacement of the Russian czar by a revolutionary Communist government. The United States and Japan emerged from the carnage as major world powers.

The United States joined the conflict during its final 19 months, from April 1917 through November 1918. American troops suffered 116,000 deaths (48,000 in combat, the rest from disease), or about 1.5 percent of the total military losses in the war. Yet, actions taken by the United States from the moment the war began affected the outcome of that horrific struggle. Events in Europe also affected America's economy, politics, and social system.

The Colonial Origins of the Conflict

The late 19th and early 20th centuries experienced unprecedented globalization. Writing in 1919 about how the world looked in 1914, British economist John Maynard Keynes imagined a prosperous Londoner who could "order by telephone, sipping his morning tea in bed, the various products of the whole earth." If he chose, he could invest in mines in Africa, railroads in the Americas, or plantations in Southeast Asia. Steamships carried immigrants from eastern and southern Europe to the United States, Argentina, and Australia and Chinese and Indians to Southeast Asia, Africa, and the Caribbean. Prominent American progressives such as Jane Addams and **William James** forged links to European reformers and championed efforts to promote public health, women's suffrage, temperance, and the arbitration of international disputes. The nearly free flow of capital and goods, as well as ideas, appeared normal, permanent, and likely to improve. Before August 1914, Keynes wrote, the "turmoil of militarism and imperialism, of racial and cultural rivalries, of monopolies, restrictions, and exclusion," seemed distant threats. War, the popular British writer Norman Angell declared in his book *The Great Illusion*, had become unthinkable.

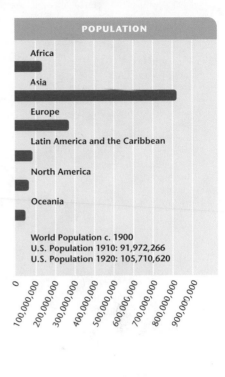

POPULATION

Africa

Asia

Europe

Latin America and the Caribbean

North America

Oceania

World Population c. 1900
U.S. Population 1910: 91,972,266
U.S. Population 1920: 105,710,620

0
100,000,000
200,000,000
300,000,000
400,000,000
500,000,000
600,000,000
700,000,000
800,000,000
900,000,000

Despite such optimism, bitter national rivalries persisted. Major European powers along with Japan hoped to expand their holdings in Asia, Africa, and the Middle East. Because most of the world was already under the control of one or another empire, acquiring new colonies meant grabbing one from a rival—as the United States had done by taking the Philippines and Puerto Rico from Spain in 1898. Competition for trade and territory sparked an arms race between nations such as Great Britain and Germany, each of whom sought to build dominant land and sea forces. To preserve a precarious balance of power in Europe and other parts of the world, each of these nations forged alliances with other states. This complex alliance system culminated as Great Britain, France, Russia, Japan, and (after the war began) Italy became known as the Allies; and Germany, Austria-Hungary, and Ottoman Turkey became known as the **Central Powers** (Map 21.1).

Strident nationalism—an extreme emphasis on national or ethnic identity—made the situation even more unstable. In the Balkans, various Slavic groups, such as Serbs and Croats, along with local Muslims contended for power as the once dominant Ottoman and Austro-Hungarian empires lost their grip over the region. Rival nationalisms led to several small Balkan wars in the years leading up to the Great War. Some of the worst tension existed between independent Serbia, with visions of dominating the Balkans, and Austria-Hungary, which controlled Bosnia, a province with a large Serb minority.

In June 1914, a teenage Serb nationalist named Gavrilo Princip assassinated the Austrian heir to the throne, **Archduke Franz Ferdinand**, as he visited the city of Sarajevo in Bosnia. When Austria threatened retaliation against Serbia (which supported the terrorist group the Black Hand, to which Princip belonged), Russia pledged to defend

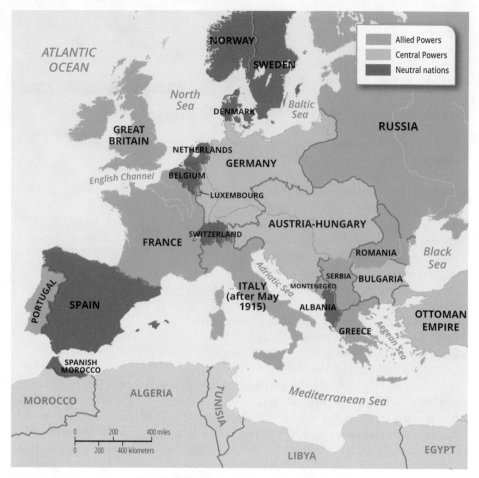

MAP 21.1 European Political Boundaries Before World War I The German, Austro-Hungarian, czarist, and Ottoman monarchies dominated most of Europe and the Middle East.

its fellow Slavs in Serbia. Germany, which feared Russia's expanding reach in Europe and the Middle East, backed its German-speaking ally, Austria-Hungary. France had already allied itself with Russia to balance the threat it saw from Germany. Concerned that German military and industrial power would dominate Europe and threaten its overseas empire, Great Britain supported France and Russia against Germany. By August these rival coalitions had mobilized their forces and rushed troops and heavy weapons by train to forward positions. Generals and political leaders convinced themselves that only by going on the offensive and striking first could they achieve a quick and certain victory.

Past predictions that world trade, the intertwined lineages of European royalty, and the interconnectedness of modern life made war between advanced nations unthinkable proved mistaken. So were assurances by European socialists and labor leaders that workers in, say, France would never take up arms against German workers. In the end, conservative capitalists and socialist factory workers enthusiastically joined forces behind their own national armies.

A War of Attrition

In August 1914, German armies struck first, overrunning neutral Belgium to outflank French and British forces deployed in northern France. They seized much of eastern France, which they held for the next four years. To the east, German and Austrian armies inflicted major defeats on Russian and later Italian forces. American press accounts of the fighting focused mainly on western Europe. However, the carnage on the eastern and southern European battlefields was at least as severe. During the first six months of combat in western Europe, nearly two million soldiers were killed or wounded. In Italy later in the war, one-half of the entire army was killed or wounded for an advance of 12 miles into Austria. The scale of death was unprecedented, and battles descended into what Woodrow Wilson called a "vast, gruesome contest of systematized destruction."

German armies won most of the initial battles but failed to achieve the quick knockout blow that would enable Berlin to dictate peace terms. Instead, by the end of 1914, German, French, and British troops had hunkered down in 400 miles of parallel trenches in eastern France—known as the "Western Front"—that stretched from Switzerland to the North Sea. Military strategists hoped, incorrectly, that trench warfare would be less lethal than the mobile attacks that led to staggering losses in the first months of combat. Millions of frontline troops lived in these hellholes for weeks or months at a time.

Once the opposing armies settled in, battle followed battle with deadly repetition. In just a matter of hours, trains and motorized vehicles moved large numbers of soldiers and vast quantities of war supplies from factories toward the frontlines. Newly

WORLD WAR I SOLDIERS WEARING GAS MASKS IN TRENCHES Terror weapons, such as poison gas, made soldiers' lives in the trenches hell.

image analysis

Photos of the Western Front (1914–18)

invented airplanes scouted the countryside. Offensives often began with one side's artillery pounding the trench line of the other for hours or even days. As artillery laid down a covering barrage, officers blowing whistles led their men "over the top" by the thousands to charge across the few hundred yards of so-called no man's land that separated the parallel trench lines. Advancing infantry often became entangled in barbed wire barriers. At this point, enemy artillery and machine guns, most of which survived the bombardment, mowed down the attackers.

New weapons, such as machine guns, high-explosive shells, and poison gas, made warfare especially lethal. Still, generals on all sides hoped that throwing additional troops into combat would eventually overwhelm their foe (Table 21.1).

The epic battles of 1914–1917 were seared into European memory. At the First Battle of the Marne in September 1914, about 250,000 German and French soldiers perished. During the siege of the French fortress of Verdun in 1916, casualties totaled nearly one million. Along the Somme battlefront, the war claimed another million. Slaughter on the eastern front and in Italy was nearly as lethal (Map 21.2).

Soon, the ostensible causes of the struggle, such as Balkan rivalries, mattered less. Instead, leaders of the warring nations anticipated a victory that would give them new territories and influence. They savored the prospect of slicing up the Middle East, Africa, and parts of China.

America's Response to War

Prominent Americans often spoke of an obligation to serve as a model of peaceful capitalist progress. For decades, the United States had policed the Western Hemisphere

Table 21.1 Deaths in World War I

Although the numbers are approximate, between 8 and 10 million soldiers died during World War I, along with about 7 million civilians.

	POPULATION (MILLIONS)	MILITARY (MILLIONS)	DEAD
Central Powers			
Austria-Hungary	52.0	7.8	1,200,000
Germany	67.0	11.0	1,800,000
Turkey		2.8	320,000
Bulgaria		1.2	90,000
Allies			
France	36.5	8.4	1,400,000
Britain	46.0	6.2	740,000
British Empire		2.7	170,000
Russia	164.0	12.0	1,700,000
Italy	37.0	5.6	460,000
United States	100.0	5.0	115,000

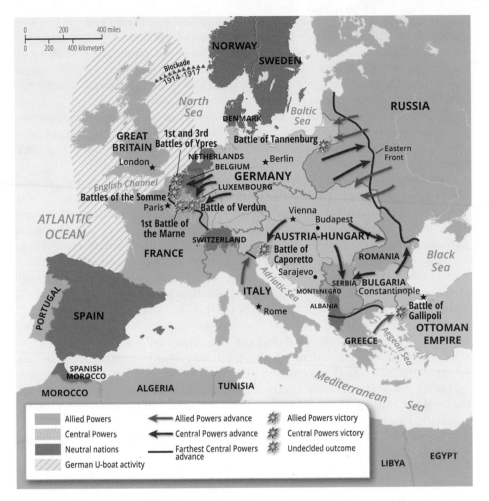

MAP 21.2 Battles of World War I The battle lines of World War I stretched from the English Channel to the steppes of Russia, and from the North Sea to the Italian Alps. Many of the most destructive battles between 1914 and 1917 were fought along a front that ran through eastern France to northern Italy.

to prevent instability that might provoke European meddling. U.S. investments in Latin American mines, railroads, and plantations were a source of enormous profit; in addition, they were seen as a way to uplift and civilize what were often described as backward races. To distinguish these actions from those of other imperialist nations, Congress took pride in its passage of the two Jones Acts of 1916 and 1917 that conferred partial rights of U.S. citizenship on the people of the Philippines and Puerto Rico.

Most Americans interpreted the war in Europe as proof of their own wisdom in contrast to other people's violent passions. As an editorial in the *Grand Forks Herald* of North Dakota remarked on the murder of the Austrian heir, "To the world or to a nation . . . an archduke more or less makes little difference." Some American business interests saw the conflict as an opportunity to displace British and German exports to

Latin America. President Woodrow Wilson reacted to the outbreak of fighting by issuing a neutrality declaration that called on Americans to stay neutral "in thought as well as in deed." Although Wilson admired Great Britain's institutions, he considered all the warring nations partly at fault for their greed, competing alliances, and aggressive nationalism. He particularly detested German militarism and its effort to acquire new territories and influence in Latin America.

Most Americans harbored a wide range of sentiments toward the warring powers. Those in the upper class identified closely with the British and French. At the same time, Irish, eastern European, and German immigrants scoffed at the notion that Great Britain or czarist Russia fought for democracy.

President Wilson, along with most business leaders, believed that American security and prosperity required close ties to the British and French. Since the Civil War, the export of grain, cotton, and minerals to western Europe and British investments in the United States had provided the capital to spur economic growth. If the war in Europe stopped exports, the United States would suffer immense harm. Factory owners and mill workers, prosperous farmers and tenant sharecroppers, would all suffer if the war closed the Atlantic sea-lanes. As a sign of solidarity and with government approval, major New York banks loaned nearly $2.5 billion (worth over $50 billion in 2017 dollars) to the British and French during the first two and a half years of the war.

Appealing to both international law and self-interest, Wilson spoke for most Americans when he insisted that a neutral United States had the right to export nonmilitary goods to all the warring powers and to have its citizens safely travel on passenger ships, including those owned by belligerent, or warring, nations. Although he agreed there was no right to sell contraband—weapons of war—to warring Europeans, the president insisted the United States had every right to sell them raw materials and non-military products.

Britain's Royal Navy dominated the Atlantic Ocean from the time the war began. After sweeping the sea of German cargo ships, the Royal Navy imposed a blockade against all neutral shipping bound for German-controlled ports in Europe. British warships either turned back or impounded cargo carried by neutral merchant ships, including U.S. vessels, attempting to deliver food or raw materials to Germany. Germany retaliated by declaring the waters around Britain and France a war zone and threatened to attack any ship, Allied or neutral, in the area.

At the start of the Great War, international law specified that when a naval vessel encountered an unarmed enemy cargo or passenger ship, it should be stopped, boarded, and its crew and passengers offloaded—before it was sunk or seized. But the submarine, or "U-boat," a new weapon in the German arsenal, was effective only if it attacked without warning. A U-boat that surfaced to identify or board a cargo ship could easily be rammed or sunk by small-arms fire.

Wilson condemned British interference with U.S. merchant ships bound for German ports. But because the blockade did not kill Americans or destroy their property (the British often paid for confiscated cargo), these violations of international law elicited diplomatic protests—not threats of violent retaliation. In contrast, Germany's seemingly indiscriminate use of submarines to attack merchant ships headed for Great Britain or France shocked most Americans. In May 1915, a U-boat torpedoed the huge British liner *Lusitania*, en route from New York to England, off the Irish coast. At the time, it was not known that the doomed ship secretly carried weapons purchased in the United States. The attack killed 1,200 of the 2,000 passengers and crew, including 128 Americans. Newspaper headlines and many public officials condemned this as a "terrorist attack." Rejecting advice from his own secretary of state that Americans should not be selling goods to warring nations or traveling on their ships, President Wilson warned Germany that the United States would take action unless it ceased U-boat attacks on all civilian vessels.

Front page of *New York Tribune* newspaper announcing sinking of *Lusitania*

In mid-1915, Germany possessed only about two dozen submarines, too few to stop all Atlantic shipping. Rather than risk war with the United States, the German government agreed to restrict U-boat attacks on merchant and passenger ships. But with an eye to the future, the German navy accelerated submarine construction. During 1915 and 1916, U-boats several times attacked British and French passenger ships, some of which caused American deaths. But when Wilson threatened to sever diplomatic relations with Germany, a prelude to a declaration of war by the United States, Germany again apologized and backed off.

Meanwhile, the fighting in Europe took a ghastly human and economic toll. To feed, equip, and move their armies, the Allies borrowed billions of dollars from American banks and used the funds to buy vital raw materials. In 1914, the value of goods that Britain and France bought from the United States totaled about $754 million. By 1916, the value had more than tripled, to $2.75 billion. With this influx of capital, the United States displaced Britain as the world's leading creditor nation, a rank it held until the 1980s. At the same time, because of the British blockade, Germany's transatlantic purchases dwindled from $345 million in 1914 to almost nothing by 1916. Enraged German leaders saw Wilson as a hypocrite for tacitly accepting the British naval blockade, which harmed civilians as well as soldiers, while condemning German naval warfare as piracy.

STUDY QUESTIONS FOR THE SHOCK OF WAR

1. What were the main causes of the Great War?
2. What new technologies made the war so deadly?
3. How did U.S. economic policy and trade affect the war in Europe?

quiz

❥ THE U.S. PATH TO WAR, 1914–1917

Between August 1914 and the spring of 1917, the United States maneuvered to stay out of the European conflict even while it benefited from what it saw as the world's folly. Divided economic interests, ethnic loyalties, and partisan politics pulled at the fabric of American society. Strident nationalists criticized Wilson for not confronting Germany more forcefully or providing greater encouragement to the Allies. America must rearm, they insisted, to avoid or win an eventual war. Progressive social reformers complained that military spending and growing intolerance toward immigrants and labor unions undercut the progress made in recent years in creating a more just society and mitigating the untrammeled power of corporations. President Wilson tried to placate both camps while attempting to mediate an end to the slaughter across the Atlantic. Partly to demonstrate his determination to defend national interests, he sent military forces to intervene in internal disorders in both Haiti and Mexico. The results of those limited military campaigns foretold some of the difficulties faced by Americans when they entered the European war and tried to formulate a lasting peace.

National Security and the Push Toward Americanization

Former president and Republican presidential hopeful Theodore Roosevelt typified those who accused Wilson of endangering the nation by leaving it a weak and vulnerable target for Germany or other aggressors. Roosevelt issued calls for the federal government to boost military preparedness, drastically restrict immigration, and implement compulsory "Americanization" programs to curb the influence of ethnic groups whose loyalty could not be counted on. He described Wilson's effort to stay out of the war as the actions of a coward who pursued a policy of "national emasculation."

Roosevelt's allies, such as Massachusetts senator Henry Cabot Lodge and General Leonard Wood, supported nongovernmental organizations such as the Immigration Restriction League, the **National Security League**, and the American Defense Society, which warned against foreign threats and advocated military training for young men along with efforts to enforce proper "social order" among working-class and ethnic Americans. Wealthy donors funded private training of college students at a camp in Plattsburgh, New York, in hopes that they would become future officers. Several thousand Americans joined the Canadian, French, and Italian armed forces.

In 1914, a group of wealthy industrialists, including auto manufacturer **Henry Ford**, members of the chemical-producing DuPont family, and railroad magnate E. F. Harriman, organized the National Americanization Committee to promote what they called the "civilian side of national defense." They pushed to "Americanize" eastern and southern European immigrants by teaching English to non-native speakers; promoting Protestant social and religious values among these largely Catholic, Eastern Orthodox, and Jewish groups; and encouraging prohibition. These industrialists embraced "race consciousness," the notion that white Anglo-Saxons and "Nordics" (northern Europeans) had to defend themselves against inferior racial groups. In 1916, **Madison Grant** expressed this idea in a popular book, *The Passing of the Great Race*, which warned that waves of swarthy immigrants would swamp white America. Pro-defense, anti-immigrant advocates insisted that sympathy for Great Britain was patriotic, but pro-German sentiment was anti-American. Partly to refute charges of labor's disloyalty, and also to limit the ranks of the unskilled who competed for jobs, Samuel Gompers, head of the American Federation of Labor (AFL) and himself an immigrant, joined those calling for strict limits on immigration. He complained that the "low-wage races" of eastern Europe undermined the livelihood of Americans.

Excerpt from Madison Grant, *The Passing of the Great Race* (1916)

Unlike Roosevelt and his circle, progressive reformers such as the philosopher **John Dewey** and peace activist and social worker Jane Addams rejected the insinuation that immigrants were disloyal. They also praised the diverse origins and cultural pluralism of the American population. Some progressives organized the American Union Against Militarism, which opposed talk of a peacetime draft and rejected calls to enter the war on the side of the Allies.

Social Reform, the Election of 1916, and Challenges to Neutrality

Appalled by the carnage in Europe, President Wilson and several prominent private citizens pursued unsuccessful peace initiatives during 1915 and 1916. Henry Ford chartered an ocean liner, dubbed the "Peace Ship," to sail to Europe to urge a cease-fire. Wilson early in 1916 sent his close aide, **Edward M. House**, to London, Paris, and Berlin to discuss a possible settlement. But neither side had much interest in American mediation. Meanwhile, the grim news from Europe affected the presidential campaign of 1916. The Republicans rejected the divisive Theodore Roosevelt in favor of a unifying figure, former New York governor and then-current Supreme Court justice **Charles Evans Hughes**.

Wilson insisted that his record showed him to be strong on both defense and social reform. He backed up the claim by pressing Congress to pass the National Defense Act of 1916, which doubled the size of the army to 200,000 men. Wilson created a new federal agency, the Council for National Defense, to coordinate the nation's response to the war in Europe. The magazine the *New Republic*, one of the most influential voices for social reform, applauded what it saw as Wilson's balanced preparedness campaign and urged him to organize a "league for peace" that might eventually intervene to stop the war.

To further bolster his standing among progressives in both parties before the November election, Wilson secured congressional approval of the Keating–Owen Act limiting child labor and the **Adamson Act** granting railroad workers an eight hour workday. The **Tax Act of 1916** increased levies on the wealthy in accord with the just-ratified Sixteenth Amendment, which permitted a graduated income tax. These legislative accomplishments—along with a snappy reelection slogan, "He Kept Us Out of War!"—helped Wilson win a narrow victory in November.

Intervention in Latin America

President Wilson also demonstrated his commitment to national security by deploying military force in the Caribbean and Latin America. He sent Marines and naval vessels to intervene in Nicaragua, Honduras, the Dominican Republic, and Cuba, where internal power struggles threatened American investments and the repayment of past loans.

Disorder in Haiti, the mostly black republic that shared the island of Hispaniola with the Dominican Republic, especially concerned Americans. The United States had few commercial interests in Haiti, but Wilson worried that its chaotic political and economic problems might tempt Germany to seize a naval base that could threaten U.S. control of the recently completed Panama Canal. (Similar concerns prompted the purchase of the Danish West Indies, better known as the Virgin Islands, in 1917.) When in 1915, Haitians resisted a U.S. plan to take over and stabilize the country's finances, Wilson dispatched 300 Marines to seize key locations. In addition to the perceived German threat, Wilson justified his action by labeling nonwhite countries as living in the "childhood of political development." Advanced powers, he insisted, had the right, even the duty, to manage their progress. In 1918, when Haitians rose up against the foreign presence, Wilson sent a larger force. About 2,000 Haitians died fighting the Americans. During the occupation, U.S. officials wrote a constitution for Haiti, supervised construction of some roads and schools, and retained military control of the country until 1934.

The Mexican Revolution, which began in 1910 and continued for a decade, posed greater challenges to the United States. Fighting between various armed factions pushed hundreds of thousands of Mexicans into the American Southwest. In 1911, a coalition of Mexicans overthrew the long-serving dictator Porfirio Díaz, who had welcomed foreign investors into the mining, oil, railroad, and agricultural sectors. His successor, a reformer named **Francisco Madero**, questioned the validity of foreign-owned mineral resources and the large landholdings of the Catholic Church. Just as Wilson took office in 1913, one of Díaz's former generals, **Victoriano Huerta**, seized power and, with what many Mexicans believed was the tacit approval of the U.S. ambassador, murdered Madero.

Wilson, in fact, supported the goals of moderate reform in Mexico and was stunned by Madero's murder. He denounced Huerta as a "butcher" and undertook various efforts to drive him out and bring to power moderate reformers who would stabilize the country and cooperate with the United States. His goal, Wilson told friends, was to "teach the South American Republics to elect good men."

Like many Americans, Wilson's understanding of events in Mexico was influenced by graphic accounts published by John Reed in *Metropolitan Magazine*. Reed, the adventurous son of a wealthy Oregon family and recent Harvard graduate, rode on horseback beside **Francisco "Pancho" Villa**, a sometime bandit, sometime revolutionary, who led a band of peasant insurgents in northern Mexico. He described a battalion of 2,000 Indian-looking soldiers, many of them teenagers, who galloped into battle, "their serapes flying out behind, their mouths one wild yell." Whatever the rebels lacked in discipline, they made up for in spirit. Reed quoted one of Villa's lieutenants as predicting "when we win the revolution" Mexico "will be governed by [ordinary people] not the rich."

Excerpt from Johm Reed, *Insurgent Mexico* (1916)

Reed's stories were reprinted in a popular book, *Insurgent Mexico* (1914) and became the basis for a movie, *The Life of General Villa*, which combined real battle scenes with recreations filmed in Bakersfield, California, with a cast of thousands, many of them refugees from the fighting south of the border. Wilson consulted with the young journalist about how to respond to the Mexican Revolution and for a while supported Villa and his "people's insurgency."

In April 1914, as part of the effort to force Huerta from power and to prevent a shipment of German weapons from reaching him, Wilson ordered naval forces to occupy the city of Veracruz on the Gulf of Mexico. The fighting there killed 126 Mexicans and 19 Americans. A few months later, after Huerta fled Mexico, the path to power opened for Venustiano Carranza, leader of the reformist Constitutionalist Party. Although he was pleased to be rid of Huerta, Wilson found Carranza's talk of nationalizing foreign-owned land and mineral rights deeply disturbing. Mexico's seizure of foreign property, he worried, might spread to all Latin America and beyond.

As a counter to Carranza, Wilson gave tentative backing to Pancho Villa. In spite of this assistance, Carranza's army defeated Villa and pushed his remaining forces north toward the U.S. border. After Wilson cut off aid to Villa, the insurgent retaliated in March 1916 by attacking the town of Columbus, New Mexico, and killing 19 Americans. Villa went on to raid several other border towns between Arizona and Texas.

PHOTOGENIC GENERAL The flamboyant and elusive General Francisco "Pancho" Villa strikes a pose for photographers.

MUCKRAKER John Reed—muckraking journalist and American radical who reported on and participated in the Mexican and Russian revolutions.

He probably hoped to provoke U.S. retaliation and then gain renewed popular support among Mexicans by resisting the Yankee invaders.

Wilson, stung by critics who accused him of failing to defend American soil, dispatched nearly 12,000 troops under the command of General John J. "Black Jack" Pershing to subdue Villa. During the next nine months, Pershing futilely chased the "bandit general" deeper into Mexico. Eventually, American troops clashed with soldiers sent north by Carranza, who guessed that Pershing's hunt for Villa was a pretext to defend foreign oil leases against Mexican plans to nationalize them. German spies in Mexico who witnessed the bungled campaign to catch Villa assured Berlin that American soldiers would be ineffective if they fought in Europe.

In July 1916, to avert a wider war that neither wanted, Wilson and Carranza agreed to submit grievances to a joint commission. By early 1917, when negotiations deadlocked, the confrontation with Germany had pushed Mexican problems aside. Germany, hoping to starve Britain and France of American supplies, unleashed its U-boats against all shipping in the Atlantic.

Decision for War

By the end of 1916, the European conflict had become a total war. John Reed, now reporting on the war for the left-wing magazine *New Masses*, recounted the sickening slaughter. In place of dashing Mexican rebels, he described endless corpses with "holes torn in bodies with jagged pieces of melanite shells, . . . sounds that make you deaf, . . . gases that destroy eye-sight, . . . wounded men dying day by day and hour by hour within forty yards of 20,000 human beings who won't stop killing each other long enough to gather them up." Nearly all able-bodied men had been drafted to replenish the ranks of the fallen, most industrial production went to the war effort, and military commanders overshadowed civilian leaders. In Germany, for example, the military high command, rather than the weak civilian government or even **Kaiser Wilhelm**, made all key decisions.

The German general staff feared that the British sea blockade would soon starve both troops and civilians, making it impossible to continue fighting. However, by unleashing its now expanded force of 120 U-boats against all merchant shipping in the Atlantic, Germany could starve Britain and France and initiate a win-the-war ground offensive before the United States became much of a military factor in Europe. The risky plan seemed the only chance for victory. On January 31, 1917, Germany informed the United States it had ordered its U-boats to sink any ship—American or otherwise—supplying the Allies.

To improve their odds, German strategists hoped to incite war between Mexico and the United States and thereby limit America's ability to fight in Europe. In mid-January, German undersecretary for foreign affairs **Arthur Zimmerman** cabled instructions to the German ambassador in Mexico City to propose to Carranza that if Mexico joined Germany in a war against the United States, a victorious Germany would return to Mexico the lost territories of Texas, New Mexico, and Arizona.

Wisely, the Mexican government shunned this proposal. But British intelligence agents had intercepted the so-called Zimmerman Telegram, held it for a month, and then passed it to American officials in late February 1917, just as German U-boats resumed their attacks on all shipping. Evidence of Germany's deceit and designs on U.S. territory outraged Americans. Wilson ordered the arming of American merchant ships and awaited the inevitable U-boat attacks. In late March, German submarines sank five American ships, killing dozens of sailors and wounding many more.

On April 2, 1917, Wilson asked Congress to declare war against Germany for what he described as unprovoked attacks on American lives and property. The United States, he declared, fought not for territory or material gain but to create a "world made safe for democracy." Despite concerns voiced by some progressives in Congress that war would kill reform, on April 6, 82 senators voted for war and just 6 voted against. In the House, the vote was 373 to 50.

STUDY QUESTIONS FOR THE U.S. PATH TO WAR, 1914–1917

1. How did Wilson prepare the country for war?

2. Why did the United States intervene in the Mexican Revolution?

3. Why did Germany choose to risk war with the United States in 1917?

quiz

⊙ AMERICA AT WAR

The decision to fight shaped both domestic policies and the international role of the United States. After April 1917, the nation raised an army of five million men in a year and sped military and financial assistance to the Allies. Although American troops did not "win" the war, they played a critical role by bolstering the Allies and blunting the last German offensive. During the war, the federal government assumed a major role in managing the economy, mobilized public opinion in support of the war, and began planning for an expanded role in the world community. The eventual disillusion felt by many of the war's initial supporters affected the international policies of the United States for two decades after the victory over Germany.

Proclamation from Woodrow Wilson (April 16, 1917)

Mobilizing People and Ideas

The federal government worked hard to generate enthusiasm for the war. Wilson appointed the progressive journalist George Creel to head the Committee on Public Information (CPI), an agency tasked with promoting the war at home and abroad as a democratic crusade. Creel and his staff "sold" the war to consumers by using innovative marketing methods. CPI provided newspapers and magazines with prewritten war information and distributed pamphlets, books, cartoons, posters, billboards, and even films directly to the public. The materials were presented in multiple languages and formats to appeal to recent immigrants and specific subgroups of Americans, such as workers, farmers, adolescents, and so forth. CPI also opened information bureaus in Latin America, Asia, Africa, and the Middle East to communicate directly to millions of people abroad and hosted foreign journalists on study tours to the United States.

FILM PROPAGANDA Recruiting poster for the U.S. Army announcing the release of the first World War I morale film, *Pershing's Crusaders*.

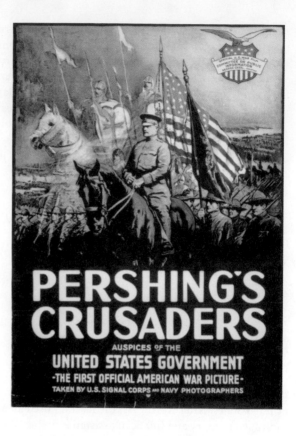

PERSHING'S CRUSADERS

AUSPICES OF THE
UNITED STATES GOVERNMENT
·THE FIRST OFFICIAL AMERICAN WAR PICTURE·
TAKEN BY U.S. SIGNAL CORPS AND NAVY PHOTOGRAPHERS

Excerpt from George Creel's memoir on the CPI

Creel recruited thousands of volunteer "Four Minute Men" to deliver patriotic talks at public gatherings, screen pro-war films at nearly all movie theaters, and distribute posters that often portrayed German soldiers as fanged beasts or apes. Pro-war posters often depicted Allied soldiers as medieval Christian knights.

Many leading Progressives such as educator and philosopher John Dewey, journalist **Walter Lippmann**, women's rights campaigner **Carrie Chapman Catt**, along with George Creel, became formal or informal employees of wartime federal agencies. The nation's foremost African American intellectual, NAACP founder, and editor of the *Crisis*, W. E. B. Du Bois, expressed hope that the war overseas for democracy would improve race relations at home. When Treasury Secretary William Gibbs McAdoo announced a series of "liberty loan" bond drives to raise money for the war, women's clubs and labor unions joined the sales effort, which raised about $16 billion of the $24 billion cost of the war. In addition to direct defense expenditures, the U.S. government—supplanting the role of private banks—loaned the Allies $11 billion, more than $200 billion in today's value.

To enlist support from college students, the Wilson administration created a Student Army Training Corps (SATC—forerunner of the Reserve Officers' Training Corps [ROTC]) at 500 colleges. Professors helped federal officials to develop a national "war issues course" whose syllabus stressed the "supreme importance to civilization of the cause for which we are fighting." These wartime offerings evolved into the "Western civilization" sequence taught at most American colleges for the remainder of the 20th century.

Social scientists also helped the war effort. Psychologist Robert M. Yerkes persuaded the War Department—which appointed him an army major—that he could develop an intelligence test that would sort out the most gifted recruits from those less mentally fit. Yerkes created standardized "IQ" tests whose results were interpreted as proof that native-born whites were smarter than African Americans or eastern and southern European immigrants, many of whom Yerkes classified as "morons." These deeply flawed studies were cited to justify emergency wartime immigration restrictions and, after the war ended, became a basis to establish strict quotas against "undesirables."

Controlling Dissent

As the United States mobilized millions of soldiers to protect victims of German aggression, it began restricting many of those victims from entering this country. Anti-German sentiment often became redirected at recent immigrants, pacifists, and labor activists. As the war began, Congress moved to exclude groups now dubbed "undesirables." By an overwhelming vote in 1917, it passed the **Literacy Act**, barring the entry of any persons unable to read in their own language. Other restrictive legislation included the Espionage Act of 1917 and the Trading with the Enemy and Sedition Acts of 1918. These laws expanded the definition of treason to prohibit most public and private utterances of words or ideas deemed interference with the war effort. The U.S. Post Office banned delivery of letters, magazines, or newspapers that questioned the justice of the war and the draft or criticized America's allies. The Justice Department and local authorities accused organizations and individuals of subversion if they spoke against the war. Former heroes such as Jane Addams and antiwar representative Jeannette Rankin were ridiculed as "a couple of foolish virgins" for questioning the nation's foreign policy.

Federal or state authorities arrested over 2,000 war critics and sentenced 1,200 of them to prison. Among those convicted for criticizing the draft and the "capitalist" war that benefited "plutocrats" and killed workers were Socialist Party and labor union leaders **Eugene V. Debs** and **William D. "Big Bill" Haywood**. Sometimes unintentional critics suffered the government's wrath. For example, movie producer Robert Goldstein received a 10-year prison sentence for "attempting to cause insubordination in the armed forces" by releasing a film about the American Revolution called the *Spirit of '76* in which British redcoats were depicted as the enemy.

Speech by Eugene Debs challenging the war (1918)

Despite such incidents, one measure of the war's underlying popularity was the large voluntary network that assisted the Justice Department. This included 250,000 members of the **American Protective League (APL)**, which had branches in most cities. APL "special agents" wearing official-looking badges opened mail, wiretapped telephone conversations, and conducted raids against newspapers and bookstores. APL members formed squads looking for slackers, a term applied to young men who avoided the draft. In one raid in New York City in 1918, APL vigilantes rounded up 50,000 suspects. Raids also took place in Chicago and other cities.

German Americans and German culture were frequently targeted by vigilantes. Delicatessen owners were ordered to rename sauerkraut "liberty cabbage" and frankfurters "liberty sausages." Symphony orchestras were pressured to drop performances of music composed a century before by Ludwig von Beethoven. Half of the states passed laws banning speaking German in public or over the telephone and forbade teaching it in schools.

US government poster depicting Germany as the "Hun"

The Civil Liberties Bureau, a predecessor of the American Civil Liberties Union, challenged these repressive activities without much success. In 1919, after the war ended, the Supreme Court unanimously upheld the constitutionality of the Espionage Act in the case of *Schenck v. United States*. Schenck had been convicted for distributing antidraft pamphlets and had challenged this as a violation of his free speech rights. Justice **Oliver Wendell Holmes, Jr.**, wrote that the Constitution did not protect the "clear and present danger" posed by "a man falsely shouting fire in a theater and causing a panic." In the related case of *Abrams v. United States*, the court ruled that in wartime, no citizen had the blanket right to criticize the government or advocate a strike by munitions workers.

Mobilizing the Economy

Mobilizing the economy for war production proved challenging. In 1917, production for the Allies and for the first phase of domestic rearmament meant that factories already operated near full capacity. The War Department relied on outmoded procurement methods that created production and transport bottlenecks. Food, munitions, coal, and other vital supplies were often stuck at depots for weeks while ships waited idly for cargo. To remedy this, the federal government created new regulatory agencies with broad powers over the economy. These included the War Industries Board, the Railroad Administration, the Food Administration, and the Fuel Administration. Many of those chosen to oversee regulatory boards were business executives hired by the government for nominal salaries and dubbed "dollar-a-year-men."

Just as the citizen's groups assisted the Justice Department in rooting out war opponents, private organizations promoted production. Among these was the Woman's Land Army. It worked with the Department of Labor to mobilize as farmhands over 20,000 young, single women, many of them enrolled in college and active in suffrage and other reform movements. Dubbed "farmerettes," they moved from cities to rural areas, where they plowed fields, drove farm equipment, and harvested crops on farms throughout the nation.

To mobilize workers in support of the war, Wilson created the National War Labor Policies Board. It drew membership primarily from the ranks of pro-war unions such as the AFL. The board discouraged strikes and pressed workers to forgo some benefits in return for pledges of full employment at wages above peacetime levels.

Some unions rejected patriotic appeals. Especially in the West, the Industrial Workers of the World (IWW), a labor union that reached out to unskilled workers, led strikes in mining towns such as Bisbee, Arizona, to demand higher wages. They complained that whereas large companies profited hugely from military contracts, workers received token increases. Local vigilantes, mine guards, and federal agents responded violently. During the summer of 1917, for example, over 1,000 striking IWW miners were rounded up, placed in railroad boxcars, and abandoned in the New Mexico desert. Most survived the ordeal after being rescued by sympathetic ranchers. Meanwhile, copper production continued in Bisbee.

Women Suffragists

The war created special challenges and opportunities for women. As five million men entered military service and most immigration ceased, paid employment opportunities

VOTING RIGHTS Suffragists demonstrate in front of the White House in 1917, trying to shame President Wilson into supporting a woman's right to vote.

expanded for women and minorities who had usually been relegated to work in agriculture, in service jobs, or as household domestics. However, politically active women had for decades created an array of local, state, and national organizations to promote suffrage. By 1917, 11 states, nearly all in the West, allowed women to vote. In the House, the first woman was elected to Congress, Republican **Jeannette Rankin** of Montana. Wilson weakly favored women's suffrage but did not press Congress to pass a constitutional amendment. He insisted that the right to vote was a state, not a federal, issue. In holding that voting rights were a state prerogative, Congress and the president dodged the fact that many states barred voting not only by women but also by African Americans.

Women's organizations, including the National American Woman Suffrage Association (NAWSA), endorsed the war in the hope that their support would also build national support for voting rights. NAWSA leaders pointed out that millions of women had assumed new and vital roles in manufacturing, transportation, agriculture, and government bureaus. Nearly 25,000 women served as army nurses in Europe. Thousands of others drove ambulances, staffed canteens for soldiers in the field, or worked as military clerks. More radical suffragists, such as National Woman's Party founder **Alice Paul**, defied bans on demonstrations by staging vigils in front of the White House with signs ridiculing talk of a democratic war in a country that barred half its population from voting.

The political winds shifted in favor of suffrage when in 1917, New York State granted women the vote. Finally embarrassed by charges that he failed to honor his ideals about self-determination, Wilson in 1918 endorsed a suffrage amendment that Congress soon passed and sent on to the states for ratification. By August 1920, enough states had ratified the Nineteenth Amendment to allow women to vote in that year's presidential election. British suffragists also used the war as a mobilizing tool in their reform campaign, and by 1918, most British women had won the right to vote.

The Great Migration

The wartime economic boom, the millions of men who entered military service, and the cessation of transatlantic immigration created labor shortages that pulled African

Americans out of the rural South. Around a half-million blacks quit agricultural work and domestic labor to seek jobs in southern and northern cities in a diaspora that contemporaries called the **Great Migration**. Black-oriented newspapers such as the *Chicago Defender* called this an "exodus" comparable to the Hebrews fleeing slavery in Egypt. Sharecroppers who made about 50 cents a day left for factory jobs that paid $3 per day.

Silent protest parade in New York City against the East St. Louis riots, 1917

The migrants headed for cities such as Atlanta, St. Louis, Chicago, Detroit, and New York. Some were specifically recruited by factory owners as strikebreakers, fueling white, working-class hostility to the new arrivals. Racism, along with competition for scarce housing and better-paying jobs, contributed to major outbreaks of violence during and just after the war. Race riots occurred in East St. Louis in 1917, in rural Arkansas in 1919, and in Chicago in 1919. In each of these incidents, dozens of blacks were killed and thousands were left homeless. In the aftermath of the violence in East St. Louis, the NAACP organized a silent protest in which 8,000 black demonstrators in New York marched to the sound of muffled drums, carrying signs that resembled those of the suffragists, asking "Mr. President, Why Not Make America Safe for Democracy?"

African American leaders and organizations such as W. E. B. Du Bois and the NAACP supported the war despite Wilson's dismissal of blacks as an "inferior race." They hoped that the struggle for democracy abroad would spur progress at home. Du Bois urged black Americans to set aside their "special grievances" and "close . . . ranks with . . . white fellow citizens." In the future, Du Bois believed, black veterans would become domestic freedom fighters. Wartime service, many black leaders hoped, would promote reforms giving the "American Negro . . . the right to vote and the right to work and the right to live without insult." A war for democracy, they believed, would also help people of color around the world. For example, in 1918, Du Bois wrote in the *Crisis,* "This war is an end and also a beginning. Never again will darker people of the world occupy just the place they had before." The war, he predicted, would help create an independent China, self-governing India and Egypt, and "an Africa for the Africans."

STUDY QUESTIONS **FOR AMERICA AT WAR**

quiz

1. How did the U.S. government "sell" the war to the public, and was it successful?

2. What methods did the government use to boost war production?

3. What legal and informal means did the government use to silence war critics?

⊙ OVER THERE

The U.S. Army numbered about 200,000 men in April 1917, a tiny fraction of the size of its enemies. Over the next 19 months, it grew to over five million men. To achieve this extraordinary growth, the government encouraged volunteers and Congress passed a selective service (draft) law that required men aged 18 to 31 to register with local draft boards that determined who would be conscripted into service.

Under the command of General John J. Pershing, the **American Expeditionary Force (AEF)** trained, transported to France, and led into battle millions of men—dubbed "doughboys"—drawn from all walks of life. Training camps taught both moral and physical lessons to recruits before they entered the hell of trench warfare. The AEF entered the war at a critical time, just as Germany launched a massive offensive to break the deadlock on the western front. The AEF arrival in France, along with the increased military aid to the Allies that accompanied them, blunted the German onslaught. Americans not only faced death on the battlefield but suffered the ravages of a little understood influenza pandemic that killed about as many of them as did enemy bullets.

Building an Army

To promote enlistment, the War Department distributed millions of posters and pamphlets encouraging voluntary service. These included an iconic image of Uncle Sam saying "I Want You," images of U-boat victims and children mutilated by German troops, and a poster of a winsome young woman dressed in a sailor's suit declaring "Gee!! I Wish I Were a Man—I'd Join the Navy." Some posters were quite gruesome, including one of a Belgian woman crucified against a wall with blood dripping down her body.

United States Navy recruiting poster, 1917

For those not sufficiently motivated to enlist, there was the draft. About 24 million men registered, an overwhelming percentage of those required to, and about 10 percent of these were chosen by local boards to enter military service. The law permitted the 65,000 "conscientious objectors" who opposed war on religious grounds to perform noncombat work as medics or orderlies in hospitals. However, those who refused to do so because their beliefs did not permit any cooperation with the military were labeled "enemies of the republic" and given stiff prison sentences.

About 70 percent of the five million Americans in uniform were native-born whites, one-fifth foreign born, and nearly 10 percent African Americans. All of the nearly 400,000 blacks served in segregated units, mostly in labor battalions under white officers. Only 1,000 blacks received officer rank.

French civilian and military authorities, who had long relied on service by their own African colonial troops, resented efforts by American officers to enforce rigid segregation on foreign soil. U.S. officers insisted that the French military *not* treat black soldiers as equals, never praise them in front of white troops, and keep them away from white French women.

The War Department and voluntary groups such as the YMCA that worked closely with conscripts during their training and deployment often appeared more concerned about the troops' moral health than with their fighting aptitude. In U.S. training camps and later in France, many young men frequented brothels during their time off. Patriots condemned beer, especially when brewed by companies founded by German immigrants, as a product unfit for real Americans. AEF commander General Pershing, who himself had taken a French mistress, declared brothels off limits to U.S. troops and threatened to court-martial soldiers infected with venereal disease because the affliction had debilitated so many of them. French officials considered the U.S. obsession with sex, alcohol, and segregation bizarre. To protect soldiers' health and calm American fears, French premier Georges Clemenceau offered to create medically inspected brothels for use by American troops. Astounded by this proposal, Secretary of War Newton Baker told an aide, "For God's sake . . . don't show this to the President or he'll stop the war." Army and YMCA officials fretted that soldiers returning from

Europe might transmit "degenerate" French sexual practices. Ultimately, better hygiene and threats of court-martial reduced infection rates.

With access to alcohol and women restricted, tobacco—especially cigarettes—became a common vice among soldiers. Before the war, most tobacco was either chewed or smoked in cigars. Sixteen states had previously outlawed cigarettes as a health threat. Anti-alcohol groups planned to begin a national antismoking crusade, dubbed "Nicotine Next," once Congress and the states ratified the Eighteenth Amendment. But in the trenches, soldiers enjoyed the camaraderie of a quick smoke. General Pershing declared cigarettes as vital for the troops as bullets and issued an appeal for Americans to send "smokes" to the boys. Groups such as the YMCA, Red Cross, and Salvation Army, which had condemned cigarettes as a moral and health hazard, became the largest tobacco distributors in the world during the war. This led one frustrated anticigarette crusader to publish a pamphlet titled *Kaiser Nicotine,* predicting that over time, tobacco would kill more soldiers than would German bullets.

Joining the Fight

General Pershing insisted that American troops deployed in Europe fight as freestanding units under U.S. command—not as replacements for badly depleted French and British ranks. Pershing made one major exception to this rule, granting the French request to have the 92nd Division of black troops fight alongside their soldiers. Elements of the 92nd Division spent more days in battle than any other American unit during the war. But when French officers presented these brave soldiers with medals, Pershing chastised them for "spoiling the Negroes."

American troops, like their European counterparts, discovered that life in the trenches was cold, wet, and terrifying. Food rations often failed to reach frontline soldiers, and they frequently had to drink rainwater collected in shell holes, spreading dysentery. After German mustard gas attacks, many men suffered temporary blindness. Nearly all those in the trenches were covered by lice. The term "basket case" entered the language in reference to soldiers who had lost limbs and were confined to a basket in a hospital.

By the end of the war, about 100,000 American soldiers had been admitted to field hospitals suffering from what doctors then called "shell shock." The symptoms, already common among British and French troops, included staring eyes or a frozen, terrified look; violent tremors; and cold and sometimes blue extremities. Some victims became blind, hysterical, or paralyzed. Doctors suspected that high-explosive shells rattling the brain caused the condition. In addition, emotional strain caused by long periods in the trenches alternating with intense combat took its toll. In Vietnam and later wars, these symptoms have often been called post-traumatic stress disorder, or PTSD. About half the victims returned to duty after a brief hospitalization, but many remained under care. Symptoms of shell shock sometimes reappeared months or even years later among those who had seemingly recovered.

Political and Military Complications

Around the time the Americans entered the war, events in Russia created new problems on the western front. Since the overthrow of Czar Nicholas in the spring of 1917, Russian armies had largely stopped fighting. In November, the Bolsheviks, or Communists, led

AFRICAN AMERICAN "DOUGHBOYS" ON PATROL IN FRANCE, 1918 Unlike most of their peers, this unit was armed for combat and not confined to service work.

by Vladimir Lenin, seized power from the pro-Allied but ineffective regime that had briefly replaced the czar. In the spring of 1918, Lenin approved the Treaty of Brest-Litovsk with Germany and formally pulled Russia out of the war. This allowed German commanders to transport hundreds of thousands of troops from eastern to western Europe. In March, the expanded German forces in the west launched a major offensive designed to overrun France before more American supplies and soldiers could arrive. The onslaught carried German armies within 50 miles of Paris.

At this point, a growing number of American troops joined the battle and blunted the German advance along the Marne River at Chateau Thierry. By the summer and fall of 1918, hundreds of thousands of additional doughboys had helped push back the Germans in the battles of Chateau Thierry and Belleau Woods in June and the 2nd Battle of the Marne in July and August (Map 21.3). The intense fighting during the 10 months of combat in 1918 killed nearly 50,000 Americans and wounded many more. The infusion of fresh forces bolstered Allied morale while the desperate Germans used up nearly all their reserve forces and war materials by October. To make matters worse, Germany's Austrian, Turkish, and Bulgarian allies quit fighting.

Within Germany hunger and war-weariness sparked riots. Leftists, inspired by Bolshevik Russia, agitating among German civilians and soldiers called for a revolution against the old order. Fearing an Allied push into Germany and the possible seizure of power by Communists, German commanders insisted that the country's civilian politicians seek a U.S.-brokered cease-fire.

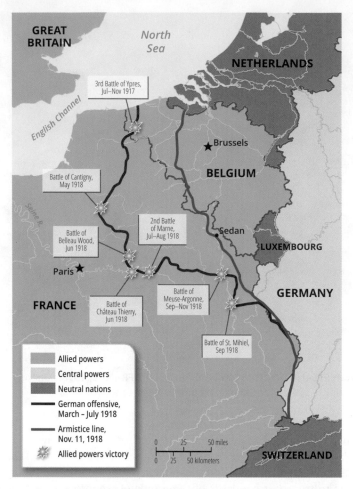

MAP 21.3 America Joins World War I, 1917–1918 U.S. armed forces entered European combat in large numbers during 1918. They played an important role in breaking the stalemate on the western front.

German moderates embraced the opportunity to end the war and create a democratic regime. They hoped that Wilson's Fourteen Points, promising fair treatment for postwar Germany, would serve as a framework for an armistice and peace agreement. However, Wilson rejected a cease-fire until the Kaiser abdicated and German troops agreed to evacuate all occupied territory and to surrender their heavy weapons.

Germany had to swallow another bitter pill. Following an armistice, the Allied food blockade would continue—victimizing mostly civilians—until Germany signed a final peace treaty, a process that might last months. Germany's democratic politicians who were eager to stop the killing and reform their government deeply resented these terms but had few options. Early in November, Kaiser Wilhelm fled to Holland, and a new civilian government accepted the harsh armistice terms. Anxious to shift the pain of defeat to the shoulders of others, German military leaders promptly accused liberals, socialists, and Jews of a "stab in the back" that betrayed the fatherland, an absurd charge later amplified by Adolf Hitler. The guns of war fell silent at 11:11 AM on November 11, 1918, but peace remained elusive.

Influenza Pandemic

During the last half of 1918 and into 1919, a global epidemic, or pandemic, added to the world's misery. As if the huge wartime toll were not terrible enough, millions more died from an especially virulent influenza virus. The "flu," an annual arrival, usually resembled a bad cold. Because the flu virus mutates quickly, immunity seldom carried over from one year to the next.

Scientists now understand that occasionally the virus mutates dramatically or "jumps species." A swine or bird flu can evolve in ways that allow it to infect humans and cause a more severe illness. Something like this occurred in 1918–1919 when otherwise healthy soldiers in the trenches of the western front came down with a severe flu that killed its victims, sometimes in a few hours. In fact, nearly half of all 116,000 U.S. military deaths in Europe resulted from the flu. The illness spread quickly in military barracks and was carried around the world by infected travelers on steamships. Unlike typical flu strains, which hit the very young and old the hardest, the 1918 variant struck healthy young adults most seriously, possibly by overstimulating those with the healthiest immune systems to inflame air passages in the lungs. Death resulted from victims "drowning" in their own phlegm.

The disease was first reported in March 1918 among soldiers based in Kansas. Troops carried it to Europe where it may have mutated further and spread quickly around the world. The virus proved even more virulent in its second appearance in the fall. Some worried that the disease was a form of germ warfare spread by German agents. By mid-1919, the virus had struck down those most susceptible to it and had possibly mutated into a less virulent strain. Ultimately, the pandemic killed about 600,000 Americans and perhaps 50 million people worldwide, with most of the deaths in China and India.

Early in the 21st century, scientists utilized new techniques to recover DNA particles from the 1918 virus lodged in the remains of victims buried in the frozen tundra of Norway and Alaska. Among their findings was the disturbing fact that only subtle mutations distinguished the "killer flu" from the mundane variety.

STUDY QUESTIONS **FOR OVER THERE**

1. What methods did the United States employ to quickly raise a mass army?
2. What impact did the arrival of U.S. troops in Europe have on the war?

quiz

⬇ MAKING PEACE ABROAD AND AT HOME

President Wilson's popularity among Americans declined after the initial enthusiasm for war. The idealistic goals he proclaimed often seemed obscured by battlefield casualties and friction with coalition partners. The president blundered badly when he

Postwar Colonialism

Despite Wilson's pledge to negotiate peace via "open diplomacy," American, British, French, Italian, and Japanese delegates did most of the important work behind closed doors, isolated from public scrutiny and with little input from other nations. They concentrated on forging a new map of Europe and the Middle East by dividing the colonial territories of the defeated powers. Efforts by stateless and colonial peoples to influence the outcome were considered a nuisance.

To press their case, the Indian National Congress, Muslim League, Korean and Chinese patriots, Zionists, Africans, Vietnamese, and even some Haitians and Dominicans, chafing under U.S. military occupation, ventured to Paris. They anticipated fierce opposition from the colonial powers but were stunned by the cold shoulder they received from Wilson and the U.S. delegation. The president confided to his aides that when he had spoken of self-determination, he had been thinking primarily of eastern Europeans, such as Czechs and Poles, not the "many nationalities which are coming to us day after day" from Asia, Africa, and the Middle East. Freedom for these people lay decades ahead, after tutelage by advanced nations. Secretary of State Robert Lansing remarked that democracy was too "dangerous" an idea to put "into the minds of certain

asked voters in November 1918 to make the congressional election a referendum on his leadership and plans for peace. Instead, a majority of voters blamed Democrats for a war they had grown weary of and a variety of accumulated economic grievances. After the armistice, Wilson had to deal with emboldened Republican critics who controlled Congress, Allied leaders bent on revenge, and a Communist regime in Russia trying to spread revolution. These factors complicated the president's effort to win Senate approval for a treaty that included membership in a new **League of Nations**, an organization he saw as the key to a lasting peace.

Making Peace and Fighting Communism

In November 1918, just before the armistice, Republicans won control of both the House and the Senate. Thus, any treaty negotiated by Wilson required substantial Republican backing in the Senate to be ratified by the required two-thirds vote. To reach this number, Wilson had to seek at least tacit support from Republicans, especially Henry Cabot Lodge, chairman of the Senate Foreign Relations Committee. Rather than reaching out to Lodge and other rivals, Wilson refused to name any prominent Republicans, or any senators at all, to the peace delegation he personally led to Europe in December 1918. The president even shunned advice from a group of technical experts, known as the Inquiry, he had previously appointed.

In December 1918, Wilson, the first sitting president to cross the Atlantic, led a peace delegation to Europe. Before going to Paris, he visited London and Rome, where adoring crowds responded to his calls for negotiating a "people's peace." Italian races" whose "state of barbarism or ignorance deprives them of the capacity" to govern themselves.

The British and French took control of much of the Middle East. Rebuffing Arab calls for independence, they appropriated from the defeated Ottoman Turks the provinces of Iraq, Palestine, Syria, Lebanon, and Trans-Jordan. Ruled by the Europeans or their local puppets, these new states jumbled together antagonistic ethnic and religious groups, a formula for future chaos. Japan, angered by Anglo-American refusal to acknowledge Japanese racial equality or immigration rights, demanded and received Western approval to retain control of Korea and parts of China. Wilson aides rebuffed efforts by Vietnamese nationalist Nguyen Tat Than (Ho Chi Minh) to deliver a petition seeking American support for his homeland's independence from France. Indian and African appeals for self-determination received similar dismissive treatment. In despair, many former moderate nationalists turned toward the promise of revolutionary change espoused by the new Communist regime in Russia. In the coming decades, uprisings against colonial masters swept much of the Middle East, Africa, and Asia. The war had not, after all, made the world safe for democracy.

- How did Wilson's wartime rhetoric inspire colonial peoples?
- Why did the Versailles Treaty shatter hopes for decolonization?

newspapers praised him as the "king of humanity," and British writer and social reformer H. G. Wells called him a political "Messiah."

Thirty-two nations, not including Germany or Communist Russia, attended the peace conference in Paris between January 18 and June 28, 1919. During the months-long deliberations in Paris, Lloyd George and Clemenceau insisted on weakening Germany by imposing strict limits on future German armaments, having France occupy some German territory along its border, and imposing a huge reparations bill designed to make Germany pay for wartime destruction (Map 21.4). The British and French also insisted that Germany accept as part of the peace treaty a "war guilt clause" in which it assumed sole responsibility for the fighting.

Even though the tone and substance of many decisions made at the conference violated the spirit of his Fourteen Points, Wilson needed French and British support. He spent months in Paris drafting plans for a League of Nations.

Woodrow Wilson, Address on the Fourteen Points for Peace, January 8, 1918; excerpts from the Treaty of Versailles (1919)

Wilson insisted that future peace and prosperity required the United States and the world's major powers to accept Article 10 of the proposed League's covenant or charter. This established a system of "collective security" that pledged all League members to safeguard the territory and independence of all other members.

Wilson had another reason for accommodating the wartime Allies. Like the British, French, and Japanese, he feared the spread of revolution from Russia and wanted quick, cooperative action to stifle the Bolshevik regime. In mid-1918, following Lenin's peace deal with Germany that took Russia out of the war, the United States and the Allies had sent troops to northern Russia, ostensibly to keep war supplies stored there out of German hands. In fact, the foreign armies assisted the "Whites," as the

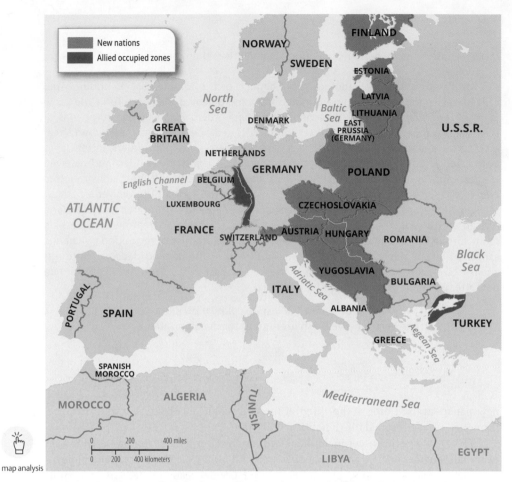

map analysis

MAP 21.4 European Political Boundaries After World War I The breakup of the German, Austro-Hungarian, Ottoman, and Russian empires gave rise to a dozen or more new nations in eastern europe and the Middle East.

anti-Communists were known, in what became a brutal three-year civil war with the Bolsheviks. Wilson sent additional troops to Siberia, where they joined Japanese and European forces in a vain effort to hold the vast region against the Communists.

Around the time of Germany's surrender in November 1918, Communist groups inspired by the Bolsheviks briefly seized power in Berlin and other German cities and in Hungary. To counter this threat to central and eastern Europe, the Allies provided support to local anti-Communist forces, who quickly regained power. The concern with halting the spread of communism from Russia contributed to the decision at Paris to create a buffer of anti-Communist states—Finland, Poland, Estonia, Latvia, and Lithuania—out of what had been the western fringe of czarist Russia.

The victors completed drafting the peace treaty in June, nearly eight months after the armistice, and presented it to Germany on a nonnegotiable basis. On June 28, 1919, with its ports still blockaded, with its economy in ruins, and amid threats of uprisings by left-wing revolutionaries or right-wing militarists, the German government accepted the harsh terms.

Red Scare

The political and economic climate in the United States had changed dramatically by the time the peace treaty came back to Washington for Senate ratification in the summer of 1919. The cancellation of most war contracts triggered a sharp recession. Economic uncertainty coincided with a growing fear of Bolshevism abroad and at home, especially the belief that Communist agents—referred to as "Reds"—either caused or planned to take advantage of labor unrest to seize power. During 1919, major employers cut workers' wages and hours, prompting a nationwide wave of labor unrest. Although the Communist movement inside the United States was tiny, it was often portrayed as the tip of the Bolshevik lance and held responsible for strikes and acts of violence.

In January 1919, unions in Seattle called a general strike that briefly shut down the city. During May and June, several prominent government officials and financiers received bombs in the mail, apparently sent by an anarchist group. Several exploded, killing innocent bystanders rather than their intended targets. These, along with later bombings, convinced many Americans that labor activists and Communists were little more than terrorists. In the fall, Boston police officers went on strike, prompting Massachusetts governor Calvin Coolidge to send in the National Guard as replacements. Coolidge became a national celebrity by declaring, "There is no right to strike against the public safety by anybody, anywhere, anytime." In September, over 300,000 steel workers walked out when the big mills tried to restore the 12-hour day, seven-day work-week at reduced wages. Industry executives denounced the strikers as revolutionaries and hired many replacement workers, including 30,000 African Americans, as strike-breakers. The walkout collapsed in January 1920.

Hostility toward minorities merged with antilabor sentiment in rural Arkansas when a group of sharecroppers, attempting to organize a union, gathered in a church in the fall of 1919. When armed whites attacked the meeting, the black sharecroppers fought back and killed several whites. Bands of white vigilantes responded by shooting, hanging, and even roasting to death between 100 and 300 African Americans in nearby towns, most of whom had nothing to do with the union. Another 300 blacks were beaten, denied lawyers, and jailed. Over 100 were convicted of serious crimes, and 12 were sentenced to death in trials that lasted 10 minutes or less. Scipio Africanus Jones, a local black attorney, assisted by the NAACP, appealed the convictions before the Supreme Court. The Court's 1923 decision, *Moore v. Dempsey*, overturned the convictions, calling them the product of mob rule, and freed the condemned men.

Attorney General **A. Mitchell Palmer** declared that these events taken together revealed that a "blaze of revolution" had engulfed the nation. Palmer appointed a young protégé, **J. Edgar Hoover**, to lead the intelligence division within the Justice Department to track radicals. In 1919, Hoover compiled lists of thousands of suspects, many of them immigrants, who belonged to groups such as the IWW and the newly organized Communist Party. In December, about 250 of these noncitizens were seized and deported to Communist-ruled Russia. In January 1920, the attorney general authorized a broader sweep. The so-called **Palmer Raids** occurred in 33 cities where federal agents

Excerpt from A. Mitchell Palmer, "The Case Against the 'Reds," (1920)

interactive timeline

TIMELINE 1913–1920

AMERICA	YEAR	THE WORLD
Mar Woodrow Wilson inaugurated as president	**1913**	
Apr U.S. naval force occupies Mexican port of Veracruz after "insult" to flag **Aug** Wilson issues neutrality declaration, allows non-military trade with warring nations	**1914**	**Jun** Archduke Franz Ferdinand assassinated in Bosnia, sparking crisis among European rivals **Aug** World War I begins in Europe as Allies confront Central Powers **Aug** Panama Canal opens
Jul U.S. Marines occupy Haiti and remain until 1934	**1915**	**May** British passenger liner *Lusitania* sunk by German U-boat, killing over 1,000, including more than 100 Americans
Mar Pancho Villa attacks several U.S. towns along Mexican border **Mar** General John J. Pershing leads punitive military expedition into Mexico to catch Villa, leading to U.S.–Mexican confrontation **May** U.S. Marines occupy Dominican Republic until 1924 **Nov** Wilson reelected president in close contest with slogan "He Kept Us Out of War"	**1916**	Massive slaughter on western and eastern battlefronts in Europe Abortive mediation efforts by private Americans and Wilson administration
Jan Zimmerman Telegram sent by German government to Mexico proposing joint war against United States **Feb** German navy resumes unrestricted submarine warfare against U.S. ships supplying Allies **Mar** U.S. merchant ships sunk by U-boats with loss of American lives **Apr** U.S. Congress declares war on Germany, endorsing Wilson's call to make the world "safe for democracy"; federal agencies established to regulate agricultural and industrial production and transportation **May–Jul** East St. Louis race riots **Jun** Espionage Act passed, restricting antiwar speech and activities	**1917**	**Mar** Russian Czar Nicholas overthrown by moderate democratic reformers **Nov** Bolsheviks, led by Lenin, seize power in Russia

without warrants broke into homes and meeting halls to arrest over 4,000 people on charges of subversion. About 600 of those seized were later deported.

Although President Wilson tacitly approved Palmer's harsh methods, the attorney general overreached. In the spring of 1920, he claimed to have uncovered a "Red" plot to seize national power on May 1 and deployed troops to protect government buildings and officials. When the day passed peacefully, and Palmer could not show evidence that such a plot had actually existed, his credibility—and presidential hopes—dissolved. However, his young assistant, J. Edgar Hoover, survived the episode. An exceptionally skilled bureaucrat, Hoover stayed on after the Republican sweep in 1920 and in 1924 became director of the Justice Department's Bureau of Investigation (later renamed the Federal Bureau of Investigation, or FBI), a job he held for nearly 50 years.

Ironically, an actual terror attack, about which he knew nothing, took place after Palmer's disgrace. On September 16, 1920, an anarchist group exploded a large bomb in front of the offices of J. P. Morgan Company on Wall Street in New York City. The explosion—the deadliest terror incident on American soil until the Oklahoma City bombing of 1995—killed 38 people and wounded 400 others. Like earlier attacks, the victims were mostly working people, not powerful bankers. Instead of promoting

AMERICA	YEAR	THE WORLD
Jan Wilson issues Fourteen Points peace plan directed at Germany, Allies, Bolsheviks, and colonial peoples **Nov** Republicans win midterm congressional elections **Nov** Armistice signed, ending fighting in Europe; Allied blockade of Germany continues along with anti-Communist effort in Russia	**1918**	**Feb** Bolsheviks sign Brest-Litovsk Treaty with Germany and quit war **Mar** Global influenza pandemic begins **Jul** Allied armies, joined by the United States, begin military intervention in Russia that lasts into 1920 **Oct–Nov** German kaiser abdicates and German civilian government seeks cease-fire
Jan Paris Peace Conference, attended by President Wilson, begins with Germany and Bolsheviks excluded **Jan** Eighteenth Amendment (Prohibition) ratified **May–Jun** Anarchist bombings in United States promote conservative backlash **Jun** Peace treaty ending Great War signed at Versailles despite Wilson's misgivings **Jul** Chicago race riots **Sep** Elaine, Arkansas, race riots **Nov** Palmer Raids against radicals begin with roundup of several thousand immigrants	**1919**	**May** Chinese May Fourth movement rallies patriots against Allied decision to give Japan control of former German-held territory in China
Mar U.S. Senate rejects Versailles Treaty by failing to muster two-thirds vote **Aug** Nineteenth Amendment ratified, giving women right to vote **Sep** Wall Street bombing kills dozens **Nov** Republican Warren G. Harding elected president with pledge to restore "normalcy"	**1920**	

revolution, the attack frightened ordinary Americans and contributed to a more conservative drift in national politics.

The Fight for the Treaty

Even before Wilson formally submitted the Versailles Treaty for ratification, 39 senators—more than the one-third needed to defeat it—signed a petition demanding that the League of Nations recognize that the Monroe Doctrine gave the United States preeminence in the Western Hemisphere. When the treaty reached the Senate in the summer of 1919, Senator Lodge bitterly criticized it. He argued that Article 10 of the League Covenant, the basis for collective security, unfairly restricted America's freedom of action and might oblige the country to engage in unwise military ventures without congressional approval. Other critics warned the League might interfere with immigration policies or require that U.S. officials accept African or Asian equality. Some progressive critics of the treaty complained that it was too conservative and locked the United States into defending British, French, and Japanese colonial holdings while treating Germany unfairly.

Wilson stubbornly rejected all criticism of the Versailles Treaty, arguing that reopening negotiations would only make things worse and that any problems could be solved once the League of Nations began operating. To bolster public support for ratification, he launched an arduous speaking tour in September 1919. He collapsed on September 26 at the end of a speech in Pueblo, Colorado, and soon suffered a nearly fatal stroke. After partially recovering, Wilson became even less willing to compromise. He insisted that Senate Democrats prove their loyalty by voting *against* an amended treaty even if they agreed with the changes. As a result, three times between November 1919 and March 1920, the Senate voted down the treaty, with and without amendments. If Wilson had allowed Senate Democrats to vote in favor of the amended treaty, it would likely have passed.

The rejection of the Versailles Treaty and League membership signified a deep division among American leaders. Some, like Wilson, believed the Great War proved the United States must join formally with other nations in managing world trade and enforcing peace. Critics of the League argued that membership would needlessly entangle the United States in European conflicts and restrict America's freedom to act. Both sides of the debate actually agreed that the nation had global interests and could not isolate itself from world affairs. But they disagreed strongly over how the United States should exercise its power and defend its interests, collectively through the League of Nations or unilaterally by picking and choosing issues and nations with whom it would cooperate. During the next decade, U.S. policymakers devised a variety of diplomatic, trade, and military agreements to accomplish many of Wilson's goals without joining the League.

STUDY QUESTIONS FOR MAKING PEACE ABROAD AND AT HOME

quiz

1. What compromises did Wilson make in negotiating peace and why?

2. Why did many liberal and conservative senators oppose the Versailles Treaty?

3. What 1919–1920 events in Europe and at home created fear of domestic radicalism?

Summary

- The outbreak of war in 1914 shocked Americans, who tried to avoid involvement while they benefited from exporting raw materials to the warring nations.
- Expanding economic links to the Allies and growing fears of German militarism gradually moved the United States toward direct involvement.
- Once in the war, the government used its new power to raise a mighty army, boost production, and stifle dissent.
- As large numbers of American troops joined the fighting early in 1918, they played a decisive role in defeating Germany.
- In 1918–1919, an influenza pandemic killed millions of people worldwide.
- Wilson personally negotiated the peace treaty, hoping to use it as a vehicle to create a League of Nations that would ensure future peace and prosperity.
- Support for the treaty, and for liberal policies, was undermined by a wave of strikes, bombings, and fears of terrorism during 1919–1920.

Key Terms and People

audio
flashcards

Reviewing Chapter 21

1. How did the war in Europe impact the United States early on?
2. What were President Wilson's major war aims?
3. How did the federal government suppress wartime dissent?
4. What international and domestic events complicated Wilson's efforts to control the peace settlement?
5. What unresolved problems from the war contributed to postwar instability?

Further Reading

Bristow, Nancy. *American Pandemic: The Lost Worlds of the 1918 Influenza Epidemic.* New York: Oxford University Press, 2012. Explores the impact and legacy of the pandemic on American society.

Clark, Christopher. *The Sleepwalkers: How Europe Went to War in 1914.* New York: Harpers, 2013. Both intense local nationalism as well as Great Power schemes of expansion fueled the drive toward war that each side felt justified in fighting.

Freeberg, Ernest. *Democracy's Prisoner: Eugene V. Debs, the Great War, and the Right to Dissent.* Cambridge, MA: Harvard University Press, 2008. Debs had several careers as a labor organizer, Socialist leader, and principled opponent of the war. His prosecution revealed the extent to which the Wilson administration went in stifling peaceful dissent.

Gardner, Lloyd. *Safe for Democracy: The Anglo-American Response to Revolution, 1913–1923.* New York: Oxford University Press, 1984. Amidst the carnage of the Great War, British and American leaders tried to control the social upheavals in Mexico, Russia, eastern Europe, and China.

Hastings, Max. *Catastrophe, 1914: Europe Goes to War.* New York: Knopf, 2014. Explores how the major powers blundered into war and why the fighting became so bloody.

Kennedy, David. *Over Here: The First World War and American Society.* New York: Oxford University Press, 1980. U.S. entry into the Great War set in motion economic, political, and social changes that had long-term consequences in the lives of ordinary Americans.

Knock, Thomas. *To End All Wars: Woodrow Wilson and the Quest for a New World Order.* New York: Oxford University Press, 1992. The author explains how Wilson saw American participation in the Great War as a way to reshape global politics and impose a uniquely American reform agenda on the world.

MacMillan, Margaret. *Paris 1919: Six Months that Changed the World.* New York: Random House, 2002. The author examines the personalities and politics behind the long peace conference after the Great War and evaluates the successes and failures of the peacemakers.

Manela, Erez. *The Wilsonian Moment: Self-Determination and the International Origins of Anticolonial Nationalism.* New York: Oxford University Press, 2007. Wilson's call for self-determination following World War I aroused great hopes among colonial peoples. But the failure to implement this promise pushed many Asians, Africans, and Arabs in radical directions.

Schaffer, Ronald. *America in the Great War: The Rise of the War Welfare State.* New York: Oxford University Press, 1994. American participation in the war, Schaffer explains, was made possible by the expansion of federal power early in the 20th century, and the war further enhanced that power. He also chronicles the experience of ordinary soldiers.

America in the World
GOODS, IDEAS, PEOPLE

CHAPTER 21: America and the Great War, 1914–1920

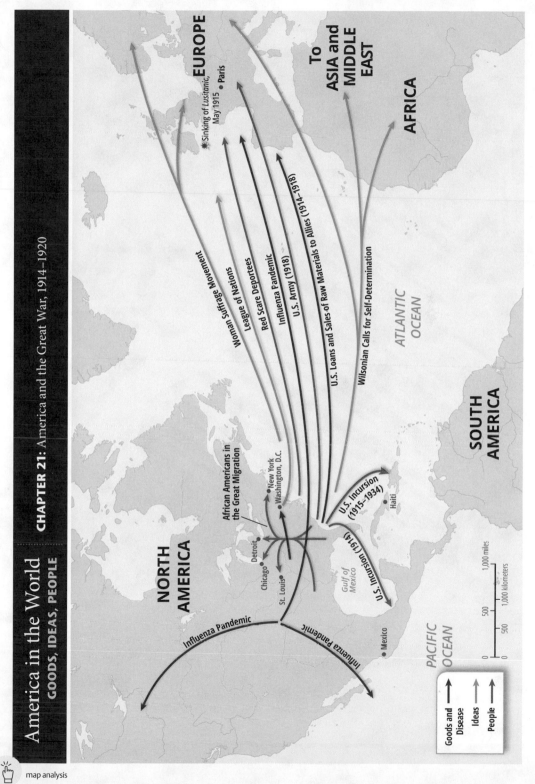

EUROPE

* Sinking of *Lusitania*,
May 1915 • Paris

To
ASIA and
MIDDLE
EAST

AFRICA

Woman Suffrage Movement
League of Nations
Red Scare Deportees
Influenza Pandemic
U.S. Army (1918)

U.S. Loans and Sales of Raw Materials to Allies (1914–1918)

Wilsonian Calls for Self-Determination

ATLANTIC
OCEAN

SOUTH
AMERICA

African Americans in
the Great Migration

• New York
  Washington, D.C.

U.S. Incursion
(1915–1934)

• Haiti

NORTH
AMERICA

• Detroit

• Chicago

U.S. Incursion (1914)

• St. Louis

Gulf of
Mexico

U.S. Incursion (1914)

Influenza Pandemic

Influenza Pandemic

• Mexico

PACIFIC
OCEAN

0   500   1,000 miles

0   500   1,000 kilometers

Goods and
Disease

Ideas

People

map analysis

Drawing in Two Colors   *Winold Re*

A New Era

O n September 26, 1925, 25 African American dancers, singers, and jazz musicians left New York for Paris aboard the SS *Berengaria*. A few weeks later, they
opened "Le Revue Nègre," a musical review featuring dancer **Josephine Baker**,
who quickly became the toast of Paris. The scantily dressed Baker, who performed an
"African" dance routine, "is knocking all Paris sideways," noted a French journalist. Born
in poverty in St. Louis, Baker soon opened up her own nightclub, Chez Josephine, in
Paris; starred in movies; hobnobbed with the rich
and famous; and lived in a luxurious apartment in the
Champs Élysées, where she kept a baby jaguar.

Baker and her fellow performers joined a small community of black World War I veterans, businessmen, writers, students, artists, and jazz musicians who made Paris
their home, seeking to escape racism and violence and
to seize opportunity unavailable in the United States.
Roughly 200,000 black soldiers served in France during
the Great War, where a grateful French public welcomed
them warmly and treated them as equals. Paris seemed
especially attractive in contrast to the racial violence faced
by blacks in the United States during the Red Summer
riots of 1919. By the early 1920s, a small African American
community had coalesced in Paris's Montmartre section.
Black soldiers first introduced jazz to France during the
war, and Parisians could not get enough of it. American
musicians and dancers, including Josephine Baker, were
at the heart of Paris culture in the 1920s.

The Great War and its aftermath left people on
both sides of the Atlantic disillusioned, their faith in
progress shattered. Jazz embodied a newfound sense of
freedom and abandon, lifting the spirits of people in
France and the United States alike. In clubs and dance
halls in both the United States and Europe, people
danced the Charleston and Black Bottom to the frenetic
beat of jazz, some seeking "authenticity" and meaning

in black culture. Radio also broadcast American jazz abroad, transforming the musical landscape around the world.

The 1920s—dubbed the "new era" by President **Herbert Hoover**—witnessed the role of radio and the movies in forging global culture at home and abroad. American music, films, celebrities, and consumer products flooded the world as never before. As jazz and Josephine Baker's suggestive dances reflected, sexual mores also shifted. This new era was marked by cultural conflict between innovation and tradition, between those who enthusiastically embraced change and social critics and religious leaders who decried the new culture as vulgar and immoral.

JOSÉPHINE BAKER
- Folies-Bergère -

JOSEPHINE BAKER Dancer Josephine Baker and other African American artists and musicians helped ignite the Jazz Age in Paris, where they found opportunities unavailable to them in the United States.

⊘ A NEW ECONOMY FOR A NEW ERA

In the decade after World War I, the spread of new technologies increased U.S. engagement with the world. Business also became more international than ever before. People around the globe bought American products, listened to American music, and watched American movies. At the same time, many Americans tried to isolate the country from the rest of the world. Hostility to outsiders led to harsh restrictions on immigration. Parts of the United States and the world economy thrived, but the widening gap between rich and poor, and the unhealthy economic legacy of the war, eventually led to a long depression. Modern advertising encouraged demand for newly available goods, and Americans borrowed billions of dollars to buy modern marvels such as cars, radios, and electrical appliances. Many in the United States reveled in this consumer culture and were proud that people around the globe sought to emulate it. Others, however, decried modern mass consumption as boorish and hollow.

Wireless America

Radio developed into one of the most popular modes of communication in the 1920s. By the end of World War I, the technology and the corporate structure were in place for a revolution in communication that would allow listeners easy access to information and entertainment created halfway around the world. Early radios were sold as kits assembled at home and often modified and improved by builders. These radios quickly captured the imagination of inventive Americans eager to tinker with the shoebox-sized contraptions.

Commercial radio broadcasting started on the night of November 2, 1920. A small audience of "wireless" enthusiasts in the Northeast tuned in to hear East Pittsburgh's new station KDKA broadcast the **Warren Harding** and James

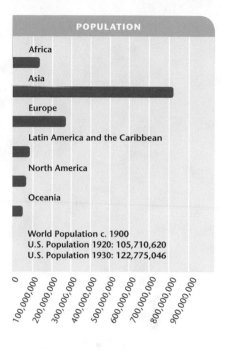

Cox presidential election returns. Two years later, 500 radio stations had mushroomed around the country, with radios in three million U.S. homes and President Harding's office. The hobby of the few had become a national obsession and a $60 million a year business. Radio broadcasts quickly spread worldwide. U.S. companies battled each other over patent rights and engaged in a heated rivalry with British allies over who would control the airwaves. Woodrow Wilson deemed U.S. supremacy in radio technology important enough to help convince General Electric (GE) to reassign patent rights and establish the Radio Corporation of America (RCA). Rapidly evolving technology spawned a powerful communications industry, and RCA emerged as the dominant company. In 1926, it created the National Broadcasting Corporation (NBC), the first countrywide network of radio stations. The next year, another company, the Columbia Broadcasting System (CBS), starting broadcasting nationwide. By 1922, the radio was the most sought-after consumer product in the nation (Map 22.1). In Europe, radio broadcasts were the most significant form of mass culture and played a major role in spreading U.S. culture worldwide. First broadcast in France from the Eiffel Tower in 1921, radio introduced American jazz to a broad spectrum of the population, and it soon became the most popular music in clubs and dance halls. By the end of the decade, the radio had profoundly altered patterns of daily life, as families reorganized their habits to catch favorite shows.

Radio changed the way people thought and bought. As radios became increasingly elaborate and expensive, consumers often had to buy their sets on credit. For rural Americans, the radio provided a vital link to the broader civic and cultural life of the nation that justified the purchase.

Radio and rural America in the 1920s

Some traditionally minded critics disapproved of the open access of the airwaves, fearing that it fostered immorality. Like other popular media of the 1920s, radio openly expressed the sexual desires of the age. Songs like "Burning Kisses," "I Need Lovin'," and "Hot Lips" floated on the air, easily accessible to young people, who gravitated to the new technology with a fervor that frightened many religious and community

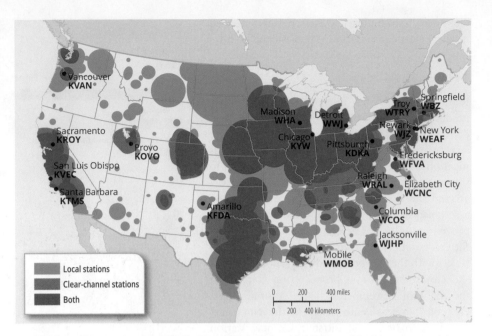

MAP 22.1 The Reach of Radio by 1939 Beginning with KDKA and its first commercial radio broadcast in 1920, radio stations mushroomed around the country, with 550 in existence by 1923. By 1930, 60 percent of Americans had purchased radios and taken advantage of the powerful clear-channel stations that broadcasted news, music, and dramatic programs from cities hundreds of miles away.

leaders. For African Americans, radio perpetuated old stereotypes through wildly popular shows such as *Amos 'n' Andy* in which white actors portrayed black characters as good-natured, submissive fools.

Car Culture

Along with the radio, the growth of the automobile industry had a profound effect on U.S. society in the 1920s. **Henry Ford** adopted mass-production techniques with the introduction of the moving assembly line in 1903. This method, soon dubbed "Fordism," allowed Ford to manufacture his Model T quickly, efficiently, and cheaply in his Highland Park, Michigan, plant. With the Model T, automobiles for the first time became affordable, versatile, and relatively reliable. Sales of Ford's "Tin Lizzie" soared. Car purchases from General Motors (GM) and the third of the "Big Three," Chrysler, multiplied as well. In 1918, 1 out of every 13 families owned a car. By 1929, four out of every five families were car owners. By 1930, Los Angeles, with a population of under two million, contained more cars than all of Asia with its more than 800 million people.

Cars changed the ways Americans viewed consumption in fundamental ways. In the mid-1920s, **Alfred P. Sloan**, chairman of GM, attacked Ford's dominant market position by introducing new GM models every year. Sloan's notion of "planned obsolescence" boosted sales, luring consumers into purchasing new cars before their old ones wore out. GM also increased sales by offering installment purchasing and promoting the idea of a product ladder with different grades of cars pegged to different incomes. By 1927, two-thirds of car buyers used the installment plan, as they sometimes spent above

La nuova Ford, guida interna a due porte è uno dei modelli più eleganti, in cui la linea allungata e bassa si accorda insuperabilmente col comfort e la massima comodità. Prezzo di vendita L. 22.400, franco Trieste, sdoganato, con 5 ruote gommate con pneus balloon.

Il nuovo coupé Ford è un esempio perfetto e caratteristico dell'eleganza e massimo comfort delle nuove carrozzerie Ford. Prezzo di vendita L. 22.400, franco Trieste sdoganato, con 5 ruote gommate con pneus balloon.

FORD'S GLOBAL ENDEAVORS Henry Ford marketed his affordable and reliable cars not only to Americans but also to consumers around the world. This 1928 ad featured two types of Fords available in Italy.

their means to participate in the car craze. In late 1927, Ford responded to GM's innovations; their rollout of the more comfortable Model A to replace the Model T resulted in a frenzy of interest from the media and the public.

Cars revolutionized mobility. Farmers and their families could now easily travel to town to shop, eat, and enjoy other recreational opportunities. Urban families took leisurely Sunday drives through the countryside. Some grabbed food at the new drive-in restaurants. Closed cars served as "mobile bedrooms" for teens and young adults who wished to escape their parents' watchful eyes. Car owners embarked on long-distance vacations, staying at auto camps or one of the new motels popping up on the highways. Along the way, drivers could fill up at one of the new gas stations or stop at one of the tourist attractions that dotted the roads.

Excerpt from Robert Lynd and Helen Lynd, *Middletown: A Study in Contemporary American Culture* (1929)

Cars and better roads also facilitated the rapid growth of suburban communities on the outskirts of the nation's major cities (Map 22.2). The population of Grosse Pointe, outside of Detroit, increased 724 percent throughout the 1920s; Shaker Heights, near Cleveland, grew 1,000 percent; and the Los Angeles suburb of Beverly Hills swelled by 2,485 percent. Open spaces and comfortable homes attracted middle-class families to the new residential communities.

By the mid-1920s, automobile manufacturing was the country's fastest-growing industry and provided much of the decade's labor growth and prosperity. One out of every five dollars spent by consumers went toward automobiles. By 1929, the industry employed almost 13 percent of all manufactures. The financial health of other industries, such as petroleum, steel, glass, and rubber, relied on the auto industry.

Automakers also sold their products abroad, modifying their cars for foreign tastes, establishing subsidiaries, and building plants outside the United States. By 1928, American multinational firms in France and Germany had outpaced production by domestic auto industries in those countries. By the mid-1930s, Ford and GM had assembly operations in nearly every major market worldwide. U.S. production plants popped up in Australia, Japan, and even the Communist Soviet Union.

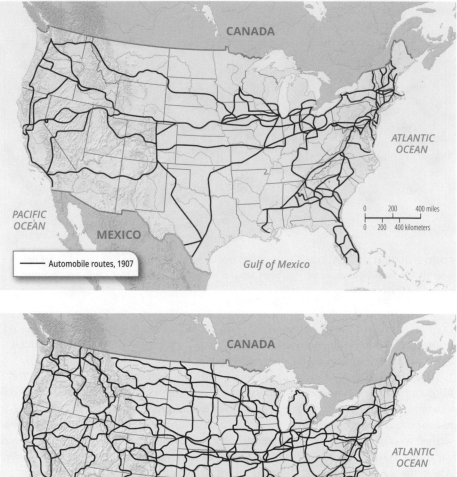

map analysis

MAP 22.2 Automobile Roads, 1907 and 1920 Highway construction exploded in the first decades of the 20th century, with roadways lacing nearly every part of the nation.

Advertising for Mass Consumption

In the 1920s, advertising took on new importance as mass consumption drove the U.S. economy. American business, perfecting methods to make people believe that they needed new goods, created sophisticated campaigns in print and on radio airwaves. Ads aimed to show how a product could reshape a consumer's image and even enhance social standing. They frequently employed movie stars and other popular personalities to endorse mundane products. By gargling with the same brand of mouthwash as movie idol Rudolph Valentino, consumers were promised a new status and even happiness as the result of a simple purchase. Cigarette makers encouraged women to "reach for a Lucky instead of a sweet." Ads also heightened demand for amazing new home appliances such as electric washers, stoves, refrigerators, and vacuum cleaners.

"Admen" of the 1920s perfected methods that drew on insights from psychology and anthropology to shift Americans away from the traditional value of thrift toward borrowing and spending on nonessential personal items. Savvy "copy writers" used market research to understand what they called the "mass mind" and the "typical consumer." Edward Bernays, a nephew of the newly popular psychoanalyst Sigmund Freud, pushed for explicitly sexual appeals in ads. Ads in magazines and newspapers, on roadside billboards, and on the radio raised awareness of personal health, hygiene, and appearance. Dramatic ads, warning of the shame of bad breath and the dangers of bad manners, gen-

THE IMPACT OF ADVERTISING Lucky Strike's ad campaign "Reach for a Lucky Instead of a Sweet," introduced in the 1920s, appealed to women who wished to stay thin.

erated remarkable sales for products as different as mouthwash and self-improvement guides. By 1927, U.S. corporations spent more than $1.5 billion on advertising annually.

STUDY QUESTIONS FOR A NEW ECONOMY FOR A NEW ERA

1. What new goods became available to Americans in the 1920s?
2. What impact did these goods have on Americans' lives and U.S. engagement with the world?
3. How did modern advertising promote the desire for new goods?

quiz

⊙ SEXUAL, RACIAL, AND ETHNIC DIVIDES

In addition to the technological and economic changes sweeping the country, the decade of the 1920s witnessed a rebellion against traditional values. Young women challenged the propriety of their mothers' generation, wearing short skirts, cutting their hair, and smoking cigarettes in public, causing a backlash against their overt sexuality. Neighborhoods in New York City, such as Greenwich Village and Harlem, touted sexual freedom and tolerance; each had gay and lesbian enclaves and was well known for cultural experimentation. Many of these rapid social and economic changes provoked resistance from some traditional-minded Americans. Some of them focused resentment on recent immigrants and people of color who they believed threatened harmony and order. Immigrants became special targets, and new laws restricted immigration into the United States.

Challenging Sexual Conventions

Just as jazz signified the 1920s, the "flapper" symbolized the "**new woman**" of that decade. She wore short skirts, cultivated a boyish figure, rouged her cheeks, bobbed her hair, and turned down her flesh-colored stockings. She smoked cigarettes in public, drank alcohol, danced "the shimmy" in jazz clubs, and flirted openly with her male playmates. Her behavior, scandalous by her mother's standards, represented "feminism—new style," according to an observer. Often indifferent to the women's organizations and causes such as suffrage that had helped bond her mother's generation, the **flapper** stressed her individuality and freedom. **Clara Bow**, who was known as the "It Girl," epitomized the flapper/new woman of the 1920s. "It" was a quality of magnetic personality and physical attraction as well as self-confidence. With boyishly tousled bobbed hair, big brown eyes, and heart-shaped mouth, she was the biggest Hollywood star of the era, and women in the United States and abroad copied her "jazz baby" style. The flapper became a Jazz Age female ideal replicated around the world—especially through movies such as *Rolled Stockings* (1927) and broadly circulated American magazines such as *Judge, Puck, Vanity Fair,* and *Life.*

NEWFOUND SEXUALITY Flapper fashions, featuring hemlines above the knees and rolled-down hose, spread around the world, as young women displayed a new sense of freedom and sexuality unknown to their mothers' generation.

The pleasure-seeking flapper embodied a new understanding of female sexuality in the 1920s. As youth culture expanded, with more young men and women attending high schools and coed colleges and universities, young Americans developed new ways of dating and interacting. New theories of sexuality, such as those posited by Sigmund Freud, stressed female pleasure and condemned "inhibitions" as unhealthy. Birth control also became more accessible. Liberated from the supervision of parents and chaperones, young men and women exercised their sexual freedom, engaged in "petting parties," and enjoyed the privacy of automobile backseats. Despite her rebellious image, the new woman of the 1920s continued to embrace many traditional values. Marriage generally remained her end goal, the means to personal fulfillment.

As women contended to land a husband, female relationships often became rivalries. Advertisements, which used female sexuality to market all kinds of items, accentuated female competition. Ads, for example, tried to convince women to purchase beauty products to vie successfully for a husband—and to keep him. Sales of cosmetics exploded in the 1920s. The "Miss America" beauty contest, first held in 1921, also embodied the competitive dimension of new womanhood, as young women contended to represent the American ideal of beauty.

Notions of marriage also changed significantly in the 1920s. "Companionate" marriage emphasized husbands and wives as friends. In addition, romance and sexual pleasure were viewed as necessary ingredients for a successful marriage. For the first time, sex manuals—rejecting older notions that sex for women was a necessary evil to be endured—stressed female pleasure.

Despite her pervasive image, the flapper was not the only new woman in the 1920s. Movies and magazines also glamorized the modern "working girl." Secretarial work, once the province of young businessmen on their way up the corporate ladder, now became a respectable job for young, middle-class, white women. But this kind of work was viewed not as a career but as a temporary phase before marriage and a return to the home.

Women office workers, 1924

For working-class women, the carefree flapper, the college coed, the glamorous working girl, or even the contented housewife rarely reflected their lives. Most working women in the 1920s remained in the occupations they had held previously: domestic service, agricultural labor, and certain manufacturing jobs. White women from the southern countryside labored in increasingly harsh conditions in textile mills. Most black women toiled in domestic service jobs. Puerto Rican and Cuban women produced clothing and cigars in urban sweatshops, whereas most Mexican immigrant women worked as domestics or agricultural workers. Yet even among women in remote parts of the country, the flapper made an impact. Southern mill girls, for example, bobbed their hair, listened to jazz on the radio, danced the shimmy, and saved their money for cosmetics and stylish dresses.

Almost all Americans considered "normal" sex to be heterosexual and occurring within marriage. But after World War I, major cities offering anonymity and freedom of expression developed well-known gay enclaves with restaurants, clubs, theaters, and speakeasies. New York's Greenwich Village not only emerged as the center of the city's gay life but also attracted others interested in challenging traditional culture, politics, and sexuality. Harlem and Chicago's Bronzeville, predominantly black neighborhoods, also featured visible gay culture, with same-sex clubs and drag balls. Gay culture was generally tolerated by working-class residents in black neighborhoods but often targeted for criticism by the middle class, especially ministers, such as Harlem's Adam Clayton Powell.

African American Renaissance and Repression

To escape the Jim Crow South, African Americans continued their massive migration from the southern countryside to northern cities. Continuing the flow of the half million who migrated during World War I, one million blacks left the rural South in the 1920s. At the end of the decade, 40 percent of black Americans lived in cities, compared to 25 percent in 1910. New York's diverse neighborhood of Harlem came to epitomize the vibrant black artistic and literary culture that flowered in the 1920s.

A product of the ongoing migration of blacks, both from the South as well as from the West Indies, the **Harlem Renaissance** helped construct a new identity for black Americans: the New Negro who exuded self-confidence, bowed to no one, and confronted racism head on. Writers and artists of the Harlem Renaissance disagreed about the nature of art: Should it be a weapon in the battle for civil rights? Or should artists be free to create as they pleased? This creative tension helped to produce a wide range of artistic creations, some of which are considered masterpieces of art and literature, and moved the black experience to the mainstream of American culture.

Langston Hughes on black artists and the racial "mountain" (1926)

Thrill-seeking whites sought out Harlem, especially its nightclubs, which featured jazz. The product of black migration and the cross-fertilization of musical styles carried to the nation's cities, jazz captured the mood of the 1920s. "The music from the trumpet at the Negro's lips is honey mixed with liquid fire," wrote African American poet **Langston Hughes** about this new musical form. The Cotton Club, Harlem's most famous nightclub, catered to people's fascination with "exotic" and "authentic" black culture, as packaged by white club owners. But these clubs were segregated: for white customers only. Blacks in Harlem, as in nearly every U.S. city, patronized their own jazz clubs, often small speakeasies. Jazz clubs also flourished in European cities, such as Paris and Berlin, where they did not enforce a color line for black patrons. Conservative leaders, both white and black, however, criticized jazz as decadent, immoral music performed in sinful settings.

Even as black culture flowered in the United States and spread around the world in the 1920s, African Americans enjoyed a smaller share of the decade's prosperity. Fluctuations in wage work created depression conditions for many blacks before the **Great Depression** of the 1930s. Competing against white workers for industrial jobs, blacks usually found themselves relegated to the dirtiest, most dangerous, lowest-paid, unskilled positions. But African Americans did find some new opportunities, most notably at the Ford Motor Company, which employed 5,000 black workers by 1923, compared to 50 in 1916, although they lived in a segregated town called Inkster. Although most black women remained mired in domestic service jobs, they also made some inroads in better-paying jobs in food industries, commercial laundries, and the needle trades. In 1925, angered at exclusion from white unions, Pullman railway porters organized the Brotherhood of Sleeping Car Porters, headed by **A. Philip Randolph**, and played an active role in asserting black civil rights.

But large-scale racial violence overshadowed advances. In 1923, white mobs from rural counties in Indiana and North Carolina drove hundreds of black families out of their homes. Two of the most brutal assaults of the era occurred in Oklahoma and Florida. In May 1921, a white mob of around 5,000 men attacked a prosperous black neighborhood in Tulsa, Oklahoma. The mob gathered to lynch a black teenager accused of assaulting a white woman; they soon torched homes and businesses, burning some alive

THE COTTON CLUB   The world-famous Cotton Club, opened in the heart of Harlem in 1923, featured some of the greatest jazz and blues artists of the day, including Duke Ellington and Cab Calloway, but allowed only white patrons.

and shooting others. By the time the National Guard restored order, about 300 blacks had been killed. The thriving, mostly black mill town of Rosewood, Florida, suffered a similar fate in January 1923. Hundreds of white men from nearby towns descended on Rosewood's 700 residents and, setting fire to homes and businesses, forced them to flee. Officially, six blacks died, although the actual tally was probably much higher.

Black International Movements

Faced with ongoing oppression at home, some black Americans began to reach out internationally. **Pan-Africanism** aimed to unite peoples of African descent around the world to seek equal rights and cast off white supremacy and colonialism. Harlem, home not only to U.S.-born blacks but also to West Indians and Africans, provided fertile ground for pan-Africanism. "The pulse of the Negro world has begun to beat in Harlem," writer **Alain Locke** declared in 1925. Pan-Africanism received a major boost with the 1919 Versailles Peace Conference and plans for decolonization. Political activist and author W. E. B. Du Bois organized the Second Pan-African Congress, held in Paris in 1921, which attracted delegates from 15 countries and demanded "the development of Africa for the Africans and not merely the profit of Europeans."

An alternative and controversial Pan-Africanism emerged under the leadership of **Marcus Garvey**, a Jamaican immigrant to New York. His **Universal Negro**

Improvement Association (UNIA) became the largest black nationalist movement in history. The charismatic Garvey captured the imagination of the masses in the United States and abroad. The UNIA, insisting on black separatism and calling for "Africa for Africans," claimed that 400 million people of African descent could free Africa from white imperialists and create their own nation. The UNIA also established black-owned and black-operated businesses, most notably the short-lived and ultimately bankrupt

Marcus Garvey, "If You Believe the Negro Has a Soul" (1921)

Black Star shipping line. Garvey inspired his followers around the world to think of themselves as a nation with a proud past and a sparkling future. He even created a national anthem, a flag, and a diplomatic corps, claiming for himself the title "Provisional President of Africa." The UNIA drew members from all over the world, including Africa, the Caribbean, and Canada. UNIA membership far outstripped that of other black organizations, such as the NAACP.

Garvey's movement inspired many followers but also generated fear and ridicule. Mass rallies and parades of UNIA members in crisp military uniforms frightened many white observers. Critics mocked Garvey's grandiose plans and Napoleonic attire. Garvey brought criticism on himself through questionable business and political tactics, such as meeting with the Imperial Wizard of the KKK as a fellow racial separatist. Black critics, especially Du Bois, found him both embarrassing and threatening and supported a "Garvey Must Go" campaign. Cooperating with the federal government, especially fearful of "negro agitation," these critics helped bring about Garvey's demise. He was convicted of mail fraud in 1923, imprisoned, and deported in 1927. Although Garveyism faded as a force in the United States, its appeal remained strong in Jamaica and throughout the Caribbean, where it helped foster national independence movements from European colonial control.

Immigration Restriction

Rapid social and economic change and challenges to the status quo for women, gays and lesbians, and African Americans led to a backlash from Americans who felt that they were losing control of their country and its traditions. The 1920s began with ominous signs that Americans were hardening their views about who could enter the United States. Immigration had stopped during World War I, and "nativists" and "restrictionists," active since the late 19th century, now added new reasons for limiting immigration when the war ended: the dangerous political ideas that influenced immigrants, especially through the successful Communist Revolution of 1917 in Russia. In 1921, some Americans expanded their campaign to limit immigration.

An economic downturn and rising numbers of immigrants converged in 1920–1921, and long-simmering racial tensions and religious prejudices catalyzed legislative change. Debates during this time revealed a particular bias against "new immigrants" from areas in eastern Europe hardest hit during the war. Immigration restrictionists especially condemned Polish Jews, who they believed came as Communists.

Research in **eugenics** supported the nativism of the early 1920s. The massive death toll of World War I energized eugenicists who feared that the "inferior" racial stock of southern and eastern Europe threatened to dilute the "superior" attributes of northern Europeans. The zoologist **Madison Grant**'s 1915 book, *The Passing of the Great Race*, popularized the "Nordic theory" of Anglo-European superiority over groups such as

Africans, Asians, and eastern and southern Europeans. In the postwar years, the new science of eugenics seemed to support some of his later discredited ideas.

Eugenics fused racism with science to provide "evidence" of the inferiority of new immigrants for those eager to justify ethnic and racial immigration restrictions. Prominent researchers produced considerable literature, which appeared in biology curricula and textbooks, on the importance of heredity over environment in shaping ability. They warned against "lower" and "degenerate" races who would spread disease and immorality to the rest of the nation. Compulsory sterilization of the "unfit"—often immigrants, the poor, and women of color—was upheld by the U.S. Supreme Court in *Buck v. Bell* (1927) as necessary, the Court claimed, "for the protection and health of the state." An estimated 65,000 sterilizations took place between 1900 and 1970.

With the passage of the **Emergency Immigration Act of 1921**, Congress created specific immigration limitations based on national origin. The act banned all immigration from Asia and placed quotas on European immigration but allowed free immigration from the Western Hemisphere, as the Southwest depended on Mexican and Latin American labor. Three years later, immigration quotas became permanent under the **National Origins Act of 1924**, which limited immigration to only 120,000 Europeans per year and favored countries such as England and Germany, drastically cutting quotas for eastern and southern Europe by 97 percent (Figure 22.1). The allotment for Catholic Italy, for example, dropped from 42,057 to 3,912. The National Origins Act established an annual ceiling on legal immigration and national quotas. Biased against all but northern Europeans, the act would remain the basis of immigration policy until 1965. It created the U.S. Border Patrol and required foreigners to carry passports and visas to enter the United States. Notably, other countries followed this model in restricting immigration on the basis of national origin. Australia banned immigration from Asia, and Germany barred entry from Poland.

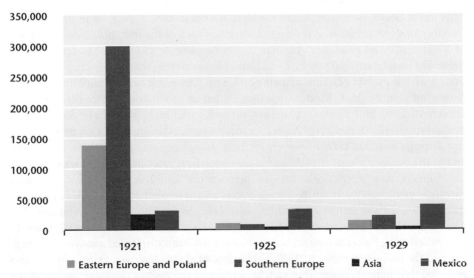

FIGURE 22.1 The impact of immigration restrictions Immigration restrictions in the 1920s, which targeted specific ethnic groups, drastically diminished the number of immigrants, from 805,000 in 1921 to 280,000 in 1929.

The passage of the National Origins Act also incited global protests. After 1924, Japanese Americans rightly feared they would remain targets of persecution in years to come. The anti-Asian sentiment of the Origins Act contributed to souring relations with Japan during the decades leading to World War II. Even more disturbing, the United States denied approximately 300,000 potential Jewish immigrants entry in the 1920s and 1930s, among them Jews who might have escaped the horrors of the coming Holocaust.

To the United States from China through Mexico

The only groups of immigrants to benefit from the 1924 restrictions were Mexicans and Latin Americans. Exempted from quotas, hundreds of thousands moved to the southwestern United States. During the early 1920s, approximately half a million Mexicans crossed the border. Many came to stay, becoming Mexican Americans rather than working as guest workers and returning home. With the support of both southwestern agribusiness and to some extent the Mexican government, approximately 800,000 Mexicans moved to the Southwest during the 1920s. By 1930, 1.4 million Mexicans resided in the United States. Although Mexicans legally entered the country, they often experienced humiliating measures not applied to European immigrants, having, for example, to strip and be deloused by immigration authorities.

Prior to 1920, the Mexican government, concerned with preserving the "cultural integrity" of Mexicans in the United States, established a network of consulates in the Southwest primarily to encourage return migration. Beginning in 1920, the consulates recognized that most emigrants planned to stay; they focused their attention on aiding Mexican Americans by sponsoring patriotic celebrations, organizing educational conferences, and advocating bilingual programs. The consuls also sought to capture migrants' dollars and loyalties partly because the new revolutionary regime of Mexican president Alvaro Obregon (1920–1924) recognized that its political legitimacy rested on how well it protected the inhabitants of what was termed "Mexico de afuera [Mexico abroad]."

"Sons of America," a Mexican-American community organization, Corpus Christi, TX (ca. 1929)

Although welcomed for their labor, these new permanent residents faced racial discrimination and anti-immigrant hostility. Mexican American children were sometimes segregated into special schools, and workers faced abrupt firings. Like African Americans in the South, they often found the legal system stacked against them. More subtle threats came from sympathetic Anglo-Americans such as the Pomona College "Friends of Mexicans," who promoted Americanization efforts. In cities such as Los Angeles, these new immigrants built vibrant and lasting communities that blended familiar traditions with the evolving culture of their new home. The result was a distinctive Mexican American identity. Most Mexican families settled in urban areas where their children attended school, built Catholic churches, formed social and political associations, and avidly supported role models of American success such as boxing sensation Bert Colima. But during the 1920s, fears of mass migration shaped popular perceptions, and by the end of the decade, "illegal aliens" had become popularly associated with "Mexicans."

Despite new restrictions, fear of immigrants' political radicalism continued throughout the 1920s. In 1920, **Nicola Sacco** and **Bartolomeo Vanzetti**, two Italian immigrants with anarchist sympathies, were arrested for killing two payroll clerks in Massachusetts the previous year. They were convicted in 1924 and sentenced to death. After their trial, Harvard Law School professor Felix Frankfurter led a movement questioning the judge's fairness. In 1927, as the date of their execution approached, it was revealed that Judge Webster Thayer, who sentenced the men to death, remarked at the time of their trial, "Did you see what I did with those anarchistic bastards the other day? I guess that will hold them for a while! Let them go to the Supreme Court now and see what they can get out of them!" Nevertheless, the Court denied their appeal and Sacco and Vanzetti were put to death. The execution of the two political radicals convicted in an obviously biased trial provoked demonstrations of outrage in the United States and around the world, including London, Paris, Tokyo, Buenos Aires, and Johannesburg.

The Ku Klux Klan

Racism merged with anti-immigrant sentiment in a revived **Ku Klux Klan (KKK)**. The Klan of the Reconstruction era resurfaced on a large scale in the 1920s with a new anti-immigrant, anti-Catholic, anti-Jewish message. Moreover, anti-urban and anti-modern, the Klan upheld what it deemed traditional values. The appearance in 1915 of a block-buster film about Reconstruction, *The Birth of a Nation,* helped spur the revival. The movie, a technical marvel of early cinema, depicted the Klan as a heroic organization saving civilization by rescuing white women from brutal, sex-crazed black men.

As one leader declared, the Klan opposed the "Jew, the [whiskey] Jug and the Jesuit" and claimed to be the defender of what it called "100 percent Americanism." Depicting Jews as dangerous radicals with an inordinate influence in banking and business, the Klan insisted that Catholics also threatened the nation, as the pope planned to take over the country, and it warned against the "rise of Catholic power." But the Klan also aimed its wrath more broadly at the larger revolution in manners and morals that marked the 1920s. Klansmen whipped or mutilated alleged bootleggers; adulterers, both white and black; wife beaters; abortionists; and those guilty of "race mixing."

The ranks of the Klan, restricted to native-born Protestants, swelled after 1920, more in the Midwest than in its original birthplace in the South. It even spawned imitators abroad. In Cuba, for example, a Ku Klux Klan Kubano arose to enforce segregation and "protect" white women. Dues and the sale of robes, hoods, and whips generated an estimated $75 million in profits for Klan leaders. White women formed the Women of

RACISM AND NATIVISM RESURFACE This ad for a KKK picnic and celebration in Girard, Illinois, in 1924 shows the support of local business "boosters" for this anti-Catholic, anti-Jewish, nativist organization.

the KKK. Motivated by many of the same fears as male members, Klan women advocated for the protection of "Pure Womanhood" and "the sanctity of the American home."

Klan membership peaked in 1925 at about five million. That year 40,000 robed members paraded down Washington's Pennsylvania Avenue. Their visibility and tactics provoked an anti-Klan backlash. Angered by the Klan's bigotry, a coalition of Catholic and Jewish leaders and civil libertarians organized to oppose its activities. Klan membership hemorrhaged in the final years of the decade, shaken by scandal. The Grand Dragon of Indiana committed a series of highly publicized sexual assaults; additional cases of assault, drunkenness, and financial fraud undermined the group's credibility. The passage of the 1924 quota bill, which ended most immigration from southern and eastern Europe, deprived the Klan of its major issue. Fears of labor violence and communism also faded as the prosperity of the middle 1920s spread.

STUDY QUESTIONS FOR SEXUAL, RACIAL, AND ETHNIC DIVIDES

quiz

1. How did women's lives change during the 1920s? How did their lives remain the same?
2. How and why did New York City become the capital of a black Atlantic world during the 1920s?
3. What were the immediate sources of the National Origins Act?
4. What challenges did Mexican immigrants face in the 1920s?

A NATIONAL CULTURE: AT HOME AND ABROAD

The Harlem Renaissance and Pan-Africanism reflected just one aspect of a broader cultural awakening. News traveled fast in the 1920s, and new means of communication hastened the spread of a national culture. Across the country people attended the same movies, read the same books, followed the same sports teams, and cheered the same instant heroes. The new technologies of radio and the movies helped spread U.S. culture around the globe. Especially in Europe, Asia, and the Western Hemisphere, new media fortified people's ideas of the United States as a huge, rich land. The new culture may have been highly popular, but many Americans were dismayed by the new trends. Some religious people expressed disappointment and outrage at what they considered to be the immorality of the modern age.

Popular Entertainment: Movies, Sports, and Celebrity

Interest in popular entertainment rose to unprecedented levels in the 1920s. By the end of the decade, movies were the fifth-largest industry in the nation. Each week nearly as many Americans attended movies as lived in the entire country. Movie theaters, occupying lavish spaces, offered prestige, glamour, and comfort to moviegoers, all at an affordable price. The 1927 film *The Jazz Singer* marked the greatest technological breakthrough of the decade as the first "talkie" with extended dialogue.

Many movies of the 1920s reflected the tensions of the "new era." As films provided a glimpse into the lives of the rich and famous, Hollywood soon began to shape national and international perceptions about fashion, etiquette, morals, and success. The movies' portrayal of wealth and high fashion may have had an even greater impact on people's ideas of American life around the globe than it did in the United States. At home, at least, people could compare their own rather ordinary lives to the images on the screen. They enjoyed the fantasy, but they knew it was just that, an unrealistic depiction of life. Internationally, American movies offered a tantalizing glimpse of a rich land populated with beautiful people wrapped in finery. Westerns and romances featuring beautiful young city dwellers proved especially popular abroad.

Movie idol **Rudolph Valentino**, one of film's first male sex symbols and international stars, epitomized shifting moral values and tastes. Born Rodolfo Alfonso Raffaello Piero Filiberto Guglielmi in Italy, he arrived in New York in 1913, changed his name to Rudolph Valentino, and soon appeared in bit parts in Hollywood gangster movies. His dark complexion, coal black eyes, and slicked-black hair stood in sharp contrast to the country's fair-skinned, light-haired standards of male beauty. In 1921, he starred in *The Sheik* as a half-Arab, half-European who abducts and seduces an adventurous Englishwoman.

Rudolph Valentino movie poster (1926)

Not everyone appreciated the effect cinema's popularity had on traditional values. Facing pressure from conservative groups, in 1921, the movie studios appointed Postmaster General Will Hays to censor their films. Hays prohibited risqué content on the screen and monitored appropriate behavior for actors and actresses off the screen.

An unparalleled interest in sports skyrocketed several athletes into superstardom during the 1920s. **Babe Ruth** of the New York Yankees established himself as a larger-than-life figure as fans flocked to professional baseball games. Hitting 60 home runs during the Yankees' dominant 1927 season, the "Sultan of Swat" set a record that would stand for over 30 years. His gregarious personality off the field likewise endeared him to fans. Professional football player Harold "Red" Grange, boxer Jack Dempsey, tennis player William Tilden, and golfer Bobby Jones likewise drew millions of fans during the decade.

Huge crowds turned out for college football games. To the dismay of those who worried that too much attention to athletics would sidetrack the academic mission of higher education, several universities—including Yale, Ohio State, and Stanford—began building stadiums that held 60,000 people or more. By the end of the decade, more fans attended college football games than professional baseball games. With more leisure time on their hands and money in their pockets, many sought to emulate their favorite athletes by participating in sports as well as by watching them. For example, by 1927, the United States had approximately 5,000 golf courses and two million players.

The 1920s was also a decade of instant celebrity. No one symbolized the spirit of the new era better than the boyishly handsome 25-year-old **Charles Lindbergh**, who collected a $25,000 prize for being the first aviator to fly solo across the Atlantic Ocean in 1927. Radio reporters breathlessly announced every minute of his 33-hour flight from Long Island to Paris in May of that year, and he became an international hero. Millions turned out for a ticker-tape parade down New York's Fifth Avenue in honor of "the Lone Eagle." This outpouring of pride in U.S. technical prowess and individual derring-do was the largest mass assembly since the New York victory parade had welcomed the doughboys home from the Great War in 1919. As a goodwill ambassador, Lindbergh, or

Hollywood Sells America to the World

In October 1923, Will H. Hays, head of the newly formed Motion Pictures Producers and Distributors of America, stated, "We are going to sell America to the world with American motion pictures." By the mid-1920s, Hollywood dominated the global film industry, with its films saturating markets in Europe, Latin America, and Asia, often making up 75 to 90 percent of movie releases around the world. Hollywood movies had so invaded world culture that the London *Morning Post* noted, "If the United States abolished its diplomatic and consular services, kept its ships in harbor and its tourists at home, and retired from the world's markets, its citizens, its problems, its towns and countryside, its roads, its motor cars, counting houses and saloons would still be familiar in the uttermost corners of the world. The film is to America what the flag was once to Britain."

World War I greatly hampered the European film industry, and Hollywood stepped into the breach. Like many other U.S. industries in the 1920s, the movie industry targeted global markets. The U.S. government, through both the State and Commerce departments, supported Hollywood's efforts, realizing the potential to portray American culture to the rest of the world. Movies proved to be powerful advertisements for products, fashions, and fads. An industry spokesman likened movies to "an animated catalogue for ideas of dress, of living, of comfort." Movies spurred orders for American cars, clothes, furniture, and appliances all over the world. For example, Brazilian imports of a stylish American car increased by 35 percent after it appeared in a popular film. Movies, an industry executive boasted in 1928, "may be called the most important and significant of America's exported products."

But many world leaders pushed back against Hollywood's "Americanization." They viewed American films as a destructive force that annihilated their own cultures.

"Lucky Lindy," as he was called, promoted U.S. aviation around the world. Lindbergh's reputation suffered a severe blow in the late 1930s when he sympathized with Nazi Germany and opposed American entry into World War II.

The New Skepticism

Despite the general prosperity of the 1920s, not all Americans considered the United States a happy home. Some lost faith in traditional values and grew alienated after the experience of World War I. Many writers and artists fled to Europe, especially France, where they hoped to live a more authentic existence. Other intellectuals remained in the United States but wrote scathing critiques of what they saw as the emptiness of mainstream, middle-class American culture.

Many of the intellectuals who left the United States for Europe in the 1920s, the so-called Lost Generation, had become disillusioned with society and ideas of progress. In his 1929 book *A Farewell to Arms*, **Ernest Hemingway** wrote, "The war annihilated all reason, virtue, and human compassion." Additionally, Hemingway and those who joined him in Paris, most notably **F. Scott Fitzgerald**, found life in the United States stifling, puritanical, driven by big business, and full of hypocrisy. In Paris, they directly challenged those values, enjoyed a less inhibited lifestyle, partied, and began writing

Some expressed horror at the widespread adoption of American hairstyles, clothing, and slang, especially among young people. A British official blamed the decline of the "King's English" on American movies. Moreover, many European governments feared that Hollywood movies undercut their hold on their colonies, as movies, they argued, often mocked white authority figures. Finally, many movies reinforced negative ethnic stereotypes. The Mexican government protested the common portrayal of Mexicans as villains and briefly barred U.S. films. China excluded *Welcome Danger* (1929) for its depiction of Chinatown residents as gamblers and opium smugglers. After the release of *Scarface* in 1932, Italy's ambassador to the United States complained about the film's representation of Italians as inherently criminal and violent. In response, filmmakers created more generic "foreigners" and promoted characters such as Dracula, who, according to a film executive, "is not really a human being so he cannot conceivably cause trouble."

In addition to protesting the influence of Hollywood films and in an attempt to protect their own film industries, Germany, Great Britain, and France all created quota systems to restrict the number of American movies that could be imported. But these systems soon collapsed as U.S. filmmakers bought into the flagging European film companies and produced cheap, low-quality "quota films" that were seldom even released. The global impact of Hollywood, a process begun in the 1920s, continues to this day.

- Why did the federal government support and encourage the American film industry's distribution of movies abroad?
- What criticisms did foreign governments direct at the U.S. film industry? How did filmmakers respond?

some of the decade's most influential works. African American writers also fled to Paris, joining black musicians and performers. Langston Hughes, **Claude McKay**, and **Nella Larsen** carried the Harlem Renaissance overseas, deeply influenced by the city's innovative spirit and racial tolerance.

The 1920s were also a time of great artistic creativity in the United States. In 1920, **Sinclair Lewis** began the charge by attacking small-town life in *Main Street*. His incisive criticism of the bigotry and shallowness of middle-class America struck a chord, and the novel became a national bestseller. In 1922, Lewis followed with *Babbitt*, an even greater success that satirized business culture. F. Scott Fitzgerald also addressed the hollow lifestyle of the rich in *The Great Gatsby* (1925).

Excerpt from Sinclair Lewis, *Babbitt* (1922)

The loudest voice of social criticism during the 1920s came from Baltimore-based journalist **H. L. Mencken**. In 1924, he launched *American Mercury*, a magazine that served as the vehicle for Mencken's piercing attacks on rural life, popular culture, religion, democracy, politicians, and the "booboisie." Mencken coined the derogatory moniker "Monkey Trial" for the Scopes evolution trial in Dayton, Tennessee, in 1925 (see following) and led the charge of journalists there to create a circus-like atmosphere. He was especially popular among college students, who imitated his irreverence. One Harvard student remarked: "The *American Mercury* was our Bible, and Mencken our God."

Religion and Society

Early in the 20th century, as the nation became more urban, industrial, and commercial, old religious patterns frayed. Especially after 1890, millions of Catholic, Eastern Orthodox, and Jewish immigrants from eastern and southern Europe brought new religious traditions to America. In the 1920s, Protestants debated how to respond to the new industrial order with its extremes of wealth and poverty and to the waves of immigrants professing new faiths.

Broadly speaking, Protestant denominations split into two groups, often called **Modernists** and **Fundamentalists**. Modernists, influenced by the Social Gospel movement of the late 19th century as well as Darwin's theory of evolution and archaeological discoveries, believed Christianity should respond positively to new knowledge and social conditions. Fundamentalists, in contrast, interpreted the Bible literally and rejected the notion that traditional faith should enter a dialogue with science and popular culture. They saw the Bible as the only path to truth and a bulwark against a corrupt, mostly urban, world. Fundamentalists condemned alcohol, tobacco, Hollywood films, and much of popular culture as sinful and subversive of traditional values.

Fundamentalist ministers, such as **Aimee Semple McPherson**, achieved fame and large followings in the 1920s by employing new technologies, such as radio and film. "Sister Aimee" became an international celebrity, opening Angelus Temple in Los Angeles, an early "megachurch" that accommodated 5,000 followers. She preached good times ahead for those who accepted Jesus, whom she presented as a real person whose love could solve all problems. Thousands claimed to have been cured of disease and disabilities by McPherson. Sister Aimee also broadcasted her sermons over her own radio station, KFSG, heard throughout the West as well as Mexico and Canada. She traveled around the country in her "gospel car" and flew from city to city by airplane. She also invoked faith to justify a political agenda, including tighter immigration laws and strict enforcement of Prohibition.

Fundamentalism also impacted education. In the summer of 1925, a prosecutor in Tennessee indicted a high school science teacher, **John Scopes**, for violating a state law that barred teaching "any theory that denies the story of the divine creation of man as taught in the Bible and teaches instead that man has descended from a lower order of animals." The World Christian Fundamentals Association recruited William Jennings Bryan as a special prosecutor for the **Scopes Trial**. Bryan feared that irreligion, symbolized by evolution, threatened the soul of America. The people of Tennessee, he argued, through their legislature had decreed what could and could not be taught. Scientists had no right to question that decision. In response, Clarence Darrow, America's most prominent trial lawyer, volunteered to head the defense team. An avowed agnostic, he represented the urbane, worldly, sophisticated type that infuriated fundamentalists.

After the judge barred testimony from scientists, a frustrated Darrow called Bryan to testify as a biblical authority. On the stand, Bryan defended the Bible's accounts of creation and miracles despite many apparent lapses and contradictions in the text. Regardless, the jury took only nine minutes to convict Scopes, who was fined $100. The state supreme court later overturned the conviction on a technicality.

Although fundamentalists took heart in the initial verdict, Bryan was left a broken man who died soon after. The national press, led by H. L. Mencken, portrayed Bryan and his supporters as small-minded, ignorant "boobs." Urbanites and college students gleefully repeated Mencken's jibes, whereas rural southerners deeply resented being the butt of jokes. Several European reporters covering the trial made it an international sensation.

Excerpts from H. L. Mencken's coverage of the Scopes Trial (1925)

Prohibition

Conflicts over the prohibition of alcohol became another flashpoint of the cultural divisions of the 1920s. The Eighteenth Amendment, which went into effect in January 1920, forbade the "manufacture, sale or transportation" of intoxicating liquors. Although Prohibition put neighborhood saloons out of business, illegal "speakeasies" flourished. Nevertheless, "drys" defended Prohibition for driving down the rate of alcohol consumption. "Wets" countered that Prohibition drove drinking underground and penalized those unable to afford the high prices charged by speakeasies. Prohibition also, they argued, encouraged the consumption of hard liquor over beer and wine and promoted the rise of organized crime and violent criminals such as Al Capone, who supplied booze to a thirsty public.

Despite the controversy, Prohibition grew into an international movement. Several Canadian provinces restricted the consumption of alcohol at roughly the same time as the United States, but cries for repeal arose more quickly there. Prohibition also changed U.S. relations with its neighbors. Tourists flocked to Cuba to patronize casinos and brothels owned by American gangsters and well stocked with liquor. Mexico and Canada became sources for smuggled whiskey. The province of Ontario, as well as Quebec, which did not ban alcohol, became major suppliers of Canadian whiskey.

PROHIBITION RAID New York City deputy police commissioner John A. Leach watches agents pour liquor into a sewer following a raid during Prohibition.

Distilleries north of the border produced liquor that was smoother tasting and not as physically harmful as some of the deadly concoctions made by American bootleggers.

Americans remained sharply divided over Prohibition throughout the 1920s. Many Protestants supported what they called the "noble" or "great social experiment," whereas most Catholics and Jews condemned it as an assault on their culture and personal liberty. Republicans, along with many southern and western Democrats, generally supported Prohibition. Drys often identified with the anti-immigrant, anti-Catholic, anti-Semitic, anti-Hollywood views of groups like the Ku Klux Klan. Northern Democrats, exemplified by New York governor **Al Smith**, bitterly opposed both Prohibition and nativism.

By 1928, Prohibition had become an intensely partisan issue. The northern, urban wing of the Democratic Party, led by its presidential nominee, Al Smith, supported repeal of the Eighteenth Amendment. Republican Herbert Hoover defended Prohibition as a "noble experiment" and won the presidential election. But in 1933, the new Democratic president, Franklin D. Roosevelt, mobilized Congress and the states to repeal Prohibition.

STUDY QUESTIONS FOR A NATIONAL CULTURE: AT HOME AND ABROAD

quiz

1. How did new forms of mass entertainment help create a national culture?
2. On what grounds did some authors and religious Fundamentalists criticize American society in the 1920s? How and why did prominent authors and religious Fundamentalists agree or disagree?

POST–WORLD WAR I POLITICS AND FOREIGN POLICY

Even as they embraced controversial new modes of cultural expression, Americans sought a return to placidity in politics. Republican presidential candidates won three consecutive elections in the 1920s with promises of reversing Progressive reforms, promoting the interests of business, and advancing the fortunes of what the last of them, Herbert Hoover, called "rugged individualism." In the aftermath of the presidential election of 1920 Americans turned their back on Woodrow Wilson's vision of a peaceful world with the United States leading the League of Nations. Although the United States did not join the League, it remained an active, albeit independent, world power throughout the 1920s. The promotion of international trade became a major government initiative. The United States also worked to stabilize the international economy in the wake of the destruction of the Great War. By slowly moving away from the interventionist policies and military occupations of the early 20th century, the United States also sought to improve relations with the people of the Western Hemisphere.

Government and Business in the 1920s

In the presidential election of 1920, Ohio Republican senator Warren Harding faced a fellow Ohioan, Democratic governor **James M. Cox**. Harding ran a "front porch campaign" in which celebrities visited his home in Marion, Ohio. Silent films showed him joking with movie stars Al Jolson and Mary Pickford, industrialist Henry Ford, and inventor Thomas Edison. Voters appreciated his promise of "less government in business and more business in government." He mocked Woodrow Wilson for offering "nostrums," or fraudulent remedies, with his plans for international reform, as he promised to return the country to "normalcy." Harding won easily. He captured 16.1 million votes (60.1 percent) and 404 electoral votes, whereas Cox gained only 9.1 million votes (34.1 percent) and 116 electoral votes. Socialist candidate Eugene V. Debs, imprisoned since 1919 for opposing the draft during the war, won 914,000 votes (3.4 percent).

Harding, a friendly, handsome man, enjoyed the company of his buddies over cards and whiskey, a practice he continued during Prohibition. He had little knowledge of or interest in the details of public policy. He began his administration with some surprises. He disappointed conservatives by commuting the sentence of Socialist leader Debs. He appointed some talented cabinet secretaries. **Henry A. Wallace**, the former editor of an Iowa farm magazine read by millions in rural America, became secretary of agriculture and developed programs to lessen the effect of a farm depression. **Andrew Mellon**, of a prominent Pittsburgh banking family, became secretary of the treasury. **Charles Evans Hughes**, former Supreme Court justice and the 1916 Republican presidential candidate, served as an active and accomplished secretary of state. Herbert Hoover, who had achieved international fame and gratitude for organizing food relief for Belgium and Russia during and after the Great War, was secretary of commerce.

The thievery and corruption of hundreds of Harding's other appointments, however, quickly overshadowed the achievements of more talented and ethical cabinet members. In the summer of 1923, as Congress prepared to investigate corruption in high places, Harding sought relief by taking a trip to Alaska. He fell ill on the return voyage and died in San Francisco on August 2.

In 1924, congressional investigations and criminal indictments revealed the broad extent of corruption in the Harding administration. Attorney General Harry Daugherty was accused of taking bribes and offering protection to bootleggers. Interior Secretary Albert Fall, an old Senate friend of Harding's, accepted bribes of $400,000 in return for granting lucrative secret leases to private oil companies on government-owned land in California and Wyoming. The episode became known as the **Teapot Dome scandal**, after the Wyoming property. Fall was fined $100,000 and went to prison for one year.

Coolidge Prosperity

Harding's successor, **Calvin Coolidge**, had won his place on the 1920 Republican ticket by breaking the Boston police strike of 1919 when he was governor of Massachusetts. Highly unpopular with the public, the strike led to fears of increased crime and anarchist activity. Coolidge, like Harding, relied on Treasury Secretary Mellon and Commerce Secretary Hoover to promote the interests of large corporations and expand the economy. Mellon encouraged Congress to lower income taxes, especially for the rich, and balance the federal budget. Mellon and Hoover also advocated high tariffs to protect domestic manufacturers. In 1922, Congress enacted the Fordney–McCumber Tariff, which made it harder for overseas manufacturers to export their products to the United States.

Hoover energetically promoted American business at home and abroad. The Commerce Department helped form trade associations, collected vast amounts of data, and sponsored conferences of business leaders across the country. Hoover also assigned hundreds of commercial attachés to U.S. embassies and consulates abroad to promote American products in countries as far away as Malaya and Iran, China, Brazil, and

Argentina. American money amounting to $12 billion—a combination of purchases of foreign goods, money sent to relatives abroad, tourism, investments in foreign firms, and overseas lending—also flowed overseas in the 1920s. In the world's industrial economies, American firms created local subsidiaries to market cars, electrical equipment, and processed food, and U.S. oil companies sold their products to car owners around the globe. U.S. mining and petroleum companies extracted raw materials in Latin America, Asia, and the Middle East.

Republican Coolidge sought election in his own right in 1924 on a platform of "Coolidge Prosperity," as Democrats collapsed into disarray. The southern wing of the Democratic Party supported former treasury secretary William Gibbs McAdoo, Woodrow Wilson's son-in-law. The southerners, along with McAdoo and many midwestern Democrats, supported Prohibition and white supremacy. Many had ties to the Ku Klux Klan, which the convention refused to condemn. Northeastern delegates to the Democratic National Convention supported New York governor Al Smith, a Catholic son of Irish immigrants who advocated the repeal of the Eighteenth Amendment. Deadlocked after an unprecedented 103 ballots, delegates settled on a compromise candidate, **John W. Davis**, a Wall Street lawyer.

The fall election was a three-way race among Coolidge, Davis, and Wisconsin Republican senator Robert La Follette, who ran as a candidate of a newly reconstituted Progressive Party. Coolidge easily won the election with 16 million votes (54 percent) and 382 electoral votes to Davis's 8.3 million votes (28 percent) and 136 electoral votes. La Follette tallied 4.8 million votes (16.6 percent) and 13 electoral votes, primarily from Democrats disillusioned with the chaos and conservative drift of their own party.

Coolidge Prosperity continued through 1928, although wealth was spread unevenly. Urban laborers and farmers suffered through lean times. Unions had trouble recruiting members in the face of stiff opposition from industry and the courts. Prices for farm products fell throughout the decade. Deeply indebted farmers tried to recover by growing more crops and raising more animals, which only drove prices down further. In 1927 and 1928, Congress offered relief by passing the **McNary–Haugen Acts**. These laws required the government to support crop prices by buying basic farm commodities. Coolidge vetoed both bills as unwarranted government interference in the economy.

The Election of 1928

In 1928, Coolidge announced, "I do not choose to run" for president. The Republicans then nominated Commerce Secretary Herbert Hoover, popular for his work in the Commerce Department. His 1922 book *American Individualism* explained how business leaders should foster "welfare capitalism," voluntary cooperation between business and labor. Hoover enhanced his status as a decisive leader ready to deploy the resources of the federal government by organizing relief for victims of the Great Mississippi Flood of 1927. Incessant rains in late 1926 caused the Mississippi River to flood parts of six states. Seven hundred thousand poor farmers, nearly half of them African Americans, fled to 154 hastily constructed relief camps. Taking charge of organizing the relief efforts in the camps, Hoover won praise for his effective action.

Hoover faced New York governor Al Smith in the election. The Democrats' battles over the Klan and Prohibition were over, and Smith easily won the nomination, becoming the first Roman Catholic to run for president. Urban residents, immigrants, Jews, and Catholics shared Smith's opposition to Prohibition and enthusiastically supported his candidacy. But their backing was not enough to overcome widespread public satisfaction with the country's prosperity and widespread anti-Catholic sentiment. Some of Smith's critics charged that he would take orders from the pope, who would move his headquarters from Vatican City to the United States if Smith were elected. Hoover won an overwhelming victory with 58 percent of the vote and 444 electoral votes to Smith's 41 percent and 87 electoral votes (Map 22.3).

Independent Internationalism in the 1920s

Despite the Senate's rejection of the Versailles Treaty and League of Nations in 1919, government and business retained a keen interest in foreign affairs. Disarmament was one international reform that survived into the Republican era. An arms race among naval powers active in the western Pacific threatened the peace. The arms buildup was also extremely costly and threatened to disrupt Treasury Secretary Andrew Mellon's plans to balance the federal budget. In 1921, Secretary of State Charles Evans Hughes convened an international conference on naval disarmament to determine the future of East Asia. It met from November 1921 to February 1922. The three treaties in which the conference culminated, maintained the territorial status quo in East Asia and set limits on the size of the navies of the United States, Great Britain, Japan, France, and Italy.

A peace movement also gained strength in the 1920s. The Women's International League for Peace and Freedom founded by reformer Jane Addams during World War I pressed for disarmament and the end to all wars. Universities across the country

Candidate (Party)	Electoral Vote (%)	Popular Vote (%)
Hoover (Republican)	444 (82%)	21,391,993 (58%)
Smith (Democratic)	87 (17%)	15,016,169 (41%)
Thomas (Socialist)		267,835 (1%)
Minor parties		62,890 (-)

MAP 22.3 Presidential Election of 1928 Republican Herbert Hoover won a landslide victory over his Democratic opponent Al Smith, as voters continued to place their trust in Republican presidents who presided over the economic boom of the 1920s.

introduced courses in international relations, many of which were devoted to explaining the causes of the Great War and exploring ways to avoid future armed conflicts. When the Columbia University professor of international law James T. Shotwell won an essay prize with a proposal to declare war illegal, Secretary of State Frank Kellogg (1925–1929) embraced the idea. Kellogg saw it as a way for the United States to tactfully decline urgent requests from France for a military alliance. In 1928, Kellogg proposed to French foreign minister Aristide Briand that the two nations agree to outlaw war instead of signing the formal alliance France had requested. In August 1928, the United States and France promised not to use war as an instrument of national policy, and they invited other nations to join them. Most countries worldwide signed the **Kellogg–Briand Pact**, although many officials remained skeptical of its effectiveness. Although the pact did not prevent the outbreak of future war, Americans later opposed German, Italian, and Japanese aggression during World War II based on their violations of the Kellogg–Briand treaty.

American bankers cooperated with the Coolidge administration to minimize the hardships caused by the Great War. The Allies owed the United States approximately $10 billion in addition to interest for war loans. They delayed repaying the Americans until Germany paid its reparations of over $100 billion. But Germany considered the bill too high and refused to pay. France, a major recipient of reparations, responded by sending soldiers to occupy the German industrial territory of the Ruhr. As a result, Germany's economy collapsed in an unprecedented wave of inflation. In the summer of 1923, a loaf of German bread sold for one billion marks. Worthless money and life's savings gone in an instant embittered millions of middle-class Germans. Coolidge appointed a commission of three American bankers to help restart German payments, which would in turn encourage European repayments on American war loans. The **Dawes Plan**, named after Charles Dawes, the chairman of the commission, provided a $110 million loan from private American banks to Germany. With Germany's currency stabilized, reparations and repayment of American war loans resumed. American firms invested heavily in Europe, fueling the continent's recovery from the war. In 1929, Owen Young, another American banker, sponsored a plan to further reduce Germany's reparations payments. It seemed as if cooperation between the American government and U.S. banks had returned prosperity to Europe. But the economic expansion rested on continued American loans and transatlantic trade. The Great Depression, which began in the fall of 1929 and dried up lending and international commerce, destroyed hopes for prosperity built on the partnership of government officials and private bankers.

The United States and Instability in the Western Hemisphere

Republican presidents of the 1920s backed away from justifications made earlier in the century for U.S. intervention in the Western Hemisphere to contain destabilizing nationalist revolutions. Still, the U.S. government remained committed to maintaining preeminence in the Western Hemisphere and to promoting the interests of private U.S. business and investors.

Faced with growing hostility to military interventions at home and abroad, the United States gradually ended its occupations of countries in Central America and the Caribbean. In 1924, after the U.S. Navy trained a local National Guard, the Coolidge administration withdrew the military from the Dominican Republic. But next door to the Dominican Republic in Haiti, American Marines continued their occupation throughout the 1920s. U.S. forces trained the Haitian National Guard and built roads, bridges, schools, and power stations. Cruelly mistreating the Haitians, they introduced racial segregation and favored the lighter-skinned mulatto elite over the darker-skinned majority. In 1919, Haitians resisted American efforts to press them into chain gangs, and the Marines began a counterinsurgency war that killed over 2,000 Haitians. Street protests erupted again in 1929, and in 1934, President Franklin D. Roosevelt finally withdrew the last of the American forces from Haiti.

The United States also moved haltingly to end the occupation of Nicaragua begun in 1910. Senator Robert La Follette's Progressive Party demanded the withdrawal of U.S. troops from Nicaragua during the election campaign of 1924, and the next year Coolidge withdrew American forces. In 1926, however, a civil war erupted between the Conservative Party, which supported the Catholic Church, and the anti-clerical Liberal Party. The United States sent 5,000 Marines back to Nicaragua, along with former secretary of war Henry Stimson, who arranged a peace agreement among the factions. The Marines supervised elections in 1928, 1930, and 1932. The Liberal Party then split into two factions. One, led by General **Cesar Augusto Sandino**, denounced Stimson's peace plan as an attempt to impose Yankee control. Sandino led several thousand guerrillas into the hills to conduct a war against another Liberal Party general, **Anastasio Somoza**, the commander of the U.S.-trained National Guard. In January 1933, President Hoover removed the last of the U.S. Marines. Shortly thereafter, Somoza and his family began a 45-year-long dictatorship.

In Mexico, the United States reached an uneasy understanding with new leaders. American mining and petroleum companies insisted that the Harding administration demand that Mexico compensate them for raw materials leases it had confiscated from U.S. mining and petroleum companies. In 1923, Mexico agreed to acknowledge the right of exploration by U.S. firms on land leased before Mexico adopted its 1917 constitution. But in 1925, Mexican president Plutarco Calles renounced the 1923 agreement because it placed over half of Mexico's petroleum in the hands of U.S. firms. Coolidge named Dwight Morrow, an old college friend and a banking partner of J. P. Morgan, as the U.S. ambassador to Mexico. In 1928, Morrow negotiated a 10-year deal with Mexico recognizing the ownership rights of U.S. oil companies to land acquired before 1917 and acknowledging their leases of oil fields acquired after 1917.

Latin American nations mounted pressure on the United States to renounce its policy of unilateral intervention in the Western Hemisphere. In 1930, the State Department adopted a memorandum on the Monroe Doctrine. The memorandum repudiated President Theodore Roosevelt's 1904 corollary to the Monroe Doctrine. It stated that neither the Monroe Doctrine nor international law authorized unilateral military intervention in the Western Hemisphere. Although the United States did not end military interventions, after 1930, Washington regularly sought the agreement of other countries in the region before sending troops.

Excerpt from the Clark Memorandum on the Monroe Doctrine (1928)

STUDY QUESTIONS FOR POST–WORLD WAR I POLITICS AND FOREIGN POLICY

1. Why were Republican presidents and their policies popular in the 1920s?

2. What was "independent internationalism"?

3. How did the growing U.S. role in the global economy shape U.S. foreign policy in the 1920s?

quiz

◆ THE CRASH

President Herbert Hoover took office in a buoyant mood on March 4, 1929. The world and the American economy seemed on a path toward permanent prosperity. He proclaimed in his inaugural address, "We have reached a higher degree of comfort and security than ever existed before in the history of the world." Yet the prosperity of the 1920s was built on sand. Debts that never could be repaid piled up across the globe. The safety and even existence of banks in New York, London, and Paris, the major financial centers of the day, depended on dubious projects that they had financed. By the end of 1929, the world had plunged downward into the Great Depression, the worst economic catastrophe of the modern era. The Depression spread to every corner of the country, wrecking lives and leaving people homeless, hungry, and desperate for work.

The End of the Boom

The 1920s seemed to many people to be an era of limitless economic opportunities. One and a half million Americans invested in the stock market in the 1920s, and millions more invested indirectly as banks put their deposits into stocks. Prices soared in 1928. General Motors rose 75 points on the stock exchange in two months. RCA stock was at 85 at the beginning of 1928; at the end of the year, it reached 420 and sold for $505 a share. Many people bought stock on "margin," putting down 10 percent of the purchase price and borrowing the rest from brokerage houses. Banks bought stock, and companies loaned banks money to buy more. When prices rose, people thought they were making money. However, if stock prices fell, borrowers could not pay off their loans with their stock. But few foresaw a stock market crash, and companies issued more and more shares to take advantage of ever-rising stock prices. Minimal government regulation allowed companies to issue shares with no underlying value; they were not required to certify the financial worthiness of investment holding companies or of banks that owned stock in major companies.

The Florida land boom and bust provided a foretaste of the catastrophe awaiting Wall Street in 1929. Cheap land, warm weather, and zealous promoters encouraged real estate developers to invest heavily in the Sunshine State in the early 1920s. Entrepreneurs promoted it as a vacation destination and for investors looking to get rich off its new popularity. Most investors simply intended to resell their property for a profit. Thousands of people paid increasingly outlandish sums for "fifty feet in paradise." Speculation caught up with Florida by 1926. Investors discovered to their chagrin that much of the land they had bought was swampland or permanently underwater. Many began pulling their money out of the state. The cost of living also skyrocketed after a devastating hurricane in September 1926.

In addition to irresponsible speculation, income disparities and rampant use of credit also destabilized the economy. In the 1920s, the income of the wealthiest 1 percent of Americans doubled, while the income of the bottom third rose only 6 percent. Income tax cuts returned money to the wealthy but did little for the middle class or the poor. Although rich Americans could keep on buying washing machines, refrigerators, radios, and cars, the bottom two-thirds found themselves stretched to the limit. By 1929, U.S. factories, like farms, were guilty of overproduction. Manufacturers cut prices and then reduced their output. They laid off workers, who in turn cut back on their purchases. Borrowers stopped paying their consumer loans, leaving banks and stores with millions in bad debt.

Imbalances in international trade and finance intensified the economic strains of 1928 and 1929. High tariffs in the United States barred many European manufacturers from the American market. Europeans borrowed from American banks to pay reparations and war debts. They tried to expand their domestic markets and forgo imports. As American industry and agriculture found it harder and harder to sell abroad, surpluses of American goods and farm products increased.

The Great Depression

Wild speculation, inequities of wealth, massive consumer borrowing, lax government regulation, international trade barriers, and excessive international lending culminated in a perfect storm on Wall Street. Stock prices hit a peak in September 1929 and then drifted lower. On Thursday, October 24, prices fell sharply in the morning. At noon, bankers met at the offices of J. P. Morgan and announced they would step in to buy shares that afternoon, and prices stabilized. But on Monday, October 28, prices fell again, and then on "**Black Tuesday**," October 29, the bottom dropped out of the market. Everyone wanted out, as banks and brokerage houses demanded the sale of stock to pay off margin debt. By the end of the day, 16 million shares, three times the normal number, had traded hands. The stock market ticker, the record of trades, fell hours behind. All the gains of 1929 had been wiped out. By the end of November, stock prices had fallen to half of what they had been at their height.

By 1930, people began to talk of a major economic depression. In 1929, the unemployment rate was a low 3.2 percent, but it shot up to 8.7 percent the following year. Government policies made the Depression worse. Secretary of the Treasury Mellon thought the downward economic spiral would correct itself. "Liquidate labor, liquidate stocks, liquidate the farmers, liquidate real estate," he advised. "It will purge the rottenness out of the system."

The **Smoot–Hawley Tariff of 1930** made it even harder for international manufacturers to sell products in the United States. When other countries raised their tariffs in retaliation, the volume of international trade dropped from $2.9 billion in 1929 to $2.1 billion in 1930 to $1.6 billion in 1931. The Federal Reserve made matters worse by raising interest rates and shrinking the money supply, devastating the nation's banks. More than 1,600 banks failed during 1930 alone, and millions of homeowners lost their houses to foreclosure. Hoover tried to arrest the slide by encouraging voluntary actions to relieve the suffering of the unemployed. He insisted that "the fundamental business of the country . . . is on a sound and prosperous basis." But by 1931, few Americans believed the president, and there was a widespread fear that this economic downturn would be worse than any previous one.

STUDY QUESTIONS FOR THE CRASH

1. What caused the Great Depression?

2. What made the early years of the Depression so severe?

quiz

interactive timeline

TIMELINE 1920–1930

AMERICA	YEAR	THE WORLD
Jan Eighteenth Amendment begins Prohibition **Aug** First International Convention of the Universal Negro Improvement Association **Nov** KDKA makes first commercial radio broadcast	**1920**	**Aug** Mahatma Gandhi begins movement to boycott all British goods
Oct *The Sheik* is released, starring Rudolph Valentino **Nov** The Washington Naval Conference begins; conference ends in February with treaties reducing naval arms and recognizing China's borders	**1921**	
Sep Publication of Sinclair Lewis's *Babbitt* **Sep** Fordney–McCumber Tariff raises duties on imports	**1922**	**Oct** Benito Mussolini and Fascists seize control of Italian government **Dec** Union of Soviet Socialist Republics (USSR) officially established
Aug President Warren Harding dies; succeeded by Calvin Coolidge	**1923**	**Oct** Modern Turkey founded as a republic **Nov** Inflation in Germany hits 1 million percent Adolf Hitler arrested and imprisoned after "Beer Hall Putsch," Nazis' failed attempt to seize Munich government
Jan First issue of the *American Mercury*, edited by H. L. Mencken **Jan–May** Teapot Dome Scandal reveals corruption in Harding administration **Apr** Dawes Plan created to reduce Germany's reparation payments **May** National Origins Act sets immigration quotas **May** Formation of U.S. Border Patrol **Nov** Calvin Coolidge elected president	**1924**	
Apr Publication of F. Scott Fitzgerald's novel *The Great Gatsby* **Jul** Scopes Trial in Dayton, Tennessee, reveals deep division between Christian Fundamentalists and Modernists over Charles Darwin's theory of evolution **Aug** 40,000 Ku Klux Klansmen march in Washington **Aug** Withdrawal of U.S. Marines from Nicaragua	**1925**	**Jul** Volume 1 of Hitler's *Mein Kampf* published

Summary

- Americans enjoyed unprecedented prosperity in the decade after World War I.
- The rapid social changes of the 1920s provoked resistance from Americans who believed that immigrants and people of color threatened harmony and order.
- New means of communication such as radio and motion pictures hastened the spread of a national culture in the 1920s.
- The Republican presidents of the 1920s promised to reverse Progressive reforms and promote the interests of business.
- The United States remained an active, albeit independent, world power throughout the 1920s.
- By 1930, America and the world were plunging downward into the Great Depression, the worst economic catastrophe of the modern era.

AMERICA	YEAR	THE WORLD
Aug Funeral of Rudolph Valentino **Nov** National Broadcasting Company (NBC) launches first major radio network **Dec** U.S. Marines return to Nicaragua	**1926**	
Apr The Great Mississippi Flood reveals deep discrimination against African Americans **May** Charles Lindbergh completes flight across Atlantic **May** The Supreme Court upholds compulsory sterilization in *Buck v. Bell* **Aug** Execution of Sacco and Vanzetti provokes international demonstrations **Oct** Release of movie *The Jazz Singer*, the first talking motion picture **Dec** Deportation of Marcus Garvey	**1927**	
Nov Herbert Hoover elected president	**1928**	**Jul** Women in the United Kingdom granted full suffrage
Jun Young Plan further reduces Germany's reparation payments from the Great War **Sep** Publication of Ernest Hemingway's novel *A Farewell to Arms* **Oct** Black Tuesday stock market crash on Wall Street	**1929**	**Oct–Dec** Onset of the global Great Depression **Dec** Street protests take place against Marines in Haiti
Mar Renunciation of Roosevelt Corollary to Monroe Doctrine **Jun** Smoot–Hawley Tariff raises duties on imported manufactured goods	**1930**	**May** Gandhi arrested by British officials after his "Salt March" protesting Britain's salt monopoly

Key Terms and People

◁))) audio flashcards

Reviewing Chapter 22

1. In what ways was the decade of the 1920s a "new era" in U.S. history?
2. How did technological innovation shape life in the United States in the 1920s?
3. How did the U.S. role in the global economy change in the 1920s?

Further Reading

Brinkley, Douglas. *Wheels for the World: Henry Ford, His Company, and a Century of Progress*. New York: Penguin Books, 2003. A thorough exploration of the history of the Ford Motor Company from 1903 to 2003, which highlights not only founder Henry Ford and his many innovations but also his workers.

Cohen, Warren I. *Empire Without Tears: American Foreign Relations, 1921–1933*. Philadelphia: Temple University Press, 1987. A study of foreign policy during the Harding, Coolidge, and Hoover administrations that explores the way Republican policymakers worked with business to ensure stability for U.S. economic interests.

Evans, Sara M. *Born for Liberty: A History of Women in America*. New York: Free Press Paperbacks, 1997. Both concise and comprehensive, this book examines the history of American women from the colonial period to the present, with a chapter devoted to women in the 1920s.

Hirsch, James S. *Riot and Remembrance: America's Worst Race Riot and Its Legacy*. New York: Mariner Books, 2003. An in-depth look at the 1921 Tulsa race riot that explores how authorities covered up the riot and the ways that victims and their descendants fought for justice.

Iriye, Akira. *The Cambridge History of American Foreign Relations*, Vol. 3: *The Globalizing of America, 1913–1945*. New York: Cambridge University Press, 1993. Explores the United States' emergence as a global power with a discussion of the "Americanizing" of other nations.

Okrent, Daniel. *Last Call: The Rise and Fall of Prohibition*. New York: Scribner, 2010. A lively, engaging look at America's experiment with Prohibition from 1920 to 1933 and its impact on nearly every aspect of society and culture.

Stovall, Tyler. *Paris Noir: African Americans in the City of Light*. New York. Houghton Mifflin, 1996. An in-depth account of the experiences of African American expatriates in Paris in the 1920s and beyond.

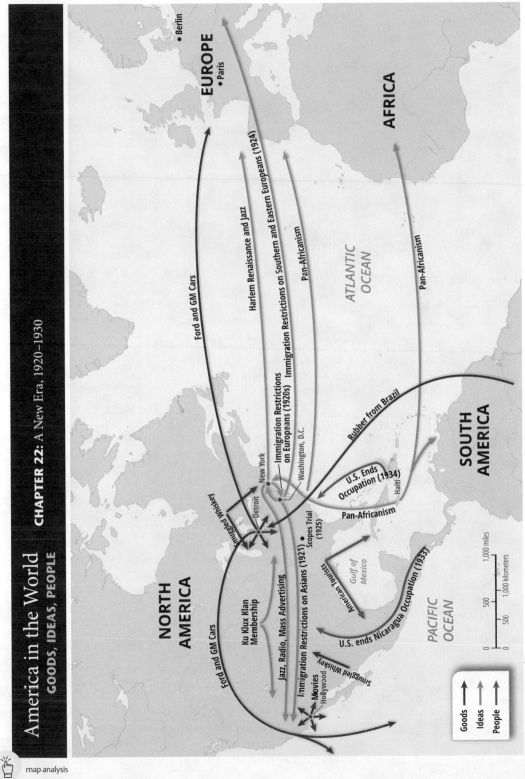

America in the World
GOODS, IDEAS, PEOPLE

CHAPTER 22: A New Era, 1920–1930

Berlin

EUROPE
Paris

AFRICA

Ford and GM Cars

Harlem Renaissance and Jazz

Immigration Restrictions on Southern and Eastern Europeans (1924)

Pan-Africanism

ATLANTIC
OCEAN

Pan-Africanism

Immigration Restrictions
on Europeans (1920s)

Washington, D.C.

New York

Detroit

Rubber from Brazil

U.S. Ends
Occupation (1934)

Haiti

Smuggled Whiskey

Pan-Africanism

SOUTH
AMERICA

Scopes Trial
(1925)

NORTH
AMERICA

Ku Klux Klan
Membership

Jazz, Radio, Mass Advertising

Immigration Restrictions on Asians (1921)

Gulf of
Mexico

American Tourists

Ford and GM Cars

Movies
Hollywood

Smuggled Whiskey

U.S. ends Nicaragua Occupation (1933)

PACIFIC
OCEAN

0	500	1,000 miles
0	500	1,000 kilometers

Goods
Ideas
People

map analysis

July 1932: Unemployed World War I veterans rally in Washington, DC, to demand that Congress provide them with financial aid.

A New Deal for Americans

1931–1939

During June 1932, 20,000 unemployed World War I–era veterans—calling themselves the Bonus Expeditionary Force (BEF)—and many of their families, totaling about 45,000, descended upon the nation's capital and set up makeshift encampments (dubbed **"Hoovervilles"**) on vacant land and in abandoned buildings. They demanded that Congress authorize payment of a $1,000 veterans benefit (worth $16,000 in today's dollars), or bonus, originally promised for 1945. The Senate balked and instead offered the veterans bus or train tickets home. One despondent BEF member remarked, "We were heroes in 1917," but now "we are bums." Over the next month, about half the "Bonus Army," as they were called in the media, drifted away, but nearly 10,000 remained in downtown Washington and more in tents and shacks across the Anacostia River.

Frustrated by this grim reminder of his failed policies and worried by claims from army chief of staff General **Douglas MacArthur** that Communist agitators planned "revolutionary action," on July 28 President Herbert Hoover ordered the city cleared of protestors. In the resulting melee, a policeman shot and killed two veterans.

MacArthur assembled nearly a thousand troops to assault the BEF camps in Anacostia. His aide, Major Dwight D. Eisenhower, later told a friend the "dumb son-of-a-bitch" believed his own fabricated claims about "incipient revolution in the air." As the troops burned ramshackle camps, they accidentally killed an infant.

Around the same time, delegates to the Democratic Party Convention gathered in Chicago to select a candidate to challenge Hoover. The nominee, New York governor **Franklin D. Roosevelt**, called on government to help the "forgotten man" and pledged to deliver a "new deal for the American people." In a private conversation with his advisors later that summer, Roosevelt

described MacArthur as "one of the two most dangerous men in the country." Just as in Germany, where
Adolf Hitler was poised to take power as the nation's
savior, many "Nazi-minded" Americans, Roosevelt
claimed, craved salvation from "a man on horseback"
like MacArthur. Roosevelt stressed the need to "tame
these fellows and make them useful to us."

Fear of looming dictatorship was not merely a rhe-
torical flourish. As the economy spiraled downward be-
tween the November 1932 election and Roosevelt's inauguration in March 1933, one
survey of influential Americans reported their agreement with Italian dictator Benito
Mussolini's boast that "democracy was destined to perish." A wide array of politicians
urged the president-elect to assume dictatorial power, or, in the words of a Senate resolution, "unlimited power."

The audience at Roosevelt's inaugural speech on March 4 responded tepidly to
what later generations considered his most memorable phrase—that Americans "had
nothing to fear but fear itself." But they wildly cheered his promise to seek "broad executive power to wage a war against the emergency," which he compared to a foreign invasion. First Lady **Eleanor Roosevelt** told a friend she feared that ordinary Americans, like
those in Germany and Italy before them, were so desperate "they would do anything"
and follow anyone who promised work and food.

⊘ THE NEW DEAL

Over the next 12 years, Roosevelt devoted his presidency to promoting democratic
reform and economic security at home and, later, to resisting totalitarian aggression
abroad. Determined to safeguard both democracy and capitalism, he dramatically expanded the power of the federal government, especially its ability to regulate banking,
Wall Street, and agriculture and to assist the unemployed. More than any president
before him, Roosevelt placed government in the service of small farmers, industrial
workers, the unemployed, and the elderly. Most Americans celebrated these changes,
but others condemned the **New Deal** for eroding both personal liberty and market
freedom.

From Prosperity to Global Depression

In 1929, President Hoover and the Republican Party took credit for eight years of
economic growth that produced what they called a "new era" in which poverty would
be banished. Instead, by the end of 1932, gross annual domestic investment had fallen
from $16 billion to $1 billion and stocks had lost almost 90 percent of their value.
Residential and business construction, steel production, and automobile output had
fallen by half. At least 20 percent of workers, 12 million, were unemployed. The overall
economy had shrunk by 33 percent.

About 40 percent of Americans still lived in rural areas, and one-quarter of the workforce held jobs related to agriculture, such as farming, food processing, building farm implements, and so forth. By 1932, prices for grain, cotton, dairy, and livestock had fallen to half their 1926 levels; farm income had declined from $12 billion to $5.3 billion; and one million farms had been seized in foreclosures. On one day in 1932, one-fourth of the farmland in Mississippi was sold at auction.

The United States did not lack raw materials, labor, or capital. But investment and commerce had completely stalled. Instead of taking advantage of bargains as economic theorists predicted, nervous investors and banks stopped putting money into consumer industries such as automobiles and electric appliances because of declining demand. As unsold inventories mounted and investment funds dried up, factories laid off more workers, further driving down demand.

As the economy shrank, U.S. banks and investors ceased making foreign loans, and by 1933, international trade had declined by two-thirds from its 1920s peak. In a futile effort to boost domestic sales by walling off imports, Congress in 1930 adopted the Smoot–Hawley Tariff that hiked duties on foreign goods. Most other countries enacted similar protectionist measures to shield home industry and agriculture from imports. As national income declined, Germany first reduced, then—under Hitler—simply ceased paying, World War I reparations to Britain and France. Britain and France, in turn, stopped paying their war debts to Washington.

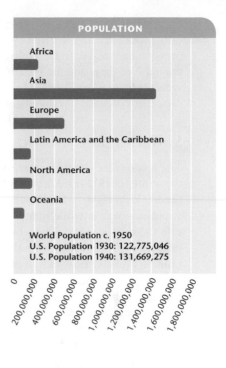

POPULATION

Africa
Asia
Europe
Latin America and the Caribbean
North America
Oceania

World Population c. 1950
U.S. Population 1930: 122,775,046
U.S. Population 1940: 131,669,275

0
200,000,000
400,000,000
600,000,000
800,000,000
1,000,000,000
1,200,000,000
1,400,000,000
1,600,000,000
1,800,000,000

Spiral of Decline, 1931–1933

It took three years after the stock market crash of October 1929 for the economy to hit rock bottom. Industrial production, employment, investment, and farm prices declined gradually. Meanwhile, most politicians, the heads of the Federal Reserve System, economists, and business leaders predicted that after a couple of tough years, the economy would recover. Downturns were simply part of a natural "business cycle" in which periodic panics drove out speculators and lowered wages and the price of goods in preparation for renewed growth. The Federal Reserve, the nation's central bank, shared the belief of bankers in Europe that the most important thing to do in any economic crisis was to maintain the gold standard that linked a nation's currency to its supply of gold and prevent inflation. Accordingly, the Federal Reserve raised interest rates and reduced the cash available to banks and other parts of the credit system. As one historian put it, "Central bankers continued to kick the world economy while it was down until it lost consciousness." When, in 1930–1931, President Hoover brought together business leaders to discuss ways to boost employment and stabilize tumbling prices, most economists criticized this as misguided "activism" that might delay recovery by undermining faith in the dollar's link to gold.

Fortune magazine article attacking Hoover's policies: "No One Has Starved" (September 1932)

During 1931, executives from U.S. Steel, the Ford Motor Company, and the New York Stock Exchange, buoyed by a brief economic uptick, declared the worst of the Depression had passed. In December, President Hoover assured Congress that the "fundamentals" of the economic system were sound and that only "dislocations, shocks, and setbacks from abroad" delayed recovery. Soon after this, the economy collapsed and the capitalist system, at home and abroad, broke down almost completely.

Suffering in the Land

The scope of the Great Depression revealed the stark reality of poverty in America. By the winter of 1932–1933, around 15 million mostly white, urban males—25 percent of the workforce—were chronically unemployed. Millions more worked reduced hours at cut-rate wages, while many sharecroppers and tenant farmers lived entirely outside the cash economy. Many businesses and local governments fired married women workers to preserve jobs for male heads of households. Out of a total population of 126 million, probably close to half of all Americans lived a hand-to-mouth existence. Conditions were so bad that crowds routinely gathered at municipal dumps to rummage through garbage for food.

African Americans, who comprised about 10 percent of the population and lived mostly in the rural South, faced more dire conditions. As cotton prices fell, landowners threw many families off the small plots they tilled. In the North, blacks worked mainly in the lower rungs of industry or in service and domestic jobs. Factory owners replaced many blacks with downwardly mobile white workers, while struggling, middle-class, white families fired black women who worked as cooks, cleaners, and nannies. About two-thirds of the black workforce in New York and Chicago, the centers of African American population in the North, had no jobs.

To get by, many families who owned homes or had apartments took in boarders. Families substituted Spam, a processed "food product," for real meat, and retailers sold individual cigarettes, "loosies," for a penny to smokers unable to afford a pack. Younger people deferred marriage and lived with parents. Even so, by 1933, half of all home mortgages were in default. Birth rates decreased sharply, and anecdotal evidence suggests that pregnant women had more frequent abortions during the 1930s. These conditions badly strained marriages. Because divorce was costly and difficult in many states, rates of desertion by unemployed husbands climbed sharply. At least two million men and one-quarter of a million boys under age 14 simply took off, riding freight trains and roaming the countryside as tramps or "hobos," dependent on odd jobs and handouts.

The Hoover administration sought to reduce surplus labor in the Southwest by deporting large numbers of Mexican nationals. With little or no aid from federal or state agencies, local governments and private charities were overwhelmed. By law, most state and city governments had to balance their budgets. When local property taxes declined, cities and states fired municipal workers and reduced already meager social service budgets. Private charities run by religious and voluntary groups such as the Salvation Army and the Red Cross were equipped to assist individual hardship cases or emergency victims of floods or fires but not millions of long-term unemployed workers and their families. By one estimate, private charities could help only about 5 percent of those in need. Governments at all levels provided almost no assistance to the poor and unemployed.

Henry Ford, "On Self Help" (1932)

The Failure of the Old Deal

Treasury Secretary Andrew Mellon assured President Hoover that the only way to restore economic growth was to "liquidate labor, liquidate stocks, liquidate the farmers, liquidate real estate ... and purge the rottenness out of the system." Declining employment and wages would force people to work harder and live a more moral life. However, in 1932, Hoover made some attempts to stanch the economic hemorrhaging through limited government intervention. He persuaded Congress to create the **Reconstruction Finance Corporation (RFC)** to loan money to struggling banks, railroads, manufacturers, and mortgage companies. As a lender of last resort, the RFC tried to keep private companies afloat. But these initiatives were too small to provide much of a cushion.

Despite this aid to business, Hoover rejected pleas that he spend federal funds to directly assist the unemployed. Decrying this as a "raid upon the treasury," the president insisted that the federal government had no obligation to unemployed individuals and that providing assistance would only create dependency, not jobs.

The Coming of the New Deal

Franklin Delano Roosevelt was born in 1882 into a wealthy family in Hyde Park, New York, on an estate in the Hudson River valley. Like his distant cousin Theodore, he entered politics and won a seat in the New York legislature in 1910, running as a Democratic Progressive who favored conservation and opposed corruption.

In 1905, Roosevelt married his fifth cousin, Eleanor, with whom he had six children. Before her marriage, Eleanor had attended a progressive school in England that introduced her to European socialist ideas. Later, she worked in a New York City settlement house and formed close friendships with women active in the labor and suffrage movements.

During the Great War, Roosevelt served as assistant secretary of the navy. In 1920, he ran as vice president on the unsuccessful Democratic ticket headed by Ohio governor James C. Cox. The next year, Roosevelt suffered a crippling attack of polio. For the rest of his life, he required help getting in or out of bed, dressing, or standing up. By wearing heavy steel braces, he could stand upright as long as he had someone or something to lean on. He could imitate walking for short distances by thrusting his hips forward while holding someone's arm. Roosevelt learned to use his upper body strength, exaggerated hand and head movements, and a broad smile to divert attention from his crippled lower body. Coping with his disability transformed Roosevelt from a dilettante into someone who related to the everyday problems of ordinary people. During his long recovery in the 1920s, he drew closer to several of Eleanor's feminist and labor activist friends. Through them, Roosevelt gained greater insight into the lives of working people. **Frances Perkins**, a veteran of Jane Addams's Hull House who had known Roosevelt since 1911 and later as secretary of labor became the first female cabinet member, remarked that after polio, "he was serious, not playing now" at politics. "He had become conscious of other people, of weak people, of human frailty."

Roosevelt ran successfully in 1928 for governor of New York. Despite his victory, he feared that if the full extent of his paralysis became known, he would have difficulty winning elections or governing. To shape press coverage, as governor and later as president, he worked hard to woo journalists, often by giving them easy access to his office and by holding frequent press conferences.

FDR'S FIRESIDE CHAT   Roosevelt delivers a fireside chat to a radio audience numbering in the tens of millions.

By 1932, Roosevelt was recognized as the nation's most prominent liberal Democrat. Unlike the passive Hoover, he recognized the Depression as the greatest crisis since the Civil War. The unemployed were not slackers, as Hoover implied, but victims of "complex and impersonal forces" over which individuals had no control. He called on states and the federal government to create work relief programs, unemployment insurance, and old-age pensions. In addition to **Harry Hopkins**, a social worker who had headed a New York State agency that had hired the unemployed to work on public projects, and Eleanor Roosevelt, Roosevelt relied for ideas on three academic lawyers and economists from Columbia University: **Raymond Moley**, **Rexford Tugwell**, and **Adolph Berle**. They advocated increased regulation of business and greater government economic planning to salvage capitalism from its follies. Journalists called them the "Brains Trust."

After Roosevelt secured the Democratic presidential nomination in the summer of 1932, he spoke of rebuilding the economy from the bottom up by helping the "forgotten man." He pledged to use federal power to ensure a more equitable distribution of income and promised "bold experimentation" in pursuit of what he called a "new deal" for Americans. On November 8, 1932, Roosevelt trounced Hoover, winning nearly 58 percent of the popular vote. Democrats took control of the House by a margin of 310 to 117 and the Senate by 60 to 35.

Roosevelt's landslide victory in November signaled hope, but no quick change. Nearly everything got worse between November 1932 and the inauguration in March 1933, including the weather. A drought that already afflicted the upper South spread west into Kansas, Colorado, Oklahoma, and Texas, carving out what would soon be known as the **Dust Bowl**. Farmers not hurt by the drought faced shrinking markets and prices for their produce. In August 1932, a group of irate Iowa farmers formed the Farm Holiday Association and declared a 30-day ban on marketing agricultural products as a way to limit supply and drive up prices. As the movement spread through the Midwest and then to other regions, farmers set up roadblocks to prevent trucks from hauling grain and dairy products, sometimes overturning the vehicles and destroying their cargo.

Franklin D. Roosevelt, First Inaugural Address (March 3, 1933)

Elsewhere, groups of farmers disrupted bank and sheriffs' auctions to block foreclosures and evictions. In many large cities, Unemployed Councils held rallies to demand work and often prevented evictions of families from apartments where the rent had not been paid.

Hoover, now a lame duck, spent the time from November through March calling in vain on the president-elect to endorse his discredited economic policies. What remained of the banking system virtually collapsed in the early months of 1933.

There were approximately 25,000 banks in the United States at the onset of the Depression. Many were small institutions with limited assets that could not survive the downturn without an infusion of cash from the Federal Reserve or the Treasury Department. Without that assistance, about 5,000 small banks failed before the 1932 election, and another 5,500 went under by March 1933. Because deposits were not insured, and ordinary Americans had no idea which banks to trust, early in 1933, millions of small savers rushed to withdraw billions of dollars from their accounts. This panic threatened to bring down even large, well-managed banks. When Hoover refused to intervene, most state governors imposed "bank holidays." They ordered banks to shut their doors to prevent mass withdrawals and inevitable collapse. By March 4, 32 states had suspended all banking activity, and the economy was paralyzed.

STUDY QUESTIONS **FOR THE NEW DEAL**

1. How did economic hardship affect ordinary American families in the early 1930s?

2. What did President Hoover do and not do in response to the economic calamity?

3. How did Roosevelt's personal and political background shape his view of the crisis as he assumed the presidency?

quiz

⊗ RECONSTRUCTING CAPITALISM

Roosevelt came of age in the Progressive era and saw government as a positive force to mitigate the excesses and inequalities of the new industrial order. He believed that government could help preserve individual liberty and enhance opportunity. New Dealers often disagreed among themselves on details of policy. Some favored balanced budgets, whereas others insisted that running deficits promoted growth. Some advocated central economic planning; others retained faith in free markets. One group of New Dealers urged redistributing wealth to those at the bottom of the economic pyramid, while others insisted that government could help the poor most effectively by promoting overall growth. New Dealers generally sympathized with the efforts of workers to organize unions but hesitated to intervene on their behalf. Most New Dealers agreed that "underconsumption" by poorly paid workers and farmers along with selfish actions by financial institutions had caused the Depression. Recovery would require active federal regulation of capital markets, assistance to farmers and businesses, and increased government spending to boost production and consumption. They considered the gold standard a straitjacket that inhibited efforts to counter the Depression. Although many conservatives condemned them as radicals, neither the president nor his top advisors considered themselves socialists or enemies of capitalism.

The First Hundred Days

In his inaugural speech on Saturday, March 4, 1933, Roosevelt condemned "unscrupulous money changers" who had "fled from their high seats in the temple of our civilization." Moments after taking the presidential oath, FDR invoked emergency powers to issue a proclamation closing all national banks effective Monday, March 6. He then called Congress into special session on Thursday, March 9.

In less than a day, the president persuaded Congress to pass an **Emergency Banking Relief Act**. This created a system to audit, loan funds to, and reopen banks under Treasury Department supervision. On the evening of March 12, Roosevelt explained the procedure to an anxious public in a 14-minute radio address, the first of three dozen "**fireside chats**" he delivered on policy issues over the next 12 years. Half of all American adults listened to the president as his reassuring voice described the causes of the banking crisis, the procedures to audit and reopen sound banks, and the steps regulators would take to safeguard future deposits. "Let us unite in banishing fear," he declared. "We have provided the machinery to restore our financial system; and it is up to you to support and make it work." The public was impressed that such an important person seemed to be speaking directly to them.

Franklin D. Roosevelt, fireside chat on banking (March 12, 1933)

On the morning of Monday, March 13, a near economic miracle occurred. For the first time in months, ordinary Americans retrieved cash from under mattresses and began depositing it in newly reopened federally supervised banks. In June, Congress enacted the **Glass–Steagall Banking Act**, which established strict guidelines for banking operations and expanded the power of the Federal Reserve System. The law closed many small banks and forced several thousand others to merge with larger, more stable institutions. It also separated risky commercial and investment banking from ordinary banking, a firewall that lasted until 1999. The new Federal Deposit Insurance Corporation (FDIC) helped restore faith in banks by guaranteeing individual deposits for up to $5,000, an amount raised gradually over time.

The new administration also moved quickly to prevent the kind of wild speculation that led to stock market booms and busts. The **Securities Act of 1933** required companies selling stock to the public to register with a federal agency and provide accurate information on what was being sold. The subsequent **Securities Exchange Act of 1934** created a Securities and Exchange Commission (SEC) to regulate stock markets and

Table 23.1 Major Laws and Programs Passed in the First Hundred Days

In just over the first three months of the Roosevelt administration in 1933, a period known as the "First Hundred Days," Congress passed a remarkable number of laws that stabilized and regulated the nation's faltering economic system.

LAW	DATE
Emergency Banking Act	March 9
Economy Act	March 15
Volstead Act modified to allow beer and wine	March 22
Civilian Conservation Corps	March 31
Agricultural Adjustment Act	May 12
Farm Mortgage Assistance	May 12
Federal Emergency Relief Act	May 12
Tennessee Valley Authority	May 18
Securities Act of 1933	May 27
Home Owners Loan Corporation	June 13
Public Works Administration	June 16
Railroad Coordination Act	June 16
National Industrial Recovery Act	June 16
Glass–Steagall Banking Act	June 16

activities by brokers. As with banking reform, this left the basic operation of capital markets in private hands but imposed rules and supervision.

Between March and June 1933, often dubbed the "**First Hundred Days,**" Roosevelt prevailed on Congress to pass 14 major pieces of legislation, a record never duplicated and a testament to both presidential leadership and the country's desire for change (Table 23.1). Congress enacted bills to raise agricultural prices, put the unemployed to work, regulate the stock market, reform banking practices, and assist homeowners and farmers in paying mortgages. At Roosevelt's urging, Congress amended the Volstead Act to allow sales of beer and wine, while the states moved to ratify the Twenty-First Amendment that repealed Prohibition.

J. Frederick Essary, "The New Deal for Nearly Four Months" (july 1933)

Except for the Economy Act, which modestly cut the salaries of federal workers and veterans' pensions, all the new legislation expanded the size, scope, and spending of the federal government. To meet the challenge of youth unemployment, Congress created the Civilian Conservation Corps (CCC). Within a few months, it enrolled 275,000 men, mostly in their 20s, in 1,300 labor camps. In 1935, at its peak, 500,000 men worked on CCC projects; by the time the program ended in 1942, about three million men had served in the corps. Besides good pay and wholesome meals, volunteers received literacy and vocational training. In addition to conservation work, the CCC constructed the infrastructure of the national park system.

Other innovations included the Federal Emergency Relief Administration (FERA), the Public Works Administration (PWA), and the Tennessee Valley Authority (TVA).

THE GRAND COULEE DAM   As one of the largest federal construction projects undertaken during the New Deal, the Grand Coulee Dam, seen here under construction in 1937, comprised part of the multidam effort to "tame" the Columbia River in the Pacific Northwest. Like the Tennessee Valley Authority in the Southeast, the river's power would be used to generate electricity for industry and to irrigate farms. The project's administrator hired folk singer Woody Guthrie to compose several ballads, including "Roll on Columbia," that memorialized the effort.

FERA, headed by Harry Hopkins, began with a $500 million appropriation to provide matching funds to states to hire the unemployed to work on public projects. PWA, managed by Interior Secretary Harold Ickes, spent over $3 billion in its first three years building large public works projects such as dams in the Pacific Northwest, highways, and public buildings.

The TVA represented a vast experiment in regional planning. It built a network of dams and hydroelectric projects to control floods, generate power, and promote growth in a chronically poor area of the South. Cheap electricity generated by the TVA dramatically improved life for millions of southerners, and it still plays a major role in the region.

Lorena Hickock reports on federal relief efforts (November 1933)

In 1933, the newly created **Agricultural Adjustment Administration (AAA)** and the related Commodity Credit Corporation provided credit, loans, and other subsidies to farmers. Secretary of Agriculture **Henry A. Wallace** oversaw financial incentives distributed to farmers who agreed to limit production of corn, wheat, cotton, tobacco, and livestock. Participating farmers who could not sell their crops above a certain price point could transfer them to the Commodity Credit Corporation, which would hold them as collateral for loans given to the farmers. The program's costs were paid by taxing food processors. Conservative critics of the program condemned it for interfering with the free market and for taxing nonfarmers to pay for it. Liberals complained that the crop support payments went disproportionately to large-scale farmers and did little or nothing to help tenants or sharecroppers. After the Supreme Court overturned the original AAA law in 1936, it was replaced by a modified program in 1938. Between 1933 and 1940, farm income doubled.

Early New Deal industrial policy had less success. The National Industrial Recovery Act created the **National Recovery Administration (NRA)**, famous for its blue eagle logo. The NRA resembled World War I programs that brought together industry leaders and labor groups to boost production. NRA wrote "production codes" for each industry that encouraged cooperation among competing businesses to set stable prices and wages and bar cutthroat competition. Roosevelt hoped these measures would stabilize the economy and prompt private business to hire more workers. Neither occurred, and NRA failed to address the biggest impediment to recovery—the lack of new private investment funds and the large pool of unemployed workers who lacked the money to buy goods. In 1935, the Supreme Court declared the NRA an unconstitutional overreach of federal authority, and it came to an unlamented end.

Today we know that full economic recovery did not occur until the United States entered World War II. Critics cite this as proof that the New Deal failed. Several other industrialized nations, including Germany, Italy, and Japan, pursued stimulus programs that resembled and often went beyond American efforts. Before they took the path of primarily military spending in the late 1930s, the German and Japanese economies achieved greater success in alleviating unemployment. The common element among these economic strategies was adoption of ideas resembling those formulated by British economist John Maynard Keynes. During hard economic times, **Keynesian economics** stipulated that governments should initiate countercyclical deficit spending to stimulate demand and create jobs. They could build roads, schools, or battleships. As the private sector recovered, deficit spending could be reduced and taxes collected to pay for public debt.

Although not perfect, the New Deal's prewar achievements were substantial. Between 1933 and 1940 (except for the recession of 1937–1938, discussed below), the economy grew at the historically high rate of 8–10 percent annually. By the end of 1937, the gross domestic product (GDP) had recovered to its 1929 level. But growth varied from year to year, bypassed some key industries, and failed to solve the unemployment problem. Private sector employment did not reach the 1929 level until 1943. In the interim, government work relief projects gave jobs to many of the unemployed. If the New Deal erred before 1941, boosters argue, it did so by spending too little, not too much. Sympathizers believe that wartime events affirmed New Deal principles: large-scale government spending (which grew from 8 percent of GDP in 1938 to 40 percent in 1943), along with targeted investments in new industries and technologies, revitalized the economy and distributed wealth more evenly. In an economy dominated by powerful business interests, New Dealers hoped to mitigate concentrated corporate power by creating what economists called "countervailing powers." For example, industrial labor unions could balance the influence of big business and promote workers' welfare. Electric power generated by government-built dams in the Tennessee valley and Pacific Northwest and distributed by consumer-owned cooperatives would compete with private utilities and pressure them to improve service and reduce rates. Agencies to regulate banking and the stock market would empower private investors to take informed risks and small depositors to put their money in banks where it could be loaned out to promote economic expansion. Government-administered pensions funded by workers' and employers' contributions would provide the elderly a decent retirement and make them less dependent on the whims of their employers. Agricultural price supports to farmers would provide a cash flow that made them less vulnerable to market blips or the power of large food processors.

Roosevelt told Labor Secretary Frances Perkins at one point, "We are going to make a country in which no one is left out." In a speech near the end of his life, he added that "true individual freedom . . . cannot exist without economic security and independence."

Voices of Protest

Between 1933 and 1935, the New Deal saved democratic capitalism by stabilizing the banking system, regulating stock markets, protecting property owners, helping farmers, and providing emergency relief to the unemployed. Ironically, many of the Republican politicians and business executives who in 1933 had urged Roosevelt to assume dictatorial power now complained that he had—and used it against them. Critics on the left accused the New Deal of doing too little to ensure social justice, assist labor unions, and redistribute wealth.

Several small fascist movements developed in the United States during the 1930s, but none gained national traction. The Communist Party, whose membership had increased from 9,000 to about 100,000, generally supported New Deal reforms. Roosevelt's most powerful critics often struck a populist tone that defied easy characterization.

In January 1934, Dr. **Frances Townsend**, health commissioner of Long Beach, California, founded a group named "Old Age Revolving Pensions Limited." It called on the federal government to impose a 2 percent income tax on all workers to finance monthly payments of $200 to everyone over age 60, as long as they spent all the money within

HOLY CRITICS Father Charles Coughlin, the popular "radio priest" from Royal Oak, Michigan, attracted millions of listeners in the mid-1930s. Although he initially supported Roosevelt's New Deal, like fellow demagogue Senator Huey Long, by 1935 he had become a fierce critic. Coughlin's so-called Social Justice movement borrowed a theme from Adolf Hitler. He blamed Jews for the nation's economic woes and claimed they conspired to rule the world. Embarrassed church authorities silenced Coughlin in the late 1930s. He lived in obscurity until 1979.

30 days. **Upton Sinclair**, muckraking author of the 1906 novel *The Jungle*, ran for governor in 1934 on the EPIC (End Poverty in California) platform that called on the state to hire the unemployed and put them to work in idle fields and factories.

Louisiana Democratic senator **Huey Long** announced the creation in 1934 of the "Share Our Wealth Society." Long blamed the Depression on a conspiracy by the rich. Under the banner "Every Man a King," he proposed to expand Townsend's ideas beyond the elderly by "soaking the rich" with taxes and giving every family a grant of $5,000 to buy a house and a guaranteed annual income of $2,500. Long's appeal spread quickly in the South and attracted a national following among the lower middle class and small farmers. By 1935, Share Our Wealth clubs claimed 27,000 chapters and five million members.

Speech to members of the Share Our Wealth Society, 1935

A Catholic priest from Royal Oak, Michigan, Father Charles Coughlin, also attacked the New Deal. Coughlin, a Canadian immigrant, broadcast radio sermons on social and political issues. At first a supporter of the New Deal, the so-called radio priest complained that it had become a tool of special interests. Coughlin charged that "Franklin Double-Crossing Roosevelt" did the bidding of Wall Street, foreigners, and an "international conspiracy of Jewish bankers." His radio rants reached an estimated 30 million, mostly Catholic, listeners each week. Coughlin organized the "National Union for Social Justice."

Townsend, Sinclair, Long, and Coughlin all highlighted real problems—the meagerness of aid to the poor, the insecurity of old age, and the maldistribution of wealth. But they offered simplistic alternatives and demonized scapegoats. In September 1935, a Louisiana doctor, angered by Long's strong-arm tactics in state politics, shot and killed the senator. Several influential Catholic Democrats, including Joseph Kennedy, convinced the Church hierarchy that Coughlin had become an embarrassment. In 1936, his superiors ordered him to cease inflammatory broadcasts, although he resumed anti-Semitic diatribes in 1938. Townsend's following waned with passage of the Social Security Act in 1935.

Several corporate opponents of the New Deal organized the Liberty League in the mid-1930s. The group accused Roosevelt of promoting class warfare and wrecking the economy. They particularly accused First Lady Eleanor Roosevelt of damaging the nation.

On the left side of the political spectrum, many industrial workers also grew frustrated with the slow improvement of wages and working conditions under the New Deal. During 1934 and 1935, industrial unions such as the United Mine Workers and United Automobile Workers broke away from the cautious American Federation of Labor (AFL) and created a more radical umbrella group, the **Congress of Industrial Organizations (CIO)**, led by John L. Lewis, head of the United Mine Workers. Although Roosevelt sympathized with the goals of organized labor, at this point he still hoped that management–union cooperation—rather than labor militancy—would boost the economy. Because most industrial employers refused to recognize or bargain with unions, however, cooperation proved impossible.

During 1934, militant truck drivers in Minneapolis and longshoremen in San Francisco battled transportation companies that refused to recognize their unions. In September, 400,000 textile workers in mills throughout New England and the South went on strike in the biggest labor action since 1919. State governors called in the National Guard to break the strikes and keep factories open.

STUDY QUESTIONS FOR RECONSTRUCTING CAPITALISM

1. What did the New Deal do to stabilize the financial system in 1933?

2. What early New Deal programs specifically helped workers and farmers?

3. What faults with the New Deal did critics on the left identify?

THE SECOND NEW DEAL

Partly in response to his critics, on June 28, 1934, in a fireside chat, Roosevelt renewed his promise to promote additional "social insurance" measures to improve living standards for ordinary people. He warned that Republicans and others would attack his initiatives, labeling them as "fascism . . . or Communism . . . or Socialism."

He then began an extended sea voyage, traveling through the Panama Canal and visiting several Latin American capitals to highlight his Good Neighbor Policy that treated hemispheric neighbors as equals. After a stop in Hawaii, he sailed back to the Pacific Northwest. From there he traveled by train back to the East Coast, making side trips to visit many big federal construction projects underway, such as the dams being built along the Columbia and Missouri rivers. These massive public works, FDR asserted, would provide millions of American households and businesses with inexpensive and reliable electricity, control floods, and relieve droughts.

In the congressional elections of November 1934, not only did Democrats hold on to their large majorities, but liberal Democrats increased their numbers in both the House and Senate. The president then launched a new burst of reforms, known as the Second New Deal, or Second Hundred Days (Table 23.2).

Early in 1935, Roosevelt introduced legislation to expand temporary work relief programs for the unemployed and to create a permanent economic security program

Table 23.2 Major Laws and Programs of the Second Hundred Days

In a period of time during 1935 dubbed the "Second Hundred Days," President Roosevelt proposed and Congress passed far-reaching reform legislation, including Social Security, the National Labor Relations Act, and the vast Works Progress Administration employment program.

LAW	DATE	PURPOSE
Emergency Relief Appropriation Act	April 8	Funds for work relief
Resettlement Administration	April 30	Aid to migrant farmers
Works Progress Administration	May 6	Mass hiring of unemployed
Rural Electrification Administration	May 11	Power to rural areas
National Labor Relations Act	July 7	Workers' right to unionize
Social Security Act	August 14	Pensions/social programs
Public Utilities Holding Company Act	August 26	Regulation of utilities

A FARMER'S LIFE African American sharecroppers during the Great Depression.

image analysis

for the aged and sick. Roosevelt opposed the notion of giving cash payments—known as the dole—to the unemployed. Instead, he proposed expanding government-funded work relief for the jobless. Congress responded by passing a $5 billion Emergency Relief Appropriation Act in April, funding projects for both urban and rural Americans.

The new Resettlement Administration (RA) supervised rural relief activities. Its head, Rexford Tugwell, a member of the original Brains Trust, pushed for assistance to tenant farmers and sharecroppers—groups ignored by earlier farm aid programs. But opposition by southern Democrats, who opposed anything that might alter the system of racial and class hierarchy in the rural South, and Republicans limited RA efforts. Only about 5,000 poor farm families were placed on better land. In 1937, the Farm Security Administration (FSA) replaced the RA. The new agency assisted about 20,000 tenant farmers to purchase their own land. It also constructed model housing camps for migratory farm workers.

The Rural Electrification Administration (REA) benefited millions of Americans. Because 90 percent of farms had no electricity in 1935, REA loaned money to locally owned nonprofit cooperatives to build rural power grids. One Arkansan from the Ozarks described the day in 1940 that the "lights came on." "I remember my mother smiling . . . when they came on full, tears started running down her cheeks. . . . It was a day of celebration." Within five years, nearly half of all farms had electric power, and by 1950, 90 percent were on the power grid. This advance created huge demand for home appliances and new farm equipment.

In 1935, FDR tasked Harry Hopkins to manage the largest of the new programs, the **Works Progress Administration (WPA)** (Table 23.3). Hopkins believed that work relief would prevent social unrest by giving the unemployed meaningful labor. The tools and raw materials used on WPA projects, along with the wages paid, would also stimulate the private economy. As an additional impetus to long-term growth, the projects would produce vital infrastructure, such as roads, bridges, libraries, airports, and schools.

Table 23.3 Major WPA Construction Projects, 1935–1941

Between 1935 and 1941, the WPA revolutionized the national infrastructure, constructing parks, roads, dams, irrigation projects, airports, schools, and government buildings. It also employed artists, musicians, writers, and actors in a remarkable variety of public arts projects.

572,000 miles of rural roads; 67,000 miles of city streets; 31,000 miles of sidewalks

122,000 bridges and 1,000 tunnels

1,050 airfields and 4,000 airport buildings

500 water treatment plants and thousands of miles of sewer lines and water lines

3,300 sports stadiums; 5,000 athletic fields; 12,800 playgrounds

36,900 school buildings and 1,000 public library buildings

2,552 hospitals; 2,700 firehouses; 900 armories; 760 prison buildings

19,400 state and local government buildings

416 fish hatcheries; 7,000 miles of firebreaks

WPA
posters

The WPA reached out not only to laborers but to artists, sculptors, musicians, playwrights, novelists, dancers, and actors as well. Between 1935 and 1942, about 8.5 million Americans worked for the WPA. When World War II began in 1941, the WPA helped construct military facilities. Thousands of WPA workers wrote letters expressing thanks. A girl from Illinois wrote, "My father immediately got employed in the WPA. This was a godsend. This was the greatest thing. It meant food, you know. Survival, just survival."

Social Security

In 1935, the Roosevelt administration proposed a national plan for unemployment and disability insurance, aid to dependent children, and pensions for the elderly. Most western European nations had begun such programs decades earlier, but in the United States, only a few states offered assistance to unemployed workers. Only one in seven private sector workers had any sort of pension. Most workers kept at their job as long as physically able.

The president assigned Labor Secretary Frances Perkins to supervise the drafting of the **Social Security Act**. Perkins proposed a government-administered system funded primarily by contributions—payroll taxes—from workers and employers, not general tax revenues. In this sense, it resembled an insurance program more than a welfare program.

Retirement pensions, normally paid beginning at age 65, would come from a fund into which workers and employers each contributed 1 percent of a salary. Each generation of younger workers contributing to the system financed the retirement benefits received by older workers, and they, in turn, would benefit on their reaching 65.

The proposal encountered fierce opposition from business owners, commercial farmers, and doctors. Some business owners objected to paying taxes that benefited workers, whereas others denounced government involvement in employer–employee relations. Republican politicians worried that those receiving pensions would all become loyal Democrats. The idea of including a modest health insurance plan within Social Security elicited such intense denunciations of "socialized medicine" by the American Medical Association that the administration dropped the plan. To placate commercial farmers and wealthier Americans who objected to paying taxes on hired help, the law exempted most agricultural and household domestic laborers. Many government workers, teachers, waitresses, and employees of nonprofit agencies were also denied coverage. These exemptions had the perverse effect of excluding half of all African American and women workers. The proposal as passed in 1935 included provisions to assist laid-off and injured workers, surviving dependents of dead workers, and single mothers with young children. During the next three decades, laws were extended to include more workers, and payments rose from their meager early levels.

Labor Activism

Until the mid-1930s, craft unions representing trades such as carpenters, plumbers, and electricians dominated the largest labor organization, the AFL. They largely ignored the plight of lower-paid industrial workers, excluded minority laborers, and often supported Republican candidates. This dynamic changed in 1935 when Congress passed and Roosevelt signed the National Labor Relations Act, or Wagner Act, named for its primary author, Senator **Robert Wagner**, Democrat of New York. The Wagner Act established the National Labor Relations Board (NLRB), empowered to protect the right of workers to form unions and to require employers to negotiate labor contracts with those unions. This gave a tremendous boost to steel, automobile, and mine workers whose past efforts to organize had been thwarted by violent company resistance.

During 1935, newly energized unions representing industrial workers formed the CIO. Most CIO-affiliated unions accepted black and other minority workers and campaigned for Roosevelt's reelection in 1936. In December 1936, and continuing through 1937, the United Automobile Workers (UAW) seized control of several General Motors and Ford plants in Flint and Detroit, Michigan, by staging "sit-down strikes." They demanded that the companies negotiate with union representatives on behalf of workers. For weeks at a time, strikers occupied the auto plants while their wives and women supporters braved a gauntlet of company-hired thugs to bring food to them.

In most past labor conflicts, state and federal authorities had sent in police or federal troops to roust strikers and reopen factories. But this time, Michigan governor **Frank Murphy** (whom FDR later named to the Supreme Court) and Roosevelt refused to send police or troops to retake the factories. Instead, they urged GM and Ford to negotiate with union officials. Over the next two years, first automobile and then steel workers, through their unions, negotiated contracts with manufacturers.

Between 1930 and 1940, the percentage of factory workers in labor unions tripled, from under 8 percent to 23 percent. By 1945, a historically high 25 percent of nonfarm laborers were union members. Unionized blue-collar workers enjoyed steadily rising levels of pay and benefits from the late 1930s through the mid-1970s. In effect, skilled workers entered and expanded the American middle class. In spite of his initial reluctance to support it, Roosevelt became a champion of the Wagner Act, or National Labor Relations Act, and organized labor became a pillar of the Democratic Party. Roosevelt described the right to join a union and bargain collectively as fundamental to social justice and a "right that means the difference between despotism and democracy."

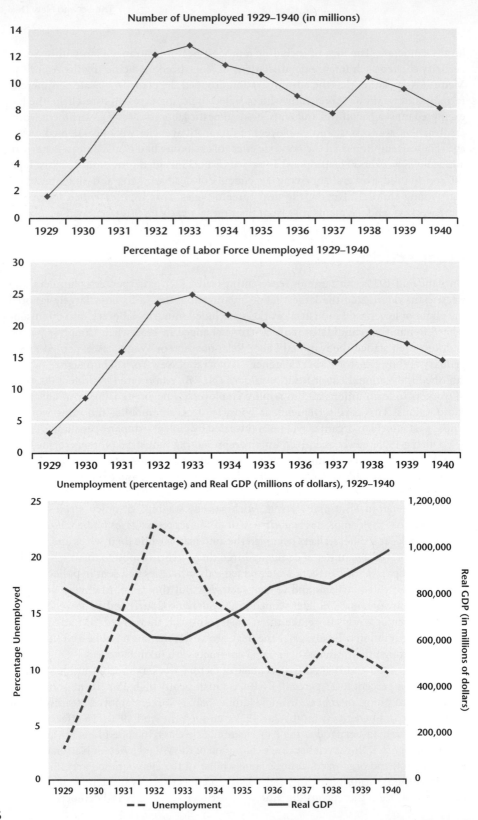

Number of Unemployed 1929–1940 (in millions)

Percentage of Labor Force Unemployed 1929–1940

Unemployment (percentage) and Real GDP (millions of dollars), 1929–1940

Percentage Unemployed

Real GDP (in millions of dollars)

– – Unemployment   —— Real GDP

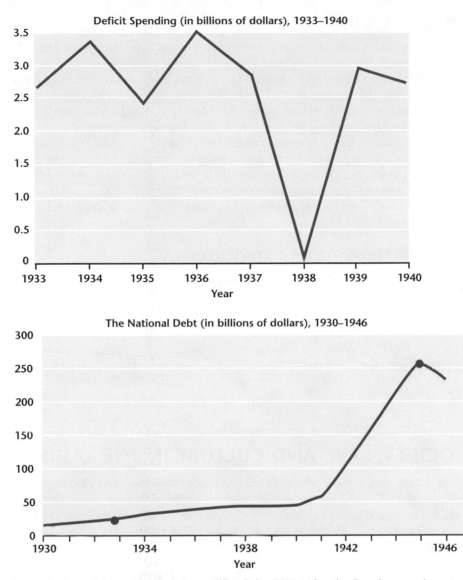

FIGURE 23.1 **National economic profile of the 1930s** After the dismal economic decline between 1929 and early 1933, the nation's GDP improved dramatically during the first five years of the New Deal. The ranks of the unemployed shrank substantially. The economy nosedived in 1937–1938 when President Roosevelt reduced federal spending but recovered when he expanded job-creating programs. Overall levels of federal spending and debt were moderate during the New Deal, rising steeply when the United States entered World War II.

The 1936 Election

Franklin D. Roosevelt, Second Inaugural Address (January 20, 1937)

The election of 1936 served as a national referendum on the New Deal (Figure 23.1). The Democrats mobilized millions of new supporters among unionized workers, farmers who received crop support, ethnic voting blocs such as Catholics and Jews, and African Americans who had migrated north. Roosevelt skillfully dubbed his Republican opponents and corporate critics "economic royalists" who opposed the New Deal not because its policies were faulty but because they feared losing their grip on power.

In 1936, Republican presidential candidate Alf Landon attacked Social Security along with most other New Deal programs as attacks on freedom by an incumbent who threatened the American way of life. Despite these claims, in November, Roosevelt won a resounding second-term victory by defeating Landon in every state except Maine and Vermont. Roosevelt received 60 percent of the popular vote to Landon's 36.5 percent.

STUDY QUESTIONS FOR THE SECOND NEW DEAL

quiz

1. What major new programs were adopted during the "Second New Deal," and how did they differ from earlier reforms?

2. How did Social Security create a national retirement system for many U.S. workers? Who was left out of it, and why?

3. In what ways did the New Deal support industrial labor unions, and how did this alter the power of industry?

⊘ SOCIETY, LAW, AND CULTURE IN THE 1930S

In their daily lives, millions of Americans found relief from the Depression in popular entertainment. Cultural initiatives celebrated the common man. Breaking with tradition, Roosevelt and his policies reached out to Catholics, Jews, African Americans, immigrants and their children, and women. The New Deal transformed society, law, and culture.

Popular Entertainment

Newspapers, magazines, and especially radio and movies informed and entertained the public. Inexpensive radio receivers were nearly ubiquitous by the late 1930s, helped by New Deal construction of rural electrical grids. With the arrival of sound and color, movies became an even more popular escape. Americans traveled less abroad but streamed into national parks, many of which had cabins and campsites built by the CCC. Trains still carried most long-distance travelers, but flying became more common with the introduction of the first modern passenger plane, the DC-3, in 1937.

During the first half of the 1930s, fear of violence gripped the nation. Although overall crime rates did not rise during the Depression, high-profile criminals, especially bank robbers, dominated newspaper headlines. John Dillinger, Baby Face

Nelson, Bonnie and Clyde, Machine Gun Kelly, and Ma Barker gained celebrity status. Some gangsters achieved a kind of "Robin Hood" aura when they gave away some of the money they robbed from banks. At the same time, the public sought reassurance that the forces of law and order would prevail.

Roosevelt sensed that launching a "war on crime" would enhance public faith in the New Deal's battle against economic hardship. He and Attorney General Homer S. Cummings designated J. Edgar Hoover, head of the Justice Department's small Bureau of Investigation (renamed the FBI in 1935), to lead the campaign. Hoover relished the chance to burnish his agency's image as the focal point of scientific crime fighting. However, the crime films so popular in the era, such as *Little Caesar, The Public Enemy*, and *Scarface* (reportedly Al Capone's favorite), depicted ruthless and violent men who gained wealth and power by breaking the law. In 1934, after Hoover's so-called G-men killed Dillinger, Nelson, and Floyd, Hollywood studios bowed to government pressure and adopted a production code that barred the sympathetic portrayal of gangsters. *G-Men*, released in 1935, followed by six FBI-centered films in 1936, featured Hoover's agents as symbols of rectitude who "always got their man." Overnight, the illusory "crime wave" ended, and Hoover secured his job as FBI director until his death in 1972.

Musicals also found large audiences among a nation that savored an escape from hard times. Debonair dancers Fred Astaire and Ginger Rogers charmed moviegoers. Comedy films starring the Marx Brothers, the Ritz Brothers, and W. C. Fields, along with cartoons produced by the Disney and Warner Brothers studios, also entertained the public. Spunky child actress Shirley Temple proved the biggest box office draw of the decade. Even when these films acknowledged the country's hard times, their plucky stars had an uncanny ability to triumph over adversity.

On the radio, daytime melodramas—called soap operas because of their sponsorship—appealed to women working at home. Late afternoon programs targeted school-age children, dinnertime broadcasts provided highlights of the day's news, and evening shows played big band music and original comedy and drama. Broadcasts of baseball games were also popular. The New York Yankees, with their colorful roster of Babe Ruth, Lou Gehrig, and Joe DiMaggio, had a national fan base.

Two of the era's most popular radio shows had ethnic themes. *Amos 'n' Andy*, a comedy in which white actors depicted two gullible African Americans scheming to strike it rich, was immensely popular. Nearly as many Americans tuned in to follow *The Goldbergs*, a comedy-drama set in a Bronx, New York, tenement. Actress Gertrude Berg played Mollie Goldberg, the matriarch of a Jewish family whose signature line was to lean out of her apartment window and call out "yoo-hoo" to neighbors with whom she gossiped.

Amos 'n' Andy advertisement, 1935

Radio sometimes provided a more serious forum for African Americans than the patronizing parodies of *Amos 'n' Andy*. Beginning in 1938 and continuing until 1947, over 100 CBS radio stations broadcast the weekly performance of a gospel choir group called Wings Over Jordan. The show also presented talks by black educators, writers, and politicians.

Black athletes also captured national attention. Both white and black Americans followed closely the remarkable achievements of runner Jesse Owens at the 1936 Olympics in Berlin. His four gold medals left Nazi officials fuming at his defeat of their "master race" of athletes. Black boxer Joe Louis, dubbed the Brown Bomber, also became a hero with his spectacular achievements in the ring after 1934 and his self-effacing personality. Louis's two fights against German Max Schmeling became proxy contests between the two nations. After Louis's disappointing loss to the German fighter in 1936, they fought a much-anticipated rematch in 1938 dubbed "the fight of the century." During a prefight visit to the White House, President Roosevelt told Louis, "Joe, we need muscles like yours to beat Germany." Louis, who said he felt the "whole damned country was depending on me," knocked out Schmeling (who was not a Nazi sympathizer) in the first round.

Theater owners showed newsreels as well as cartoons before or between feature films. *The March of Time*, beginning in 1934, contained vivid footage of current events, natural disasters, and celebrity sightings.

Newspapers remained the predominant form of journalism during the 1930s, but they faced competition from magazines. *Reader's Digest*, which reprinted articles from various magazines, became the nation's most widely circulated periodical by 1938. Newsweeklies such as *Time* and *Newsweek* also gained large readerships, and *Life* magazine won acclaim for its stunning photography. In the heartland, readers particularly liked the *Saturday Evening Post*. Hard times pushed down overall book sales, but the literate public snapped up "tough guy" detective fiction. The modern comic book made its first appearance in 1938 when Action Comics introduced Superman. The wildly popular character was supplemented by a radio version of the "man of steel" and in 1939 by other superheroes introduced by Marvel Comics. Superman, like Captain America and Batman, threw off his meek identity to lead battles against criminals at home and aggressors abroad. Wonder Woman joined the superhero ranks in 1941.

Superman's comic book debut, June 1938

In 1934, the Treasury Department funded a one-year Public Works of Arts Project that employed nearly 4,000 painters and sculptors who produced over 15,000 works of art displayed in public buildings. This became a model for the much larger Federal Arts, Music, Dance, Theater, and Writers Projects, all WPA programs created in 1935.

As a devoted stamp collector, Roosevelt had a special interest in the postal service. Post offices in small towns and large cities, he believed, served as a focal point of democracy where rich and poor alike mingled. At the president's direction, the postal service and the WPA collaborated in hiring architects to design graceful new buildings and commissioned artists to paint over 1,000 murals in them.

The WPA employed thousands of struggling artists to paint murals in other public buildings and teach art classes in public schools. Thirty-eight symphony orchestras received support to perform free concerts nationwide. The Writers Project employed 10,000 people who traveled around the country recording regional music and folk stories, writing local histories and travel guides, and interviewing former slaves for a massive oral history. The Federal Theater Project hired writers, directors, and actors to stage plays for the public. Productions included classics such as *Macbeth* and *The Mikado* as well as social dramas about the Depression and the threat of fascism such as *The Cradle Will Rock*, *Living Newspaper*, and Sinclair Lewis's *It Can't Happen Here*. These plays, like many of the murals painted in public spaces depicting workers and farmers, and photographs of the rural poor taken for the FSA, promoted a populist vision of culture that celebrated the "common man." They also provoked a backlash. When conservative Democrats and Republicans in Congress gained influence during 1939, they criticized these arts programs as left-wing propaganda and cut off funds for the Federal Theater and other cultural projects.

Women and the New Deal

Women played a larger role in the Roosevelt administration than they had in any previous period, despite the fact that few New Deal programs specifically targeted women. Eleanor Roosevelt had no formal government job, but she transformed the traditional role of First Lady from hostess to social crusader. The handicapped Roosevelt called her his "legs," and she helped him forge the New Deal agenda. Eleanor maintained a circle of feminist friends and social workers concerned with the well-being of working-class women and their families. Through this network and her own travels, she provided her husband with insights into a world he barely knew. Trade unionists, sharecroppers, and African Americans considered her their pipeline to the administration. Eleanor also arranged meetings between the president and labor activists. In 1937, she began writing a nationally syndicated newspaper column, "My Day."

On average, Eleanor Roosevelt traveled 200 days per year to inspect federal projects and the living conditions of ordinary Americans. Once she trudged across a half mile of mud to visit the shack of a tenant farmer. When she knocked on the door, the laborer opened it and with only a hint of surprise said, "Oh, Mrs. Roosevelt, you've come to see me." A few months later the First Lady, wearing a hard hat, descended into a West Virginia coal mine to inspect conditions.

Secretary of Labor Frances Perkins held the highest formal position among female New Dealers. Like Eleanor Roosevelt, she became politically active as a Progressive era reformer promoting causes such as women's voting rights and industrial safety. As secretary of labor, Perkins pushed legislation to improve conditions for all workers, not just women. She played a key role in formulating the Social Security system. Several hundred women were hired as middle-level administrators in federal agencies, an improvement from the past. Nevertheless, most New Deal employment and relief programs adopted a traditional view of the male head of household as breadwinner who should be helped to support his family.

A New Deal for Blacks

African Americans, whether sharecroppers in the South or service workers in the North, suffered some of the worst ravages of the Depression. A few advisors close to the president, such as Eleanor Roosevelt and Interior Secretary Ickes, urged him to support civil rights and openly assist blacks. Roosevelt, weighing his political options, judged it more important to maintain good political relations with powerful southern Democrats in Congress, most of whom strongly opposed any kind of "outside" interference in the rigidly segregated world of the South.

Black community leaders wrote directly to Roosevelt and Harry Hopkins demanding that African Americans be included in federal work relief programs. A number of black officials created a "Federal Council on Negro Affairs." Educator Mary McLeod Bethune served as the informal head of the group. Eleanor Roosevelt arranged for periodic meetings between Bethune and the president.

Because employment policies were often set locally, WPA administrators in the South and Southwest agreed to hire blacks, Hispanics, and Native Americans but paid them lower wages than whites received and assigned them menial tasks. By the late 1930s, most federal work relief programs allocated about 10 percent of their budget to

European Refugees

The New Deal addressed only indirectly the social problems faced by ethnic Americans of European descent. Most recent immigrants and second-generation Americans lived in cities and worked in blue-collar jobs. New Dealers believed that general economic recovery as well as work relief programs would provide basic assistance to these groups. Harry Hopkins and Harold Ickes, both of whom abhorred racism and relished diversity, tried to ensure that the WPA and PWA employed talented administrators and manual laborers of all backgrounds. The president, like many who shared his background, had common social prejudices. But he often reached out to Catholics, Jews, and the descendants of recent immigrants to work closely with him.

Because of hard economic times and lingering antiforeign sentiment, neither members of Congress nor the Roosevelt administration pushed to revise the restrictive National Origins Act of 1924. That law barred most immigration from eastern and southern Europe, as well as all Asian immigration. The prohibition was especially hard on Jewish refugees attempting to flee Nazi and other anti-Semitic campaigns in Europe during the 1930s. Right through the end of World War II, most Americans were more concerned with excluding refugees than with welcoming them. Despite his sympathy with the plight of the oppressed, Roosevelt recognized the unwillingness of Congress to ease entry into the United States and declined to challenge these entrenched views.

AFRICAN AMERICAN ROUNDTABLE   First Lady Eleanor Roosevelt meeting with Mary McLeod Bethune and other African Americans who comprised the informal "black cabinet."

In an era when prejudice lay close to the surface, as seen in Father Coughlin's popular radio rants, anti-Semites bristled at Roosevelt's hiring of several Jewish advisors. Stung by accusations that his name was really "Rosenfeld" and that he came from "Jew York" to lead a "Jew Deal," the president declined to confront the widespread hostility toward immigrants and left in place the barriers that restricted their entry.

A few high-status European refugees, both Jews and Christians, were permitted to enter the country. As discussed in later chapters, dozens of accomplished physicists, including Albert Einstein, Edward Teller, Enrico Fermi, and Leo Szilard, found positions at leading American universities and eventually played critical roles in developing the atomic bomb. When the acclaimed Italian orchestra conductor and fervent antifascist Arturo Toscanini fled to the United States in 1938, the NBC radio network created an orchestra for him to direct. The New School for Social Research in New York City became known as the "university in exile" when, beginning in 1933, it offered faculty positions for hundreds of academics fleeing Nazi persecution. Nearly a thousand Jewish and non-Jewish German film directors, screenwriters, cinematographers, and actors secured visas to work in Hollywood after the Nazis declared them disloyal and purged them from the film industry. These luminaries, including Billy Wilder, Marlene Dietrich, Fritz Lang, Fred Zinnemann, Peter Lorre, and Ernst Lubitsch, deeply influenced American cinema. But the majority of less prominent Europeans, especially Jews, fleeing terror before 1939, found their entry to America barred.

- How did U.S. law ignore the plight of refugees?
- What categories of refugee found safety in the United States?

minority employment. This matched the African American portion of the population, although blacks comprised about 20 percent of the poor. In the South, blacks usually worked in segregated teams doing the most unpleasant jobs. In the North, projects were gradually integrated. In 1939, about one-third of all black households received some income from the WPA.

Simple acts by New Dealers carried great symbolic weight. For example, when Eleanor Roosevelt attended a meeting in a segregated Alabama auditorium, she insisted on sitting in the "coloreds only" section. When Harold Ickes abolished segregated food lines in the Department of Interior cafeteria, the story made national headlines. In 1939, after the Daughters of the American Revolution refused to allow black opera singer Marian Anderson to perform in its Washington, DC, concert hall, Eleanor Roosevelt resigned from the group. She and Ickes arranged for Anderson to perform on the steps of the Lincoln Memorial before a crowd of 75,000.

Roosevelt would not challenge segregation directly nor even endorse a federal anti-lynching law for fear of alienating southern Democrats whose votes he needed in Congress. But over time, the New Deal record on race improved. Roosevelt appointed many federal judges who sympathized with minority aspirations. Among the eight judges FDR appointed to the Supreme Court between 1937 and 1944, several eventually played roles in the effort to dismantle the legal framework of segregation.

Although three-fourths of blacks still lived in the South and had no voting rights, New Deal policies paid a big political dividend to the Democratic Party in the North.

In 1932, most northern blacks remained loyal to the party of Lincoln and voted for Hoover and his fellow Republicans. By 1936, blacks had switched overwhelmingly in favor of Roosevelt and the Democratic Party. During World War II, as large numbers of African Americans moved north, they became committed Democratic voters and have remained so.

Hispanics and the New Deal

The Depression decade proved especially hard on Mexican nationals and other Hispanics living in the West and Southwest. Although the 1924 immigration law placed no formal quota on Mexican migration, under Hoover, border agents blocked most new Mexican immigration and assisted state officials in deporting about 25,000 Mexican nationals and some Mexican Americans. After 1933, state and federal authorities rounded up and sometimes forcibly deported tens of thousands of additional Mexican nationals and Mexican Americans from California and the Rocky Mountain West. Some were shipped south in guarded trains departing from Los Angeles and Denver. By 1935, nearly half a million Mexicans, about as many as had migrated to the United States during the 1920s, had been forcibly sent back to their homeland.

Hispanic woman weaver on a WPA project, New Mexico, 1939

Mexican nationals and those of Mexican descent who avoided deportation lived mainly in California, Texas, and other states in the Southwest. Many worked as migrant agricultural laborers on large commercial farms or on railroads. New Deal agricultural policies did little to help these and other landless farm workers. Instead, federal crop support payments and subsidized irrigation projects helped large landowners. As in the South, commercial farmers often used the payments to mechanize their operations and reduce their need for migrant labor.

The Indian New Deal

Federal policy toward American Indians changed dramatically during the 1930s. Since passage of the Dawes Act in 1887, about two-thirds of tribal lands had been sold off or confiscated; thus, many who lived on reservations became essentially landless. Pressure for them to assimilate into white society continued. During the 1920s, the notoriously corrupt Bureau of Indian Affairs (BIA) extended its ban on Native religious ceremonies and pressed families to send their children to distant boarding schools that discouraged traditional language and culture.

These policies outraged Interior Secretary Harold Ickes. He named **John Collier**, a professional social worker, to head the BIA. In the 1920s, Collier had visited Taos, New Mexico, and became entranced by the culture of the nearby Pueblo tribe. Collier persuaded the CCC to create an Indian division; convinced the Agriculture Department to fund projects on reservations and hire Indians as workers; and lobbied Congress to pass the Pueblo Relief Act in 1933, which compensated the tribe for past land seizures. Congress also approved the **Johnson–O'Malley Act of 1934** that encouraged states to provide better health care and education to Indian tribes. Collier increased the number of Indian BIA employees from a few hundred to over 4,000. He replaced many boarding schools with community day schools, lifted the ban on Native religious ceremonies, and created an Indian Arts and Crafts Board to promote and market traditional handicrafts. In 1934, Congress replaced the Dawes Act with the **Indian Reorganization Act**.

This action slowed the division of reservation land into small plots, encouraged tribal self-government, and established Indian-run corporations to control communal land and resources.

Many western landowners objected to newly imposed limits on mining, grazing, and farming on or around reservations. Some Christian groups resented losing their religious monopoly on reservations. Even some Indians complained that Collier's reverence for tradition was forcing them to "return to the blanket" and that he did not comprehend the diversity among various tribal groups. By the time he left office in 1945, not all tribes had agreed to reorganize themselves under the scheme of self-government he promoted. Nevertheless, the reforms ended several of the worst policies inflicted on Native peoples and provided a guide for greater tribal rights.

Nature's New Deal

New Deal environmental policies pulled in various, sometimes contradictory, directions. To assist commercial farming in the Pacific Northwest and California, federal agencies constructed irrigation canals and dams on the Colorado and Columbia rivers. These heavily subsidized water projects boosted production on arid land otherwise unfit for large-scale agriculture. The massive TVA also relied on dam construction for flood control and power generation. Other New Deal projects undertaken by the CCC and WPA promoted reforestation and virtually created the infrastructure of the national park system.

Elsewhere, New Deal programs tried to ameliorate the consequences of overdevelopment. Decades of corn and wheat cultivation on the Great Plains, the destruction of native grasses, and prolonged drought created the Dust Bowl, a major ecological disaster (Map 23.1). Beginning in the early 1930s and continuing for much of the decade,

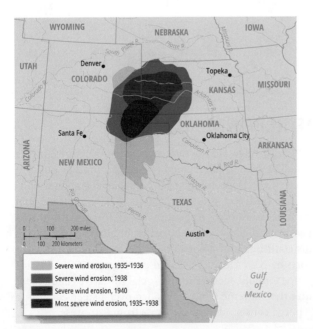

MAP 23.1 The Dimensions of the Dust Bowl in the 1930s The Dust Bowl of the mid-1930s affected parts of Colorado, Kansas, New Mexico, Texas, and Oklahoma. Its economic and social impact was even wider, as millions of farmers from this region sought work along the West Coast.

map analysis

fierce windstorms blowing from west to east picked up dry topsoil and darkened the sky, sometimes for days. Millions of tons of Plains soil landed on the East Coast and some across the Atlantic. Oklahoma balladeer Woody Guthrie described these storms in haunting songs. In his 1939 novel *The Grapes of Wrath,* John Steinbeck immortalized the Joads, a mythical family of "Okies," poor farmers driven from Oklahoma by hard times and bad weather. Like the Joads, over two million people fled the Plains states, many traveling Route 66 to California seeking work as migrant laborers.

Roosevelt took a personal interest in solving these problems. Much of the early effort by the CCC was directed toward rural conservation projects in the West. At Roosevelt's personal direction, for example, young volunteers planted over 200 million trees as part of a 3,600-mile, north-to-south system of windbreaks, or "shelter belts," in the Midwest and Great Plains. Many experts scoffed at this idea, but over time, the windbreaks worked as the president hoped. Other federal programs limited grazing on public lands and replanted native grasses.

Aerial view of Boulder (Hoover) Dam (1934)

On a per capita basis, the West received more federal payments for development than any other region of the country during the 1930s. Much of the Western infrastructure built during the 1930s, such as dams, irrigation networks, electric grids, and roads, played a major role in speeding military production during World War II and regional growth afterward. The Grand Coulee Dam, for example, supplied electrical power to produce the aluminum that went into constructing military aircraft and ships along the West Coast.

STUDY QUESTIONS FOR SOCIETY, LAW, AND CULTURE IN THE 1930S

quiz

1. How did New Deal reforms help or ignore problems faced by women and minorities during the Depression?

2. Did popular culture in the 1930s reflect social concerns or provide audiences with an escape from reality?

3. What impact did New Deal programs have on the American West?

❂ THE TWILIGHT OF REFORM

Excerpt from Norman Thomas, *After the New Deal, What?* (1936)

Early in 1937, Congress convened with huge Democratic majorities: 331 to 89 in the House and 76 to 16 in the Senate. The New Deal seemed poised for another burst of social activism. Yet, once the worst of the Depression crisis had abated, national politics reverted to its more conservative tradition. Southern Democrats, who feared that liberal New Dealers would promote racial reform, frequently joined forces with northern Republicans, who opposed additional economic regulation, to block expansion of social programs. After 1938, this coalition, along with the gathering clouds of war in Europe and Asia, frustrated efforts by New Dealers to build on their previous accomplishments. By the end of 1938, hope for bold economic and social initiatives had faded. Roosevelt lost a fight to reorganize the Supreme Court, presided over a steep economic downturn, and failed in a bid to purge conservative Democrats from Congress.

The New Deal and Judicial Change

Between 1934 and 1936, a five-vote conservative majority on the nine-member Supreme Court struck down as unconstitutional key pieces of New Deal legislation, including the NRA and AAA. The conservatives ruled that the interstate commerce clause of the Constitution granted Congress and the president very limited power to regulate the economy, set wages, or impose workplace rules. Some of their decisions even questioned whether state governments could regulate business within their borders. These actions, Roosevelt complained, created a "no-man's land where no government—state or federal—can function" or impose any meaningful regulation on business behavior or other aspects of the economy. With the Court poised in 1937 to strike down such New Deal pillars as the Social Security and National Labor Relations acts, the president and his supporters expressed growing frustration.

Several of the most conservative Supreme Court justices were elderly men appointed decades earlier who saw themselves as guardians of property rights. To "ease the burden" on these elderly jurists, in 1937 Roosevelt asked Congress to pass a Judiciary Reorganization Act. It would dilute the conservative bloc by allowing him to appoint additional justices for each member of the high court over age 70.

The Constitution allowed Congress to adjust the size of the Supreme Court. But the number had settled at nine after the Civil War. When Roosevelt tried to push this change through Congress without much consultation, he alienated members of both parties, who complained about what they called the "**court packing scheme**." The president dropped the plan at a substantial cost to his reputation.

However, the Supreme Court soon swung around to support the New Deal. One conservative justice switched sides, joining the four liberals in voting to sustain key laws. Over the next few years, several other conservative justices retired. By 1944, Roosevelt had appointed a total of eight Supreme Court justices.

This new majority supported the president's belief that the Constitution gave the federal government broad authority to regulate business, the economy, labor conditions, and the environment. The Supreme Court upheld minimum wage laws, workplace regulations, production limits on farmers, Social Security, and the government's right to require that businesses recognize labor unions. During the 1940s and early 1950s, several of these justices joined in landmark civil rights decisions that began dismantling the framework of racial segregation enshrined since the 1890s.

Recession

Even after the Supreme Court upheld the New Deal, new economic and political constraints stifled reform efforts. Midway through 1937, a severe recession shook confidence in Roosevelt's leadership and prompted a conservative resurgence. The economy had grown rapidly between 1933 and 1937. Although many workers still sought jobs, the rate of unemployment had declined from 25 to about 14 percent. Roosevelt and Treasury Secretary Henry Morgenthau considered this evidence that the economic emergency had passed and the time had come to balance the budget. With their consent, Congress reduced federal spending by about 10 percent, eliminating funding for many WPA-related jobs programs. At this same time, workers began paying the new Social Security tax, which pulled about $2 billion out of circulation. The Federal Reserve

interactive timeline

TIMELINE 1931–1939

AMERICA	YEAR	THE WORLD
Jan–Jul The Great Depression becomes more severe as businesses and banks fail and millions of workers lose jobs and savings **Jul** President Hoover is discredited after he orders Bonus Army dispersed in Washington by police and troops; Democratic Party nominates Franklin D. Roosevelt as its candidate for president with promise of a "new deal" for the American people and concern for the "forgotten man." **Nov** Roosevelt elected president by a wide margin and Democrats dominate new Congress **Nov 1932–Mar 1933** Depression worsens in five months between Roosevelt's election and inauguration; thousands more banks fail, and unemployment rate rises to 25 percent, with another 25 percent working part-time for reduced wages	**1932**	**Jan–Dec** Most of Europe, Asia, and Latin America succumb to the Depression
Feb–Mar Banking system virtually closes down throughout United States; many politicians urge Roosevelt to assume dictatorial powers **Mar** Roosevelt inaugurated; proposes series of government initiatives to deal with economic crisis; begins speaking directly to public through "fireside chats" broadcast over the radio **Mar** United States abandons the gold standard **Mar–Jun** "First Hundred Days" of legislative reform enacted by Congress, including bank regulation, farm aid, and emergency relief appropriations for the unemployed; Prohibition repealed by constitutional amendment	**1933**	**Jan** Adolf Hitler becomes German chancellor and soon assumes dictatorial power
Apr Indian Reorganization Act passed by Congress **Jun** Securities and Exchange Commission created, regulating stock market	**1934**	
Spring–summer Second Hundred Days of reform legislation begins **Apr** WPA created to employ millions of jobless laborers and to work on federal projects **Aug** Social Security Act passed, creating old-age pension system and programs to assist injured workers	**1935**	

further stressed the economy by tightening credit rules for the nation's banks, an action that made loans more expensive.

This combination of spending cuts, tax hikes, and credit reduction sharply reduced consumer purchasing power and pushed the still fragile economy into a steep decline. Five years of steady stock price increases reversed and unemployment surged. Conservative economists urged Roosevelt to make steeper cuts to balance the budget. New Deal liberals, influenced by Keynes's landmark book *The General Theory of Employment, Interest, and Money* (1936), argued in favor of increased federal spending to stimulate economic growth.

Keynes and his American disciples considered the events of 1937 as proof that the private economy had only partially recovered from the trauma of the Depression and still required a big federal stimulus. Roosevelt dithered for months before taking action. In the spring of 1938, he abandoned his quest for a balanced budget. He persuaded Congress to fund a $5 billion spending program to resume hiring the unemployed and increase mass purchasing power. This new spending, along with military orders placed in American factories from Great Britain and France in response to the German threat in Europe, restored economic growth.

In June 1938, Roosevelt won congressional approval for what turned out to be the last major New Deal reform before World War II, the **Fair Labor Standards Act**. The law banned child labor, established a federal minimum wage starting at 40 cents per

AMERICA	YEAR	THE WORLD
Nov Roosevelt reelected in a landslide; large Democratic majorities elected to Congress **Dec** Automobile workers' sit-down strikes begin in Michigan, demanding union recognition	**1936**	**Feb** Keynes publishes *The General Theory of Employment, Interest, and Money,* describing how government spending could stimulate economic growth
Feb Roosevelt proposes Judicial Reorganization Act to enlarge Supreme Court by adding liberal judges, but Congress rejects his plan **Jul** Roosevelt agrees to reduce federal deficit spending to balance the budget, triggering a steep recession and a surge in unemployment	**1937**	**Jul** Japan invades China
May Congress creates House Committee on Un-American Activities to investigate left-wing influence in New Deal agencies **Spring–summer** Roosevelt resumes deficit spending on federal projects, restores economic growth **Jun** Congress enacts Fair Labor Standards Act, last major New Deal reform before World War II **Jun–Nov** Roosevelt fails in effort to "purge" mostly southern conservative Democrats from Congress by endorsing liberal opponents in party primaries **Nov** Following midterm elections, conservative southern Democrats and an increased number of northern Republicans in Congress join forces to block further New Deal reforms	**1938**	**Sep** Munich Conference sacrifices Czechoslovakia **Nov** Nazis step up attacks on German Jews
	1939	**Sep** War begins in Europe after Hitler's armies invade Poland

hour, and set the standard workweek at 40 hours, with extra pay for overtime. But to secure the votes of southern Democrats, Roosevelt agreed once again to exempt from coverage most agricultural and domestic workers, whose ranks included a high proportion of women, blacks, and Hispanics.

Political Setbacks

Another New Deal stumble followed the court packing fiasco and recession of 1937–1938. Frustrated by the continued opposition to his policies by conservative Democrats mostly from the South, Roosevelt tried to reshape the party. In the 1938 Democratic primary elections, he campaigned on behalf of liberals who ran against entrenched anti–New Deal Democrats. Despite his effort, most of the old guard survived the challenge. In the South, incumbents stoked fear among poor whites that Roosevelt intended to challenge segregation and empower blacks.

The congressional election of 1938 brought more bad news for Roosevelt. Republicans picked up 81 additional House and 8 additional Senate seats. This enhanced GOP minority frequently joined forces with southern Democrats to block New Deal proposals. Conservatives in both parties renewed demands to balance the federal budget, to curb the power of labor unions, and to spend less on the unemployed. The conservative coalition killed proposals to restructure the tax code, reorganize the executive branch, and create additional TVA-like regional development programs. Congress even created a House Committee on Un-American Activities to probe alleged Communist penetration of the labor movement and New Deal agencies. At the end of 1938, Roosevelt told an aide that it was sad but true that the economy and Democratic Party would benefit from the global slide toward war. "Foreign orders for armaments . . . mean prosperity in this country and we can't elect Democrats unless we get prosperity." The president also recognized that to win broad support for a policy of resisting Germany and Japan, he needed to improve ties to the business community as well as to conservatives in both parties. The outbreak of war in Europe in September 1939 pushed social reform further into the background, as Roosevelt prepared the nation to confront the gathering threat from abroad.

STUDY QUESTIONS FOR THE TWILIGHT OF REFORM

quiz

1. What issue led Roosevelt to clash with the Supreme Court in 1937?

2. Why did the economy suffer a setback in 1937–1938?

3. How did the New Deal lose political support after 1938?

Summary

- The Depression grew steadily worse between 1929 and early 1933.
- Both the new urban poor and rural farmers received little help.
- The Hoover administration provided modest assistance to business but none directly to the unemployed.
- Franklin Roosevelt took an innovative approach to unemployment while he was governor of New York and brought this view to the presidency in 1933.
- The New Deal involved a series of regulatory reforms to stabilize the private economy and several programs to assist the unemployed and the rural poor.
- Critics on the right and on the left attacked the New Deal for doing either too much or too little.
- Roosevelt implemented additional radical social and economic reforms between 1935 and 1938.
- New Deal construction projects reshaped the American landscape.
- New Deal programs reached out to many groups previously ignored by government and built a political coalition that included organized labor, ethnic Americans, African Americans, and women.
- Throughout the 1930s, conservatives in Congress and on the Supreme Court opposed New Deal reforms and limited their scope.
- By 1938 a coalition of conservative Democrats and Republicans had stymied further social and economic reform.
- Although the private economy did not fully recover until World War II, the New Deal helped preserve both capitalism and democracy in a world where both were endangered and developed infrastructure vital to both defense production during World War II and economic growth after 1945.

Key Terms and People

Agricultural Adjustment Administration (AAA) 798

Berle, Adolph 794

Collier, John 814

Congress of Industrial Organizations (CIO) 801

court packing scheme 817

Dust Bowl 795

Emergency Banking Relief Act 796

Fair Labor Standards Act 818

fireside chats 796

First Hundred Days 797

Glass–Steagall Banking Act 796

Hitler, Adolf 790

Hoovervilles 789

Hopkins, Harry 794

Indian Reorganization Act 814

Johnson–O'Malley Act of 1934 814

Keynesian economics 799

Long, Huey 801

MacArthur, Douglas 789

Moley, Raymond 794

Murphy, Frank 805

National Recovery Administration (NRA) 799

New Deal 790

Perkins, Frances 793

Reconstruction Finance Corporation (RFC) 793

Roosevelt, Eleanor 790

Roosevelt, Franklin D. 789

Securities Act of 1933 796

Securities Exchange Act of 1934 796

Sinclair, Upton 801

Social Security Act 804

Tennessee Valley Authority (TVA) 797

Townsend, Frances 800

Tugwell, Rexford 794

Wagner, Robert 805

Wallace, Henry A. 798

Works Progress Administration (WPA) 803

Reviewing Chapter 23

1. How did the Depression worsen in the months after the 1932 election?
2. What were several early New Deal recovery measures?
3. What major new reforms did the New Deal implement in 1935–1936?
4. What were some of the failures of the New Deal?
5. After 1938, what political barriers emerged to further reform?

Further Reading

Badger, Anthony. *The New Deal: The Depression Years, 1933–1940*. New York: Macmillan, 1989. Badger examines the dire economic conditions and social malaise that afflicted American workers and farmers as the Depression ravaged their lives.

Breitman, Richard, and Lichtman, Allan. *FDR and the Jews*. Cambridge, MA: Belknap Press, 2013. Examines Roosevelt's efforts—both compassionate and pragmatic—to respond to the plight of those suffering Nazi persecution while constrained by domestic politics and wartime imperatives.

Brinkley, Alan. *Voices of Protest: Huey Long, Father Coughlin, and the Great Depression*. New York: Knopf, 1982. Long and Coughlin were revered—and despised—by millions of Americans when they proposed radical solutions to the nation's distress.

Cohen, Lizabeth. *Making a New Deal: Industrial Workers in Chicago, 1919–1939*. New York: Cambridge University Press, 1990. Cohen explains how blue-collar workers and their unions pressed for economic reform before the 1930s and pushed the often cautious New Deal in more radical, pro-labor directions.

Cowie, Jefferson. *The Great Exception: The New Deal and the Limits of American Politics*. Princeton, NJ: Princeton University Press, 2016. Examines the political forces that enabled liberals to forge the New Deal while also limiting the scope and duration of domestic reform.

Downey, Kristin. *The Woman Behind the New Deal: The Life and Legacy of Frances Perkins.* New York: Nan A. Talese, 2009. As the first female cabinet member, Secretary of Labor Frances Perkins shaped the nation's welfare policies and was the principal architect of the New Deal's best-known innovation, Social Security.

Katznelson, Ira. *Fear Itself: The New Deal and the Origins of Our Time.* New York: Liveright, 2013. Southern politicians, and their commitment to segregation, both shaped and limited the reform dimensions of the New Deal. At the same time, white southerners favored a more militant foreign policy that carried the United States into the Cold War.

Kennedy, David. *Freedom from Fear: The American People in Depression and War, 1929–1945.* New York: Oxford University Press, 2001. A panoramic overview of the Depression and New Deal era that highlights the nearly unimaginably complex challenges faced by the Roosevelt administration at home and abroad.

Patel, Kiran Klaus. *The New Deal: A Global History.* Princeton, NJ: Princeton University Press, 2016. Examines the ways in which New Deal reforms were influenced by developments in Europe and Latin America and how Roosevelt's ideas were received abroad.

Philips-Fein, Kim. *Invisible Hands: The Businessmen's Crusade Against the New Deal.* New York, Norton, 2010. Chronicles the effort by big business since the 1930s to oppose and roll back New Deal reforms.

Sitkoff, Harvard. *A New Deal for Blacks.* New York: Oxford University Press, 1978. Long oppressed by racial injustice, no group of Americans suffered more from the Depression than African Americans. New Deal reformers were among the first national leaders to attempt to ameliorate these wrongs.

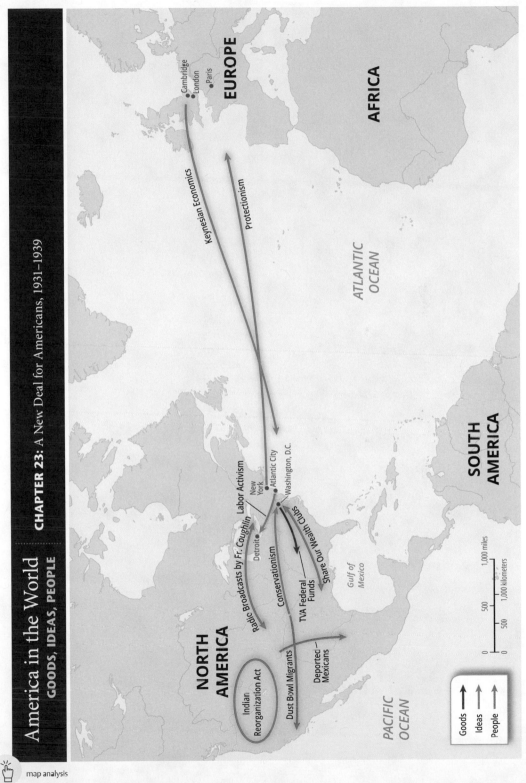

America in the World
GOODS, IDEAS, PEOPLE

CHAPTER 23: A New Deal for Americans, 1931–1939

EUROPE

Cambridge
London
Paris

AFRICA

Keynesian Economics

Protectionism

ATLANTIC OCEAN

NORTH AMERICA

Labor Activism

New York

Atlantic City

Washington, D.C.

Radio Broadcasts by Fr. Coughlin

Detroit

Conservationism

TVA Federal Funds

Share Our Wealth Clubs

Gulf of Mexico

SOUTH AMERICA

Indian Reorganization Act

Dust Bowl Migrants

Deported Mexicans

PACIFIC OCEAN

Goods
Ideas
People

0   500   1,000 miles
0   500   1,000 kilometers

map analysis

President Franklin D. Roosevelt studying a giant globe shortly after the United States entered World War II.

CHAPTER 24

Arsenal of Democracy: The World at War

1931–1945

On the night of June 22, 1941, as a million soldiers in Germany's *Wehrmacht* (army) invaded the Soviet Union, **Adolf Hitler**'s propaganda minister, **Joseph Goebbels**, joined other top Nazis in watching a special screening of the American film *Gone with the Wind*. Nazi leaders often expressed admiration for the Old South and lamented the defeat of the Confederacy. The Union's victory, Hitler rued, had destroyed a "great new social order based on the principle of slavery and inequality." After 1865, Hitler believed, immigration from eastern Europe had created a "decadent" America (he singled out Miami as the worst of cities), "half Judaized and the other half negrified," that worshipped the dollar and corrupted everything it touched.

Nazi leaders saw a glimmer of hope in the American South. There state eugenics laws—eagerly copied by the Nazi regime—allowed sterilization of "defectives," while the Ku Klux Klan defended white supremacy against blacks, Jews, and Catholics. Hitler thought the Klan might even become a vanguard of German influence. He encouraged Nazi journalists to praise the racist organization for sharing what he called his "progressive" views of racial hierarchy, such as lynching blacks and attacking Jews.

Several months later, the *führer*, as Hitler was called, expressed glee over Japan's bold attack on the U.S. Pacific Fleet in Hawaii on December 7, 1941. He predicted this would force the United States to defend the Pacific coast and reduce America's ability to assist Great Britain and the Soviet Union. Convinced now that Germany could not lose, on December 11, Hitler, along with his Italian ally Benito Mussolini, declared war on the United States.

Japanese military leaders also viewed *Gone with the Wind*, after capturing a copy when their troops overran Singapore in February 1942. Unlike their Nazi allies, however, Japanese militarists were deeply troubled by the movie. Could Japan, they asked themselves, defeat a nation that had produced such a technologically advanced film?

World War II was the most destructive human-caused event of the 20th century. Around 70 million people, mostly civilians in Europe and Asia, perished in battles and firebombed cities, from war-caused famines and epidemics, or in industrial-scale death camps like those set up by the Nazis in eastern Europe (Table 24.1). When the killing stopped in 1945, the United States—which suffered about 400,000 military deaths—with just 6 percent of the world's population, produced half of the world's goods. This relative level of economic power has never been surpassed. As one American veteran noted, "While the rest of the world came out bruised and scarred and nearly destroyed, we came out with the most unbelievable machinery, trade, manpower, and money." It seemed, in the confident words of *Time-Life* magazine publisher **Henry Luce**, the beginning of the "first great American Century."

Table 24.1 Deaths in World War II

As many as 70 million people died globally during World War II. At least as many civilians as soldiers perished, especially in eastern Europe and China, where German and Japanese armed forces killed large numbers of noncombatants and prisoners of war. The numbers are estimates.

COUNTRY	MILITARY DEAD AND MISSING	CIVILIAN DEAD	JEWISH HOLOCAUST VICTIMS	TOTAL DEAD AND MISSING
United States	420,000	1,700	—	421,700
United Kingdom	383,600	66,400	—	450,000
France	250,000	350,000	90,000	690,000
Soviet Union	13,600,000	13,000,000	1,720,000	28,320,000
China	3,500,000	16,000,000	—	19,500,000
Germany	5,500,000	2,500,000	170,000	8,170,000
Italy	300,000	155,500	15,000	470,500
Japan	2,100,000	500,000	—	2,600,000
All other participants	1,180,000	4,690,000	3,998,000	9,868,000
Total	27,233,600	37,263,600	5,993,000	70,490,200

THE LONG FUSE

Several of the issues that sparked World War I—competing nationalism, drive for colonies, rival alliances—continued to fester during the 1920s and 1930s. Many Germans felt betrayed by the harsh peace settlement at Versailles. Italy and Japan resented the limited territories they had gained from victory. France remained terrified of a revived Germany. A financially strapped Great Britain resolved to avoid a land war in Europe while preserving its overseas empire. The Soviet Union, born from the ruins of czarist Russia, remained an international outcast that preached a doctrine of world revolution. Most Americans regretted the failure of the Great War to "make the world safe for democracy" and resented the lives lost and money spent that had achieved so little.

By the time of Roosevelt's inauguration in March 1933, dictators on the left and right ruled several major nations. Various forms of fascism—an authoritarian political movement that linked militarists, big business, extreme nationalists, religious conservatives, and racial purists—dominated Italy and Germany and had footholds elsewhere in Europe and Latin America. In the Soviet Union, **Joseph Stalin** established a dictatorship under the banner of the Communist Party. In Japan, power slipped away from the elected parliament and into the hands of the emperor and a coalition of military extremists and industrial tycoons who envisioned taking control of all Asia. Nazi dictator Adolf Hitler, who came to power at almost the same time as Roosevelt, spoke of creating a "Greater Germany" in control of central and eastern Europe, whereas Italy's **Benito Mussolini**, in power a decade longer, called for rebuilding a "Roman Empire" in the Mediterranean and northern Africa. To various degrees German, Italian, and Japanese leaders justified their plans with a mystical belief in racial superiority and a willingness to dominate or even exterminate what they called inferior peoples.

POPULATION

Africa

Asia

Europe

Latin America and the Caribbean

North America

Oceania

World Population c. 1950
U.S. Population 1930: 122,775,046
U.S. Population 1940: 131,669,275

0
200,000,000
400,000,000
600,000,000
800,000,000
1,000,000,000
1,200,000,000
1,400,000,000
1,600,000,000
1,800,000,000

Mussolini on fascism (1932)

Isolationist Impulse

Franklin Roosevelt, like most Americans, looked on events in Europe and Asia with a mix of detachment and disgust. He could scarcely believe that 15 years after Wilson's prediction of a "new world order," militarism again threatened peace. Americans, however, looked skeptically at any proposal to become militarily or politically involved abroad.

Even during the good times of the 1920s, the United States had pursued a unilateral, or go-it-alone, approach to many aspects of world affairs. Americans profited from foreign trade, and Washington negotiated arms limitation pacts. But Congress put a tight lid on immigration and shunned most cooperation with the League of Nations and other international organizations. Many scholars and journalists argued that in 1917 the United States had been hoodwinked by the British and French into fighting to protect their empires, not to defend American security or promote democratic ideals. Popular novels by Ernest Hemingway and John Dos Passos echoed this theme.

As the Depression took hold, Americans turned increasingly inward. A prominent Democrat, Pennsylvania governor George Earle, proclaimed in 1935, "If the world is to become a wilderness of waste, hatred, and bitterness, let us all the more earnestly protect and preserve our own oasis of liberty." Membership surged in antiwar groups such as the Women's International League for Peace and Freedom. Thousands of college students pledged not to fight in another war, whereas others mocked politicians by organizing a group called Veterans of Future Wars. Congressional committees issued reports blaming bankers and munitions manufacturers—so-called merchants of death—for duping Americans to fight in 1917.

Excerpt from Aldous Huxley, *An Encyclopedia of Pacifism* (1937)

Although Roosevelt had served as assistant secretary of the navy during World War I and had campaigned in 1920 for membership in the League of Nations, by 1933 he had opted not to challenge this isolationist tide. Shortly after becoming president, he refused to join an international effort to restore the gold standard and cut the budget for the already tiny U.S. Army.

Roosevelt promoted a few noncontroversial foreign policy initiatives. These included implementing a "**Good Neighbor Policy**" to cease bullying Latin American nations. In December 1933, the United States informed the Pan-American Conference in Uruguay that it agreed that no nation, large or small, had the right to interfere militarily in the affairs of other hemispheric states. In 1934, after two decades of occupation, Roosevelt withdrew Marines from Haiti and canceled the Platt Amendment, a law enacted after the Spanish-American War asserting the United States' right to send troops into Cuba. The only risky diplomatic initiative the president took came in November 1933 when he extended diplomatic recognition to the Soviet Union, an action opposed by religious and political conservatives.

Disengagement from Europe

Most politicians opposed even modest engagement in world affairs. For example, early in 1935 the Senate, encouraged by an isolationist press, rejected a treaty proposed by Roosevelt to allow the United States to participate in the World Court, a largely advisory body. In August 1935, Congress passed and Roosevelt signed the first of five restrictive **Neutrality Acts**. These laws reassured German, Italian, and Japanese leaders that the United States was unlikely to impede their actions.

The Neutrality Act of 1935 stipulated that once war began between foreign nations, the U.S. government must impose an embargo on arms sales to both sides and stop U.S. citizens from traveling on their ships. The law made no distinction between "aggressor" and "victim."

The impact of this policy was apparent in October 1935 when Mussolini's Italian army invaded Ethiopia, one of only two independent nations in Africa. The Italians used airplanes, poison gas, and heavy artillery to kill thousands of Ethiopian civilians and lightly armed soldiers. This brutality appalled many Americans. Even though oil and other raw material sales were not covered by the embargo provisions of the neutrality law, Roosevelt requested that U.S. exporters impose a "moral embargo" restricting oil sales to Italy. However, chasing profits, few companies complied.

Congress expanded the scope of the Neutrality Act in February 1936. New provisions barred private and government loans and credits, as well as arms sales, to warring nations. Once again the law did not restrict sales of raw materials. A month later, in March 1936, when Hitler marched troops into the Rhineland, German territory along the French border that by treaty was supposed to remain demilitarized, Britain and France acquiesced. France turned its attention to constructing the Maginot Line, an expensive and ultimately useless system of fixed border fortifications.

Emboldened by their success, on November 1, 1936, Italy and Germany announced the creation of an alliance they called the Rome-Berlin Axis. Soon after, Germany, Japan, and Italy signed the **Anti-Comintern Pact**, an anti-Communist alliance. In September 1940, Germany, Italy, and Japan created the so-called Axis alliance, a promise of military cooperation should any of them be attacked.

The outbreak of the **Spanish Civil War** in July 1936 prompted Hitler and Mussolini to rush military aid to General Francisco Franco, a Spanish Fascist who led his troops in revolt against the leftist but democratic Spanish Republican government. Stalin, too, dispatched some military aid and advisors to assist the Republic. Several thousand Americans volunteered to fight on behalf of the Republic, their experience described in Hemingway's 1940 novel, *For Whom the Bell Tolls*. Fighting in Spain prompted Congress to pass a third Neutrality Act in January 1937. This extended the existing ban on loans and arms sales to cover civil wars. In another twist, Congress decreed that warring nations could continue to buy U.S. raw materials, but they had to pay cash and transport the goods in their own ships. This "cash and carry" provision once again implicitly helped Germany, Japan, and Italy, which, unlike most of their victims, had cash, ships, and factories to purchase, transport, and process American raw materials.

Guernica (1937)

Disengagement in Asia

Japanese nationalists also nursed dreams of empire. In 1931, Japan's army had seized Manchuria and set up a puppet state called Manchukuo. Although this action violated treaty pledges Japan had signed with the United States a decade earlier, the Hoover administration responded with only a declaration by Secretary of State **Henry L. Stimson** that the United States would not recognize the legality of Japan's conquests. When the League of Nations condemned Japanese aggression, Tokyo, like Germany, quit the organization.

In mid-1937, the rival Chinese Communist and Chinese Nationalist parties halted their civil war and formed an anti-Japanese United Front. Japan responded in July by invading China with the aim of incorporating it into what it later called the "Greater East Asia Co-Prosperity Sphere"—a euphemism for Japanese control of Asia and the Pacific.

By the close of 1937, Japanese armies controlled most of coastal China. China's large but poorly equipped forces fled inland, trading space for time. When Japanese troops captured the capital city of Nanking (Nanjing) in December 1937, they slaughtered between 200,000 and 400,000 civilians, an outrage soon known as the Rape of Nanking.

Although such mass terror appalled Americans, a Chicago newspaper headline typified public sentiment: "We Sympathize, But It Is Not Our Concern." Even the sinking of a U.S. Navy ship, the *Panay*, on China's Yangtze River in December 1937 by Japanese planes failed to arouse Americans. Shortly before this Japanese attack, Roosevelt gave a speech proposing that democratic nations cooperate to "quarantine" aggressors. After being labeled a "warmonger" by many newspapers and his Republican opponents, he dropped the idea.

Appeasement

Doubting their own capacity to resist Hitler, and with little prospect of U.S. support, the governments of Great Britain and France adopted a policy known as appeasement. Although this term later became an epithet hurled at politicians who caved to threats, it initially implied compromising with rivals to avert war. European conservatives, who feared Soviet communism nearly as much as Nazi Germany, saw another benefit to appeasement. By accommodating Hitler's expansion into eastern Europe, they might turn him against the Soviet Union and spare themselves.

Appeasement not only failed a moral test, but, as Britain's future prime minister **Winston Churchill** noted, it had a basic practical flaw: in theory, as he put it, "jaw, jaw" (negotiations) was better than "war, war," except that Hitler intended to go to war eventually to secure what he called *Lebensraum,* or living space. He would settle for nothing less than a Greater Germany that dominated central Europe and annexed most of eastern Europe and Russia, from which subhuman "races," such as the Jews, Poles, Slavs, and Gypsies, would be removed and killed. Appeasement reached its peak during 1938. In March, Hitler again defied the Versailles Treaty by annexing Austria. In September, he demanded that Czechoslovakia, a nation created in 1919 from the disbanded Austro-Hungarian Empire, turn over its Sudetenland region that had a large German-speaking population. British prime minister **Neville Chamberlain** and French leader Édouard Daladier again caved to Hitler's demands, despite earlier pledges to defend the Czechs. Appeasement, Chamberlain claimed, had secured "peace for our time." A few months later, the Nazis seized the remainder of Czechoslovakia.

A year later, Hitler targeted Germany's eastern neighbor, Poland. The British and French governments finally recognized the futility of appeasement and resolved to fight. Soviet dictator Joseph Stalin secretly negotiated his own self-serving deal with Hitler. The German–Soviet Non-Aggression Pact, signed in August 1939, provided for joint German–Soviet partition of Poland, Soviet delivery of raw materials to Germany, and a German pledge not to attack the Soviet Union. Hitler approved of Stalin's seizing the Baltic states of Lithuania, Latvia, and Estonia, which had been stripped from Russia after World War I, and Stalin agreed that Hitler could take whatever territory he wanted in southeastern Europe.

Having neutralized the Soviet Union, Hitler attacked Poland on September 1, 1939. German forces quickly overpowered the courageous but outmatched Poles, who sent waves of cavalry in futile charges against *panzers* (tanks). Meanwhile, Soviet forces occupied the eastern portions of the country. Stunned by the cunning showed by both Hitler and Stalin, Great Britain and France declared war on Germany on September 3, 1939.

Speech by Hitler after the invasion of Poland (September 19, 1939)

NAZI PROPAGANDA Adolf Hitler and Neville Chamberlain on the steps of the Berghof in Obersalzberg, on September 15, 1938. In the background is the interpreter Paul Schmidt.

America at the Brink of War, 1939–1941

As required by law, Roosevelt responded to the European war by declaring American neutrality. But unlike Wilson in 1914, he did not ask Americans to remain neutral in their thoughts or passions. Roosevelt made it clear he believed the United States must do more to assist those who stood up to Axis aggression, and the public increasingly shared his view. But how to do so? The U.S. Army, with only 175,000 enlisted men in 1939, could not provide much help to anyone. Roosevelt hoped that the U.S. Navy could shelter the nation as the army rebuilt its strength. U.S. military spending in 1939 was barely one-tenth of Germany's. Meanwhile, Roosevelt prodded a reluctant Congress in November 1939 to permit arms sales to Britain and France, and then only if they paid cash and transported the weapons on their own ships.

In the spring of 1940, Germany launched a series of rapid attacks in western Europe, dubbed a "Blitzkrieg," or lightning war. During May and June, German forces overran France. Marshal Philippe Pétain, a hero of World War I, formed a pro-German government, known as Vichy, in the southern half of the country. The surrender stranded

300,000 British troops along with some French forces loyal to General Charles de Gaulle on the beaches at Dunkirk. A heroic rescue by British fishing boats and the Royal Navy saved most of the troops but not their equipment.

After the fall of France, British resolve wavered. Key government officials, many of them advocates of the discredited appeasement policy, favored making peace with Hitler, leaving him in control of Europe if he allowed Britain to keep most of its empire. Only the ironclad determination of Britain's new prime minister, Winston Churchill, sustained morale and held peace advocates at bay during the summer of 1940. Churchill's description of the rescue of British soldiers at Dunkirk turned a near military disaster into a psychological victory. In his first and best-remembered speech to the House of Commons, he grimly declared that he had nothing to offer but "blood, toil, tears, and sweat," but that no matter what Nazi Germany did, Britain, unlike France, would "never surrender."

The prime minister directed his pledge at the United States as well as his own people. Churchill and Roosevelt had barely known each other before the war, but they gradually formed a close personal bond through their exchange of frank and frequent messages. Churchill acknowledged that without massive U.S. aid, his nation was doomed. Roosevelt understood that if the Nazis conquered Britain and its colonies, they would dominate the Atlantic Ocean, the Mediterranean region, and the Middle East, making them nearly unbeatable.

During 1940, Congress acceded to Roosevelt's pleas to boost military spending and authorized a peacetime draft. In September, Roosevelt used his executive power to transfer to the Royal Navy 50 World War I–era U.S. destroyers in return for granting the United States naval base rights in the British West Indies. Roosevelt then pulled back from providing more assistance to Britain. He had decided to run for an unprecedented third term in November 1940 and feared his opponents would paint him as a warmonger.

Anti-interventionist groups accused Roosevelt of planning to enter the war if reelected. Among his critics was aviation hero Charles Lindbergh, who praised Nazi accomplishments and promoted the America First Committee, founded in 1940 with the backing of several wealthy anti–New Deal corporate donors. Lindbergh warned that British imperialists and a shadowy group of Jews were behind efforts to fight Germany. Even more vicious attacks came from the pro-Nazi German American Bund, whose leaders denounced Roosevelt as a traitor under the thumb of powerful Jewish interests.

Radio address by Charles Lindbergh (April 1941)

During the summer and fall of 1940, Germany's Luftwaffe relentlessly bombed British cities, factories, and airfields in preparation for a cross-channel invasion. Americans closely followed the Battle of Britain in radio broadcasts on the CBS network, narrated by journalist **Edward R. Murrow**. Reporting from rooftops and air-raid shelters, with audible explosions in the background, he opened with the words: "This . . . is London." These reports deepened popular support for the British people.

A secret technological breakthrough, along with heroic efforts by the Royal Air Force (RAF) and Royal Navy, sustained Britain. British mathematicians at Bletchley Park constructed a primitive computer that helped decipher coded messages sent on the German Enigma machine used to direct air and submarine attacks. Code-named ULTRA, this project revealed which cities or airfields the Germans had targeted for attack, giving the outnumbered RAF a defensive edge. Later in the war, they also cracked German naval codes revealing where U-boats lurked in the Atlantic. Along with innovations such as radio detection and ranging (RADAR) and other new forms of electronic detection, ULTRA enabled the outnumbered RAF to concentrate on defending key targets.

In October 1940, the badly mauled Luftwaffe cut back its attacks, compelling Hitler to postpone and then cancel the invasion of Britain. Germany now attempted to starve the British into submission by sending so-called wolf packs of U-boats to sink merchant ships carrying food and other supplies from the United States. Hitler turned his gaze eastward, redeploying German ground forces for a planned invasion of his nominal ally, the Soviet Union.

In the run-up to the 1940 election, Roosevelt blunted criticism about his military policies by appointing several prominent Republicans to powerful cabinet positions. He named the widely respected Wall Street lawyer Henry L. Stimson, who had served as President Hoover's secretary of state, as secretary of war. Most Americans preferred Roosevelt to his little-known Republican challenger, corporate executive **Wendell Willkie**, and he won reelection to an unprecedented third term in November.

Once reelected, Roosevelt acted more forcefully. When he learned in December that Britain would soon run out of cash to purchase American weapons, he conceived a plan to provide vital assistance free of charge. In a fireside chat on December 29, 1940, he called for the United States to become the great "Arsenal of Democracy." To keep Britain in the fight against Germany and to support China in resisting Japan, Roosevelt proposed "loaning," rather than selling, weapons and raw materials. In January 1941, Roosevelt submitted his so-called **Lend-Lease proposal** to Congress. He linked aid to the Allies to preserving what he called the **Four Freedoms**—freedom of speech and of religion, freedom from fear and from want. American freedom and the New Deal, he argued, depended on the survival of freedom abroad. Congress passed the **Lend-Lease Act** in March and funded it at a cost of $7 billion, an amount nearly as large as that year's entire federal budget.

Franklin D. Roosevelt, "The Four Freedoms," January 6, 1941

During 1941, British and U.S. military planners informally agreed that their first priority should be the defeat of Germany, followed by Japan if it attacked in the Pacific. When Germany invaded the Soviet Union in June 1941, Roosevelt and Churchill agreed that despite their past dislike of Stalin and his recent cooperation with Hitler, victory over Germany required that they assist the Communist nation with Lend-Lease. If Hitler gained control of Russian oil, coal, steel, and grain, his well-provisioned armies could be redirected against Britain and the Middle East. Roosevelt and Churchill solidified their partnership at a shipboard meeting off the coast of Canada in August. At the president's insistence, they issued the **Atlantic Charter**, a pledge to defeat aggressors and create a "permanent system of general security" based on the Four Freedoms, open trade, and the "right of all peoples to choose the form of government under which they will live."

The Atlantic Charter, August 14, 1941

During the final months of 1941, Roosevelt deployed U.S. warships to escort British Lend-Lease merchant ships more than halfway across the Atlantic. German U-boats attacked and even sank several American vessels assisting the British in what amounted to an undeclared naval war.

Day of Infamy

Although Roosevelt and his military advisors considered Germany the greater threat to U.S. security, war came first with Japan. Since 1938, the United States had tried to restrain Japan by providing assistance to China and gradually imposing trade sanctions on Tokyo. The armies of Chinese leader **Jiang Jieshi (Chiang Kai-shek)** and the guerrilla forces of the small Chinese Communist Party won few battles, but they tied down at least two million Japanese troops simply by not surrendering. To keep China fighting, the United States provided first economic assistance and then military aid.

But after German armies overran France and Holland in mid-1940, the Japanese demanded greater access to French Indochina and the Dutch East Indies. In July 1941, Japanese forces seized control of most of French Indochina. The United States responded by enlarging the size of the Pacific Fleet at Pearl Harbor in Hawaii, sending several dozen new B-17 bombers to bases in the Philippines, and blocking all U.S. exports to Japan. This halted the sale of petroleum on which the Japanese navy depended, as the country produced no oil of its own. The Japanese made it clear that unless oil sales resumed by December 1941, they would seize oil fields in Southeast Asia by force.

During the last months of 1941, Japanese and American diplomats discussed ways to avert war. Roosevelt rejected the idea of temporarily relaxing the oil embargo after reviewing secret messages exchanged between leaders in Tokyo, such as prime minister and general **Tojo Hideki**, and Japanese negotiators in Washington. U.S. naval intelligence, in a remarkable operation code-named MAGIC, had built a machine resembling that used by the Japanese for secret radio transmissions. This allowed Americans to decrypt diplomatic communications (military codes were not broken until later), which revealed that Japan's military leaders were unlikely to agree to or honor any compromises reached by civilian negotiators.

After talks broke off at the end of November, U.S. officials expected a Japanese attack within two weeks and sent warnings to commanders throughout the Pacific. Unfortunately, MAGIC did not reveal the exact timing or the target of Japan's battle fleets. U.S. intelligence analysts guessed Japan would first strike in Southeast Asia. Hawaii seemed beyond the effective range of Japanese power.

Japanese admiral **Yamamoto Isoroku** calculated that crippling the Pacific Fleet at Pearl Harbor would set U.S. Navy operations back at least one year. By then, Japan should control China and resource-rich Southeast Asia. If, as seemed likely, Germany defeated the Soviet Union, Roosevelt would be compelled to focus on defending the Atlantic, giving Japan a free hand in the Pacific. Hitler, as noted, thought the opposite: a Japanese attack would force the United States to focus on the Pacific.

Franklin D. Roosevelt, "Address to Congress Requesting a Declaration of War with Japan," December 8, 1941.

Yamamoto understood that attacking the United States entailed a terrific gamble. He recognized that if Germany failed to defeat the Soviet Union, the British and Americans would be able to fight in *both* Europe and the Pacific. U.S. supplies would keep China fighting and would tie down millions of Japanese troops. In that case, Yamamoto conceded, Japanese forces would be able to "run wild" in the Pacific for a year or two but would then be overwhelmed by superior American military power.

Early on December 7, 1941—a date that Roosevelt declared would "live in infamy"—Japanese carrier-based aircraft mounted a surprise attack on ships and planes in Hawaii. Attacks in the Philippines and Southeast Asia began several hours later. The death of almost 2,400 sailors and soldiers at Pearl Harbor and nearby bases made it the deadliest single attack on American soil until the terrorist attacks of September 11, 2001. The Japanese sank or damaged eight battleships and many other

"A DATE WHICH WILL LIVE IN INFAMY"   A scene of devastation at Pearl Harbor, Hawaii, shortly after the Japanese attack on the Pacific Fleet on December 7, 1941.

vessels and destroyed several hundred planes. By chance, the Pacific Fleet's aircraft carriers were at sea on maneuvers and avoided destruction; they proved crucial for subsequent battles. Afraid to risk a second air strike after the successful first wave, Japanese commanders passed up the chance to destroy vital repair facilities and fuel storage tanks in Hawaii.

At Roosevelt's request, Congress promptly declared war on Japan. Great Britain, whose Asian colonies had also been attacked, followed suit. On December 11, after deciding that with Japan as an ally "it was impossible" for Germany to lose, Hitler, followed by Mussolini, declared war on the United States.

America's British, Chinese, and Soviet allies expressed relief that the United States had joined the war. Commenting on what he considered Japan's monumental folly and Britain's good fortune, Winston Churchill declared, "So we had won after all! . . . Hitler's fate was sealed. Mussolini's fate was sealed. As for the Japanese, they would be ground to powder."

STUDY QUESTIONS **FOR THE LONG FUSE**

1. How did the Axis nations threaten world peace after 1931?

2. Why were most Americans "isolationists" during the 1930s?

3. Between 1939 and 1941, how did Roosevelt seek to help Great Britain and China? Why did he feel this was vital to U.S. security?

quiz

⊘ A GRAND ALLIANCE

During the first months after the Pearl Harbor attack, Americans heard nothing but bad news. Along with a string of defeats in the Pacific, German submarines sank dozens of U.S. merchant ships within sight of ports stretching from Miami to New York. But Roosevelt calmed public fears by speaking frankly. The struggle would be long and difficult, he explained, but by attacking America, its enemies had sowed the seeds of their destruction.

On New Year's Day 1942, the United States, Great Britain, the Soviet Union, China, and two dozen smaller partners issued a "Declaration of the United Nations," a pledge to fight for victory. The United States provided substantial military aid to this so-called Grand Alliance, recognizing that it would be a year or more before large numbers of American troops could engage the enemy. Meanwhile, Lend-Lease would help British, Chinese, and especially Soviet armies keep fighting. Because Soviet forces engaged nearly two-thirds of all German troops until 1944, Roosevelt and Churchill promised Stalin that as soon as possible they would open a second front against Germany by invading western Europe. Meanwhile, U.S. and British naval and ground forces, with an assist from China, would hold a defensive line against Japan until German defeat appeared certain.

As the U.S. military grew from a few hundred thousand to over 12 million, the command structure changed dramatically. Roosevelt encouraged the chiefs of the separate military services to meet jointly, later formalized by the creation of the Joint Chiefs of Staff. Army chief of staff General **George C. Marshall** and Navy commander Admiral **Ernest J. King** assumed unparalleled authority over their respective services. The service chiefs and their large staffs moved into an immense new headquarters in Arlington, Virginia, the Pentagon, whose very name came to symbolize American power.

War in the Pacific

In the first six months of fighting, Japan's Imperial Army and Imperial Navy overran Burma, Hong Kong, Malaya, Singapore, the Philippines, the Dutch East Indies, and many Pacific islands and prepared to invade India and Australia. Asian peoples gazed in wonder as the Japanese rolled over British, Dutch, and American forces defending colonial outposts. These victories impressed nationalists, such as **Mao Zedong** in China, **Ho Chi Minh** in Vietnam, **Mohandas Gandhi** in India, and Sukarno in the East Indies. Like most Asians, however, they rejected Japanese claims to be liberators. Communists such as Mao and Ho fought the Japanese and sought to cooperate with the United States, hoping to secure American support in their future quest for power.

On the Bataan Peninsula and the island fortress of Corregidor in the Philippines, U.S. and Filipino troops held out against Japanese invaders, under dire conditions, until May 1942. The Japanese forced many of the desperately ill 10,000 Americans and 60,000 Filipinos who surrendered to trek 80 miles to a prison camp. The so-called Bataan Death March claimed the lives of over 600 Americans and 10,000 Filipinos and came to symbolize Japanese brutality toward surrendered Americans, even though most of its victims were Filipinos fighting for the United States. Mostly to bolster civilian morale, early in 1942 Roosevelt approved a small, largely symbolic, raid against the Japanese home islands. On April 18, a handful of B-25 bombers under the command of

Lieutenant Colonel **James H. Doolittle** flew off the deck of the aircraft carrier *Hornet* on a 650-mile, one-way run. The planes dropped a few bombs on Tokyo and then flew off to crash land on the China coast, where Chinese soldiers rescued most of the crewmen. Several others were captured and executed by the Japanese. Although the Doolittle raid did little physical damage, it cheered the American public and provoked the Japanese into a disastrous retaliatory strike.

In early May 1942, Australian troops blocked a Japanese effort to seize Port Moresby in New Guinea, intended as a jumping-off point for a Japanese invasion of Australia. Around the same time, a joint U.S.–Australian naval force at the Battle of the Coral Sea turned back a Japanese naval force attempting to occupy other parts of New Guinea. Even though Japan enjoyed superior naval strength, in 1942, U.S. codebreakers deciphered a key Japanese naval code. This coup gave the outmatched U.S. Navy a critical edge in subsequent battles.

To eliminate the threat still posed by the U.S. Navy, Japanese strategists planned to draw the bulk of the diminished Pacific Fleet into a decisive battle. They sent several aircraft carriers to attack Midway Island, at the far western end of the Hawaiian chain. The Japanese expected the Americans to defend Midway because losing it would place in jeopardy Hawaii and the entire U.S. position in the Pacific.

The plan made good sense—except that U.S. intelligence had prior warning through decoded radio intercepts and had positioned the United States' own aircraft carriers near Midway so their planes could pounce on the unsuspecting Japanese. On June 4, 1942, U.S. aircraft destroyed four of Japan's six large aircraft carriers, along with hundreds of planes and skilled pilots. The U.S. Navy lost just one carrier, *Yorktown*. This one engagement shifted the balance of power in the Pacific dramatically in favor of the United States. During the next two years, Japan built only a handful of new aircraft carriers and never replaced many of its skilled pilots. In contrast, U.S. shipyards launched dozens of new aircraft carriers, replete with planes and pilots, providing the navy with a great advantage.

In mid-1942, American soldiers and Marines began a prolonged fight to control Guadalcanal, part of the Solomon Islands near New Guinea, and Australia. The bloody, hand-to-hand combat and associated sea battles lasted from the summer of 1942 through February 1943.

Throughout the fighting in the Pacific, racial and cultural conflict brought a special brutality to the warfare. Japanese military culture and training infused a belief that soldiers should never surrender—they must fight till death. Fearing that any Japanese prisoners of war might turn on their captors, American units took few prisoners. For their part, Japanese commanders considered captured Americans as totally dishonored for not having fought to the death, and this philosophy often served as a justification for them to treat prisoners of war brutally. The intensity of combat, and its racial dimension, is illustrated in one Marine's diary entry: "I wish we were fighting Germans. They are human beings like us. But the Japanese are like animals."

American ashtray depicting Tojo Hideki as a rat

During 1943, Roosevelt approved a two-pronged strategy against Japan. Admiral **Chester Nimitz** led a naval offensive in the central Pacific to destroy enemy shipping and seize islands close enough to Japan to permit bombing by land-based aircraft. Simultaneously, army general **Douglas MacArthur,** who had been sent to Australia to head the southwest Pacific theater of war, was tasked with pushing the Japanese out of New Guinea and the chain of Japanese-held islands leading to the Philippines. American strategists who hoped that China would fight the millions of Japanese troops on the Asian mainland more effectively were disappointed. Chinese leader Chiang Kai-shek proved more interested in hoarding U.S. aid to fight his Communist rivals than in opposing the invaders.

With exceptions such as Guadalcanal and New Guinea, most of the battles fought on Pacific islands from 1942 to 1944 were bloody but short. The intensity and duration of fighting increased when U.S. forces invaded the Philippines in October 1944. It took months of heavy combat to liberate the archipelago, and some Japanese troops fought on until August 1945. The battles for Iwo Jima, in February–March 1945, and Okinawa, in April–June 1945, proved even more difficult and took a heavy toll of lives.

The closer the Americans came to Japan, the more fiercely the Japanese fought. As its military resources dwindled at the end of 1944, Japan unleashed kamikaze (suicide) planes loaded with explosives against U.S. ships and troops (Map 24.1). The high casualties suffered in the fights for the Philippines, Iwo Jima, and Okinawa weighed heavily on the minds of U.S. planners as they prepared for a final assault on Japan and weighed the arguments for and against using the atomic bomb.

By early 1945, the U.S. Navy had severed Japan's economic links to Southeast Asia and China. The several million Japanese soldiers on the Asian mainland were cut off

Excerpts
from the
diary of a
US seaman
serving in
the Pacific
(1944–45)

map analysis

MAP 24.1 Map of the Pacific Theater of War (World War II) The war in the Asia-Pacific region was fought at sea, in jungles, and on countless islands. Most Japanese troops remained in China and Southeast Asia during the war. By early 1945, the United States had begun to bomb the Japanese home islands, attacks that culminated in the dropping of two atomic bombs in August 1945.

from home and supplies. That spring the U.S. Army Air Forces, operating from newly captured bases on Saipan and other Pacific islands, began massive air raids on Japan. Eventually, as many as 1,000 giant B-29 bombers at a time dropped explosives and incendiary bombs that destroyed most of Japan's cities and factories and killed between 500,000 and 700,000 civilians. A single firebomb raid against Tokyo in March incinerated as many as 100,000 residents. Japan was beaten, but its leaders refused to surrender.

The War in Europe

In 1942, Roosevelt and Churchill promised Stalin they would soon open a second front in western Europe to relieve pressure on the Soviets. But the competing needs of the global war made it difficult to keep the promise. Recalling the slaughter of World War I, Churchill feared high casualties from an early invasion of France and favored attacks in peripheral areas such as North Africa and Italy.

PACIFIC THEATER DESTRUCTION Tokyo after the U.S. firebombing of March 1945 that killed an estimated 100,000 civilians.

In November 1942, U.S. forces invaded North Africa with the goal of linking up with British troops in Egypt. In May 1943, after months of desert combat, British and U.S. armies at last defeated German forces commanded by General Erwin Rommel, which earlier had nearly overrun the vital Suez Canal and jeopardized Allied access to Iraqi and Iranian oil.

After securing North Africa, Allied forces invaded the island of Sicily and then moved on to the Italian mainland. Churchill had pressed for the Italian campaign, insisting it would be a relatively easy fight that would weaken Germany without risking the heavy casualties of an early invasion of France. In fact, fighting in Italy proved long, difficult, and costly. Although Mussolini's government collapsed in 1943, the Wehrmacht remained entrenched in northern Italy until 1945, and the entire campaign had little effect on ultimate victory.

The Soviet Red Army, more than any single factor, ensured Hitler's doom. In the first six months of fighting, June to December 1941, the Wehrmacht literally reached the gates of Moscow before winter weather and Soviet resistance stopped their advance. During the first two years of the war, the Red Army lost nearly as many soldiers as the total number of Americans—12 million—who served in the U.S. armed forces. Fighting on the eastern front killed 4 million German soldiers, nearly 10 times as many as died fighting the British and Americans.

Ultimately, between 20 million and 30 million Soviet civilians and soldiers died in what the government called the Great Patriotic War (Map 24.2). Writing of these events, one historian explained the Allied victory in this way: by not surrendering in 1940–1941, "Britain provided the time." Between 1941 and 1945, America provided the "money and weapons," while "Russia supplied the blood."

The tide of battle turned early in 1943 when the Red Army defeated a large German force at Stalingrad, a city on the Volga River named after the Soviet leader. During the two years after Stalingrad, the Wehrmacht fought a slow but brutally effective retreat back across Russia and eastern Europe toward Berlin.

After nearly two years of delay, the **D-Day** invasion of France finally occurred on June 6, 1944. By then, most German forces in the east had been pushed out of Russia. The Anglo-American armies that invaded France under the command of General **Dwight D. Eisenhower** trapped the Wehrmacht in an unbreakable vise. German commanders

Photograph of the D-Day invasion

MAP 24.2 Map of the European Theater of War (World War II) The European theater of war stretched across the Atlantic, as far north as the Arctic Circle, as far east as the Ural Mountains, and south into North Africa. The heaviest fighting—that claimed tens of millions of lives—occurred in eastern Europe and the Soviet Union.

and troops fought skillful rearguard battles to slow both the Soviet and Anglo-American offensives; they even managed to launch large counterattacks, such as the **Battle of the Bulge** in Belgium, at the end of 1944, which temporarily stopped the Allied momentum. But the overwhelming power of the two-front Allied offensive drove steadily toward Berlin.

The Holocaust

Among the many horrors of war, none exceeded Nazi efforts to systematically murder whole categories of "inferior" people. Anti-Semitism had a long history in Germany and much of Europe. In the late 1930s, Nazi hostility toward Jews turned to violent persecution, and by 1942 Hitler had sanctioned the mass extermination of "undesirables." German doctors had earlier assisted the Nazi regime in killing tens of thousands of fellow Germans who suffered from physical deformities and mental illness. Nazi ideologues then expanded the category of those to be eliminated, adding Jews, Gypsies, homosexuals, and then Poles and Soviet prisoners of war. According to this plan, Germans would be resettled in eastern Europe and western Russia once the Slavs and the approximately 10 million Jews living in German-occupied eastern Europe and the Soviet Union were cleared. Ultimately, about six million Jews were killed.

Special German military and police units, sometimes aided by local militias, began shooting and clubbing to death large numbers of Jews and many Slavs after the occupation of Poland in 1939. The process accelerated after June 1941 when the Wehrmacht invaded the western Soviet Union, home to around four million Jews, most of whom were killed. Early in 1942, Nazi leaders approved a so-called Final Solution

LIBERATION   Survivors of a Nazi concentration camp in eastern Europe at their liberation in the spring of 1945.

Varian
Fry, "The
Massacre of
the Jews,"
(December
21, 1942

that envisioned concentrating all of Europe's surviving Jews and other undesirables in large-scale death camps and eliminating victims through the use of poison gas and other means. During the next three years, about two million additional Jews deported from western Europe, along with five million Poles and Soviet prisoners, died in these killing centers.

When, in 1944, the possibility arose of bombing the rail lines that serviced death camps such as Auschwitz, British and American military strategists rejected the idea as a "diversion" from the central task of defeating the Wehrmacht and destroying war production. In addition, anti-Semitism remained common in the United States. Wartime polls revealed that a majority of Americans distrusted Jews and opposed providing them a safe haven. Because leaders of Jewish-American organizations feared a backlash if they spoke out forcefully on behalf of European Jews, they lobbied quietly if at all.

During the war, Congress maintained rigid immigration restrictions that barred entry for most European Jews and other victims of Nazism. Lawmakers even rebuffed efforts to allow some Jewish children into the United States on an emergency basis or shelter those few Jews who escaped Nazi clutches. Ironically, dozens of Jewish scientists, such as Albert Einstein and Edward Teller, who had fled Nazi persecution before the outbreak of war, made vital, although secret, contributions to Allied victory through their work developing the atomic bomb.

In 1944, President Roosevelt, who sympathized with the plight of those victimized by the Nazis but whose powers were constrained by Congress, created a War Refugee Board to establish temporary havens in neutral countries or liberated territories overseas. These centers saved the lives of about 200,000 refugees. But during the entire war, fewer than 1,000 European Jews were permitted to enter the United States, and most of these were confined to a fenced-in camp in rural Oswego, New York.

STUDY QUESTIONS **FOR A GRAND ALLIANCE**

quiz

1. Why did the United States pursue a "Europe First" war strategy?

2. Why did U.S. strategists consider it vital to aid the Soviet Union?

3. How did U.S. officials and the public respond to the Holocaust?

⊘ BATTLE FOR PRODUCTION

Shortly after the Republicans scored big gains in the 1942 congressional elections, Franklin Roosevelt told journalists that "Dr. New Deal" had been replaced by "Dr. Win-the-War." The wartime Congress terminated several New Deal programs such as the WPA and CCC, but it left intact many others, including Social Security, farm price supports, and minimum wage laws. Ultimately, the war acted as a catalyst for social and economic changes that enshrined the New Deal in American life. The war improved life for most Americans, ended unemployment, increased mobility, and laid a foundation for a postwar economic surge.

War Economy

America's enemies and allies recognized the importance of its war production. In December 1941, even as Hitler belittled the United States, his foreign minister, Joachim von Ribbentrop, warned that Germany had at most "one year to cut off Russia from her American supplies." If U.S. weapons were placed in the hands of Russian soldiers, "the war would be difficult to win." Soviet leader Joseph Stalin agreed. At his first meeting with Roosevelt in 1943, he declared that the "most important thing in this war are machines. The U.S. is a country of machines." Stalin offered a toast to the city of Detroit, whose workers and factories produced the tanks, trucks, and airplanes that were "winning the war." Detroit, in fact, ended the war as one of America's wealthiest cities.

Speaking to the nation in January 1942, Roosevelt set ambitious goals for war production (see Table 24.2 and Figure 24.1). During the next three and a half years, the share of the gross national product devoted to military spending rose from under 2 percent in 1939 to 43 percent in 1944.

German and Japanese engineers excelled at designing advanced weapons that outclassed many of those in Allied arsenals. But these weapons were so complex and costly that Germany and Japan could produce them only in limited numbers. Lumbering American B-17 or B-24 bombers seemed primitive compared to a jet-powered Messerschmitt fighter plane, but German factories produced only a handful of these marvels compared to the tens of thousands of U.S. aircraft that dominated the skies over Europe by 1944. By 1943, U.S. shipyards were producing merchant vessels, so-called Liberty Ships, faster than Germany and Japan's excellent submarines could possibly sink them. At Ford's Willow Run plant outside Detroit, 40,000 workers laboring three shifts a day on a mile-long production line produced a B-24 bomber every 60 minutes.

To mobilize industry, labor, capital, and public support for the war, FDR created agencies that resembled those used to fight the Depression. These were loosely supervised by the War Production Board (WPB). Prices, profits, and wages were capped;

Table 24.2 Military Production in the United States, 1942–1945

The surge in U.S. military production during World War II gave the Allies at least a 3:1 advantage over their Axis enemies.

297,000 aircraft

193,000 artillery pieces

86,000 tanks

2.4 million military trucks and jeeps

1,200 combat vessels

8,800 total naval vessels

87,000 landing craft

3,300 merchant ships and tankers

14 million shoulder arms

5 million pounds of bombs

40 billion bullets

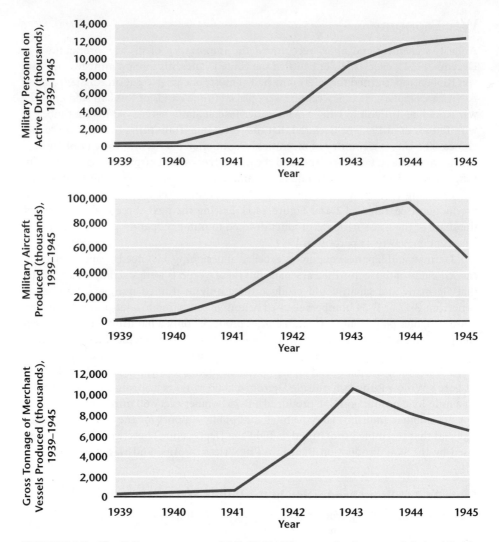

FIGURE 24.1 **The U.S. war economy, 1941–1945** Military production surged during World War II, as the federal government invested heavily in factories and new technologies. This gave U.S. armed forces, and those of its major allies, a sizeable advantage over the Axis powers in terms of aircraft, ships, tanks, artillery, and so forth.

commodities, crops, and consumer goods were rationed. Most war orders went to large manufacturers, such as General Motors, Ford, General Electric, and U.S. Steel. Companies producing weapons were guaranteed profits through "cost plus" contracts. At the end of the war, many of these manufacturers received valuable government-funded equipment in return for a token payment. By 1945, corporate profits had nearly doubled from the 1940 level.

Wartime spending boosted paid employment by 11 million workers. They included 3.5 million who came of age during the war and 7.5 million first-time adult workers, half of them women. With full employment, families began saving money for the first time since the early 1930s. In fact, savings increased 10-fold during the war years. To attract workers, large employers provided a range of benefits, including job-based health insurance. The number of families with annual incomes below $2,000 fell by half, whereas those earning over $5,000 increased fourfold. By 1945, full employment and rising wages had created a taxpaying base of 42 million Americans. Income taxes, now automatically deducted from wages, covered about half the $350 billion cost of the war. Sales of war bonds made up the rest.

Labor leaders, with the exception of the combative head of the United Mine Workers, John L. Lewis, issued a "no strike" pledge once the United States entered the war. The employment boom along with a government policy of encouraging union membership led to a steep increase in workers carrying union cards. By 1945, 15 million Americans belonged to labor unions, including one-third of all nonfarm workers—a historic high in percentage terms.

High demand for food for soldiers and workers at home and abroad rescued American agriculture from the decades-long problem of overproduction and underconsumption. New Deal policies had helped cash-strapped farmers during the 1930s. Wartime procurement and new technologies proved even more important. As the government purchased all that the land could produce, the cash inflow promoted farm mechanization, which reduced production costs and the need for manual labor. Wartime research produced new chemical herbicides, pesticides, and fertilizers that further increased yields. In addition, improved refrigeration technology boosted the domestic and foreign markets for meat and dairy products. By 1959, U.S. farms produced 60 percent more than they had in 1941.

A Government-Sponsored Technology Revolution

As part of the effort to spur production, the federal government boosted funding of scientific research from zero to about $1.5 billion annually. Money provided by the War Department's Office of Scientific Research and Development (OSRD) led to the construction of plants that produced synthetic rubber and fibers, advances in radar and other electronic weapons systems, and the development of antibiotic drugs as well as computers, jet engines, and guided missiles. Academic laboratories at the Massachusetts Institute of Technology and the California Institute of Technology pioneered research that eventually led to microwave ovens and rocket propulsion. Wartime research resulted in techniques to produce abundant quantities of formerly scarce penicillin as well as antimalarial drugs vital to troops fighting in the tropics.

Letter from Albert Einstein to President Roosevelt on nuclear warfare (August 2, 1939)

OSRD also spent $2 billion developing the atomic bomb. The work took place in three new "atomic cities." Special facilities in Oak Ridge, Tennessee, and Hanford, Washington, processed uranium ore into fissionable bomb material. In remote Los Alamos, New Mexico, at the site of a former boarding school, nuclear physicists under the direction of **J. Robert Oppenheimer** designed and assembled the secret weapon. Nearly 150,000 people, ranging from distinguished nuclear physicists to anonymous Navajo miners in Arizona, worked on the so-called **Manhattan Project**. In July 1945, their efforts culminated in the successful test of the atomic bomb in New Mexico. After the war, Los Alamos became one of several federal laboratories that conducted both military and civilian research.

A Battle of Books and Ideas

In May 1933, theaters in the United States showed newsreels of mobs of university students in Berlin burning piles of books. Mobilized by the new Nazi government's minister of public enlightenment, Joseph Goebbels, the students targeted authors who "injured the German spirit." Among the first books burned were works by Albert Einstein, Sigmund Freud, Helen Keller, and Ernest Hemingway. Henceforth, books in Germany would stress "race science" rather than ideas spread by "Jewish and Negro" writers. Similar purges followed in nearly 100 German universities.

The orgy of destruction appalled many Americans. The *New York Times* labeled it a "literary holocaust" and collective "insanity." *Time* magazine described it as a "bibliocaust." These reactions marked one of the first times the term "holocaust" appeared in public discourse. The attack evoked the somber prediction by 19th-century German poet Heinrich Heine that "where they burn books, at the end they will also burn people."

When war erupted in Europe in September 1939, Nazis extended their war of ideas. By 1945, they had destroyed half of all books in Poland and Czechoslovakia and 55 million volumes in the Soviet Union. Elsewhere in occupied Europe, librarians rushed to hide forbidden books. Even so, by 1945 the Nazis had destroyed an estimated 100 million books.

President Franklin D. Roosevelt urged Americans in 1942 to help fight the "war of ideas" by donating books to soldiers. He remarked that "books cannot be killed by fire." No "man nor force could put thought in a concentration camp forever," and in the war against fascism, "books are weapons." In response, American writers, librarians, publishers, and military officials pledged to supply soldiers, sailors, Marines, and airmen—who often wrote home appealing for reading material—with books.

Public libraries turned into collection centers for a "Victory Book Campaign." In one year, this voluntary drive gathered over six million books. But this was inadequate because many well-meaning donors had simply emptied home shelves of unwanted publications, such as instruction manuals or cookbooks.

To meet this demand, in mid-1943, the War and Navy departments teamed up with over 70 publishing companies to form the Council on Books in Wartime (CBW).

The Draft

Thirty million American males, aged 18–26, were draft eligible during the war. A voluntary network of 6,500 local boards administered the system. Two million farm laborers and nearly four million industrial workers received blanket exemption from military service. Married men, especially those with children, were initially draft exempt, but they later became combat eligible. Ultimately, about 16 million men, or one in nine Americans, served in the military, and the armed services reached a peak size of 12 million. By 1945, one in five families had a son, a husband, or a brother in uniform.

Although women were draft exempt, about 350,000 volunteered for special units. Approximately 140,000 served as WACs (Women's Army Corps), 100,000 as WAVES (Women Accepted for Voluntary Emergency Naval Service), 13,000 as Coast Guard

The CBW devised ways to produce tens of millions of books cheaply and sized to fit into a soldier's vest or pants pocket. The innovative Armed Services Editions (ASE) cost less than a dime to produce and were supplied free to military personnel. By 1945, the armed forces had distributed 123 million ASE books.

The military editions included contemporary fiction, historical novels, mysteries, humor, and westerns, as well as poetry and classics by Dickens and Shakespeare. *The Great Gatsby*, by F. Scott Fitzgerald, had been largely forgotten before it was reissued as a wartime paperback and became a perennial bestseller. The 1944 novel *A Tree Grows in Brooklyn* became a surprising favorite among combat Marines. Author Betty Smith received thousands of letters from Marines who described the solace they found in the heroine's perseverance.

Books were often shipped as priority items to combat units around the world. Officers compared the value of the books to penicillin in maintaining troop morale. ASE volumes were routinely shared among soldiers, and an unwritten code specified none should be thrown away.

As the war in Europe ended in May 1945 and the ASE program wound down, soldiers donated many of their ASE books to depleted European libraries. As they returned home, servicemen received a copy of the ASE title *Going Back to Civilian Life*. It explained where veterans could turn for personal counseling, career guidance, and medical care and how to utilize the generous educational, loan, and employment benefits available from the new GI Bill of Rights. Many veterans enrolled in colleges and universities in record numbers following the world's most destructive war.

The popularity of ASE paperbacks transformed the publishing industry. From a tiny prewar niche, in 1943, partly because of wartime rationing and paper shortages, nonmilitary consumers purchased 40 million paperbacks. After 1945, the market for inexpensive editions exploded. In 1947, readers bought 95 million paperbacks; by 1952, that figure had risen to 270 million. Wartime readership contributed to the creation of a more literate postwar American middle class.

- Why were books seen as vital to the war effort?
- How did wartime publishing change the postwar book industry?

SPARs (after the Guard's motto, *semper paratus* or "always ready"), and 1,000 as WASPs (Women's Air Force Service Pilots), who flew planes in noncombat zones. About 75,000 female nurses also served in the military. In addition, 350,000 women volunteered to work for groups such as the Red Cross and the United Service Organization (USO), which assisted troops.

Shared experiences of training and combat eroded many ethnic barriers among whites in the military. Wartime mixing encouraged more open housing and employment patterns in the postwar era. The black–white racial barrier proved harder to crack. Although the United States fought enemies who exterminated "inferior races," it did so with rigidly segregated armed forces that relegated all-black units mostly to noncombat duty under the command of white officers.

◉ ON THE MOVE: WARTIME MOBILITY

The war dramatically affected where Americans lived and worked. Sixteen million soldiers, sailors, and Marines were deployed throughout the country and around the world. In addition, 15 million civilians, or one in eight Americans, relocated between 1941 and 1945. They included midwestern farmhands heading to factory jobs in Detroit and Chicago, black sharecroppers going north for war work, Mexican nationals recruited back into the Southwest after a decade of expulsion, Mexican Americans leaving the rural Southwest for cities such as Los Angeles, women shifting from unpaid domestic work to paid employment, and over 100,000 Japanese Americans forcibly relocated from the West Coast to desert internment camps.

The warm, coastal states of the South, Southwest, and West Coast, later called the Sunbelt, grew rapidly during the 1940s. The federal government invested $2 billion in developing western infrastructure such as roads and water projects and spent at least $30 billion purchasing products from the region. Two million war workers moved to California alone between 1942 and 1945, and the state had grown 72 percent by the end of the decade.

U.S. EMPLOYMENT SERVICE POSTER, 1943

Wartime Women

During the war, the number of women working for wages increased from 12 million to about 19 million. Previously, aside from being teachers and nurses, women worked mostly in service jobs segregated along gender and racial lines. These included restaurant and secretarial work, domestic employment, and jobs in textile mills. Typically, single rather than married women worked outside the home. Wartime labor shortages changed public policy and attitudes toward women in the workforce, especially in jobs traditionally held by men in shipyards, on assembly lines, and in aircraft factories. The Office of War Information (OWI) released radio plays, films, and posters that encouraged women to join the industrial workforce. Before the war, 80 percent of the public told pollsters they disapproved of wives working outside the home. By 1942, 80 percent said they approved.

Yet business and political leaders frequently urged women to think of factory work as a temporary status. They should keep their focus on the home and prepare to resume their lives as homemakers and mothers when the war ended. After 1945, the number of women in industrial jobs fell precipitously, returning to prewar levels. This resulted from the return of men to the workplace and ongoing gender discrimination, as well as rapidly rising marriage and pregnancy rates among American women. In fact, the post-war "baby boom" actually began in 1944 and continued for the next 20 years.

Recollec-
tions of a
"Rosie the
Riveter"

Mexican Migrants, Mexican Americans, and American Indians in Wartime

Wartime labor shortages ended the policy of expelling Mexican nationals. With so many Anglos entering the armed services or taking industrial jobs, farm managers in the Southwest had too few workers to harvest crops. Under the so-called **Bracero Program**, Spanish slang for "strong arm," U.S. authorities recruited Mexican farm and railroad workers. Puerto Ricans, who were citizens, were also encouraged to seek work on the mainland. This action marked the beginning of a large population transfer from the island.

IMMIGRANT LABOR The Bracero Program recruited several million Mexican agricultural laborers to work on U.S. farms between the 1940s and 1960s.

By 1945, about 300,000 braceros had entered the United States; they worked first in the Southwest and then throughout the country. The program, which continued until 1964, in total recruited an estimated four million Mexican laborers. Despite promises of fair treatment and payment of 30 cents per hour, some braceros earned as little as 35 cents per day, and many lived in terrible housing. Schools, housing, and employment were often segregated for the two million or more Mexican Americans. Social tensions flared in cities such as Los Angeles and Chicago, which experienced a rapid influx of southern whites, blacks, and Mexican Americans. Some Mexican American youth dressed in flamboyant outfits called zoot suits. Police and white servicemen frequently harassed them, sometimes cruising barrios in search of "zoot-suiters" whom they attacked and humiliated by stripping off their clothes.

Racial violence exploded in Los Angeles in June 1943 when hundreds of Marines and sailors on leave joined local police in attacking Latino youths as well as blacks and Filipinos. Military police had to restore order. In spite of these difficulties, the war years also brought some important advances for Mexican Americans. Because they were classified by the army as "white," the half million or so Mexican Americans in uniform were not assigned to segregated units. Military service provided many young Mexican Americans with a sense of power and personal worth as well as new skills. Like white and black soldiers, they also benefited from the postwar GI Bill. After the war, many of these Latino veterans joined groups such as the League of United Latin American Citizens (LULAC) and the American GI Forum, both of which mounted campaigns against discrimination in the Southwest.

When the war began, most American Indians lived on reservations created in the late 19th century. About 25,000 Indians entered military service, including some 400 Navajo code talkers who participated in many of the bloodiest battles in the Pacific. These specially trained soldiers and Marines provided vital assistance to their comrades by communicating battlefield information over the radio in the Navajo language. Many Indians who served in uniform continued their education or started businesses with benefits from the GI Bill. A large number of Indians left the reservations for factory and service jobs in cities such as Los Angeles, Phoenix, Denver, and Chicago. The outbound path continued after 1945, and by the mid-1960s, nearly half of the U.S. Indian population had left reservation life.

African Americans in Wartime

The war years held both new promises and old challenges for the nation's 12 million African Americans. In 1941, three-fourths of all African Americans still lived in the South under conditions of rigid segregation. Only one-fourth graduated high school, while a third of the black population still worked as sharecroppers or tenant farmers. State laws and intimidation kept most people of color from voting.

On the threshold of war, some black leaders envisioned military service and defense work as ways to break the stranglehold of poverty. In late 1940, **A. Philip Randolph**, head of the Brotherhood of Sleeping Car Porters, a union composed of mostly black railroad workers, met President Roosevelt and pressed him, without success, to desegregate the armed forces. African American leaders complained to federal officials that even as war production expanded, skilled factory jobs were reserved for whites. Randolph made plans for a "march on Washington" to bring 100,000 African Americans to the capital on July 1, 1941. Roosevelt urged Randolph to cancel

A. Philip Randolph, *Why Should We March?* (1942)

the protest, but he refused, saying the president must first act to bar discrimination in defense work.

On June 25, 1941, a week before the march, Roosevelt issued Executive Order 8802 that barred racial discrimination in defense industries or government employment, although it did not end segregation in the military. The president created a Fair Employment Practices Commission (FEPC) to investigate complaints and take remedial action. Over the next four years, the number of blacks working in defense plants nearly tripled, from 3 percent to 8 percent, totaling 600,000. A typical African American cook or maid who earned $3.50 per week in Georgia in 1941 could earn $48 weekly at a Lockheed plant in Los Angeles. The number of blacks in the federal civil service tripled to 200,000. Nearly three-quarters of a million African Americans responded to these new employment opportunities by leaving the rural South for northern cities. Reflecting the surge in employment and the more tolerant politics of the North, membership in the NAACP grew 10-fold, to 500,000, during the war.

The U.S. military remained segregated but eventually recruited a squadron of 1,000 combat pilots and 15,000 support personnel, known as the Tuskegee Airmen, from their training facility at the famous Alabama college. It also formed several black ground combat units. In 1940, the army had five black officers, but by 1945, the number had risen to 7,000. In addition, hundreds of thousands of black recruits learned to read in the army and picked up valuable job skills they utilized after the war.

Most black political and social organizations supported the war, but they also championed what they called a double victory, or Double V, campaign against fascism abroad and racism in America. Black servicemen were startled when they witnessed German and Italian prisoners of war who worked in southern towns being served in restaurants or admitted to movie theaters that barred blacks. As NAACP leader **Walter White** remarked during a fact-finding trip to the Pacific, African American soldiers knew the "real fight for democracy will begin when they reach San Francisco on their way home."

Black migration north and west sometimes provoked urban violence as blacks sought homes in formerly all-white neighborhoods and began working alongside whites in factories. For example, a fight among blacks and whites in a park sparked the 1943 Detroit violence. In Harlem, the shooting of a black soldier by a white policeman led to rioting. Federal troops were required to stop the violence in Detroit.

During the war years, however, blacks achieved some important legal victories. Texas, like most southern

AFRICAN AMERICAN AIR SUPPORT African American pilots who were members of the famed Tuskegee Airmen during World War II.

states, used a variety of schemes to bar African Americans from voting, including an all-white Democratic primary. White supremacists claimed the party was a private club that could deny nonwhites the right to vote. Whoever won the primary in southern states was virtually guaranteed election. Lonnie Smith, a black Texan, challenged the law as racially biased. **Thurgood Marshall**, a young African American lawyer working for the NAACP, argued Smith's case before the Supreme Court in 1944. The justices ruled, eight to one, in *Smith v. Allwright* that white primaries were an unconstitutional denial of equal voting rights. Although other impediments prevented most blacks from voting in the South until the 1960s, the ruling showed that the Supreme Court was re-thinking its role in civil rights cases.

Japanese American Internment

Japanese Americans were singled out for official persecution during wartime. Not only was Japan an enemy nation that inflicted a humiliating defeat at Pearl Harbor, but the United States had a decades-long legacy of anti-Asian agitation, especially in the West. The intensity of these feelings showed in popular songs during the war, with typical lyrics that declared, "I'm gonna find me a fella who is yella and beat him Red, White, and Blue!"

Hawaii had the largest concentration of Japanese Americans, about 200,000, almost a fourth of the territory's population. They comprised such a vital part of the local economy that, aside from arresting a few ethnic Japanese who supported Tokyo's policies, authorities left the rest alone.

The 120,000 ethnic Japanese living on the West Coast experienced harsher treatment. Japan's rapid military victories in the Pacific inflamed public opinion and fueled exaggerated fear of an attack on California. Prominent journalists and public officials called for placing all ethnic Japanese "under guard." Representative Leland Ford of California insisted that Japanese Americans prove their loyalty by "submitting them-selves to a concentration camp." General John DeWitt, head of the Western Defense Command, declared in a logic-defying statement that the absence of sabotage on the West Coast constituted proof of a conspiracy among ethnic Japanese.

On February 19, 1942, President Roosevelt issued Executive Order 9066, giving federal authorities power to exclude anyone it chose, whether ethnic Japanese or not or citizen or alien, from designated "military areas" within the United States. The executive order became the legal basis for interning older Japanese who were barred from citizenship, known as *issei*, and their American-born, citizen children, called *nissei*.

Technically, the exclusion order also applied to the 800,000 German and Italian nationals living in the United States. Except for a few pro-Fascist activists, however, they were generally left alone. In May 1942, the new War Relocation Authority ordered 112,000 Japanese living along the West Coast to leave in a matter of days. Japanese Americans had to report to "assembly centers" such as the Santa Anita Race Track for transport to "relocation centers." One camp was located in Arkansas, and nine others in the arid West in places such as Manzanar, California, and Gila Bend, Arizona. Nearly all Japanese complied, even though most had to abandon homes, farms, businesses, and personal property. Several U.S. allies, including Canada and Peru, also interned Japanese, placing some of them in American camps.

Excerpt from Yoshiko Uchida, *Desert Exile: The Uprooting of a Japanese American Family* (1982)

The relocation centers were nothing like Nazi extermination camps. They isolated and confined but did not kill the inhabitants. Nevertheless, the internees lived under

JAPANESE INTERNMENT
Japanese American residents of Los Angeles, California, assemble with their possessions for transportation to internment camps in 1942.

Image analysis

armed guard, behind barbed wire, in crowded conditions, and with no legal recourse—because the Supreme Court declined to rule on the issue until 1944. That year, in a case brought against **Fred Korematsu**, the high court upheld the policy of forced relocation. Korematsu, a native-born citizen of Japanese ancestry, had refused to leave a designated war zone on the West Coast. The *Korematsu* decision affirmed the government's right to exclude anyone it chose, regardless of race or ethnicity, from designated areas on the basis of military necessity. The Court dodged the fact that the government acted against only Japanese Americans. Despite harsh treatment, about 35,000 Japanese American men volunteered for military duty. Some served as translators and interpreters in the Pacific. Many fought in all-Japanese army units in Europe, such as the 442nd Regimental Combat Team, achieving recognition for their bravery. By 1943, all Japanese young men in internment camps were required to register for the draft. Those who refused because of their forced incarceration were convicted of draft evasion.

In mid-1944, with the Pacific war turning in its favor, the American government permitted about 25,000 internees to leave the camps on the condition that they relocate east of the Rockies. Shortly before Japan's surrender in the summer of 1945, all internees were allowed to return home. A few found that friends had protected their homes or businesses, but most lost the work and possessions of a lifetime. In 1948, acknowledging that "mistakes had been made," Congress offered token payments to wartime internees. A genuine apology and larger payment to survivors came only in 1988. By then, the Justice Department had opened records showing that wartime officials knew that Japanese Americans posed no threat but claimed otherwise.

STUDY QUESTIONS FOR ON THE MOVE: WARTIME MOBILITY

1. What role did women play in the new wartime economy?
2. How did the war affect the lives of African Americans and Hispanics?
3. Why were Japanese Americans singled out for punishment?

quiz

◉ WARTIME POLITICS AND POSTWAR ISSUES

In spite of events such as race riots and internment, the United States remained a democracy during wartime. Politicians, journalists, religious groups, and ordinary citizens debated and voted on issues ranging from the conduct of the war to the future role of government in the economy. Even as the nation's politics turned more conservative, Americans generally supported New Deal precepts as a reliable guide for the future.

At the international level, Roosevelt pushed plans to promote postwar prosperity and peace. In 1944, the United States hosted a conference in Bretton Woods, New Hampshire, that created several economic organizations to manage and stabilize world trade. The most important of these was the International Bank for Reconstruction and Development (later divided into the World Bank and International Monetary Fund). The **Bretton Woods agreements** also established the dollar as the world "reserve currency," or benchmark for international trade, and pegged its value at $35 per ounce of gold. The dollar dominated world trade until the early 1970s.

State Dept. map showing what the postwar world would look like (1942)

Roosevelt hoped to parlay the wartime Grand Alliance into a plan for postwar political cooperation. He outlined what became the **United Nations (UN)** organization as a forum for all nations to participate in future peacekeeping. As Roosevelt envisioned it, the UN would be dominated by the "great powers" (the United States, Soviet Union, Great Britain, China) but would allow smaller nations to cooperate in promoting world trade, disarmament, decolonization, and the rehabilitation of the defeated Axis nations along democratic lines. The UN was formally created with 50 members in April 1945, shortly after Roosevelt's death.

Right Turn

In November 1942, 22 million fewer people voted than had in the presidential race of 1940. The low turnout—caused partly by the influx of men into the military and millions of workers relocating—proved disastrous for the Democrats. Republicans gained 7 Senate seats (for a total of 43 out of 96) and 47 House seats (giving them 208 to the Democrats' 222). Nearly half the remaining Democrats came from the party's conservative southern wing. Congress soon eliminated several New Deal agencies and rebuffed efforts by liberals to simplify voting by soldiers.

Although constrained by the power of congressional conservatism, President Roosevelt remained committed to expanding liberty and security for all Americans. On January 11, 1944, he broadcast his State of the Union speech that called for enacting a "**Second Bill of Rights** . . . an economic bill of rights" that would guarantee every citizen a job, a living wage, decent housing, adequate medical care, educational opportunity, and protection against unemployment in postwar America. Yet, except for a veterans' aid program, Congress balked.

In the summer of 1944, a coalition of liberal Democrats and conservative Republicans passed the Serviceman's Readjustment Act of 1944, or GI Bill of Rights. Initially conceived as a simple pension program, the GI Bill morphed into the last major piece of New Deal legislation. Under pressure from both veterans' groups and social liberals, Congress agreed to provide returning servicemen unemployment benefits, medical coverage, home mortgage guarantees, small business loans, hiring preferences for government jobs, and generous education benefits. Because the law covered 16 million veterans and, indirectly, their spouses and families, it became after 1945 the biggest, longest-running, and perhaps most successful New Deal social program.

Many soldiers shared the experience of Jack Short of Poughkeepsie, New York. Just 20 years old when his army unit landed in France in June 1944, he and his "band of brothers" fought their way into the heart of Nazi Germany. Short's unit liberated the Nordhausen concentration camp, where they found the bodies of thousands of dead prisoners "stacked up like cordwood." In spite of this painful memory, Short felt the war transformed his life for the better. For generations his family had labored in factories, and none went beyond high school. But after the war ended, Short used his GI Bill benefits. "It paid for 99 percent of your college expenses and gave you money to live on," he recalled. In 1950, Jack Short graduated from college and found a well-paying job in an innovative company, IBM.

The 1944 Election and the Threshold of Victory

Roosevelt won renomination for an extraordinary fourth term in 1944, but to do so he had to appease conservative Democrats who disliked the liberal vice president, Henry Wallace. Wallace vigorously supported civil rights for minorities, expanded influence for labor unions, and cooperation with the Soviet Union. Roosevelt replaced Wallace with Missouri senator Harry S Truman. A political moderate, Truman had gained a measure of fame by investigating profiteering by military contractors.

Republicans nominated a moderate of their own for the presidency, New York governor Thomas E. Dewey. He attacked the Democrats as "soft on communism" and beholden to labor unions but endorsed many New Deal programs as well as Roosevelt's plans for the postwar world. In November 1944, with the war news from Europe and the Pacific mostly positive, Roosevelt won reelection. Democrats picked up 20 House seats and retained their 56 to 38 majority in the Senate.

Victory in Europe

In spite of overall wartime strategic cooperation among the Allies, many points of tension had surfaced. For example, Stalin saw the delayed opening of the second front in Europe as proof that Roosevelt and Churchill hoped to see the Soviets weakened by prolonging the war on the eastern front. Many British and American officials worried that as the Red Army pursued the retreating Wehrmacht, Stalin would annex Polish and other territories and set up pro-Soviet states in eastern Europe. These concerns were justified by Stalin's decision in 1940 to have Soviet security troops massacre around 20,000 captured Polish officers and intellectuals. In 1944, when Polish resistance fighters in Warsaw rose up against the retreating Germans, Stalin ordered his armies to halt their offensive and thus allowed the Germans to kill 15,000 armed Poles along with 200,000 civilians who might have formed a counterweight to Soviet influence in liberated Poland.

Even Roosevelt and Churchill bitterly disagreed over the future of European empires. The president insisted that after victory, the British, French, and Dutch put their Middle Eastern, Asian, and African colonies on the path toward independence, much as the United States had done with the Philippines. Unless they did so, radical nationalists, perhaps with Soviet help, would rebel against their colonial masters. But America's allies balked and set the stage for bitter conflicts in the coming decade.

By 1945, a pattern of dividing the spoils of war had emerged. As Stalin remarked, "Whoever occupies a territory also imposes on it his own social system." Between 1943 and 1945, the British and Americans, joined by General Charles de Gaulle's Free French forces, occupied and established pro-Western, non-Communist regimes in North Africa, Italy, Greece, France, and then western Germany, Japan, and southern Korea.

The U.S. forces in the Pacific took possession of hundreds of islands formerly occupied by Japan and later declared them "strategic trusteeships."

As Soviet forces pushed the Wehrmacht toward Berlin in 1944–1945, Stalin brutally imposed pro-Soviet regimes in most of eastern Europe. As long as Germany fought on and Japan remained in the war, Roosevelt refused to risk a break with Stalin over the fate of eastern Europe. In February 1945, Roosevelt, Churchill, and Stalin met together at Yalta, a Soviet city on the Black Sea. Stalin agreed to join the UN and to fight Japan soon after Germany's defeat. In return, the Soviets were promised reparations from Germany; special economic privileges in northeast China, known as Manchuria; and a good deal of political control over Poland, Bulgaria, and Romania. Critics soon labeled the Yalta accords a sellout by Roosevelt. In fact, Soviet forces already controlled much of this territory. American strategists believed that what was most important was Soviet help in defeating Japan and avoiding a rupture of the alliance.

During a side trip while returning from Yalta, Roosevelt met with King Abdul Aziz of Saudi Arabia. In 1943 the president had authorized Lend-Lease aid to the kingdom and built on that foundation in their February 1945 meeting. The two leaders informally agreed that in return for security promises, the Saudis would ensure the flow of inexpensive oil to the United States. That relationship has endured, more or less intact, for 70 years.

During April and May 1945, the Soviet offensive that ultimately captured Berlin in the face of fierce German resistance cost the Red Army hundreds of thousands of additional dead and injured. Hitler killed himself inside his bunker at the end of April. On May 8, after the remnants of the Nazi government surrendered, General Eisenhower reported tersely that the "mission of this Allied Force was fulfilled." Most Americans greeted the victory in Europe as a triumph of Allied cooperation.

Victory in the Pacific

Similar considerations guided the strategy to defeat Japan. Japanese troops and suicide pilots had inflicted heavy casualties on the Marines, soldiers, and seamen who captured the islands of Iwo Jima and Okinawa during the first half of 1945. Japan's military leadership seemed determined to fight to the bitter end and had prepared the civilian population to join the army in resisting an Allied invasion set to begin near the end of 1945. Although casualty estimates were uncertain, no one doubted that large numbers of Americans as well as Japanese would perish in the final battles. The American air campaign had already destroyed most of urban Japan and killed over half a million civilians. The naval blockade threatened to starve a large portion of Japan's 70 million residents unless the war ended quickly.

Burial at sea of US sailors of the USS *Intrepid* killed by Japanese bombs (November 26, 1944)

American strategists were prepared to invade Japan, but they hoped that some other means to compel its surrender could be found. In the summer of 1945, two alternatives to an invasion seemed possible. Stalin had promised to join the war against Japan three months after Germany's defeat, around mid-August. This would dash Japan's hope that the Soviet Union might mediate something short of an unconditional surrender. A Soviet attack would also neutralize the several million Japanese troops still deployed in Manchuria and other parts of China.

As an alternative to Soviet assistance—which would come at a price—the United States possessed a secret weapon. In mid-July 1945, at the same time as American, British, and Soviet leaders were meeting in the Berlin suburb of Potsdam to haggle over the future of Germany and eastern Europe, scientists in New Mexico successfully detonated an atomic

YALTA SUMMIT CONFERENCE The "Big Three"—Prime Minister Winston Churchill, President Franklin D. Roosevelt, and Premier Joseph Stalin— at the Yalta Summit Conference in February 1945.

bomb. If used to destroy one or two Japanese cities, military planners believed, this new weapon might shock the Japanese into surrendering and thus make both Soviet help and an invasion unnecessary. The first two atomic bombs were transported early in August to the island of Tinian in the Pacific where specially trained B-29 bombing crews readied the weapons for use. As described in the next chapter, the bombs struck Japan on August 6 and 9, and the Soviet Union declared war on Japan on August 8. A week later, Japan surrendered.

Four months earlier, on April 12, while sitting for a portrait at his beloved retreat in Warm Springs, Georgia, the president died of a cerebral hemorrhage. His passing left a void in American life. Poet Carl Lamson Carmer captured the nation's sense of loss:

> I never saw him—
> But I knew him. Can you have forgotten
> How with his voice, he came into our house,
> The President of the United States,
> Calling us friends.

STUDY QUESTIONS FOR WARTIME POLITICS AND POSTWAR ISSUES

1. What conservative political trends emerged in American politics during the war?

2. What issues created mistrust between the United States and the Soviet Union as the war ended?

3. What was the importance of the GI Bill of Rights?

quiz

interactive timeline

TIMELINE 1929–1945

AMERICA	YEAR	THE WORLD
Oct U.S. stock market crash sparks global depression	**1929**	
	1931	**Sep** Japan invades and annexes Manchuria
Nov Roosevelt elected	**1932**	
Mar Roosevelt inaugurated	**1933**	**Jan** Adolf Hitler becomes German chancellor **Mar** Japan quits League of Nations **Sep** Germany quits League of Nations **Nov** U.S. recognizes Soviet Union
Aug Congress passes first of several Neutrality Acts	**1935**	**Oct** Italy invades Ethiopia
	1936	**Mar** German troops occupy Rhineland in defiance of Versailles Treaty **Jul** Spanish Civil War begins **Nov–Dec** Germany and Italy create "Axis" alliance; Germany and Japan sign Anti-Comintern Pact
	1937	**Jul** Japan invades China
Dec United States begins economic aid to China	**1938**	**Mar** Germany annexes Austria **Sep** Munich Agreement sacrifices Czechoslovakia
Aug Albert Einstein's warning to FDR about German atomic research spurs creation of U.S. atomic program **Sep** War in Europe begins; U.S. arms sales to British and French put on "cash and carry" basis	**1939**	**May** German–Italian alliance **Aug** German–Soviet Non-Aggression Pact signed **Sep** German invasion of Poland results in outbreak of Second World War
Sep United States begins peacetime draft **Sep** United States transfers warships to British navy **Nov** Roosevelt reelected to third term	**1940**	**May** German Blitzkrieg in western Europe **Jun** France surrenders to Germany **Sep** Germany, Japan, and Italy sign Tripartite Pact (Axis alliance)

Summary

- The Great Depression destabilized the world and prompted German, Italian, and Japanese aggression.
- Disillusionment with the results of World War I convinced many Americans that the nation should avoid foreign conflict, whatever the cost.
- After Japan's attack on Pearl Harbor, the United States organized a global alliance to defeat the Axis powers and, Roosevelt hoped, to secure postwar peace.
- During 1943, the Soviet Red Army blunted and turned back the German armies, while U.S. naval victories in the Pacific put Japan on the defensive.
- Tens of millions or more civilians died as a result of Nazi extermination policies in eastern Europe, while Japanese troops inflicted horrible crimes against Chinese civilians.
- Wartime mobilization included raising a vast military and retooling the economy to produce weapons. American factories turned out remarkable numbers of ships, planes, tanks, rifles, and so forth, which went to U.S. and Allied troops.
- War production vanquished unemployment and brought broad prosperity to American workers, including large numbers of women and minorities who entered the industrial workforce.
- Although business and conservative political interests regained influence, policies and programs adopted during the war years also enshrined New Deal values in American life.

AMERICA	YEAR	THE WORLD
Jan FDR delivers "Four Freedoms" speech and proposes Lend-Lease aid program **Mar** Lend-Lease passed by Congress **Jul** United States embargoes oil sales to Japan **Aug** Atlantic Charter issued by Roosevelt and Churchill **Sep–Dec** Undeclared U.S.–German naval war in Atlantic **Dec** Japan attacks Pearl Harbor **Dec** Germany and Italy declare war on United States	**1941**	**Jun** Germany invades Soviet Union
Jan United States and Allies issue "Declaration of the United Nations" and form Grand Alliance **Apr** Internment of Japanese Americans; Doolittle raid on Japan **Jun** U.S. naval victory at Midway **Nov** U.S. forces invade North Africa	**1942**	
Jan Casablanca Conference **Nov–Dec** Conferences in Cairo and Tehran	**1943**	**Feb** German forces defeated at Stalingrad **May** German and Italian troops surrender in North Africa **Sep** Italy surrenders
Jun D-Day landings in France **Jun** GI Bill of Rights passed **Jul** Bretton Woods Economic Conference **Nov** Roosevelt reelected to fourth term **Dec** Battle of the Bulge	**1944**	
Feb Yalta Conference **Feb** Battle of Iwo Jima begins **Mar** Tokyo firebombed; battle for Okinawa begins **Apr** Roosevelt dies; Harry Truman becomes president **Jun** United Nations Charter signed	**1945**	**Apr** Hitler commits suicide **May** Germany surrenders **Aug** Japan surrenders after atomic bombing and Soviet entry into war

- On the cusp of victory in the spring and summer of 1945, U.S. and Soviet leaders became increasingly suspicious of each other's postwar intentions.

Key Terms and People

Anti-Comintern Pact 829
Atlantic Charter 833
Battle of the Bulge 841
Bracero Program 849
Bretton Woods agreements 854
Chamberlain, Neville 830
Churchill, Winston 830
D-Day 840
Doolittle, James H. 837
Eisenhower, Dwight D. 840
Four Freedoms 833
Gandhi, Mohandas 836
Goebbels, Joseph 825
Good Neighbor Policy 828
Hitler, Adolf 825
Jiang Jieshi (Chiang Kai-shek) 834

King, Ernest J. 836
Korematsu, Fred 853
Lend-Lease Act 833
Lend-Lease proposal 833
Luce, Henry 826
MacArthur, Douglas 837
Manhattan Project 845
Mao Zedong 836
Marshall, George C. 836
Minh, Ho Chi 836
Marshall, Thurgood 852
Murrow, Edward R. 832
Mussolini, Benito 825
Neutrality Acts 828
Nimitz, Chester 837
Oppenheimer, J. Robert 845

audio flashcards

Reviewing Chapter 24

1. During the 1930s, why did most Americans oppose foreign military intervention?
2. After the outbreak of war in Europe in 1939, how and why did Roosevelt aid the British?
3. Why did the United States emphasize the war against Germany rather than Japan?
4. What strains existed among the Allies during the war?
5. How did Roosevelt see the Grand Alliance as a basis for postwar cooperation?
6. How did defense spending transform the American economy?

Further Reading

Adams, Michael. *The Best War Ever: America and World War II*. Baltimore: Johns Hopkins University Press, 1994. The author demythologizes the war and highlights the many contradictions between American ideals, memory, and the realities of conflict.

Breitman, Richard, and Allan Lichtman. *FDR and the Jews*. Cambridge, MA: Belknap Press, 2013. The authors examine U.S. refugee policy both before and during the war. They conclude that fierce domestic political opposition to immigration blocked Roosevelt's modest efforts to help refugees and that after 1941 there was relatively little that could be done to save the Jews.

Dallek, Robert. *Franklin D. Roosevelt and American Foreign Policy, 1932–1945*. New York: Oxford University Press, 1979. A comprehensive study of the diplomacy that led up to the outbreak of war and the ways in which Roosevelt tried to shape the postwar agenda.

Dower, John. *War Without Mercy: Race and Power in the Pacific War*. New York: Pantheon, 1993. The author shows that the ferocity of fighting in the Pacific reflected the racial hostility between Japan and the United States.

Goodwin, Doris Kearns. *No Ordinary Time: Franklin and Eleanor Roosevelt: The Home Front in World War II*. New York: Simon and Schuster, 1995. Examines how the president and first lady struggled to defend liberal values and the New Deal during wartime.

Overy, Richard. *Why the Allies Won*. London: Jonathan Cape, 1995. An incisive analysis of the economic, material, and political factors that ensured an Allied victory over the Axis powers.

Roberts, Andrew. *The Storm of War: A New History of the Second World War*. New York: HarperCollins, 2011. A highly readable narrative history of the global conflict that examines both military and political elements.

Sherwin, Martin. *A World Destroyed: The Atomic Bomb and the Grand Alliance*. New York: Knopf, 1975. A fast-paced history of how the atomic bomb affected wartime strategy and postwar relations.

Snyder, Timothy. *Bloodlands: Eastern Europe Between Hitler and Stalin*. New York: Basic Books, 2010. A harrowing account of the vast scale of ethnic slaughter that occurred in central and eastern Europe during the 1930s and 1940s.

America in the World
GOODS, IDEAS, PEOPLE

CHAPTER 24: Arsenal of Democracy: The World at War, 1931–1945

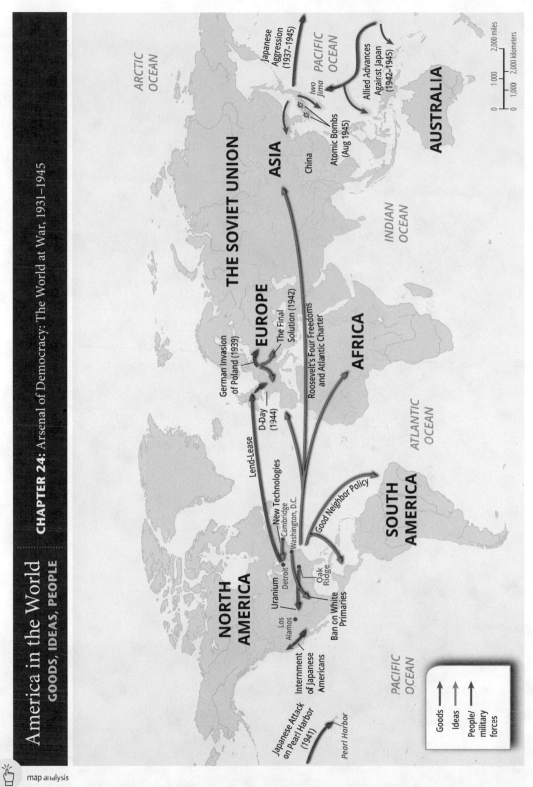

map analysis

Goods

Ideas

People/ military forces

ARCTIC OCEAN

NORTH AMERICA

THE SOVIET UNION

EUROPE

ASIA

PACIFIC OCEAN

AUSTRALIA

AFRICA

INDIAN OCEAN

SOUTH AMERICA

ATLANTIC OCEAN

PACIFIC OCEAN

Japanese Aggression (1937–1945)

Iwo Jima

Allied Advances Against Japan (1942–1945)

China

Atomic Bombs (Aug 1945)

The Final Solution (1942)

German Invasion of Poland (1939)

Roosevelt's Four Freedoms and Atlantic Charter

D-Day (1944)

Lend-Lease

New Technologies

Cambridge

Washington, D.C.

Good Neighbor Policy

Uranium

Detroit

Oak Ridge

Los Alamos

Ban on White Primaries

Internment of Japanese Americans

Japanese Attack on Pearl Harbor (1941)

Pearl Harbor

0   1,000   2,000 miles

0 1,000 2,000 kilometers

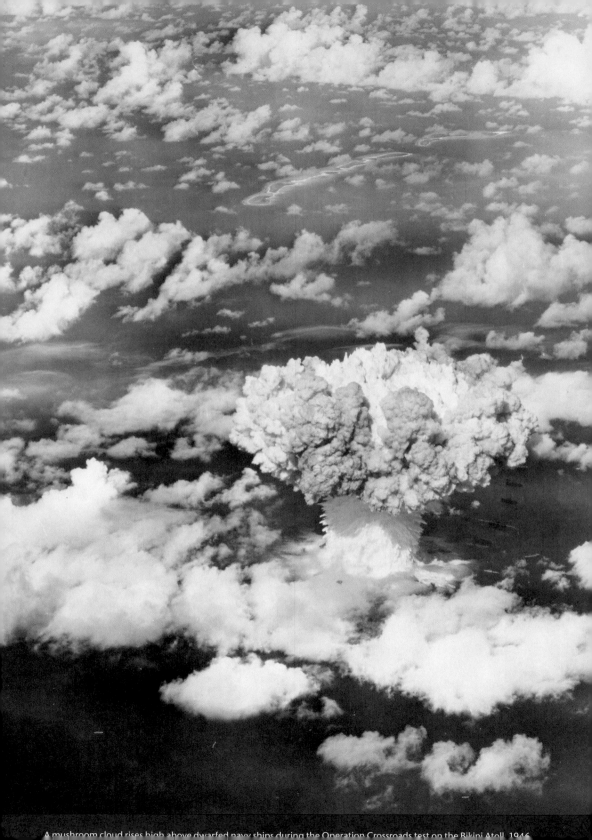

A mushroom cloud rises high above dwarfed navy ships during the Operation Crossroads test on the Bikini Atoll, 1946.

Prosperity and Liberty Under the Shadow of the Bomb

1945–1952

O n August 6, 1945, a lone U.S. bomber, the B-29 Superfortress *Enola Gay*, carrying only one bomb, named "Little Boy," flew unbothered through a cloudy early morning sky toward the Japanese city of Hiroshima. The plane was named for the mother of mission commander Paul Tibbets, who selected the plane himself for his historic mission. At 8:15 AM Japan time, the crew released their bomb. It detonated 2,000 feet above the city just as planned. The blast released energy equivalent to 16 kilotons of TNT in a millionth of a second. With the push of a button, a dozen men invisible to their enemy at 31,000 feet in the sky instantly obliterated almost five square miles of a city with a weapon. The idea that one plane with one bomb could cause so much damage shocked even hardened military leaders. At least 80,000 people were killed instantly, about 30 percent of the city's population. Another 70,000 were injured and tens of thousands contaminated by radiation in the days and weeks that followed. Radiation sickness eventually killed thousands more and left tens of thousands with lingering and often mysterious health conditions.

Few events in history have generated as much controversy as the decision to use the atomic bomb on human targets. In the 1990s, the Smithsonian Institution acquired funding to restore the once—shining silver *Enola Gay*. The American Air Force Association helped raise funds to support the restoration and presentation of the plane. Then, the Smithsonian designed an exhibition around it: "The Crossroads: The End of World War II, the Atomic Bomb and the Origins of the Cold War." In the months before the official opening of the exhibit in 1995, Pacific veterans and Republican leaders got a sneak peak ahead of the public. Many came away dismayed at the impression left by an exhibit that included graphic details of the bomb's effect on the citizens of Hiroshima. Eight thousand vets, with the support of conservatives in Congress, petitioned the Smithsonian to revise the exhibit and remove the disturbing content about bomb victims. The ensuing political fight was part of a larger **"culture war"** pitting conservative politicians and pundits against historians. Ultimately, the exhibit was curtailed, eliminating most references to the politics of war and focusing on the mechanics of the airplane and its atomic payload. The director of the Smithsonian was fired, and a heated national debate about "who owns history" made headlines and fueled discussions on radio and television. Unlike the clarity of purpose and shared sense of sacrifice of World War II, the Cold War and its nuclear escalation divided opinion and forced all Americans to rethink the relationship of the nation to the world. Atomic power brought heavy responsibility.

THE COLD WAR

Harry S Truman, the man who made the decision to use those first two atomic weapons, was still a mystery to most Americans when he became president after the sudden death of Franklin Roosevelt on April 12, 1945. Truman inherited the moral responsibility for the atomic bomb, the job of ending World War II, the management of a faltering alliance with the Soviet Union, and the drafting of American foreign and domestic policy in the dawning postwar world.

Thrust into power overnight, Truman faced some of the most vexing troubles of any 20th-century president. In an early press conference in which he asked the nation for their prayers, he said that he felt "as if the sun, moon, and the stars" had fallen on him. In the first weeks of his administration, with the war in Europe reaching its end, one of Truman's concerns was the growing rift between the United States and its wartime ally, the Communist Soviet Union. In the coming months, tensions grew in the global turmoil following the end of World War II. Strained relations led to a **Cold War** that defined domestic culture and U.S. relations with the world in the second half of the 20th century. Truman's decisions during the months and years following World War II spurred three generations of global competition with the Soviets with enormous consequences for peoples on every continent. How did wartime alliances so quickly dissolve into Cold War tensions?

The Roots of Conflict

In April 1945, British and American troops closed in on Berlin from the west, while the Soviets slugged their way toward the city in the face of dogged resistance from the east. Hours after assuming the presidency, Truman learned that Stalin was pushing his troops to capture the city ahead of the Americans. With big shoes to fill on the world stage, Truman worked to understand the complicated relationship with the Soviets. FDR had left the Yalta Conference convinced that his hard-won alliance with Stalin would help ensure that the Soviets would live up to their agreements in eastern

Europe. In his first months in office, Truman shared his predecessor's optimism. In his diaries, he described Stalin as "honest" and "smart as hell."

Briefings with Roosevelt's top military advisors tempered Truman's optimism and raised his distrust of Stalin and the Soviets. They now cautioned Truman to avoid appeasing Stalin as he gained control of eastern Europe. Truman sent top diplomat **W. Averell Harriman** to Moscow. Harriman's dispatches decried Stalin's "barbarian invasion of Europe." He warned the Soviets that Truman would not stand for Communist expansion. Forced to formulate a foreign policy strategy in less than a week, Truman latched on to the strong anti-Communist position of Harriman. The growing rivalry between the members of the Grand Alliance heated up as the final battle of the war in Europe took shape around Berlin.

By April 1945, the German army had been reduced to young boys and old men and Berlin was in ruins. Still, the fight for the city remained brutal to the end. When the Soviets reached the city first, they symbolically hoisted their red flag on the roof of the ruined Reichstag, while Hitler lay dead of a self-inflicted gunshot in his underground bunker.

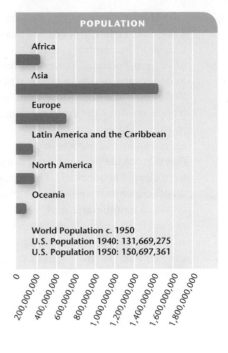

POPULATION

Africa
Asia
Europe
Latin America and the Caribbean
North America
Oceania

World Population c. 1950
U.S. Population 1940: 131,669,275
U.S. Population 1950: 150,697,361

0
200,000,000
400,000,000
600,000,000
800,000,000
1,000,000,000
1,200,000,000
1,400,000,000
1,600,000,000
1,800,000,000

Managing Postwar Europe in Potsdam

Germany formally surrendered on May 8, 1945. Even as the German guns finally fell silent, it was clear that the peace would be complicated and contested. Although citizens and soldiers rejoiced, political and military leaders remained deeply concerned by news of deteriorating relations with Stalin. The Soviets occupied Berlin and controlled a vast territory stretching from the Black Sea in Romania to Poland's Baltic shores. They also controlled a large swath of eastern Germany past Berlin and up the Elbe River. The Allies had agreed at Yalta to partition Germany into occupation zones, but no formal mechanism existed for cooperation between the Soviets, the United States, and Great Britain. Tensions grew when the Soviets annexed a huge swath of eastern Poland, confirming the Poles' worst fears.

American and Soviet soldiers shake hands near Berlin, April 1945

In Washington, only 11 days after taking office, Truman faced off with Soviet foreign minister **Vyacheslav Molotov** and accused the Soviets of breaking their agreement to give Poland independence. Stalin responded by firmly maintaining they were only establishing a "security zone" in Poland and that Soviet interests in eastern Europe were more important than good relations with America's new president.

The leaders of the Alliance met for the last time in Potsdam, a suburb of Berlin. On July 15, Truman and Secretary of State **James F. Byrnes** arrived at Potsdam without a clear understanding of the extent of Stalin's expansionist ambitions and with the war in Japan entering a pivotal moment. Still hoping for Soviet assistance in subduing the millions of Japanese troops on the Asian mainland, Truman tempered his position on Poland and agreed to the Soviets' occupation of eastern Europe.

The debate about Poland symbolized the brewing ideological Cold War to come. Two years earlier, at a critical meeting of the Alliance at Tehran, Iran, Roosevelt and Churchill had secretly agreed to Stalin's demand that the Allies accept Soviet control of eastern Poland. Unaware of this agreement, Polish resistance leaders organized a massive uprising against the Germans in Warsaw with the assumption that the nearby Red Army would join the fight. In one of the bloodiest events of the war, German troops, crushing the uprising, slaughtered a quarter-million civilians, reducing Warsaw to ruins. The Soviets stayed away and allowed Warsaw to fall. Months later, Truman agreed to let the Soviets formally redraw the map of Poland—a crushing blow to the Poles. From the perspective of central Europe, the battle lines of the coming Cold War were clear. The ideological battle between the emerging superpowers would be fought on other people's territory with profound and lasting consequences for those nations.

Two months later, on Monday, July 16, 1945, Manhattan Project observers huddled in the New Mexico desert received pieces of dark welder's glass to cover their eyes and sunscreen to protect their faces. At 5:29 AM, a flash 10 times brighter than the sun lit up the night sky in three states. An eerie multicolored plasma ball formed within a millionth of a second before launching a 38,000-foot cloud of radioactive debris into the atmosphere. Far above New Mexico, radioactive isotopes floated into the atmosphere before they rained down on an area the size of Australia, showing up months later in straw grown in Maryland and in milk from cows outside of Chicago. The poisonous mix of radioactivity resulting from nuclear blasts became known as "fallout," and scientists understood from the beginning that they would never be able to fully control or contain it. **Robert Oppenheimer** recalled that first atomic explosion by citing Hindu scripture: "Now I am become death, destroyer of worlds."

BURGEONING COLD WAR TENSIONS   The utter devastation of Warsaw was one of the starkest monuments of World War II and a harbinger of emerging Cold War tensions in the waning months of the war.

At Potsdam, Truman received coded word from New Mexico of the successful "Trinity" explosion. The news, he confided to advisors, was "a great load off my mind." Truman knew the atomic bomb would change the situation in the Pacific and mentioned the news of a "new weapon of great power" to Stalin. Stalin simply nodded, having known of the Manhattan Project through an elaborate espionage operation linking New Mexico to Moscow. When he returned, Truman had to choose between a full-scale invasion of the Japanese mainland with military estimates of heavy casualties or use of the atom bombs.

The Defeat of Japan

With some confidence about the stability of Europe, Truman prepared for the final assault on Japan. Firebombings of Tokyo in March of 1945 killed more than 100,000 civilians, while desperate fighting at Iwo Jima and Okinawa left tens of thousands of U.S. casualties.

U.S. leaders feared the cost of a full-scale invasion of Japan, because the militarists in Tokyo seemed unwilling to surrender on any terms acceptable to the Allies. At Yalta and Potsdam, Stalin agreed to attack Japanese forces in northeast Asia three months after Germany surrendered. Most of Japan's army was stationed on the Asian mainland. Although Soviet military help would greatly reduce America's burden and casualties, Truman feared that if the Red Army joined the war against Japan, it would support Communist forces in China. Given this potential problem, Truman chose to use the atomic bomb: its use could shock Japanese hardliners into surrender, avoid U.S. casualties, and end the war before the Soviets could move into Japan. Furthermore, the use of the bomb would provide a graphic example of U.S. power in the Soviets' backyard.

On August 8, the day before the second atomic bomb was dropped on Nagasaki, the Soviets declared war on Japan. These combined blows finally shattered Japanese high command resistance and convinced the emperor to accept Allied demands for an unconditional surrender. The U.S. armistice terms provided that Hirohito could remain provisionally on the throne if the emperor ordered the surrender of all Japanese forces in Asia and promised to cooperate with the occupation authorities. The Japanese accepted, and armistice was declared on August 15. The occupation of Japan that followed was nominally Allied, but in practice virtually entirely U.S. controlled, through 1952.

Henry Stimson, "The Decision to Use the Atomic Bomb," February 1947

Dividing the Postwar Globe

The United States emerged from the cataclysmic war stronger and wealthier than before. Between 1940 and 1945, while U.S. enemies and allies alike endured massive physical and financial destruction, the U.S. gross national product (GNP) increased by over 170 percent. Aside from the attack on Pearl Harbor and a few Japanese incendiary bombs carried by balloon over the Pacific Northwest, the U.S. homeland remained unscathed. Its industrial complex had dramatically expanded, its navy and air force were unmatched, and its president and military leaders had sole possession of the atomic bomb. Meanwhile, the Soviet Union was devastated, with entire cities leveled and an estimated 28 million citizens dead.

Despite the relative strength of the United States compared to the USSR, concerns about the spread of communism in the aftermath of war escalated. American leaders framed the contest as a struggle between Western democracy and a global Communist conspiracy led by the Soviet Union.

The war unleashed dramatic forces of global change and created conditions for a transnational ideological power struggle. The war irreparably altered the colonial empires of European nations and enabled the rise of revolutionary nationalism in Asia, Africa, the Middle East, and Latin America. All over the world, in countries like India and French Indochina (soon to be known as Vietnam), crumbling colonial control fueled nationalist desires and demands for independence, modernization, and higher quality of life (Map 25.1). Even before the war ended, boundaries shifted, as diverse peoples searched for ideologies and leadership to enable a new phase of their history to begin. U.S. policymakers pejoratively labeled these mostly nonwhite developing nations and contested regions the "**Third World**" in contrast to the presumed civility and superiority of the "First" and "Second" nations. The assumed lack of sophistication, cultural development, and national cohesiveness in former colonies prejudiced critical Cold War decision making in the coming years, often with disastrous results.

Ho Chi Minh declares independence for Vietnam (1945)

MAP 25.1 Dividing Postwar Europe This map shows the division of Europe into spheres of influence in the early years of the Cold War. By 1950, countries across a wide swath of the globe were divided by color on maps according to their relationship with NATO allies and Warsaw Pact signers. The developing world and neutral nations were shaded according to their importance to Cold War strategies on both sides.

At the end of the war, America had a clear military and economic advantage over the Soviets. To succeed in the growing Cold War, however, Truman needed another resource: an appealing ideology to counter Communist promises that had gained popularity among those disillusioned by the democratic capitalist model. Many people in former colonies of Western powers viewed the capitalism of their colonizers as the cause of depression, war, and fascism. In the coming decades, the selling of American culture and ideology became an important weapon in the Cold War. Spreading American ideals through international marketing of everything from jeans and cars to music and movies provided the "**soft power**" behind hard-edged Cold War foreign policy.

Dulles and Murrow: Two Americans Between World War II and the Cold War

There were very real reasons to fear the expansion of communism. By 1947, alarming statistics about the growing popularity of communism across Europe had raised concerns that the Soviets would have the balance of power handed to them by nations reeling from the aftermath of war. Between 1935 and 1945, Communist Party membership increased from 17,000 to 70,000 in Greece; from 28,000 to 750,000 in Czechoslovakia; and from 5,000 to 1,700,000 in Italy. Much of this rapid growth stemmed from the key anti-Nazi role played by local Communists during the war rather than from admiration for Stalin's policies. Still, there seemed to be evidence that communism was a powerful force in the postcolonial world.

In 1946, international observers and reporters were invited to watch Operation Crossroads demonstrate the atomic bomb's destructive power on hundreds of ships anchored in the Bikini Atoll of the South Pacific. Very early in the atomic age, fear of nuclear war worked its way into American popular culture. The August 1946 publication and serialization of John Hersey's best-selling *Hiroshima* explained the devastation of the bombs and the lasting horror of radiation sickness. Operation Crossroads received more global press than any other event in 1946. Two years later, David Bradley, a doctor who witnessed the Bikini tests, published *No Place to Hide*, a riveting firsthand account. "Bikini is San Francisco Bay, Puget Sound, East River," he wrote. "It isn't just King Juda and his displaced native subjects about whom we have to think—or to forget." Wide media coverage of atomic developments and frightening doomsday scenarios made the consequences of atomic warfare more real for the American public even before the Soviets got the bomb.

No Place to Hide

BY David Bradley

What the atomic bomb can do to ships, or water, or land, and thereby to human beings, is told with clear implications for all of us by a brilliant young doctor whose job it was to watch for radioactive contamination during and after the Bikini tests.

ATOMIC PREMONITIONS David Bradley's bestseller *No Place to Hide* (1948) alerted the public about the coming atomic age. Having witnessed the first atomic tests after the war, radiation expert Bradley understood how difficult it would be to control the power of the atom.

A Policy for Containment

In 1946, Truman needed a clear policy to respond to both real and perceived changes in the global balance of power in the nuclear age. Inspiration for a critical foreign policy plan came from Soviet expert **George F. Kennan**. In 1946, he sent his analysis of the postwar Soviet Union from his post in Moscow to Washington in a widely circulated 8,000-word "Long Telegram." In July 1947, Kennan published an even longer version of his pessimistic assessment of the Soviets in the influential journal *Foreign Affairs.* Kennan argued that Soviet communism was "impervious to the logic of reason," inherently expansionist, and controllable only through "long-term, patient but firm and vigilant containment." Kennan's idea, **containment**, became the foundation of U.S. foreign policy for the next four decades.

George F. Kennan, "The Sources of Soviet Conduct," *Foreign Affairs* (July 1947)

Although Kennan's assessment was alarming, he assured policymakers that the Soviets did not want war. Instead, they hoped that economic desperation in western Europe and Japan would drive these key regions into the Soviet camp. Kennan believed that if U.S. reconstruction programs stabilized western Europe, Japan, the Middle East, and the Third World, the Soviets would be contained and ultimately destroyed without actual war.

Faced with the need to garner support for massive funding efforts to fight Communists across the globe, Truman stepped up his anti-Communist rhetoric in a stark March 12, 1947, speech to Congress. Truman told Congress and the American people, "It must be the policy of the United States to support free peoples who are resisting attempted subjugation by armed minorities or by outside pressures." This bold new commitment to fight "Communist tyranny" wherever it might appear became known as the **Truman Doctrine**.

The Truman Doctrine

Michigan Republican senator Arthur Vandenberg advised Truman to "scare hell out of the American people" so they would understand the seriousness of the threat and thus win support from a GOP-led Congress. In several speeches, Truman painted a dramatic picture of a worldwide Communist conspiracy that could be contained only through aggressive force. These warnings secured $400 million from Congress to fight communism in Greece and elsewhere while creating a high level of anxiety about communism in America.

At home, the acceptance of the Truman Doctrine required a reorganization of the government in preparation for a protracted Cold War against communism. With the creation of the Department of Defense, the **National Security Act of 1947** consolidated the U.S. military command; a representative from each military branch would now advise a newly created secretary of defense and the president through the Joint Chiefs of Staff office. The act also created a National Security Council to advise the president and the Central Intelligence Agency (CIA) to gather intelligence about hostile, mostly Communist, activities throughout the world. After Truman's election in 1948, he appointed a new secretary of state, **Dean Acheson**, a strong supporter of a formal multinational alliance against the Soviet bloc (Map 25.2).

Working closely with European allies, Acheson achieved his goal with the founding of the **North Atlantic Treaty Organization (NATO)**. All of these foreign policy mechanisms demonstrated the military and diplomatic might of the United States. Of even greater lasting importance was the soft power side of the Truman Doctrine, the **Marshall Plan**, to rebuild Germany and Japan as models of democracy and capitalism.

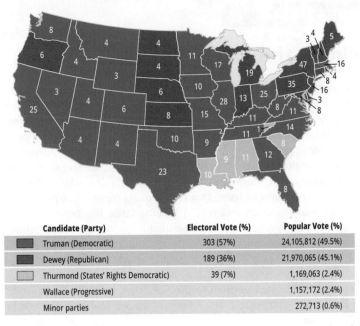

MAP 25.2 The Election of 1948 Segregationist candidate Strom Thurmond took four states in the divided South, but Truman defied expectations by carrying the day with what remained of the Roosevelt coalition.

Candidate (Party)	Electoral Vote (%)	Popular Vote (%)
Truman (Democratic)	303 (57%)	24,105,812 (49.5%)
Dewey (Republican)	189 (36%)	21,970,065 (45.1%)
Thurmond (States' Rights Democratic)	39 (7%)	1,169,063 (2.4%)
Wallace (Progressive)		1,157,172 (2.4%)
Minor parties		272,713 (0.6%)

STUDY QUESTIONS FOR THE COLD WAR

1. What does the Warsaw uprising tell us about the early Cold War?

2. In what ways did the policy of containment address U.S. fears of Soviet influence?

quiz

⊗ THE RED SCARE

At home, containment spawned a Red scare. Fear of communism led to restrictions of individual rights and the systematic persecution of diverse groups of American citizens. The decision to fight communism at all costs raised the crucial question: Under what conditions is the sacrifice of civil liberties justified in a democratic society?

A series of disturbing events between 1948 and 1950 accomplished Harry Truman's goal to "scare the hell" out of the American public. First, the Soviets caused an international crisis when they blockaded Berlin in hopes of gaining control of the divided city and thwarting U.S. efforts to rebuild a powerful West Germany. Between June 1948 and May 1949, the Soviets, locking down all roads leading to the city, forced the first showdown of the Cold War. The United States responded with the most remarkable air supply effort in history. For almost a year, U.S. transport planes carried food and coal into the city 24 hours a day. As they flew low over the city, U.S. pilots—earning the nickname "Candy Bombers"—took special pleasure in showering the children of Berlin with candy. The **Berlin Airlift** won the hearts of Berliners and humiliated the Soviets,

Rebuilding the World

Truman's new secretary of state was George C. Marshall, America's first five-star general and the top-ranking U.S. commander during World War II. In June 1947, Marshall gave a speech at Harvard University outlining what he called the European Recovery Plan (ERP). Popularly known as the Marshall Plan, this unprecedented proposal called for massive aid packages to help western Europe—including West Germany—and Japan rapidly rebuild their devastated economies, restore industries and trade, and rejoin the free world. A military man willing to use force when needed, Marshall also understood the power of economics and believed that free markets created free people. The stress on the word "free" was common and meant to emphasize the benefits of the American system as opposed to communism. The Marshall Plan dramatically expanded earlier efforts to use economic mechanisms such as the International Monetary Fund (IMF) and the World Bank to stabilize the world capitalist economy that had malfunctioned so dramatically in the 1930s, enabling the rise of totalitarian regimes in Germany, Italy, and Japan.

The United Nations was designed to provide the type of global assistance Marshall proposed. But, under Marshall's plan, America stepped ahead of the UN and became the world's banker and policeman, a broker of strategic trade relations, and the CEO of the global capitalist economy. Like the occupations of Japan and Germany, the economic dependencies forged under the Marshall Plan and approved by the U.S. Congress in March 1948 had profound and lasting consequences for U.S. foreign policy and contributed to the rise of the postwar global economy. For example, the rebuilding of western Europe required U.S. involvement in the development and protection of Middle Eastern oil reserves. However, although the reconstruction of Japan required U.S. involvement in Southeast Asia, former colonial nations could supply natural resources to Japan and counterbalance growing Communist economies in China and Korea.

Europe was the primary focus of the Marshall Plan as approved, but Japan also received extensive aid and expertise to rebuild the country's industrial complex and

who reopened the city on May 11, 1949. By then the United States had realized its goal of unifying the western zones of Germany into a pro-Western state in opposition to the Soviet-controlled eastern zones. Policymakers had only a few months to enjoy the success in Berlin, however, as the shocking news arrived on August 29, 1949, that the Soviets had successfully tested an atomic bomb. The Soviets' ability to catch up with American technology so rapidly revealed what U.S. leaders had suspected: that Communist spies had successfully infiltrated the Manhattan Project. America's monopoly on atomic power was over.

In October 1949, only one month after the stunning news about the Soviet atomic bomb, China fell to the Communists under the leadership of **Mao Zedong**. The formation of the Communist People's Republic of China especially disheartened Americans because of their long-standing charitable and missionary aid to the nation and significant diplomatic efforts by General **George Marshall** to ensure that China would remain free. Marshall had spent most of 1946 in China arranging a coalition between promote strategic trade expansion. Japan remained occupied until April 1952. The rebuilding in Japan followed a different course, but one with the same goal: using economic redevelopment and open markets as a means of blocking the expansion of communism.

The aid to European countries was a strategic necessity but also a humanitarian imperative. With war-ravaged people starving and freezing to death because of diminished food and coal reserves, aid was urgently necessary. The extent of the tragedy was well reported in the United States, as polls showed a majority of Americans supporting an extension of wartime food rationing to help the Europeans.

Fear that communism would appeal to the desperate and destitute in Europe drove rebuilding efforts and justified the unprecedented expense. Marshall's brilliant plan never mentioned these political concerns and even offered assistance to the Soviets and their satellites. By presenting a positive economic solution in a time of urgent need, Marshall deftly took the moral high ground and left the Soviets no retort in the public relations arena of the Cold War. Over the next three years, the United States appropriated over $15 billion ($145 billion in today's dollars) in aid to Europe and Japan, an unprecedented transfer of wealth that aided one of the most remarkable economic recoveries in history. As a result, Japan and Germany became the two key bastions of American power during the Cold War and today rank as the world's third- and fourth-largest economies, behind the United States and China. Further, America's liberal occupation policies created very positive images of Americans throughout the world. Marshall won the Nobel Peace Prize in 1953 for his humanitarian efforts. The Marshall Plan crushed Stalin's hopes of keeping Germany and Japan weak and at the same time demonstrated the enormous economic might and global reach of the United States.

Marshall Plan poster, 1947

- Students often wonder why the United States provided massive financial aid to Germany and Japan after spending billions to destroy them during World War II. What explains the rapid transition from spending to destroy to spending to rebuild?
- Beyond emerging politics, what explains the urgency of the Marshall Plan?

the Chinese nationalists, led by **Chiang Kai-shek**, and his Communist rivals, led by Mao. Despite Marshall's efforts, the coalition faltered. Chiang's incompetence contrasted with the Communists' rising popularity and superior organization. Full-scale civil war broke out in 1947, and by 1949, Mao led a unified China that allied itself with the Soviet Union. In the stridently anti-Communist environment of Cold War America, the fall of any Third World nation into the hands of communism became ammunition for domestic political rivalries. Republicans quickly blamed Truman for the "loss of China."

Americans worried that the new alliance between Stalin and Mao threatened to spread communism more widely in Asia. All of these events in 1949 raised U.S. fears and seemed to confirm the basic premise of the Truman Doctrine that Communist revolutionaries threatened freedom around the globe. Any doubts about a world Communist conspiracy faded with the news of a Communist North Korean invasion of South Korea on June 25, 1950.

War in Korea

The North Korean attack turned the Cold War hot. In a limited "proxy" or "brush fire" war, distant rivals served as substitutes for the Americans and Soviets, who stood behind or beside them. In Korea this stance was put to the test.

At the close of World War II, the Soviets and Americans agreed to the temporary North–South division of Korea, a Japanese colony since the early 20th century. The United States and the USSR agreed to divide Korea into occupation zones at the 38th parallel. Northern Korea had strategic importance for the Soviets, who considered the peninsula key to blocking future Japanese influence in the region and a counterweight to continued U.S. occupation of Japan. Between 1945 and 1950, the Soviets sponsored the creation in the north of the Democratic People's Republic of Korea under **Kim Il-sung**. The United States backed a separate government in the south, the Republic of Korea, headed by the conservative nationalist **Syngman Rhee**, who had lived in the United States for decades. Both of these new states experienced political insecurity and violence, with an estimated 100,000 people killed during constant internal struggles.

The rivalry between the North and the South intensified throughout the late 1940s. Both shared much in common despite their opposing political views. Repressive autocratic leaders controlled both sections of divided Korea, and both were willing to use violence against their own people and expend massive resources on the military to prevent unification on any terms but their own. In a precedent-setting decision, the U.S. Joint Chiefs of Staff concluded as early as 1947 that Korea had little strategic value to the United States but abandoning the unstable South Korean regime would almost certainly lead to war between the U.S.-supported South and the Soviet-supported North.

By 1950, U.S. leaders had growing concerns that Communist China would join the fight as well. Under the logic of containment, this potential spread of communism was unacceptable, even if it meant supporting South Korea—a repressive malfunctioning government in a country known to few Americans with no significant strategic value.

On June 25, 1950, the Soviet-supplied North Korean army launched a large-scale invasion across the 38th parallel. The well-organized assault drove quickly through South Korea and into the capital city of Seoul, forcing the U.S.-backed government to flee. Stunned by the remarkable success of the invasion, Truman worried that this major Communist incursion into a "free" state might allow Communists in Asia to "swallow up one piece after another." Two days after the invasion, the **United Nations Security Council**, with the Soviets absent so they could not veto the move, met and voted to authorize a U.S.-led coalition of forces to push the Communists back across the 38th parallel. Truman named General **Douglas MacArthur**, chief of the American occupation force in Japan, as U.S./UN theater commander in Korea.

From its onset, the Korean War tested not only U.S. Cold War foreign policy but also the ability of the United Nations to create coalitions of supporters willing to fight for collective rather than national goals (Map 25.3). During the conflict, 17 UN member nations from four continents sent troops to Korea, but U.S. troops far outnumbered those of all other nations combined. By the end of the war, the United States had sent over 500,000 troops; the British sent approximately 65,000, and other nations contributed as few as 400.

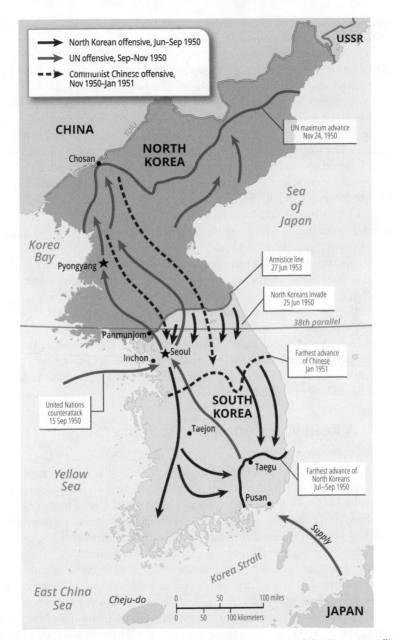

Legend:
→ North Korean offensive, Jun–Sep 1950
→ UN offensive, Sep–Nov 1950
--▶ Communist Chinese offensive, Nov 1950–Jan 1951

USSR

CHINA

NORTH KOREA

Yalu

Chosan

UN maximum advance Nov 24, 1950

Sea of Japan

Korea Bay

Pyongyang

Armistice line 27 Jun 1953

North Koreans invade 25 Jun 1950

38th parallel

Panmunjom

Inchon

Seoul

Farthest advance of Chinese Jan 1951

United Nations counterattack 15 Sep 1950

SOUTH KOREA

Taejon

Yellow Sea

Taegu

Farthest advance of North Koreans Jul–Sep 1950

Pusan

Korea Strait

Supply

East China Sea

Cheju-do

0   50   100 miles
0   50   100 kilometers

JAPAN

map analysis

MAP 25.3 The Deceptive Complexity of Proxy War This map of the Korean conflict looks simple, North versus South, but the war was vexingly complicated on every front. Maps similar to this appeared on the front pages of newspapers throughout World War II, offering the public a means to gauge progress. However, the back-and-forth struggle in Korea, changing cast of key players, and ultimate stalemate indicated that the Cold War would be harder to map than previous conflicts.

After North Korean forces pushed coalition troops to a small foothold in South Korea, MacArthur staged a dramatic counterattack at Inchon on the northwestern coast of South Korea on September 15, 1950. Pushing rapidly across the peninsula and liberated Seoul, U.S. and UN troops drove hundreds of thousands of North Korean troops north and won back the South in one sustained assault.

This surprisingly easy victory inspired both Truman and MacArthur to expand the war. Instead of simply restoring South Korea, the United States announced a new goal: destroying the North Korean regime and unifying the country under Syngman Rhee. In just a few weeks, the coalition reached the northern capital city of Pyongyang and seemed poised to retake the entire country. In the flush of apparent victory, both Truman and MacArthur ignored Chinese warnings that its forces would intervene to defend North Korea, especially if U.S. troops approached the Yalu River that separated Korea from China's industrial heartland in Manchuria. MacArthur's forceful personality convinced Truman that China was bluffing and that both the president and general would share in the glory of "rolling back" communism.

Chinese poster, "Resist America, Aid Korea" (1951)

When a quarter-million Chinese troops swarmed across the border and quickly pushed the United States all the way back to the 38th parallel, that assumption was dramatically proved wrong. With U.S. troops in retreat, MacArthur and Truman accused each other of incompetence and political posturing. In April 1951, Truman fired MacArthur for insubordination. The 38th parallel was the focal point of three more years of protracted and bloody fighting with no decisive objective other than holding the line. The demilitarized zone (DMZ), or no-man's-land, splitting Korea at the 38th parallel became a Cold War icon: a symbol of stalemate and a persistent reminder that proxy wars could lead to seemingly infinite conflict.

NSC-68: A Cold War Containment Policy

A top-secret 1950 National Security Council document known as NSC-68 supported Truman's decisive military response in Korea. Early Cold War containment policy focused on building allies through economic programs such as the Marshall Plan. By 1950, events had led State Department officials like **Paul H. Nitze** to suggest that economic diplomacy was not enough and that countering Soviet and Chinese actions in places such as Korea required direct use of U.S. military force. Although never fully implemented, NSC-68 painted a graphic picture of a fanatically expansionist USSR bent on world domination and demonstrated a willingness to consider radical options to combat communism. The document concluded with a strong recommendation for massive military spending and decisive military response to any and all Soviet actions around the globe. NSC-68 further warned that the Soviet Union was "animated by a new fanatical faith" and ready to "impose absolute authority over the rest of the world."

Paul H. Nitze, "A Report to the National Security Council— NC-68," (April 1950)

NSC-68 called for expanding annual military spending from about $13 billion to $50 billion to accomplish these goals. Part of the increase would fund more and bigger nuclear weapons. This dramatic increase in military spending and the resulting military-industrial complex precipitously and permanently increased the costs of government. Beyond the military buildup and financial cost, NSC-68 completely changed the tone of American Cold War culture. Recommendations from the NSC included extensive propaganda campaigns to sell ideological war to the American people: programs to quell dissent, foster loyalty, and create consensus even at the cost of hard-won social welfare programs. Even before the Korean War, government and elected officials who believed that national security depended on a stronger military ratcheted up anti-Communist rhetoric, fanning the flames of a long-simmering Red scare.

Fears of communism and Red scares were not new to the postwar era. During World War I, in the aftermath of the 1917 Communist Revolution in Russia, Americans worried about the global appeal of communism. Liberals and conservatives alike defined communism as the opposite of democracy and the economic collectivism of the new Soviet state as the antithesis of free market individualism. Political tensions in the 1930s energized American conservatives, who linked liberalism and communism and railed against the "creeping socialism" of New Deal social programs.

Systematic government efforts to enforce conformity in support of containment began before the end of World War II. Starting in 1944, the **House Committee on Un-American Activities (HCUA)** made the search for Communists and conspiracies within the United States the centerpiece of a domestic containment policy. Between 1944 and 1946, the vehemently racist and anti-Semitic **John E. Rankin**, a Democratic congressman from Mississippi, used the committee as a forum to attack liberal causes under the guise of fighting Communists. From his seat on HCUA, Rankin railed against Jews and linked the "mongrelization" of the races with anti-Christian communism. Rankin's ravings enhanced a link in American culture between any perceived cultural, racial, or religious differences and communism.

The Color of Difference Is Red

The linking of cultural difference with communism opened a Pandora's box. Emboldened conservative government investigations soon cast an ever-widening net of suspicion over a range of "liberal" civic activities from civil rights to poverty relief, which they linked to the global Communist conspiracy. Virtually any advocacy or protest could be linked to communism and encourage a pernicious climate of mutual suspicion. Although many Americans rejected this notion outright, the fear of communism caused significant numbers to acquiesce and agree to dramatic restrictions of civil liberties.

In 1946, responding to fears of Communist infiltration of the U.S. government, Truman issued Executive Order 9835, which launched the Federal Employee Loyalty Program that by 1950 had investigated over five million workers. Government employees were subjected to intense questioning about their behavior and beliefs. Membership in a long list of broadly defined "subversive" groups was grounds for dismissal. Even the flimsiest hearsay evidence about an employee's inclinations or beliefs could lead to summary firing and brand him or her as a Red. Proving one's loyalty in the face of often unfounded accusation was often extremely difficult.

In the course of loyalty investigations, 91 homosexual State Department employees were fired. In the following years, homosexuals became the target of editorials, congressional debates, and intense media scrutiny, leading to 600 dismissals. In the coming years, Jews, immigrants, and even five-star generals were also labeled Communists based on broad assumptions about subversion in the atomic age.

In 1940, Congress passed the Smith Act, which made advocating the overthrow of the U.S. government a federal offense. The act was widely interpreted as a tool for arresting suspected Fascists and Communists. That year, 11 members of the American Communist Party were arrested for discussing the overthrow of the government; they were prosecuted and convicted under the new act despite the lack of evidence suggesting they were plotting any action. The U.S. Supreme Court upheld the constitutionality of the act in 1951 in *Dennis v. United States*. The ruling demonstrated that there was consensus, across all three branches of the federal government, that communism was inherently subversive and that Communists lurked in the United States itself.

Hollywood and the Pumpkin Papers

Starting in 1944, Hollywood became the focal point of a series of dramatic HCUA hearings when actors, directors, and writers were subpoenaed to appear before Congress. Friendly witnesses, such as future president Ronald Reagan and screenwriter Ayn Rand, identified individuals they thought might be associated with Communist activities. Most witnesses were horrified to be called to Washington, and many argued for protection of free speech under the First Amendment or chose to exercise their Fifth Amendment right to remain silent rather than "rat out" their friends and colleagues. Those who refused to cooperate were convicted of contempt of Congress and sentenced to a year in federal prison.

HCUA gained even more attention in 1948 when it investigated *Time* editor **Whittaker Chambers**. Chambers claimed that he had been part of an elaborate Soviet spy ring funneling U.S. secrets to the Soviets throughout the 1930s. He confided this story to a young congressman from California named **Richard M. Nixon**. In August 1948, Chambers provided dramatic testimony to HCUA and named **Alger Hiss**, the head of the Carnegie Endowment for International Peace and a former State Department official, as a collaborator and Communist spy. Hiss sued Chambers for libel and the case became a national sensation. Chambers responded with a remarkable tale of secrets passed by Hiss during the 1930s, copies of which Chambers kept in a hollowed-out pumpkin on his Maryland farm. The FBI determined that the "Pumpkin Papers," as they were dubbed, contained a variety of records, including some decade-old State Department documents retyped on a typewriter owned by the Hiss family. The United States tried Hiss, but the jury was unable to agree on a verdict. Charged a second time with perjury for lying about knowing Chambers, Hiss was convicted and sentenced to prison.

STUDY QUESTIONS FOR THE RED SCARE

1. How did NSC-68 change American Cold War policy? How did it affect domestic policy and culture?

quiz

2. Why was the Korean conflict called a "proxy war"?

A NEW AFFLUENCE

Cold War anxieties seemed at odds with rising domestic prosperity in the aftermath of World War II as programs such as the GI Bill and Truman's **Fair Deal** created avenues to middle-class status for many Americans. The Cold War fostered a period of unprecedented economic growth in global capitalism. Military spending on new technologies led to advances in domestic production and consumer goods. These twin engines of economic growth created an extended period of domestic prosperity and more widely spread affluence than at any other time in American history.

Saturday afternoon street scene, West Virginia, August 24, 1946

This new prosperity depended on the globalization of the international economy. U.S. Cold War policies fostered free trade and the free flow of goods and capital among friendly nations. American business took advantage of these trends. The creation of powerful new multinational corporations resulted in an unprecedented global exchange of technologies and institutional practices. Further, philanthropic and international organizations became enormously influential during this period. Powerful and wealthy **nongovernmental organizations (NGOs)** supported American foreign relations and fostered the growth of global capitalism. Those Americans who supported the agenda of the New Deal saw the postwar boom as an opportunity to expand the scope and reach of social welfare programs.

The Fair Deal

On September 6, 1945, President Truman sent Congress an ambitious 21-point domestic agenda. He worked to secure the domestic goals of his predecessor while establishing a domestic program distinctly his own. Truman faced strong resistance to his domestic program from the first Republican majority in Congress since the Hoover administration. Despite their differences on domestic policy, however, the national security imperatives inherent in the Truman Doctrine fostered a level of consensus and cooperation rarely seen in the U.S. Congress.

Undeterred, Truman pressed his domestic agenda through speeches to Congress and to the people through national radio addresses. By 1946, the outlines of his Fair Deal had begun to emerge. Truman offered some bold and controversial expansions of the New Deal. The 21-point program called for an increase in the minimum wage, comprehensive housing legislation for returning veterans, full employment and expanded unemployment benefits, permanent federal farm subsidies, expanded public works projects, and expanded environmental conservation programs. Most controversially, Truman proposed a comprehensive federal health insurance program and restructuring of Social Security programs.

Some of Truman's proposals were hard to oppose. With the memories of the ecological catastrophe of the Great Plains Dust Bowl still fresh, Truman's recommendations on the environment resulted in expanded conservation programs, new funding for national parks, and water reclamation projects in the West and South. Likewise, the return home of millions of soldiers caused a crisis in both employment and housing so severe that there were fears the nation might descend back into depression. Congress responded with the Veterans Emergency Housing Act and a series of reforms aiding the transition of soldiers to citizens.

The GI Bill

As the war wound down, concern for returning soldiers came from every quarter. Memories of inadequate treatment for veterans of World War I still resonated. FDR called for an "economic bill of rights," framing GI rights in the context of the New Deal. In

1944, Congress passed the Servicemen's Readjustment Act, or GI Bill, with the support of liberals who saw it as a much-needed social welfare program and conservatives who considered it a patriotic vote of thanks. This enlightened legislation produced dramatic changes in American society. The GI Bill expanded access to higher education, enabled homeownership for a much wider segment of society, and helped create a climate of success for returning veterans.

Operating as a comprehensive welfare program, the GI Bill provided returning veterans temporary unemployment assistance; government backed, low-interest loans to start businesses or buy homes; hiring preferences for civil service jobs; and extensive health services. The bill provided living stipends and tuition to all universities, colleges, and vocational schools.

The billions of dollars Congress authorized to fund the umbrella of support programs jump-started millions of veterans toward a higher standard of life. The impact on American higher education was equally dramatic. In the years following the war, over two million men and 64,000 women veterans found open doors at public and private colleges and universities.

Greater access to higher education during the 1940s and 1950s provided American industry with the best-educated white-collar workforce in the world. Another six million men used the GI Bill for technical and vocational training, building an army of highly trained workers for expanding American industries. After signing the GI Bill into law on June 22, 1944, President Roosevelt said the bill gave "emphatic notice to the men and women in our armed forces that the American people do not intend to let them down." The programs of the GI Bill guaranteed a higher quality of life for many veterans while highlighting social and racial disparities for others.

A US Army sergeant explains the GI Bill to members of his company (1945)

Educational and housing opportunities for blacks in the South remained severely restricted by legal segregation and existed in the North in more subtle ways. The desire for equal opportunity in education played a large role in directing civil rights efforts after the war, as African American vets watched their former comrades at arms prosper while they faced the same grinding poverty and inequality they had since the 1870s. For women of all backgrounds, the return of the soldiers raised questions about their role in peacetime.

Working Women

For the soldiers who benefited from education and preferential hiring policies, advantages often came at the expense of their wives, sisters, and mothers. In the years following the war, women were expected to move from their wartime identity as heroic "Rosie the Riveters" back to traditional roles as wives at home. Lower-income and minority women were forced back to the lower-paying, limiting jobs they had held before the war. Many women resisted this trend, but employers, with support from the government, required most to leave lucrative jobs and abandon hard-earned skills.

During the war, the percentage of married women and mothers entering the workforce had increased from 13.9 percent to 22.5 percent and 7.8 percent to 12.1 percent, respectively. Wartime polls showed that between 60 percent and 80 percent of these women wanted to keep their jobs when the war ended. When the war ended, however, women workers faced pressure from a new wave of government propaganda encouraging them to hand their jobs back to men.

Sisters under the apron—Yesterday's war worker becomes today's housewife.

What's Become of Rosie the Riveter?

WHEN a character captures the imagination of the American public, its ups and downs are followed with an interest that sometimes surpasses avidity. Thus it is with Rosie the Riveter, who symbolized to America the effort of all women workers toward winning the war.

Her numbers reduced by millions since July, she is involved in a tremendous reshuffling.

By FRIEDA S. MILLER,
Director, Women's Bureau, United States Department of Labor

CHANGING ROLES This image from the June 1946 *New York Times Magazine* accompanied an article titled, "What's Become of Rosie the Riveter?" Unlike their Soviet counterparts, U.S. women were expected to leave the workforce after their exceptional wartime efforts. Government officials and industry leaders worked to convince American women that they could best support democracy and capitalism as mothers, housewives, and consumers.

WOMEN WORKERS This Soviet propaganda poster emphasized not only "more bread for the front and the rear: bring in the whole harvest!" but the role of women as workers. During the Cold War, the Soviets never missed a chance to point toward gender or racial inequalities in the United States as signs of flawed democracy.

image analysis

The systematic removal of women from the industrial workforce was more than a practical response to the return of male veterans: it became a Cold War imperative. Government Cold War propaganda stressed that American women could best fight the Communist ideological menace by being homemakers. Comparisons between women's work in the Soviet Union and women's work in the United States became important points of differentiation for the two systems. The Soviets celebrated women workers as symbols of Socialist equality. American politicians pointed to Soviet women workers as an example of the backward Communist system that required all to slave away in service of the state. Images of well-dressed American housewives surrounded by new appliances became standard U.S. propaganda tools.

Globally, the United States and the USSR fought for the "hearts and minds" of developing world women through competing organizations. The UN-supported International Council for Women (ICW) advocated for democracy and freedom for women and children. The Soviet-backed Women's International Democratic Federation (WIDF) supported nationalism and colonial independence and the fight against fascism and racial discrimination around the globe. In the international arena, the WIDF's pro-nationalist message had great appeal, whereas the ICW could point to the rising standard of living for women in America and U.S.-occupied Germany and Japan as evidence of the benefits of capitalism.

STUDY QUESTIONS FOR A NEW AFFLUENCE

1. How did the GI Bill benefit the United States in the transition from World War II to the Cold War?

2. Was the GI Bill an expansion of the social programs of the New Deal? Why or why not?

quiz

◉ POSTWAR MIGRATIONS

In the searing heat of August anywhere in the South or Southwest, temperatures reach dangerous levels. For centuries, weather limited the design and scope of cities and settlements in these hottest regions of the nation. Following World War II, the availability of millions of cheap window-unit air conditioners enabled places such as scorching Phoenix, Arizona, to attract businesses and people. Retirees and winter-weary migrants moved in record numbers from the North and the Midwest to the Sunbelt. Migrants to the Southwest assumed that the engineering marvels of the Hoover Dam and complex system of reclamation projects on the Colorado River had permanently turned the desert to a garden. Migrant workers moving north from Latin America through the United States ensured a supply of cheap labor. Libertarian-leaning western state governments allowed lax environmental standards, limited regulation, and low taxation for entrepreneurs and companies looking to build on the industrialization of the war.

Ongoing internal migrations of African Americans to the urban North played a major role in changing the demographic character of American cities and industries. Renewed migrations of Mexicans north into the American Southwest built on long-established patterns but surpassed older trends in both numbers and reach. Across the country, suburban growth fueled by these migrations and the GI Bill caused fundamental changes in American life. Finally, millions of Americans took to the road on

COOKIE-CUTTER HOMES   William Levitt became the Henry Ford of housing when he perfected mas-production methods for suburban development. This image shows the best-known of the Levittowns, on Long Island, New York, May 14, 1954.

seasonal migrations to national parks, historic sites, and vacation spots. These leisure travelers elevated tourism to one of the most important sectors of the postwar economy.

The entire United States experienced significant demographic shifts during and after World War II, but the newly industrialized American West and South saw the greatest changes. Both regions benefited from the war mobilization that redistributed tens of millions of soldiers and support staff and billions of dollars to massive new military installations in these regions. In prewar 1939, the United States maintained a standing army of 200,000 men. By 1945, that number had increased to 8,266,000 in the army and 12,294,000 in the combined armed forces. This increase resulted in the most significant federally organized movement of people and resources in U.S. history. The U.S. Air Force (still part of the army during the war) alone required the construction of 500 new airfields and support facilities to build and service over 70,000 aircraft.

Military-Industrial West and South

Military leaders favored the South and West as locations for wartime mobilization for the regions' warm weather, clear skies, and wide-open spaces. Air bases were built in the desert Southwest where the climate was perfect for both training and storage, but the South got the lion's share of new air bases (Map 25.4). Plentiful cheap labor and land combined with powerful southern politicians explain the clustering of air bases throughout the Southeast. The demographic and economic impact in areas surrounding military bases was immediate.

Cold War imperatives ensured the continued growth of the military-industrial complex. Racial segregation ensured that white workers benefited from new federal opportunities in the South, whereas black workers, including veterans, suffered from high rates of unemployment. White southern politicians used their new Cold War political influence to garner a large share of federal programs. At the same time, they maintained and even expanded the Jim Crow system to make sure that the South played by

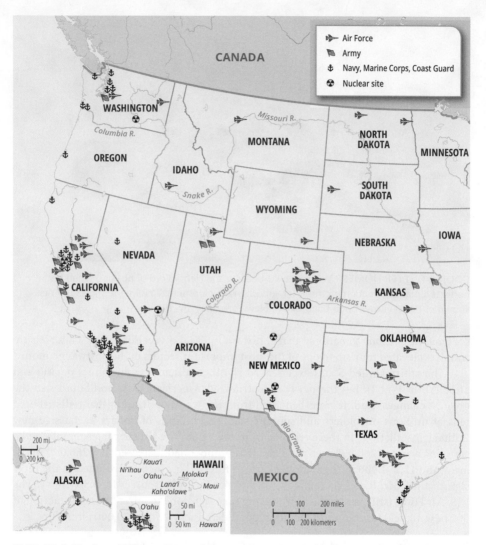

MAP 25.4 Modern Military West This map shows the extent of military development in the West during World War II and the Cold War. The West was transformed by the construction of the military-industrial complex.

its own rules, even as military and economic developments brought the region more closely into the fold of the nation.

For those working on America's new nuclear-industrial complex, the West afforded vast tracts of remote lands where large military bases could be hidden. Only one major atomic installation was built in the South, at Oak Ridge, Tennessee. The rest of America's atomic complex was scattered across the West in New Mexico, Washington, California, and Nevada. Los Alamos, New Mexico, hosted the international brain trust at the center of the Manhattan Project. White Sands, outside of Alamogordo, New Mexico, was used for the Trinity test. In Albuquerque, a series of laboratories, eventually consolidated as Sandia National Labs, grew next to Kirtland Air Base. In California, both the California Institute of Technology and, starting in 1952, Lawrence Livermore National

Laboratory became important centers of atomic research. Argonne, Brookhaven, and coalitions of eastern universities too came together in a system of national laboratories that formalized wartime relationships.

During World War II, Nellis Air Force base in Las Vegas, Nevada, used the largely unpopulated Mojave Desert as an extensive bombing range. The remoteness of the location, federal control of the lands under the Bureau of Land Management, and assumptions about the general worthlessness of desert lands made Nevada a logical choice for a continental nuclear testing facility. Starting in 1951, the Nevada Proving Ground, only 90 miles from Las Vegas, replaced remote Pacific islands as the site where the United States perfected its nuclear arsenal. Dramatic nuclear tests became a regular feature of Las Vegas life, with mushroom clouds clearly visible from the city. On the other side of town, the Basic Magnesium facility employed 15,000 workers refining the "wonder metal" of modern aeronautics. Similarly extensive industrialization efforts such as the Kaiser Ship Works in Long Beach, California, transformed the West from an extractive economy to a highly urbanized industrial powerhouse.

Atomic bomb blast, Yucca Flats, Nevada (1951)

The military-driven industrialization of the West dramatically expanded the political and cultural importance of the region. Between 1910 and 1950, migrations to the West led to significant congressional reapportionments resulting in a net gain of 28 new seats in Congress. California alone gained 19 new seats during this time. In the coming decades, California produced two presidents, completing the shift in the West from the frontier periphery to a vital center of American culture and politics.

Hispanics Move North

The ebb and flow of immigrants from Mexico and Latin America helped boost the health of the U.S. economy. During good times such as the 1920s, Mexican immigration was loosely regulated and strongly encouraged by American industries that benefited from influxes of cheap labor. The crackdown on Mexican immigrants during the Depression years, however, resulted in a dramatic reduction of migration and a 60 percent decline in persons listing Mexico as their place of birth on the 1940 census.

World War II once again changed needs and attitudes. By 1942, U.S. war industries and the military had absorbed a huge percentage of the workforce. Like African Americans and women of all backgrounds, Mexicans found closed doors suddenly open. Both in the military and in wartime industry, Mexican immigrants, like other U.S. minorities, saw an opportunity to prove their worth to a nation that had offered

IMPORTED WORKFORCE

Identified only as "Mica from El Paso," this Bracero worker used his ID card to legally work in the Southwest. During periods of economic prosperity, political and industry leaders collaborated to facilitate mass migrations from Mexico and Latin America to meet labor demands. When labor markets tightened, these workers were no longer welcome.

them only grudging respect during the best of times. A Mexican song of the war years, "*Soldado raso*," captured the goal with lyrics proclaiming, "*Les probaré que mi raza, sabe morir dondequiera*"—"I will prove my people know how to die anywhere."

In 1942, the United States and Mexico reached an agreement on a regulated worker immigration program to encourage Mexican workers to move north to jobs abandoned by the millions of American workers occupied by the war effort. The Emergency Farm Labor Supply, or Bracero Program, granted annual entry to hundreds of thousands of seasonal agricultural workers. Control of the border was generally loosened, and hundreds of thousands of other Mexicans were lured north by growing opportunities in other areas of the greatly expanding U.S. economy. This shift in attitudes and policy led to a fourfold increase in the Mexican-born population of California alone and permanently transformed the demographic character of the Southwest.

Mexican Women Railroad Workers, San Bernardino California, 1944

Between 1940 and 1950, the U.S. Census recorded 450,000 Mexican-born resident aliens and 2.69 million Spanish-surnamed citizens. Census figures, however, never fully documented the extent of the flux of migration across the southern border and remain contested to this day. Many Bracero workers stayed beyond the season, moving throughout the West and in increasing numbers to the North to work in nonseasonal industrial jobs. Labor agents hired by American corporations operated ahead of or against official U.S. policy, pulling immigrants to the United States in large numbers unrepresented in census figures.

The return of millions of U.S. soldiers to civilian life once again drew attention to the Mexican migrant workforce. Created in 1924, the U.S. Border Patrol facilitated the Bracero Program during the war. In the early 1950s, responding to concerns about the extent of illegal migration, the patrol stepped up efforts to apprehend "wetbacks" (slang for illegal immigrants crossing into the United States over the Rio Grande River) and workers without proper documents. For Hispanic immigrants and their descendants, their indispensable work in wartime industry and their valiant service during the war were rewarded with widespread distrust and contempt.

As with all domestic issues during the period between 1945 and 1952, the Cold War affected immigration policies. Since the passage of the National Origins Act of 1924, strict quotas had regulated the flow and character of U.S. immigration. In the aftermath of war, the need to admit displaced persons from eastern Europe fleeing the aftermath of Nazi brutality or the onset of Soviet control sparked debate about quotas. Truman argued for a less restrictive system able to cope with the global movement of peoples. In 1948, Congress passed the Displaced Persons Act that allowed about 100,000 (out of several million) refugees into the United States. There was also a gradual erosion of policies barring entry of Asian immigrants.

Organizations such as the Daughters of the American Revolution, however, linked immigrants with the spread of communism and encouraged severe restrictions. Senator Pat McCarran of Nevada engineered such restrictions with his sponsorship of the Immigration and Naturalization Act that became law on December 24, 1952, over Truman's veto. The **McCarran International Security Act** reinforced perceptions of immigrants as a source of radicalism during the Cold War and set the tone for a contentious debate about immigration in the coming decade. The new law retained all the worst features of the 1924 quota system and added new categories of "undesirables" barred from the United States.

Mobile Leisure

During World War II, rationing severely restricted gasoline, rubber, metal, and all of the components needed for auto travel. Bald tires became a symbol of wartime sacrifice on the home front. As troops returned home to a revitalized economy, however, auto travel expanded drastically. (In Chapter 26, we explore the huge impact of the Interstate Highway system launched by the Eisenhower administration.) Even before the dramatic expansion of the interstates, Americans took to the road in search of leisure, learning, and fun. For families who had endured almost two decades of hardship, the family vacation became the ultimate expression of freedom and affluence. Automakers rapidly retooled factories from military to domestic production and promoted ownership and travel. Along with the single-family home, car ownership marked a family's successful rise to the middle class, and personal mobility became a symbol of American freedom during the Cold War. Manufacturers promoted auto travel with catchy ad campaigns such as "See the USA in your Chevrolet." Americans responded by purchasing cars in unprecedented numbers. Cold War patriotism inspired widespread interest in historic sites and boosted efforts to preserve America's heritage. The Gettysburg historic battlefield and other iconic historic sites sprouted "gateway" villages with miles of nearby motels catering to a new breed of "heritage tourist."

The GI Bill ensured that millions of Americans learned more about their history, and all forms of cultural resources benefited from an educated middle class with the time and the means to visit museums and cultural sites around the country. The rise of an outdoor industry provided new recreational opportunities while dramatically expanding the popularity of pursuits such as hunting and fishing, skiing, and hiking. Starting in the late 1940s, newsstands from Manhattan to Los Angeles carried a wide array of magazines such as *Field and Stream* and *Sports Outdoors* for the growing numbers of outdoor and "armchair" enthusiasts.

Businesses recognized the seemingly unlimited economic opportunities presented by an expanding middle class obsessed with travel and recreation. Companies such as Ford capitalized on the popularity of outdoor recreation with advertising campaigns showing their vehicles loaded with camping gear and parked alongside a lake or in a mountain meadow. Cigarette companies eager to keep wartime smokers buying at home shifted from advertising that depicted dapper smokers in urban settings to ads showing rugged men and outdoorsy women enjoying a smoke around the campfire. Between the end of the war and the mid-1950s, wartime-boosted products and technologies moved into the general marketplace with far-reaching consequences for American culture and the economy.

1949 Lucky Strikes cigarette advertisement

For those who could afford it, the vacation retreat to the slopes, the woods, or the beach provided a welcome distraction from Cold War anxiety. This relief was not shared equally. Carefully monitored visitor statistics in the national parks showed that less than 1 percent of tourists were African American, and, even in the Southwest, the numbers for Hispanics were equally low. In the 1950s, the world of recreational travel was almost exclusively white.

But after World War II, many people of color were on the move in search of work, opportunity, and greater racial equality.

◉ LAYING THE FOUNDATIONS FOR CIVIL RIGHTS

In the sweltering July heat of 1946, African American veteran George Dorsey, his wife Mae, his brother-in-law Roger and his wife Dorothy were tied to trees and executed by a mob in Monroe, Georgia. The bodies were dismembered by hundreds of bullets fired from the crowd. Dorsey was castrated. The lynching in Monroe was one of many across the South during that summer. Several of the most vicious murders were sparked by whites offended by the sight of a black man in uniform. Veteran status ensured that African American soldiers were heroes abroad, but those who returned to the South found their standing unchanged or worse. For millions of Americans, the simple dream of a family life was out of reach. African Americans were constantly reminded that the new affluent America had little room for them. Veterans and workers who tasted freedom during the war and hoped for new access to freedom at home would energize the civil rights movement.

Between 1945 and 1952, African American civil rights advocates mounted challenges to racial discrimination and mobilized for a massive expansion of the movement in the coming decades. In the fight for equality, African Americans needed leadership, legal resources, strategic alliances with whites, and a unifying philosophy to propel their movement forward. Many of these core resources came together during and immediately after the war.

James G. Thompson, "Should I Sacrifice to Live 'Half-American?'" *Pittsburgh Courier,* January 31, 1942

During the war, the NAACP launched a widely publicized "Double V" campaign against the twin evils of fascism and racism; it was their hope that the racism of the Nazis would open American eyes to inequality at home. When Harry Truman became president, he brought an ambivalence about race not uncommon to politicians of his day. Despite personal uncertainties about racial equality, however, Truman made civil rights part of his domestic agenda at great political cost.

First Steps

In 1946, Truman established the President's Committee on Civil Rights and supported its controversial 1947 report "To Secure These Rights." Truman's most significant civil rights achievement was the desegregation of the military. When leading civil rights leader and labor organizer **A. Philip Randolph** threatened to organize a boycott to protest segregation in the military, Truman responded quickly and courageously. On July 26, 1948, Truman issued **Executive Order 9981** declaring, "There shall be equality of treatment and opportunity for all persons in the armed services without regard to race, color, religion, or national origin." The military took almost six years to implement Truman's policy, but the desegregation of the military set a critical precedent; at least on paper, it erased one of the most glaringly contradictory policies of the leading nation of the "free world" during the Cold War.

At home and abroad American leaders reinforced the notion that the Cold War was a fight to protect the "free world." At the same time, during the 1940s and 1950s, the repressive and violent racism of the South and institutional racism throughout the nation contradicted U.S. foreign policy rhetoric. Conservative citizens' groups and politicians justified racism by equating civil rights with radical liberalism and communism. Despite these strident voices, a slowly growing national consensus about the importance of civil rights in the fight against the world Communist conspiracy emerged in the postwar years. For many white Americans, pragmatic responses to racial inequality grew into genuine humanitarian concerns as they learned more about their fellow African American citizens from their war experiences and from the national media spotlight thrown on exceptional African American individuals.

Jack Roosevelt Robinson

No one changed public opinion more significantly in the early postwar fight for civil rights than **Jack Roosevelt "Jackie" Robinson**. During his childhood, Robinson's family moved from Georgia to southern California. A good student and gifted athlete, Robinson attended the University of California, Los Angeles, and starred in several sports. As an officer during World War II, Robinson refused to move to the back of a bus, and he gained notoriety by defending himself in a military court martial. Honorably discharged, Robinson resumed his athletic career. At the same time, civil rights supporter and Brooklyn Dodgers owner Branch Rickey was looking for an opportunity to challenge segregation in professional baseball. In 1945, he offered Robinson a contract for the Dodgers' minor league team.

In April 1947, after an exemplary season, Rickey sent Robinson up to the major leagues. When Jackie Robinson walked on to the field wearing the Dodgers uniform, he took center stage in an early battle to win American hearts and minds in the battle against racism. In his first season, he experienced constant racial slurs hurled from the stands, protests by opposing teams who threatened to boycott the Dodgers, and a steady stream of death threats. When the team traveled, Robinson, not allowed to stay in segregated hotels, was forced to search for places to sleep on his own. Responding stoically, he played despite the controversy swirling around him, focusing on the game and demonstrating his remarkable talent and ability. His outstanding first season won him the National League Rookie of the Year award and legions of fans of all races who admired his excellence on the field and personal bravery in the face of racial hatred. Robinson scored two victories: one for baseball and another in the public relations campaign for civil rights.

Other black players soon followed Robinson into the major leagues. In the coming years, African Americans used sports and entertainment to cross the color line and win the admiration of white fans who often became allies in the fight for equality.

BREAKING THE COLOR BARRIER
Brooklyn Dodger Jackie Robinson poses in his batting stance in March 1953. Robinson's determined expression in this image reflects his grace under fire at the plate and as the spearhead of racial integration in major league baseball.

The Influence of African American Veterans

America's critical role in World War II and Truman's strong assertion of American leadership in the postwar world ensured a much higher level of international scrutiny of American culture. The United Nations, headquartered in New York City, brought thousands of international diplomats and media representatives to the United States, where American life, warts and all, was plainly on view. Entrenched American racism, legal segregation in the South, and obscene levels of racial violence became international news.

The foreign policy implications of this new global attention were immediate and vexing. In an early 1946 exchange about Soviet denial of voting rights in eastern Europe, a U.S. official faced quick questions from Soviet reporters about the complete denial of voting rights for blacks in the American South. Stumped, he was unable to respond. Over the next few years, Soviet reporters and officials and representatives of Third World nations constantly questioned U.S. officials about racism. The inability of diplomats to respond to reasonable questions about American racial inequality was more than an embarrassment; it represented a serious threat to the very foundations of U.S. foreign policy during a vital period of global change.

Civil rights leaders were well aware of how the Cold War could aid their cause. The NAACP, growing dramatically during and after the war, increased its membership from 50,000 in 1940 to 450,000 by 1946. America's leading black intellectual, **W. E. B. Du Bois**, captured the NAACP philosophy at the dawn of the atomic age with his influential address to the United Nations, *An Appeal to the World* (1947). In *An Appeal*, Du Bois warned, "It is not Russia that threatens the United States so much as Mississippi." Du Bois's *Appeal* presented American racism and Cold War hypocrisy in such rich detail and with eloquence and insight that could not be easily dismissed. His credentials as a longtime advocate of pan-Africanism made his devastating critique all the more worrisome to U.S. officials concerned about nationalist movements in Africa and all the more welcome by Soviet propagandists. The harsh light of international attention in the early years of the Cold War led to a series of judicial victories setting the stage for a major legal assault on segregation in the mid-1950s.

For African Americans, the oppressive ironies of the Cold War South seemed unbearable. They had served the United States with great distinction during World War II. They were treated as heroes in France and other liberated countries where, often for the first time in their lives, they were identified as Americans, not blacks. Southern African Americans fought for freedom during World War II knowing freedom at home only as an ideal never fully realized. Despite wartime civil rights efforts like the "Double V" campaign, veterans came home to a segregated southern power structure more racist and conservative than when they left. Revelations of Nazi racism and the Holocaust drew global attention to the brutal realities of racial hatred in all its forms. In the American South, however, black veterans discovered that civil rights activists were branded as subversives in the southern media, linked with communism, hounded by FBI and other federal officials, and even murdered by fellow Americans.

Stories of black veterans beaten, gunned down, or lynched after simply attempting to register to vote became international news. Veterans such as Medgar and Charles Evers, who spoke out about the absurdity and moral perversion of racism in a country fighting for global freedom, faced coercion and violence from all levels

UNJUST FUNERAL
Mrs. Medgar Evers with her children at Medgar Evers's grave in Arlington National Cemetery in June 1964. Evers's murder at the hands of southern racists highlighted the violence and injustice of the segregated South.

of southern authorities and the resurgent Ku Klux Klan. Medgar Evers repeatedly tried to register to vote only to be chased by a violent mob threatening death. But he refused to give in. Stories such as these disturbed a growing number of white Americans while providing powerful ammunition to the Soviets and anti-American forces around the world.

American racism posed a serious problem for Cold War efforts to win the loyalty of the nonwhite Third World. Global ideological competition with the Soviet Union required America's political leaders to demonstrate the appeal of the American life in opposition to the Communist system. The existence of Jim Crow put America at a decided disadvantage, forcing reluctant national leaders to take a stand against segregation in the next decade in the name of national security if not decency and respect.

Black Migration and the Nationalization of Race

The treatment of African Americans during World War II and the early Cold War demonstrated to the world the nature and extent of American racism. Within the United States, a migration of African Americans during and after the war forced millions of Americans into closer contact with blacks and made it increasingly difficult to think of racism as a southern issue. Between 1946 and the 1960s, many African American southerners, responding to disheartening postwar racism, fled the South for new opportunities in booming cities of the North and West.

Despite wartime movement and a major migration in the earlier part of the century, 77 percent of African Americans still lived in the South at the beginning of World War II; 49 percent of those lived in the rural South. By 1970, only half of America's African Americans lived in the South.

In the 1940s, the demographic character of cities and industries changed, and angry whites worried about the effect of race and cheap black labor on the character

1950 map of the US showing distribution of African American population

interactive timeline

TIMELINE 1945–1952

AMERICA	YEAR	THE WORLD
Mar Tokyo firebombings kill more than 100,000 **Mar** Tens of thousands of U.S. troops killed or wounded in Iwo Jima and Okinawa **Apr** FDR dies; Harry S Truman becomes president **May** Germany formally surrenders **Jul** First atomic bomb successfully tested in New Mexico desert **Aug** Hiroshima and Nagasaki are first targets of atomic bomb **Aug** Victory in Japan Day (VJ Day)	**1945**	**Apr** U.S. and Soviet troops race toward Berlin **Jul–Aug** Potsdam Conference sets stage for Cold War **Dec** International Monetary Fund (IMF) formally created to aid global economic stability and prevent another world war
Feb George F. Kennan's "Long Telegram" outlines new Soviet strategy **Mar** Truman signs Executive Order 9835, launching Federal Employee Loyalty Program **Aug** John Hersey's essay, "Hiroshima," published by the *New Yorker*, raises nuclear fears **Dec** Truman establishes President's Committee on Civil Rights	**1946**	**Jul** Dramatic demonstrations of new atomic bombs in Bikini Atoll in Pacific cause global fallout concern **Jul** Treaty of Manila grants independence to Philippines
Mar Truman Doctrine explained in congressional speech **Apr** Jackie Robinson desegregates major league baseball **Jun** George C. Marshall announces European Recovery Plan (Marshall Plan) **Jun** Taft–Hartley Act rolls back Wagner Act protections for unions **Jul** George F. Kennan outlines containment policy **Jul** National Security Act signed by President Truman, creating National Security Council, Department of Defense, and Central Intelligence Agency **Sep** HCUA subpoenas 41 suspected American Communists **Oct** W. E. B. Du Bois gives UN speech, *An Appeal to the World*, linking civil rights and Cold War politics	**1947**	**Aug** India and Pakistan gain independence **Aug** Jawaharlal Nehru becomes first Indian prime minister

of their communities. Often they responded with violence. In the spring of 1943, race riots in Harlem killed 5 people, injured 400, and caused millions in damage. Similar riots in Detroit led to significant violence, creating lasting racial tensions in the city that came to represent the best and worst possibilities of the black migration. In many cases, white southern workers who had migrated north to work in the war industry clashed with blacks who had done the same. Across the nation, white neighborhoods responded with racial covenants or "redlining" of cities, creating a de facto system of segregation enforced by markets if not by law.

Between 1945 and 1952, progress in civil rights built a foundation for the dramatic expansion of the movement that would occur in the 1950s and 1960s, when civil rights moved to the center of American politics and became part of a broader struggle to redefine American culture and values.

STUDY QUESTIONS FOR LAYING THE FOUNDATIONS FOR CIVIL RIGHTS

quiz

1. What was the relationship between Cold War foreign policy and civil rights activism in America?

2. Why was baseball player Jackie Robinson's rise to national prominence important to early civil rights?

AMERICA	YEAR	THE WORLD
Jan Truman signs Smith Act **Jul** Truman issues Executive Order 9981, desegregating U.S. military **Aug** Whittaker Chambers provides dramatic testimony to HCUA against Alger Hiss **Aug** David Bradley's *No Place to Hide* raises nuclear concerns	**1948**	**Apr** North Atlantic Treaty Organization (NATO) founded
	1949	**Aug** Soviets successfully test atomic bomb, ending U.S. monopoly **Oct** U.S. ally Chiang Kai-shek becomes leader of Chinese Nationalists People's Republic of China formally established by Mao
Feb Joseph McCarthy announces list of Communists in U.S. State Department **Apr** NSC-68 initiates a more confrontational Cold War strategy	**1950**	**Jun** North Korea invades South Korea, initiating Korean War **Nov** Chinese forces enter Korea **Sep** MacArthur stages dramatic counterattack at Inchon
Jan Nuclear testing begins at Nevada test site **Jun** *Dennis v. United States*	**1951**	**Jan** Seoul falls to Chinese People's Volunteer Army
Apr Truman relieves MacArthur of command **Dec** McCarran Immigration and Naturalization Act restricts immigration	**1952**	

Summary

- Successful development of the atomic bomb shaped the U.S. military, diplomacy, and culture.
- Postwar geopolitics created tensions between the United States and the Soviet Union, leading to the Cold War.
- Cold War fears spawned a Red scare that forced Americans to grapple with issues of individual rights versus conformity.
- Government programs such as the GI Bill and Truman's Fair Deal provided new access to middle-class status for many Americans.
- Economic opportunity spurred mass migrations from within and to the United States.
- Civil rights advocates mounted challenges to racial discrimination in the early postwar years.

Key Terms and People

Acheson, Dean 870
Berlin Airlift 871
Byrnes, James F. 865
Chambers, Whittaker 878
Chiang Kai-shek 873
Cold War 864
containment 870

culture war 864
Du Bois, W. E. B. 890
Executive Order 9981 888
Fair Deal 878
Harriman, W. Averell 865
Hiss, Alger 878

audio
flashcards

Reviewing Chapter 25

1. Between 1945 and 1952, much of U.S. foreign policy involved discussions of the "Third World" (now known as the developing nations). What was this "Third World"? Why were these nations important during the very early years of the emerging Cold War?
2. The 1950s are often remembered as a time of great prosperity. What trends and programs contributed to the growth of affluence during the postwar years?
3. How did developing Cold War foreign policies contribute to rising concerns for civil liberties at home?

Further Reading

Borstelmann, Thomas. *The Cold War and the Color Line: American Race Relations in the Global Arena.* Cambridge, MA: Harvard University Press, 2001. Deeper context on the relationship between Cold War politics and civil rights.

Boyer, Paul. *By the Bomb's Early Light: American Thought and Culture at the Dawn of the Atomic Age.* New York: Pantheon Books, 1985. A wonderfully detailed study of Cold War popular culture.

Casey, Steven. *Selling the Korean War: Propaganda, Politics, and Public Opinion in the United States, 1950–1953.* New York: Oxford University Press, 2008.

Cohen, Lisabeth. *A Consumer's Republic: The Politics of Mass Consumption in Postwar America.* New York: Vintage, 2003. A detailed and compelling analysis of the transformative power of mass consumption.

Costigliola, Frank. *Roosevelt's Lost Alliances: How Personal Politics Helped Start the Cold War.* Princeton, NJ: Princeton University Press, 2012. New perspective helps understand the transition from FDR to Truman and the role of culture and personality in national security decisions during this period.

Gutierrez, David G. *Walls and Mirrors: Mexican Americans, Mexican Immigrants, and the Politics of Ethnicity.* Berkeley: University of California Press, 1995. A different perspective on immigration and race.

McGirr, Lisa. *Suburban Warriors: The Origins of the New American Right.* Princeton, NJ: Princeton University Press, 2001. The rise of the Sunbelt and politics in southern California, the author argues, produced a new kind of American conservatism during the 1950s and 1960s.

Nash, Gerald D. *The American West in the Twentieth Century: A Short History of an Urban Oasis.* Albuquerque: University of New Mexico Press, 1977. A classic study of the West in the 20th century.

Rhodes, Richard. *The Making of the Atomic Bomb.* New York: Simon & Schuster, 1995. A Pulitzer Prize–winning account that proves that truth is stranger than fiction.

America in the World
GOODS, IDEAS, PEOPLE

CHAPTER 25: Prosperity and Liberty Under the Shadow of the Bomb, 1945–1952

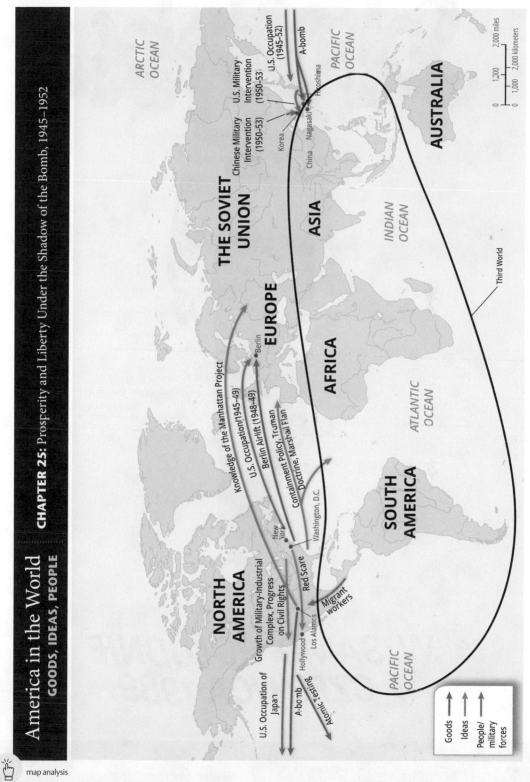

map analysis

**W SAMO POŁUDNIE
4 CZERWCA 1989**

The Dynamic 1950s

1950–1959

A middle-aged man walks alone down a dusty street in a western town circa 1870. Sheriff Will Kane, played by actor Gary Cooper, wears a classic western lawman's outfit with a white shirt and gold star. As the film begins, the focus shifts to a clock ticking on the wall showing one hour to noon. The movie continues in real time, with each minute of film time taking one minute of real time building toward a dramatic showdown with an off-screen bad man who has come to seek revenge on the man and town that sent him away. The drama of the film comes from this showdown but also from Kane's increasingly futile efforts to muster support to fight against an impending wrong from the townspeople who gave him his badge. As the minutes tick away, it becomes clear to the viewer that the sheriff will stand alone against the forces of evil, whether they are the bad guys waiting in the wings or the complacent masses of the town unwilling to stand up for freedom in the face of tyranny.

High Noon (1952) won Cooper the Oscar for Best Actor, was widely hailed by critics in the 1950s, and is considered a classic of the western genre. The film was directed by Fred Zimmerman and written by prominent screenwriter Carl Foreman. Foreman missed the Oscars in which his film ultimately won four awards because he had fled in exile to London after being blacklisted by the House Committee on Un-American Activities (HUAC). While the film was in production, Foreman was called to testify before HUAC, where he explained that he had been a member of the American Communist Party in his youth. When Foreman was asked to name other Communists he knew he refused. Like all others who testified but declined to name names, Foreman was labeled an "uncooperative witness" and placed on the Hollywood blacklist, preventing him from working for any studio. Critics and viewers of *High Noon* interpreted the film as a metaphor for the U.S. Red scare when citizens accepted great restrictions on personal liberties in exchange for security.

High Noon was screened around the world and was especially popular in Eastern bloc countries like Poland where the message of bravery in the face of near-certain doom resonated with those fighting for freedom. An American film depicting a mythic 1870s West was a distinct artifact of the Cold War 1950s. In the 1980s, the iconic image of Cooper as Sheriff Will Kane was adopted by the Polish Solidarity movement and used on posters members plastered across the country on the night of June 3, 1989. Bold red letters backed Gary Cooper's image, with the Solidarity badge replacing the gold star on his chest; text below that read simply, "High Noon 4 June, 1989," announcing the day of reckoning when the Solidarity leaders would attempt to seize the government. American popular culture in the 1950s reflected the concerns of U.S. citizens and resonated with people around the globe as they grappled with the complicated realities of the Cold War.

❂ THE EISENHOWER ERA

In 1952, Republicans nominated retired five-star U.S. Army general, supreme Allied commander during World War II, head of NATO, and president of Columbia University **Dwight D. Eisenhower** as their candidate for president. Eisenhower was a very popular choice with the American people. Few, however, knew much about his political views. Both the Democratic and Republican parties courted him as a potential candidate in 1948 before he revealed himself a Republican.

In 1952, when Eisenhower accepted the Republican nomination, the Korean War was stalled in a bloody stalemate. Senator Joseph McCarthy still terrified the nation with his charges of Communist conspiracies inside the government. The United States was on the verge of testing a hydrogen bomb, and an ailing and unpredictable Joseph Stalin controlled the USSR. The U.S. economy, transitioning from war to peace with the help of government programs in areas such as education, transportation, and social services, created jobs and opportunities not seen for a generation. Still, global Cold War uncertainties and Red scare fears contributed to widespread support for a military hero as presidential candidate. To bolster his anti-Communist credentials among right-wing Republicans, Eisenhower selected the 38-year-old senator Richard M. Nixon of California as his vice presidential running mate.

Shortly after the nominating convention, Republicans revealed their campaign slogan as "K_1C_2." This was shorthand for Korea first, then Communism and Corruption. Republicans argued that the Democratic Truman administration had been lax in its prosecution of the Korean War, had dropped the ball on China, and had allowed subversives and corruption to run rampant in Washington and throughout the nation. Although Eisenhower stayed above the fray, he pledged to root out these "evils."

Although effective in his political attacks, Nixon soon found himself in danger of costing Eisenhower the election and being removed from the ticket. On September 18, 1952, the *New York Post* reported that 60 Californians had set up a secret slush fund of $18,000 for Nixon during his tenure as senator. Nixon denied that he received any secret gifts and called the charge a "Communist smear." In an emotional televised speech, a somber Nixon defended the secret fund and made a public accounting of his rather modest finances, admitting only one gift—to his daughters: a black and white cocker spaniel named Checkers. Claiming that his opponents would surely come after Checkers too, Nixon defiantly pledged to keep the dog.

The 1952 campaign was the first TV election. Eisenhower's decisive victory ensured that presidential campaigning would never be the same. "Ike" used the powerful new media more effectively than his opponent, and Nixon used it to save his political career. Eisenhower alone made 40 televised speeches. Stevenson, too, made TV speeches, but unlike Eisenhower's generally upbeat "sound bites," they were long, detailed, and intellectual presentations that stressed the nation's difficulties and lack of easy answers. Nixon's "Checkers Speech," drawing the largest viewing audience of any television broadcast to that date, demonstrated the critical new role of television in American politics. Liberals ridiculed Nixon for ignoring the key allegations against him, but he persuaded most viewers that he was an "ordinary" American.

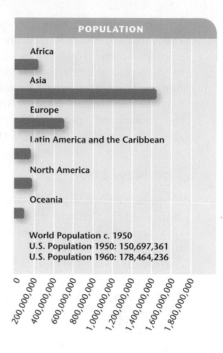

POPULATION

Africa
Asia
Europe
Latin America and the Caribbean
North America
Oceania

World Population c. 1950
U.S. Population 1950: 150,697,361
U.S. Population 1960: 178,464,236

0
200,000,000
400,000,000
600,000,000
800,000,000
1,000,000,000
1,200,000,000
1,400,000,000
1,600,000,000
1,800,000,000

The End of the Korean War

On November 29, 1952, Eisenhower traveled to Korea to fulfill a campaign pledge. Voters assumed that the seasoned general and leader of the D-Day invasion had a plan for victory when in fact he had no secret plan. The bloody stalemate dragged on for another seven months. Eisenhower asked military advisors to study the use of atomic weapons in Korea, something Truman had considered. Advisors told both presidents that Korea had few targets appropriate for atomic attack, and use by the United States would only escalate the conflict and possibly undermine the impact of the bomb as the "ultimate weapon." Eisenhower privately accepted the argument against atomic warfare, but he leaked rumors of plans to escalate the war or even use atomic bombs in the hope of pressuring the Chinese Communists, whose troops made up the bulk of those fighting the Americans, to negotiate a settlement.

The atomic threats proved unnecessary after Stalin died on March 5, 1953, just weeks after Eisenhower took office. The absence of Stalin and the resulting confusion over his succession contributed to the Soviets' eagerness to see the Korean situation brought to a quick end. Further, the Chinese, weary of the costly war, were seeking better relations with the West. It was these factors, along with a Sino-American compromise over the return of prisoners, that led to the end of the war rather than Eisenhower's atomic saber rattling.

On July 27, 1953, a cease-fire was finally achieved at Panmunjom, a village astride the North and South Korean divide. The agreement created a heavily fortified "demilitarized zone" (DMZ), or no-man's-land, splitting Korea at the 38th parallel, close to where the fighting began in 1950. The cost of this first proxy war was high. Ten million people, or one-tenth of the population of North and South Korea, had been killed, wounded, or declared missing. Another five million people had been dispossessed of their homes and uprooted. The inconclusive end to the war left troubling questions about the containment strategy in the complicated postcolonial world.

The New Look

Korea highlighted the need for new Cold War tools. The Eisenhower administration authorized the Central Intelligence Agency (CIA) to carry out covert military operations against unfriendly regimes. General James Doolittle had warned the president that a Cold War had "no rules" and that Americans "must learn to subvert, sabotage and destroy our enemies by more clever and sophisticated" means than in the past. Doolittle further cautioned that "accepted norms of human conduct" no longer applied. During his two terms, Eisenhower expanded the mission of the CIA far beyond intelligence gathering and analysis. He authorized it to conduct secret operations across the globe. The CIA conducted experiments with chemical weapons, tested LSD on unsuspecting U.S. citizens to see if the hallucinogenic drug could be used to dope the Soviets, plotted assassinations, and conducted elaborate surveillance of Communists in allied and enemy states alike. During this time, the CIA played a critical role in America's efforts to win control of the developing world, most significantly in the overthrow of the Iranian nationalist **Mohammed Mossadeq**, who threatened U.S. oil companies and consulted with the Soviets.

SUPERIOR AIR POWER B-29 Superfortress bombers featured a pressurized cabin for high-altitude flying and excelled at delivering huge payloads of bombs across vast distances.

With Mossadeq out, the United States reinstalled ally Shah **Mohammed Reza Pahlavi**. Similarly, the CIA helped overthrow the government of **Jacobo Árbenz Guzmán** in Guatemala in 1954. CIA actions would be harshly criticized later, but at the time, Eisenhower and his advisors believed that spying at home and abroad helped avert total nuclear war. The CIA was also fighting a nasty opponent in the Soviet Secret Service (KGB). The KGB regularly used murder, torture, and vicious tactics, terrorizing the USSR's own citizens and those of other nations they sought to control. The battle between the CIA and KGB raised questions about how far U.S. agencies would go to compete with the Soviets in the deadly game of Cold War espionage.

The Rise of the Developing World

In the aftermath of World War II, the map of the globe changed dramatically with the collapse of the European colonial system. Former colonies across the

POSSIBLE DESTRUCTION   The horror of nuclear war was brought home to Americans as part of a special issue of *Collier's* Magazine, "Hiroshima, U.S.A.," published on August 5, 1950. The graphic depiction of a hypothetical American nuclear holocaust emphasized that civilians would be the primary targets of atomic war.

image analysis

globe sought and gained their independence from western European colonial powers. This trend, especially evident in Africa and Asia, figured heavily in U.S. foreign policy during the 1950s.

Decolonization coincided with the Cold War, and the United States and the USSR each sought to influence the politics of the newly independent nations (Map 26.1). The U.S. policy of containment assumed, often correctly, that former colonial nations would gravitate toward communism or toward a neutral stance between the Cold War camps. As former wards of capitalist countries, many developing world countries were wary of the intentions of the United States and its Cold War allies. Between 1945 and 1960, 37 nations gained independence, and a majority leaned toward or openly embraced communism. Most of these new nations were nonwhite, preindustrial, and poor. Further complicating the picture, many of these nations emerged with festering internal guerrilla insurgencies or outright civil war. During the 1950s alone, there were 28 prolonged insurgencies in the developing world. Protests by Puerto Rican nationalists across the U.S. commonwealth and in Washington, DC, brought these concerns very close to home.

Nationalist leaders such as India's prime minister, **Jawaharlal Nehru**, stated, "We do not intend to be the playthings of others." The determination by the United States and USSR to treat these new nations as pawns in a fight between capitalism and communism led to profound misunderstandings about the power and extent of nationalism. While critics like Nehru derided the policies of containment, other developing nations

Mao Zedong, "The Chinese People have Stood Up!" (1949)

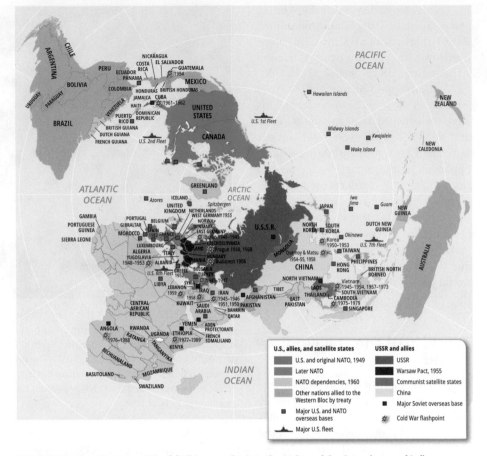

MAP 26.1 The Postwar World This map depicts the U.S. and Soviet spheres of influence during the Cold War. Debate over the concept of "spheres of influence" dominated the final days of World War II. The Soviets occupied a massive swath of eastern Europe by the time they reached Berlin, whereas the Americans and Allies controlled all of western Europe and territories across the globe. The rapid remapping of the globe in the aftermath of war was supposed to be temporary but lasted for decades, as Cold War conflict solidified the lines on the map.

exploited the Soviet–U.S. competition by playing one against the other to gain increased aid or to remove political enemies.

The Eisenhower administration viewed the developing world as vital to maintaining a world balance of power with the Soviets. But economic and domestic political concerns also drove efforts to keep these countries from Soviet domination. Having inherited many of the world's postwar markets, the United States sought international stability and the protection of raw material sources. Vast developing world oil reserves, in particular, elevated the strategic importance of emerging markets for U.S. policymakers.

U.S. intervention in the developing world often took the form of massive financial aid, behind-the-scenes diplomatic pressure, and both direct and covert military action. By 1960, the United States was sending $4 billion annually to developing nations around the globe.

Hungary and the Suez, 1956

In Hungary and Poland, the Soviet Union brutally crushed nationalist uprisings that gained momentum after the death of Stalin and the relaxation of some controls by his successors. In the Middle East, Egypt sought to throw off the last vestiges of colonialism through the nationalization of the Suez Canal.

On October 23, 1956, Hungarian students flooded the streets in a show of solidarity with Polish protestors seeking removal of the Soviet-controlled government. Twelve days later, Soviet tanks rolled in and brutally crushed the demonstrations, ending the revolt. Despite having urged the uprising on Radio Free Europe, the Eisenhower administration backed away from a direct challenge to the Soviets within their eastern European sphere. The best the United States had to offer the fleeing Hungarian freedom fighters was "displaced persons" status—first applied as a precedent in the late 1940s to Jews escaping the Nazis.

While the eyes of the world were on eastern Europe, Israel, and then France and Great Britain, launched an effort to retake the Suez Canal from the Egyptians. Nationalist Egyptian leader **Gamal Abdel Nasser**, who had recently deposed Egypt's decadent monarchy, sought to unify all Arabs under his banner by expropriating the canal from its British owners. Nasser saw the canal as a humiliating reminder of colonial control, a revenue source, and a potential instrument of power, as half the world's oil supply passed through its waters. For the latter reason, Israel, Great Britain, and France were unwilling to allow it to fall under Egyptian control. In addition, all had unstated reasons to risk war. Israel wanted to intimidate Nasser for launching raids from Gaza and to undermine his pan-Arab appeal. Britain wanted to regain the canal, and France hoped to lessen the appeal of Algerian revolutionaries.

Gamal Abdel Nasser, speech on the nationalization of the Suez Canal (1956)

Having advised the British not to react militarily in Suez, Eisenhower was outraged when word reached him of the invasion. He had no love for Nasser but feared that any military action and occupation would only disrupt oil supplies, inflame Arab passions against Western nations, and possibly enable the Soviets to gain a foothold in the vital region.

As the fighting shut off traffic through the canal and strangled western Europe's oil supply, Eisenhower refused to open American oil supplies to the British, and instead of the aid the British expected, Eisenhower threatened additional oil sanctions if the involved nations did not remove all troops. Still, when the Soviets rattled their atomic sword at the British and French "aggressors," Eisenhower assured his Soviet counterpart that should London and Paris be attacked, Moscow would be devastated "as surely as night follows day."

By early December, French and British troops had withdrawn from the canal region and been replaced with UN peacekeepers. The last Israeli troops left the Sinai soon afterward. By publicly siding with Arab nationalists and against European colonizers, the United States gained considerable goodwill in the Arab world that served U.S. oil companies well. Eisenhower had carried the day but also committed the United States to a dramatically expanded role in Middle Eastern politics with far-reaching consequences.

France's Vietnam War

At the end of World War II, Vietnam epitomized the complexity of rapidly evolving postwar geopolitics. After the war, the French regained control of their sphere of influence in Southeast Asian "Indochina"—composed of Vietnam, Cambodia, and Laos.

Vietnamese nationalists led by **Ho Chi Minh** had fought the Japanese in hope of winning U.S. backing for postwar independence. Instead, under Truman, Washington supported French efforts to reassert control. As a result, in 1946, Ho's followers, the Vietminh, launched a guerrilla war against the French. In the southern part of the colony, where the Vietminh had less strength, the French created a puppet government led by a pliant playboy-emperor named Bao Dai.

The outbreak of the Korean War increased U.S. interest in the surrounding region. As a result, the Truman administration dispatched eight cargo planes of military supplies to French troops in Vietnam and thus began a pattern of direct military aid. The conflict in Indochina is seen as a parallel to the Korean War. When Truman left office in early 1953, the conflict ranked second only to Korea in terms of U.S. military aid. That year, the United States covered 40 percent of French war costs. Shortly before Eisenhower's inauguration, outgoing secretary of state Dean Acheson informed him that if the French situation in Vietnam deteriorated, the United States must be prepared to act decisively. Heeding Acheson's words, Eisenhower accepted the recommendations of the National Security Council "124/2" directive, which stated that the loss of any of the countries of Southeast Asia "would probably lead to relatively swift submission" by the remaining countries to Chinese Communist control. This concept soon became known as the domino theory and provided a rationale for American involvement.

In February 1954, the faltering French, with the urging of the United States, agreed to enter into negotiations with the Vietminh in Geneva in April. In the meantime, the French decided to strengthen their bargaining position by airdropping 12,000 troops into a valley in northwestern Vietnam called Dien Bien Phu. The troops were met, surrounded, and soundly defeated by 50,000 Vietminh forces. During the battle, as French defeat became certain, Eisenhower's advisors briefly considered the use of tactical nuclear weapons against the Vietminh positions.

President Eisenhower on the "domino theory" and Indochina (April 1954)

On July 24, 1954, at the Geneva Conference, Vietnam was temporarily divided into North and South segments, with Ho Chi Minh in control of the North and Bao Dai's government in control of the South. The accords called for popular national unity elections in 1956. By 1956, Bao had been replaced by the U.S.-backed Ngo Dinh Diem, who quickly staged a pair of rigged elections, with U.S. backing, to create an independent Republic of Vietnam, or South Vietnam. The United States quickly recognized Diem's republic and began sending expanded military and economic aid and technical advisors.

On February 12, 1955, Eisenhower deployed the first U.S. military advisors to the region to bolster the democratic South against the Communist North. Between 1955 and 1960, billions of dollars of U.S. military and economic aid flowed to South Vietnam while U.S. military advisors trained South Vietnamese troops. Ho Chi Minh fumed at this division of Vietnam but could do little to oppose it. Until a rebellion erupted in the South in 1960, most Americans considered the result a successful case of anti-Communist "nation building."

McCarthyism and the Red Scare

Red scares at home in part fueled the need to be tough on Communists abroad. When Eisenhower took office in 1953, the Red scare was at its height. The House Committee on Un-American Activities (HCUA) hearings and the sensational Alger Hiss case had been eclipsed by the astonishing rise to power of an obscure junior senator from Wisconsin named **Joseph McCarthy**. "Tail Gunner Joe" already had a sleazy reputation for his mean-spirited Senate campaign in 1946. As a struggling senator, McCarthy capitalized on anti-Communist hysteria to advance his career from the "worst senator" to one of the most powerful and feared men in America. McCarthy's rise began on February 9, 1950, when in a minor speech to a group of Republican women he made a startling claim about Communist spies in the State Department. McCarthy said he had a secret list of 205 known Communists working at the highest levels of U.S. government and whose names were known by President Truman and Secretary of State Acheson.

Joseph McCarthy, speech in Wheeling, West Virginia (February 9, 1950)

This stunning announcement, garnering extensive press coverage as McCarthy repeated the story over the coming weeks, launched him from obscurity and failure to America's leading Communist hunter. In some ways McCarthy's charges were so outlandish it was impossible to disprove them. More responsible Republicans knew he peddled hot air, but they found him a useful wrecking ball to batter the Democrats. Between 1950 and 1954, McCarthy dominated a national Communist witch hunt so completely that his name became synonymous with a dark chapter in American civil liberties. Of course, there were spies on all sides during the Cold War. McCarthy, however, had little interest or ability to find them; instead, he sought headlines that would undermine Democrats. **McCarthyism** represented a sinister turn in government efforts

A FAILING IMAGE Senator Joseph McCarthy fared much worse in the new media of TV, where he often appeared disheveled and far less convincing than when his words and tactics were interpreted in the print media.

1954 comic book depicting Captain America smashing communists

to control communism within the United States. McCarthy's rise raised serious questions about the ability of the government to reconcile Cold War imperatives with American democratic traditions.

Although Eisenhower disliked McCarthy, he did not criticize the senator during his campaign in 1952. McCarthy's wild smears included Eisenhower's friend and political ally, retired general and former secretary of state **George Marshall**, whom McCarthy accused of perpetrating a "conspiracy so immense as to dwarf any previous such venture in the history of man." A series of sensational espionage cases aided McCarthy's rise to power. First, **Klaus Fuchs**, a theoretical physicist involved with the Manhattan Project, confessed to British intelligence officers in January 1950 that he had spied for the Soviet Union. His confession drew much publicity in the United States and led to a 14-year prison sentence.

The furor over domestic Communist conspiracies grew even stronger when, on March 6, 1951, **Julius** and **Ethel Rosenberg** went on trial for conspiring to provide the Soviet Union with U.S. atomic secrets. A jury convicted the couple of this charge and sentenced them to death. The Rosenbergs had two young sons, and the death sentence caused an international outcry for clemency for Ethel. Despite the protests and serious questions about Ethel's participation, on June 19, 1953, the Rosenbergs became the first American civilians executed for espionage.

In 1953–1954, the Senate launched a new televised inquiry into alleged Communist influence in the army and questions about Eisenhower's own record of "coddling" the Reds. McCarthy seized the opportunity to escalate his investigations to the highest levels of U.S. military and government. This bizarre investigation prompted Ike, who knew he was the real target, to encourage army leaders, behind the scenes, not to cooperate with McCarthy and to warn the senator to reconsider his attack. Undeterred, McCarthy forged on. Twenty million people watched the Army–McCarthy hearings, as most got their first clear look at the tactics of the ranting rogue senator. TV was not kind to McCarthy. On the small screen he came across as a thuggish bully, appearing disheveled and less than credible when compared to the distinguished military leaders he accused.

The hearings, along with a brave attack by TV journalist **Edward R. Murrow** on his show *See It Now*, led to Senate disciplinary hearings, and in December 1954, the Senate publicly denounced McCarthy for "unbecoming conduct." Politicians from both parties celebrated the demise of the feared McCarthy, but his rise to power would not have been possible without the support of powerful cultural and political leaders. Before it faded, McCarthyism undermined basic constitutional principles, destroyed careers and lives, terrified millions of Americans, and gave ammunition to the Soviets and other adversaries who used the authoritarian McCarthy as an example of American hypocrisy.

STUDY QUESTIONS FOR THE EISENHOWER ERA

quiz

1. What was the "developing world"? Why did these nations gain significance during the Eisenhower administration?

2. Why did Americans tolerate McCarthy's tactics? How does one person gain so much power in a democracy?

⊘ A DYNAMIC DECADE

In his farewell address to the American people on January 17, 1961, a thoughtful President Eisenhower cautioned listeners to strive for balance and restraint in the "ever growing smaller" world of the future. Wary of overconfidence in the stability and equity of American affluence at home, he advised his fellow citizens to "avoid the impulse to live only for today, plundering for our own ease and convenience the precious resources of tomorrow." Uneasy about the future of the technocratic Cold War globe he helped design, Ike left office with "a definite sense of disappointment." "As one who has witnessed the horror of war," and "as one who knows that another war could utterly destroy this civilization," the general knew the agony of war and dangers of militarization, and as a retiring president, he had learned the complexity and fragility of prosperity.

President Eisenhower's "military-industrial complex" speech, January, 1961

Those Americans who listened to Ike's final speech might have been surprised by the tone considering the remarkable statistics of the 1950s. During the decade, the United States led the world in economic growth. Fueled by the Cold War "military-industrial complex," vastly increased consumer spending, a "baby boom," suburbanization, and government social programs like the GI Bill, the American economy grew to new heights.

Despite some short recessions in the 1950s, consumer spending remained strong throughout the decade and reached the $300 billion per year mark in 1959. Combined with a low unemployment average of 4 to 6 percent for the decade, the United States was becoming, in the words of economist John Kenneth Galbraith, an "affluent society."

The Baby Boom

Unprecedented population growth was the most dramatic sign of American affluence in the 1950s. After a decade of declining birth rates during the Great Depression, population growth escalated modestly during World War II before soaring upward in 1947. Escalations of population following war were not uncommon, but this boom was unprecedented in scope. By 1958, a British tourist remarked while on vacation in the United States, "Every other young housewife I see is pregnant." The tourist witnessed the apex of a demographic trend so significant it became known as the **baby boom** (Figure 26.1). This remarkable spike was part of a larger transnational trend that saw a dramatic increase in fertility rates in many western European nations, including Britain and France. Because of devastating population losses during the war, the postwar population boom in the Soviet Union resulting in the "*Sputnik* Generation" was celebrated as an important victory by Communist leaders. Australia and New Zealand also experienced population spikes during this period. Population growth became a measure of success and power during the Cold War. Likewise, population statistics were vital indicators of recovery in Germany and Japan, where sharp percentage declines from war casualties required dramatic birth rates just to achieve prewar population levels.

When the American baby boom began in 1946, it caught forecasters by surprise. American demographers viewed the trend as a temporary result of the end of the war and predicted a modest five million births by decade's end. Their estimate quickly proved far too low. In 1948 alone, American mothers had a baby every eight seconds on average. By the year's end, four million births almost matched the experts' prediction for the entire four-year period. By 1950, the total number of births had surpassed nine

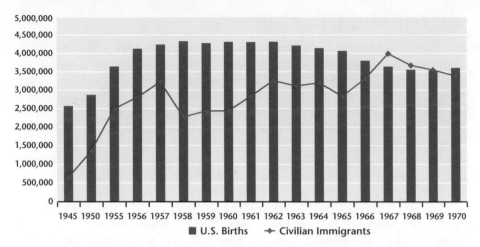

FIGURE 26.1 **Population boom** Unprecedented population growth was the most dramatic sign of American affluence in the 1950s. After a decade of declining birth rates during the Great Depression, population growth escalated modestly during World War II before soaring upward in 1947, peaking in 1958. Despite Cold War restriction, foreign immigration increased during the 1950s from wartime and Depression era lows.

million. By 1959 children under the age of 14 accounted for 50 million or approximately 30 percent of the nation's population.

There is no simple explanation for this dramatic birth rate increase. Affluence, health improvements, and an extended period of peace, interrupted only by the 1950–1953 Korean War, all contributed. Americans tended to marry at a younger age and extended their childbearing years. The federal government, through the GI Bill and Federal Housing Administration loans, shared some responsibility for helping to create an affluent and secure environment conducive to childbearing. Likewise, an emerging suburban culture celebrated by government leaders actively promoted a "procreation ethic." The mass media and popular culture honored and celebrated motherhood. Applied science, especially in medicine, led to massive public health campaigns to eliminate polio and other infectious diseases and to discourage dangerous behaviors such as smoking. During the 1950s, public health groups such as the American Cancer Society, along with government researchers, used new statistical techniques to reveal and publicize the link between cigarettes and lung cancer. Scientists, including Dr. **Jonas Salk,** who perfected the polio vaccine in 1954, became international heroes. The development of "miracle drugs" such as penicillin, discovered in the 1930s and mass-produced during World War II, and the polio vaccine made the American children of the baby boom the healthiest generation in history.

Suburban Migrations—Urban Decline

Millions of those with the financial capacity moved to dramatically expanding suburbs. By the end of the 1950s, nearly half of the U.S. population, most of whom were white, lived in new suburbs, whereas people of color increasingly populated inner cities (Figure 26.2). America reached its peak as an urban nation in the early 1950s. In the early

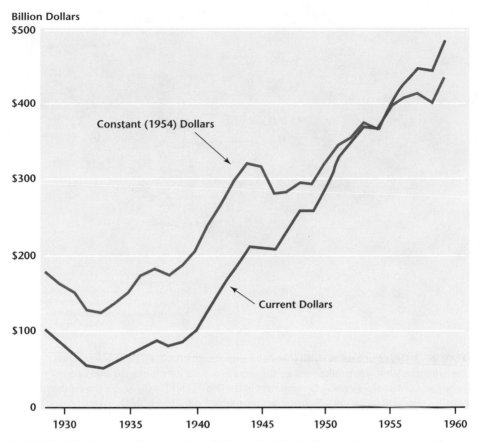

Billion Dollars

FIGURE 26.2   Gross national product (GNP) This critical indicator of economic growth increased steadily during World War II and dramatically throughout the 1950s.

postwar period, American cities remained dynamic places full of busy sidewalks, cafes, office buildings, and bustling neighborhoods connected to downtowns. Urban railways ran full schedules, with cars often packed to capacity. By 1960, these urban railways had disappeared from all but the largest American cities. Former rail and mass-transit patrons embraced the automobile to ferry them to and from increasingly distant suburban homes. Eisenhower's 1956 Federal Highway Act, also known as the **Interstate and Defense Highways Act**, the largest public works program in American history, facilitated the growth of suburbs and the complex of industries that sustained them (Map 26.2).

After 1956, wide concrete highways funneling people to and from suburbia bisected once-vital neighborhoods and soared over other areas of town. Increasingly, as professionals and businesses left for the suburbs, the decline of downtowns was evident in abandoned buildings, deteriorating neighborhoods, and increased crime. Perceptions of the inner city as crumbling, dangerous, and depressed only increased "white flight."

Those left behind were often minorities and working-class whites with limited access to the jobs that fueled the affluent society. Blacks, Jews, and others were often explicitly denied the suburban dream by discriminatory loaning practices, redlining, and racist housing covenants in new neighborhoods. The U.S. Supreme Court outlawed

Mexican Americans being evicted from their homes to make way for Dodger Stadium, Los Angeles, 1959

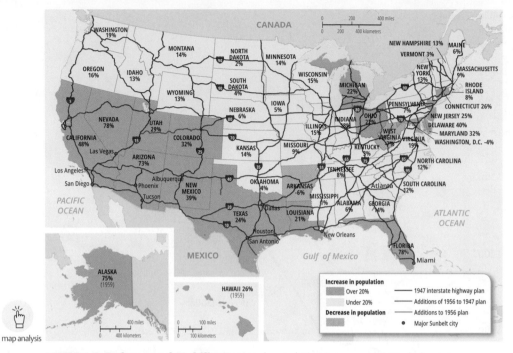

map analysis

MAP 26.2 Defense and Mobility Regional population increases, particularly across the American West, were influenced by the growth of interstate highways that opened lightly populated areas to new development in the 1950s and 1960s. Across the nation, the construction of the Interstate Highway system enabled suburban growth, created markets for a new roadside economy, and split cities, obliterating centuries-old patterns of urban development.

racial covenants in *Shelly v. Kraemer* (1948), but they persisted in practice throughout the 1950s. Suburbs across the country used neighborhood and homeowner associations to restrict access on the basis of race, ethnicity, and religion.

In the South, racial segregation, supported by law, remained entrenched. In the North, racism could be overt, with posted signs informing blacks, Jews, or others they were unwelcome. Increasingly affluent Jewish Americans founded mainly Jewish suburbs in response to discrimination. Other communities across the United States were "sundown towns," where minorities were welcomed during daytime as workers but warned by posted signs: "N___'s! Don't Let the Sun Set on You in This Town!" Other communities used less obvious means to warn minorities of all backgrounds to look elsewhere. In whatever form, racism ensured that most suburbs outside the legally segregated South were completely white and not representative of the period's increasing racial diversity.

Suburbs grew because of demand and new technologies. The assembly-line "tract home" was the most significant innovation. Block after block of mass-produced homes, called housing tracts, transformed enormous regions of rural landscape into seas of houses linked by highways to islands of new shopping and strip malls. Suburban housing pioneers, including **William Levitt**, builder of the prototypical modern tract suburb of **Levittown** on Long Island, New York, were hailed as heroes in the years after the war when serious housing shortages left some returning war vets living with parents or

SEGREGATION LITERATURE This 1935 linoleum print from the book *Scottsboro Alabama* illustrates the idea of the "sundown town." Fifties versions of segregation like "redlining" might not have been as blatant but had the same chilling effect.

even in converted chicken coops. Using large tracts of farmland on the outskirts of big cities, Levitt built simple, four-room homes complete with the latest kitchen appliances. The homes sold for $7,990 in 1947 (roughly $88,000 in today's dollars). Suburbs filled an urgent housing need and promised a level of comfort and modernity previously unknown to most city dwellers. Snapping up the houses as fast as Levitt could build them, enthusiastic buyers drew other developers, like California's **Henry J. Kaiser**, into the business. The federal government encouraged this trend with Federal Housing Administration (FHA) and Veterans Administration (VA) loans featuring modest down payments and reasonable interest rates.

Suburbs had long been a part of American life. By 1955, however, suburban planned communities accounted for 75 percent of all housing starts. Five years later, more Americans lived in suburbs than in cities, and over one-fourth of the nation's housing stock was less than 10 years old. Suburban development was so dramatic during the 1950s that it prompted critics such as historian Godfrey Hodgson to write about a "suburban-industrial complex" comparable in scope to the "military-industrial complex" of the Cold War.

Suburbs seemed to offer a more rural, or "natural," life than Americans could find in crowded cities. Suburban growth, bringing urban Americans into closer contact with the countryside and natural areas, helped build a new power base for environmental protection. Waves of suburbanites witnessed housing developments devour an area the size of Rhode Island every year. As suburbs encroached on open spaces previously used for recreation, some Americans began to support limits on growth and protection of at least some scenic lands.

Consumer Nation

Americans in the 1950s embraced consumption as a cornerstone of quality of life and an important weapon in the battle for hearts and minds during the Cold War. After nearly two decades of material sacrifice during depression and war, Americans emerged with an appetite for consumption not seen since the 1920s. As in the 1920s, sophisticated advertisements from savvy marketers peddled a wide variety of new technological wonders. During the 1950s, more money was spent on advertising than on public education. Newly available credit cards, including the popular Diners Club, American Express, and Sears, made it easier for Americans to purchase and enjoy advertised products. By the end of the decade, there were over 10 million Sears cards in American wallets, and millions of consumers began to rely on short-term credit to outfit their new homes.

Cover of *Saturday Evening Post* (August 1959)

Actively promoted by the U.S. government as a critical attribute of good citizenship, mass consumption represented more than just an economic trend. For the first time in American history, political leaders, economists, and foreign policy experts recognized that consumption, not production, was the single most important contributor to America's economic health. Popular publications such as *Life* presented economic data suggesting the success of the postwar economy hinged on consumer purchase of new homes, appliances, and cars. Mass consumption was extolled as a virtue that would lift all Americans and provide universal employment and prosperity.

The Cold War figured prominently in both private and governmental encouragement of consumption. Mass consumption also represented American culture worldwide as American products traveled the globe (Figure 26.3). During World War II, American products from cigarettes to sodas reached the far corners of the world. By 1950, the Coca-Cola Company had 60 bottling plants on six continents. Newly opened postwar trade routes even funneled American products behind the Iron Curtain. People throughout the world came to know America through its material culture, exported by the millions of tons. Some embraced these material ambassadors and the culture they represented. Others viewed the tidal wave of American products in global markets with intensified anti-American animosity and felt these spearheads of American capitalism threatened the nature of their societies.

1958 newspaper ad in Ghana, Africa for Ford automobiles

The global spread of U.S. culture during the late postwar period through Hollywood films, TV, music, and consumer products was so successful that American "cultural imperialism" caused tensions even between Cold War allies. The governments of France and Italy both worked to block importations of Coke during the fifties. But in the United States, the global spread of consumer culture was celebrated. *Life* magazine publisher Henry Luce proclaimed the postwar period the "American Century." Luce and others articulated a market version of containment, one in which American culture peacefully won the hearts and minds of people across the globe.

Corporate Order and Industrial Labor

Increasingly powerful American corporations fostered the 1950s culture of consumption. Large national corporations, seeing a repeat of pre-Depression business trends, consolidated production and distribution networks and perfected national and international marketing techniques. Most significantly, U.S. corporations began

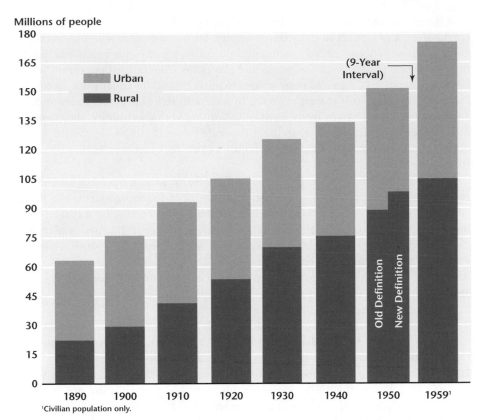

Millions of people

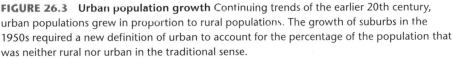

FIGURE 26.3 Urban population growth Continuing trends of the earlier 20th century, urban populations grew in proportion to rural populations. The growth of suburbs in the 1950s required a new definition of urban to account for the percentage of the population that was neither rural nor urban in the traditional sense.

diversifying their holdings across the spectrum of the consumer economy to create conglomerates of dizzying size. Thus, corporations such as General Electric produced hundreds of different products from light bulbs to televisions to military equipment. GE diversified its product lines while acquiring companies that made food, clothing, and products of all sorts. Through expansion and consolidation, GE became America's fourth-largest company in the 1950s; with 136 factories in 28 states, it was the nation's third-largest employer. As corporations became conglomerates, they spread their risk while increasing profits to record levels. The huge American corporations of the 1950s were also better able to take advantage of expanding global markets. U.S. exports, doubling during the decade, left the nation with a $5 billion trade surplus in 1960.

Consumers were often unaware that these new giants gained political power as they forged a powerful new postwar business model. Those who worked for the corporations clearly understood the significance of the transformation of American business during this time. Giant corporations required a dramatically expanded workforce with a large managerial class and a tightly managed labor force. For millions of World

War II vets, college educated with the help of the GI Bill, corporations offered lifetime employment and a ticket to the affluent society. Such companies, with bureaucracies as big as many nations, needed a seemingly endless supply of young executives to man thousands of offices around the nation and the globe. Unparalleled opportunities allowed a generation of men and some women to move into white-collar work. In return, these mostly male workers were expected to adhere to strict corporate codes of dress and behavior. Often moved from one state to another with short notice, they contributed to the transience of suburban life. Corporate life in the 1950s demanded a level of conformity that many men and their families came to resent even as they benefited from higher incomes.

Workers and labor unions prospered in the affluent society, but labor leaders had reason to wonder how long it might last. The culture of consensus during the 1950s, characterized by economic growth, wider spread prosperity, and the fight against communism appeared to ease relations between business and labor. Business leaders and chambers of commerce touted this perception but with a clear bias toward employers. Programs such as Junior Achievement promoted the ideal of "free enterprise" among American youth, while free market thinkers such as economists Friedrich von Hayek and Milton Friedman argued that universal employment and "people's capitalism" made unions obsolete.

Union membership remained steady through the decade. The nation's two largest unions, the **American Federation of Labor (AFL)** and the **Congress of Industrial Organizations (CIO)**, ended their long rivalry and united to form the AFL-CIO. However, by 1960, union workers comprised a smaller overall percentage of workers than they had in the 1950s. Moreover, high employment rates did not translate to economic equality. As the United States entered the 1960s, 5 percent of Americans controlled half the wealth of the nation. A close look at U.S. economic statistics reveals startling poverty rates in the "other America." For many elderly, minority, and rural Americans, the affluent society remained out of reach as American corporations, through conservative groups such as the American Enterprise Association, actively worked to undermine the social safety net of the New Deal.

Even though blue-collar unionized workers did not gain any real control of the workplace during the prosperity of the 1950s, they did benefit materially through steady pay increases and significant expansions of job benefits, such as medical insurance, paid vacations, and retirement benefits. Big corporations provided these benefits in exchange for agreements like the "Treaty of Detroit" in 1955, when the powerful United Auto Workers (UAW) agreed to take labor radicalism off the table if the company expanded the benefits packages.

Excerpt from Vance Packard, *The Status Seekers* (1959)

STUDY QUESTIONS **FOR A DYNAMIC DECADE**

quiz

1. By the end of the 1950s, nearly half of the U.S. population lived in new suburbs. What factors contributed to this change?

2. In what ways was the 1950s consumer culture linked to Cold War politics? What impact did the goods and mass media that the United States exported have on the image of the United States internationally?

◉ THE FUTURE IS NOW

With dramatic music blaring in the background, headlines flashed across the movie screen: "Cities Alerted for Final Stand Against Fantastic Invader" and "Nation Maps Fight Against Unknown Terror!" The scene shifted to the New Mexico desert and the blinding flash of an atomic bomb before turning to the stern TV reporter who revealed that out of that explosion arose a mutant terror that threatened to destroy all humanity. In 1954, movie audiences gasped in terror at *Them!* They knew this was fiction, of course, but weirdly plausible fiction that resonated with very real concerns about the pace of technological development and the power of science in the postwar world.

America has always been a nation obsessed with the future and with progress. The astonishing technological advances of the postwar period enhanced this tradition. Medical breakthroughs, nuclear science, labor-saving devices, and innovations in transportation and communication all created a sense of accelerating progress. Many of these advances, related to the Cold War, created a tension between fear that technology would run wild and the optimistic belief that technology was the cornerstone of an affluent future. Some Americans insisted that new technologies would usher in a period of unprecedented personal freedom and new standards of health and quality of life for everyone. Others worried about the pace of change. The wildly popular genre of science fiction exploited technological fears with films such as *Them!* and *Godzilla* (1954), which showed mutants of technology turning on humanity.

Whether they feared it or celebrated it, Americans could not escape the reshaping of U.S. culture and geography by new and improved technologies. None was more important than the car. The rise of the corporation, the growth of suburbs, and 1950s consumer culture all depended on the automobile industry.

Auto Mania

By the 1950s, the automobile had long been deemed by Americans a necessity. Since the introduction of Ford's Model T in 1908, the automobile had provided the average American with affordable individual transportation and occupied a central place in American culture and economy. The Great Depression and the wartime shortages that followed forced many Americans to give up the freedom of the family car. But in 1945, when scarcity began to fade, Americans lined up at dealerships to order the first new models in a generation. During the next decade, the American automobile industry matured, influenced policy, and became the critical link in the postwar consumer economy.

In 1955, the United States produced two-thirds of the world's supply of automobiles. Trends toward consolidation left the mature American automobile industry in the hands of three big producers. General Motors (GM), Ford, and Chrysler accounted for 94 percent of American automobile output. GM, under the dynamic leadership of Alfred P. Sloan, elevated the auto industry to unprecedented influence in American life. Between 1945 and 1955, GM's marketing strategies were so successful that "Sloanism" became a widely emulated business model. Sloan's philosophy was simple: use extensive marketing and constant design changes to convince Americans to buy new cars regardless of need. Sloan created a "ladder of consumption" with different brands of cars tailored to different income levels. The strategy was so successful that the family car became the most important marker of American success among all classes during the 1950s. No

The International Geophysical Year

In 1957, scientists from around the world were working on projects for the International Geophysical Year (IGY), a global celebration of modern technology. The United States planned to launch a three-pound satellite into the earth's orbit as part of the event. The IGY represented an opportunity for international cooperation in technology, especially in the new realm of space. Scientists were hopeful that space exploration might open new avenues for research cooperation during a period of secrecy and competition surrounding weapons technology. This hope faded on October 4, 1957, with the stunning news of the successful launch and orbit of the Soviet satellite *Sputnik*.

The launch of *Sputnik* came as a shock to the Western world, where it was assumed the United States was far superior to the Soviets technologically. *Sputnik* offered a dramatic illustration of Soviet technological advancement. As *Sputnik* circled the globe, it beamed a radio beep back to Earth. Astonished Americans listened to the Soviet beeps on radios as the satellite sped through space directly over their heads. Only the size of a basketball, the little space ball caused an international uproar and instigated an unprecedented peacetime technological race.

In the United States, *Sputnik* raised concerns about a "**science lag**," an education crisis, and a "missile gap." The Soviet victory in the first battle of space exploration forever linked the "space race" with the Cold War. On November 7, 1957, just weeks after *Sputnik* stunned the world, an influential report, "Deterrence & Survival in the Nuclear Age," drafted by the chairman of the President's Science Advisory Committee, **Horace Rowan Gaither**, explicitly linked science, space exploration, military capacity, capitalism, and democracy. This report built on an earlier influential 1949 report, also drafted by Gaither, who was then chairman of the Ford Foundation board.

The Ford Foundation's "Gaither Report," as it came to be known, explained how powerful private foundations, like the Ford and Rockefeller groups, could use their power and vast resources to spread democracy and capitalism throughout the world to counter

1954 Cadillac convertible

longer the stripped-down utilitarian transportation devised by Henry Ford, American cars now came loaded with push-button transmissions, radios, powerful engines, and futuristic tailfins. Automakers used gadgets and "custom" features to encourage rapid obsolescence and generate demand for new models. Automakers also successfully convinced suburban Americans that they needed two cars to support their lifestyle.

The results were dramatic. During the 1950s, auto production increased to 8 million units annually, and by 1960, there were over 70 million cars on the roads. In 1955, GM became the first U.S. company to make over $1 billion in a single year. By 1960, it had become the world's largest corporation, surpassing in income the GNP of many nations.

The auto mania that transformed cities and enabled the suburban revolution grew from near-total consensus by the American public. Everyone from corporate executives to union leaders celebrated the dramatic rise of the auto industry and supported federal programs to improve America's highway system. By 1956, when Eisenhower signed the communism. The Gaither Report offered a far-reaching vision of globalism in which "traditional concepts such as sovereignty will be subject to scrutiny and redefinition." By 1957, with the release of "Deterrence & Survival in the Nuclear Age," preeminence in science and space had become a cornerstone of the larger mission to spread democracy throughout the globe. *Sputnik* provided powerful motivation for cooperation between private foundations, the United Nations, American universities, and the federal government in the coming years.

Sputnik posed no actual danger but raised the specter of a future in which nuclear missiles could rain down on America from space and provided evidence of the global nature of the Cold War. Eisenhower responded by increasing federal science funding and working with Congress to create the National Aeronautics and Space Administration (NASA). Congress then quickly passed the National Defense Education Act (NDEA), which provided federal funds to local school districts for practically the first time in the nation's history. Books such as *Why Johnny Can't Read and Ivan Can* fueled fears about the baby boom generation's ability to compete with the Communists. Eisenhower's Soviet counterpart, **Nikita Khrushchev**, reveled in the public relations victory.

The Ford Foundation, among others, worked in private to support the policies of the federal government and used its great wealth in support of a wide range of efforts to help support and stabilize the developing world and ally its countries with the United States. "In an era when both problems and solutions disdain national boundaries," the foundation explained, we all "must be prepared to act globally." By 1960, the United States was spending billions on rocket science in a full-fledged space race with the Soviets as the Cold War moved beyond the confines of Earth and into the final frontier.

- What is the meaning of globalism? How was this idea linked to military, political, and scientific policies in the 1950s?
- The International Geophysical Year began with enthusiasm for science and technology but ended with fears and concerns about both. In what ways were these shifting opinions linked to events in the Cold War?

Interstate Highway Act, the auto industry and web of connected ventures dominated the American economy.

The Interstate Highway system was the most significant transportation project since the Transcontinental Railroad. The 1956 act authorized construction of 40,000 miles of new highways at a cost of $50 billion. Auto industry taxes paid part of the bill, and the government picked up the rest of the tab. Still, by the middle of the decade, there were signs that the U.S. industry's growth was not unlimited.

Oil Culture

Oil companies were the big winners in the Interstate era and enjoyed record profits in the 1950s. Cars accounted for the bulk of oil consumption in the United States after World War II, but from the farm to the factory, and even in the suburban home, oil was essential. New innovations such as petroleum-based plastics also contributed to skyrocketing oil demand during the 1950s. During the war, chemists had perfected polyethylene, a versatile petroleum-based plastic used as insulation for radar and radio cables. After the war, DuPont researchers explored plastics for domestic use, and soon plastic was used to make millions of new products from milk jugs and food storage to televisions and satellite components. By 1960, virtually every product sold in the United States was affected by oil supplies and prices.

Millions of Americans worked to produce oil or oil-dependent products and materials. Providing jobs, goods, and fuel, the oil culture underwrote the decade's affluence. It also made the stability of the American oil supply a critical issue. If the second half of the 20th century marked the beginning of the "oil age," then national security and economic stability depended on plentiful supplies.

Prior to World War II, the United States had relied primarily on its own oil reserves for cheap fuel. After the war, U.S. companies took advantage of newly opened world markets in the Persian Gulf and Arabian Peninsula to secure external sources. The Eisenhower administration worked to keep prices low, oil-producing regions stable, and global sources flowing. Thus, areas of the world previously insignificant to the United States suddenly took on great importance. In the years that followed, this dependence on cheap sources of oil became problematic. Like the policies of containment, the oil culture of the 1950s permanently linked the United States to the rest of the world and made the isolationism of past decades impossible.

Television

The meteoric rise of television in the 1950s as the preeminent source of information and entertainment was one of the most significant developments of the century. Television changed American culture, lifestyles, family dynamics, and economics and broadcast American culture to most of the world.

Invented in 1928 by **Philo Farnsworth**, television remained an obscure technology through World War II. Wartime improvements in electronics and plastics made the rapid rise of television possible during the postwar period. Television became second only to the car as the most important appliance of affluence. By 1953, two-thirds of American households had television sets. At the end of the decade, 94 percent owned sets. Almost overnight television became the most popular entertainment medium.

Family watching television during Thanksgiving dinner (1949)

Americans of the 1950s embraced television with open arms. By the end of the 1950s, the average American watched approximately five hours of television each day. By the 1960s, Americans spent nearly as much time on average watching TV as working. The federal government, through the Federal Communications Commission (FCC), gave television an important boost. In the early 1950s, FCC streamlining of the license procedure helped local channels to air even in the smallest markets.

American corporations quickly adapted radio-marketing models to the new media. In the early years of TV, sponsors actually produced shows as vehicles for advertising. *Texaco Star Theater* and the *Goodyear TV Playhouse*, for example, built shows around their products with no clear line between content and advertisement. Cigarette companies such as Philip Morris sponsored many popular shows including *I Love Lucy* and incorporated their products directly into the show as mass appeal drove prices down. Television was the ultimate mass medium, but marketers quickly realized the potential for "narrowcasting" to new audiences. Daytime shows sponsored by appliance and soap

CROSS-CULTURAL ICON A Latin American version of *The Howdy Doody Show, La Hora de Jaudi Dudi,* aired on CMQ-TV in Cuba in 1953 featuring Jaudi and his new sidekick, "Don Burro." Popular *Domingos Alegres* comics followed in 1954.

makers targeted housewives. Children's programming especially interested TV sponsors and advertisers. The most popular show of the decade, *The Howdy Doody Show,* was a prized advertising venue. Welch's juice sponsored *Howdy Doody,* and kids from the "peanut gallery" singing catchy Welch songs were woven into the show to great effect. *Howdy Doody* was also the first American TV show to go international, with popular offshoots broadcast in Cuba and Canada during the 1950s.

STUDY QUESTIONS FOR THE FUTURE IS NOW

1. What impact did the rise of the auto industry have on America in the 1950s?

2. What was the significance of TV in the 1950s?

quiz

⊘ CONFORMITY AND REBELLION

An estimated 6,000 people spilled out of the "Canvas Cathedral" in Los Angeles. Billy Graham, the forceful young preacher with the wild, sweeping mop of hair, pointed to the audience and said, "You know there's a man in this audience tonight . . . who knows this is the decision he should make. . . . *This* is your moment of decision." The preacher was reaching out to potential converts but could have been speaking for millions of 1950s Americans who felt alienated by the dominant trends and culture of their time and thought that it was truly a national "moment of decision."

The 1950s are often remembered as an age of consensus, conformity, and prosperity following the trials and tribulations of the Great Depression and World War II. Rising salaries, greater access to education, and high rates of employment all support this perception. Not all Americans, however, shared in the prosperity of the decade, and many who did were disturbed by the culture of conformity that came with prosperity during the Cold War. Although much of the popular culture of the time celebrated conformity, examples of growing discontent were easy to find. Writers such as Europeans Oswald Spengler, T. S. Eliot, and Aldous Huxley and American conservative William F. Buckley railed against excessive materialism and "spiritual collapse." Cartoonists in *Mad* magazine ridiculed politicians, the Cold War, and television. Frightening government civil defense programs spawned a bomb-shelter industry as communities and individuals prepared for possible nuclear attack. In American schools, children practiced "duck-and-cover" drills that caused deep anxiety about human helplessness in the face of new technologies of mass destruction.

Psychologists worried about rising rates of depression and clinical anxiety among suburbanites, corporate executives, and middle-class women, all beneficiaries of the postwar "good life." Suburban housewives, often overextended through domestic work and unrealistic expectations of domestic bliss, suffered high rates of depression. Likewise, parents and community leaders worried as never before about children rebelling and becoming juvenile delinquents.

Family in an underground bomb shelter, Long Island, NY (1955)

Old-Time Religion

Religion took on increased importance in public life during the 1950s, with American spirituality contrasted with what opponents characterized as godless communism. Politicians paid homage to their faith while religious leaders such as Cardinal Francis Spellman, Norman Vincent Peale, Billy Graham, and Bishop Fulton Sheen became media stars and presidential advisors.

Billy Graham rose from obscurity to national prominence by explicitly linking the ideology of containment with religious salvation. Graham began his rise to national prominence in the fall of 1949 when he launched a series of nightly revivals in his Los Angeles "Canvas Cathedral."

The 30-year-old Graham started his crusade after learning that the Soviets had the atomic bomb. In his fiery sermons, he focused on world events and warned increasingly large audiences that nothing short of religious conversion could save America from nuclear apocalypse. Graham told his followers that Communists had "declared war against Christ, against the Bible, and against all religion!" By the early 1950s, Graham had appeared on the covers of *Time* and *Newsweek*, met the president, and toured the world meeting with political leaders. Through the medium of television, the message of the "New Evangelical" movement spread widely. Graham, however, was only the most visible representative of a dynamic "plain folk" evangelical movement that linked politics and religion during the Cold War and laid the foundation for a new conservatism.

The warnings of Graham and others who linked religion and geopolitics fell on fertile ground. Religious participation surged during the 1950s. In 1950 alone, membership in

STADIUM PREACHING   Evangelist Billy Graham opened his eight-day Washington, DC, crusade in Griffith Stadium before an estimated crowd of 16,000 on June 19, 1960.

Protestant denominations increased by 4 percent, while the number of American Roman Catholics grew by 2 percent. This trend accelerated throughout the decade, as church membership increased from 58 percent of the population in 1950 to 63 percent by 1959. Denominational change was equally dramatic. Evangelicals gained millions of converts during the 1950s, especially in the transient Southwest. Graham built his career in Los Angeles on the western revivalist tradition begun by radio pioneer Aimee Semple McPherson in the 1920s. By 1959, Americans invested $935 million annually in new church construction, much of it in Los Angeles and other rapidly growing western cities.

Religious fervor wedded to Cold War ideology served the goals of the federal government. Political leaders from both parties allied themselves with popular religious movements, and the line between church and state blurred. That religion was seen by many Americans as a weapon in the Cold War led Congress to pass an act making "In God We Trust" the nation's official motto and featuring it on all U.S. currency. During the 1950s, the U.S. dollar replaced the British pound as the global currency of choice, and the message that the United States was a nation "under God" spread around the world. So, too, the sentiment became ritually reinforced at home after 1954 when Congress added the phrase "under God" to the U.S. Pledge of Allegiance. These changes marked a distinct politicization of religion. Many later falsely assumed that these mottos were an American tradition or part of a deeper colonial history, not modern artifacts of the Cold War.

Women in the 1950s

The linkage of religion and politics had special implications for American women. Social values appeared to veer off in contradictory directions in the 1950s. Even as a growing number of women attended college and worked outside the home, opinion leaders, popular TV shows, and advertisers began celebrating "traditional families" or "nuclear families" anchored by a working husband and homemaker wife.

Adlai Stevenson, "A Purpose for Modern Women," (September 1955)

The 1950s white suburban housewife and mother became a Cold War icon as powerful as Rosie the Riveter had been during World War II. Suburban culture and the changing nature of men's work forced many middle-class women to manage the family's needs while husbands were away at jobs, sometimes far from home. Advertisers, religious leaders, and politicians encouraged domestic consumption as the best means for suburban women to participate in public life and to fight communism.

Modern labor-saving appliances provided the centerpieces of suburban households in the 1950s. The newest percolator, range, or vacuum cleaner, advertisements promised, would shave time off of a housewife's busy daily routine. The purchase and use of appliances took on a major role for the 1950s housewife. Whereas the husband often earned the income, the wife at least exercised authority over many household purchases. More than consumers, many suburban women became active dealers of appliances and household goods. Women sold the multicolored plastic Tupperware that filled 1950s cabinets and refrigerators door to door or through Tupperware parties in homes. Most of the female sales staff received their pay in Tupperware, not cash, whereas their male regional managers pocketed large cash commissions. Likewise, as masters of households, women moved into real estate in increasing numbers and in effect transformed that industry. Thus, women of the 1950s often used their domestic status to open new career paths directly tied to the most significant economic trends of the day. At home or in new careers, middle-class women felt pressure to live up to an idealized vision of patriotic femininity. TV moms such as *Father Knows Best*'s Margaret Anderson (played by Jane Wyatt) presented pictures of perfection as they cooked breakfast in designer dresses and were always ready to tend to their family's needs. Despite all of the talk of motherhood and the home in the 1950s, many women, especially minority mothers, remained in the workplace, often at low-paying jobs, while others entered the workforce for the first time. In 1960, twice as many women held jobs outside the home as they did in 1940. Of women with children aged 6 to 17, 39 percent held paying jobs at the end of 1959.

Professional women faced challenges gaining entrance to the best graduate schools and landing good jobs even with advanced degrees. Even the most accomplished women, such as scientist **Rachel Carson**, whose prize-winning books *The Sea Around Us* and *Silent Spring* became environmental classics, faced prejudice. In Carson's case, industry critics used the media to paint Carson as an "emotional woman" who worried too much about plants and animals.

Women's magazines provided some balance for most American women who did not fit popular stereotypes. *Ladies' Home Journal* was the most popular magazine in the world in the 1940s and 1950s, and other women's magazines, such as *McCall's, Redbook,*

CONSUMERISM AS ART Both women and consumption are idealized in this Tupperware party advertisement from 1950. The elevation of food containers to art reflected pressure for women to create a distinctly American form of domesticity as a response to communism.

and *Better Homes and Gardens*, sold millions. Although filled with advertisements supporting the woman-as-consumer message, these magazines also offered a forum for more serious discussions of women's issues. Editors such as **Gertrude Lane** of *Women's Home Companion* respected readers as "intelligent and clearheaded" and tried to provide content aimed at serious issues facing working women and housewives.

Many women found public outlets for their skills and opinions through volunteer societies such as the influential League of Women Voters. The LWV and other organizations, often at the request of the U.S. government, went beyond mere domestic activity to take on a role in international affairs. The LWV also hosted foreign dignitaries visiting the United States and helped to shape the politics of the decade. Behind what writer **Betty Friedan** later named the "feminine mystique" of vacuous suburban domesticity, American women of the 1950s forged new opportunities for themselves while raising awareness of issues that were specific to women and those that reached far beyond the stereotypical suburban household.

Ladies' Home Journal interview with four suburban housewives (February 1956)

Organization Men

Life in the 1950s was hardly ideal for males of the suburban castle—the army of new corporate executives. Sociologist **David Reisman** uncovered widespread unhappiness in his study of corporate culture, *The Lonely Crowd* (1950). Reisman worried that Americans had lost what German sociologist Max Weber referred to as the Protestant work ethic: the moral drive to prosper through one's own individual hard work that had accounted for the greatness of America.

Journalist **William H. Whyte, Jr.**, published similar results in his widely read study *The Organization Man* (1956). Whyte discovered much anxiety among white-collar workers who were disengaged from their families and traditional social structures by rigid corporate work lives and long commutes. Whyte's contentions buttressed concerns on the part of religious leaders that increased affluence did not necessarily translate into universal happiness and social well-being. Novels such as Sloan Wilson's 1955 bestseller *The Man in the Grey Flannel Suit*, which painted a disturbing picture of mind-numbing conformity in corporate America, helped popularize these concerns.

By the time these studies appeared, major demographic and social changes had transformed life for American men. In 1957, white-collar workers outnumbered blue-collar workers for the first time in American history. For critics these corporate strivers represented the apex of a conformist society. Directed to dress in uniform suits, they commuted on crowded trains or highways and worked long hours on bureaucratic tasks. To climb the company ladder, they were expected to move often and to conform without question to corporate rules of behavior.

Teens, Rebels, and Beats

Middle-class affluence and extended education created a new category in American life in the 1950s, the teenager, who had money to spend and the power to influence popular culture. During the 1950s, teenagers emerged as a distinct consumer group. By the decade's end, this influential demographic actively shaped American culture.

The word "teenager" first came into popular usage in the United States during World War II. In the 1940s, many more adolescents than ever before found themselves grouped together in high schools. During and after the war many states passed mandatory school attendance statutes that resulted in a dramatic expansion of attendance and graduation figures. In 1930, only 50 percent of America's 14- to 17-year-olds attended high school; by 1950, this number had climbed to 73 percent. The percentage escalated throughout the 1950s as baby boomers entered their teens.

American businesses understood the potential buying power of this new group. As early as 1944, with the publication of *Seventeen* magazine, ads aimed specifically at teens began to appear regularly. By the 1950s, teens—driving sales of records and fashion—were the most sought-after market segment. By the 1960s, with an average income of $10 per week, teens contributed over $10 billion to the U.S. economy. Early teen advertisements and TV shows tended to portray teens as clean-cut, wholesome, middle class, and white. Although marketers embraced these new consumers, cultural critics, parents, and law enforcement officials worried about the growing cultural influence of teenagers and their rebellious tendencies.

Excerpt from H.H. Remmers and D.H. Radler, "Teenage Attitudes," *Scientific American* (1958)

The high energy and open sexuality of rock 'n' roll fueled anxiety about a brewing youth rebellion. Rock 'n' roll emerged in the early 1950s as Chuck Berry, Fats Domino, Little Richard, and other black musicians mixed the musical traditions of gospel and rhythm and blues into a unique new form of distinctly American music. Black musicians, gaining popularity among white teens, launched a musical revolution with lasting social consequences.

By the mid-1950s, young white men such as **Elvis Presley** and **Jerry Lee Lewis** had repackaged the music emerging from the black community and made it acceptable for a much wider white audience. Elvis Presley's meteoric rise began at the humble Memphis Sun Records in 1955. By September of the next year, he had been signed to RCA's label and was selling records by the millions. Early media reactions to Elvis ranged from characterizations of him as "vulgar" and "suggestive" to racially coded claims that he was a purveyor of an "aborigines' mating dance." Parents, along with religious and political leaders, viewed the music and the reactions it caused as dangerously subversive. Despite concerted community and national efforts to ban the new music, teens embraced the rebellious and sexually charged rock 'n' roll with fanatical fervor. Fears of juvenile delinquency and racial mixing over the unsegregated radio airwaves fueled protest against the new music.

Popular films of the 1950s dramatized teenage troubles and contributed to popular anxieties about youth. Movies, especially *The Wild Ones* (1953), *Rebel Without a Cause* (1955), and *Blackboard Jungle* (1955), marked a stark departure from the patriotic offerings of the war years. Featuring Marlon Brando, James Dean, and Sidney Poitier as angry nonconformists, these films celebrated rebellion as well as contempt for parents and social institutions. Likewise, Leonard Bernstein's Broadway hit *West Side Story* (1957) celebrated ethnic diversity and youth rebellion. Mild by later standards, these productions, along with books such as J. D. Salinger's hugely popular *Catcher in the Rye* (1951), frightened critics who rightly assumed that the buying power and sheer numbers of teenagers had led to the creation of an influential subculture.

Teenagers were not alone in using popular culture to express their discontent with Cold War culture. Much like the Lost Generation writers of the 1920s, Beatniks or Beat (slang for "down and out") writers such as Jack Kerouac, Allen Ginsberg, and William S. Burroughs looked at postwar American society and did not like what they saw. Beats celebrated nonconformity and experimentation in their lives. Sexual experimentation, rootless travel, and anger permeated Kerouac's *On the Road* (1957) and Burroughs's *Naked Lunch* (1959). Even more disturbing was Allen Ginsberg's shocking "Howl," which gave poetic voice to the statistics of discontent compiled by sociologists Reisman and Whyte. Ginsberg's lament, "I saw the best minds of my generation destroyed," spoke to a growing number of alienated dissenters in a society obsessed with materialism and anticommunism. The poem caused considerable controversy also because of its overtly homosexual references. Photographer Robert Frank added visuals to the critique with his bleak 1959 portrait of the nation, *The Americans*.

Beat literature, 1950s films, and rock 'n' roll all revealed the diversity of American culture brewing beneath the conformity of the decade. The American culture of rebellion traveled the globe and circled back with new ideas from abroad. The 1950s critics helped link the Western world's postwar generation and bring in some new voices from the developing world. This fusion of global concern established the foundation for the cultural revolutions of the 1960s. By calling into question America's traditional values, 1950s nonconformists took the first steps toward a critical collaboration between alienated progressive whites and black civil rights activists. Throughout the 1950s, new advocates and old asked the question, "What resources do we need to mobilize to achieve civil rights?"

⊗ LAYING THE FOUNDATION FOR CIVIL RIGHTS

In 1959, jazz musician Miles Davis was rich and famous. His shows drew eager multiracial crowds to his New York City gigs, and his landmark contribution to modern musical history, *Kind of Blue*, topped the jazz charts. Leaving the upscale Birdland jazz club in August of that year, Davis was approached by two New York City police officers, who beat him severely with a blackjack after a brief and seemingly benign exchange of words. Covered with blood, Davis was arrested and thrown in jail. Pictures of the brutally beaten famous musician were in the news the next day. Though he was later acquitted of all charges, the incident demonstrated the racism that even the most successful African Americans living outside the South faced on a daily basis.

Davis was a smoky-voiced iconoclast whose direct contributions to the civil rights movement included a few significant benefit concerts but little political advocacy or action. The scowling and quintessentially hip Davis couldn't have been more different from figures like the Reverend **Martin Luther King, Jr**. But there would not have been a successful civil rights movement without the diversity of opinion and action represented by Davis and King. Despite their obvious differences, King and Davis confronted the same question facing all civil rights advocates in the 1950s: Play slowly by the rules? Or take a stand against the law now regardless of the consequences?

The civil rights revolution confronted all aspects of segregation and racism in the 1950s. The movement was not monolithic, and from the beginning fundamental tensions divided its proponents. The Cold War had added another layer of complexity to the basic fight for racial equality in the United States. The civil rights movement gained some support from federal officials aware that in the contest for the loyalty of the emerging nations of Africa, the Middle East, and Asia, "American apartheid" gave the Soviet Union a powerful Cold War propaganda tool.

By 1954, the civil rights movement had divided over the best means to attack the pervasive racism that denied blacks access to the affluent society and basic human rights. Some activists felt that change should come rapidly through dramatic mass action. Others, including members of the NAACP, argued that gradual change brought about by strategic challenges to the legal system offered the best chance of long-term success.

Brown and the Legal Assault

The NAACP worked to mobilize the resources needed to launch an assault on *Plessy v. Ferguson* and the separate-but-equal doctrine of segregation. The legal fight required the NAACP to train talented black lawyers, raise money to fund cases, and build coalitions of progressive black and white researchers who could provide hard sociological data to undermine the premise of "separate but equal." The legal battle to overturn *Plessy* began in the 1930s when Charles Hamilton Houston, dean of Howard Law School, offered special classes, developed strategies, and trained a generation of talented lawyers.

The best-known opportunity to test the method came when the Supreme Court agreed to hear the case of ***Brown v. Board of Education of Topeka, Kansas.*** A compilation of multiple cases of educational discrimination, *Brown* was brought before the Supreme Court by NAACP Legal Defense Fund lawyer **Thurgood Marshall**. Marshall and NAACP colleagues George E. C. Hayes and James Nabrit, Jr., mounted a stunningly complete argument against segregation. Using sociological data, extensive research, and the Fourteenth Amendment, they dismantled the basis of legal segregation. On May 17, 1954, Chief Justice Earl Warren's Court ruled unanimously that separate educational facilities for blacks and whites resulted in inherently unequal education. In his new role as chief justice, Warren was determined to use judicial power to help the powerless. The opinion of the Court, read by Warren, was decisive and powerful: "We conclude that, in the field of public education, the doctrine of 'separate but equal' has no place. Separate educational facilities are inherently unequal." This long-awaited decision set the precedent for the eventual desegregation of all public institutions, but the actual decision called for "all deliberate speed" only in the desegregation of schools.

Excerpt from court opinion in *Brown v. Board of Education of Topeka Kansas* (1954)

The Warren Court's strongly worded unanimous opinion came at a moment of great concern regarding international attention to the American civil rights movement. By the early 1950s, the inability of U.S. officials to respond to America's racial inequality was more than an embarrassment; it represented a serious threat to the very foundations of U.S. foreign policy during a vital period of global change. Warren was keenly aware of how segregation undermined the U.S. position in the Cold War just as African and Asian liberation movements were gaining traction. The NAACP and other civil rights organizations used the Cold War rhetoric of freedom and democracy for all as a powerful tool to motivate rapid action on long-festering issues such as segregation.

Opposition to *Brown v. Board* ("Southern Manifesto," 1956)

The *Brown* decision opened the door, albeit slowly, for the nation's 11.5 million black children to receive an education equal to that of their white peers. The case helped move the nation further along the road to human rights than ever before. However, the battle against racism in schools was far from over.

Showdown in Little Rock

The first real test of the *Brown* ruling came in 1957 in Little Rock, Arkansas. That September, nine black students, armed with a federal court order, attempted to desegregate the city's Central High School. Governor Orval Faubus, responding by calling out the Arkansas National Guard to block their way, directly challenged the authority of the federal government.

On September 23, the situation escalated when the nine young students attempted to enter the school. Television cameras recorded the well-dressed students as they walked a gauntlet of abusive white students, parents, and community members, who spat and hurled obscenities at the "Little Rock Nine." School officials forced the children to withdraw from classes for their own safety. Governor Faubus promised to chain himself to the high school doors if the students returned, while the **Ku Klux Klan** made threats of violence against the Little Rock Nine and their supporters. Watching this dismal scene unfold on the Oval Office TV, President Eisenhower stepped in.

Careful, the Walls Have Ears
Reprinted with permission from *Arkansas Democrat-Gazette*

Eisenhower, who had spent his entire career in a segregated army, was ambivalent about civil rights but not about states' rights over federal authority. Ike's lukewarm response to the *Brown* decision had encouraged segregationists such as Faubus, who assumed the president would stay out of the fight. Faubus was wrong. Under pressure from a slowly changing tide of public opinion in the North and Cold War advisors who recognized the international public relations implications, Ike reluctantly sent federal troops to secure the students' safe passage into their school. Soldiers with the 101st Airborne escorted the children to class and stayed in Little Rock for the entire school year. This was the first time a Republican president had sent federal troops into the South since Grant in 1874. Eisenhower followed the strong showing in Little Rock with support for a civil rights bill sent to Congress in 1957. The bill included controversial provisions for voting rights that even Eisenhower questioned. The Civil Rights Act of 1957 expanded voting rights on paper but once again failed to deal with the question of enforcement.

During the showdown at Little Rock, television contributed to shifting the balance of power in the fight for civil rights. The glare of TV lights laid bare to the world the harsh tactics of the segregationist movement. Millions of white American viewers who watched the drama unfold converted to the cause of civil rights as they witnessed the calm dignity of the Little Rock Nine in the face of unfiltered racial hatred.

Boots on the Ground

During the long years of preparation for the legal assault on segregation, other civil rights activists mobilized to attack racism through direct protest. This movement gained momentum on December 1, 1955, after a humble protest by a tired seamstress and local NAACP member named Rosa Parks. On that evening, Parks refused to give up her seat for a white passenger on a Montgomery bus as she traveled home from work. "My feet hurt," she recalled, and she was ready to learn "once and for all what rights I had as a human and citizen." Local segregation laws and bus company policy required that when whites boarded a bus and needed seats, any blacks on the bus had to move to seats in the rear. After she refused to move, police arrested Parks.

The Montgomery Women's Political Council (WPC) seized on the arrest of the upstanding Parks as an example of racial injustice. Working with local NAACP leader E. D. Nixon, they launched a campaign against discriminatory practices on public transit. After securing legal representation for Parks, Nixon and the WPC assembled a critical coalition of local ministers to lead a boycott of the bus system.

Excerpts from Rosa Parks and E.D. Nixon on the creation of the Montgomery Improvement Association

To oversee the boycott, the ministers set up the **Montgomery Improvement Association (MIA)**. They named 26-year-old minister Martin Luther King, Jr., as its head. King was chosen as the association's leader largely because he was new to town and an eloquent speaker. On the first night of the boycott, King pushed his way through a tightly packed crowd in the Holt Street Baptist Church to address the gathered crowd. "We are here," he told the audience, because "there comes a time when people get tired of being trampled over by the iron feet of oppression." In the months that followed, he became the face and strategist of the boycott. Most importantly, he refined a philosophy of nonviolent protest for boycotters. The boycott lasted a year and sparked violence against King, Nixon, and other leaders, but it demonstrated the power of collective community action. During the 381 days of the boycott, Montgomery's protestors walked miles to work every day, were threatened with violence, and were arrested without cause. In the end, the Supreme Court struck down the city's bus segregation.

The significance of the Montgomery boycotts spread well beyond Alabama. The boycott revealed that grassroots protest with thoughtful leadership could succeed. The victory in Montgomery provided national recognition for Martin Luther King, Jr., and it highlighted the role of religious leaders, women, and ordinary people in the coming fight for civil rights.

MLK and the Philosophy of Nonviolence

Leading a national civil rights movement with global consequences was not what Martin Luther King, Jr., had in mind when he moved to Montgomery in 1955. The young minister summed up his feelings in a conversation with friends in early 1956: "If anybody had asked me a year ago to head this movement, I would have run a mile to get away from it." But, thanks largely to his role as leader of the successful boycott, King emerged as the movement's public face.

King, along with NAACP associates **Bayard Rustin** and **Ralph Abernathy**, decided that he would lose an invaluable opportunity if he did not seize the momentum generated by the bus boycott to work in changing the South and the nation. They scheduled

interactive timeline

TIMELINE 1950–1959

AMERICA	YEAR	THE WORLD
Jan Klaus Fuchs confesses to being a Soviet spy **Feb** Joseph McCarthy announces list of Communists in U.S. State Department	**1950**	**Jun** North Korea invades South Korea, initiating Korean War Coca-Cola completes 60th international bottling plant **Oct** Puerto Rican National Party stages uprising **Nov** Chinese forces enter Korea
Jan Nuclear testing begins at Nevada test site **Feb** 22nd Amendment to the U.S. Constitution ratified	**1951**	**Aug** United States Information Agency (USIA) created to coordinate efforts to reach developing nations with pro-U.S. programming
Jun National Security Council memo 124/2 outlines "domino theory" in Southeast Asia **Jul** The *New York Post* reports questionable contribution to Richard Nixon's California campaign funds **Nov** Dwight D. Eisenhower defeats Adlai Stevenson for U.S. presidency **Nov** President Eisenhower travels to Korea	**1952**	**Nov** United States detonates first hydrogen bomb "Mike" on the Eniwetok Islands in South Pacific
Mar Jonas Salk announces first successful polio vaccine **Jun** Julius and Ethel Rosenberg executed	**1953**	**Mar** Death of Joseph Stalin **Jul** Cease-fire achieved; DMZ is created at Panmunjom, Korea *La Hora de Jaudi Dudi* premieres in Cuba
Jan *Hernandez v. Texas* extends 14th Amendment protection to ethnic groups as well as racial **Mar** Broadcast journalist Edward R. Murrow attacks Joseph McCarthy on *See It Now* **Apr** President Eisenhower delivers "domino theory" speech **Apr–Jun** U.S. Army and McCarthy hearings **May** *Brown v. Board of Education of Topeka, Kansas* decision **Jun** "Under God" is added to U.S. Pledge of Allegiance	**1954**	**May** French defeated at Battle of Dien Bien Phu **May** Mexican government works with United States to repatriate migrant workers under "Operation Wetback" **Jul** Geneva Conference partitions Vietnam into North and South **Oct** Algerian War for Independence begins

a conference of black ministers and community activists for January 10 and 11, 1957, in Atlanta, Georgia. This meeting, called the "Southern Negro Leaders Conference on Transportation and Nonviolent Integration," resulted in the Southern Christian Leadership Conference (SCLC). Electing King as its head, the SCLC quickly became one of the greatest forces for change in the civil rights movement.

Although not universally supported by his fellow activists, King proved such an effective spokesman that he was able to unify previously divided factions. As an expert in using the media, and TV in particular, King reached out to a much broader audience of supporters in America and abroad. A master orator with a doctorate in theology from Boston University, King was a deep thinker who crafted an effective and appealing ideology of peaceful mass resistance. Influenced by his readings of Henry David Thoreau's "Civil Disobedience" and Mahatma Gandhi's accounts of nonviolent protest in India, King strategically combined boycott and protest. After Montgomery, King preached about "militant nonviolence" and encouraged blacks and whites to confront racism everywhere. King warned segregationists, "We will soon wear you down by our capacity

AMERICA	YEAR	THE WORLD
Feb U.S. president Eisenhower sends first military advisors to South Vietnam **Apr** Polio vaccine introduced to public **Aug** Emmett Till murdered in Mississippi **Dec** Rosa Parks arrested, marking beginning of Montgomery Bus Boycott **Dec** GM becomes first U.S. company to make over $1 billion in a single year	**1955**	
Jun Federal Highway Act enacted **Jul** Congress authorizes "In God We Trust" as national motto **Nov** Eisenhower reelected as U.S. president **Dec** Montgomery Bus Boycott ends	**1956**	**Jul** Egypt nationalizes Suez Canal **Nov** Hungary revolts against Soviet rule **Oct** Britain, France, and Israel launch military attacks against Egypt **Dec** Britain and France withdraw troops from Suez
Jan Southern Christian Leadership Conference (SCLC) founded **Apr** Allen Ginsberg's "Howl" seized by U.S. Customs officials on grounds of obscenity **Sep** Jack Kerouac's *On the Road* released **Sep** Little Rock's Central High School desegregated	**1957**	**Jul** International Geophysical Year begins hopeful cooperation between 67 countries on range of science and technology development **Oct** Soviets successfully launch *Sputnik*
	1958	**Mar** Nikita Khrushchev becomes premier of Soviet Union
Aug Hawaii becomes 50th U.S. state	**1959**	**Jul** Nixon and Khrushchev's "Kitchen Debate" at Soviet National Exhibition Radio Free Dixie broadcasts in Cuba to promote pan-African civil rights By end of year, 37 developing world nations achieve independence

to suffer, and in winning our freedom we will so appeal to your heart and conscience that we will win you in the process."

The idea of massive resistance to segregation through militant nonviolence was ingenious and bold. It called on blacks of all ages to place their lives in danger and exercise a phenomenal level of willpower. King rightly concluded that if demonstrators refrained from violence, even in self-defense, the moral compass of world opinion would swing in their direction. In the age of television and worldwide media, recurring images of brutality used against groups and individuals peacefully demonstrating for their human rights gave protesters the high ground and forced political leaders to act. "This is the beauty of nonviolence," King said later. "It says you can struggle without hating. You can fight war without violence." Through the waning years of the 1950s, King and a growing army of brave protestors perfected the method of nonviolent resistance. Across the South, protesters as young as 10 and as old as 80 filled jails, stopped traffic, crippled businesses, and drew increasing numbers of reporters to the Deep South to witness and publicize their fight.

At a time when the United States was engaging in a daily struggle to project images of equality, freedom, and Christian values, civil rights protesters drew attention to systematic racial oppression and discrimination. These activists knew that the world was watching. The impact of growing civil rights protest on global politics was not lost on national political leaders, who were aware that people of color made up most newly independent developing world nations critical to the Cold War balance of power.

The actions of African Americans fighting legal segregation in the South and whites awakening to the hypocrisy of American race relations inspired soul searching about inequality for all those seeking freedom. Just as the NAACP mobilized the black fight for equality in 1954–1955, over one million Mexicans and Mexican Americans were deported from the United States during Operation Wetback. Under the direction of U.S. Immigration and Naturalization Service director General Joseph Swing, Operation Wetback raided Mexican American neighborhoods across the Southwest and Southeast, rounded up entire families, and deported parents and their native-born children who were American citizens. In some cases, "Mexican-looking" American citizens were deported. In the United States and abroad, critics accused the United States of "police-state" methods similar to those in Communist nations. Latinos throughout the southern swath of the nation fought for their rights and won some early victories with cases such as *Hernandez v. Texas* (1954).

By the close of the 1950s, the resources for an all-out multifront civil rights battle were in place. In the coming decade, Americans would finally face the stain of racial inequality head-on and end a century of shameful denial and inaction.

STUDY QUESTIONS FOR LAYING THE FOUNDATION FOR CIVIL RIGHTS

1. What was the relationship between expressions of cultural dissent and civil rights activism?

2. What was the significance of the *Brown v. Board of Education* decision?

quiz

Summary

- Cold War diplomacy shaped domestic life.
- American culture traveled the globe.
- The space race intensified the Cold War.
- The United States led the world in economic growth fueled by the "military-industrial complex," vastly increased consumer spending, and the baby boom.
- American corporations consolidated production and distribution networks and perfected national and international marketing techniques.
- Applied science, especially in medicine, led to massive public health campaigns to eliminate infectious diseases such as polio.
- Uneven economic prosperity and racial, gender, and generational tensions made the 1950s a time of affluence and anxiety.
- A civil rights revolution confronted all aspects of segregation in the 1950s, which led to critical legal victories and the rise of a widespread grassroots movement with dynamic leadership.

Key Terms and People

🔊))

audio
flashcards

Reviewing Chapter 26

1. What was the "science lag"? Why did science take on new significance during the Cold War?

2. What factors contributed to the massive demographic changes of the 1950s? How did the changes in the United States compare to the rest of the world?

3. Why did millions of Americans leave cities for rapidly growing suburbs? What trends and policies supported this migration?

4. Some consider the 1950s to be the pivotal decade in the creation of an "oil culture" in the United States. What developments and policies elevated the importance of oil during this time? How did demand for oil redirect the flow of people, goods, and ideas during the period?

Further Reading

Brown, Kate. *Plutopia: Nuclear Families, Atomic Cities, and the Great Soviet and American Plutonium Disasters*. New York: Oxford University Press, 2013. Fantastic transnational history of how the Soviets and Americans came to resemble each other even as they fought the Cold War.

Dochuk, Darren. *From Bible Belt to Sunbelt: Plain-Folk Religion, Grassroots Politics, and the Rise of Evangelical Conservatism*. New York: W. W. Norton, 2011. Carefully explains the rise of one of the most influential postwar movements.

Friedan, Betty. *The Feminine Mystique*. New York: W. W. Norton, 1963. The book that helped spark a movement.

Harvey, Mark T. *A Symbol of Wilderness: Echo Park and the American Conservation Movement*. Albuquerque: University of New Mexico Press, 1994. Explains the surprising 1950s origins of the wilderness movement.

McDougall, Walter. *The Heavens and the Earth: A Political History of the Space Age*. New York: Basic Books, 1985. An award-winning account of the space race in Cold War context.

Mulroy, Kevin. *Western Amerykanski: Polish Poster Art & the Western*. Seattle: University of Washington Press, 1999. Beautiful collection of western film posters from Poland with insightful commentary.

Rome, Adam. *The Bulldozer in the Countryside: Suburban Sprawl and the Rise of American Environmentalism*. Cambridge, UK: Cambridge University Press, 2001. The rise of suburbia creates environmental problems and inspires new types of environmental protection.

Scott, Felicity. *Outlaw Territories: Environments of Insecurity/Architectures of Counterinsurgency*. New York: Zone Books, 2016. A meticulous history linking Cold War politics with the rise of globalism and neoliberalism as revealed even by the architecture of postwar America.

Tyson, Timothy B. *Radio Free Dixie: Robert F. Williams and the Roots of Black Power*. Chapel Hill: University of North Carolina Press, 2001. Reveals the borderless nature of radio and shows how the technology extends American civil rights into other nations.

America in the World
GOODS, IDEAS, PEOPLE

CHAPTER 26: The Dynamic 1950s 1950–1959

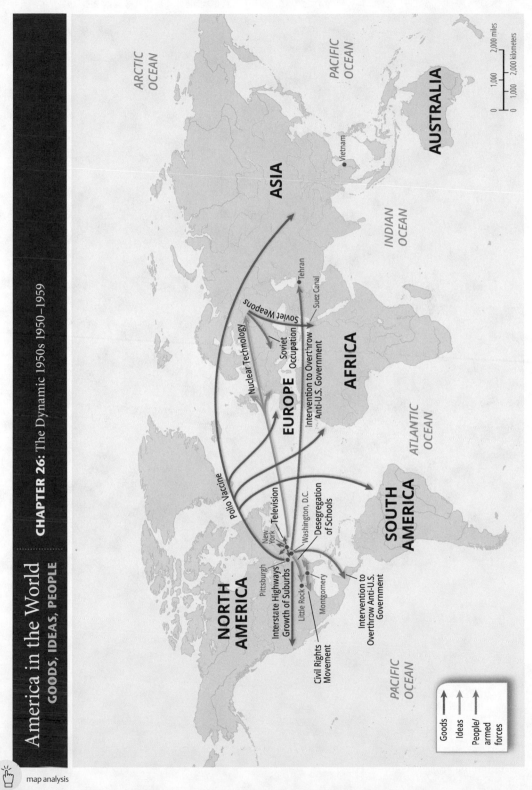

ARCTIC OCEAN

PACIFIC OCEAN

AUSTRALIA

ASIA

• Vietnam

INDIAN OCEAN

Tehran •

Suez Canal

Soviet Weapons

Nuclear Technology

Soviet Occupation

EUROPE

Intervention to Overthrow Anti-U.S. Government

AFRICA

ATLANTIC OCEAN

Polio Vaccine

New York • Television

Washington, D.C. •

Desegregation of Schools

SOUTH AMERICA

NORTH AMERICA

Pittsburgh

Interstate Highways Growth of Suburbs

Little Rock •

Montgomery •

Intervention to Overthrow Anti-U.S. Government

Civil Rights Movement

PACIFIC OCEAN

Goods

Ideas

People/ armed forces

0   1,000   2,000 miles
0   1,000   2,000 kilometers

map analysis

The Optimism and the Anguish of the 1960s

1960–1969

O n Christmas Eve, 1968, the crew of NASA's *Apollo 8* mission was orbiting the Moon. Astronauts James Lovell, Bill Anders, and Frank Borman were survey- ing the Moon in preparation for a future landing. These hardened test pilots were galactic Cold Warriors on the front lines of the space race. As the capsule made its fourth orbit, the normally cool and collected Borman yelled, "Oh my God! Look at that picture over there! Here's the Earth coming up. Wow, that is pretty!" The others jostled to see and agreed that the sight was incredible.

From the vantage point of the Moon they watched in awe as the brilliant blue and white Earth rose on the horizon, the only colorful thing in an otherwise inky black and lifeless space. Borman was the first human to ever see Earth rising over the barren Moon, and he realized instantly that this image of a living planet so alone and so small would change history. "It was the most beautiful thing there was to see in all the heav- ens. People down here don't realize what they have—it really is 'one world.'"

When Borman's brilliant color photos of **"Earth- rise"** became public, the effect was immediate and just as he assumed. The astronauts had gone to explore the frontier of space, but it was the images of our global home that captivated the world. These first high- quality color photos of Earth from distant space con- firmed what proponents of the ecology movement had been saying for years. The world was small and fragile, its resources precious and unique in the solar system. "Nationalistic interests, famines, wars, pestilence don't show from that distance," Borman said later. "We are one hunk of ground, water, air, clouds, floating around in space."

The effort to be the first nation to reach the Moon embodied the ideal of space as the final frontier. This particularly American view of Earth reflected the spirit of the Kennedy administration's push into space as a continuation of American history and new battlefront in the Cold War. The "Earthrise" image, however, de-centered national interests, replacing them with a truly global perspective of our shared reliance on a single, fragile natural environment. The emotional reaction of even the normally unsentimental astronauts was a har-binger of changing views about the environment. The image of our shared Earth with the barren Moon in the foreground forced all who saw it to think holistically.

⊘ THE NEW FRONTIER

The 1960s had started with widespread optimism. Many Americans believed that the prosperity of the 15 years after World War II could be widely shared, and they worked to remove the stain of racial discrimination. Most Americans followed their political leaders' call for greater efforts to contain Soviet communism in the Cold War. People in other countries saw a United States more deeply engaged in international affairs. The hopes of the early years of the decade became strained after the assassination of President **John F. Kennedy** in November 1963, a horrifying murder that shocked and saddened people around the globe. His successor, **Lyndon B. Johnson**, pursued an ini-tially popular program of domestic social and economic reform. By 1966, however, Americans had become deeply divided and angry with one another. Some, especially among the young and people of color, embraced change and worked to help engineer transformations of politics, culture, and life. Others—mainly older, white Americans—believed that movements for social justice had turned violent and destructive and that the emerging counterculture was the product of a spoiled generation unfamiliar with the hardship of depression and war. They feared that advances toward racial equality and other forms of political and cultural transformation came at their expense.

JFK's New Frontier

The decade began with the election of 43-year-old Massachusetts Democratic sena-tor John F. Kennedy as the nation's first Roman Catholic president. Many Americans thrilled at his vibrant youth and his idealistic appeals to serve the public good. During the fall campaign of 1960, Kennedy challenged voters to explore and conquer a **New Frontier**. Although he offered few specifics, he inspired millions of Americans to be-lieve they could improve their country. They expected to expand economic and social opportunities for those who missed the prosperity of the 1950s and, at the same time, wage the Cold War against the Soviet Union and its allies more energetically.

Excerpt from John F. Kennedy's inaugural address, January 20, 1961

As president, Kennedy exuded youth, confidence, and fitness. The public thought they knew him better than almost any previous occupant of the White House, largely because he mastered the new medium of television. His quick wit and bright smile endeared him to White House reporters and millions of citizens who watched live broadcasts of his dazzling press conferences. Pictures of him sailing off of Cape Cod with his beautiful and talented young wife, Jackie, and their two young children reinforced the view that he, like the nation he led, was ready to take on any challenge. Befriending movie stars and popular singers, the president suggested to a celebrity-struck public that he could move gracefully in the currents of popular culture. Few knew the full extent of Kennedy's chronic bad back and Addison's disease, a serious adrenal disorder that left him in almost constant pain and sometimes even threatened his life. Fewer still, only his closest friends and a few reporters, knew at the time that he conducted a series of sexual affairs, both inside and out of the White House. Although the public's idealized image glossed over his troubled marriage and serious health problems, while he lived and in the years that followed, many Americans viewed his administration "the age of Camelot."

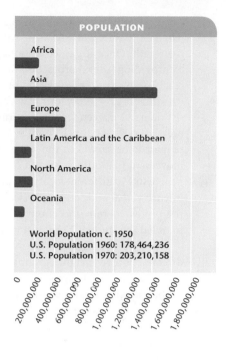

The Challenge of Racial Justice

The hopes inspired by Kennedy's call to conquer a New Frontier represented one part of a more widespread sense that the time was ripe to remake the United States into a more just and more prosperous society. The African American struggle for civil rights inspired millions of Americans, black and white, to join a mass movement for racial equality.

MEETING THE PRESS   Reporters surround President-Elect John F. Kennedy outside the White House after Kennedy met with President Dwight D. Eisenhower on December 6, 1960.

image analysis

The grassroots movement that reached a critical turning point in the early 1960s originated in hundreds of African American churches, high schools, and colleges across the South. Once it gained national visibility, the Kennedy administration responded by providing federal protection to embattled civil rights advocates and introducing far-reaching civil rights legislation in Congress.

Martin Luther King, Jr. on the sit-in movement (April 1960)

In February 1960, four black college students at North Carolina A&T State University demanded an end to segregation. These young men entered a Woolworth's in Greensboro, sat down on lunch counter stools reserved for whites, and asked to be served. Their request to be served in the same way as white customers was what started the "sit-in" movement that quickly spread throughout the South and eventually numbered 70,000 people in 150 different locations. Sit-in participants faced the threat of arrest along with intense verbal and, often, physical abuse from whites. No matter how harsh the abuse, the protestors remained nonviolent. Encouraged by their involvement, sit-in veterans founded the Student Nonviolent Coordinating Committee (SNCC) in April 1960.

Student Non-Violent Coordinating Committee, Statement of Purpose, April 1960

In 1961, SNCC joined the initiative of CORE (Congress of Racial Equality), another direct-action civil rights group, to test court-ordered integration along interstate bus travel and in bus stations. The first "freedom ride" traveled from Washington, DC, to Alabama, where mobs of angry whites attacked a small group of interracial activists and burned a bus (Map 27.1). Local law enforcement rarely provided protection for the riders. In Birmingham, Alabama, police commissioner "Bull" Connor allowed the Ku Klux Klan to attack the riders with clubs and chains. The national and international media, however, gave the riders extensive, sympathetic coverage.

President Kennedy at first found the freedom riders too militant. He wanted racial justice to come about gradually. Although his brother, Attorney General **Robert F. Kennedy**, ordered U.S. Marshals to protect the riders when no other authorities would, he called for a "cooling off" period for the freedom rides and suggested that the racial

FREEDOM RIDERS BEING ATTACKED IN BIRMINGHAM, MAY 15, 1961 Dramatic images such as this achieved the goal of the freedom rides to use the media to undermine the credibility of southern segregationists, who lived up to low expectations at every stop along the way.

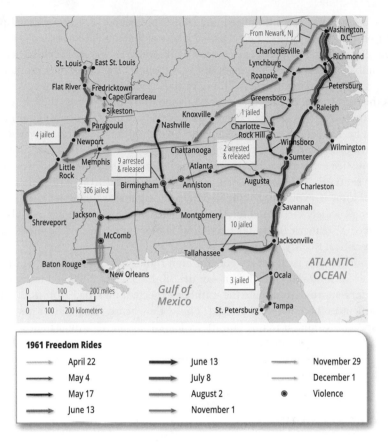

1961 Freedom Rides

⟶	April 22	⟹	June 13	⟶	November 29
⟶	May 4	⟹	July 8	⟶	December 1
⟶	May 17	⟹	August 2	◉	Violence
⟹	June 13	⟹	November 1		

MAP 27.1 Freedom Riders This map details routes taken by freedom riders in 1961. All of the freedom riders knew that they were placing themselves in harm's way. The trips were punctuated by escalating violence as the buses moved deeper into the segregated South.

map analysis

tension at home would embarrass the president at his upcoming summit meeting with Soviet premier Nikita Khrushchev. One civil rights leader replied, "Doesn't the Attorney General know that we've been embarrassed all our lives?" The freedom riders continued on to Mississippi, where they were arrested. Finally, in September 1962, the Interstate Commerce Commission enforced desegregation of bus facilities.

The challenge of integrating public education after the Supreme Court's 1954 decision in *Brown v. Board of Education* continued in the South. In the fall of 1962, Air Force veteran **James Meredith**—with a federal court order in hand—sought to become the first black student to attend the University of Mississippi. In response, thousands of whites rioted. Robert Kennedy again ordered federal marshals to shield Meredith. They were attacked, and 160 of the marshals were wounded, several by gunfire. President Kennedy then ordered the National Guard to the university campus to defend the marshals and restore order. Much to the dismay of the white supremacists, Meredith attended the university and graduated in 1963.

In early 1963, civil rights leaders in the Southern Christian Leadership Conference (SCLC), including **Martin Luther King, Jr.**, focused their efforts on Birmingham,

Alabama, a hotbed of racism. Police chief Bull Connor and his force sprayed protest-ers with powerful fire hoses and turned dogs loose on the demonstrators, including children. Outrage and disgust peaked when four young girls were killed in September after a bomb exploded in the basement of the Sixteenth Street Baptist Church, a center for civil rights organizing. Images of these brutal attacks received global coverage, and news of the Birmingham protests energized a wider movement across the United States. Martin Luther King was arrested during a nonviolent protest in Birmingham in April 1963. From his jail cell, he wrote an eloquent open letter on the margins of newspapers left on the floor explaining his evolving civil rights philosophy. "Injustice anywhere is a threat to justice everywhere," King wrote at a moment when civil rights were moving fast from a southern issue to a national issue. King's "Letter from a Birmingham Jail," as it became known, explained his philosophy after eight years' experience of successful protest. King's widely circulated letter and images of the violence against black pro-testors forced all Americans to take civil rights more seriously as the movement ap-proached a critical turning point.

Martin Luther King, Jr., "Letter from Birmingham Jail" (1963)

The effort to gain national support for civil rights culminated with the **March on Washington** for Jobs and Freedom on August 28, 1963. Over 200,000 black and white demonstrators, more than double the number expected, marched from the Washing-ton Monument to the Lincoln Memorial. There, they heard King deliver his "I Have a Dream" speech. Although Kennedy initially feared the march might turn violent and provoke an anti–civil rights backlash among whites, he soon supported it. The large turnout, peaceful demonstration, and positive media coverage gave his proposed civil rights bill even higher priority.

Cold War Tensions

Many advocates for civil rights saw the struggle for racial equality inside the United States as a way to win friends in the global Cold War competition with the Soviet Union, especially in the developing world. Kennedy devoted more attention toward winning the Cold War than to any other subject. During the 1960 campaign, Kennedy advocated more assertive U.S. action in the Cold War; he charged that Eisenhower had allowed a "missile gap" to grow between the Americans' and the Soviets' arsenals. In his inaugural address, he called on Americans to "pay any price, bear any burden, meet any hardship, support any friend, oppose any foe to assure the survival and success of liberty." In June 1961, Kennedy met in Vienna with Soviet Communist Party chair-man Nikita Khrushchev to discuss the Berlin question. The status of Germany had never been resolved after World War II, and its division was a central question of the Cold War. The country remained split into two states, the pro-West Federal Republic of Germany (FRG) and the Soviet satellite the Democratic Republic of Germany (DRG). Berlin, inside the DRG, was also divided into Western and Communist halves. Each week more than 4,000 people fled East Berlin for West Berlin in search of a better life—a sensitive subject to Khrushchev. At the summit he threatened to make a separate peace with the DRG, depriving the Western powers of their legal right to station military forces in Berlin, if the Western powers did not leave West Berlin by the end of the year.

Kennedy felt bullied by Khrushchev at Vienna. After he returned to the United States, the president went to great lengths to demonstrate his commitment to Berlin. He asked Congress for a $3.25 billion increase in the defense budget, recalled thousands of military reserves to active duty, and more than doubled draft calls. In August, the Soviets responded by building a wall separating the two Berlins and preventing passage to the West. Later, in 1963, JFK went to Berlin to smooth things over, declaring to a receptive crowd, "*Ich bin ein Berliner*" ("I am a Berliner"). Actually it meant in German "I am a jelly doughnut"—but it endeared Kennedy to the Germans. The Berlin Wall remained standing for 26 years, a symbol of East–West tensions and of East German repression of its citizens.

To foster legitimate governments and prosperous, growing economies, Kennedy advocated nation building. He created the Peace Corps, which sent thousands of idealistic young American volunteers to teach; give vaccinations; and build wells, schools, and hospitals throughout the developing world. In Latin America, in particular, Kennedy hoped to counter the appeal of communism and **Fidel Castro**'s successful revolution in Cuba in 1959 by initiating in March 1961 the **Alliance for Progress**, a multibillion-dollar aid program for Latin America.

Fidel Castro's revolution in Cuba had inspired interest in Latin America by offering an alternative approach to the political and economic promises of the United States. Castro had overthrown a pro-American government that allowed gambling, prostitution, and narcotics sales to flourish and held ties to organized crime and American business. Eager to see Castro removed from power, Kennedy approved a CIA plan in January 1961 initiated by the Eisenhower administration to train approximately 1,500 Cuban exiles to invade the Bay of Pigs in southern Cuba (Map 27.2). When

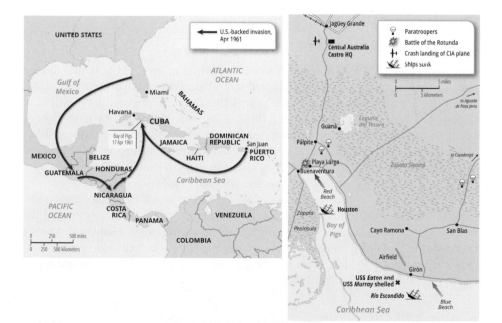

MAP 27.2 The Bay of Pigs This map shows the Bay of Pigs invasion and training sites. JFK and other supporters were confident the invasion was well planned and supported sufficiently at home to succeed. Later critics pointed to the treacherous nature of the bay and other miscalculations as insurmountable weaknesses.

the raid began on April 17, Kennedy refused to approve any further assistance to the invaders, and the Cuban army quickly captured the U.S.-sponsored guerrillas. After the **Bay of Pigs invasion**, the CIA, through Operation Mongoose, continued attempting to overthrow or assassinate Castro. These unsuccessful efforts managed only to push Castro more firmly into the Soviet camp.

A little over a year after the Bay of Pigs fiasco, in October 1962, the installation of Soviet missiles in Cuba prompted the **Cuban missile crisis**, the most dramatic nuclear standoff of the Cold War. By early October, Kennedy knew that the Soviets had built a missile base in Cuba, only 90 miles off the coast of Florida. Kennedy decided to initiate a blockade, or "quarantine," to stop future nuclear weapons from reaching Cuba and demanded that the Soviets withdraw the missiles already there. JFK was under heavy pressure from the military high command to strike first, with both air strikes and a sea invasion. Kennedy resisted this dire option, hoping for a diplomatic solution that might avoid the clash with the Soviets that would surely follow an invasion of Cuba. Anxiety rose across the nation as adults stocked up on groceries and schoolchildren practiced air-raid drills. On October 28, the Soviets, to Castro's dismay, pledged to remove the missiles in return for an American promise not to invade Cuba. The United States also secretly agreed to remove its own obsolete Jupiter missiles aimed at the Soviet Union from Turkey and not to invade Cuba or support an invasion like the Bay of Pigs.

President John F. Kennedy, "Radio and Television Report to the American People on the Soviet Arms Buildup in Cuba" (October 22, 1962)

After the close call of the Cuban missile crisis, Kennedy and his team grew more willing to ease relations with the Soviet Union. The Americans and Soviets set up a "hot line" between the White House and the Kremlin in case of future emergencies. In August 1963, the United States and the Soviet Union signed a **Limited Test Ban Treaty**, ending above ground atomic testing but allowing continued testing underground.

Kennedy Assassination

How Kennedy would have responded to developments in the Cold War will forever remain unanswerable, as he was murdered in Dallas, Texas, on November 22, 1963. When the president's open motorcade passed the Texas Book Depository early that afternoon, Lee Harvey Oswald—firing three shots from the building's sixth floor— killed Kennedy. Police quickly apprehended Oswald. Over the next four days, millions of Americans remained glued to their TVs, mourning and watching intently as news-casters provided new information. They also witnessed Oswald's own assassination by Dallas nightclub owner Jack Ruby on live television on November 24. The country united as it viewed Kennedy's emotional state funeral, at which Kennedy's three-year-old son, John Jr., saluted his father's casket. People wept openly on streets around the world when they heard the news and saw the funeral on television. Many of Kennedy's backers, as well as those who had been lukewarm supporters or even critics, almost im-mediately romanticized his tenure in office. Later observers viewed his presidency as one full of promise tragically cut short.

STUDY QUESTIONS FOR THE NEW FRONTIER

1. How did the Kennedy administration promote a sense of optimism in the United States?

2. What events caused Cold War tensions to rise in the early 1960s?

quiz

◉ THE GREAT SOCIETY

The early 1960s were years of enormous promise, temporarily dimmed, but not extinguished, by Kennedy's assassination. Optimism reflected the enduring appeal of political liberalism, the belief in using the power of the federal government to promote economic growth and social harmony. By the end of the 1960s, however, much of the hopefulness had soured, and many Americans had become frustrated and angry with their leaders and most public institutions. Many rejected liberalism as a failed approach that raised false hopes.

From 1964 to 1966, President Lyndon B. Johnson pressed Congress to enact a series of social and economic reforms designed to promote what he called the **Great Society**. At first the public supported action to end racial discrimination, expand educational opportunities, end hunger and poverty, and make health care available for all. Public approval of the Great Society faded, however, as the war in Vietnam expanded and many white Americans became angry and frightened by African American demands for civil rights. Johnson, once feared as one of the toughest politicians of his generation, seemed to wither as he struggled with the impossible decisions of supporting Vietnam or the Great Society, or, as reporters put it, "Guns or butter?"

President Lyndon B. Johnson, commencement address at the University of Michigan (May 1964)

Civil Rights Laws

On November 22, 1963, Johnson was sworn in as president aboard Air Force One as Jacqueline Kennedy, her clothes stained with her husband's blood, stood by his side. In the days immediately following the assassination, Johnson implored Kennedy's top aides to remain. They did so out of a sense of duty, but most left over the next 18 months, unable to overcome their grief and the sense that Johnson was an unworthy successor to their hero.

Almost immediately President Johnson expressed impatience with America's racial injustice. He told a grieving Congress the day before Thanksgiving, "We have talked long enough in this country about equal rights. We have talked for a hundred years or more." Johnson's addresses to Congress in 1963 and 1964 called on the country and lawmakers to enact Kennedy's unfinished agenda. He emphasized the need to eliminate the blight of poverty. He declared "unconditional war on poverty in America. . . . [W]e shall not rest until that war is won."

Johnson threw himself into the struggle to enact the civil rights law Kennedy had introduced in the summer of 1963. In the first six months of 1964, he pleaded with and badgered members of Congress to pass the law. He overcame the inclination of some Republican senators to join with southern Democrats to filibuster the bill when he told Everett Dirksen, the Republican Senate leader, that the party of Abraham Lincoln could not be seen as standing in the way of civil rights. In July, Johnson signed the most sweeping civil rights law since Reconstruction, the **Civil Rights Act of 1964**. It outlawed segregation in restaurants, overnight accommodations, and transportation. It created the Fair Employment Practices Commission that could sue to guarantee equal opportunity in hiring and promotion in private firms with more than 99 workers. The law gave the Justice Department the power to file a suit when a person's civil rights were violated. The law also outlawed discrimination on the basis of sex as well as race.

Enactment of the Civil Rights Act occurred as the presidential election campaign got underway. Johnson—who easily defeated the Republican candidate, Arizona senator **Barry Goldwater**—campaigned, he said, to become "president of all the people." Johnson won 61.1 percent of the popular vote (43.1 million) and 486 electoral votes to Goldwater's 38.1 percent (27.2 million) and 52 electoral votes. The president carried every state with the exception of Goldwater's Arizona and five states in the Old Confederacy.

Barry Goldwater's acceptance speech, Republican National Convention, July 1964

On election night, it appeared as if Johnson and the Democrats had cemented a durable majority in favor of political liberalism and an active federal government. Despite the size of Johnson's victory, however, there were ominous signs for the future of the Democrats as the majority party and portents of hope for Republicans. Goldwater's nomination represented the triumph of newly assertive western conservatism. Unlike the Republican presidential nominees from 1940 to 1960, who had endorsed the idea of a federal government that would take responsibility for the country's economic and social well-being, Goldwater and his supporters considered the federal government an adversary of personal liberty. Western conservatives chafed at the extent of federal ownership of millions of square miles of the West and railed against the federal land managers. Control of federal lands became a cornerstone of broader arguments against federal power in the coming decades.

After the election, Johnson pressed forward with voting rights laws. In the spring of 1965, Martin Luther King, Jr., and SNCC led demonstrations in Selma, Alabama, to demand the right to vote. Fifteen thousand voting-age African Americans lived in Selma, but only 355 were registered voters. Would-be African American voters faced the prospect of losing their jobs or homes or even their lives if they applied to vote. Those brave enough to attempt registering faced hostile officials who rejected voter application forms if the would-be black registrant failed to cross a *t* or dot an *i*. Registrars asked black, but not white, applicants complicated questions, such as, "What two rights does a person have after being indicted by a grand jury?" or "How many bubbles are there in a bar of soap?"

Over 3,000 demonstrators demanding the right to vote were arrested in January and February 1965. Sheriff's deputies knocked a woman to the ground and singed the skin of demonstrators with electric cattle prods. In response to the brutality, King and **John Lewis** of SNCC planned a 56-mile march from Selma to Birmingham. On Sunday, March 7, with television crews filming, 600 demonstrators assembled at the Edmund Pettis Bridge at the edge of Selma, where they faced dozens of sheriff's deputies. Sheriff Jim Clark gave the demonstrators two minutes to disperse before ordering horse-mounted deputies into the crowd. They fired tear gas and swung bullwhips and rubber tubes wrapped with barbed wire at the demonstrators.

On March 15, Johnson addressed Congress on the need for voting rights. He recalled his days as a schoolteacher in rural Texas in 1928 where his poor, mostly Mexican American students often arrived without breakfast. "They knew even in their youth the pain of injustice. . . . Somehow you never forget what poverty and hatred can do when you see its scars in the hopeful face of a young child." He called on Americans to "overcome the crippling legacy of bigotry and injustice" and demand that Congress pass the Voting Rights Act.

In the summer of 1965, Congress responded to the widespread public revulsion at the displays of racism by enacting the Voting Rights Act. Under its terms, which

Table 27.1 African American Voter Registration

This chart shows 1960s changes in African American voter registration. No single issue sparked more intense civil rights activism and opposition than the simple effort to register African American voters. Segregationists feared the inevitable transformation of regional politics that would follow full democratic participation across the South. Grassroots civil rights activists put their lives on the line demanding this fundamental right.

| | BLACK | | WHITE | |
	REGISTERED	VOTED	REGISTERED	VOTED
1964	Not available	58.5	Not available	70.7
1966	60.2	41.7	71.7	57.0
1968	66.2	57.6	75.4	69.1

outlawed literacy tests to vote, the Justice Department had the power directly to register voters in districts where discrimination existed. Justice Department officials also monitored the conduct of elections on polling days. The **Voting Rights Act of 1965** succeeded in dramatically increasing African American voter participation (Table 27.1). In fact, such supervision of the polls became a common international practice over the next decades. Independent election watchers representing international organizations, nongovernmental organizations, and the U.S. and other governments observed elections in countries new to electoral politics or with histories of voting rights abuses.

Passage of the Voting Rights Act also deepened the racial divide between the major parties. Newly registered African American voters overwhelmingly voted for Democratic Party candidates. In the Deep South, white voters increasingly voted Republican rather than Democratic. From the 1980s to the early 21st century, southern states became the most heavily Republican region of the country.

Great Society Programs

In his first State of the Union address in January 1964, President Johnson declared "unconditional war on poverty." Later, during the 1964 election campaign, he painted a glorious vision of a Great Society where there was "abundance and liberty for all . . . an end to poverty and racial injustice . . . a place where every child can find knowledge to enrich his mind and to enlarge his talents." The Congress that convened in January 1965 had the largest Democratic Party majority since 1937. Over the next two years, it enacted the most far-reaching economic and social laws since the New Deal.

In 1948, President Harry Truman had proposed government-sponsored universal health insurance, similar to government-sponsored health plans that had been enacted in western Europe. The medical profession strongly opposed Truman's plan, and it was never approved. By the 1960s, elderly Americans were among the poorest people in the country, primarily because of their mounting health bills. In 1965, Congress passed **Medicare**, a health plan providing universal hospital insurance for Americans over 65. Medicare also included voluntary insurance to cover doctors' fees and nursing home charges. In 1966, Congress created **Medicaid**, a system in which the federal government provided states matching grants to pay for medical costs of poor people of all ages.

Medicare helped reduce poverty among the elderly, and both programs narrowed the gap in health care between the rich and the poor.

In 1965 and 1966, Congress enacted a wide array of programs designed directly to eliminate poverty. It created the Office of Economic Opportunity, headed by Sargent Shriver, the first director of the Peace Corps, to supervise the war on poverty. Congress also created food stamps to feed people whose income fell below the government-calculated poverty level. A later study concluded that federal food programs had been "almost fully effective in reducing flagrant malnutrition." Congress created the Head Start program to provide preschool for children of poor families. The Job Corps, modeled on the Civilian Conservation Corps of the New Deal, employed 100,000 poor young men and women during its first eight years. Volunteers in Service to America (VISTA), patterned on the Peace Corps, recruited people to work in poverty-stricken areas in the United States. An ambitious **Model Cities** program was designed to encourage physical and economic revitalization of the nation's poorest urban areas; however, infighting among local and federal officials and lack of funds caused by the growing Vietnam War hampered its success. Congress created the cabinet Department of Transportation and Department of Housing and Urban Development to oversee programs to improve urban life.

Great Society programs also addressed the quality of life of middle-income and wealthy Americans. The National Foundation for the Arts and Humanities, patterned on the larger National Science Foundation created in 1950, provided federal grants to individuals and institutions such as universities, museums, theaters, orchestras, ballet companies, and local arts councils. Congress created the Corporation for Public Broadcasting (CPB). It provided funds for notable television series such as *Sesame Street* (translated into many languages and broadcast around the world), *Nova*, and *The American Experience*.

In 1965, Congress ended the national quota system for immigration in place since the 1920s. After World War II, advocates for refugees denounced the quota system for denying Jews entry into the United States before the war—a stance that led to their eventual murder. Nevertheless, in 1952, in the midst of fears of communism, Congress passed, over President Truman's veto, an immigration law that retained the quotas and added restrictions on the entry of political radicals. The 1965 immigration law replaced that system and allowed 170,000 immigrants from the Eastern Hemisphere and 120,000 from the Western Hemisphere to enter the United States each year. When Johnson signed the bill, he said it ended "the harsh injustice of the national origins quota system," which was "a cruel and enduring wrong."

The 1965 law changed the source of U.S. immigration from Europe to Asia and the Western Hemisphere (Figure 27.1). A provision, little noticed at the time, permitted an unlimited number of visas for family unification. An immigration chain developed. An international student would earn an advanced degree in the United States, which entitled him or her to bring siblings, parents, a spouse, and children. These, in turn, could ask that their relatives be granted visas. Before passage of the law, Europe and Canada contributed nearly half of the immigrants to the United States. By the late 1970s, Europe and Canada accounted for 20 percent of legal immigrants, whereas Latin America and Asia made up 77 percent of immigrants.

Great Society reforms were popular at first, but enthusiasm faded in the last two years of Johnson's presidency. African American uprisings against police brutality,

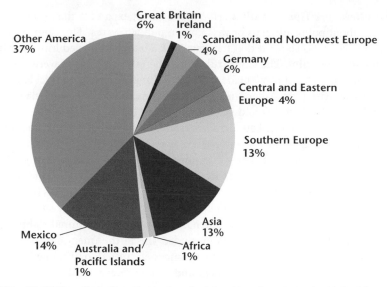

FIGURE 27.1 **1960s immigration** Countries of origin of immigrants to the United States after 1965. The 1965 immigration law reversed the harsh quota system that had limited immigration for half a century. The law enabled a new wave of immigration from Asia and the Pacific Rim and Latin America.

poverty, and continuing racial discrimination in major cities left dozens dead at the hands of police and National Guard units sent in by governors to quell the violence. Nearly all the dead were African Americans. The scenes of burning stores and sounds of gunshots and police sirens, played endlessly on television news, alarmed many whites. They expressed this "white backlash" by rejecting the Great Society and voting for Republican candidates who promised to restore law and order. Republicans replaced Democratic majorities in the congressional election of 1966. During the rest of his term, Johnson was able to persuade Congress to pass only one more major piece of social reform legislation. In 1968, after the Federal Commission on Civil Disorders reported that the United States was in danger of becoming two nations, one white and one black, separate and unequal, Congress passed the Fair Housing Law banning racial discrimination in public and private housing.

Marian Wright testifies to Congress on the war on poverty (1967)

The Supreme Court and Rights and Liberties

The Supreme Court played a major role in expanding civil rights and liberties to people and groups formerly ignored or excluded from the protection of the Constitution. It broadly defined the rights of expression, defined the rights of criminal defendants, and enhanced the right of privacy. The Court's 1960s decisions coincided with popular movements for greater personal freedom. The rulings also provoked significant resistance from many Americans who believed that they undermined the authority of police or religious institutions. Opposition to the Warren Court's expansion of rights and liberties became a significant element of the renewal of conservatism during the later 1960s.

In *New York Times v. Sullivan* (1964), the Court expanded the rights of news media to write about public officials or well-known public figures. The Court ruled against a public official who claimed that the *New York Times* had libeled him by printing false statements about him. The Court ruled that the false statements were trivial and only "recklessly false statements" made with "actual malice" violated libel laws. The Court also clarified the First Amendment's "establishment of a religion" clause with *Engel v. Vitale* (1962), which banned governments and local school boards from requiring prayers in public schools. Later in the decade, it ruled that schools could not require devotional readings of the Bible.

Several decisions of the 1960s expanded the rights of criminal defendants. In *Mapp v. Ohio* (1961), the Court declared that state and local courts must exclude from trial evidence gathered outside the terms of a search warrant. In *Gideon v. Wainwright* (1963), it ruled that a defendant was entitled to a defense lawyer; if he or she could not afford one, the state would provide one. The most controversial criminal rights decision was **Miranda v. Arizona** (1966), which expanded the Fifth Amendment's prohibition on self-incrimination. The Court held that someone arrested for a crime had to be clearly informed of the right to remain silent and to be represented by a lawyer. The Court also determined that the Constitution protected an inherent right to privacy; thus, in *Griswold v. Connecticut* (1965), the Court made ownership of contraceptives legal as a private matter.

Johnson appointed liberal justices committed to the Warren Court's expansion of civil rights and liberties. In the summer of 1967, he nominated **Thurgood Marshall**, who became the first African American Supreme Court justice in U.S. history. Even at the time of Marshall's confirmation, however, a backlash against the Supreme Court was underway. Conservative legal scholars and political activists argued that recognition of rights for people formerly excluded from protection harmed the majority. Future presidential appointments to the Supreme Court ignited angry controversies, as conservatives sought to reverse the Court's expansion of rights and liberals tried to maintain them.

The United States and the World Beyond Vietnam

The rise and fall of the Great Society and growing controversies over the war in Vietnam absorbed most of President Lyndon Johnson's attention. Still, he tried with mixed success to continue the efforts of earlier administrations to project American power around the globe and to expand Kennedy's efforts to reduce tensions with the Soviet Union. As a result, the United States became involved in regional disputes in Latin America, the Middle East, and Europe.

In Latin America, the Johnson administration minimized Kennedy's efforts to foster social reform. It supported military governments if they faced Communist insurrections. In April 1965, the United States intervened militarily in the Dominican Republic to support a military government that had ousted a popularly elected president, Juan Bosch. The U.S. embassy in Santo Domingo, the capital city, falsely claimed that 58 "identified and prominent Communist and Castroite leaders" were maneuvering to bring Bosch back from his temporary exile in Puerto Rico. Johnson ordered the Marines to the Dominican Republic to put down Bosch's supporters and bolster the military government. He explained that "people outside the Dominican Republic are seeking to gain control."

The military intervention set off protests throughout Latin America and in the United States. Bosch complained, "This was a democratic revolution, crushed by the leading democracy in the world." In the United States, liberals decried the military operation as a throwback to the bad old days of gunboat diplomacy of the late 19th and early 20th centuries. Combined with growing anxieties over the expanding U.S. role in fighting the Vietnam War, these misgivings undermined trust in Johnson's truthfulness.

American preoccupation with the Vietnam War contributed to the outbreak and bitter aftermath of the Six-Day War of June 1967 between Israel and the Arab states of Egypt, Syria, and Jordan. In the spring of 1967, Egyptian president Gamal Abdel Nasser insisted that the United Nations remove its forces from the Sinai Peninsula, which had separated Israel and Egypt since Israel's attack on Egypt in 1956. After the UN force withdrew, Nasser closed the Strait of Tiran to ships bound for Israel. The Johnson administration urged Israel not to respond until the United States could organize an international naval force to open the strait. European nations, declining to join, believed that the United States, preoccupied in Vietnam, would not open the strait. The Israelis grew impatient with the delay and on June 5 launched a preemptive strike against Egypt. Jordan and Syria then entered the war against Israel. In six days, Israel took Sinai and the Gaza Strip from Egypt, the West Bank of the Jordan River and East Jerusalem from Jordan, and the Golan Heights from Syria. The United Nations Security Council called for Israel to withdraw from captured territories in return for peace and security within recognized borders. It also called for a settlement of the Palestinian problem.

The aftermath of the war did bring Soviet prime minister **Alexei Kosygin** to New York for a special session of the UN General Assembly. Kosygin then met with Johnson in the first summit conference since Kennedy and Khrushchev met in Vienna in June 1961. Johnson pressed Kosygin for help in ending the Vietnam War, but the Soviet leader declined. He was competing with the People's Republic of China for the favor of the North Vietnamese. He did not wish to appear less committed to North Vietnam's war aims than were the Chinese.

Johnson and Kosygin agreed to intensify their efforts to end the competition in intercontinental ballistic missiles. In August 1968, the Johnson administration was preparing to announce that the president would visit Leningrad in September to confer on arms control. On August 20, however, the Soviet Union sent its armed forces into Prague, Czechoslovakia, to stop Czechoslovakia's efforts to loosen Communist controls. *Pravda*, the newspaper of the Soviet Communist Party, justified the invasion and occupation of Czechoslovakia as an act of solidarity designed to prevent a friendly Communist state from falling "into the process of antisocialist degeneration." European and American newspapers called this reasoning the "Brezhnev Doctrine," after Soviet Communist Party chairman **Leonid Brezhnev**. Johnson canceled his visit to the Soviet Union, and the efforts to relax tensions with the Soviet Union once more failed.

STUDY QUESTIONS FOR THE GREAT SOCIETY

1. What factors led to the passage of the civil rights and voting rights laws?
2. Explain the rise and the subsequent decline of support for the Great Society.
3. In what ways did the Johnson administration continue, and in what ways did it alter, the foreign policies of the Kennedy administration?

quiz

⚙ A ROBUST ECONOMY

In the early and mid-1960s, the economy of the United States boomed, technology advanced, and the quality of life for many Americans rose steadily. Between 1961 and 1965, average yearly economic growth exceeded 5 percent. Unemployment dropped to under 4 percent by 1966. By the end of the decade, however, the public's mood had soured as economic growth fell to under 4 percent and inflation, tame since the late 1940s, exceeded 6 percent per year. Many Americans feared that the prosperity of the early part of the decade would not last. Their pessimism that their children's lives would not be better than their own intensified racial, regional, and class tensions.

Technological Change, Science, and Space Exploration

Technological innovations, from space travel to domestic marvels, gave many Americans a sense that they were living in the golden age of the Industrial Revolution. Color television and other new electronics transformed home entertainment for the average American. By 1970, 96 percent of families had at least one TV at home. Satellites originally developed as part of the space program provided the infrastructure for telephone systems, television networks, military surveillance, and weather forecasting. By the end of the decade, the integrated circuit microchip began to appear, although it would have its greatest impact on the personal computer revolution of a later period. And, in the later 1960s, government scientists developed an early version of the Internet, which promoted communications inside the Defense Department and among government research labs.

The American economy, growing every month from 1961 to 1969, enhanced the material well-being of many at home, whereas it sparked an economic nationalist backlash in other countries. The stock market also performed remarkably in the first half of the decade. American industrial exports surged. Chrysler, the third-largest U.S. automaker, sold more cars in France than did all French car manufacturers combined. In 1967, French journalist Jean-Jacques Servan-Schreiber published *The American Challenge*. Translated into many languages and widely read throughout Europe, *The American Challenge* predicted that Europe was becoming an economic and cultural satellite of the United States.

The 1950s marked a high point for American faith in science, and Americans continued to value scientific and technological advancement through the 1960s. In other ways, though, they grew more skeptical. Americans celebrated the discovery of pulsars, quarks, and quasars—even if they had little practical impact on daily life, and many did not really understand what they were. They were also encouraged by medical breakthroughs such as the first successful heart transplant, improved vaccinations for children, and the possibility of new treatments for cancer, diabetes, and kidney disease.

Yet American confidence in science and technology began to waver over the course of the decade. Again, the Vietnam War played a critical role. Superior technology could not deliver victory on the battlefield, where the military unleashed the latest innovations. As had occurred after the use of the atomic bomb during World War II, some citizens expressed concern over the ways scientific knowledge and academic research were being used to bring death and destruction. Other skeptics thought that unquestioned reliance on scientific or technological solutions had created a dehumanized "technocracy" that failed to address serious social problems. Many also began to worry about the scale of government-funded science and the rise of what historian and philosopher

Lewis Mumford called "megamachines": systems in which humans were simply life-less components in staggeringly complex technological societies. Mumford had warned Americans about "technocracy" in the 1930s and more forcefully in his 1967 classic, *The Myth of the Machine*. Starting in the late 1950s, a back-to-the-land movement eventually sent millions in search of a simpler and more natural life in communes, on farms, and in rural hinterlands. The National Book Award–winning *Whole Earth Catalog* (1968) was a bible for these modern frontier people, advising on simple living and promoting tools and small-scale "appropriate technologies" such as solar water heaters.

One area where scientific and technological advancement enjoyed continued popularity was the "space race" between the United States and the Soviet Union. Americans saw the space race as a vital arena in the Cold War. Americans were still reeling from the embarrassment caused by *Sputnik*, the first successful satellite in space, launched by the Soviets in 1957. A nervous Congress responded in 1958 by creating the National Aeronautics and Space Administration (NASA) to coordinate U.S. efforts. Despite NASA's Mercury program, which concentrated on sending an American astronaut into outer space, the Soviet Union once again beat the United States to the punch when cosmonaut Yuri Gagarin became the first person to reach outer space and the first to orbit Earth in April 1961. Only in February 1962 did the Americans match this feat when astronaut Alan B. Shepard became the first American in space and astronaut **John Glenn** successfully orbited Earth.

Still, both *Sputnik* and Gagarin's successful trip raised the political stakes. Early in his presidency, Kennedy addressed the competition for space supremacy by promising to land a man on the Moon by the end of the decade. In May 1961, he told a joint session of Congress that it was "time for this nation to take a clearly leading role in space achievement, which in many ways may hold the key to our future on earth." The Apollo program, responsible for achieving Kennedy's goal, garnered a $20 billion budget and captured the public imagination. On July 20, 1969, in the midst of the tumultuous late 1960s, the nation rejoiced when the crew of the *Apollo 11* mission touched down on the Moon. Astronaut Neil Armstrong became the first human to set foot on another part of the solar system. His first words echoed across the Earth, "That's one small step for man, one giant leap for mankind." The symbolic planting of the American flag on the Moon staked out new territory for the Cold War, but the astronauts also placed a coded silicon disc with a message of peace from 73 nations of Earth.

President John F. Kennedy, "Special Message to the Congress on Urgent National Needs" (May 1961)

LUNAR SALUTE Edwin "Buzz" Aldrin salutes the U.S. flag on the surface of the moon during the *Apollo 11*, mission on July 20, 1969.

The Rise of the Sunbelt

The space race also accelerated a shift in the nation's population and its political and economic strength from the North and East to the South and West, a region called the Sunbelt (Map 27.3). During World War II, western states had benefited from over $30 billion in defense contracts and more than $2 billion in federal investment. Heavy military spending continued in the West during the Cold War, and it expanded to the South, with its hospitable climate, through the construction of new military bases. Together with huge NASA-related expenditures, such as space centers in Houston and near Cape Canaveral, Florida, these developments quickly reshaped the regions.

In addition to the new aerospace and defense jobs, related booms in computer and other high-tech firms, along with accompanying boosts in the service and banking industries, combined to make the **Sunbelt** the fastest-growing section of the country (Figure 27.2). The West had 75 percent of the country's 30 most rapidly developing urban areas during the 1950s and 50 percent in the 1960s. The West, already the most urbanized part of the country, experienced a huge increase of urban residents. Moreover, between 1950 and 1970, median family income in western metropolitan areas almost tripled.

Developers and local politicians attracted business to the Sunbelt by highlighting the cheap, nonunion labor; available land; low taxes; and minimal regulation in the region. Air-conditioned homes and numerous recreational options also attracted retirees from the North and Midwest to the Sunbelt. Workers moved to the Sunbelt to find new manufacturing or white-collar jobs. Development in the South and West came at significant cost to the natural environment. Hundreds of thousands of acres of farmland and forest disappeared as suburbs expanded outward and towns grew into major cities. The explosive population growth demanded new water projects for irrigation and electricity. Dams and reservoirs across the Sunbelt permanently flooded thousands of acres of virgin land, changed the source of ancient rivers, and endangered hundreds of plant and animal species.

Excerpt from Neil Morgan, Westward Tilt: The American West Today (1963)

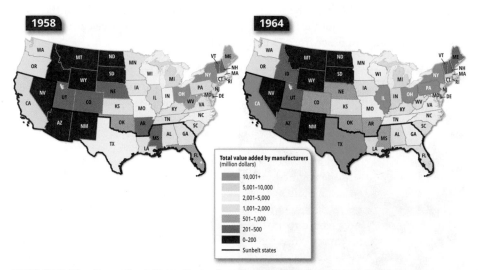

MAP 27.3 The Growth of Manufacturing in the Sunbelt This map indicates the industrial and economic growth in the Sunbelt states during the 1960s.

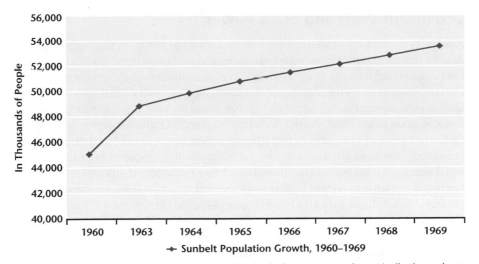

FIGURE 27.2   Sunbelt population growth The Sunbelt states grew dramatically throughout the 1950s–1960s. World War II industrialized the West and sparked a mass migration to the Sunbelt states of the West and South. Generally low taxes, business-friendly politics, and sunny weather attracted corporations, retirees, and workers, shifting the economic and political balance of the nation. Growing opportunity and influence pulled millions of legal and illegal immigrants to these states, sparking another wave of debate about immigrants, labor, and the law.

STUDY QUESTIONS FOR A ROBUST ECONOMY

1. Why did the U.S. economy expand briskly in the 1960s?

2. Who benefited from the decade's legal precedents?

3. Why did the Sunbelt grow in the 1960s?

quiz

RACE, GENDER, YOUTH, AND THE CHALLENGE TO THE ESTABLISHMENT

American culture, social life, and politics underwent a radical transformation during the 1960s. Groups that traditionally had little power challenged traditional authorities and ways of ordering work, education, families, and private life. People of color insisted on civil rights. They also forged new ethnic and racial identities. A new feminist movement arose to demand economic and social equality and sexual freedom for women. Opposition to the war in Vietnam, which reached a crescendo during the climactic year of 1968, profoundly influenced the course of other protest movements.

Many young people came to see themselves as constrained by an uncaring society dominated by a self-satisfied establishment. Their exuberant flowering of racial, gender, sexual, and cultural protest—a **counterculture**—excited millions. The counterculture also provoked a fierce backlash from an equal if not larger number of Americans.

Urban Uprisings and Black Power

Advocates for civil rights altered their tactics during the 1960s. In the beginning of the decade, traditional civil rights organizations such as the NAACP and the National Urban League employed lawsuits, sit-ins, and mass demonstrations to highlight the moral injustices of segregation. By the middle of the decade, the focus had shifted from the struggle against legal segregation in the South to other forms of racial discrimination across the country. Many urban blacks outside the South felt that civil rights legislation failed to solve their most pressing problems. Young African Americans believed racial discrimination prevented them from fair access to jobs, housing, credit, transportation, education, and equal treatment from police. They thought that traditional civil rights organizations paid too much attention to ending legal segregation and too little to the crushing burden of poverty. More militant African American groups such as the Congress of Racial Equality, the Student Nonviolent Coordinating Committee, and the Nation of Islam rejected the style of traditional civil rights leaders as weak, accommodating, and unsuccessful. More militant, often younger African Americans advocated what they called **Black Power**—a

RACE RIOTS An army vehicle patrols 12th Street in Detroit, Michigan, during a race riot on July 25, 1967; 43 people died in race riots during the miserable summer of 1967. Images of military vehicles and combat troops in the streets of burning American cities demonstrated the fragility of the social coalitions that had so recently united in support of civil rights.

combination of racial pride and forceful, even violent resistance to anti-black violence. This more militant assertion of rights and willingness to use "whatever means necessary" split the civil rights coalition. It also produced and intensified the white backlash against political, social, and economic gains by African Americans.

The civil rights movement experienced a major turning point in 1965. On August 11, five days after Johnson signed the Voting Rights Act into law, violence broke out in the Watts neighborhood of Los Angeles. A crowd protesting the arrest of a young African American driver began to throw rocks and bottles at police in the streets of this poor, African American section of the city. For the next six days, thousands of residents set fires, looted white-owned businesses, attacked white drivers, and fought the more than 15,000 police and National Guardsmen requested by California officials to restore order. The outburst resulted in 34 people dead, nearly all of them African American, over 1,000 injured, and more than 4,000 arrested. The shocking violence of Watts terrified and confused white Americans, but many African Americans understood the frustration and rage that was expressed there.

Rioting continued in major American cities throughout the rest of the 1960s. In 1966, the National Guard patrolled Cleveland, Chicago, Milwaukee, and other cities. In 1967, a particularly "long hot summer" resulted in 164 conflicts, including eight major riots. The most intense clashes occurred in Newark and Detroit, where 43 people died, most of them shot by police or National Guardsmen. The *Washington Post* lamented, "In Detroit this week, America lost what was left of her innocence. . . . [C]ivil society fell apart." Conservative and middle-class whites, often blaming the riots on outside agitators and undisciplined black youth looking for a thrill, wanted police to act forcefully against rioters. They turned against the urban social programs of the Great Society, which they thought rewarded rioters and threatened their suburbs.

By the mid-1960s, some younger civil rights activists had grown frustrated with the nonviolent, integrationist approach of moderate leaders. Continued violence against blacks, extreme poverty, and the slow pace of change drove them to embrace more radical measures. In 1966, SNCC leader **Stokely Carmichael** announced, "The only way we gonna stop them white men from whuppin' us is to take over. We've been saying *freedom* for six years—and we ain't got nothin'. What we gonna start saying now is 'Black Power!' '!"

Carmichael and others turned to the black nationalist ideas of the minister **Malcolm X** for inspiration. After his release from prison in 1952 for petty larceny, Malcolm had joined the Nation of Islam, often referred to as the "Black Muslims." Malcolm promoted separatism because, he believed, white racism would never end. He also encouraged pride in African Americans' cultural heritage, supporting black businesses and self-defense. Later, Malcolm left the Nation of Islam, embraced traditional Islam, moderated his anti-white stance slightly, and formed the Organization for Afro-American Unity. What he might have accomplished will never be known because in early 1965 he was assassinated by three Black Muslims who were angry that he had left their organization.

Malcom X, "The Negro Revolt, and Where Do We Go From Here?" (1964)

Although SNCC served as the early leading Black Power group, the **Black Panther Party** gained the most notoriety. Founded in Oakland in 1966 by Huey Newton and Bobby Seale, members of the Black Panthers advocated black self-determination and armed self-defense against police brutality. Their shootouts with police—which resulted in several deaths on both sides—captured the close attention of the media and frightened many whites. Although they also developed health, education, and nutrition programs, their influence faded by the early 1970s.

STOKELY CARMICHAEL GIVING BLACK POWER SPEECH, JULY 24, 1967 Disenchanted with violence in Vietnam and incomplete civil rights achievements at home, Carmichael helped found the Black Power movement advocating more radical means of achieving racial equality. Speaking about Vietnam and civil rights in New York City, he said, "Bigotry and death over here is no different than bigotry and death over there." In dress and message, Black Power advocates like Carmichael were completely different from MLK. They offered a powerful image to those activists ready to forcefully demand their rights while frightening some of the moderates who had supported the earlier movement.

Excerpt from Stokely Carmichael (Kwame Touré), *Stokely Speaks: Black Power to Pan-Africanism* (1971)

The civil rights struggle and the Black Power movement had worldwide impact. After Carmichael stepped down as the chairman of SNCC in 1967, he traveled widely in Africa and married the South Africa singer Miriam Makeba, an outspoken opponent of apartheid, South Africa's policy of legal segregation. Carmichael eventually settled in the West African country of Guinea, where he became an advisor to the nation's prime minister. He changed his name to Kwame Toure, in honor of two heroes of African decolonization, Kwame Nkrumah of Ghana and Sekou Toure of Guinea. The black majority of South Africa took special notice of both the nonviolent and the militant forms of the American civil rights movement. The brutality of apartheid attracted the attention of American civil rights advocates. In June 1966, Robert F. Kennedy, now a senator from New York and growing ever more estranged from Lyndon Johnson over the Vietnam War, visited South Africa and denounced apartheid. He urged racially mixed audiences to follow the nonviolent approach of the protesters of the early 1960s.

Many African Americans who subscribed to "Black Power" took a less violent approach than the Black Panthers. In 1968, soul singer James Brown encouraged listeners, as his song title indicates, to "Say It Loud—I'm Black and I'm Proud." African Americans celebrated their heritage through the cultural nationalism of the Black Arts movement. The "Afro" hairstyle became a way for blacks to distinguish themselves from mainstream white fashion standards and declare, "Black is beautiful." A large number of whites, however, perceived Black Power only in its most sensational forms, which alienated them from supporting African American efforts and spawned the "white backlash" mentioned previously.

Latinos and Indians Struggle for Rights

The energy of the African American civil rights movement inspired members of other traditionally excluded groups to demand equality. Latinos and Indians began the decade with moderate tactics of strikes, boycotts, and demonstrations. Later in the 1960s, each group developed its own versions of protest inspired by the militancy and energy of the Black Power movement.

The economic situation of Latinos was at least as dire as that of African Americans. In 1960, one-third of Mexican Americans lived below the poverty line, and the unemployment rate for Latinos was double that of whites. Latino children attended some of the country's worst schools, where few of the teachers spoke or understood Spanish.

The movement for rights for Mexican Americans burst into international prominence in 1965 when 5,000 members of the National Farm Workers Association (NFWA) joined a *huelga*, or strike, against grape growers in Delano, California. **Cesar Chavez** and **Delores Huerta**, two charismatic leaders of the NFWA, led a nationwide boycott of the purchase of grapes to force the growers to recognize the union. The grape boycott spread across the Atlantic to the United Kingdom. The strike went on for five years until the growers signed a contract recognizing the NFWA as the pickers' representative. Chavez became an international leader for newly empowered Mexican Americans. His marches drew hundreds of sympathetic whites. He became a close friend of Robert F. Kennedy. Chavez, like Martin Luther King, Jr., used Christian imagery and nonviolent tactics. He saw himself as part of an international Catholic movement for social justice.

CESAR CHAVEZ, ORGANIZER AND LEADER OF THE NATIONAL FARM WORKERS ASSOCIATION, AT A SAFEWAY BOYCOTT   Chavez successfully called for a nationwide boycott of nonunion-picked grapes and helped launch a civil rights movement.

Flag of the National Farm Workers Association

The NFWA's standard bore a stylized drawing of a black Aztec eagle, which became a symbol of Mexican American pride. Other Latinos advocated cultural nationalism similar to the Black Power movement. They found Chavez too committed to nonviolence and too eager to gain support from sympathetic white liberals. They described themselves as **Chicanos**, appropriating what traditionally had been an ethnic slur used against them. In the late 1960s, the Chicano movement grew across the Southwest and West.

In New Mexico, **Reies Lopez Tijerina** formed the *Alianza Federal de Mercedes* (Federal Alliance of Land Grants) in 1962 to demand that the government make good on its promise in the 1848 Treaty of Guadalupe Hidalgo to respect Mexicans' rights to land annexed by the United States. In June 1967, Tijerina led Chicano protesters into the federal courthouse in Rio Arriba County. In the gun battle that followed, two police officers were wounded. Tijerina was arrested and the *Alianza* broke up.

Ethnic identity and militancy also spread among Puerto Ricans, both on the island and in the cities of the Northeast where hundreds of thousands of Puerto Ricans lived. Some militant young Puerto Ricans described themselves as *boricua*; this term of ethnic pride, too, had previously been hurled as a racial insult at Puerto Ricans. In the mid-1960s, Puerto Rican activists in New York City created the Young Lords, patterned on the Black Panthers.

Indians were among the poorest Americans in 1960. About 200,000 Indians left reservations for cities after President Dwight Eisenhower ended "the status of Indians

ACTIVIST OCCUPATION Indian activists occupying Alcatraz in 1969. The abandoned prison off the coast of San Francisco was claimed by a coalition of Indian rights activists and student protestors in an effort to symbolically call attention to the occupation of Indian lands. They held the island for almost two years, bringing new attention to another "century of dishonor" in U.S. Indian policy.

as wards of the government" in 1953. This policy of termination stopped federal aid to reservations but did not replace it with support for Indians who moved to cities. In June 1961, 700 representatives from 64 different Indian nations met in Chicago to draft the Declaration of Indian Purpose. It stated that "we have the responsibility of preserving our precious heritage." The declaration marked the beginning of the Red Power movement.

The **American Indian Movement (AIM)** formed in Minneapolis in 1968. The organization was inspired by the November 1969 occupation of Alcatraz Island in San Francisco Bay, when hundreds of young Indian activists demanded that the federal government turn over ownership of the land. In the 1970s, AIM and other Indian advocacy groups staged several well-publicized protests. In November 1972, they took over the offices of the Bureau of Indian Affairs (BIA) in Washington, DC. In February 1973, AIM activists occupied the site of the 1890 Battle of Wounded Knee on the Pine Ridge Sioux Indian reservation of South Dakota. Richard Wilson, the president of the Oglala Sioux, denounced AIM as a band of "social misfits" and banned them from Pine Ridge. AIM, in turn, denounced Wilson and his tribal government as corrupt and vowed to stay at Wounded Knee until the federal government investigated what it called wholesale thievery and mismanagement at the BIA and in tribal councils. Federal marshals and AIM protesters faced off for 71 days. A gun battle in which two AIM activists were killed and a marshal was wounded ended the protest. Hundreds were arrested, and both sides claimed victory. Although the government agreed to investigate claims of corruption, it did so only decades after the occupation at Wounded Knee.

The New Feminism

Women also demanded greater equality in both public and private life. Many middle-class white women believed their lives were constrained amid the prosperity of the post–World War II boom. In 1963, writer **Betty Friedan** gave voice to these concerns in her book *The Feminine Mystique*. She identified "the problem that has no name," and she described how educated, middle-class women felt isolated and useless in the "comfortable concentration camp" of the suburban house. She argued for meaningful work for educated women at equal pay with men. The disaffection of middle-class housewives in the United States and Europe sparked fears of epidemic alcoholism and drug use, a concern widespread enough that it was the subject of the 1966 Rolling Stones hit song "Mother's Little Helper." In 1966, Friedan helped found the **National Organization for Women (NOW)**, which advocated an end to laws that discriminated against women, opportunity to work at any job, and equal pay for equal work. Some women veterans of the civil rights movement came to see the situation of women as resembling that of blacks.

National Organization of Women, "Statement of Purpose" (1966)

Changes in attitudes toward marriage and divorce enhanced the appeal of the new feminism. The family no longer seemed to be a safe haven from the heartless world of the 1960s. Divorce became more commonplace. Social workers and psychologists spoke out against violence by husbands against wives. Toward the end of the decade, analysts began to discuss a hitherto taboo subject—sexual abuse of children by older males in homes.

In 1967, women's rights activists began calling opposition to women's rights "sexism," similar to racism, and described "male chauvinism" as a key element blocking women's equality. They called for "women's liberation." NOW advocated the ratification of the Equal Rights Amendment (ERA) to the United States Constitution. First proposed

BETTY FRIEDAN ANNOUNCING A BOYCOTT OF PRODUCTS INSULTING WOMEN IN THEIR ADVERTISEMENTS, AUGUST 1970 In 1966, Friedan helped found the National Organization for Women (NOW) and became one of the most forceful advocates for meaningful work for educated women at equal pay with men.

in 1923, the ERA was a short declaration banning the denial or abridgment of rights on the basis of sex. Congress eventually adopted the ERA and sent it to the states for ratification; 35 states ratified the amendment, but it failed to achieve approval of the minimum of 38 state legislatures before a 1982 deadline. The new, or Second Wave, feminism inspired a global movement for women's rights. Large marches and rallies for gender equality occurred in cities such as Toronto, London, Berlin, Buenos Aires, Tokyo, and Sydney.

But feminism also encountered stiff opposition. Men who thought they might lose privileges, some middle-class housewives who worried that they would lose legal protections, and some traditional Christians who believed that the Bible sanctioned male leadership in the home resisted the new feminism. Conservative activist **Phyllis Schlafly**, one of Barry Goldwater's earliest supporters for the presidency, organized a grassroots movement opposed to ratification of the ERA. Many African American women and Latinas considered the push for women's rights a white middle-class movement that did not understand the problems of domestic workers or farmworkers raising children on their own.

Despite derision and the failure to ratify the ERA, women advanced in education and the workplace. In the 1970s and 1980s, courts struck down numerous statutes and regulations that limited women's rights to property, employment, and reproductive choices. By 1990, women held about half the nation's jobs, and they had moved in large numbers into professions such as law, medicine, dentistry, higher education teaching, and accounting. In most professions, the wage gap between men and women narrowed but remained. In 1970, women earned 59 cents for every dollar earned by men; by 2000, they earned 76 cents for every dollar, leaving much room for improvement. Even as some women with postgraduate degrees moved into highly paid occupations, however, the poverty rate for single mothers increased in the decades after the 1960s and remains a serious issue.

Environmentalism

During the 1960s, scholar activists exposed problems in the way citizens and corporations interacted with the natural environment. Scientist **Rachel Carson**'s bestseller *Silent Spring* (1962) alerted readers to the harmful effect of pesticides on bird and animal populations. Dramatic environmental disasters during the decade captured the public's attention. In 1969, the heavily polluted Cuyahoga River in Ohio caught fire. Oil fouled California beaches and smog blanketed cities across the country, causing health emergencies. Environmentalists focused on grassroots efforts and lobbying through long-established conservation groups such as the Sierra Club and new ones such as the Environmental Defense Fund, formed in 1967. New understandings of ecology and widespread public concern sparked political action. Congress passed the Wilderness Act in 1964, the National Wildlife Refuge System Administration Act in 1966, and the National Wild and Scenic Rivers Act and National Trails Act in 1968. It also enacted laws aimed at limiting pollution, such as an amendment to the Clean Air Act and the Water Quality Act in 1965.

On April 22, 1970, 20 million supporters gathered in cities across the country for the first Earth Day, the biggest public event in American history. Even President Richard Nixon and major corporations supported the initiative. During the Nixon administration, Congress created the Environmental Protection Agency (EPA) and Occupational Safety and Health Administration (OSHA) in 1970 to regulate and propose solutions, while environmental activists continued working both inside and outside of government channels. Increased awareness of environmental and behavioral threats to health affected government health programs. In January 1964, the U.S. Surgeon General confirmed the long-suspected belief that smoking increased the risk of lung cancer and heart disease. Over the next generation, the federal government gradually increased efforts to discourage tobacco use.

Earth Day poster, 1970

Countercultures

During the 1960s, young people played a larger role in the political, cultural, and social life of the United States than at any time before. Before 1965, a small minority of college students expressed their dissatisfaction with the political status quo and with college administration. By the end of the decade, student activism, deeply enmeshed in opposition to the war in Vietnam, had rocked campuses across the country. Young people also profoundly influenced trends in popular culture. Many experimented with alternative lifestyles during the second half of the decade. The most disaffected joined the commune movement, abandoning the status quo altogether in hopes of building a new society and new way of life, whereas thousands of other young Americans joined an international tribe of nomads on the "hippie trail" that led them across Europe to Turkey, India, and Nepal. Others simply wanted to have a good time wherever they were. Nearly everything they did startled or upset the older generation.

The most influential of the early student groups was Students for a Democratic Society (SDS), founded at the University of Michigan in 1960. Inspired by the protests of the civil rights movement, members of SDS advanced the idea of "participatory democracy" and militant nonviolence. They envisioned a society shaped by a far greater range of voices in both local and national decisions. SDS advocated grassroots activism to bring economic and racial justice to the United States and desired a less confrontational approach to the Cold War. The society's organizing principles, the "Port Huron Statement," adopted in 1962, began with this: "We are people of this generation, bred in at least modest comfort, housed in the universities, looking uncomfortably to the world we inherit." SDS led the **New Left**, groups of young activists who intentionally

The Republic of Rock

The remarkable rise of rock music demonstrated the power of the global youth movement. By the early 1970s, rock records made up 80 percent of all U.S. music sales and dominated the charts in Europe. In rock and roll, young people found a cultural medium that allowed them to rebel against traditional values. Rock music provided a rebellious soundtrack for the Vietnam War, both at home and in-country. Young Vietnamese who grew up surrounded by Americans adopted rock music and founded popular bands. Rock music became a powerful transnational "sonic space" transcending old cultural and political boundaries. These global connections were reflected in the "British Invasion" of the 1960s.

On February 7, 1964, the Beatles landed at Kennedy International Airport in New York and were greeted by several thousand screaming teenage girls. Two days later, the band from Liverpool, England, played to a hysterical studio audience on CBS's *The Ed Sullivan Show*. Seventy million people—still reeling emotionally from John F. Kennedy's assassination—tuned in to watch John Lennon, Paul McCartney, George Harrison, and Ringo Starr perform on television, which equaled more than 60 percent of the nation's television viewers. A similarly enormous television audience watched the Beatles' follow-up performance in Miami on the next week's *Ed Sullivan Show*. Before returning to England, where they were already adored, the band also played two sold-out concerts in New York and Washington, DC. In the span of nine days, Americans bought more than two million Beatles records and spent over $2.5 million on Beatles merchandise.

"Beatlemania" erupted in the United States in early 1964. Millions of Americans, particularly teenage girls of the baby boom generation, were smitten with the band's catchy songs; romantic lyrics; fashion sense; and wholesome but sexualized image, wit, and charm. Young men started growing their hair longer to copy their new idols and began wearing "Beatle boots." *A Hard Day's Night*, a film starring the band released in the summer of 1964, furthered their already extraordinary popularity and their reputation as likable young men. The Beatles seemed to represent freedom and fun to a generation of youth. For their part, the Beatles had found American music—especially Elvis Presley, Chuck Berry, rhythm and blues, and rockabilly—an escape from working-class life in postwar England.

The Beatles' popularity, paving the way for many other British rock bands, opened the insular American music market and initiated the "British Invasion." Throughout the

distanced themselves from the ideological infighting, communism, and labor organizing of the Old Left. International in its scope, the American New Left was heavily influenced by Socialist thinkers in Britain, France, and West Germany and by the Cuban revolution.

The New Left and the wider student movement grew slowly at first on campuses around the country and around the world. After the Free Speech movement at Berkeley in the fall of 1964, more students began to echo the same complaints toward their own universities. In addition to free speech, free political activity, curriculum reform, and opposition to the "military-industrial complex," students took on *in loco parentis*, decade, British bands thrived in the United States. Some drew their inspiration from Chicago blues artists such as Muddy Waters and Willie Dixon. The Rolling Stones, who took their name from a Waters song, became the most famous of these blues-based groups. Encouraged by their manager, who wanted people to think "the Stones were threatening, uncouth, and animalistic," the band adopted a rougher, more rebellious image than the Beatles. Another band, the Who, brought London's "mod" fashion scene to Americans, and the Animals had a number one hit in the United States and Great Britain with a reworked version of an American folk song, "The House of the Rising Sun." Ironically, American guitarist **Jimi Hendrix** had to establish himself in England before he gained recognition in the United States.

British and American musical artists fueled each other's creativity. American folk-singer Bob Dylan decided to "go electric" after hearing the Beatles. Dylan introduced the Beatles to marijuana and encouraged them to branch out musically and write more introspective lyrics. The result was the album *Rubber Soul* (1965), which inspired Brian Wilson of the Beach Boys to create the musically experimental *Pet Sounds* (1966). That album, a departure from the Beach Boys' earlier, more innocent songs in turn pushed the Beatles to produce their psychedelic *Sgt. Pepper's Lonely Hearts Club Band* in 1967. It was popular worldwide. A journalist reported that "in every city in Europe and America the stereo systems and the radio played ['Lucy in the Sky with Diamonds' from the album]. For a brief while the irreparably fragmented consciousness of the West was unified, at least in the minds of the young." *Sgt. Pepper* became part of the soundtrack of the so-called Summer of Love for the counterculture in San Francisco.

This artistic competition, as well as the growing influence of older blues and rock-and-roll musicians, created an international music scene that deeply affected popular culture on both sides of the Atlantic and around the globe. The historian Terry H. Anderson has noted that the British Invasion "demonstrated that rock and roll—although a uniquely American invention—was becoming the music of the international postwar baby boom: The sixties would not just be an American phenomenon."

- Beyond their catchy tunes, what explains the American embrace of the British Beatles?
- How was the emerging culture of rock music linked to global demographic trends?

the idea that colleges and universities acted in the place of one's parents. In particular, students rallied for changes—with moderate success—in old-fashioned rules regarding curfews, visiting hours, and housing organized by gender.

Mario Savio, "An End to History" (1964)

In the second half of the 1960s, young people unnerved mainstream society outside politics as well. Some rejected establishment values by advocating personal freedom above the older generation's emphasis on collective responsibility and materialism. Inspired by the Beats of the 1950s, their vanguard rejected the security and boredom of middle-class life to pursue a liberated, often hedonistic, lifestyle. These diverse counterculturalists also launched a significant resettlement of the West. Communes and

interactive timeline

TIMELINE 1960–1969

AMERICA	YEAR	THE WORLD
May FDA approves oral contraceptive pill Enovid for use as birth control **Feb** Sit-in at Woolworth's lunch counter, Greensboro, North Carolina **Nov** John F. Kennedy elected president over Richard M. Nixon	**1960**	**Dec** Creation of National Front for the Liberation of Vietnam (the Viet Cong)
May First freedom rider buses leave Washington, DC, heading across the South	**1961**	**Apr** Soviet cosmonaut Yuri Gagarin orbits Earth **Apr** Bay of Pigs invasion fails **Jun** Kennedy meets Khrushchev in Vienna **Aug** Construction of Berlin Wall begins
Feb U.S. astronaut John Glenn orbits Earth **Jun** Publication of Students for a Democratic Society's "Port Huron Statement" **Jun** Supreme Court ruling in *Engel v. Vitale* banning prayer in public schools **Sep** Publication of Rachel Carson's *Silent Spring* **Oct** James Meredith successfully integrates University of Mississippi **Oct** Cuban missile crisis	**1962**	**Oct** Soviets install missiles in Cuba
Feb Publication of Betty Friedan's *The Feminine Mystique* **Mar** Supreme Court ruling in *Gideon v. Wainwright* **Aug** March on Washington **Sep** 16th Street Baptist Church bombed in Birmingham, Alabama **Nov** Assassination of John F. Kennedy	**1963**	**May–Jun** Buddhist crisis in South Vietnam **Jun** Kennedy gives "*Ich bin ein Berliner*" speech in Berlin **Nov** Military coup deposes South Vietnamese president Ngo Dinh Diem
Jan Surgeon General says smoking causes lung cancer, beginning a decades-long antismoking movement **Mar** Supreme Court ruling in *New York Times v. Sullivan* **Jun–Aug** Mississippi Freedom Summer **Jul** Civil Rights Act bans racial discrimination in public accommodations **Oct–Dec** Free Speech movement at University of California, Berkeley **Nov** Lyndon Johnson elected president over Barry Goldwater	**1964**	**Feb** Beatles land at JFK International Airport, launching "British Invasion" **Apr** Malcolm X travels to Middle East and Mecca

settlements sprang up in and around towns such as Bolinas, California, and Taos, New Mexico. Hippies worked with locals to revive traditions with a psychedelic twist. Interesting coalitions between disaffected young people and local communities were common, but the influx of communards often strained local economies and created tensions with law enforcement. Ultimately, the counterculture migration fostered gentrification in towns like Aspen, Colorado, pushing out traditional residents. In cities, counterculturalists moved into blighted urban areas, setting the stage for historic preservation and urban gentrification in the coming decades.

Mind-altering drugs played a significant role in the countercultural awakening. Timothy Leary, a former professor of psychology at Harvard, promoted the use of the hallucinogenic drug LSD, commonly called acid, to help people "turn on, tune in, and drop out." The drug had first been tested by the U.S. military as a way to expand the minds of soldiers. Members of the counterculture, labeled "hippies" by the mainstream media, smoked marijuana and experimented with a wide range of drugs, new and old. They ushered in a "sexual revolution," celebrating casual sex and rejecting traditional Protestant prudishness, a development facilitated by the availability of the birth control pill in 1960. They sometimes grew their hair long and dressed flamboyantly in colorful

AMERICA	YEAR	THE WORLD
Feb–Mar Civil rights demonstration at Selma, Alabama **Feb** Murder of Malcolm X **Jun** Supreme Court ruling on *Griswold v. Connecticut* **Jul** Passage of Medicare **Aug** Passage of Voting Rights Act **Aug** Watts racial uprising	**1965**	**Apr** U.S. invasion and occupation of Dominican Republic
Jun Supreme Court decides *Miranda v. Arizona* **Jun** Robert F. Kennedy visits South Africa **Jun** Founding of NOW **Oct** Creation of Black Panthers **Oct** SNCC leader Stokely Carmichael calls for Black Power	**1966**	**May** Great Proletarian Cultural Revolution begins in China
Jun Release of the Beatles' *Sgt. Pepper's Lonely Hearts Club Band* **Jun–Aug** Summer of Love in San Francisco **Jun** Reies Tijerina leads raid on federal courthouse in Rio Arriba County, New Mexico **Jul** Detroit racial uprising increases racial divide **Aug** Thurgood Marshall becomes first African American Justice of Supreme Court **Sep** Formation of Brown Berets	**1967**	**May** Jean-Paul Sartre organizes International War Crime tribunal to judge U.S. conduct in Vietnam **Jun** Six-Day War between Israel, Egypt, Jordan, and Syria **Oct** Publication of Jean-Jacques Servan-Schreiber's *The American Challenge*
Apr Passage of Fair Housing Act **Aug** Woodstock music festival **Nov** Indian activists begin occupation of Alcatraz	**1968**	**Aug** Soviet invasion of Czechoslovakia in response to Prague uprisings **May** Student uprising in Paris leads to crippling nationwide general strike **Oct** Mexican troops kill hundreds of young people protesting the Olympic Games in Mexico City

clothes and beads. There was no typical "hippie," and the movement was far more complicated and diverse than the popular media or conservative critics presumed. For every hippie in psychedelic costumes there were hundreds of ordinary-looking Americans across the country who more quietly adopted the values and sensibilities of the counterculture.

Although countercultural communities developed in many cities and college towns, the Haight-Ashbury district of San Francisco served as the epicenter of the movement. In 1967, during the "Summer of Love," young men and women flocked to the Haight for free drugs, free music, and free love. By the end of the summer, however, serious problems had developed. The streets became overcrowded with drunk or stoned hippies, enterprising drug dealers, prostitutes, young runaways, and panhandlers. There were rapes, muggings, and chaos, all observed by thousands of tourists and locals who also flocked to the area to watch the weirdness. The dark side of the counterculture was immortalized in films such as Dennis Hopper's *Easy Rider* (1969), which showed both the hope and the despair of utopian escape in all its forms. As with earlier generations, the fantasy of new beginnings and escape proved hard to achieve.

Journalist Hunter S. Thompson describes Haight-Ashbury in 1967

TRIPS FESTIVAL Wes Wilson's op art Trips Festival poster perfectly captured the convergence of technological enthusiasm and psychedelic culture for an iconic countercultural event. The festival launched the careers of the Grateful Dead, master rock promoter Bill Graham, *One Flew over the Cuckoo's Nest* author and acid test promoter Ken Kesey and his Merry Pranksters, and Stewart Brand, publisher of the *Whole Earth Catalog*.

As the utopianism of the early counterculture faded, a generation of inventive counterculture veterans turned their energies to creating the framework of the new economy in the information age of the 1980s and 1990s. Computer pioneers like **Steve Jobs** used the creative energy of LSD and the counterculture to devise new products and business models. Others worked on sustainable energy technologies and ecological design.

Most teenagers and college students in the late 1960s, however, stayed away from radical politics and never committed to the more extreme countercultural rejections of mainstream society. Hollywood and savvy marketers catered to the youth market and cashed in on the popularity of countercultural ideas and imagery to sell their products.

STUDY QUESTIONS FOR RACE, GENDER, YOUTH, AND THE CHALLENGE TO THE ESTABLISHMENT

quiz

1. How did changes in the movement for the rights of African Americans affect other groups' struggles to advance their status in U.S. society?

2. Why did the counterculture appeal to millions of Americans?

3. Who opposed the increasing assertiveness of people of color, women, and youth?

Summary

- The 1960s began with great optimism that a prosperous country would solve long-standing problems of racial injustice and end poverty.
- The Kennedy and Johnson administrations continued earlier administrations' confrontation with the Communist world in the Cold War.
- President Lyndon B. Johnson's administration enacted an ambitious program of social reform.
- Science and technological innovation sparked a widespread economic boom.
- People of color, women, youth, and students created a robust counterculture as they challenged traditional authority.
- Public enthusiasm for social reform dissipated toward the end of the decade as more conservative Americans became alarmed at the culture of protest and rejected many of its aspects.

Key Terms and People

◁)))
audio
flashcards

Alianza Federal de Mercedes 960
Alliance for Progress 943
American Indian Movement (AIM) 961
Bay of Pigs invasion 944
Black Panther Party 957
Black Power 956
Brezhnev, Leonid 951
Carmichael, Stokely 957
Carson, Rachel 962
Castro, Fidel 943
Chavez, Cesar 959
Chicano 960
Civil Rights Act of 1964 945
counterculture 955
Cuban missile crisis 944
Earthrise 937
Friedan, Betty 961
Glenn, John 953
Goldwater, Barry 946
Great Society 945
Hendrix, Jimi 965
Huerta, Delores 959
Jobs, Steve 968

Johnson, Lyndon B. 938
Kennedy, John F. 938
Kennedy, Robert F. 940
King, Martin Luther, Jr. 941
Kosygin, Alexei 951
Lewis, John 946
Limited Test Ban Treaty 944
Malcolm X 957
March on Washington 942
Marshall, Thurgood 950
Medicaid 947
Medicare 947
Meredith, James 941
Miranda v. Arizona 950
Model Cities 948
National Organization for Women (NOW) 961
New Frontier 938
New Left 963
Schlafly, Phyllis 962
Sunbelt 954
Tijerina, Reies Lopez 960
Voting Rights Act of 1965 947

Reviewing Chapter 27

1. Why were many Americans hopeful about the possibility of reforming their society in the 1960s?
2. What actions did Americans take to reform society in the 1960s?
3. Explain why and how millions of Americans opposed the challenges to traditional authority posed by the social change movements of the 1960s.

⌄

Further Reading

Branch, Taylor. *Parting the Waters: America in the King Years, 1954–65*. New York: Simon & Schuster, 1999. Multivolume history of the civil rights movement.

Braunstein, Peter, and Michael William Doyle. *Imagine Nation: The American Counterculture of the 1960s and 1970s*. New York: Routledge, 2002. Insightful essays on counterculture in all its varied forms.

Dallek, Robert. *An Unfinished Life: John F. Kennedy and His Times, 1917–1963*. New York: Little, Brown and Company, 2003. A respected biography of the president who helped define the times.

Farber, David, and Beth Bailey, eds. *The Columbia Guide to America in the 1960s*. New York: Columbia University Press, 2001. Comprehensive collection of essays on the decade.

Kramer, Michael J. *The Republic of Rock: Music and Citizenship in the Sixties Counterculture*. New York: Oxford University Press, 2013.

Lewis, John L., Andrew Aydin, and Nate Powell. *The March*. Vols. 1, 2, and 3. Marietta, GA: Top Shelf Productions, 2013. Powerful series of graphic novels tell the story of Lewis's life of civil rights protest.

Lassiter, Matthew D. *The Silent Majority: Suburban Politics in the Sunbelt South*. Princeton, NJ: Princeton University Press, 2006. Insightful study of the shifting power base in politics in the 1960s.

Poole, Robert. *Earthrise: How Man First Saw the Earth*. New Haven, CT: Yale University Press, 2008. The remarkable story of how humanity first saw Earth from space and how that image launched an environmental revolution.

Rome, Adam. *The Genius of Earth Day: How a 1970 Teach-In Unexpectedly Made the First Green Generation*. New York: Hill & Wang, 2013. Engaging narrative that explains how Earth Day served as a tipping point and passing of the torch for the environmental movement.

America in the World
GOODS, IDEAS, PEOPLE

CHAPTER 27: The Optimism and the Anguish of the 1960s, 1960–1969

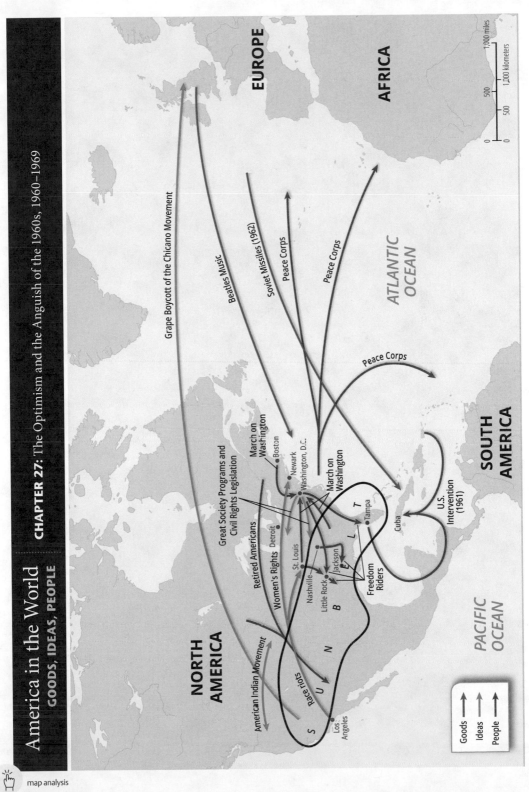

EUROPE

AFRICA

NORTH AMERICA

SOUTH AMERICA

ATLANTIC OCEAN

PACIFIC OCEAN

Grape Boycott of the Chicano Movement

Beatles Music

Soviet Missiles (1962)

Peace Corps

Peace Corps

Peace Corps

Peace Corps

U.S. Intervention (1961)

Cuba

Great Society Programs and Civil Rights Legislation

March on Washington

Boston

Newark

Washington, D.C.

March on Washington

Retired Americans

Detroit

Women's Rights

St. Louis

Nashville

Jackson

Little Rock

Freedom Riders

Tampa

American Indian Movement

Race riots

Los Angeles

S U N B E L T

Goods
Ideas
People

0   500   1,000 miles
0   500   1,200 kilometers

map analysis

American troops in action, Vietnam, 1968–1969.

The Vietnam Era

O n June 8, 1972, a plane from the South Vietnamese air force dropped napalm (jellied burning gasoline) on a group of Vietnamese fleeing from a North Vietnamese attack on the village of Trang Bang in southeast Vietnam. Several villagers were killed. Kim Phuc, a nine-year-old girl, had her clothes burned off and was photographed running naked down the road. She screamed, "Nong qua, nong qua [too hot, too hot]." Associated Press cameraman Nick Ut won the Pulitzer Prize for the picture, which became an iconic image of the brutality of the war. When President Richard M. Nixon saw the photograph, he falsely speculated that it had been doctored by antiwar activists to make more Americans want to end U.S. involvement in Vietnam.

Ut took Phuc and other burned children to a Saigon hospital. Doctors thought she would not survive, but after 17 operations over 14 months, she returned to her village. Following the Communist victory in 1975, North Vietnamese government officials publicized Phuc's suffering to demonstrate the barbarity of the defeated South Vietnamese and their American pa-trons. She became angry that officials took her from her studies to become a propaganda symbol against the anti-Communist regime. In 1986, she left Vietnam for medical school in Cuba. There she met Bui Huy Tuan, another Vietnamese student. The couple married and asked for and received asylum in Canada.

Phuc practiced medicine in Ontario and became an international advocate for reconciliation. On Veterans Day 1996, one year after the United States and Vietnam restored diplomatic relations broken in 1975, she spoke at the Vietnam Veterans Memorial in Washington, DC. She said, "We cannot change history, but we should try to do good things for the present and for the future to promote peace." She forgave an American veteran who believed he had helped the South Vietnamese air force select its target on that June day.

Kim Phuc, for decades called the Girl in the Picture, symbolized the human cost of the Vietnam War. Vietnamese and Americans suffered physical and psychological wounds that took decades to heal. A key battleground of the Cold War, Vietnam had repercussions around the globe.

THE TERROR OF WAR, 1972 Nick Ut's Pulitzer Prize–winning photo shows Kim Phuc running naked down the highway on June 8, 1972. No single picture better captured the horror and confusion of the Vietnam War.

BACKGROUND TO A WAR, 1945–1963

The United States' interest in events in Indochina developed gradually. Before World War II, few Americans knew much about the culture, history, or politics of Vietnam or its neighbors, Cambodia and Laos, the three states that comprised the French dependencies of Indochina. As the Cold War developed in Asia, top American officials became increasingly concerned with the growing conflict between France and a Communist insurgency led by **Ho Chi Minh**. The United States provided money and arms to France, but that aid proved insufficient to prevent Ho's Vietminh, a Communist-led coalition of anticolonial forces, from defeating France in 1954. That year Vietnam was divided into two states, a Communist North Vietnam and a non-Communist South Vietnam.

Ho Chi Minh, "The Path Which Led me to Leninism" (1960)

For the next several years, the United States helped the government of South Vietnam establish itself as a legitimate force worthy of the allegiance of its people. Those efforts failed, and beginning in 1960, a revived Communist insurgency challenged the authority of an unpopular and often corrupt South Vietnamese government. The administrations of Dwight D. Eisenhower and John F. Kennedy considered Vietnam to be an important bulwark against the spread of Communist-led governments in the rest of Southeast Asia. They sent millions of dollars in military and civilian aid and thousands of uniformed military advisors to help South Vietnam, but the American support could not stop the Communist gains. By the time Kennedy was assassinated in 1963, the Communist forces were winning the war against South Vietnam.

Vietnam and the Cold War

From the earliest days of the Cold War, the United States had backed alternatives to the Democratic Republic of Vietnam (DRV) proclaimed by Ho Chi Minh on September 2, 1945. In late 1946, war broke out between the Vietminh and France, which sought to re-establish its control over its colonies of Vietnam, Cambodia, and Laos. During the war, the United States backed France to encourage that country to be a strong ally in the struggle against communism.

By 1954, the United States was paying 70 percent of France's war costs against the Vietminh, yet France was unable to defeat the Communists. In the spring of 1954, Vietminh fighters, supported by troops from the People's Republic of China, surrounded a French outpost at Dien Bien Phu in northwest Vietnam. President Dwight D. Eisenhower viewed Vietnam as an important arena of the Cold War. He likened it to the first of a row of dominoes stretching throughout Southeast Asia to Australia and Japan.

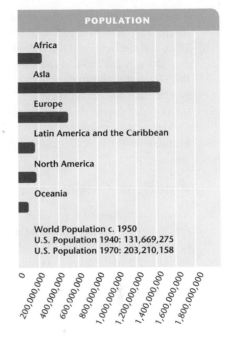

POPULATION

Africa

Asia

Europe

Latin America and the Caribbean

North America

Oceania

World Population c. 1950
U.S. Population 1940: 131,669,275
U.S. Population 1970: 203,210,158

0, 200,000,000, 400,000,000, 600,000,000, 800,000,000, 1,000,000,000, 1,200,000,000, 1,400,000,000, 1,600,000,000, 1,800,000,000

HO CHI MINH DECLARING THE INDEPENDENCE OF THE DEMOCRATIC REPUBLIC OF VIETNAM, SEPTEMBER 2, 1945 The United States steadfastly opposed efforts to establish an independent Vietnam, supporting France's fight against Ho Chi Minh that began the year after Ho Chi Minh's declaration.

This domino theory later became a vivid fear of Communist expansion in which the last domino to fall would be the United States itself. But the Korean War had ended in July 1953, and the president did not want to send U.S. troops to fight in another war in Asia.

On July 24, 1954, at the Geneva Conference, Vietnam was temporarily divided at the 17th parallel into North and South segments, with Ho Chi Minh in control of the North and Bao Dai's government in control of the South (Map 28.1). The accords called for popular national unity elections in 1956. The United States attended the Geneva Conference as an observer, but it did not sign the agreements. Instead, it supplanted France as the principal backer of the non-Communist South.

American Commitments to South Vietnam

Washington helped Ngo Dinh Diem, a Vietnamese nationalist who had spent several years in a New Jersey Catholic monastery, become prime minister of the state of Vietnam. U.S. officials hoped his Roman Catholic faith and his American experience would make him a reliable ally. In 1955, Diem deposed the emperor Bao Dai, established the Republic of (South) Vietnam, and seized the position of president. The United States supported his decision not to allow the 1956 nationwide unification elections promised by the Geneva accords. Despite the trappings of democracy in South Vietnam, Diem ruled as a virtual dictator. His domestic support came from a minority of upper-class Catholics, landlords, and businesses. The United States helped Diem build the Army of the Republic of Vietnam (ARVN) and a national police force. South Vietnam adopted democratic trappings but functioned as a dictatorship. The South's military and police forces arrested 20,000 and killed over 1,000 former members of the Vietminh who remained in the South after 1954. Yet Diem's forces could not eliminate all of the former Vietminh fighters, who regrouped with supplies from the North. The American press ignored Diem's weak base of support and his authoritarian rule. They praised South Vietnam and post–World War II Japan as two American successes in Asia.

Ngo Dinh Diem on the challenges facing South Vietnam (1957)

Full-scale civil war erupted in South Vietnam in late 1960. Diem's government, which relied heavily on the support of the small Catholic minority in South Vietnam, had grown increasingly unpopular with the Buddhist majority, who made up over 80 percent of the population. On December 20, 1960, Le Duan, the leader of the Vietminh in the South, established the National Front for the Liberation of Vietnam (NLF), a Communist-led coalition that included Buddhists, students, and nationalists opposed to Diem. NLF fighters, derisively called the Viet Cong, or Vietnamese Communists, by the ARVN, attacked government positions across the South, and by mid-1961, the NLF controlled about 58 percent of South Vietnamese territory.

The new Kennedy administration feared that the deteriorating situation in Vietnam put the United States at a disadvantage in the global fight against communism. American officials considered Soviet Communist Party chairman Nikita Khrushchev's promise to support wars of national liberation around the world as a direct challenge to the United States. Consequently, Kennedy increased military aid to South Vietnam. He dispatched 400 Army Special Forces, known as Green Berets for their distinctive headgear, to help 9,000 mountain tribesmen stop the infiltration of pro-NLF fighters from North Vietnam to help the NLF. Thus, in 1962, over 9,000 American military personnel were in Vietnam.

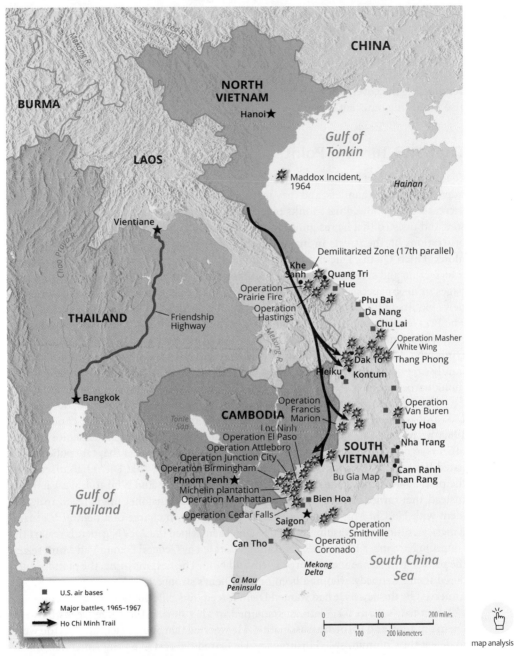

MAP 28.1 Divided Vietnam This map of Indochina shows the division of North and South Vietnam after the Geneva Conference. Maps of Vietnam distributed to soldiers and printed by the American media oversimplified the political and military situation of Vietnam, where a line on the map meant little to troops on the ground.

The Americans helped the ARVN move hundreds of thousands of Vietnamese peasants from their traditional villages into larger strategic hamlets—small villages protected by fences and guard towers. Once the hamlets were created, the ARVN bombed the countryside to crush the NLF and killed thousands of civilians. The hamlets proved to be a catastrophe for the ARVN. The NLF won adherents to its cause by denouncing the government for forcibly removing farmers from their beloved land and also for killing innocent civilians.

The 1963 Turning Point

Diem's government became increasingly unpopular in early 1963. Peasants hated being moved to strategic hamlets, and they resented Diem's ties to landowners who demanded increasing rents. Buddhist monks objected to Diem's reliance on a few Catholic advisors and insisted that he resign. In May and June, Buddhists led antigovernment demonstrations on the streets in major South Vietnamese cities. On June 11, 73-year-old monk **Thich Quang Duc** poured gasoline on himself in the midst of a busy Saigon intersection and set himself on fire. Pictures of his ritual suicide appeared on the front pages of newspapers around the world. When Kennedy saw the picture, he said, "No news picture in history has generated so much emotion around the world as that one." The People's Republic of China distributed millions of copies of the picture in Asia and Africa to highlight what it called the crimes of American imperialism. Madame Ngo Dinh Nhu, Diem's sister-in-law who acted as South Vietnam's first lady, muddied her family's reputation more when she said she would happily "clap hands at seeing another monk barbecue show."

Thich Quang Duc in flames (1963)

The Kennedy administration lost faith in Diem over the summer of 1963. A new U.S. ambassador, **Henry Cabot Lodge**, the Republican vice presidential candidate in 1960, arrived in Saigon in August. He immediately encouraged some senior ARVN officers to oust Diem and his brother, Ngo Dinh Nhu, the head of the state police and a hated figure for the Buddhists. The ARVN generals, fearful that Diem had discovered the plot, aborted their plans. U.S. officials pressured Diem and Nhu to leave Vietnam. Instead, they turned on their American patrons and hinted that they might reach an agreement with Ho Chi Minh that would leave their family in charge of a neutral Vietnam. American officials in Washington and Saigon then helped the ARVN generals restart the coup. On November 1, 1963, ARVN commanders led by General Duong Van Minh seized the presidential palace and captured Diem and Nhu. The next morning, the plotters murdered them. Kennedy, who had been one of Diem's strongest backers in the 1950s, was unnerved by the news. He had wanted Diem forced into exile but not killed.

Kennedy's plans for Vietnam remained in flux during the three weeks between Diem's murder and his own assassination. He worried that South Vietnam was too weak to defeat the Communist-led insurgency. He feared the cost of a fully American war to save Vietnam, and he speculated about reducing the American commitment after he won reelection in 1964. Some of Kennedy's trusted advisors later said he would not have committed the United States to fight in Vietnam as his successor, Lyndon B. Johnson, did. Although Kennedy believed a successful South Vietnam was necessary to counter the Soviet Union, he also had grown increasingly hopeful of reducing tensions with the Soviets in the year since the Cuban missile crisis, and he was beginning to believe that Vietnam mattered less to the United States than it had before the crisis.

STUDY QUESTIONS FOR BACKGROUND TO A WAR, 1945–1963

1. What effect did the Cold War have in shaping U.S. policy toward the conflict in Vietnam?
2. What did the Vietnamese think of the governments in North and South Vietnam? How did Americans perceive this division?
3. Why did the administration of John F. Kennedy increase America's commitment to the government of South Vietnam?

quiz

AN AMERICAN WAR, 1964–1967

As the new president, Lyndon Johnson vowed to continue Kennedy's policies in Vietnam, just after Kennedy had expressed misgivings about fighting there. Johnson anguished over Americanizing the war, but he decided to do so to avoid appearing weak. He feared that Communist success in Vietnam would be as costly to him and the Democratic Party as the Communist victory in China's civil war had been to President Harry Truman in the 1940s and early 1950s. He worried that an angry debate over "who lost Vietnam" would drain public support for the Great Society, his cherished program of domestic economic and social reform. From 1964 to 1967, the United States gradually sent more than 500,000 troops to fight against the insurgency in the South. After 1964, the Americans continuously bombed North Vietnam in a futile effort to stop Ho Chi Minh from sending supplies and troops to the South. The war devastated the land and people of both North and South Vietnam. Hundreds of thousands of civilians died, and millions became refugees. The war strained U.S. relations with traditional allies, and it halted progress in dampening Cold War tensions.

Decisions for Escalation, 1964–1965

Ill at ease in dealing with international issues, President Johnson relied on a corps of advisors inherited from John F. Kennedy, most of whom were committed to South Vietnam despite Kennedy's concerns. In late November 1963, the new president told an American diplomat in Saigon, "Lyndon Johnson is not going down as the president who lost Vietnam." He demanded that his advisors reach consensus on a strategy to prevent a Communist victory before the American election of 1964.

The United States slowly increased its military commitments to Vietnam in 1964 (Figure 28.1). In January, the CIA helped General **Nguyen Khanh** ost General. Minh, who was preparing to negotiate with North Vietnam. Khanh wanted American help in invading the North, a move Johnson resisted. He feared provoking Chinese intervention in the war, as had occurred in Korea. But Goldwater also goaded Johnson by suggesting that American field commanders in Vietnam had the right to use tactical nuclear weapons.

In the summer of 1964, U.S. naval vessels escorted South Vietnamese ships inside North Vietnam's declared 12-mile coastal limit to attack northern ports. On the night of August 2, North Vietnamese patrol boats attacked the *Maddox*, a U.S. electronic surveillance ship in the Gulf of Tonkin. Two nights later, the commander of another

Conversation between President Johnson and Senator Richard Russell on the situation in Vietnam (May 1964)

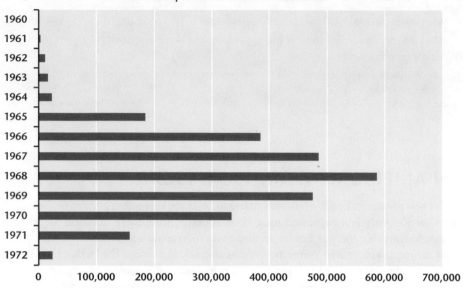

U.S. Troop Levels in Vietnam 1960–1972

FIGURE 28.1 Troop escalation This graph shows the numbers of U.S. troops in Vietnam from 1961 to 1972.

destroyer, the *C. Turner Joy*, believed the North Vietnamese had attacked his ship. The *C. Turner Joy* fired its guns into the night but hit nothing because, in fact, no North Vietnamese boats were attacking. Nevertheless, Johnson ordered U.S. Navy planes to attack North Vietnamese radars and ports. He also asked Congress for authorization "to take all necessary steps, including the use of armed force, to assist" Southeast Asian countries requesting military aid from the United States. On August 7, Congress passed the **Gulf of Tonkin Resolution** with little debate and minimal opposition.

A few years after the Gulf of Tonkin Resolution passed Congress, it became clear that the North Vietnamese attacks either had not occurred or had been provoked by the U.S. Navy. The resolution, however, justified Americanizing the fighting. Support by Republican presidential candidate Barry Goldwater removed Vietnam as an issue in the 1964 election. Johnson appeared as the more moderate candidate. He said that "only as a last resort" would he "start dropping bombs around that are likely to involve American boys in a war in Asia with 700 million Chinese."

Safely reelected, Johnson proceeded to make Vietnam an American war. South Vietnamese forces continued to suffer losses against the NLF, and the South Vietnamese government grew ever more desperate and pleaded for Americans to send ground troops and attack the North. On February 7, 1965, NLF fighters attacked the American air base at Pleiku. They killed eight American airmen and destroyed 10 planes. In retaliation, Johnson authorized Operation Rolling Thunder, the sustained bombing of North Vietnamese military installations, roads, rail lines, bridges, power plants, and fuel depots. Rolling Thunder disappointed advocates of air power because the North Vietnamese quickly rebuilt. The thick cloud cover and heavy foliage helped them hide the thousands of tons of supplies, arms, and soldiers they had infiltrated from the

MAP 28.2 Ho Chi Minh Trail The Ho Chi Minh Trail linked the North and the South while circumnavigating American defenses. The ability of the Viet Cong to resupply via the trail despite massive bombing campaigns vexed American military leaders and contributed to the sense at home that the war was unwinnable.

North to the South through Laos and Cambodia on a complex system of hundreds of miles of hidden roads, bridges, tunnels, camps, and paths called the Ho Chi Minh Trail (Map 28.2).

From March to July, Johnson made the final decisions to escalate the war. In March, American Marines waded ashore at Da Nang to provide added protection to the American forces in Vietnam. In April, General William Westmoreland, the U.S. commander in Vietnam, wrote the president that the United States had to "put our own finger in the dike" or the South would lose the war. In April, the general asked for another 150,000 American troops in addition to the 90,000 already there to fight a ground war throughout South Vietnam.

Lyndon B. Johnson, "Peace without Conquest" (April 1965)

In July, Johnson settled on sending another 100,000 American troops by the end of 1965. This policy of gradual escalation prevented a quick Communist victory. But it did not lead to an American and South Vietnamese triumph. The war went on

Lyndon B.
Johnson,
"Why
Americans
Fight in
Vietnam"
(1965)

inconclusively for the remainder of Johnson's term. Meanwhile, the public was growing disillusioned with the war, with the president, and with Johnson's Great Society.

Ground and Air War, 1966–1967

In 1966 and 1967, the United States escalated the number of troops in Vietnam from 190,000 to 535,000. It took over the bulk of fighting from its South Vietnamese allies. The Americans tried to apply the lessons learned in World War II and Korea: use the modern technology of warfare—withering firepower, tank and heavy artillery attacks, bombing from the air—to defeat a more numerous, less well-equipped enemy. But this reliance on technology grossly misjudged the abilities of North Vietnamese and NLF forces to outlast the better-armed Americans. The Communists avoided fighting the U.S. forces in large battles where superior American firepower could overwhelm them. Instead, the Communist forces chose their battles carefully.

General Westmoreland advocated a strategy of attrition to wear down the number of NLF and North Vietnamese fighters until they were no longer capable of continuing the fight. Americans used helicopters to ferry soldiers into the field on search-and-destroy missions designed to kill as many enemy fighters as possible. The body count of dead NLF and North Vietnamese served as a measure of military success for the American public at home (Figure 28.2). Reliance on these numbers rather than territory captured encouraged inflated reports about the number of enemy killed and the

U.S. HELICOPTERS LIFT OFF AS THEY GO OUT ON A SEARCH-AND-DESTROY MISSION, SEPTEMBER 1967 "Search and destroy" became a metaphor for the unclear mission in Vietnam. Military leaders hoped the nimble craft would turn the tide, but the slow-moving copters were easy targets. Between 1962 and 1972, the United States lost over 4,800 helicopters.

Killed in Action

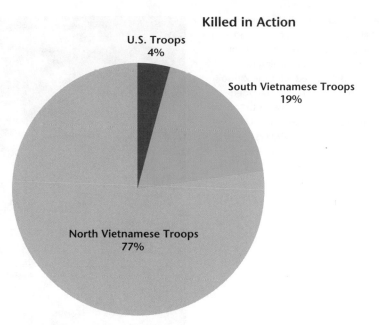

U.S. Troops
4%

South Vietnamese Troops
19%

North Vietnamese Troops
77%

FIGURE 28.2 Vietnam death toll This graph includes figures for U.S., North Vietnamese, and South Vietnamese deaths in Vietnam from 1961–1975.

inclusion of dead civilians in the body count. Dismal nightly reports on American and enemy dead did little to convince the American public that the war was going well. The NLF did not wear uniforms, and American soldiers could not distinguish them from the South Vietnamese peasants whom the Americans presumably were helping. Atrocities occur in all wars, but the emphasis on the body count enhanced brutality. Some soldiers, including Americans, even dismembered the bodies of enemy fighters and kept their ears for trophies.

At its peak, the United States dropped more bombs on North and South Vietnam than fell on Europe during all of World War II. Initially, bombing terrified the NLF and North Vietnamese. But they soon realized that the Americans bombed at the same time each day, and they retreated into deep tunnels. They used unexploded bombs to improvise booby traps that killed more than 1,000 U.S. troops in 1966 alone.

Americans and their South Vietnamese allies continued to conduct huge search-and-destroy operations in late 1966 and 1967. They warned peasants to leave their villages for the cities and declared vast stretches of Vietnam free-fire zones. Anyone who remained in them would be considered an enemy fighter and would be shot and killed. American and ARVN troops sometimes used flamethrowers or cigarette lighters to burn down villages in "Zippo raids," named after a popular cigarette lighter. The U.S. Army also dropped over one million pounds of defoliants, often called Agent Orange, on the forests of Vietnam to deny the enemy the invisibility provided by the leaves. The defoliants destroyed over half of South Vietnam's trees, killed peasants' livestock, and caused birth defects among their children, all of which turned more Vietnamese into supporters of the NLF. The horrific environmental and health effects of the defoliation campaign lasted for decades.

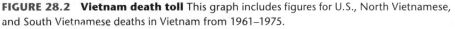

Newspaper cartoon contrasting Vietnamese guerrilla warfare against American firepower

VIETNAM ZIPPOS In 1965, journalist Morley Safer and his CBS crew filmed U.S. soldiers torching the grass huts of Vietnamese villagers. Disturbing footage of "Zippo raids," named after the Zippo lighters issued to U.S. troops, enraged LBJ and supporters of the war effort and fed growing public concern over U.S. involvement in Vietnam. Soldiers engraved their Zippo lighters with messages of hope and despair.

image analysis

The sustained bombing of the Ho Chi Minh Trail achieved minimal results. North Vietnamese trucks carrying supplies hid under camouflage and jungle cover during the day and traveled at night to avoid firepower. Thousands of mostly female Vietnamese peasants helped maintain the trail by staying at campsites along the route every nine miles. Russian and Chinese engineers also helped repair the trail.

North Vietnam faced the most devastating air attacks of the war. Bombing destroyed homes and schools and killed tens of thousands. Health care, food supplies, and education suffered. Between 1965 and 1967, the United States dropped almost 650,000 tons of bombs. The bombing infuriated the Vietnamese. One North Vietnamese soldier recalled that after assaults, "the people got very mad and cursed the Americans. . . . To them the Americans were the cruel enemy who had [bombed] the civilians."

The United States looked for ways to increase faltering public support for its war efforts. American officials tried to reassemble the multinational coalition that had joined the UN forces in repelling the North Korean attack in 1950. Yet none of the European allies agreed to send troops. Relations between the United States, France, Great Britain, and West Germany, where antiwar sentiment ran high, grew tense. Australia and New Zealand did send about 10,000 troops to fight alongside the Americans. The largest contingent of troops from other nations fighting alongside the ARVN came from the Republic of (South) Korea. About 50,000 South Korean forces, paid for by the United States, joined the fighting.

With no victory in sight, the Johnson administration explored negotiations with North Vietnam. In late summer and early fall, Harvard professor **Henry Kissinger**, a private citizen acting on behalf of the U.S. government, secretly informed unofficial

North Vietnamese representatives that the Johnson administration would temporarily suspend bombing North Vietnam if the North would agree to hold talks with the United States about ending the war. The United States would not insist, as it had earlier, that the North remove its troops from the South before talks could begin. Johnson directly addressed Ho Chi Minh in a widely publicized speech on September 28. He proclaimed, "I am ready to send a trusted representative of America to any spot on this earth to talk in public or private with a spokesman of Hanoi." But these overtures failed. The United States did not suspend the bombing as it promised, and the North Vietnamese continued to denounce the war as illegal.

The War at Home

After 1965, the Vietnam War grew increasingly unpopular in the United States. Protests against the war combined with the movements for civil rights, the empowerment of youth, and Second Wave feminism opened deep divisions in American society. Opposition to the war mounted in Congress, and hundreds of thousands of Americans took to the streets in unprecedented protests of the war's physical, financial, and moral costs. Television showed gritty examples of the war, often at odds with the optimistic government declarations of progress toward creating a stable, legitimate, and self-reliant government of South Vietnam. Journalists in Vietnam spoke contemptuously of a credibility gap between what government officials from President Johnson on down were saying about the war and what actually was taking place in Vietnam.

Domestic opposition to the war grew steadily. In February 1966, the Senate Committee on Foreign Relations held televised hearings on Vietnam. **George F. Kennan**, the

ORGANIZED OUTRAGE The intersections of counterculture and Vietnam protest are clear in this c. 1966–1968 lithographic poster by artist Nancy Coner. Posters were a common tool for protest, and examples like this used iconic forms and colors from rock music advertisements to draw attention to the serious issues featured in the center circle.

Global Disruption

Students, politicians, radicals, and typical citizens around the world condemned American involvement in Vietnam. Antiwar rallies took place in several European capitals during the International Days of Protest in October 1965 and March 1966. At other times they protested outside U.S. embassies or military bases. In Japan, a student group organized thousands of protesters in 1968 to prevent a U.S. aircraft carrier from entering a Japanese port. Protests by Japanese students dissuaded the government from providing financial support to the American war effort. Frequently, the protests, taking their own form, targeted issues within the respective countries' cultural, social, and political structures in addition to the more narrow antiwar and anti-American critiques. American and European activists looked to one another for encouragement. Antiwar protests played a significant part in what one historian has called the "global disruption" of 1968. The mass student movement that arose in France in the spring had its roots in a protest of the Vietnam War. Protesters in West Germany, moreover, stressed the need for Germany to come to terms with its guilt for the Holocaust and to prevent what they viewed as another genocide in Vietnam from continuing.

Speech by Ernesto "Che" Guevara on US imperialism in Vietnam (April 1967)

The Eastern bloc countries supported the cause of the North Vietnamese. So did Third World revolutionaries, who looked toward the NLF's struggle for inspiration. **Ernesto "Che" Guevara**, the Cuban revolutionary hero, called for "one, two . . . many Vietnams." American radical activists themselves raised the ire of most Americans when

father of the containment doctrine, opposed deeper American involvement in Vietnam because, he said, "unbalanced concentration of resources and attention" on the war diverted American resources from more important foreign policy concerns in Europe. Senator J. William Fulbright, the committee's chair, emerged as one of the Senate's most prominent doves, people who sought a quick, peaceful end to the war. He rejected assertions by hawks, advocates of a military victory in Vietnam, such as Secretary of State Dean Rusk, that Vietnam "is a clear case of international Communist aggression." Instead, Fulbright said that he agreed with other nations that considered Vietnam to be "a civil war in which outside parties have become involved."

A citizens' peace movement made up of liberals, pacifists, and radicals emerged to oppose the war. It organized antiwar marches that drew thousands at first. In 1965, opponents of the war held the first of hundreds of teach-ins at college campuses across the country. In 1967, Students for a Democratic Society sponsored a Vietnam Summer, modeled on the 1964 Mississippi Freedom Summer. In October 1967, over 100,000 antiwar demonstrators converged on Washington, DC, to demand an end to the fighting and an American withdrawal from Vietnam. Some publicly burned their draft cards in open defiance of the law.

Martin Luther King, Jr., "A Time to Break the Silence" (April 1967)

The draft galvanized opposition to the war. All men aged 18–26 faced the possibility of conscription. But the government applied the draft haphazardly. Fewer than half of draft-age men served in the military during the Vietnam era. Fewer still went they traveled to conferences in these countries to meet with North Vietnamese and NLF officials. They failed to gain any wider sympathy with the larger public with their provocative statements of solidarity at such events.

Beginning in 1966, the Great Proletarian Cultural Revolution, directed by Mao Zedong himself, convulsed China. Millions of young Chinese Red Guards took to the streets to denounce and assault thousands of teachers, village leaders, and Communist Party officials who had incurred Mao's displeasure. Opposition to the U.S. role in Vietnam played only a minor role in the Cultural Revolution. But the international publicity given to the world's most populated nation upended by millions of young revolutionaries aroused protesters worldwide. At the same time, scenes of the Cultural Revolution also fortified the resolve of the Johnson administration to prevail in Vietnam.

The global antiwar movement elevated anti-Americanism to new levels in many parts of the world. It also subsequently eroded the prestige that the United States had held on the world stage after World War II. But Daniel Cohn-Bendit, one of the leaders of the student movement in France, summed up a common sentiment: "It started with bombings on Vietnam. . . . Marching left and right, saying: stop it, stop it!—and nobody stops, and it doesn't stop."

- How did opponents of U.S. policies in Vietnam express their dissent?
- In what ways did international protests of the Vietnam War contribute to the global disruptions of the 1960s?

to Vietnam. An array of draft deferments, exemptions, and military alternatives to Vietnam was available, especially to more educated and wealthier young men, who managed to avoid service in Vietnam or military service altogether. Many Americans came to see selective service or the draft as unfair. The inequities of the draft heightened popular distrust of the government and intensified opposition to the war.

Large demonstrations and the coverage of the fighting changed Americans' perceptions of the war. Scenes of battles appeared on the evening news within 24 hours. The sight of American soldiers burning villages proved deeply troubling to many. In 1967, the proportion of Americans who believed American involvement was a mistake rose from 33 percent in January to 46 percent in October. That fall, only 28 percent of the public approved of Johnson's handling of the war. The bulk of the public were neither hawks nor doves; they wanted only to see progress.

A husband and wife watch television news coverage of the war in Vietnam

STUDY QUESTIONS FOR AN AMERICAN WAR, 1964–1967

1. Why did President Lyndon B. Johnson decide to Americanize the Vietnam War?

2. What were American tactics in Vietnam? What were the consequences of these tactics?

3. Why did opposition grow to the war in Vietnam at home and abroad?

quiz

⊗ 1968: TURMOIL AND TURNING POINTS

The war in Vietnam reached its climax and American society came close to a breaking point in 1968. Public unhappiness with the course of the Vietnam War combined with other 1960s social movements to make 1968 one of the most tumultuous years in American history. Two political assassinations, the bloodiest urban uprisings of the 1960s, and a tumultuous presidential election campaign shook American self-confidence. Protests against the war in Vietnam and against other government policies erupted around the world. It appeared to many thoughtful people that the world teetered on the brink of revolutionary upheaval. These protests sparked resistance from people opposed to radical change and from authorities. Conservatives eventually prevailed at home and internationally.

The Tet Offensive

In October 1967, North Vietnamese leaders decided to launch a nationwide offensive throughout South Vietnam during the annual cease-fire for the lunar new year celebration of Tet. U.S. and South Vietnamese intelligence saw signs of a massive increase in North Vietnamese forces in the South in December 1967, but neither foresaw a coordinated attack. Instead, the Americans worried that North Vietnamese forces would assault Khe Sanh, a Marine base in northwest South Vietnam. President Johnson believed the North Vietnamese wanted to reenact the defeat of the French at Dien Bien Phu by capturing Khe Sanh, and he ordered that the base be held at all costs and had a model of it constructed in the White House so he could follow the battle.

With American attention distracted at Khe Sanh, in the early morning hours of January 31, 1968, the North Vietnamese and NLF attacked throughout South Vietnam. The Tet Offensive began when 19 NLF fighters blasted through the thick wall surrounding the U.S. embassy in Saigon and fought with Marine guards for the next six hours. The Americans killed all 19 commandos, none of whom entered embassy buildings. The daring raid coincided with attacks on the South Vietnamese presidential palace, Saigon's airport, radio stations, and 36 of 40 district capitals.

Bloody battles occurred for the next six weeks. **Nguyen Ngoc Loan**, chief of the national police force, publicly executed a captured NLF fighter on a Saigon street on February 1. Pictures of blood spurting from the prisoner's head sickened the American public. The ARVN and U.S. forces, applying massive firepower, killed about 40,000 NLF and North Vietnamese troops, while they lost 3,400 of their own. As many as one million South Vietnamese were forced to flee their homes. The bitterest fighting took place in the old imperial capital of Hue, which the NLF controlled for three weeks in February. American and ARVN bombs and artillery leveled much of the city's core; they left it, as one U.S. soldier recalled, "a shattered, stinking hulk, its streets choked with rubble and rotting bodies." After the battle, ARVN soldiers discovered a mass grave of 2,800 South Vietnamese officials murdered by the NLF.

Walter Cronkite, "We are Mired in Stalemate" (February 27, 1968)

On March 16, American troops committed their grossest atrocity of the war in the village of My Lai. Company C of the American division entered the village at dawn after being told that it was a major sanctuary for the NLF. Instead of finding enemy fighters, however, the Americans found only old men, women, and children. In the words of an eyewitness, the American soldiers "went berserk, gunning down unarmed men, women, children and babies. . . . Those who emerged with hands held high were murdered." The Americans raped women and mutilated dead bodies. All told, soldiers killed 504 Vietnamese. The carnage stopped only when one heroic U.S. Army helicopter pilot threatened to turn his chopper's guns on the rampaging soldiers. The **My Lai Massacre** remained a secret in the United States for over a year. When knowledge of it leaked in late 1969, opposition to the war intensified. Only one soldier, Lieutenant William Calley, was punished for the massacre, and he served less than two years in prison.

American public opinion turned sharply against President Johnson and his handling of the war in the wake of Tet; 78 percent of the public said the United States was not making progress, and only 2 percent approved of Johnson's handling of the war. As Tet revealed the vulnerabilities of the South, Westmoreland requested an additional 206,000 U.S. troops. Johnson asked the new secretary of defense, Clark Clifford, to review Westmoreland's request. The president reluctantly accepted the once-supportive Clifford's new advice to begin deescalating the war. On March 31, hoping to begin peace negotiations with Hanoi, he announced a halt to the bombing of North Vietnam north of the 19th parallel. He also shocked the nation by announcing that he would not seek reelection in November.

The Agony of 1968

Johnson's withdrawal from the presidential race shook up an already turbulent contest for the Democratic Party's presidential nomination. In the fall of 1967, antiwar Democrats encouraged Minnesota senator **Eugene "Gene" McCarthy** to challenge Johnson for the nomination. McCarthy's campaign attracted little interest until the Tet Offensive undermined support for the war. In February, thousands of college-age volunteers cut their long hair, shaved their beards, and wore shirts and ties or skirts and sweaters to become "clean for Gene" as they campaigned for him in the New Hampshire primary against Johnson. The Minnesotan had come within a few hundred votes of defeating Johnson before he withdrew and actually gained 20 of the 24 delegates at stake.

The next few months were among the most turbulent in the 20th century both in the United States and around the world. On April 4, Martin Luther King, Jr., was murdered in Memphis, where he had gone to support the nearly all-black garbage workers in a strike. King's assassination set off waves of black rage across the country. Uprisings occurred in more than 100 cities across the country. The police, the National Guard, and the regular army, called in to quell the violence, killed 37 people. Later in April, student uprisings erupted. Members of the Students for a Democratic Society at Columbia University, occupying several classroom buildings, demanded that the university stop construction of a gymnasium in Morningside Park, which separated the mostly white Ivy League university from largely African American Harlem. University administrators called in the police after eight days. They cleared the buildings by swinging their clubs and fists. Pictures of bloodied student demonstrators invoked some sympathy, but many Americans were frightened by the protests. French students had grievances of their own against a paternalistic university system where they were forced to stand or sit in the aisles of overcrowded lecture halls. The rigid curriculum allowed almost no opportunity to explore contemporary issues. Thousands walked out of classes across Paris. The government sent police with clubs against the protesting students, who then set up barricades in the city's Latin Quarter. In May, the students joined a general

Statement from the coordinating committee of the Columbia University student strike (1968)

NEW YORK CITY POLICE BEATING COLUMBIA UNIVERSITY STUDENT STRIKERS, APRIL 1968 Scenes of violence in the streets contributed to the bleak mood of 1968.

strike of workers throughout France. Marching through the capital, over one million demonstrators demanded the resignation of President Charles de Gaulle and his government. Some supporters thought that the country was experiencing a new revolution. De Gaulle sought refuge in a military command post as the crisis grew. Public opinion turned against the strikers, however, and de Gaulle won a resounding victory in special parliamentary elections.

Student demonstrations and strikes also shook authorities elsewhere in Europe and in Latin America. In West Germany, New Left students occupied university buildings in sympathy with their fellow students in France. Uprisings were especially dramatic in Communist-ruled eastern Europe. Polish students briefly took to the streets against the Communist government. The deepest challenge to Communist rule in eastern Europe occurred in Czechoslovakia. There the Prague Spring began in January with student protests against authoritarian university rules. The experiment with a nonrepressive style of socialism called "socialism with a human face," by the new Czech leader **Alexander Dubček**, lasted until the Soviet Union invaded Czechoslovakia in August. However, the most brutal suppression of student protests occurred in Mexico City in October. Students closed the university with demands for reforms similar to the student demands in France. They also protested the government's flattening of poor neighborhoods to make way for the Olympic Games. The government, unwilling to have protests anywhere near the site of the Games, cracked down with brute force. The Mexican army shot and killed over 1,000 demonstrators the week before the Games began.

Other shocking events from June through August further unnerved Americans. A few days after the New Hampshire primary, Senator Robert Kennedy entered the race to challenge Johnson. After Johnson withdrew, a three-way battle ensued among Senators

McCarthy and Kennedy and Vice President **Hubert Humphrey**. Kennedy pulled ahead of McCarthy by winning the California primary on June 5. In the early morning hours of June 6, as Kennedy declared his victory, Sirhan Sirhan, a Palestinian angered by the senator's support for Israel, shot and killed him. The country, hardly recovered from the grief of King's murder, was stunned and depressed. Even for his detractors, the killing of RFK so soon after King added to the sense of chaos and disorder that seemed to be escalating.

Events at the Democratic convention in Chicago in late August added to the sense of chaos. Antiwar protesters vowed to come to the Chicago convention to undermine what they called the "party of death." They were joined by the Yippies, or members of the Youth International Party, who vowed to disrupt conventional politics with antic street theater. Chicago's Democratic mayor, Richard J. Daley, swore that the demonstrators would not interrupt the convention. He ordered his 12,000-member police force to work 12-hour shifts and had the governor send 6,000 National Guard troops to the city. President Johnson sent 7,500 regular army soldiers to patrol the African American community. On the night of August 28, when the convention nominated Humphrey, police and National Guardsmen clubbed and tear-gassed a crowd of demonstrators outside the Hilton Hotel in downtown Chicago. Through the eerie fog of tear gas, the protesters shouted, "The whole world is watching!" Tanks and soldiers with assault rifles drove back the chanting protestors while the national media recorded the action live on TV. Opinion surveys following riots showed that the American public sided with the police by a margin of two to one. But the turmoil of America's culture war was disheartening to all.

Testimony from a protester who demonstrated at the Democratic National Convention (1968)

Humphrey left the convention trailing former vice president **Richard M. Nixon**, the Republican nominee, by more than 20 points. A third candidate, Alabama Democratic governor **George C. Wallace**, also polled strongly with about 20 percent in early September. Wallace appealed to white working-class voters, mostly but not exclusively in the South, who had left the Democratic Party over its support for civil rights for African Americans.

Nixon and Wallace both opposed Johnson's handling of the war. The Republican nominee, a veteran anti-Communist, had been a hawk on Vietnam. During the campaign, he avoided specifics, while calling for "peace with honor," a formulation that appealed both to those who wanted the war to end soon and to those who craved an American victory. Wallace implied he would end the war more quickly than either Humphrey or Nixon by adopting the toughest tactics.

Nixon also campaigned against civil rights activists and antiwar protesters. He adopted a "southern strategy" designed to transform the traditionally Democratic South into a Republican stronghold. He decried "crime in the streets," code for the African American urban uprisings after the assassination of Martin Luther King, Jr., and the antiwar protests he despised. He tapped deep strains of white racial anger, in both North and South, with promises to prevent local school districts from busing students to achieve desegregation.

Richard Nixon, "What Has Happened to America?" Reader's Digest (October 1967)

Humphrey's campaign picked up support after he distanced himself from Johnson on September 30 and offered a total halt to the bombing of North Vietnam as "an acceptable risk for peace." Progress in the peace talks between the United States and North Vietnam in Paris also helped Humphrey. For months the North Vietnamese refused to engage directly in talks with representatives of South Vietnam. But the pace of negotiations quickened in late October. The North Vietnamese indicated that they would hold meaningful talks if the United States halted the bombing. Johnson was loath to agree to such a step, which he feared would allow the North to reinforce its positions in the South. But the weekend before the election, Johnson announced a total bombing halt. Serious negotiations would begin on Thursday, November 7, two days after the election.

The announcement of the bombing halt was not quite enough to turn the election to Humphrey. Members of Nixon's campaign, including Henry Kissinger, alerted representatives of South Vietnam president **Nguyen Van Thieu** about the proposed bombing halt. Thieu denounced it and said his government would not attend the talks. Humphrey's surge stalled, and Nixon won a close election by 512,000 votes (Nixon: 31,783,000 votes, 43.6 percent, 301 electoral votes; Humphrey: 31,271,000 votes, 42.9 percent, 191 electoral votes; Wallace: 9,901,000 votes, 13.5 percent, 46 electoral votes). The narrow difference between Nixon and Humphrey masked the extent of the public's turn against Johnson, the Great Society, the Vietnam War, and political liberalism. Together Nixon and Wallace, the two conservative candidates, received over 56 percent of the popular vote. The Democratic Party's share of the vote fell from 60.5 percent in the landslide election of 1964 to under 43 percent. Nixon's victory began more than two decades of nearly uninterrupted success for Republican presidential candidates.

STUDY QUESTIONS FOR 1968: TURMOIL AND TURNING POINTS

1. The Tet Offensive appeared to be a decisive victory for the U.S. military. Why then was the American public so profoundly shocked and disillusioned by this event?

2. How did opponents of U.S. involvement in the war in Vietnam express their dissent, both at home and abroad?

3. Why was the presidential election of 1968 so tumultuous? Why did Richard Nixon win it?

quiz

NIXON AND THE WORLD

Richard Nixon came to the presidency vowing to restore America's badly damaged credibility in world affairs. Together with Henry Kissinger, his national security advisor and later secretary of state, Nixon engineered some of the most dramatic diplomatic changes in the 20th century. From 1969 to 1973, the United States reduced its forces in Vietnam and in 1973 signed a cease-fire agreement with Hanoi. Although the Paris Peace Accords were hailed at the time, they did not last, and in 1975 the Communist side won the Vietnam War.

Nixon, pursuing **détente,** or the relaxation of tension with the Soviet Union, had more success in calming the Cold War. Nixon also visited the People's Republic of China (PRC) and thus ended a more than two-decades-long estrangement between the two countries. Nixon and Kissinger conducted foreign affairs in secret, however, and often expressed contempt for the public, Congress, and other government officials. Their maneuverings cost them widespread support for their foreign policies.

From Vietnamization to Paris

The Nixon administration managed to divert public attention from the Vietnam War, beginning a process of Vietnamization of the war in 1969. The United States gradually reduced its ground forces in Vietnam and provided more arms and training for the ARVN. Nixon met South Vietnam's President Thieu in June 1969 and informed him that he planned to remove 25,000 U.S. forces from Vietnam. Nixon also promised that after the war ended, the United States would continue to aid Asian countries to resist Communist revolutions, but it would expect them to assume the "primary responsibility of providing the manpower for [their] own defense." As U.S. troop levels fell, monthly draft calls declined; as a result, draft protests lessened, but tensions remained high.

At the same time, the United States increased the pace of bombings in South Vietnam and in neighboring Cambodia. Nixon hoped to keep the bombing of Cambodia a secret to preserve a fiction that it was a neutral country. When the *New York Times* published news of the attacks, Nixon suspected the leak came from members of Kissinger's staff at the National Security Council and complained that he was "being sabotaged by bureaucrats." Despite removing an additional 150,000 troops from Vietnam in 1970, the United States expanded the ground war into neighboring Cambodia. On April 30, U.S. and South Vietnamese troops entered Cambodia to bolster the fortunes of a new anti-Communist government and to destroy the headquarters of the NLF they believed were located near the Cambodian and South Vietnamese border. The invasion was a disaster. The South Vietnamese were unprepared and outmatched and never found the rumored headquarters.

The expansion of the war into Cambodia ignited some of the largest antiwar demonstrations of the Vietnam era. On college campuses and in high schools across the country, students rallied against the Cambodian invasion. The protests turned deadly at **Kent State** University in northern Ohio when National Guardsmen, called in by the governor to stop the demonstrations, shot and killed four demonstrators. After the violence at Kent State, student strikes shut down hundreds of universities and colleges. Over 100,000 young people descended on Washington to petition Congress to end the war. Congress repealed the Gulf of Tonkin Resolution and tried unsuccessfully to cut off funds for fighting in Cambodia.

Iconic photo of a student demonstrator killed at Kent State University (1970)

Public confidence in the government's handling of the war was shaken further in June 1971 when the *New York Times* published excerpts from the **Pentagon Papers**, a collection of government documents outlining U.S. decision making in Vietnam dating as far back as World War II. Daniel Ellsberg, a once-hawkish former Defense Department advisor who now opposed the war, leaked copies to the newspaper. He hoped that the documents' record of successive administrations' misstatements and outright lies about the war would persuade more Americans to demand a quick end to the fighting. The Nixon administration reacted furiously to the leak and obtained an injunction forbidding the *New York Times* from further publication of the papers. The Supreme Court, overturning the restraining order, ruled that the Nixon administration had not proved that publication would harm national security.

John Ehrlichman, Nixon's chief domestic policy advisor, responded to the Court's rebuff by assembling a team of "White House Plumbers," so named because they plugged leaks, to embarrass Ellsberg. E. Howard Hunt, the head of the unit, organized a break-in at Ellsberg's psychiatrist's office to find information to "destroy his public image and credibility." A year later, veterans of the Plumbers' operation broke into the offices of the Democratic National Committee at the Watergate office complex in Washington in an attempt to steal campaign secrets. Their actions set in motion the scandal that forced Nixon's resignation in 1974.

For the next eight months, Henry Kissinger conducted secret talks in Paris with North Vietnam's **Le Duc Tho**. Kissinger and Nixon publicly supported South Vietnam's President Thieu. Privately, however, they favored an end to the war and the withdrawal of U.S. forces, followed by a decent interval before the Communists took over. They wanted to give South Vietnam a chance to succeed, but if it lost the war, the failure would be Saigon's, not Washington's.

North Vietnam launched a major offensive across the border into South Vietnam in April 1972. The United States responded by resuming bombing over all of North Vietnam and by mining the harbor of the port of Haiphong. Still, Kissinger continued to negotiate with Le Duc Tho. In October 1972, less than two weeks before the U.S. presidential election, Kissinger, announcing that he and Tho had reached a breakthrough, declared that "peace is at hand." President Thieu, furious at the deal, refused to accept it. The announcement of an impending peace helped Nixon coast to a landslide victory over Democratic presidential candidate **George McGovern**. Nixon won 47.1 million votes, 60.7 percent, and 520 electoral votes; McGovern received 29.1 million votes, 37.5 percent, and 17 electoral votes.

The United States initiated the heaviest bombing campaign of the war over North Vietnam in December 1972 to persuade President Thieu to accept a settlement and to convince him that the United States would come to his assistance if the war resumed. The agreements signed at Paris on January 27, 1973, were almost the same as the deal hammered out in October. The United States agreed to withdraw all of its troops from Vietnam. North Vietnam would keep a force of 200,000 in the South, but Thieu agreed not to increase this. Prisoners of war would be returned within 60 days. North Vietnam dropped its key demand that Thieu and his administration resign. Thieu remained in power, but the accords called for the eventual creation of a government of national reconciliation.

The End of the Vietnam War

The cease-fire promised by the Paris Accords never held. President Thieu ordered the ARVN to attack in March 1973. He hoped renewed fighting would encourage Washington to honor its pledge for increased military support. But he badly misjudged American public opinion, which was heartily sick of the war. Once 591 American prisoners of war returned home in March, Americans shifted their attention to the growing **Watergate scandal**. In the fall of 1973, Kissinger and Le Duc Tho won the Nobel Peace Prize for their negotiations ending the war. Kissinger was lauded at home as a miracle worker, whereas Tho refused to accept the prize because peace had not come to his land.

Nixon resigned in August 1974, and Vice President **Gerald R. Ford**, who succeeded Nixon as president, had little desire to reengage in Vietnam (more following). A Democratic Party sweep in the 1974 congressional elections further weakened Ford's standing.

In early 1975, North Vietnam launched a final offensive to defeat Thieu. After North Vietnamese forces captured the coastal city of Da Nang in March, ARVN troops retreated in terror. Many threw down their weapons and shed their uniforms. Hundreds of them fought with thousands of desperate refugees for places on helicopters, planes, trucks, and buses to flee the Communist advances. On April 29, the last Americans departed from Saigon on a helicopter that lifted off from the roof of a building near the embassy. Although the Americans helped about 150,000 Vietnamese who had worked for the Americans or supported the South Vietnamese government escape, they left hundreds of thousands behind. On April 30, 1975, the government of South Vietnam surrendered to the NLF, and the capital city of Saigon was renamed Ho Chi Minh City.

The Vietnam War ended at enormous cost. Over two million Vietnamese and 58,000 Americans died. The war wrecked the Vietnamese countryside and created over three million Vietnamese refugees. Vietnam also exacted a heavy price on American outlook and optimism. The attitude of most Americans changed from trust to skepticism to eventual outright disbelief as the credibility gap widened throughout the Johnson and Nixon administrations. The victory of the Communists in Vietnam caused many Americans to lose faith in their country's ability to fashion a world according to its liking.

Reduction of Cold War Tensions

In 1969, Henry Kissinger opened secret backchannel negotiations with the Soviet ambassador to the United States, Anatoly Dobrynin. The United States and the Soviet Union conducted arduous secret negotiations for three years. In May 1972, Nixon traveled to Moscow for a summit meeting with Soviet Communist Party secretary **Leonid Brezhnev**. The two leaders signed three important agreements: an anti-ballistic missile (ABM) treaty limiting each country to only two missile sites; an interim agreement on limitations of strategic armaments (SALT I), which limited the number of each side's nuclear missiles and promised a treaty with greater limitations within five years; and "Basic Principles of Relations Between the United States of America and the Union of Soviet Socialist Republics," a document promising that each nation would deal with the other on "the principle of equality."

Richard Nixon makes the case for détente (July 1971)

Nixon and Kissinger came back from the Moscow summit lauded as masters of foreign policy. Détente with the Soviet Union won praise from old adversaries astonished that Nixon, the veteran Cold Warrior, had succeeded in reducing the conflict with the Soviets after his predecessors had failed. Brezhnev returned Nixon's visit with visits to Washington and California in June 1973, and Nixon went back to Moscow in June 1974. By that time, however, Nixon's presidency was nearing its end as his reputation became destroyed by the Watergate scandal. By 1974, détente had also lost much of its early allure. Many officials in the Department of Defense and their supporters in Congress and the press claimed that arms control agreements gave the Soviet Union a military advantage. Advocates for human rights complained that Nixon and Kissinger ignored the Soviet Union's mistreatment of its own people.

Nixon's most astonishing foreign policy reversal was opening the frozen relations between the United States and the People's Republic of China. In July 1971, Kissinger secretly traveled to Beijing to meet China's premier, Zhou Enlai, whom he called "one of the two or three most impressive men I have ever met. Urbane, infinitely patient, intelligent, subtle." The two agreed that Nixon would visit China in 1972 and spoke of the threat of Soviet domination of Europe and Asia. Nixon made a celebrated five-day visit to China in February 1972. He toasted Chairman Mao, and he and his wife Pat visited the Great Wall. He ended his visit in Shanghai, where the two nations issued a carefully crafted declaration of what they had accomplished. The Shanghai Communiqué announced that each country would open "interests sections," embassies in all but name, in each other's capitals. The United States would maintain its embassy on the island of

MEETING OF THE MINDS Henry Kissinger and Soviet ambassador Anatoly Dobrynin in 1974.

Taiwan, the Republic of China. The communiqué stated that all Chinese on both sides of the Straits of Taiwan must formally affirm that China was a single country, a key issue for the PRC. Nixon's visit to China and his 1972 summit in Moscow indicated that the Vietnam War no longer paralyzed U.S. foreign policy as it had in 1968. In December 1972, *Time* named Nixon and Kissinger their Men of the Year because détente with the Soviet Union and the new relationship with China had been "the most profound rearrangement of the earth's political powers since the beginning of the Cold War."

Crises in Latin America and the Middle East, however, eroded Nixon's and Kissinger's reputation for foreign policy success. In September 1973, Kissinger became secretary of state and retained the position of national security advisor. Days before Kissinger was sworn in, the commander of Chile's army, General **Augusto Pinochet**, overthrew the democratically elected government of Socialist president **Salvador Allende**. The United States had tried to thwart Allende for years. In 1970, before Allende was elected in the last of his four tries for the presidency, Kissinger told an interagency intelligence group, "I don't see why we have to let a country go Marxist just because its people are irresponsible."

After Allende's inauguration, the United States cut off economic aid to Chile and the CIA spent $20 million supporting his political opponents. In August 1973, the economy plunged and strikes paralyzed the country. After Pinochet seized power, the military murdered Allende, although they claimed he committed suicide. The military government killed hundreds, arrested over 20,000 of Allende's supporters, and forced thousands to flee into exile. The thousands of presumed dead militants became known

Salvador Allende, " Last Words to the Nation" (August 1973)

as the "disappeared." The "Madres of the Plaza de Mayo" protested steadfastly in the streets for decades demanding an end to the violence and information on the locations of the bodies of their murdered children. The Nixon administration ignored the human rights abuses and restored economic and military aid to Chile. Pinochet ruled a police state for the next 17 years.

On the afternoon of October 6, 1973, the Jewish holy day of Yom Kippur, war broke out in the Middle East. Egypt and Syria launched coordinated attacks on Israeli military positions. The Egyptian and Syrian forces made major gains. Egypt's army captured hundreds of Israeli soldiers in the Sinai Peninsula, and Syria recovered much of the Golan Heights. Shaken by the success of the attackers in this conflict known as the Yom Kippur War, Israeli prime minister **Golda Meir** begged the United States to resupply tanks, arms, planes, and ammunition lost in the first days of the war. The United States responded with an airlift of military equipment that enabled Israel to counterattack. Egypt's president, **Anwar Sadat**, who had evicted Soviet advisors from his country in 1972, now called on Moscow for military aid. Nixon and Kissinger worried that Soviet intervention threatened superpower détente, so Kissinger traveled to Moscow to arrange an end to the fighting. He and Soviet foreign minister **Andrei Gromyko** jointly called on the UN Security Council to sponsor a cease-fire.

Kissinger achieved his highest level of international celebrity after the Yom Kippur War. *Time* wrote that "no other Secretary of State in U.S. history has ever carried so much power, so much responsibility, or so heavy a burden." He traveled back and forth between Israel's capital of Jerusalem and Cairo and Damascus, the capitals of Egypt and Syria, respectively. This shuttle diplomacy resulted in the disengagement of the nations' military forces. Israel moved its forces east of the Suez Canal and thus enabled Egypt to open the important waterway. Israel also withdrew from some, but not all, of Syrian territory on the Golan Heights. Shuttle diplomacy diminished the threat of the resumption of the war, and it began a peace process that led eventually to direct talks and a treaty between Israel and Egypt. It did not, however, address the complex issue of a Palestinian demand for an independent state.

During the Yom Kippur War, members of the **Organization of Petroleum Exporting Countries (OPEC)**, an oil cartel formed in 1960, supported Egypt and Syria. Angered at the West's backing of Israel, OPEC boycotted the sale of oil to the United States, western Europe, and Japan. Because the United States imported less of its oil from the Middle East than did Europe or Japan, it agreed to make up some of its allies' shortfall by reducing its own oil supplies to 80 percent of their customary levels. After the price of a barrel of oil shot up by 400 percent, from two to eight dollars a barrel, the industrial world sank into the gravest economic recession since the Great Depression. The next year, unemployment in the United States rose from 5 percent to 7 percent, and the price of a gallon of gasoline more than doubled from 45 cents to one dollar.

President Richard Nixon, television address concerning national energy policy (November 1973)

STUDY QUESTIONS **FOR NIXON AND THE WORLD**

1. How did the Nixon administration reduce the public's interest in the Vietnam War?

2. How and why did the Communists prevail in the Vietnam War?

3. What were the successes and the failures of the Nixon administration's foreign policy? Explain why some policies succeeded and others did not.

quiz

◉ DOMESTIC POLICY AND THE ABUSE OF POWER

An enormous gulf separated the Nixon administration's rhetoric from the reality of its actions. It cut back but did not eliminate Great Society programs of social reform. Nixon appointed conservative justices to the Supreme Court, but they too did not alter the Court's expansion of individual rights and liberties. His southern strategy encouraged the movement of whites in the Old Confederacy and border states toward the Republican Party, especially as regarded the presidential elections. In 1972, he won one of the most lopsided electoral victories in U.S. history, yet his suspicious nature proved to be his undoing. From 1971 to 1973, numerous White House operatives committed a series of illegal acts known as Watergate, a scandal that forced Nixon to resign from the presidency in August 1974.

Curtailing the Great Society

When Nixon campaigned for the presidency in 1968, he endorsed the Great Society's goals of eliminating poverty and racial discrimination. However, he criticized the Johnson administration's conduct of the war on poverty as inept and inefficient. Congress, controlled by Democrats, reluctantly accepted Nixon's plan to transfer control over antipoverty programs to the states. In return, they prevailed on the Nixon administration to enact laws protecting the environment, workers, and consumers.

In 1971, responding to the growing environmental movement, Congress created the Environmental Protection Agency. The EPA brought hundreds of lawsuits against polluters and set emissions standards for cars and power plants. Congress also addressed issues of worker and consumer protection by creating the Occupational Safety and Health Administration (OSHA) and the Consumer Products Safety Commission (CPSC). OSHA leaders wrote rules for workplace safety and sent inspectors into factories, stores, and offices. Their actions reduced workplace accidents and injuries, but business groups complained that the regulations raised costs and made them uncompetitive. The CPSC's reports on toys and on children's clothing safety were highly popular with parents. Manufacturers, however, resented the regulations; they argued that the additional costs of compliance made their products unaffordable.

International pressures forced Nixon to break with conservative economic orthodoxy. From 1969 to 1971, the economy nearly stagnated while inflation increased. This combination defied the expectations of economists, who called it **stagflation**. Nixon believed the hard economic times endangered his chances for reelection in 1972. In the summer of 1971 European governments that owned U.S. dollars threatened to redeem their greenbacks for gold. When Undersecretary of the Treasury Paul Volcker heard the news on Friday, August 13, he telephoned Treasury Secretary John Connally to tell him that "a major crisis [was] developing in the world's monetary exchange system." On August 15, Nixon announced his "New Economic Policy," the wording of which he borrowed from Democratic Party liberals. He imposed a three-month freeze on wages and prices and announced that the United States would no longer redeem its dollars for gold. This policy began a process under which governments around the world no longer fixed the value of their currency to the value of the dollar. By 1972, currencies floated, with their value being determined in foreign exchange markets. The more cohesive exchange rates that followed helped create a unified global market for goods to flow more freely across national boundaries.

During the election campaign of 1968, Nixon promised to appoint conservative justices to the Supreme Court. When Nixon became president, he appointed **Warren Burger**, a moderately conservative Minnesota federal judge, as chief justice. As part of Nixon's southern strategy of encouraging Democrats in the states of the Old Confederacy to cross over to the Republican Party, he tried to make good on a promise to appoint a southerner to the Court. This effort failed, however, when the Senate defeated the confirmation of Clement Haynsworth and G. Harrold Carswell on the grounds that each had supported racial segregation in the past. Harry Blackmun and **William Rehnquist** joined the Court instead. As part of his judicial strategies, Nixon also initiated a series of domestic "wars," with lasting consequences. After decades of war—including the Cold War—it became common for politicians to use military language to sell social policy. LBJ declared a "war on poverty," and Nixon launched "wars" on drugs and cancer. Nixon justified big federal spending by calling policies "wars," in effect substituting narcotics and malignant cells for Reds and Viet Cong. The war on drugs continued for over forty years, costing billions of dollars and resulting in over 40 million arrests. Medical wars remain big-ticket items in federal budgets.

Despite liberals' fears and conservatives' hopes, the Burger Court did not sharply reverse the Warren Court's expansion of civil rights and liberties. In some notable cases it even went beyond its predecessor. In *Swann v. Charlotte-Mecklenburg Board of Education* (1971) and *Keyes v. Denver School District No. 1* (1973), the Court upheld the use of buses to transport students throughout a school district to achieve racial balance. The decisions provoked angry outbursts. Whites burned school buses in southern states but also generally more moderate cities such as Denver, Colorado, and Pontiac, Michigan. In Boston, white mobs attacked black schoolchildren who under Court order attended previously all-white schools. In 1974, Congress stipulated that busing should be used only as a last resort.

The Court also advanced women's rights. In 1971, it held in *Phillips v. Martin Marietta* that companies could not discriminate against women with small children in their hiring practices. In *Frontiero v. Richardson* (1973), the Court required the military to provide women the same pension rights as men. In *Roe v. Wade* (1973), the Court decided that the right to privacy extended to "a woman's decision whether or not to terminate her pregnancy." It therefore concluded that states could not limit the right to an abortion during the first trimester, or about 13 weeks of a pregnancy. States could regulate, but not outlaw, abortion in the second 13 weeks. Only in the last trimester could states ban abortion.

"The Soiling of Old Glory," a photograph taken during the Boston busing crisis (1976)

Watergate

Richard Nixon constantly felt he was being unfairly attacked by the media, intellectuals, and Democratic Party officials. He treated his domestic political opponents as not merely rivals but enemies. As he prepared for his reelection campaign, he authorized an illegal plot against the Democratic Party designed to undermine its presidential candidates and assure his reelection. Nixon relied on a team of operatives called the "White House Plumbers" he had originally recruited to attack the antiwar movement.

At 1:40 A.M. on June 17, 1972, seven men working for G. Gordon Liddy, an employee of the **Committee to Reelect the President (CREEP)**, broke into the headquarters of the Democratic National Committee to repair an illegal bug, or listening device, they had installed in May. A night watchman called the police, who arrested the burglars and discovered the White House telephone number of E. Howard Hunt, one of the Plumbers who had broken into Daniel Ellsberg's psychiatrist's office in 1971. When Liddy heard of the arrest, he telephoned John Ehrlichman at the White House. Ehrlichman relayed the message to Nixon's chief of staff, **H. R. Haldeman**. The president and his chief of staff immediately began a cover-up of White House involvement in bugging the Democrats' headquarters. Nixon told Haldeman to have the CIA make the FBI "stay the hell out of this" and not investigate any White House ties to the break-in. Nixon put his legal counsel **John Dean** in charge of the cover-up.

Dean's efforts were successful for nearly six months. Few Americans paid attention to articles by *Washington Post* reporters **Bob Woodward** and **Carl Bernstein** that sought to expose the money trail leading from the Watergate burglars to the White House. Democratic presidential candidate George McGovern made little headway with voters when he characterized Nixon as leading "the most corrupt administration in history." In November 1972, Nixon easily defeated McGovern in a landslide election, winning all but Massachusetts and the District of Columbia. Early in 1973, however, the Watergate cover-up began to unravel. The Senate appointed a Select Committee on Presidential Campaign Activities, chaired by North Carolina Democrat Sam Ervin. As the committee prepared for hearings on how Nixon had raised money for his reelection, federal judge **John Sirica** threatened the Watergate burglars with long sentences unless they revealed who had ordered the break-in. Nixon urged his underlings to do whatever they could to maintain the cover-up. The burglars, who had been receiving money from Dean to keep quiet, demanded more. Dean found it increasingly difficult to provide hush money, and he told Nixon that there was a "cancer growing on the presidency." In April, prosecutors began questioning Dean about his role. Dean agreed to cooperate in return for immunity, and he told Ervin and committee staff members all he knew. On April 30, Nixon fired Dean and accepted the resignations of Haldeman and Ehrlichman, who had also been part of the break-in and its cover-up aftermath. Hoping to buy time, Nixon appointed Harvard Law School professor **Archibald Cox** as a special independent prosecutor to investigate Watergate.

In the spring and summer of 1973, the Senate Watergate Committee held televised hearings on events surrounding the break-in and cover-up. The public watched in fascination and disgust as witnesses outlined the millions raised in cash, the administration's dirty tricks against political adversaries, and the extent of the cover-up. The climax came in July when White House aide **Alexander Butterfield** revealed that Nixon had secretly taped his conversations since 1970. All the officials investigating Watergate now wanted the tapes to determine Nixon's role.

Meanwhile, another scandal hit the White House in August when the *Wall Street Journal* reported that Vice President **Spiro T. Agnew** was being investigated for taking bribes when he served as governor of Maryland. Agnew made a deal with prosecutors to avoid jail time and resigned in October. Nixon then appointed House Minority Leader Gerald R. Ford, untainted by Watergate, to replace Agnew.

In October, special prosecutor Cox asked Judge Sirica to order Nixon to provide him with the tapes. Instead, Nixon fired Cox and closed the office of the independent counsel. The public responded with a deluge of outraged telegrams and phone calls to Congress demanding that the House of Representatives begin impeachment proceedings against Nixon. In the first six months of 1974, the Judiciary Committee built a case against Nixon. In July, the committee approved three articles of impeachment against him for obstruction of justice, abuse of power, and an illegal disregard of congressional

Sam J. Ervin, "Final Report of the Senate Select Committee on Presidential Campaign Activities" (1974)

WATERGATE SPECIAL PROSECUTOR ARCHIBALD COX MEETING THE PRESS ON JUNE 4, 1973 A former law professor at Harvard, Cox left the university to take the lead in the investigation of President Nixon's connections to and cover-up of the Watergate events. Nixon ordered Cox be dismissed, leading to resignations of top Justice Department officials who refused to do so. When Cox was finally reluctantly dismissed, it helped turn the legal tide against Nixon.

subpoenas. Nixon continued to deny wrongdoing until the Supreme Court unanimously ordered him to release the tapes of 64 conversations. One of them contained the "smoking gun" conversation in which he and Haldeman conspired to use the CIA to cover up the burglary at the Watergate. With the release of that tape, Nixon lost all of his remaining Republican congressional support, and he resigned on August 9, 1974.

Nixon's resignation temporarily unified the country. Americans were outraged by the abuses of power, but they felt relieved that Congress, the court system, and the press had worked together to reveal the extent of the misconduct. Most agreed with President Ford, who exclaimed after he took the oath of office, "Our long national nightmare is over."

STUDY QUESTIONS **FOR DOMESTIC POLICY AND THE ABUSE OF POWER**

1. What domestic goals did the Nixon administration pursue?
2. Where was the Nixon administration successful, and where did it fail in changing the direction and scope of the Great Society programs of the Johnson administration?
3. What threats to constitutional government did the Watergate scandal represent?

quiz

interactive timeline

TIMELINE 1945–1975

AMERICA	YEAR	THE WORLD
	1945	**Apr** U.S. and Soviet troops race toward Berlin **Jul–Aug** Potsdam Conference sets stage for Cold War **Sep** Ho Chi Minh declares independence of Democratic Republic of Vietnam **Dec** International Monetary Fund (IMF) formally created to aid global economic stability and prevent another world war
	1946	**Jul** Dramatic demonstrations of new atomic bombs in Bikini Atoll in Pacific cause global fallout concern **Jul** Treaty of Manila grants independence to Philippines **Dec** War begins between France and the Vietminh
Apr President Eisenhower decides against American military operation to relieve French at Dien Bien Phu **May** Mexican government works with United States to repatriate migrant workers under "Operation Wetback"	**1954**	**May** French defeated at Battle of Dien Bien Phu **Jul** Geneva Conference partitions Vietnam into North and South **Oct** Algerian War for Independence begins **Nov** Hungary revolts against Soviet rule
	1956	**Oct** Britain, France, and Israel launch military attacks against Egypt **Dec** Britain and France withdraw troops from Suez
	1957	**Jul** Egypt nationalizes Suez Canal **Jul** International Geophysical Year begins hopeful cooperation between 67 countries on range of science and technology developments **Oct** Soviets successfully launch *Sputnik*
	1960	**Dec** Creation of National Front for the Liberation of Vietnam (the Viet Cong)
	1963	**May–Jun** Buddhist crisis in South Vietnam **Jun** Kennedy gives "*Ich bin ein Berliner*" speech in Berlin **Nov** Military coup deposes President Ngo Dinh Diem
Feb Beatles land at JFK International Airport launching "British Invasion" **Aug** Congress adopts Gulf of Tonkin Resolution	**1964**	**Apr** Malcolm X travels to Middle East and Mecca
Mar First anti-Vietnam teach-in at University of Michigan **Jul** President Johnson makes final decision to Americanize the Vietnam War	**1965**	

Summary

- From 1945 to 1963, the United States supported anti-Communist forces in Vietnam as part of the Cold War competition with the Soviet Union and Communist China.
- From 1964 to 1967, the administration of President Lyndon B. Johnson Americanized the Vietnam War. By 1968, approximately 500,000 U.S. forces were fighting in Vietnam.
- After 1965, opposition to the war grew at home and abroad.
- The climactic year of the war was 1968. Assassinations, urban uprisings, and protests shocked Americans and led to the election of Richard M. Nixon as president.

AMERICA	YEAR	THE WORLD
	1966	**May** Great Proletarian Cultural Revolution begins in China
Oct Over 100,000 people join antiwar march on Washington	**1967**	**May** Jean Paul Sartre organizes International War Crimes Tribunal to judge U.S. conduct in Vietnam **Oct** Publication of Jean-Jacques Servan-Schreiber's *The American Challenge*
Jan Tet Offensive begins **Mar** My Lai Massacre **Mar** Johnson announces he will not seek Democratic Party presidential nomination **Apr** Martin Luther King, Jr., assassinated **Apr** Student demonstrations at Columbia University **Jun** Robert F. Kennedy assassinated **Aug** Demonstrations at Democratic National Convention in Chicago **Nov** Richard Nixon defeats Hubert Humphrey and George Wallace for presidency	**1968**	**Jan–Aug** Prague Spring in Czechoslovakia **May** Student uprising in Paris leads to crippling nationwide general strike **Oct** Mexican troops kill over 1,000 young people protesting Olympic Games in Mexico City
Nov American Indian Movement occupies Alcatraz	**1969**	**Mar** Vietnamization begins
May National Guard kills four protesters at Kent State University	**1970**	**Apr** U.S. and South Vietnamese invasion of Cambodia
Feb Nixon visits the PRC **Jun** Publication of the Pentagon Papers **Jul** Henry Kissinger secretly visits the People's Republic of China	**1971**	**Jan–Apr** U.S. and South Vietnamese invasion of Laos ends in failure
Jun Watergate break-in that eventually leads to Nixon's resignation **Nov** Nixon reelected in landslide	**1972**	**Feb** Nixon makes landmark trip to China toasting Chairman Mao **May** Nixon visits Soviet Union, furthering détente between the world's two nuclear superpowers; two leaders sign SALT I nuclear arms limitations
May Senate Watergate hearings begin **Oct** Spiro Agnew resigns as vice president **Dec** Gerald R. Ford becomes vice president	**1973**	**Oct** Yom Kippur War erupts across Middle East **Oct–Mar** Mideast Arab oil embargo against United States and other supporters of Israel; sharp international economic recession follows
Jul House Judiciary Committee approves three articles of impeachment against Richard Nixon **Aug** Nixon resigns as president	**1974**	
	1975	**Mar** North Vietnamese and NLF forces capture Da Nang **Apr** Communist forces win Vietnam War

- President Nixon and national security advisor Henry Kissinger engineered dramatic reversals in American foreign policy toward the Soviet Union and China.
- The Paris Peace Accords of 1973 ended U.S. involvement in the Vietnam War. The Communist North won the war in 1975.
- The Nixon administration curtailed but did not eliminate the Great Society programs of the Johnson administration.
- The Watergate scandal was the gravest constitutional crisis of the 20th century for the United States. It led to President Nixon's resignation in 1974.

Key Terms and People

Reviewing Chapter 28

1. How did the war in Vietnam affect U.S. foreign policies?
2. How did growing dissatisfaction with the war in Vietnam contribute to wider disillusionment with public institutions and officials?
3. How did the actions of the Nixon administration, at home and abroad, affect public attitudes toward government and public institutions?

Further Reading

Buchanan, Sherry. *Vietnam Zippos: American Soldiers' Engravings and Stories, 1965–1973.* Chicago: University of Chicago Press, 2007.

Farber, David R. *Chicago '68.* Chicago: University of Chicago Press, 1988. An innovative study of a critical turning point in history.

Herring, George C. *America's Longest War: The United States and Vietnam, 1950–1975.* New York: McGraw-Hill, 2002. A detailed yet readable account of the uncertain U.S. entry, often-perplexing escalation of involvement, and painful exit from Vietnam.

O'Brien, Tim. *The Things They Carried.* New York: Houghton Mifflin, 1990. An award-winning collection of stories based on the author's actual experience in Vietnam.

Schulzinger, Robert D. *A Time for War: The United States and Vietnam, 1941–1975.* New York: Oxford University Press, 1997. Insightful analysis of the war from the perspective of a leading diplomatic historian.

Small, Melvin. *Antiwarriors: The Vietnam War and the Battle for America's Hearts and Minds.* New York: Rowman & Littlefield, 2002. A critical analysis of the antiwar movement in politics and culture.

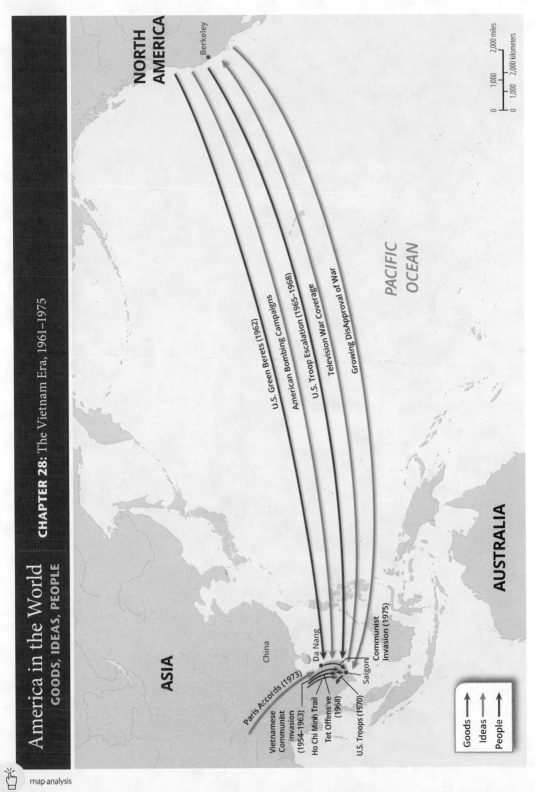

America in the World
GOODS, IDEAS, PEOPLE

CHAPTER 28: The Vietnam Era, 1961–1975

map analysis

NORTH AMERICA

Berkeley

PACIFIC OCEAN

ASIA

China

Da Nang

Saigon

AUSTRALIA

U.S. Green Berets (1962)

American Bombing Campaigns

American Troop Escalation (1965–1968)

U.S. Troop Escalation

Television War Coverage

Growing DisApproval of War

Paris Accords (1973)

Vietnamese Communist Invasion (1954–1963)

Ho Chi Minh Trail

Tet Offensive (1968)

U.S. Troops (1970)

Communist Invasion (1975)

Goods
Ideas
People

0   1,000   2,000 miles
0   1,000   2,000 kilometers

Morning Again in America: With the first lady at his side, Ronald Reagan waves to supporters after being sworn in as president, January 20, 1981.

Conservatism Resurgent

1973–1988

n June 1984, President Ronald Reagan assembled his top foreign policy advisors, Vice President George H. W. Bush, CIA Director William Casey, Secretary of State George Shultz, Secretary of Defense Caspar Weinberger, and National Security Advisor **Robert McFarlane** to discuss funding the right-wing **"Contra"** guerrillas fighting against the leftist Sandinista regime in Nicaragua. The public admired Reagan's success in restoring national pride and Congress generally supported Reagan's muscular foreign policy, but both opposed direct involvement in Central America's brutal civil wars. In reaction to Contra attacks on Nicaraguan civilians in 1984, Congress barred all military aid to the guerrillas. Condemning congressional interference, Reagan praised the Contras as "freedom fighters" and ordered his subordinates to work around the aid ban. They asked friendly foreign governments, such as Taiwan, Israel, Brunei, and Saudi Arabia, to funnel money to the Contras, with repayment by the United States. Reagan knew the plan was a ruse that violated the law. If the "story gets out," he quipped, "we'll all be hanging by our thumbs in front of the White House."

Over the next two years, several foreign governments funded the Contras. But when the money proved inadequate, the president authorized an even more brazen scheme that linked the fighting in Central America to the cauldron of the Middle East. Reagan directed the National Security Council (NSC) staff to arrange secret arms sales to the Islamic Republic of Iran, then at war with Iraq, and a sworn enemy of the United States. In return for the weapons, Iranian intermediaries (who claimed to be "moderates" seeking improved relations with the United States) promised to help free several Americans held hostage by pro-Iranian militias in Lebanon. By overcharging Iran for the weapons, the NSC would generate profits to finance the Contras.

This violated several laws and mocked Reagan's pledge to "never to negotiate with terrorists."

The scheme imploded in October 1986 when a CIA-chartered plane ferrying arms to the Contras was brought down. The surviving American pilot disclosed the illegal gun-running scheme, and Iranian and Lebanese sources then revealed their roles. Reagan's aides justified the arms sales by claiming they were cultivating ties with Iranian moderates, who proved to be hard-liners loyal to Ayatollah Khomeini. Reagan had achieved a dubious trifecta: he had broken laws that barred aid to the Contras *and* arms sales to Iran, effectively paid ransom to terrorists who kidnapped Americans, and made the United States appear ridiculous.

The president's aides destroyed incriminating documents and falsely claimed he knew few details about what was called the **Iran-Contra scandal**. Probes by Congress, a special prosecutor, and journalists revealed many details of the bungled operation. Reagan deflected tough questions about his own involvement by repeatedly claiming he had "forgotten" most details. In the cynical words of NSC staffer Colonel **Oliver North**, "The president didn't always know what he knew."

Reagan survived the Iran-Contra scandal, which had one positive consequence. To salvage his badly tarnished image, Reagan fired nearly all the hard-line conservative advisors he had relied on since 1981. He delegated responsibility for foreign and domestic affairs to moderates such as George Shultz, Frank Carlucci, Howard Baker, and Colin Powell. They steered the United States away from bizarre entanglements and, more importantly, encouraged Reagan to cooperate with Mikhail Gorbachev, the new reformist leader of the Soviet Union.

⌄ BACKLASH

The political upheaval of 1980—signified by a resurgent conservative movement under the banner of the Republican Party—was the culmination of a decade-long erosion of public faith in government at all levels. The chaotic end of the war in Vietnam; Nixon's lawbreaking; the perceived failure of his two successors to manage the economy or protect the nation; rising rates of crime, welfare, and divorce; slow economic growth; high inflation; and gasoline shortages seemed proof that misguided government policies either caused major problems or could not alleviate them. Stand-up comedians joked that the 10 most frightening words in English were "I'm from the government and I'm here to help you." Conservatives charged that although Nixon and his successors promoted détente with the Soviets, the Kremlin increased its strength and meddled in Central America, Africa, and the Middle East. They spoke of an affliction Reagan dubbed the "Vietnam syndrome": U.S. fear of defending its allies or resisting its foes. As they saw it, this weakness made the seizure of Americans in Iran inevitable.

Nixon's resignation in August 1974 relieved the acute pain of the Watergate crisis, but his exit left unresolved problems. The Vietnam War had fractured the national consensus over the value of containing communism everywhere. The opening with China and the pursuit of détente with the Soviets blurred the certainties of the Cold War. Despite these initiatives, the arms race continued, insurgencies spread in the Third World, terrorist attacks on Americans and allies such as Israel became more frequent, and access to Middle Eastern petroleum became less secure.

In the 1970s, the civil rights movement continued to make gains for new segments of the population. Congress addressed the marginalization of disabled youth in the landmark Disabilities Education Act of 1975. It mandated that schools and other institutions "mainstream" physically and mentally disabled children in the "least restrictive environment" possible. In 1978, responding to pressure from Native American activists in groups like AIM (American Indian Movement), Congress enacted the Indian Self-Determination and Education Act. The government officially abandoned its 25-year effort to "terminate" tribal sovereignty and instead bolstered tribal authority over reservation land and resources.

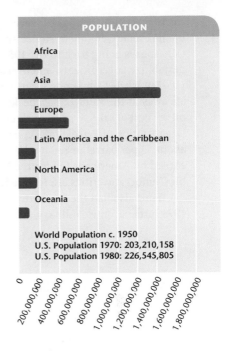

POPULATION

Africa

Asia

Europe

Latin America and the Caribbean

North America

Oceania

World Population c. 1950
U.S. Population 1970: 203,210,158
U.S. Population 1980: 226,545,805

However, many Great Society programs that had begun with hope had lost support due to mounting costs, limited progress, and the difficulties imposed by an economic slowdown lasting much of the 1970s. For the first time in living memory, the economy experienced slow growth combined with steep inflation, a phenomenon dubbed "stagflation."

An Accidental President

Nixon's two successors, the appointed Gerald Ford and the elected **Jimmy Carter,** both began with the good wishes of the electorate but soon squandered that trust. Ford struck a healing tone as he entered the Oval Office in August 1974 after Nixon resigned. Personally untainted by Nixon's crimes, he assured the nation that the "long national nightmare" of Watergate had ended. But after his decision a few weeks later to pardon Nixon—conceived as an act of mercy but seen by many as an unwarranted "get out of jail free" pass—a majority of Americans lost confidence in his judgment. The new president's approval rating plummeted from 72 percent to 49 percent and never recovered.

Ford then angered conservatives by appointing former New York governor **Nelson Rockefeller,** a Republican moderate, as vice president. Subsequent remarks made by First Lady Betty Ford endorsing abortion rights, the Equal Rights Amendment, and premarital sex incurred the wrath of religious conservatives, some of whom called her "a disgrace."

The lingering shadow of Watergate, the weak economy, and Republican disarray produced big Democratic gains in the 1974 midterm election. In the wake of the election, Democrats passed several campaign reform bills and investigated misdeeds by the executive branch. House and Senate committees mounted several inquiries into CIA abuses going back to the 1950s, including attempts to assassinate foreign leaders, destabilize governments, and overthrow Chilean president Salvador Allende in 1973.

But while Democrats scrutinized past misdeeds, job losses mounted and inflation ate away at the value of paychecks. Since the October 1973 Arab-Israeli War, the Arab oil boycott of sales to pro-Israeli nations, along with effective marketing controls by the Organization of Petroleum Exporting Counties (OPEC), had pushed oil prices up from about $3 per barrel to $30 by the end of the decade (Figure 29.1). In 1975, hourly wages earned by Americans fell for the first time in 25 years. But neither President Ford nor his Democratic critics offered credible proposals to solve these problems.

Ford also had the misfortune to deal with the collapse of South Vietnam. In April 1975, after a quick military offensive, North Vietnamese troops overran the South.

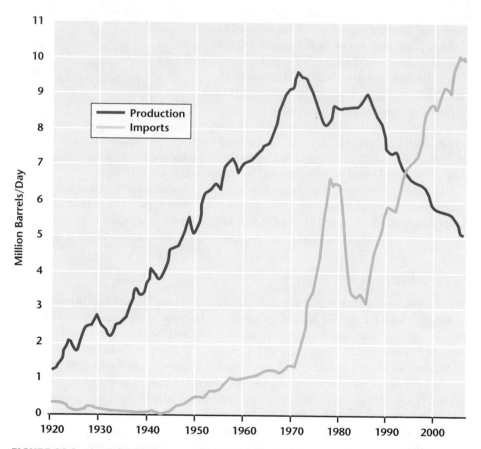

FIGURE 29.1 America's energy use and sources Petroleum production in the United States peaked in the early 1970s (new fracking technology boosted output after 2010), even as demand increased. For the past 40 years, the United States has imported half or more of its oil requirements. Most of the imports come from Canada, Mexico, Saudi Arabia, Venezuela, Colombia, and Nigeria. Aside from Saudi oil, the United States imports relatively little petroleum from the Middle East.

Henry Kissinger, who stayed on as Ford's national security advisor and secretary of state, had attempted to manage the Cold War by negotiating arms control deals with the Soviet Union and restoring ties to China. But by the mid-1970s, a chorus of critics from both parties was complaining that détente with the Soviets had failed. Democrats who criticized détente—later known as **neoconservatives**—charged the Soviets with cheating on arms control and continuing to oppress political and religious dissidents. Republican critics of détente, like Ronald Reagan, also charged that the Soviets had armed insurgent groups in Latin America, Africa, and the Middle East. When Ford negotiated the SALT II agreement with Soviet leader Leonid Brezhnev in late 1974, the Senate refused to ratify the pact. Critics accused Ford of cutting a deal that strengthened the Soviet nuclear arsenal while further diminishing American strength.

A Polish student's view of the Cold War (1973)

Ford attempted to improve Soviet–American ties when he met with Brezhnev in Finland in 1975. They signed the so-called **Helsinki Accords**, a set of principles that accepted the post-1945 division of Europe into East–West spheres. American conservatives viewed the accords as a cave-in.

To win over conservative delegates at the Republican nominating convention in the summer of 1976, Ford adopted more conservative positions. He reduced Kissinger's role; replaced Vice President Rockefeller with a sharp-tongued conservative senator from Kansas, **Robert Dole**; suspended talks with Panama on a new canal treaty; promised to reduce taxes and government spending; and endorsed constitutional amendments to ban abortion and permit school prayer. Even so, Ford barely edged out Reagan for the nomination.

Democrats selected as their nominee Jimmy Carter, a former governor of Georgia. Carter graduated from the Naval Academy at Annapolis and served on a nuclear submarine before returning home to manage his family's peanut farm near Plains, Georgia. He was elected governor as a segregationist sympathizer, but on taking office, he pledged to end discrimination.

Carter's campaign stressed his evangelical religious beliefs and status as a Washington "outsider." He took centrist stands on controversial issues such as abortion and school busing for racial balance. He personally opposed both, but he also rejected calls for amending the Constitution to ban either practice. To reassure northern Democrats, Carter selected Minnesota senator **Walter Mondale**, a traditional liberal, as his running mate.

Ford and Carter both ran lackluster campaigns that failed to energize the public. Just over half of eligible voters went to the polls in November, the lowest number in any presidential election since World War II. Carter won by a narrow margin.

The Politics of Limits and Malaise

Some of the very characteristics that helped Carter get elected, such as his lack of Washington experience, his disdain for many politicians, and his focus on technical expertise, made it hard for him to govern or build alliances in Congress. For example, he angered powerful members of Congress by abruptly canceling 19 dam and irrigation projects in the South and West, on the mostly accurate grounds that they were both costly and bad for the environment. He seemed indifferent to the fact that they had promoted these projects as ways of ensuring political support.

As president, Carter attempted to tackle "big" issues, including energy shortages and the Middle East peace process, but stumbled when trying to explain these policies to ordinary people or to get Congress to act. By frequently saying there were "no easy answers," he made it sound as if he had no answers. Many politicians agreed that although Carter was extremely smart, he was completely inept at passing legislation.

Despite signs of public restiveness, Carter believed that his commitment to principles of "good government" would win wide backing. His administration supported affirmative action. Race-preference policies, begun under Nixon, aimed to redress past discrimination by giving minorities and women preferential treatment in hiring, school admission, or receiving government contracts. Although these preferences had a very modest impact, the policy struck many Americans as conflicting with the ideal of equality for all, regardless of race. When the Voting Rights Act of 1965 was extended in 1975, a new provision included Latinos and Asians, many of whom had arrived after passage of the initial law. The law stipulated that in districts with high concentrations of non-native English speakers, voting materials be made available in languages such as Spanish and Chinese. This provision provoked an "English-only" movement that criticized "special privileges" for minorities and gathered strength over the next decade.

The Supreme Court ruled on race-based preferences in 1978 in the case of *University of California Board of Regents v. Bakke*. Allan Bakke, a white male, had been denied admission to medical school. He argued that California's affirmative action program was a form of reverse discrimination because it led to the admission of less-qualified black applicants. A five-justice majority of the Court ruled that Bakke should be admitted to medical school and that rigid racial quotas were forbidden. However, the majority also stated that race could be used as a factor in admission and hiring decisions so long as it was not the only factor.

Carter tried, without much success, to solve America's chronic energy dilemma. In 1950, the United States produced about 50 percent of the world's petroleum. That had fallen to 20 percent by 1972. By the late 1970s, the United States imported 43 percent of the 17 million barrels of oil it consumed daily and the costs were steadily mounting. Carter persuaded Congress to create a new Department of Energy (as well as a Department of Education) along with programs to boost energy conservation; expand domestic drilling; and promote new energy sources, such as synthetic fuels from coal and shale and wind, solar, and nuclear energy. But when Congress finally passed an energy bill in 1978, it rejected imposing any substantial increases in energy taxes, the one thing most likely to spur conservation and encourage investment in nonfossil fuels. The new law did little to promote nuclear power, as the public had soured on this energy source both prior to and following the March 1979 near-meltdown of a nuclear reactor at Three Mile Island in Pennsylvania. But even short-term benefits from the energy bill were undermined in 1979 by the Iranian Revolution, which disrupted oil markets and drove up the price of petroleum to the then historic high of $30 per barrel. At the pump, this increase translated into nearly a tripling of the price of gasoline, from just over 30 cents per gallon to nearly one dollar.

Spiking energy prices, along with a growing foreign trade deficit and a dollar falling in value, further weakened the American economy and caused inflation to rise to crisis levels. At the time of Carter's inauguration, annual inflation hit 6 percent. In 1978, the rate hit 9 percent per year, followed by 11.3 percent in 1979 and 13 percent in 1980. Interest rates for car and home loans reached 17 percent. During the same period, the unemployment rate remained stubbornly high, 6–7.5 percent. Carter's approval rating plummeted. By July 1979, less than one-third of Americans approved of Carter's performance.

Voter frustration with the failure of politicians to solve economic problems surfaced dramatically in California. In June 1978, residents overwhelmingly approved Proposition 13, a plan to roll back the state's high property tax and require a two-thirds vote of the legislature to raise future taxes. Over the next four years, legislatures in 18 states slashed taxes.

For many Americans, taxes had become a symbol of larger problems. As wages stagnated and inflation climbed, about the only way ordinary people could see more money was by lowering taxes. Antitax activists like those promoting Prop 13 argued that cutting taxes would not only relieve the burden on middle-class homeowners but force a reduction in wasteful government welfare. In July 1979, responding to dismal poll numbers, Carter delivered a speech urging Americans to work harder, not to despair, to overcome their "crisis of confidence" through self-sacrifice, and to find alternatives to dependence on oil. Although he did not utter the word, one of his aides referred to this as Carter's "malaise speech," and the term stuck. At first the public seemed impressed by Carter's appeal for sacrifice. But it became more cynical two days later when he fired five cabinet members and seemed to blame them for the country's troubles.

President Jimmy Carter's "Malaise Speech" (1979)

To tackle inflation, Carter appointed **Paul Volcker** to head the Federal Reserve. Volcker quickly hiked interest rates above 15 percent to slow business activity by raising the cost of borrowing. Over the next three years, these high rates reduced inflation dramatically, but not soon enough to help Carter. In 1979–1980, high interest rates made jobs and mortgages harder to come by and made Carter even less popular.

A Dangerous World, 1974–1980

In spite of his domestic troubles and later failures in foreign affairs, Carter initially achieved several foreign policy breakthroughs in the Middle East and Latin America. Early in his presidency, Carter declared, "We are now free of the inordinate fear of communism which once led us to embrace any dictator." Respect for human rights, he promised, would be a foundation, not an afterthought, of foreign policy. Carter became the first president to visit sub-Saharan Africa and voice support for peaceful efforts to replace the white-ruled regimes in Rhodesia and South Africa. This emphasis on human rights inspired hope among many opponents of dictatorship, but it became a target for conservatives who considered communism still the major threat.

Carter pursued a Middle Eastern peace plan after Egyptian president **Anwar Sadat** flew to Jerusalem in November 1977 to address Israel's parliament. In 1978, the president mediated between Sadat and Israeli prime minister **Menachem Begin** during negotiations at Camp David, the presidential retreat in Maryland. Begin agreed to end occupation of the Sinai Peninsula in return for Egypt's recognizing the existence of the Jewish state. They signed a formal treaty in March 1979.

The president showed considerable skill in breaking two diplomatic logjams. In March 1978, he convinced the Senate to ratify the long-stalled treaty with Panama and gradually transfer control of the canal to Panamanians. In early 1979, following up on Nixon's breakthrough, he formally ended the long estrangement from China by severing official ties with Taiwan and extending full diplomatic recognition to the People's Republic of China.

The president attempted to salvage détente by meeting with Soviet leader Brezhnev in Vienna in June 1979. They agreed to a SALT II treaty placing caps on the number of

PEACE SIGNING President Jimmy Carter achieved a breakthrough in the Middle East when he brokered a peace between Egypt and Israel. The Camp David agreement was signed by Egypt's Anwar Sadat and Israel's Menachem Begin.

nuclear weapons and delivery systems in their arsenals. But the treaty never came up for a Senate vote. In December 1979, Soviet forces invaded neighboring Afghanistan in an attempt to shore up a teetering pro-Communist government. Like many Americans, Carter feared that the Soviets' real goal was control of the oil-rich Persian Gulf. The president suspended consideration of the SALT II treaty, pulled U.S. athletes from the upcoming Moscow Olympics, suspended grain sales to Moscow, resumed draft registration, and sharply increased military spending. Carter pledged to resist any Soviet encroachment into the Middle East (sometimes called the Carter Doctrine) and authorized the CIA to secretly aid the **Mujahideen**, Islamic guerrillas fighting the Soviets in Afghanistan.

Many Americans viewed the Afghan crisis as part of a wider Soviet offensive. During the 1970s, Brezhnev had cracked down on internal dissent and expanded nuclear and conventional forces. Although the United States maintained a large strategic advantage, the Soviets deployed new missiles in eastern Europe capable of hitting any country in western Europe and subsidized Fidel Castro's dispatch of Cuban military advisors to Angola and Ethiopia. In Central America in 1979, the leftist Sandinista guerrillas toppled the pro-American dictator of Nicaragua, Anastasio Somoza DeBayle, and allied themselves with Cuba and the Soviet Union. Critics accused Carter of doing little or nothing to counter these threats.

America Held Hostage

From the end of World War II through the late 1970s, the United States had successfully curtailed Soviet influence in the greater Middle East. Most of the Arab autocrats who ruled the region often used Islam as a cover but had little use for religion. Both these secular strongmen and the region's religious authorities tried to keep out "modern" ideas and fed their people a steady diet of very traditional Islam and conspiracy theories about the West, Israel, and Jews. The United States maintained its closest regional ties with Israel, Saudi Arabia, and Iran and through them dominated the region.

The seizure of the U.S. embassy in Tehran, Iran, and the taking of 66 diplomats and Marine guards as hostages on November 4, 1979, altered the region's power balance and soon dominated domestic politics. Tensions with Iran went back to 1953, when the CIA helped depose the government of reformer **Mohammed Mossadeq** and restored to power the pro-American Shah **Mohammed Reza Pahlavi**. As oil revenues mounted during the 1960s and 1970s, the shah, with American encouragement, built up Iran's military power and embarked on what he called a "revolution from above." He modernized schools and the agricultural system and limited the influence of Islamic clerics. Under the shah, Iran maintained fairly amicable trade relations with Israel. During a visit to Iran late in 1977, Jimmy Carter praised the monarch for making Iran an "island of stability" in a troubled region.

Many Iranians, however, detested the corruption and the lack of political freedom. Dissenters were beaten, jailed, or exiled by the secret police. American diplomats worried mostly about pro-Soviet or Communist opposition to the shah. They failed to notice that resistance increasingly centered among conservative Islamic clerics who denounced Western influence and the shah's monopoly on power. An exiled, elderly ayatollah, or religious leader, **Ruholla Khomeini**, who called the United States the "Great Satan" and favored a society based on the Qur'an (or Koran), emerged as the symbol of opposition. In February 1979, after months of street protests, the shah fled and the ayatollah returned as Iran's leader. Khomeini did not sever diplomatic ties with or halt oil sales to the United Sates. For its part, the Carter administration hoped to maintain economic ties to the new regime and wanted to avoid doing anything to imperil the 10,000 Americans (teachers, technical specialists, and businesspeople) living in Iran. About 50,000 Iranian students studied in American institutions.

Poster showing the overthrow of the shah (1980)

Relations soured in October 1979 when Carter allowed the deposed shah to enter the United States to receive treatment for an ultimately fatal cancer. The Iranian government demanded that the United States send the shah and his "stolen wealth" home. When Carter balked, on November 4 radical students seized the U.S. embassy in Tehran—which they called a "nest of spies"—and took the hostages. Of the 66 initially detained, a dozen were soon released. Ultimately, 52 were held for 444 days. The president condemned this violation of international law and pledged to free the captives. At first, the U.S. public rallied behind Carter, but as the crisis dragged on—played out day after day on television—he appeared weak.

In December 1979, after two months of medical treatment, Carter expelled the shah, who thereafter lived as a wandering exile until he died in July 1980. Beyond that, there was actually little Carter could do, since Iranian radicals believed that prolonging, not solving, the crisis increased their power. Meanwhile, also in December 1979, Soviet forces invaded Afghanistan to prop up a weak pro-Soviet regime. Carter, like many Americans, saw this as evidence of a Soviet plan to dominate the oil-rich Persian Gulf.

In April 1980, Carter approved a daring and complex raid to rescue the captives. But sandstorms damaged several of the helicopters as they flew toward their target, and Carter aborted the mission. During a refueling stop in the Iranian desert, two of the

HOSTILE TAKEOVER Iranian student radicals burn an American flag as they celebrate the seizure of the U.S. embassy in Tehran and the taking of hostages in November 1979.

President Jimmy Carter, television address on the rescue attempt for American hostages in Iran (April 25, 1980)

aircraft collided on the ground and killed eight crew members. Secretary of State Cyrus Vance, who had opposed the mission, resigned in protest. In a televised address, Carter attributed the fiasco to "mechanical difficulties." Khomeini called the sandstorms "divine intervention." As details of the botched rescue came to light, many Americans blamed Carter, not bad weather. The shah's death in July did little to solve the hostage crisis. Iran continued to demand the return of billions of dollars in blocked funds and other concessions.

Bad luck also undermined Carter's attempt to support human rights in Cuba. In March 1980, when thousands of Cuban dissidents sought refuge in foreign embassies in Havana, he offered them asylum in the United States. Fidel Castro announced that for a limited time any Cuban who wanted to leave could do so by departing from the small fishing port of Mariel. The U.S. government organized a flotilla of private boats to transport the so-called Marielitos, whose numbers totaled 130,000 by the time the boatlift ended in October. Public support for the effort faded when Castro opened jails and mental institutions and told inmates to join the exodus. Although they comprised only a few thousand of the total, the media highlighted problems caused by these undesirables. Critics claimed that a gullible Carter had allowed Castro to dump his problems on America.

In the midst of these difficulties, Carter faced a renomination challenge from Massachusetts senator **Edward "Ted" Kennedy,** who accused him of incompetence and deserting the party's liberal tenets. Although he prevailed over Kennedy, Carter could not as easily shake off Ronald Reagan. Gearing up for a run at the White House, Reagan ridiculed Carter as a "woolly-headed idealist" who had no plan to improve the economy

MARIELITOS Tens of thousands of Cuban "Marielitos" fled on fishing boats toward the United States from the small port of Mariel during the spring and summer of 1980. A small number of the refugees were criminals or mentally ill.

or reverse the nation's slide. Carter, Reagan charged, "deserted" the shah and did nothing while the Soviets surged forward and as Cuban agents took over Nicaragua and extended their reach in Africa.

A solution to the hostage crisis came from an unlikely source. In September 1980, Iraqi dictator Saddam Hussein ordered his army to invade neighboring Iran to seize oil, water, and territory. In addition to his megalomania, Saddam, a secular Sunni Muslim in a country where Shias comprised the majority, feared and despised the Shia Muslims who controlled Iran. Iraqi and Iranian armies fought bloody battles larger than any since World War II. The carnage lasted eight years and claimed one million lives on both sides.

The huge cost of the war even in its early phase made Iran receptive to trading the hostages for billions of Iranian dollars frozen in Western banks. Nevertheless, negotiations dragged on for months. To humiliate Carter, the Iranians purposely stalled until after the election, freeing the hostages on January 20, 1981, just as Reagan took the presidential oath. Iran received $8 billion in unblocked assets and the satisfaction of playing a role in bringing down a president.

STUDY QUESTIONS FOR BACKLASH

1. Why did the public quickly lose faith in President Gerald Ford?

2. What economic problems undermined the Carter administration?

3. How did the Iran hostage crisis doom the Carter presidency?

quiz

⊻ DEMOCRATIC DECLINE AND THE RISING TIDE ON THE RIGHT

Frustration with the government had become widespread by 1980. Many Americans felt that both Jimmy Carter and Democrats in Congress debated issues and passed laws unconnected to the problems of everyday life. Some believed that the government looked after the very wealthy and the chronically poor but ignored everyone in between. Conservative Republicans seized on this anger to propose what sounded to many Americans like practical solutions to economic and social problems.

The Crisis of the Democrats

During the 1970s, the liberal Democratic coalition forged in the 1930s, composed of unionized labor, blacks, Jews, and Catholics of Irish and eastern European origin, fragmented. As the nation's population moved west and south, northern cities became home to more of the poor and people of color. Rising rates of crime, divorce, drug use, and abortion—often blamed on racial minorities and, according to 83 percent of the public in a 1980 poll, liberal judges—particularly upset blue-collar, white ethnic voters. (Crime rates are more closely related to the rise and fall in the young male population than to liberal or conservative sentencing.) Membership in labor unions shrank by one-third during the 1970s, as manufacturing jobs migrated abroad or to the South where "right to work" laws kept unions weak. Once-prosperous cities such as Buffalo and Detroit lost jobs and population and became emblems of what was now dubbed the "rust belt." Unions, which had previously promoted progressive social policies, increasingly focused on efforts to preserve jobs by opposing imports. White Democrats in the South, generally more conservative than those in the North, peeled away from the party after the 1965 Voting Rights Act opened registration to millions of African Americans. The Sunbelt, a region from the Southeast through southern California, became the bastion of the increasingly conservative Republican Party.

A growing number of working and middle-class Americans viewed the Democratic Party as little more than a tax collector for the welfare state. One poll in 1980 found that about two-thirds of whites believed that elected Democrats cared mostly about minorities. At the same time, Democratic politicians muddied their brand by frequently defining themselves as primarily pro-consumer, pro-environment, pro-labor, or pro-feminist. This kind of "identity politics" left the party without a cohesive message. By 1980, except for Jews and blacks, much of the old New Deal coalition voted Republican.

Rising Tide on the Right

For decades, conservative thought had pulled in separate directions. By the late 1970s, politically energized evangelical Protestants, conservative Catholics, gun rights groups, antiabortion activists, business lobbyists, tax reformers, and advocates of a more militarized foreign policy had organized a variety of lobbying groups that effectively challenged liberal ideas and Democratic control of national politics. Calls for law and order, tax cuts, a greater role for religion in public life, and increased defense spending easily trumped muddled Democratic messages. By 1980, conservative Republicans were strong enough to vie for control of Congress and the White House.

Between the end of World War II and the early 1970s, steady economic growth had been a tide that lifted nearly all boats. Three decades of high employment, increasing productivity (the amount produced per worker), and annual GNP growth of about 4 percent made taxes and government regulation easy to live with. For example, living standards for a unionized blue-collar automobile worker or steelworker rose nearly every year, with predictable wage increases as well as paid vacations, health insurance, and pension benefits. A family with one spouse working for General Motors or U.S. Steel achieved middle-class status in a job he or she likely held until retirement.

The erosion in the value of the dollar forced the United States in 1971 to sever the dollar's link to gold. As the decade went by, an increasing volume of manufactured goods came from abroad rather than American factories, and productivity growth fell from 3 percent to 1 percent annually. The steep rise in the cost of imported oil cut in half annual GNP growth. Corporate profits also fell steeply, declining from an average of 10 percent during the 1960s to 5–6 percent during the 1970s and early 1980s.

Cartoon showing General Motors managers laying off workers (October 1974)

The traditional liberal economic tools of deficit spending to stimulate the economy did not alleviate stagflation—a slowly growing economy with high rates of unemployment and inflation. The problem lay partly with surging energy costs, which affected the global economy, and the bulge of tail-end baby boomers who entered the job market for the first time just as growth slowed. By 1980, two-thirds of Americans described themselves as worse off than they had been before 1973, and many blamed "big government" for their problems (Figure 29.2).

As government came to be seen as a drag on the economy, many ordinary Americans turned toward the idea of free markets and deregulation. The ideas of these so-called **monetarists** were widely promoted by economist Milton Friedman and others with assistance from well-funded conservative public policy groups, including the Heritage Foundation, Cato Institute, and American Enterprise Institute. These organizations received much of their support from finance, insurance, real estate, and energy companies especially eager to reduce regulations.

An even more radical group of economists, called supply siders, argued that to restore growth the government must slash taxes paid by the wealthy and by business. Rich individuals and corporations, they predicted, would then invest the money productively and benefit both themselves and the larger economy. As the economy grew, government would collect all it needed, even at lower rates. Some more cynical supply siders, such as antitax crusader Grover Norquist, privately acknowledged that lower taxes might not generate higher revenues. But this would force government to reduce spending on otherwise popular social programs. He called this tactic "starving the beast." Ronald Reagan had long complained that high tax rates and overregulation by government discouraged entrepreneurship. Supply-side economics provided a theory, however dubious, to bolster his belief. Reagan made deep tax cuts, along with deregulation, major themes of his 1980 presidential campaign.

The Religious Right and Neoconservatism

As social problems eroded faith in many traditional institutions, some Americans, dubbed the "me generation" by novelist Tom Wolfe, turned away from politics and

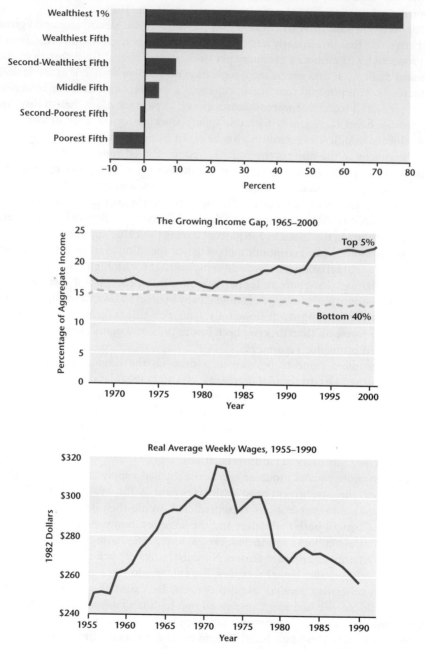

FIGURE 29.2 **Middle-class squeeze: The new wealth distribution** From the 1970s through 2000, the richest 40 percent of Americans—and especially the top 5 percent—got much richer. The bottom 40 percent of households fell increasingly behind as income equality declined. Meanwhile, annual budget deficits and the cumulative national debt grew rapidly during the presidencies of Ronald Reagan and George H. W. Bush. The budget achieved first a balance, then a surplus during the Clinton presidency.

focused on self-improvement through what they called "personal transformation." They found guidance in popular books such as *I'm OK, You're OK* or by joining group therapy programs such as EST (Erhard Seminars Training). In contrast, many other Americans, like Ronald Reagan, found solace through embracing religious orthodoxy.

These voters of faith became more politically active during the 1970s and 1980s. Protestants and Catholics had often worked against each other politically. Before the 1970s, most Catholics opposed organized prayer in public schools because the devotions were typically Protestant. Protestants generally opposed giving tax dollars to parochial schools because nearly all were Catholic. The 1973 Supreme Court decision in *Roe v. Wade*, affirming a woman's right to terminate a pregnancy, created a new interfaith coalition among Protestants and Catholics opposed to abortion. They soon discovered other areas of agreement, such as opposition to sex education in public schools and to granting legal equality to gays and lesbians. As more Protestants in the South responded to school integration by opening all-white Christian academies, they joined Catholics—whose schools were racially integrated—in seeking public funds or more generous tax benefits for these institutions.

Total rates of church membership did not change much between 1975 and 2000, but evangelical denominations grew while others lost adherents. Religious activists had also become more involved in politics by the mid-1970s. **Phyllis Schlafly**, an Illinois homemaker, lawyer, Catholic, and Republican activist, organized the Eagle Forum, an association of conservative religious women. Their immediate goal was to block state ratification of the **Equal Rights Amendment (ERA)** that Congress had passed in 1972 and sent to the states for ratification. Schlafly charged that the ERA would lead to unisex bathrooms, compulsory military service for women, and same-sex marriage. In 1979, **Beverly LaHaye** organized Concerned Women of America (CWA) to oppose laws that eased divorce and abortion or decriminalized homosexuality. CWA attracted 500,000 members, far more than its liberal counterpart, the National Organization for Women. James Dobson, an evangelical child psychologist, founded Focus on the Family in 1977, initially to stop school sex education programs.

To reach a wider audience, some ministers formed "megachurches" while others began "electronic ministries." Critics dubbed them televangelists. Among the most popular religious shows during the 1970s and 1980s were *The 700 Club*, *The PTL Club*, and *The Old Time Gospel Hour*. **Jerry Falwell**, **Pat Robertson**, Jim and Tammy Faye Bakker, and Jimmy Swaggart became religious celebrities. The Reverend **Billy Graham**, who had preached on the airwaves since the 1940s, retained a huge following; he kept his distance, however, from the more flamboyant newcomers and avoided the financial and sex scandals that later beset them.

Traditionally, white evangelicals had either voted in low numbers or supported Democrats. In 1976, for example, Jimmy Carter, a born-again Southern Baptist who proudly proclaimed his faith, received 56 percent of the white evangelical vote. But in 1978, President Carter instructed the IRS to eliminate tax breaks for segregated "Christian academies." Richard Viguerie, a fundraiser for conservative causes, described the event as the "spark" that transformed evangelical Christians into the politically engaged "religious Right." In 1979, Falwell cofounded the **Moral Majority**, a lobbying group designed to mobilize evangelicals and "get them saved, baptized, and registered" to vote. Falwell hoped to drive from office politicians "who are against . . . the Bible, moralist position." In 1980, Reagan received 61 percent of the votes of self-described

Excerpt from Jerry, Falwell, *Listen, America!* (1980)

THE FALL Televangelists Tammy Faye and Jim Bakker captivated large numbers of viewers before their fall from grace and conviction for fraud.

image
analysis

evangelicals. By 1988, 80 percent of evangelicals voted Republican, and the South had been transformed from a Democratic to a Republican stronghold.

The conservative drift among working-class and lower-middle-class whites was showcased by a popular television show first aired in 1971, *All in the Family*. Written and produced by a liberal team, the show's protagonist, Archie Bunker, a foreman at a trucking firm, epitomized white working-class resentment and anxiety in the face of economic decline, racial change, feminism, crime, and immigration. Despite his Democratic roots, by 1980, Archie had become a "Reagan Democrat."

Corporate funding helped spread these criticisms of liberalism and big government. By the end of the 1970s, corporations and their allies had lined up strongly behind Republican groups and candidates who promised to slash business taxes, reduce regulations, and curb union power. Corporations and wealthy donors provided a substantial amount of money to **political action committees (PACs)**, which could bundle donations from many sources and use the cash to assist sympathetic candidates. The number of PACs grew from 89 in 1974 to about 1,500 in the early 1980s. Conservative pro-business PACs, such as the National Conservative Political Action Committee, outnumbered and outspent liberal and pro-union PACs four to one.

Ronald Reagan proved the ideal candidate to both articulate and benefit from these trends and ideas. On the stump in 1980, he argued that the country did not have too little oil, but "too much government regulation." He blamed deficits on expensive welfare programs that aided minorities and the poor. In fact, most social spending went to two popular programs, Social Security and Medicare, which helped all Americans over age 65. Food stamps, Reagan claimed, "allowed some fellow ahead of you to buy T-bone steak" while you "stood in the checkout line with your package of hamburger." He ridiculed "welfare queens" with "eighty names, thirty addresses, and twelve Social Security Cards" whose "tax-free income alone is over $150,000." His claims, while largely fact-free, implicitly attacked minorities and resonated among economically stressed, white working- and middle-class voters.

Reagan defeated Carter by a popular vote margin of 51 to 41 percent. Independent John Anderson took the rest. Republicans won 33 new seats in the House and 12 in the Senate. This gave the GOP a 53 to 47 majority in the upper chamber. Democrats retained nominal control of the House, but enough conservative Democrats voted with the president to give Republicans a working majority.

STUDY QUESTIONS FOR DEMOCRATIC DECLINE AND THE RISING TIDE ON THE RIGHT

1. What factors drove down U.S. incomes and living standards during the 1970s?
2. What social problems emerged during the 1970s that liberalism failed to solve?
3. How did issues such as abortion rights and aid to parochial schools unify and energize religious conservatives during the 1970s?

quiz

IT'S MORNING AGAIN IN AMERICA

As a candidate and in his inaugural address in January 1981, Ronald Reagan voiced his hope to restore an era of small government, traditional cultural values, and an economy controlled by market forces. During the next eight years, he worked to roll back or reduce many New Deal and Great Society programs. Reagan pledged to shrink the social welfare system; limit the role of federal courts in promoting civil rights; reduce regulation of business and the environment; slash income taxes; and promote a conservative social ethic on issues of sex, drug use, and the role of religion in public life. The bond he established with a majority of Americans transcended specific policies and tapped a popular will to restore a sense of community, real or imagined, that had been lost since the 1960s.

Reagan's success at communicating his faith in America gave the impression that optimism, tax cuts, business deregulation, and enhanced military power had vanquished the nation's difficulties at home and abroad. But many problems, such as housing, health care, and the environment, were simply ignored by Reagan, who insisted the free market would solve them. Other policies, such as the war on drugs, made existing problems worse.

The Rise of Reagan

Reagan's election capped a long journey for the 69-year-old ex–movie actor. Born in 1911, he grew up in humble circumstances in small Illinois towns along the Mississippi River. During a visit to Hollywood in 1937, Reagan took a screen test and won a contract from the Warner Brothers film studio. For more than a decade, he had a successful career as a second-tier movie actor. Reagan was an enthusiastic and very liberal Democrat until the end of the 1940s.

As Reagan's film career waned in the late 1940s, he became active in union affairs and served as head of the Screen Actors Guild. With the onset of the Cold War, Reagan's politics became more conservative. He warned of a "communist plot to take over the motion picture business" and cooperated with studio executives and the FBI to identify and fire left-wing writers, actors, and directors. During the 1950s, Reagan hosted popular television shows and became a corporate spokesman for General Electric speaking to civic groups about the dangers of high taxes and communism. He developed an effective speaking style, blending these warnings with self-deprecating humor and a hopeful twist.

Reagan formally became a Republican in 1962 and achieved national exposure by giving a spirited televised speech in support of Barry Goldwater's doomed 1964 presidential bid. Two years later, he won election as governor of California, campaigning as "an ordinary citizen" fed up with big government. As governor from 1967 to 1975, Reagan "talked Right" but generally governed from the center. He condemned Democrats for spending and taxing too much, but as governor he doubled the state budget and raised taxes. Despite his having been divorced before he married his second wife, Nancy, and having frosty relations with his children, he spoke reverently of "traditional family values." He also signed into law a pioneering no-fault divorce statute and, in 1967, a bill that effectively legalized most abortions in California.

As president, Reagan tapped his chief rival, George H. W. Bush, as his vice president and, once elected, chose Bush's friend **James A. Baker, III**, as his chief of staff. The talented Baker convinced Reagan to focus on getting Congress to lower taxes and boost defense spending. On March 30, 1981, just six weeks into his presidency, a crazed gunman severely wounded Reagan. The good humor he displayed before going into surgery led to a surge of support for him. Congress approved Reagan's call to cut federal income taxes by about 25 percent over three years. At the same time, lawmakers voted to substantially increase military spending while leaving expenditures on large, popular social programs such as Social Security and Medicare intact.

The tax cuts proved no magic bullet, and the economy continued to slide during 1981–1982. However, by 1983, the improving economy had boosted Reagan's popularity as he faced reelection in 1984. Democrats nominated former vice president Walter Mondale to challenge Reagan. He selected New York representative **Geraldine Ferraro** as his running mate, the first woman to run for this office on the ticket of a major party. Reagan ran on a slogan borrowed from a popular ad campaign for Chrysler automobiles: "It's Morning Again in America." Most voters agreed, giving him a sweep of 49 states in November 1984 and nearly 59 percent of the vote to Mondale's 40 percent. In spite of this reelection landslide, Republicans won few additional congressional seats and in 1986 lost control of the Senate.

Reagan's second term disappointed those who saw it as an opportunity to enact many of his conservative positions. A tax reform passed in 1986 reduced the number of tax brackets, but it closed so many loopholes and tax shelters that it actually raised taxes on the rich and corporations that had benefited from tax cuts just a few years earlier.

Meanwhile, the Simpson–Rodino immigration law enacted in 1986 expanded the number of legal immigrants; by the end of the decade, nearly 8 million immigrants had arrived. About one-half of the new arrivals came from Latin America and the Caribbean and about 40 percent from Asia. In addition, an estimated 300,000 undocumented entrants came each year, primarily from Mexico and Central America. The 1986 law offered amnesty to many of the undocumented aliens living in the United States. New immigrants settled primarily in the cities of California, Arizona, Florida, Texas, New Jersey, and Illinois. But a growing number moved to midwestern cities and even southern towns.

In 1980, Congress had enacted a refugee act that offered asylum to anyone facing a "well founded fear" of persecution for religious, political, or ethnic reasons. However, the Reagan administration continued the long-standing practice of giving preferential treatment to anyone fleeing Cuba or other Communist countries. It routinely barred entry to people streaming out of Haiti or Central America even if they were fleeing brutal civil wars. In response, a so-called sanctuary movement, loosely modeled on the pre–Civil War Underground Railroad, arose among religious and lay activists who defied the law by transporting and relocating these migrants. Several communities, including San Francisco, Boston, and Tucson, declared themselves sanctuary cities where local authorities declined to cooperate with federal agents. The Justice Department brought charges against several sanctuary activists, labeling them "alien smugglers." Tensions eased in 1986 when the Reagan administration agreed to let some of the Central Americans apply for citizenship and allowed others to live in the United States until violence in their home countries subsided.

Economic Realities

Reaganomics, as journalists called the president's economic policy, is often credited with restoring the nation's economic growth after a dismal decade. Reagan condemned "big spenders" in Congress for "mortgaging our future" and pledged to halt the practice of "living beyond our means." But the two key events in stimulating recovery had nothing to do with Reagan's policies or ideas. The high interest rates imposed by Federal Reserve chairman Paul Volcker, a Carter appointee, brought the inflation rate down from 13 percent when Reagan took office to just over 4 percent by mid-decade. Similarly, global oil prices peaked in 1981 and declined sharply for most of the decade, spurring economic growth. Although it was natural for Reagan and Republicans to take credit for these successes, Reaganomics had little to do with either. Reagan is remembered for his strong advocacy of lower taxes, smaller government, and reduced spending and debt. He spoke forcefully about these policies yet generally ignored his own advice. For example, he never submitted a balanced budget proposal to Congress. Federal spending as a percentage of the GDP remained steady at about 22 percent throughout the 1980s. When Reagan endorsed a constitutional amendment to bar deficit spending, he stipulated it should apply only to future presidents. On his first day in office, Reagan issued an order freezing federal hiring. Then he quietly rescinded it. Consequently, the number of civilians employed by federal agencies rose from 2.9 to 3.1 million.

Ronald Reagan, "Address to the Nation on the Economy," February 5, 1981

After the large tax cut of 1981, the ballooning deficit forced Reagan to raise taxes and fees (which he called "revenue enhancements") about a dozen times after 1982. The total tax bite barely changed for most Americans. However, the distribution of the tax burden changed dramatically. The bulk of income tax cuts went to the wealthiest 2–3 percent of taxpayers.

Very wealthy Americans fared best of all. A typical chief executive officer (CEO) made about 40 times the salary of a worker in 1980. By 1989, the CEO made 93 times as much (the ratio had risen to 200 times as much by 2015). The share of national income going to the wealthiest 1 percent of Americans practically doubled in these years, from 8.1 percent to about 15 percent; 60 percent of income growth during the 1980s went to this richest 1 percent. Wall Street traders and real estate moguls such as Carl Icahn, T. Boone Pickens, Ivan Boesky, and Donald Trump made hundreds of millions of dollars annually in dubious deals that relied on borrowed money often secured by risky "junk bonds." Television shows such as *Dallas*, *Dynasty*, and *Lifestyles of the Rich and Famous* celebrated their wealth and material achievements. Boesky's defense of greed in a speech to business majors at the University of California in 1986 became part of popular culture when it was paraphrased as "greed is good" in the 1987 movie *Wall Street*.

Between 1982 and 1988, the economy produced around 16 million new jobs, a big improvement compared to the dismal years from 1979 to 1982. However, this was actually a *lower* rate of job creation than in most of the 1960s and 1970s or in later decades. Also, many of the new jobs, which were in the service sector, paid less than the manufacturing jobs that had been lost. Real wages—that is, the value of earnings adjusted for inflation—barely held steady or slightly declined for most Americans during the 1980s. Total household income rose slightly, usually because so many wives and young mothers joined the workforce to make ends meet. Income inequality—the gap between rich and poor—increased in the 1980s and continued doing so into the 21st century.

Reagan spoke forcefully and frequently about eliminating annual budget shortfalls and paying down the accumulated national debt of $1 trillion that he had inherited. Partly because of increased spending for the military and partly because tax cuts did not produce expected revenue, the annual federal budget deficits under Reagan grew to record levels. By 1989, the cumulative national debt had tripled to nearly $3 trillion. In less than 10 years, the United States went from the world's biggest lender to the world's biggest borrower.

The Justice Department adopted a relaxed attitude toward monopoly, dropping many antitrust suits against corporate giants and permitting more mergers. Reagan's administration sped the privatization of federal lands and lifted many restrictions on oil drilling, logging, and mining in national forests and coastal areas. A combination of regulatory and legislative changes, begun in the 1970s but accelerated under Reagan, permitted savings and loan institutions to expand their lending practices from housing to commercial real estate with little oversight and dire consequences.

Excerpt from George Gilder, *Wealth and Poverty* (1981)

Reagan described all these policies as efforts to "unleash market forces" and grow the economy. He believed that market forces could also do a better job than government programs in reducing poverty. America, he quipped, had fought a war against poverty for 20 years, and "poverty won." Reagan argued that despite spending on antipoverty programs, the overall poverty rate had not changed much since 1964. In fact, the rates had decreased, and the profile of poverty had changed dramatically. Before 1965, the poor were mostly elderly and sick Americans. Their numbers fell after the passage of Medicare, Medicaid, and the expansion of Social Security. By the 1970s and 1980s, the typical poor Americans were a single mother and her children, a phenomenon referred to as the "feminization of poverty."

Conservative Justice

As president, Reagan appointed nearly 400 federal judges—a majority of the total number of judges—to lifetime appointments. These included **William Rehnquist**, promoted from associate justice to chief justice of the Supreme Court, and three associate justices: Sandra Day O'Connor, who was the first woman on the high court; **Antonin Scalia**; and **Anthony Kennedy**. Reagan's reshaping of the judiciary in a more conservative direction proved to be one of his most lasting impacts on public policy. Rulings by the Supreme Court in the late 1980s limited protections for criminal defendants; upheld state death penalty laws; and made it harder for women, minorities, the elderly, and the disabled to sue employers for job discrimination. The Court also restricted but did not eliminate access to abortions. Many of Reagan's appointees to the Justice Department and federal commissions overseeing civil rights enforcement, such as future Supreme

Court Justice Clarence Thomas, had little interest in pursuing cases of race or sexual discrimination.

During the 1980s, Reagan as well as many members of Congress and state legislatures adopted much harsher attitudes toward crime, especially among repeat felons and drug users. Policies such as "three strikes" and mandatory sentencing laws continued for over 30 years. In 1980, state prisons held about 300,000 inmates and federal prisons about 25,000. By 2015, the number of prisoners in federal custody had topped 200,000, and those in local jails and state prisons totaled around 2 million. The price tag for direct incarceration expenses rose from about $7 billion per year in 1980 to $80 billion in 2014. The United States has the world's highest rate of incarceration and largest number of prisoners, a disproportionate number of whom are black and Latino. Prison construction became one of the nation's fastest-growing industries after 1980. Even after release, prison records often permanently barred ex-felons from voting or from many jobs. These restrictions fell hardest on minorities.

Taking its lead from First Lady Nancy Reagan, who coined the slogan "Just Say No," the Reagan administration ramped up the "war on drugs" as the Cold War faded after 1986. Federal and state authorities by 1989 spent about $10 billion annually in their effort to interdict drugs and incarcerate both small-time users and major dealers. As in earlier and later drug wars, these measures had little impact on rates of drug use but boosted rates of incarceration, especially among minorities.

STUDY QUESTIONS FOR IT'S MORNING AGAIN IN AMERICA

1. What happened to taxes, deficits, and the size of government during the 1980s?

2. In what ways did policies on justice and crime change under Ronald Reagan?

quiz

SOCIAL TRANSFORMATION AND THE TECHNOLOGY REVOLUTION

The conservative drift in national politics in the 1970s and 1980s often seemed at variance with social changes experienced by individuals and families. Also, in spite of the decline in traditional manufacturing, technological innovations originating at this time created the basis for a dynamic new economy in the 1990s and beyond.

The Rise of the "Nontraditional Family"

During the 1970s and 1980s, the nation embraced a more inclusive notion of family. In spite of the antigay and antifeminist tone of emerging conservatism, traditional gender hierarchies began to crumble, and there was real movement toward greater equality for women. By 1983, a majority of both single and married women worked outside the home in a growing variety of professions. By 1980, women comprised one-third of law school enrollees and one-fourth of those in medical school. These numbers increased steadily over time.

Second Wave feminism (as distinct from the suffragist campaign in the early 20th century) energized Congress to act. The ERA won overwhelming bipartisan congressional approval in 1971 before it went to the states for ratification. Advocates for women's equality got 47 states to adopt some form of no-fault divorce during the 1970s, and most states adopted laws recognizing the crime of spousal rape. Title 9 of the 1972 Higher Education Act focused on equality in athletics at colleges, but it had much wider ramifications for education, since it affected many programs in schools that received federal funds. In 1973, in its *Roe v. Wade* decision, the Supreme Court ruled that women had a constitutionally protected right to abort pregnancies during the first two trimesters.

In 1970, only one-fourth of adults told pollsters that premarital sex was permissible. In 1975, First Lady Betty Ford publicly approved of her adult children living with their lovers before marriage. Despite denunciations by religious conservatives, by 1979, 55 percent of adults agreed with her. Cultural conservatives, however, often lumped together gay rights, pornography, abortion, working mothers, and the ERA—which failed to win state ratification—as related moral lapses. Conservatives spoke reverently of the traditional family composed of a working husband, a homemaker wife, and the proverbial 2.2 children. But this tradition resembled a 1950s television sitcom rather than any reality. By the 1980s, about one-third of children were born to single mothers, mostly over age 19, and an even greater number to single African American and Latino women. With divorce rates at 40 percent or more, with women outliving men, and with more unmarried couples living together and postponing having children, less than one-third of households consisted of two parents and one or more minor children. More households were composed of unmarried couples, single parents, blended families, childless couples, or the elderly living alone.

During the 1980s, the Reagan administration and many in Congress promoted a conservative sexual agenda. At the president's urging, lawmakers reduced funding for international health and population control agencies that promoted birth control or even mentioned abortion. Congress funded teen "chastity clinics" that stressed abstinence before marriage as the only permissible form of birth control. This "just say no to sex" agenda mirrored the similarly ineffective anti-drug campaign. Reagan promoted, without success, a constitutional amendment banning abortion.

1984 Republican and Democratic party platforms on the American family

Gay Rights and the AIDS Epidemic

The gay liberation movement emerged from the 1969 Stonewall riots in New York City when patrons of a gay bar resisted police harassment. In 1973, the American Psychiatric Association removed homosexuality from its list of mental disorders. The U.S. Civil Service Commission in 1975 eliminated a blanket ban on employing gays, and by 1980, 12 states had repealed antisodomy laws that criminalized gay sex. In 1979, over 100,000 people marched in Washington to celebrate gay pride and demand equal rights. The next year, for the first time, the Democratic Party included a gay rights clause in its party platform.

There was also resistance to change. Singer Anita Bryant organized a successful campaign in 1977 to repeal an ordinance in Dade County, Florida, barring discrimination based on sexual orientation. Moral Majority cofounder Jerry Falwell denounced the gay pride parade as an affront to God. The Lord, he explained, had created "Adam and Eve, not Adam and Steve." In 1986, the Supreme Court upheld a Georgia law similar to those in 29 states that criminalized sexual acts between consenting same-sex adults. The ruling stood for nearly 20 years.

The appearance of acquired immune deficiency syndrome (AIDS) early in the 1980s created a health crisis that made Americans more cautious about sexual relations. The result of the human immunodeficiency virus (HIV) identified in 1984, AIDS destroyed the immune system and left patients vulnerable to many infections. HIV was transmitted through the exchange of bodily fluids, typically semen or blood. Transmission was common among gay men, intravenous drug users, and their partners. Research suggested the virus had originated in Africa decades earlier when an animal virus jumped species through human contact with meat or blood.

The spread of the illness coincided with the growth of the gay consciousness and rights movements. This prompted some conservatives such as Reagan advisor **Patrick Buchanan** to dub AIDS the "gay plague," a sort of divine retribution for immoral behavior. By the late 1980s, about 50,000 Americans had died of AIDS, and as many as one million Americans carried the HIV virus. AIDS also struck other parts of the world hard, especially countries in sub-Saharan Africa. Until 1985, when actor Rock Hudson, a closeted gay man and friend of Reagan's, died of AIDS, the president kept silent about the epidemic. He then appointed an advisory panel that joined Surgeon General **C. Everett Koop** in calling for more funds for research and a campaign to encourage sexually active Americans to use condoms, a simple way to avoid infection. Reagan expressed compassion for AIDS victims but refused to endorse condom use. Over time, improved treatment allowed many HIV-positive men and women to live longer, healthier lives.

The Disco Wars

A Health-Conscious America

At the same time that AIDS became a major concern, a broader health and wellness movement gained popularity. Many Americans shunned high-fat diets, sugar, and salt and quit smoking in growing numbers. Exercise became a national obsession (even as the nation as a whole became more obese). Some Americans joined trendy health clubs, while others jogged and bicycled. New groups such as Mothers Against Drunk Driving campaigned to stiffen penalties for driving intoxicated, and public health organizations such as the American Cancer Society pressed state and local officials to adopt restrictions on public smoking. Confessionals about drug and alcohol addiction became a staple of television and radio talk shows.

Surgeon General Koop, who took the lead in publicizing the danger of AIDS, also played a key role in reenergizing the national campaign against tobacco, which the federal government had begun in the 1960s. Ignoring Reagan's call for less regulation of business, Koop issued a series of high-profile reports during the 1980s that called smoking the nation's "chief preventable cause of death," compared nicotine addiction to heroin and cocaine use, and lobbied for state and federal regulations to create a "smoke-free society" by the year 2000. His efforts helped reduce smoking rates substantially.

High Technology

Despite the prevailing mood of economic gloom in the late 1970s and early 1980s, a wide array of new technologies emerged during these years and shaped the domestic and world economies for the next 40 years. Among the innovations were visual scanners, universal product codes (UPCs), cargo shipping containers, cable television, jumbo jets, videocassette recorders, personal computers, communication satellites, and Internet protocols, to name a few. Many of these technologies allowed individuals, government, and private businesses to generate, store, and analyze vast amounts of data. Companies such as Walmart, Federal Express, Apple, and Microsoft utilized these and related technologies to develop new products, business models, and global reach. Research also began on a variety of alternative energy technologies, including those that drew from geothermal or solar energy; electric cars; and green architecture.

STUDY QUESTIONS FOR SOCIAL TRANSFORMATION AND THE TECHNOLOGY REVOLUTION

quiz

1. During the 1970s and 1980s, how did American society become both more committed to equality and more socially conservative?

2. What dramatic changes affected family structures in the 1970s and 1980s?

3. What were several new technologies introduced in the 1970s and 1980s that shaped future economic growth?

⊘ CHALLENGING THE "EVIL EMPIRE"

Excerpt from speech by Ronald Reagan dubbing the Soviet Union the "focus of evil" (March 1983)

Reagan has been credited for "winning the Cold War without firing a shot." As a candidate, he complained that the United States suffered from a "Vietnam Syndrome," shorthand for an unwillingness to counter Soviet threats by defending allies and opposing enemies. In what was sometimes called the "Reagan Doctrine," he pledged to restore American military superiority and to support anti-Communist movements around the globe. The president called the Soviet Union the "focus of evil in the modern world" and promised, as he later put it, to consign it to the "ash heap of history."

On Christmas Day in 1991, Soviet president **Mikhail Gorbachev** issued a decree dissolving the Soviet Union and turned over power to **Boris Yeltsin**, elected leader of a democratic Russia. Although this occurred after Reagan left office, some attribute the collapse of communism in eastern Europe and Russia to Reagan's policies of tough talk, a big arms buildup, economic pressure, and covert military interventions.

A New Arms Race

Reagan argued that the United States had virtually disarmed itself even as the Soviet Union and its proxies became stronger. To restore superiority over America's enemies, the president pushed through Congress the largest ever peacetime increase in military spending. Between 1981 and 1989, the defense budget rose from about $157 billion to over $304 billion per year (Map 29.1). The money went primarily to buy new missiles, tanks, ships, and other expensive equipment designed to close a so-called window of vulnerability.

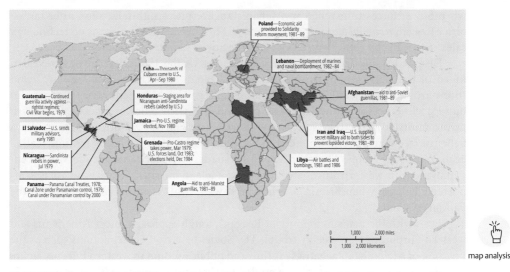

MAP 29.1 Reagan-Era Military Interventions The Reagan administration intervened with overt and covert military force throughout Central America as well as in Angola, Libya, Lebanon, Iran, and Afghanistan. Aid to anti-Soviet Afghans helped to drive out the invaders but sowed the seeds of Islamist radicalism. The most successful intervention occurred in Poland, where the United States provided economic support to the anti-Communist, pro-democratic Solidarity movement.

Shaken by events such as the Iran hostage crisis and the Soviet invasion of Afghanistan, the public shared Reagan's mistrust of the Soviets and generally supported rearmament. At the same time, many citizens, religious leaders, and members of Congress continued to fear the consequences of atomic war. In 1982–1983, a grassroots "nuclear freeze movement" urged Reagan to cap the U.S. arsenal at current levels. In November 1983, millions of Americans viewed a realistic television movie, *The Day After*, depicting the horror of life in a Kansas town following a nuclear war.

Statement from National Conference of Catholic Bishops opposing nuclear weapons and the arms race (1983)

In March 1983, Reagan revealed a program to build a "space shield" designed to render Soviet missiles "impotent and obsolete." The Strategic Defense Initiative (SDI), which critics dubbed "Star Wars," would utilize a space-based, nuclear-powered laser whose energy beams would destroy Soviet missiles before they reached U.S. targets.

Opinions vary over whether the SDI was intended as a bargaining chip, an effort to ease public fears about nuclear war, a scheme to drag the Soviet Union into a spending race it could not win, or a boondoggle for defense contractors. It probably encompassed all these elements. Despite a $20 billion investment in the 1980s, the project proved technologically unfeasible and was eventually abandoned. Even if the SDI were only partially effective, the Soviets feared it might prove good enough to destroy the handful of Soviet missiles that survived a first strike by the United States. From Moscow's perspective, the SDI seemed like an offensive, not defensive, weapon.

The Reagan administration in 1981 imposed a variety of economic sanctions on the Soviet Union, barring loans and the sale of certain high-technology products. This ban mostly affected western European and Japanese exporters. The United States sold mostly agricultural products to the Soviets. President Carter had suspended these sales when Soviet forces intervened in Afghanistan. Despite tough talk, soon after taking office Reagan *resumed* agricultural exports to Moscow. Many of the bans on technology sales were lifted by 1985, before, not after, the Soviet Union changed its behavior.

Despite his popularity at home, during most of the 1980s, survey data revealed much of the world's population considered Reagan something of a "cowboy" who threw around American weight without much regard to other countries. Reagan did build a close personal and diplomatic friendship with fellow conservative British prime minister **Margaret Thatcher**, who took office in 1979. Both leaders shared a belief in free markets and the need to build up military power. They jokingly called each other soul mates. Thatcher helped persuade skeptical NATO leaders to accept deployment in western Europe of new U.S. nuclear missiles. Reagan, in turn, supported Thatcher when Britain fought a brief war with Argentina over control of the Falkland Islands.

Even with their misgivings about Reagan's tough approach, most Americans and western Europeans were deeply troubled by Soviet behavior. Soviet actions such as the invasion of Afghanistan negatively influenced public opinion in western Europe, Japan, and the Middle East. Soviet stature eroded further in December 1981 when Brezhnev ordered the Communist Polish government to impose martial law to prevent the democratic labor movement Solidarity from taking power. Reagan denounced these "forces of tyranny" and authorized the CIA to work with the Catholic Church in Poland to provide secret funding for Solidarity.

GUERRILLA FIGHTERS　CIA-assisted Mujahideen guerrillas pose on a captured Soviet truck in the mid-1980s. Many of the Islamist fighters turned against their American patron after 1989.

Interventions

In addition to the arms buildup and economic sanctions, the Reagan administration worked to undermine Soviet power and spread democracy through open and covert use of force in the Middle East, South Asia, Africa, and Latin America. These interventions proved costly in lives and money while achieving dubious results.

In 1983, Reagan sent warships and a few thousand Marines to Lebanon, a nation engaged in a bloody civil war between several Christian and Muslim factions. U.S. forces supported Christian elements considered pro-Western and more accepting of Israel. Muslim fighters responded by blowing up the U.S. embassy in Beirut in April 1983, killing 63 people, and the Marine barracks in October, killing 241 servicemen. Reagan offered a stirring tribute to the fallen Marines and then pulled out all remaining forces. The incident impressed future al-Qaeda leader Osama bin Laden, who told his followers that another spectacular bombing might force an American retreat in the Middle East.

The ongoing war between Iraq and Iran continued to destabilize the region. Fearful of a victory by either Iraq's Saddam Hussein or Iran's Ayatollah Khomeini, the Reagan administration secretly provided aid to both nations to preserve a rough balance, even though the administration claimed to despise both. In 1983, Reagan sent former (and future) defense secretary Donald Rumsfeld as a "personal envoy" to assure Saddam of America's friendship. Meanwhile, secret U.S. arms sales to Iran generated profits that the Reagan administration illegally used to fund the anti-Communist Contra guerrillas in Nicaragua.

Terrorist airline hijackings, bombings, and kidnappings became a weapon of choice for many frustrated groups, especially in the Middle East. Although very few Americans were actually harmed before 2001, the fear of terrorism gripped the public imagination. Libya's demagogic strongman **Muammar Qaddafi** used oil profits to buy weapons from the Soviets and fund violent groups in the Middle East. In response, the United States deployed naval vessels off the Libyan coast and fought several aerial battles against Libyan planes, incidents fictionalized in the 1986 Tom Cruise film *Top Gun*. In April 1986, when Libyan agents were implicated in the bombing of a Berlin nightclub frequented by Americans, Reagan called Qaddafi a "mad dog" and sent planes to bomb

SUPPORT FOR IRAQ In 1983, President Reagan sent Donald Rumsfeld to Iraq in a show of U.S. support for Iraqi dictator Saddam Hussein. Twenty years later, Rumsfeld would be a key figure in helping to remove Hussein from power.

Bombs Away: The B-52 and America's Global Military Footprint

In 1982, as part of his administration's military buildup, President Reagan urged Congress to fund a new long-range bomber. "Many of our B-52 bombers," he remarked, "are older than the pilots that fly them." Although Congress appropriated funds for a replacement aircraft, the eight-engine B-52 Stratofortress, the largest warplane in the U.S. arsenal, was far from retirement. Designed by Boeing engineers in the wake of World War II, it became operational in 1954. Two years later, a B-52 was used to drop the first test hydrogen bomb on Bikini Atoll. B-52s were put into service most extensively during the Vietnam War, during which they flew 100,000 bombing missions. They were also employed in conflicts in the Persian Gulf, Afghanistan, and Iraq.

Originally designed to drop nuclear weapons on the Soviet heartland, the B-52 has instead dropped conventional bombs, napalm, laser-guided weapons, cruise missiles, and even propaganda leaflets. During the 1950s and 1960s, a small number of B-52s remained airborne at all times to avoid destruction in case of an enemy first strike. Many others operated on a short alert, able to fly within 15 minutes of an order.

Despite several attempts to retire the subsonic B-52, it has remained combat active for over 60 years and has outlasted many intended replacements. In the early 2000s it dropped laser-guided bombs on the Taliban hiding in the caves of Afghanistan and in 2016 attacked ISIS positions in Syria. With another generation of long-range bombers currently in the design phase, the 76 operational B-52s (down from an original force of 740, the last of which was built in 1962) will likely keep flying until 2040, an astounding eight decades of service.

The B-52 has lasted due to its rugged design and aerodynamic efficiency—and the flaws of its intended replacements. Each B-52 cost about $8 million, or about $85 million in today's dollars. It can attack from an altitude of 50,000 feet, delivering several hydrogen bombs or a conventional payload of 70,000 pounds. As a U.S. Air Force general

his residence. Qaddafi survived but in December 1988 took revenge when Libyan agents planted a bomb that destroyed a U.S. airliner flying over Lockerbie, Scotland, and killed several hundred passengers and 11 people on the ground.

As noted earlier, in December 1979, Soviet forces invaded Afghanistan to prop up a Communist regime on the verge of collapse. Russian troops became mired in a brutal war against the Mujahideen, Islamic-inspired Afghan and foreign guerrillas, who counted among their ranks Saudi fundamentalist Osama bin Laden. Carter began and Reagan expanded aid to these insurgents. U.S. weapons went through Pakistan, a military dictatorship that in return received tacit U.S. approval to develop an atomic bomb. The U.S.-backed guerrillas forced a Soviet pullout in the late 1980s. By then, Pakistan had sold nuclear weapons technology to rogue states such as North Korea and Libya. After Islamic radicals called the Taliban took power in Afghanistan after the Soviet withdrawal, they eventually played host to bin Laden.

remarked, it "cannot be seen or heard until the bombs start falling, and then it's like rolling thunder." Alternatively, it could fly close to the ground, with the roar of its engines striking terror among those on the receiving end of its bombs.

All intended replacements have fallen short. Debuting in 1988 at $283 million per plane, the B-1B was plagued by engine fires, and its radar-jamming system jammed its own radar. A decade later, the $2 billion-per-plane B-2 Spirit utilized advanced sensors and stealth technology so finicky that it initially had difficulty distinguishing clouds from mountains. Even worse, the surface coating that made it nearly invisible to enemy radar deteriorated in bad weather, making it perilous to fly in the rain. A proposed nuclear-powered aircraft, intended to fly for weeks without landing, proved too radioactive for crew safety. The dart-shaped B-58 crashed repeatedly. The especially swift B-70 was sidelined after tests revealed that it spewed toxic waste along its flight path.

The inside of the crowded B-52 cockpit resembles a 1950s Radio Shack showroom, with racks of dials, vacuum tubes, and obsolete steam gauges. Lacking a toilet, crews (originally all men) on long missions urinated through rubber hoses. Hand-operated pulleys and levers still connect some of the cockpit flight controls to the jet engines. In 2016, one B-52 pilot discovered he was flying the same aircraft flown by his grandfather. Maintenance staff often find graffiti in the plane's nooks and crannies left decades earlier.

Initially built to fly about 5,000 hours before structural fatigue set in, Boeing engineers have devised ways to keep the B-52 aloft. Cannibalized parts from decommissioned aircraft along with new structural, electronic, and avionic components have quadrupled its useful life.

The B-52's huge lift capacity and ability to fly exceptionally long distances (about 8,800 miles before midair refueling) provide an additional advantage: it can hold a position outside combat zones and function as a launch platform for a new generation of laser- and satellite-guided weapons, drones, cruise missiles, and other innovative ordnance. Simply by deploying the B-52 near a combat zone, U.S. officials can make a powerful statement.

- What war-fighting role was the B-52 originally designed to carry out?
- How has the B-52 been used in regional conflicts since the 1950s?

The CIA assisted anti-Communist forces in several conflicts, such as those in Angola, Mozambique, and Cambodia, without achieving much success. A more decisive result came in October 1983 when U.S. military forces invaded the tiny Caribbean island of Grenada after a local Marxist group seized power. Concerned that the island might become a Soviet base, the president justified action as necessary to protect some 500 American students enrolled in a Grenada medical school. Photographs of the students kissing U.S. soil were featured in Reagan's 1984 campaign ads.

Cold War Thaw

The U.S.–Soviet relationship changed dramatically after March 1985 when the relatively young, well-educated, and widely traveled Mikhail Gorbachev was chosen by the Communist hierarchy to lead the Soviet Union. Unlike his rigid predecessors,

interactive timeline

TIMELINE 1973–1988

AMERICA	YEAR	THE WORLD
Jan *Roe v. Wade* ruling by Supreme Court upholds abortion rights	1973	**Oct** Arab-Israeli War occurs, followed by oil embargo and blow to U.S. economy
Aug Nixon resigns and Gerald Ford becomes president **Sep** Ford pardons Nixon	1974	
Jan–Dec "Stagflation" worsens	1975	**Apr** North Vietnam defeats South Vietnam
Nov Jimmy Carter elected president	1976	**Sep** Chinese leader Mao dies
Jan President Jimmy Carter offers pardon to Vietnam draft resisters	1977	**Nov** Egyptian president Sadat visits Israel
Mar Senate approves Panama Canal treaties **Jun** *Bakke v. University of California* Supreme Court ruling upholds affirmative action **Jun** Proposition 13 tax cut passed in California **Sep** Camp David Accords signed between Israel and Egypt	1978	
Mar A major accident occurs with Three Mile Island nuclear reactor **Jun** Moral Majority formed **Nov** Iranian radicals seize U.S. hostages while gasoline shortages worsen **Dec** United States begins covert aid to Afghan guerrillas	1979	**Jan** Shah flees Iran, succeeded by Ayatollah Khomeini **Feb–Mar** China and Vietnam fight border war **Jul** Somoza regime overthrown in Nicaragua **Sep** Conservative Margaret Thatcher elected British prime minister **Dec** Soviet forces invade Afghanistan
Apr Attempt to rescue Iranian U.S. hostages fails **Apr–Oct** Controversial Mariel boatlift from Cuba **Nov** Ronald Reagan elected president	1980	**Sep** Iraq–Iran war begins and lasts until 1988

Gorbachev impressed foreign leaders as a dynamic reformer determined to radically alter the Soviet political and economic system.

Internal problems, more so than Reagan's hard line, motivated Gorbachev to radically alter Soviet policies at home and abroad. With its stagnant economy, backward technology, and chronic social problems, the Soviet Union—aside from its nuclear arsenal—seemed more like a Third World country than a world power. The end of the Cold War, a veteran diplomat explained, "came when a new generation of Soviet leaders realized how badly their system at home and the policies abroad had failed." The Soviets did not so much "lose" the Cold War as call it off.

Reagan had the good fortune—and sense—to respond positively to these changes even if his tough policies played only a small part in causing them. Reagan cooperated with Gorbachev partly because of his own need to demonstrate an ability to govern in the wake of the Iran-Contra scandal. Also during 1987, Reagan replaced nearly all his "hard-line" anti-Soviet advisors with moderates who favored negotiating with Gorbachev.

Between 1986 and 1991, Gorbachev attempted to save the Soviet Union through radical reform. He released political prisoners, allowed freer emigration, and lifted

AMERICA	YEAR	THE WORLD
Jan Reagan inaugurated; Iran hostages released; AIDS identified for the first time in the United States, covert aid increased to Afghan guerrillas and Contras **Aug–Oct** Congress approves Reagan tax cuts and defense increase	**1981**	**Dec** Solidarity reform movement challenges Communist control in Poland; martial law imposed
Oct Garn–St. Germain bill deregulates savings and loan institutions **Oct** Reagan declares illicit drugs "threat to national security"; Nancy Reagan calls for "Just Say No" antidrug campaign **Nov** Democrats regain some House seats **Dec** Boland amendment bars aid to Contras	**1982**	**Jun** Israel invades Lebanon **Apr–Jun** Britain and Argentina fight war over Falkland Islands
Mar Reagan unveils SDI anti-missile plan **Oct** Marine barracks bombed in Lebanon; United States invades Grenada	**1983**	
Apr HIV identified as cause of AIDS **Nov** Reagan reelected	**1984**	**Dec** Thatcher meets and praises rising Soviet leader Mikhail Gorbachev
Aug Reagan authorizes first secret arms sales to Iran **Nov** Reagan and Gorbachev meet in Geneva	**1985**	**Mar** Mikhail Gorbachev becomes Soviet leader
Jan Space shuttle *Challenger* explodes **Oct** Iran-Contra scandal erupts **Nov** Democrats regain control of Senate	**1986**	
Feb Reagan condemned by Tower Commission for his role in Iran-Contra scandal **Nov** United States and Soviets agree to treaty limiting intermediate-range missiles **Dec** Gorbachev visits United States to sign Intermediate-Range Nuclear Forces (INF) treaty	**1987**	**Jun** Reagan calls on Gorbachev to "tear down" Berlin Wall
May Reagan visits Soviet Union **Nov** George H. W. Bush elected president **Dec** Gorbachev again visits United States	**1988**	**Feb** Gorbachev announces pullout of Soviet forces from Afghanistan

press restrictions. To revive the dormant economy, he introduced market mechanisms and courted foreign capital and technology. In 1987, after two inconclusive meetings with Reagan, Gorbachev visited Washington and agreed to a treaty, largely on American terms, eliminating all intermediate-range nuclear missiles held by both sides.

Mikhail Gorbachev on the arms race with the United States (1987)

During 1988, Gorbachev proposed that as the Soviets pulled out of Afghanistan, Washington and Moscow should organize a unity government to prevent the rise of extremist groups like the Taliban. The Reagan administration ignored the idea, along with proposals to cut nuclear arsenals more deeply. In June, Reagan visited Moscow and posed with Gorbachev on top of Lenin's Tomb in Red Square. When a reporter asked about the "evil empire," Reagan said that was "another time, another era." Gorbachev appealed again for joint efforts to resolve disputes in the developing world and to speed nuclear disarmament, but Reagan did little more than smile for the cameras as he coasted toward the end of his presidency. With the mellowing of the Red Menace, and the possible onset of the dementia from which he later suffered, Reagan's interest in foreign and domestic affairs lapsed.

KREMLIN STROLL As the Cold War began to recede during 1988, President Ronald Reagan enjoyed a stroll through the Kremlin with Soviet premier Mikhail Gorbachev.

STUDY QUESTIONS FOR CHALLENGING THE "EVIL EMPIRE"

quiz

1. Why did Reagan believe the Soviet Union was "winning" the Cold War in 1980, and what policies did he adopt to reverse the trend?

2. What was the purpose behind the covert programs in Iran and Nicaragua, and how did they undermine Reagan?

3. Why were Reagan and Gorbachev able to find common ground and areas for international cooperation after 1985?

Summary

- In the 1970s, a host of social, economic, and military problems, and two "failed presidencies," left Americans mistrustful of "big government."
- Conservative religious and political groups came to dominate the Republican Party and offered appealing alternatives to liberal ideas.

- Reagan became the vehicle for conservatism and won the presidential election by promising to restore American pride, power, and prosperity.
- Actual economic performance during the 1980s was highly selective, with a small number of Americans doing very well and most merely treading water.
- Reagan's strident anti-Communism and foreign interventions achieved little success through 1986. After the Iran-Contra scandal, the president's need to compromise coincided with Gorbachev's effort to reform the Soviet Union and led to a major thaw in the Cold War.

Key Terms and People

◁))

audio
flashcards

Baker, James A., III 1024
Begin, Menachem 1013
Buchanan, Patrick 1029
Carter, Jimmy 1009
Contras 1007
Dole, Robert 1011
Equal Rights Amendment (ERA) 1021
Falwell, Jerry 1021
Ferraro, Geraldine 1024
Gorbachev, Mikhail 1030
Graham, Billy 1021
Helsinki Accords 1011
Iran-Contra scandal 1008
Kennedy, Anthony 1026
Kennedy, Edward "Ted" 1016
Khomeini, Ruholla 1015
Koop, C. Everett 1029
LaHaye, Beverly 1021
McFarlane, Robert 1007
Mondale, Walter 1011
monetarists 1019

Moral Majority 1021
Mossadeq, Mohammed 1015
Mujahideen 1014
neoconservatives 1011
North, Oliver 1008
Pahlavi, Mohammed Reza 1015
political action committees
   (PACs) 1022
Qaddafi, Muammar 1033
Reaganomics 1025
Rehnquist, William 1026
Robertson, Pat 1021
Rockefeller, Nelson 1009
Roe v. Wade 1021
Sadat, Anwar 1013
Scalia, Antonin 1026
Schlafly, Phyllis 1021
Thatcher, Margaret 1032
Volcker, Paul 1013
Yeltsin, Boris 1030

Reviewing Chapter 29

1. What domestic and foreign problems overwhelmed the Carter administration?
2. What was Sunbelt conservatism?
3. What was Ronald Reagan's criticism of liberal economic and social programs, and how did he propose to alter their course?
4. In what ways were Reagan's domestic policies successful? In what ways did they fail?
5. Why did Reagan charge that the Soviets were "winning" the Cold War?
6. Did Reagan's foreign policies alter Soviet behavior, or were other factors responsible for winding down the Cold War?

Further Reading

Alexander, Michelle. *The New Jim Crow: Mass Incarceration in the Age of Color Blindness.* New York: New Press, 2010. An exploration of how a "war on crime" hobbled black communities.

Borstelmann, Thomas. *The 1970s: A New Global History from Civil Rights to Economic In-equality.* Examines the seemingly contradictory trends toward both greater gender and personal freedom along with the growth of free market principles and conservative politics.

Dinnerstein, Leonard, and David Reimers. *The World Comes to America: Immigration to the United States Since 1945.* New York: Oxford University Press, 2013. Examines how policy changes within the United States and global economic trends transformed the patterns of immigration to the United States, especially after 1965.

Edsall, Thomas, and Mary Edsall. *Chain Reaction: The Impact of Race, Politics, and Taxes on American Politics.* New York: W. W. Norton, 1992. The authors examine how racial tension, economic frustrations, and posturing by politicians shattered the liberal consensus in post-1945 America.

Farber, David. *Taken Hostage: The Iran Hostage Crisis and America's First Encounter with Radical Islam.* Princeton, NJ: Princeton University Press, 2005. Details the political and cultural impact of the year-long hostage crisis.

Kalman, Laura. *Right Star Rising: A New Politics, 1974–1980.* New York: W. W. Norton, 2010. Social and economic pressures during the 1970s, rather than any single personality or event, realigned American politics and propelled conservatives to leadership.

Levy, Steven. *Insanely Great.* New York: Penguin, 2000. Follows the creation of the Macintosh computer in the 1980s and the rise of Apple.

McGirr, Lisa. *Suburban Warriors: The Origins of the New American Right.* Princeton, NJ: Princeton University Press, 2001. The rise of the Sunbelt and politics in southern California, the author argues, produced a new kind of American conservatism during the 1950s and 1960s.

Mickelthwait, John, and Adrian Wooldridge. *Right Nation: Conservative Power in America.* New York: Penguin Books, 2004. The authors examine how the religious, economic, intellectual, and political strains of conservatism merged into a powerful force in American society.

Moreton, Bethany. *To Serve God and Wal-Mart: The Making of Christian Free Enterprise.* Cambridge, MA: Harvard University Press, 2010. Explores the relationship among corporate capitalism, the rise of the Christian Right, and conservative politics during the 1970s and 1980s.

Oberdorfer, Don. *From the Cold War to a New Era: The United States and the Soviet Union, 1983–1991.* Baltimore: Johns Hopkins University Press, 1998. This well-sourced account by an accomplished journalist traces the ups and downs of the Cold War during the Reagan–Bush era.

Rome, Adam. *Bulldozer in the Countryside.* New York: Cambridge University Press, 2001. Chronicles the environmental cost of suburban development and efforts to mitigate degradation.

Schulman, Bruce. *The Seventies: The Great Shift in American Culture, Society, and Politics.* New York: Free Press, 2001. A reinterpretation of the "me decade" that examines the crisis of liberalism and the events that made conservative ideas appear so attractive.

Willentz, Sean. *The Age of Reagan: A History, 1974–2008.* New York: Harper, 2008. Part biography and part policy study, Willentz traces the sources of Reagan's ideas and their impact on America in the two decades after his presidency.

America in the World
GOODS, IDEAS, PEOPLE

CHAPTER 29: Conservatism Resurgent, 1973–1988

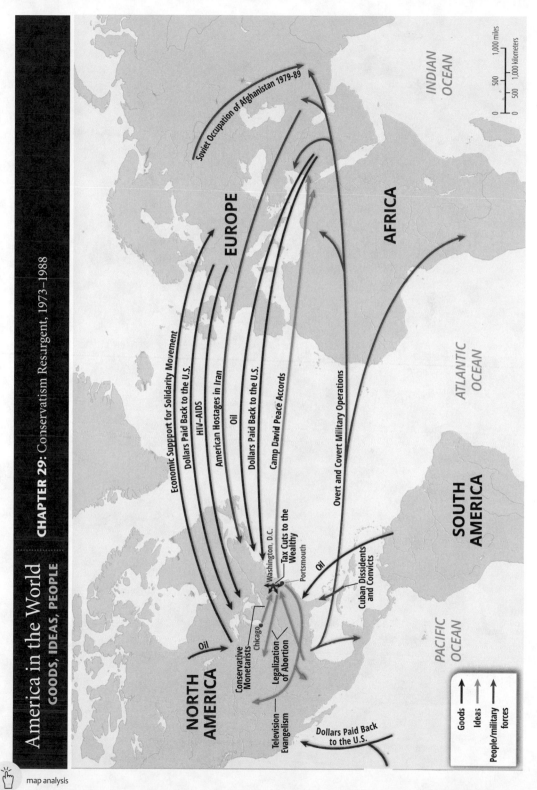

map analysis

Trading floor of the New York Stock Exchange.

After the Cold War

I n 1983, 29-year-old computer designer **Steven Jobs** persuaded John Sculley, an executive at Pepsi, to leave the soft-drink maker to become the CEO of Apple Computer, a company Jobs had helped create in 1976. Jobs asked Sculley, "Do you want to spend the rest of your life selling sugared water to children, or do you want a chance to change the world?" Jobs and other rebellious innovators in Silicon Valley were about to transform the way people around the world communicated and lived their lives. Apple produced a stunning commercial titled "1984," broadcast during that year's Super Bowl. It informed consumers that it was shaking up the stodgy corporate world ruled by IBM, the manufacturer of the personal computer, with the introduction of its Macintosh.

Jobs, eager to promote the "next big thing" and uncomfortable with Apple's new corporate structure, moved on in the mid-1980s to found NeXT Computer, which appealed to graphic designers and scientists. Jobs called his machines "interpersonal computers" because users could communicate easily with others. The machines allowed easy access to the emerging Internet and possessed other advanced features. In 1996, with California's Silicon Valley in the midst of an Internet-inspired boom, Apple bought NeXT Computer, and Jobs returned as Apple's interim CEO. The company continued to introduce innovative products for graphic designers and scientists. Jobs developed an almost cult-like following with his enthusiastic speeches, called "Stevenotes," which launched new advances to the Mac at the company's annual Macworld Expos.

Over the next decade, Apple products, including the iPad and iPhone, became global phenomena blurring the distinctions between computers, telephones, and cameras. Apple became one of the world's most profitable and admired corporations. In December 2012, on release of the iPhone 5, two million were sold in China in less than three days. Tech-savvy Chinese, like young adults around the world, measured their personal success by the acquisition of these items and enjoyed displaying them in public.

Tech companies in Silicon Valley were loose and informal places. At Apple, Jobs showed his irreverence by flying a pirate flag outside company headquarters. Software designers and hardware engineers in their 20s and 30s wore sandals and T-shirts. There were no fixed hours, but workers came in early and stayed late, seven days a week. Search engine company Google, founded in 1996, kept gourmet chefs on staff and encouraged employees to use the on-site day spa and massage service. Happy workers were expected to embrace the company's motto: "Don't Be Evil."

In contrast to these Silicon Valley offices, the facilities that actually manufactured Apple products in China and other countries offered a far less appealing ambience. In these locations, workers, typically young women recruited from the countryside, often worked long hours and lived in barracks-like dormitories so bleak that safety nets were installed in some to frustrate would-be suicides.

The IBM personal computer and the Apple Macintosh (along with other nearly forgotten machines such as the Commodore and Amiga) made computers into household appliances as common as TVs and helped spread information technology around the globe. Computer software produced by Microsoft and Google, along with agricultural products, Hollywood films, and weapons, have comprised America's major exports since the 1980s. The end of the Cold War in the early 1990s hastened the process. Instantaneous communication and access to vast amounts of information made the world seem smaller and, for a while, richer and more peaceful. Even as traditional industries shrank, high-tech entrepreneurs created hundreds of new businesses employing tens of thousands. But the rapid changes in technology and information created losers as well as winners, division as well as cohesion.

GEORGE H. W. BUSH AND THE END OF THE COLD WAR

The Cold War ended between 1989 and 1991. With the exception of Romania, peaceful uprisings swept aside Communist governments of eastern Europe in 1989, and the Soviet Union disintegrated in late 1991. President **George H. W. Bush** successfully navigated the fall of European communism. Echoing a phrase coined by Woodrow Wilson at the end of World War I, he proclaimed the dawn of a **new world order** in which the United States, the one remaining superpower, would lead multinational coalitions to enforce its standards of international behavior. Some pundits, triumphantly proclaiming the "end of history," predicted that people everywhere would soon adopt U.S. and western European values of free market capitalism, representative government, free civil institutions, and the rule of law.

In spite of these expectations, the collapse of communism in eastern Europe did not usher in an age of world peace and prosperity. The United States intervened militarily in the Western Hemisphere and fought a major war against Iraq. Long-suppressed ethnic rivalries ripped apart the former Yugoslavia and Somalia and Rwanda in Africa. Voters defeated Bush for reelection in 1992 in part because his foreign policy expertise seemed less valuable in the post–Cold War era, when ordinary Americans worried more about their economic livelihood. They replaced him with Democrat Bill Clinton, a 46-year-old governor of Arkansas who promised to revive the fortunes of the middle class.

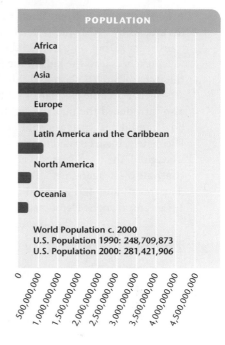

World Population c. 2000
U.S. Population 1990: 248,709,873
U.S. Population 2000: 281,421,906

The Election of 1988

At the end of the Reagan presidency, conditions looked promising for the Democratic Party to win the presidential election in 1988. After living in Reagan's shadow for eight years, Vice President George H. W. Bush had made little impression on most Americans. Conservative rivals for the nomination, including television preacher Pat Robertson, Kansas senator Robert Dole, and former secretary of state Alexander Haig, attacked him as inauthentic in light of his pre-1981 criticism of Reagan's tax proposals as "voodoo economics" and his vigorous support for government-funded contraception while a member of Congress. Bush pointed to his loyal service under Reagan and, by selecting 39-year-old first-term Indiana senator **Dan Quayle** as his own vice presidential nominee, placated enough party conservatives to secure the nomination. Bush received the loudest cheers from conservatives at the Republican National Convention when he paraphrased a line from Hollywood tough guy Clint Eastwood and proclaimed, "Read my lips, no new taxes."

The Democrats selected Massachusetts governor **Michael Dukakis** from among eight candidates. Dukakis ran as a pragmatic problem solver, responsible for the "Massachusetts miracle" of booming economic growth in the 1980s. Much of that success, however, had been the result of defense dollars that poured into Massachusetts during the Reagan arms buildup. To enhance the ticket's appeal among southerners, Dukakis chose Texas senator Lloyd Bentsen as his running mate. Bentsen had defeated Bush for the Senate in 1970.

Dukakis began the campaign in the summer of 1988 with a 17-point lead over Bush in public opinion polls. Following the advice of his campaign manager, Lee Atwater, to avoid discussing substantive economic and social policy issues, Bush ran a slashing series of negative ads against the Massachusetts governor, denouncing him as an unpatriotic "unrepentant liberal" and a "high tax, high spending, pro-abortion, card-carrying member of the American Civil Liberties Union." He criticized Dukakis for vetoing a law requiring schoolteachers to lead students in reciting the Pledge of Allegiance. He also blamed Dukakis for granting a prison furlough to Willie Horton, an African

American convicted murderer, who raped a woman while on release. Bush justified his attacks by declaring, "I don't understand the type of thinking that lets first degree murderers . . . out on parole so they can rape and plunder again, and then isn't willing to let teachers lead the kids in the Pledge of Allegiance." Dukakis responded ineptly to these charges. The "slash-and-burn" tactics used by Bush established a style of personal attack that became standard in subsequent political campaigns. News reports in 1988 also introduced the public to terms such as "sound bite" and "spin," which described how candidates' images could be manipulated through skillful media management. Ultimately, Bush coasted to an easy victory against the wooden Dukakis because times were good, the Cold War was ending, and he seemed to be the candidate most likely to continue on Reagan's path. Bush carried 40 of the 50 states. He won 48.9 million votes, 54 percent, and 426 electoral votes to Dukakis's 41.8 million votes, 46 percent, and 111 electoral votes. Democrats, however, retained control of Congress.

The Bush Presidency at Home

Despite Bush's brutal electoral tactics, he tried to govern from the center. But the new president's efforts to fulfill a promise he made at the nominating convention to promote a "kinder, gentler America" infuriated conservative Republicans—who wondered, Kinder and gentler than whom?—and failed to gain support from Democrats angry at his negative campaigning during the election.

More concerned than Reagan with the actual business of governing, President Bush supported and signed laws expanding civil rights and protecting the environment. In 1991, a new civil rights law allowed the establishment of racial and gender goals—but not quotas—in hiring. The **Americans with Disabilities Act (ADA)** of 1990 represented the culmination of years of activism on behalf of people with disabilities. As many as 45 million Americans (one-sixth of the population) were permanently or temporarily disabled. More than half of them were unemployed, and they were among the poorest people in the country. The ADA required that government, business, and educational institutions make "reasonable accommodations" so that people with mental or physical disabilities could work and have the same access as fully abled people. In March 1989, a huge oil tanker, the *Exxon Valdez*, ran aground in Alaska's Prince William Sound. Ten million gallons of oil leaked from the ship and spoiled over 800 miles of pristine coastline. Public outrage over the environmental damage led Congress to update the Clean Air and Water acts. The new laws enhanced sewage systems and set emissions standards for vehicles. By enacting the Radiation Exposure Compensation Act of 1990, Congress provided assistance to miners, millworkers, and soldiers who had been injured by uranium processing or atomic testing since the onset of the Cold War. The Native American Graves Protection and Repatriation Act, also passed in 1990, compelled museums and other institutions to return certain bones and cultural artifacts taken from tribes.

Conservatives criticized all these measures as extensions of the welfare state. They erupted in outright fury when Bush retreated from his pledge not to raise taxes. Government spending soared in 1989 as the Bush administration created the Resolution Trust Corporation to buy $129 billion in defaulted properties from savings and loans (S&Ls), banks that had made massive, risky commercial loans during the 1980s that had failed in the last year of the Reagan presidency. The federal budget deficit approached $300 billion in 1990, and the Treasury Department feared that international owners of U.S. bonds might refuse to buy more. The Democratic congressional leadership reached a deal with Bush to raise taxes modestly and make small cuts in defense and social programs. Opposition from a coalition of conservative Republicans and liberal Democrats blocked the compromise. When Bush vetoed a stopgap budget, the government shut down for three days in October. Congress then adopted another bill with tax increases for the wealthy and small spending cuts. In the aftermath, congressional Republicans condemned Bush for abandoning Ronald Reagan's supposed legacy (Bush had, of course, raised taxes 12 times after cutting them), whereas Democrats saw him as weak and ineffectual.

The Supreme Court also became a focal point of resentment and controversy in the Bush administration. Abortion was a flash point. Early in his political career, Bush had defended a woman's right to choose an abortion, but in the 1988 election campaign, he declared that "abortion is murder." In *Webster v. Reproductive Services of Missouri* (1989) and *Planned Parenthood v. Casey* (1992), the Court decided by five-to-four majorities that states could restrict but not eliminate access to abortion. The retirement of two liberal justices, William Brennan and Thurgood Marshall, raised conservative hopes that new justices would turn the Court further to the right. In 1990, Bush nominated federal judge **David Souter** to replace Brennan. Souter had not written or spoken on major constitutional issues, and he declined to tell senators how he might vote on a contentious question like abortion. He easily won Senate confirmation, and he soon astounded both Democrats and Republicans by voting with the Court's liberal minority.

Bush scrutinized his next nominee more carefully. To replace Marshall, the only African American justice, he selected 43-year-old federal judge **Clarence Thomas**. Thomas, an outspoken black conservative, had directed the office of the Equal Employment Opportunity Commission (EEOC) during the Reagan years. Bush had appointed Thomas to the federal court of appeals in 1990. Thomas frequently criticized Court decisions legalizing abortion, banning school prayer, and restricting the death penalty. Thomas's confirmation seemed assured when civil rights groups and some liberal Democrats muted their misgivings over his conservative views and endorsed him as the only African American Bush was likely to nominate. Then reports surfaced that **Anita Hill**, an African American law professor, had accused him of sexual harassment

SUPREME COURT SCANDAL   Law professor Anita Hill, a former colleague of Clarence Thomas, accused the Supreme Court nominee of sexual harassment during Senate testimony in October 1991. Thomas denied the charge, and most senators dismissed Hill's accusations as fantasy, even though several coworkers were prepared to verify her story.

when she worked for him at the EEOC. The Senate Judiciary Committee reopened its confirmation hearings. In televised testimony, Hill calmly described how Thomas had harassed her and other female workers, talked incessantly about viewing pornographic movies, and boasted of his sexual prowess. Republican senators on the committee accused Hill of making up her story. Thomas accused his opponents of conducting "a high-tech lynching for uppity blacks."

The Senate confirmed Thomas, who became the Court's most conservative member. Bush emerged from the confirmation battle weaker than ever. Many women considered the dismissive tone taken toward Hill by both senators and the administration unforgivable—especially when they later found out that other women who had worked with Thomas were prepared to confirm Hill's allegations but were never summoned to testify.

The New World Order

From 1989 to 1991, with revolutions sweeping through eastern Europe and the Soviet Union, the United States and other NATO countries provided billions of dollars to promote reform in the former Soviet empire. Bush assembled a talented team to direct foreign affairs. National Security Advisor Brent Scowcroft, Secretary of Defense Dick Cheney, Secretary of State James A. Baker, III, and Chairman of the Joint Chiefs of Staff Colin Powell had held high positions in the Ford and Reagan administrations. With the exception of Cheney, all prided themselves on being policy realists rather than reflexive ideologues. Together they helped manage the peaceful end of the Cold War, one of the most dramatic and far-reaching sets of events in the 20th century.

FALLING DIVIDE   Exuberant Germans celebrate the crumbling of the hated Berlin Wall in November 1989. The iconic Cold War symbol had divided the city since 1961.

In July 1989, Soviet president **Mikhail Gorbachev** stunned the world when he announced that his country would no longer intervene in the internal affairs of the Communist states of eastern Europe. In a dramatic reversal of 50 years of policy, the Soviet leader made clear that his country sought to cooperate with, not dominate, its neighbors, and they were free, if they liked, to form non-Communist governments. Huge peaceful demonstrations soon toppled the Communist regimes of Czechoslovakia, Hungary, and Poland. On November 9, 1989, the Berlin Wall, perhaps the most visible symbol of the Cold War, came down after months of street demonstrations rocked East Germany. Exuberant crowds used hammers, crowbars, and their bare hands to tear down the wall that divided Germans. Less than a year later, on October 2, 1990, East Germany ceased to exist, and its territory became part of the Federal Republic of Germany.

The rapid collapse of Communist regimes caught both American and Soviet leaders by surprise (Map 30.1). Bush had urged eastern Europeans to move slowly, and he endorsed gradual rather than rapid change. Only the Romanian Communist leadership used force in a vain effort to suppress the democratic tide. The political upheavals spread to the Soviet Union as well. In 1990, the Baltic republics of Latvia, Lithuania, and Estonia declared independence from the Soviet Union. Other Soviet republics also wanted independence. After an initial reluctance to engage with the Soviet leader, Bush met six times with Gorbachev in 1989 and 1990, and in November of 1990, the two men declared the end of the Cold War.

Just as Bush fully embraced Gorbachev, the Soviet leader's power waned. Orthodox Communists accused him of letting loose forces that had destroyed the Soviet empire.

map analysis

MAP 30.1 After the Fall: Russia and Eastern Europe Since 1991 Between 1989 and 1991, the Soviet empire collapsed, starting in eastern Europe and culminating in the dissolution of the Soviet Union. To Russia's west, Ukraine, Belarus, Estonia, Latvia, and Lithuania gained independence. In what had been Soviet Central Asia, a half-dozen predominantly Muslim republics emerged.

Two views of why the Cold War ended (1993)

Reformers, such as **Boris Yeltsin**, a former Communist and mayor of Moscow who was elected president of the Russian Federation in June 1991, complained that Gorbachev moved too slowly toward democratic and market reforms. In August 1991, Communist hard-liners staged a coup against Gorbachev. With Yeltsin's help, Gorbachev regained power after a few days, but his authority had evaporated. In the final months of 1991, power shifted to Yeltsin in Russia, and additional Soviet republics declared their independence. On December 25, 1991, Gorbachev proclaimed the end of the Soviet Union and peacefully handed power to Yeltsin.

Although the Cold War and the threat of instant nuclear annihilation receded, regional conflicts persisted, and in some places, such as Yugoslavia and a number of countries in Africa, they grew worse. In Latin America, however, the hostilities between U.S.-backed regimes and leftist guerrillas in El Salvador and Honduras abated. A peace settlement in Nicaragua led to elections and the replacement of the Sandinista regime. Bush used force to oust Manuel Noriega, Panama's dictator since 1983. For some time, Reagan had ignored his drug running and money laundering because Noriega cooperated with CIA efforts to aid the Contras in Nicaragua. By the time Bush became president, however, the civil wars in Central America were over, and Noriega's drug activities collided with Washington's renewed stress on the so-called war on drugs. An infuriated Noriega canceled an election in 1989 and sent club-wielding thugs to terrorize his opponents. Economic sanctions failed to drive Noriega from power, and Bush, stung by critics who said he "coddled" the dictator,

ADDRESS TO THE SOLDIERS   Saddam Hussein speaks to Iraqi troops around 1987 during the war he fought with Iran from 1980 to 1988. Nearly one million soldiers had died by the time both sides stopped fighting. Saddam soon turned his attention toward Kuwait, a small, rich neighbor that had loaned Iraq money to fight the war.

turned to force. In December 1989, the United States sent 12,000 troops to arrest Noriega and install the winner of the disputed May elections. After a few days of fighting, Noriega was captured and flown to Florida, where he was tried and convicted of drug smuggling.

The United States fought yet another war with far greater consequences after Iraqi leader **Saddam Hussein** invaded and annexed the oil-rich sheikdom of Kuwait on August 2, 1990 (Map 30.2). During the 1980s, the United States had sometimes sided with Iraq in its eight-year war with Iran. The United States had provided economic assistance to Iraq and had tacitly approved Saddam's drive to acquire chemical, biological, and nuclear weapons, some of which he used in fighting Iran and suppressing domestic opponents. In 1983, Reagan sent corporate executive and future secretary of defense Donald Rumsfeld as a special emissary to assure the dictator of Washington's support. Continuing Reagan's policy, Bush approved granting Iraq $400 million in agricultural credits shortly before Saddam seized Kuwait, an act the dictator may have interpreted as a green light because he had already threatened his neighbor.

The conquest of Kuwait, however, alarmed the richest oil kingdom, Saudi Arabia, which feared that Iraq would turn on it next. No one wanted the mercurial dictator, whom Bush now compared to Hitler, to control a major part of the world's petroleum reserve. In addition, Iraq's seizure of Kuwait clearly violated the United Nations Charter. Bush persuaded the UN Security Council to demand that Iraq quit Kuwait. He then sent 500,000 U.S. troops to protect Saudi Arabia and prevailed on 27 other countries to contribute an additional 200,000 troops to drive Iraq out of Kuwait.

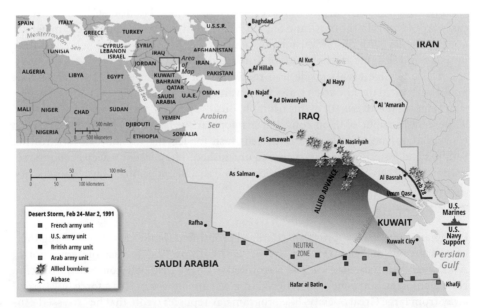

MAP 30.2 War in the Persian Gulf, 1991–1992 In 1991, President George H. W. Bush organized a broad international coalition that opposed Iraq's seizure of Kuwait and its threat to Saudi Arabia. In a short but effective air and ground war, coalition forces drove the Iraqis out of Kuwait but allowed Saddam Hussein to remain in power. Many Americans came to regret this decision.

The enormous size of the coalition forces arrayed against Saddam Hussein represented the lessons learned by Generals Powell and **H. Norman Schwarzkopf, Jr.**, the American commander in chief of the operation. They had concluded that the United States had failed in Vietnam partly because it had increased its forces gradually rather than employing overwhelming numbers of troops and firepower at the beginning of the war. In addition, this Powell Doctrine affirmed that the military objectives of any war must be clear and obtainable; public support must be sustainable; and there must be a clear "exit strategy," or way and timetable to end the fighting and bring the troops home.

President George H. Bush, "Address to the Nation Announcing Allied Military Action in the Persian Gulf" (January 16, 1991)

In January 1991, it became clear that Iraq would not leave Kuwait. Congress approved a resolution authorizing the use of force, and on January 17, the United States began bombing Iraq. When he announced the beginning of Operation Desert Storm, Bush spoke words first uttered by President Wilson during World War I. "We have before us," Bush declared, "the opportunity to forge for ourselves a new world order." U.S. and Allied planes bombed Iraq and Kuwait for five weeks before Schwarzkopf launched a bold ground assault on February 23. During the fighting, the Pentagon applied another lesson from the Vietnam War: to control the flow of information, it severely restricted the access of reporters to the battlefield. After only four days of fighting, Iraqi forces fled from Kuwait and the United States accepted Saddam's call for a cease-fire. During the brief conflict, 227 Allied troops lost their lives, while between 50,000 and 80,000 Iraqis died. The low number of American casualties became an unrealistic standard by which the public and news media would evaluate later wars. Saddam Hussein, however, remained in power. General Powell and Secretary of Defense Cheney advised Bush to cut short the war and not topple the dictator. They feared—quite accurately, it later turned out—that a prolonged occupation of Iraq would be deadly to American troops and provide an opportunity for Iran to expand its influence. However, U.S. radio broadcasts urged Kurds in the north and Shi'ites in the south to rebel against Saddam, whose power base lay with Sunni Muslims in central Iraq. Saddam's forces suppressed the uprising and slaughtered thousands of Kurds and Shi'ites.

These terrible events inside Iraq received little press coverage at the time. The public celebrated the low-cost victory in Kuwait and the apparent invincibility of American arms. In the aftermath of this triumph, Bush's approval reached an unprecedented 90 percent in public opinion polls. But his popularity was short-lived. At home, both conservatives and liberals soon criticized Bush for leaving the job of overthrowing Saddam and fostering democracy in Iraq unfinished. The onset of a steep economic recession in 1992 tarnished the glow of victory in Iraq and undermined Bush's popularity.

The Election of 1992

Bush's soaring public approval discouraged prominent Democrats from seeking their party's presidential nomination in 1992. **Bill Clinton**, the 46-year-old governor of Arkansas, eventually prevailed in a crowded primary field. Clinton called himself a New Democrat, someone who believed in government as a positive force but turned away from large Great Society–like programs. A reporter wrote that he "stressed economic mobility rather than wealth transfers, took a tough-minded line on crime, welfare dependency and international security issues, and called for a new ethic of personal responsibility to temper demands for entitlements." He was chair of the Democratic Leadership Council, a group of centrist officeholders, mostly from the South and West, who wanted to reverse their party's decades-long history of presidential electoral defeats. He chose as his vice president another centrist southerner, 44-year-old Tennessee senator **Al Gore**.

By 1992, Bush had grown increasingly unpopular. Two of his famous phrases—"Read my lips, no new taxes," and "the new world order"—became terms of derision. Conservatives resented his willingness to raise taxes to stem growing deficits. Saddam Hussein's continuation in power in Iraq—and evidence of what befell Iraqis who acted on Bush's call to overthrow the tyrant—dampened the initial enthusiasm over the war's outcome. A sharp economic downturn arising from the savings and loan crisis further eroded Bush's support. As S&Ls closed across the country, construction stopped on shopping malls, apartment complexes, and commercial buildings. Also, the so-called peace dividend of reduced military spending at the end of the Cold War initially hurt the economy. California, home to many defense-related businesses, was especially hard hit as contractors laid off well-paid engineers and skilled machinists. By February 1992, Bush's approval rating had fallen from 90 percent the previous March to 44 percent; 80 percent of the public said the country was on the wrong track.

President Bush's lethargic response to a major riot in Los Angeles in April 1992 further eroded his stature. The city erupted in flames following the acquittal of several police officers tried for the videotaped beating the year before of black motorist Rodney King. Thousands of African Americans and some Latinos went on a rampage, especially against Asian-owned retail stores in minority neighborhoods, to vent their anger at the verdict and at long-term economic problems. Over 50 people died in six days of violence, and the city sustained over a half-billion dollars in damages before National Guard troops restored calm. Bush said nothing about these events for several days, and then he waited a week before visiting the ravaged city. His rapid response to aggression in Kuwait contrasted dramatically with his lassitude toward Los Angeles.

Bush defeated a renomination challenge from former Reagan speechwriter **Pat Buchanan**, who led a revolt of angry conservatives who called for a "culture war" against feminists, homosexuals, and illegal immigrants. Their harsh rhetoric did nothing to broaden the Republicans' appeal. By the summer of 1992, Bush was running third in national polls behind Clinton and **Ross Perot**, an extremely wealthy and quirky Texan business executive who ran as an independent promising to reduce the federal budget deficit. Although Perot's campaign ignited fervent followers in the spring and early summer, his support faded as he became increasingly erratic. In the summer, he dropped out of the race only to resume his campaign several weeks later.

Clinton declared he would "focus like a laser" on repairing the economy. He promised tax cuts for the middle class; reconstruction of the nation's bridges, roads, and airports; and an ambitious plan to provide health insurance for everyone in the country. His campaign aides taped the slogan "It's the economy, stupid" to the wall of their headquarters. Bush stressed his successes in international affairs. Referring to Clinton and Gore, Bush said, "My dog Millie knows more about foreign policy than those two Bozos." Republican attacks on Clinton for avoiding the draft during the Vietnam War gained little traction. Bush also mocked Gore as "ozone man" for his commitment to the environment. Clinton, appearing knowledgeable and empathetic to the needs of ordinary Americans, did well in three presidential debates. Bush, by contrast, appeared remote and inarticulate. Perot was folksy and funny but no longer seemed a serious candidate. On Election Day, Clinton prevailed with 43 percent of the vote. Bush's share was 37 percent, the lowest Republican total since 1912. Perot received 19 percent, the highest share for a third party since 1912. Clinton won 44.9 million popular and 370 electoral votes, Bush captured 37 million popular and 178 electoral votes, and Perot obtained 19 million popular but no electoral votes. Voters admired Clinton's knowledge, curiosity, and empathy and thought he deserved a chance to put in practice his New Democratic plans.

STUDY QUESTIONS FOR GEORGE H. W. BUSH AND THE END OF THE COLD WAR

1. How did the George H. W. Bush administration respond to the end of the Cold War? In what ways were its responses successful? Where did they fall short?

quiz

2. Why did the Bush administration lose public support in 1991 and 1992?

3. Why did Bill Clinton win the 1992 presidential election?

❂ THE GOOD TIMES

In spite of the brief "Bush recession" in 1991–1992, the end of the Cold War and remarkable technological changes propelled the United States to unexpected prosperity. Between early 1992 and March 2000, the U.S. economy experienced the longest period of uninterrupted growth since the economic expansion of the 1960s. The end of communism in Europe hastened the pace of **globalization**, the knitting together of the world's economies through new information technology and the end of the artificial political barriers of the Cold War. Worldwide growth quickened. Asian and some Latin American economies boomed. They exported manufactured products to the United States, while the United States supplied the world with technical innovations, food, weapons, and cultural exports such as films and software.

The new prosperity was all the more welcome because few analysts expected it. A surge in worker productivity ignited the new growth, with the information technology industry leading the way. Workplaces led by young entrepreneurs became more informal. Millions of Americans invested heavily in the stock of new companies, and many believed an era of abundance had begun. Prosperity did not flow evenly, however, and the income gap between the rich and the poor continued to grow, with the fault lines reflecting differences in education as well as in race and gender.

Innovation and New Technology

Many technological advances in the 1990s changed the way Americans conducted business, communicated with one another, and spent their leisure time. As personal computers became more affordable and more common in homes and offices across the country, innovations in computing created new, radically faster ways to send information. The introduction of the Internet into daily life marked the most significant technological development for commerce and society in years. It also played a key role in the expansion of the economy that lasted almost the entire decade.

The Internet began when the **Defense Advanced Research Projects Agency (DARPA)**, founded in 1958 in response to the Soviet launch of *Sputnik*, experimented with ways to link networks of computers. In the 1960s and 1970s, government agencies, mostly related to the Department of Defense, along with university researchers, began sharing information on their local computers over the so-called ARPAnet. In 1991, Tim Berners-Lee, a British computer scientist, developed the World Wide Web, making the Internet more accessible. Businesses, organizations, government departments, and universities built Web sites that anyone could visit. Internet users could send messages via electronic mail addresses that delivered information instantaneously. The Global Positioning System (GPS), another offshoot of military research, soon found its way into civilian life and changed how Americans navigated in their automobiles.

Businesses eagerly embraced the new advancements in information technology. The Internet sped up the exchange of data and ideas within companies and connected them to new, previously inaccessible global markets. Telecommunications improvements also enabled U.S. corporations to reduce labor costs by outsourcing parts of their business, particularly customer service divisions, to developing countries with a pool of English-speaking workers. For example, when calling the phone company or a credit card company with a question or complaint, callers from, say, Chicago would be routed to a call center in Manila or New Delhi. The globalized economy drew criticism from those concerned with keeping jobs in the United States. Manufacturing jobs continued their decades-long decline, often replaced by lower-paying service jobs. But there were also many winners in this new economy. The Internet provided an entirely new opportunity for e-commerce

EMPLOYEES OF A SILICON VALLEY START-UP COMPANY AROUND 2000   Start-ups combined technical talent, boundless energy, and an often-chaotic lifestyle in an effort to create the next Microsoft or its equivalent.

Map of the
Internet
(2003)

by Web sites that sold goods or services. Two of the most successful online businesses proved to be online bookstore Amazon.com, founded in 1994, and eBay, a sort of electronic garage sale founded in 1995. Gambling and pornographic sites also proliferated, challenging print publications such as *Playboy* that had dominated the adult entertainment market since the 1950s. By 2001, more than 60 million of the 107 million American households had a personal computer, and 51 million of them had Internet access.

During the 1990s, the new information technology industries fueled a boom on Wall Street, where stock prices more than quadrupled as the Dow Jones Industrial Average index rose from a low of 2,588 points in January 1991 to a high of 11,722 points in January 2000 (Figure 30.1). The NASDAQ index, which included many high-tech stocks, increased 86 percent in 1999 alone. Before the tech stock bubble burst in March 2000, the decade saw rapid growth, low unemployment, low inflation, and an increase in investment in real estate. Pensions also became linked to the stock market, as many companies dropped traditional retirement programs and pushed employees into 401(k) plans, named for a provision in the tax code that linked payouts to investments. The new communications technology and global business market at the very least helped make companies more efficient and productive, even if not entirely responsible for shaping the economy as a whole.

The Internet revolution also enabled another adaptation for workers—telecommuting. Telecommuting allowed employees to work from their home through the Internet. Employees could put in eight hours of work without ever getting out of their pajamas. By 2001, more than four million people telecommuted, and many more ran their own Internet businesses.

In 1999, economic growth received a further boost from the repeal of parts of the Glass–Steagall Act of 1933, which had barred many banks from undertaking risky investments with depositors' money. The law was enacted originally to prevent the kind of wild speculation that had contributed to the Great Depression. President Clinton, who, along with congressional Republicans pushed the repeal, argued that deregulation would encourage new forms of lending and investment without increasing risk. His prediction worked—for a while.

Although new technologies such as communications satellites and the Internet were central parts of the global business environment, most global trade still relied on ocean shipping. Merchant vessels carried bulk cargo (mineral ores and grains) and high-value products such as automobiles. But high shipping costs—involving packing goods into crates, moving them to ports, loading and unloading them from ships, and delivering them to stores—made it impractical to transport many low-value-added products such as running shoes or shirts from low-cost-producing countries to wealthy consuming nations. As of 1960, the cost of shipping accounted for about 10 percent of the price of most imports and exports.

Beginning in the late 1950s and accelerating during the next 20 years, several companies devised the concept of packing goods in a sealed container at the point of production and delivering the container across the world. Costly investments in ship design, port facilities, and labor contracts were required to make the concept of "intermodal" ship truck railroad shipping work. By the 1970s, standardized 8' × 40' containers could be stacked 10 high on specialized vessels, offloaded by giant cranes, and placed directly onto trucks or railroad cars at the port of destination. Previously, it took dozens of cargo handlers a week or more to unload a large ship. Now, a single crane operator could load or offload a container ship in a day.

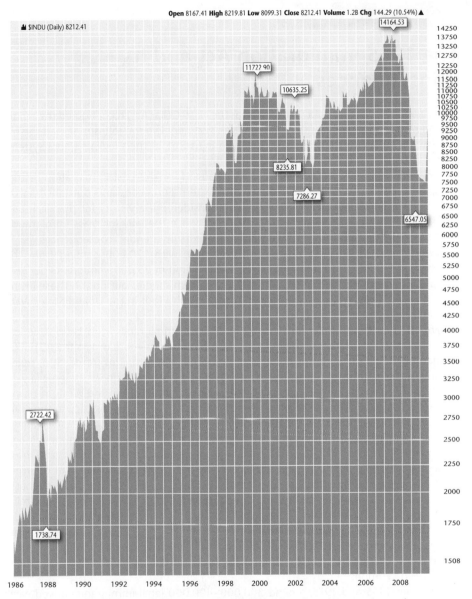

Open 8167.41 **High** 8219.81 **Low** 8099.31 **Close** 8212.41 **Volume** 1.2B **Chg** 144.29 (10.54%) ▲

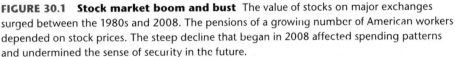

FIGURE 30.1 Stock market boom and bust The value of stocks on major exchanges surged between the 1980s and 2008. The pensions of a growing number of American workers depended on stock prices. The steep decline that began in 2008 affected spending patterns and undermined the sense of security in the future.

A factory in China or Bangladesh that produced, say, Nike running shoes would load thousands of pairs into a single container destined for a particular Walmart store in Kansas. After crossing the Pacific Ocean to Oakland or Long Beach, the container would be placed on a railcar or truck and delivered to the Walmart in Kansas City without being unpacked. The technology relied in part on optical scanners that recorded

The 1965 Immigration Act and Its Consequences

The Nationality Act of 1965 (known also as the Hart–Cellar Act) reconfigured the ethnic and racial composition of the nation. When President Lyndon Johnson signed the bill into law, he proclaimed an end to the "harsh injustice" of the previous quota system, which had been a "cruel and enduring wrong."

The bipartisan law erased the most egregious aspects of past immigration restrictions, including the 1924 meager quotas for eastern Europeans and outright ban on Asians. But even supporters of the law—who considered it a victory for pluralism and racial equality—failed to recognize how it would pave the way for mass immigration from Latin America and Asia; nor did they consider its unintended consequences.

Congress specified an annual cap of 290,000, with 170,000 coming from the Eastern Hemisphere and 120,000 from the West. A limit of 20,000 immigrants per year was placed on individual countries in the Eastern Hemisphere, but not on those in the West. Under a Cold War law, virtually all Cubans setting foot in the United States were welcomed outside of quota limits.

For the first time, there was an overall limit on immigrants from Latin America. Previously, Mexican migrants had entered the United States more or less freely, pulled by seasonal demands for agricultural labor and other opportunities. After 1965, many continued their annual migration but were classified as "illegals" under the new law. In 1976, Congress imposed the 20,000 annual cap on all countries in the Western Hemisphere. The annual demand for Mexican farm labor far exceeded this cap, so the scale of undocumented immigration rose sharply.

Several categories of immigrants were granted preference *outside* hemispheric and country quotas. These included close family members of naturalized U.S. citizens and those possessing desirable skills as varied as nuclear physicists, fashion models, and gourmet chefs. This created an unintended "brain drain" in poorer countries, with many scientists and skilled professionals migrating to the United States for higher-paying work. By the mid-1990s, a fourth of science and engineering PhDs in the United States were foreign born.

Congress originally anticipated that the family reunification provision would primarily benefit close relatives of eastern and southern Europeans who had immigrated since World War II. While true initially, over time the provision mostly benefited those coming from outside Europe.

Between 1965 and 1975, around 300,000–400,000 legal immigrants arrived each year. From 1976 to 1988, the annual number ranged from 500,000 to 650,000. In 1986, President Reagan raised quotas and granted 2.7 million undocumented immigrants amnesty and a path to citizenship. In 1990, Congress raised immigration quotas by 35 percent in response to robust economic growth and the demand for inexpensive labor. Since the early 1990s, about one million immigrants have arrived each year. About 60 percent enter under the non-quota provisions of family unification; about 15 percent are admitted with special job skills, and less than 10 percent as refugees. About 9,000 visas providing a fast track to citizenship are "sold" annually to wealthy foreigners who invest between $500,000 and $1 million in business ventures in "economically depressed areas."

Expanded immigration promoted a more diverse and multicultural society. Pre-1965 migrants came overwhelmingly from western Europe. The 1960 U.S. Census enumerated about one million people of Asian descent (mostly Chinese, Japanese, and Filipino descendants of those who came before 1924), less than 1 percent of the nation's population. Between 1970 and 2010, the Asian/Pacific Islander population increased to 6 percent, including Chinese, Vietnamese, Koreans, Thais, Indians, and Malaysians. Demographers project that Asian/Pacific Islanders may comprise 8 percent of the population by 2030.

The rise in the number of Hispanic Americans (primarily those who trace their origins to Mexico, Puerto Rico, Cuba, and Central and South America) has been even greater. In 1960, Hispanics comprised about 3.6 percent of the U.S. population. By 2010, they had increased to 16.3 percent. By 2030, nearly a quarter of the American population will likely have Hispanic roots. As the percent of "non-Hispanic whites" declines, the Census Bureau has predicted that the United States will become a "majority-minority" country by 2043. Several states, including California, Hawaii, Texas, and New Mexico, are already in this category, with others expected to soon join their ranks, as are 25 major cities, including New York, Los Angeles, Miami, Chicago, Houston, and Phoenix.

image analysis

UNDER THE EYES OF LADY LIBERTY President Lyndon B. Johnson signs the Immigration and Nationality Act on October 3, 1965, on Liberty Island, New York.

The number of illegal, or undocumented, migrants also increased rapidly. During the 1990s through 2009, the size of the undocumented population increased by about 275,000 annually, with about 80 percent coming from Mexico. For a variety of reasons, Mexican migration—both legal and undocumented—declined sharply after 2009.

Greater diversity troubled some conservatives, who complained that the new immigration eroded traditional values and distorted the nation's politics. In 1995, California tried to bar undocumented immigrants from receiving basic government social services, but a federal court blocked the attempt. Since 2000, several states have adopted laws proclaiming English the official language. Arizona tasked local law enforcement with detaining undocumented residents. The harshest measures were blocked by federal courts, which held that enforcement of immigration law remained a federal responsibility.

As of 2016, just over 40 million people born abroad now call the United States home. Three-fourths of these are legal residents. Together, the foreign born and their children comprise nearly 25 percent of the American population, near a historic high.

- What historic injustices did the 1965 law correct?
- What were the unintended consequences of the 1965 law?

UPC codes attached to each container. This reduced transportation costs by about 90 percent from 1960s levels, allowing low-wage producers to connect with bargain-hunting Walmart shoppers. While expanded global trade boosted economic growth in the aggregate, it also hurt workers, who lost jobs in U.S. factories. But even without cheap imports, many domestic manufacturing jobs were being replaced through automation.

In 1979, U.S. trans-Pacific trade for the first time surpassed transatlantic trade. By the early 21st century, cargo ships moved over 300 million containers per year. Half of all goods imported to the United States came through the ports of Long Beach and Los Angeles. Because giant container ships were too large to pass through the century-old Panama Canal, the canal had to be enlarged. The first ship to transit the expanded 50-mile waterway in 2016 was a 1,000-foot-long Chinese behemoth carrying 9,000 containers en route to California.

STUDY QUESTIONS FOR THE GOOD TIMES

quiz

1. Why did the U.S. economy expand in the 1990s?

2. Who benefited and who was left behind in the economic expansion of the 1990s?

3. In what ways did international migration and immigration alter life in the United States in the 1990s?

BILL CLINTON AND THE NEW DEMOCRATS

Bill Clinton's eight-year presidency from 1993 through 2001 raised enormous hopes of meeting domestic needs unfilled for decades. Some of these were realized, but many went unmet. As a New Democrat, Clinton tried to steer a middle course between the conservatism of the Reagan era and the liberalism of the Great Society. He ardently supported globalization. Like most economists, business executives, and financiers of the time, the president expected globalization to increase wealth as it sped the flow of information and goods.

Clinton was a highly accomplished politician who remained popular for much of his term. Intelligent, curious, and articulate, he sought advice widely. He was also impulsive, and his presidency nearly ended in disgrace because of a sex scandal. Although many Americans admired Clinton's commitment to solving the problems of ordinary people, a sizeable share of the population hated him. He became a focal point of clashes between conservatives—many of whom defended traditional religious values—and liberals who liked his embrace of new economic and cultural trends. Some conservatives considered his presidency illegitimate for interrupting the Reagan legacy, and they tried to drive him from office.

An Awkward Start

Clinton outlined a bold agenda in his inaugural address: "We must do what no generation has had to do before. We must invest more in our own people, in their jobs, in their future, and at the same time cut our massive debt." But circumstances interrupted his plans.

Clinton scaled back plans to permit gays and lesbians to serve openly in the military in the face of stiff opposition from the Joint Chiefs of Staff. Instead, Clinton fashioned a compromise in which the military would not inquire about its members' sexual preferences, and gays and lesbians could serve if they did not reveal their sexual identity. This policy, labeled "Don't Ask, Don't Tell," disappointed advocates for full equality between gays and straights and offended conservatives who opposed any relaxation of restrictions on gays serving in the military. Although Clinton intended this as an interim solution, it lasted until 2010, when Congress voted to permit gays to serve openly in the armed forces. Despite predictions of chaos in the ranks, the military adjusted to both the interim rule and the far-reaching later change.

Excerpts from the National Defense Authorization Act of 1994

Robert Rubin, the chairman of the president's National Economic Council and a successful Wall Street bond trader, persuaded Clinton to attack the budget deficit of $300 billion. Once Wall Street believed the government was going to borrow less in the future, Rubin argued, interest rates would fall, and the economy would receive the boost it needed. In February 1993, Clinton presented Congress a program of tax increases and spending cuts to reduce the federal budget deficit. Congress rejected Clinton's program to invest in infrastructure and then began a four-month debate on the tax increases and spending cuts. Georgia representative **Newt Gingrich**, the Republican House minority whip and a rising star among conservatives, insisted that Clinton's tax increases would "lead to recession . . . and will actually increase the deficit." Democrats stood by the plan, which passed the House in August by the narrowest margin of 218 to 216. In the Senate, Vice President Al Gore cast the deciding vote to break a 50–50 tie in favor of the plan. Not one Republican voted for the plan in either house. The dire predictions of economic calamity made by the law's opponents proved to be completely wrong. In fact, the federal budget deficit began a sharp decline, while business and employment grew.

After the passage of his economic plan, Clinton persuaded enough Democrats to join Republicans in voting to approve the **North American Free Trade Agreement (NAFTA)** at the close of 1993. President George H. W. Bush had negotiated this free-trade pact with Canada and Mexico, the country's two largest trading partners, but Congress had not voted on it before he left office. NAFTA was popular with business leaders, and most economists believed that reducing barriers to trade would lift living standards. Organized labor and its allies in the Democratic Party strongly opposed it, however; they feared that it would accelerate the loss of jobs to lower-wage plants in Mexico. Environmentalists also opposed NAFTA because of Mexico's poor record of environmental protection. Clinton promised to support NAFTA once labor and environmental standards were included in the pact. He achieved some of these aims and submitted the agreement to Congress in the fall. A heated debate ensued in Congress and on the airwaves. Popular sentiment gradually turned in favored of ratification, and Congress completed its approval of NAFTA in November.

Clinton advocated free trade and promoted the benefits of globalization throughout his eight years in the White House. By the late 1990s, however, a worldwide movement arose against globalization. Critics charged that it made the rich richer and the poor poorer while destroying traditional cultures. Tens of thousands of antiglobalization demonstrators came to Seattle in December 1999 to oppose Clinton's support for the World Trade Organization, which had been created in 1995 to supervise world trade.

A portrait of three families in three worlds (1993–94)

Globalization had a differential impact on many countries. Increased trade helped lift tens of millions of Indians and Chinese out of poverty. At the same time, inexpensive exports from those countries displaced many American manufacturing jobs. Expanding trade and new technology created many new jobs within the United States, but often not for those with lower skills or education who had worked in factories.

Despite many changes in the workplace, most women still had to juggle outside employment and family responsibilities. By the beginning of the 1990s, barely one in four families fit the model of the traditional family, with a breadwinner husband and homemaker wife. Many families struggled to find affordable, reliable child care. As noted previously, between one-fourth and one-half of families—varying by race, class, and education level—included children who lived with one parent or whose parents had never married. The 1993 Family and Medical Leave Act, passed during the first Clinton administration, provided some relief, as it guaranteed up to 12 weeks of unpaid leave for workers needing time off. But as of 2016, the United States remained one of the few industrial democracies that did not mandate paid leave for new parents. In 2002, women working full time still earned only about 77.5 percent of what men did working in similar positions. Few found a place in top positions at major corporations.

In September 1993, in the midst of the debate over NAFTA, Clinton returned to the subject of reforming the nation's health care system. He delivered a well-received speech favoring a continuation of the current system of private health insurance but expanding coverage for the uninsured. Private employers would be mandated to provide coverage for their workers, while other government programs would insure the unemployed. As a sign of the importance he assigned to this reform, Clinton asked his wife, First Lady Hillary Rodham Clinton, to develop and steer the proposal through Congress.

Although nearly every American had complaints about the costs and quality of health care, the reform plan encountered stiff opposition in Congress and among the public. The health insurance industry and some medical groups strongly opposed Clinton's proposals for mandating types of coverage and controlling costs. Opponents spent millions of dollars debunking the plan in radio and TV ads.

Many Americans who already had medical insurance feared that extending coverage to the uninsured would come at their expense. These doubts, and others cultivated by the insurance industry's disinformation campaign, effectively killed the Clinton proposal by September 1994, when the Senate dropped consideration of it. In the wake of this failure, many employers tried to control rapidly rising medical costs by forcing workers to enroll in health maintenance organizations, or HMOs. HMOs, often run by large insurers, earned big profits by imposing many of the restrictions on treatment and coverage that the antireform campaign had warned would come with federal oversight. During the next 15 years, health costs rose steeply and millions more working Americans lost insurance coverage.

The defeat of health reform made Republicans jubilant at the prospect of major gains in the November election. Several hundred Republican candidates, both incumbents and challengers, stood on the steps of the Capitol and signed their names to the **Contract with America**, a document conceived by Representative Newt Gingrich that promised to make Congress more accountable, balance the federal budget, reverse the tax increases passed in 1993, and reduce the capital gains tax. On Election Day, many Democrats who had voted for Clinton in 1992 stayed home. The reduced Democratic turnout resulted in Republicans capturing both houses of Congress for the first time in 40 years. They also governed 9 of the 10 most populous states.

Newt Gingrich introduces the Contract with America (September 1994)

REPUBLICAN PROMISES   Newt Gingrich, the Republican firebrand from Georgia, proclaims his "Contract with America." The campaign document helped Republicans capture control of the House of Representatives in November 1994.

Clinton's Recovery

The Republican Congress came to power in January 1995 convinced they could make Clinton irrelevant and recapture the White House in 1996. Newt Gingrich, the new Speaker of the House, was the most prominent political figure in the early months of 1995. He denounced Clinton and promoted the agenda offered in the Contract with America. To the Speaker's amazement, Clinton began a slow recovery, partly because of a tragic domestic terrorist event that wrenched the public's eye away from political squabbling in Washington. In April 1995, **Timothy McVeigh** and **Terry Nichols**, two angry army veterans who belonged to antigovernment, white supremacist militia groups, bombed the Alfred P. Murrah Federal Building in Oklahoma City. The blast killed 169 people, including federal workers, visitors, and children at a day care facility. At a memorial service, Clinton spoke movingly of the victims, and he asked Americans to reflect on whether the strident antigovernment rhetoric of conservative radio talk show hosts—along with some members of Congress—had poisoned political conversation and legitimized violence.

Clinton's confidence and popularity continued to recover after the Oklahoma City bombing. He adapted a strategy of "triangulation" in which he navigated positions between conservative Republicans and liberal Democrats in Congress. In the fall of 1995, Gingrich guessed that he could undermine public confidence in Clinton—as congressional Democrats had with Bush—by refusing to compromise with the White House on adoption of the federal budget. As a result of the House's failure to approve a new budget, the government shut down twice, first in November and then in December. But instead of focusing public resentment on the president, the shutdown backfired against Gingrich and other Republicans whose demeanor came across as petty and who seemed indifferent to the safety of the nation.

During 1996, Clinton undercut more of the Republicans' agenda. In his State of the Union message, he said, "The era of big government is over." He proposed a federal budget that would be in balance within a year and register a surplus in 1998. He compromised with Republicans on one of their perennial complaints, the cost and provisions of welfare. The welfare reform bill signed in July 1996 limited recipients to two years of lifetime cash benefits and required them to look for work while on assistance. Some of Clinton's liberal supporters considered the bill punitive and feared it would

President Bill Clinton, "State of the Union Address" (January 23, 1993)

drive millions into grinding poverty. But the booming economy and the expansion of low-skilled (but also low-paying) service jobs in the late 1990s softened the blow. Public assistance rolls fell by 25 percent by 2001, and most welfare recipients did find jobs.

The Clinton administration continued federal efforts to discourage tobacco use. The president joined with those who called nicotine an addictive drug and in 1996 approved regulations that labeled cigarettes as "drug delivery devices." Seeking to recover the health costs of treating sick smokers, nearly every state attorney general joined in a lawsuit against the tobacco industry. In 1998, the industry reached a settlement that provided payments of several hundred billion dollars to be paid over 30 years. In 1999, the U.S. Department of Justice brought a criminal suit against cigarette manufacturers for selling a dangerous product. In 2006, a federal judge ruled that the companies had misled the public about the risks of their product. By then, however, even major cigarette companies acknowledged what the public health community and most Americans had long recognized—cigarettes were a major cause of lung cancer and other diseases. In a massive change in public behavior, adult smoking rates, which had peaked at 42 percent in 1964, fell below 20 percent in the early 21st century and continued declining.

Clinton easily won reelection in 1996. He seemed far more in touch with the concerns of suburban families, the largest voting bloc, than either of his rivals, Republican senator **Bob Dole** and independent candidate Ross Perot. Dole, a 73-year-old World War II veteran, was popular with the press for his endless stream of acerbic remarks, but voters considered him a figure of an earlier era. Perot's signature issue of reducing the federal budget deficit faded after Clinton proposed a realistic balanced budget. Clinton won 47.4 million votes, 49.2 percent of the total. He captured 379 electoral votes. Dole received 39.1 million votes, 40.7 percent of those cast, and 159 electoral votes. Perot came in a distant third, with 8.08 million votes, or 8.4 percent.

Clinton's Second Term

Bitter partisan divisions continued during Clinton's second term. Despite Clinton's reelection, Republicans retained control of Congress after 1996, and they spent much of 1997 investigating the president's fundraising. The public, enjoying the economic good times, took little notice of these hearings. Then in January 1998, news of Clinton's sexual involvement with Monica Lewinsky, a 21-year-old White House intern when the liaison began in 1995, came to dominate the headlines for a year, especially on cable television, which became a major source of news and entertainment at around this time. Unrestrained by the standards of accuracy that characterized most print journalism, cable news broadcasts and commentators treated politics like a contact sport and sensationalized personal scandals.

The coarsening of culture seemed evident in the popularity of talk radio shows such as Rush Limbaugh's, on air since the late 1980s; television's *Geraldo*, beginning in 1987, and the *Jerry Springer Show* after 1991; and the Internet's *Drudge Report*, which appeared online in 1997. Previously the domain of trashy supermarket tabloids such as the *National Enquirer*, the hairstyles, marriages, divorces, sexual prowess, and crimes of the famous now became a focus of these shows. These "shock jocks" delighted in lurid details, whether they concerned the trial in 1994–1995 of former football star O. J. Simpson for the alleged murder of his ex-wife or the impeachment of President Clinton in 1998–1999 for lying about an affair with Lewinsky.

Clinton, who had a reputation for womanizing and extramarital sex going back to his days as Arkansas governor, made an easy target for what his staff called "bimbo eruptions." His relationship with Lewinsky came to light through the investigations of **Kenneth Starr**, a special prosecutor authorized by the Justice Department in 1994 to look into Bill and Hillary Clinton's involvement in a minor real estate transaction in Arkansas, known as Whitewater, 15 years earlier. After several years of probing, Starr found no illegalities in the Clintons' past business deals, but he was convinced they were lying about something. As Starr prepared to close his inquiries in 1998, lawyers for **Paula Jones**, a woman who accused Clinton of sexual harassment when he was governor, learned that the president had had an affair with Lewinsky. Jones's lawyers told Starr about the affair. Even though this transgression had nothing to do with the Whitewater investigation, Starr forced Lewinsky to divulge details of her relationship with Clinton. News quickly spread about the liaison, and reporters demanded that the president tell what he knew. During a news conference, Clinton wagged his finger at a questioner and said, "I did not have sexual relations with that woman, Monica Lewinsky." The denial fell flat as additional details emerged that Clinton and Lewinsky had engaged in sexual contact, if not intercourse, on several occasions in 1995 and 1996.

In August, after Starr forced Clinton to testify under oath, the prosecutor decided Clinton had lied about the affair. In September, Starr sent Congress a 500-page report detailing what he considered Clinton's sexual misconduct but presented nothing about any official wrongdoing. Republicans prepared to impeach the president, convinced he would either resign or be removed from office by votes in the House and Senate.

Once again, Gingrich and House Republicans badly misread public opinion. Clinton's behavior disappointed ordinary Americans, who saw it as childish and degrading. But they were even angrier at Special Prosecutor Starr and Gingrich for making a public spectacle out of what essentially were smutty details of a private affair. During the fall of 1998, Clinton's positive approval rating among the public actually improved, to 60 percent. Democrats also gained seats in the November midterm congressional elections. Stunned by these developments, Gingrich belatedly admitted that he, too, had conducted an affair with a young female staff member and resigned from Congress.

Instead of ending the crisis, Clinton's Republican opponents doubled down. In December, the House voted along party lines to impeach Clinton, making him only the second president to be impeached, as Nixon had resigned before a vote was taken. A Senate trial opened in January 1999. By then, two-thirds of the public had told pollsters they did not want Clinton removed from office. Finally getting the message, in February, the Senate acquitted Clinton.

STUDY QUESTIONS FOR BILL CLINTON AND THE NEW DEMOCRATS

1. What were the characteristics of the "New Democrats"?

2. How did President Clinton regain popularity after the Republicans won the 1994 congressional elections?

3. Why did the House of Representatives impeach President Clinton? Why did the Senate acquit him?

quiz

❤A POST–COLD WAR FOREIGN POLICY

The United States stood as the world's only superpower after the Cold War. The Clinton administration embraced knitting together the world's economy through globalization. It engaged in several humanitarian interventions, some of which involved the use of military force, and it sought to mediate some ancient regional disputes. Clinton formed a partnership with Russian president Boris Yeltsin to manage Russia's integration into the post–Cold War world. At the end of the 1990s, the United States became more alert to the danger posed by al-Qaeda and Islamist terrorism.

Intervention and Mediation

In December 1992, the defeated Bush administration sent 28,000 U.S. troops to the East African country of Somalia to distribute food to millions who faced starvation in the face of a civil war. Clinton continued this operation. In May 1993, the UN took over the relief mission, and the United States reduced its force to 4,000 in June. In October, U.S. forces tried to help UN troops arrest a Somali warlord. Eighteen U.S. Army Rangers lost their lives in a bloody firefight in which over 900 Somali fighters were also killed. Television showed Somalis dragging the corpse of one of the Americans through the streets. These graphic images quickly turned American opinion against the Somalia relief effort, and Clinton withdrew the remaining forces. The incident became the basis for a best-selling book and popular film, *Black Hawk Down*.

BOSNIAN MASS GRAVE War crimes investigators sift through the carnage created by ethnic strife in Bosnia during the 1990s.

Public resistance to additional commitments in Africa kept the Clinton administration from intervening to stop genocide in the East African country of Rwanda in 1994. That spring, the Hutu majority murdered 700,000 minority Tutsis. The U.S. and European governments declined urgent requests from a few hundred UN observers to send forces to stop the carnage. Six years later, Clinton stopped briefly in Rwanda and apologized for Western inaction during the catastrophe.

The United States intervened more forcefully in the former Yugoslavia. During the 1992 election campaign, Clinton criticized the Bush administration for doing little to stop Serbs in the former Yugoslav republic of Bosnia from their brutal **ethnic cleansing** of their Muslim neighbors. Once in office, however, Clinton concluded that the divisions between the Orthodox Christian

Serbs, Roman Catholic Croats, and Muslim Bosnians were so deep and ancient that outside intervention could not contain them. The fighting got worse in the summer of 1995 when Serb forces massacred 4,000 Muslim men and boys in the village of Srebrenica and also raped thousands of Muslim women and girls.

The United States, Britain, and France responded by bombing Serb armaments and supplies. Yugoslav president **Slobodan Milošević**, who promoted ethnic violence as a way to build support among Serbs, now feared that he might be driven from power; he consented to attend a peace conference at Wright Patterson Air Force base in Dayton, Ohio. In November, the warring sides agreed to share power in an independent state of Bosnia. The United States contributed 2,000 troops to a 6,000-member International Implementation Force (IFOR) to maintain peace and security in Bosnia. In mid-1999, the United States and its NATO allies again used air power against Yugoslavia to compel it to withdraw its troops from the largely Muslim province of Kosovo.

The Clinton administration came poignantly close to successfully mediating the half-century-long conflict between Israelis and Palestinians. In September 1993, Clinton brought Israeli prime minister **Yitzhak Rabin** and Palestine Liberation Organization chairman **Yasser Arafat** together to sign a peace agreement on the White House lawn. The PLO recognized Israel in exchange for a withdrawal of Israeli forces from the Gaza Strip and a large part of the West Bank over the next five years. Arafat would control the evacuated territory for a new Palestine National Authority. The two sides promised to reach a final peace within five years.

Hope for a settlement quickly faded. A Jewish extremist opposed to any peace with the PLO murdered Rabin in 1995. Neither Israeli nationalists who replaced Rabin nor the more moderate Labor government returned to power in 1999 reached an agreement with the PLO. Clinton hosted a meeting between Israeli prime minister Ehud Barak and Arafat in July 2000, but the sides could not agree on what land Israel would turn over to the PLO. Two months later a Palestinian uprising erupted across the West Bank against Israeli rule. Hundreds of Palestinians and dozens of Israelis were killed in the fighting.

International Terrorism

International terrorism sponsored by Islamist radicals became a significant concern of American policymakers in the 1990s. On February 26, 1993, a little more than a month after Bill Clinton became president, several supporters of **Osama bin Laden**, the Muslim extremist leader of al-Qaeda (founded in 1990) whom the Reagan administration had supported when he fought the Soviets in Afghanistan during the 1980s, drove an explosives-laden Ryder rental truck into the parking garage beneath the World Trade Center in lower Manhattan. Although the bomb failed to bring down the Twin Towers as the plotters hoped, the blast killed six people and injured over 1,000.

In 1996, bin Laden moved his headquarters from Sudan to Afghanistan, where he continued to plan attacks on American interests around the world. In 1998, he declared it was the duty of every Muslim to kill Americans anywhere in the world. His anger against the United States had been kindled by the presence of American troops in his homeland of Saudi Arabia during and after the Gulf War of 1991, U.S. support for Israel, and a sense that the United States and the West expressed contempt for Muslim civilization.

Excerpt from Osama bin Laden, "A Declaration of Jihad "(1996)

In August 1998, al-Qaeda teams detonated truck bombs outside the U.S. embassies in Nairobi, Kenya, and Dar es Salaam, Tanzania; 12 Americans and more than 200 embassy workers and visitors of other nationalities were killed, and more than 5,000 people were injured. Clinton ordered air strikes against bin Laden's Afghanistan headquarters and a Sudanese factory the CIA believed was producing nerve gas. The attacks did not seriously disrupt al-Qaeda. Clinton's Republican opponents hinted that he had ordered the air strikes to distract public attention from the Lewinsky scandal. Republicans ignored al-Qaeda but pushed through Congress the Iraqi Liberation Act of 1998, a law that offered support to those trying to depose Saddam Hussein. In October 2000, in the midst of the presidential election campaign, al-Qaedaa commandos blew a hole in the hull of the navy destroyer *Cole* in a harbor off the coast of Yemen and killed 17 sailors. Clinton pressured the Taliban-led government of Afghanistan to expel bin Laden, but Afghanistan continued to provide him sanctuary.

STUDY QUESTIONS FOR A POST–COLD WAR FOREIGN POLICY

1. What international objectives did the Clinton administration pursue?
2. Where did the Clinton administration's humanitarian interventions, peace initiatives, and antiterrorism efforts succeed? Where did they fail?

quiz

THE DISPUTED ELECTION OF 2000

The 21st century began with one of the most disputed presidential contests in U.S. history. The prosperity and peace of the Clinton years favored the prospects of Democratic vice president Al Gore. But the good times also made American voters believe that politics was not that important in their daily lives. Some Democrats and independents wanted to punish Clinton for his misconduct with Monica Lewinsky by voting for the Republican candidate, Texas governor **George W. Bush**, the son of President George H. W. Bush. Others, who believed that Gore and Bush were nearly identical centrists, voted for consumer activist **Ralph Nader**. In November, Gore received 500,000 more popular votes than Bush, but the virtually tied vote in Florida created an electoral stalemate, ultimately decided by the Supreme Court.

Bush Versus Gore

Having served as vice president for eight years and considered a "straight arrow" untainted by the Lewinsky scandal, Al Gore easily secured the Democratic presidential nomination in 2000. The Republican candidate, George W. Bush, locked up his party's nomination by winning a string of primaries.

Both Gore and Bush portrayed themselves as moderates. Consumer advocate Ralph Nader and Republican dissident Pat Buchanan also ran as presidential candidates. Nader railed against corporate greed and supported progressive causes as the nominee for the Green Party. Buchanan ran on an anti-immigrant, anti-interventionist platform for the Reform Party. Neither Nader nor Buchanan had much influence on the national vote, but their tallies in Florida had a huge impact. Although Gore had worked closely with Clinton and shared most of his policy views, the vice president felt personally betrayed by Clinton's behavior in the Lewinsky affair. Throughout the campaign, he kept the president at arm's length. Gore ignored many of Clinton's accomplishments and even sidestepped his own commitment to environmental protection. Although Bush had degrees from both Yale and Harvard, he belittled his eastern elite education. Instead, he stressed his ties to Texas along with a down-home, plainspoken style. He promised tax cuts, regulatory reform, and fewer foreign commitments. Clinton and Gore, he charged, had foolishly engaged in "nation building," the effort to construct functioning societies in places such as Haiti, Somalia, and Yugoslavia. Neither candidate inspired much enthusiasm.

The Election in Florida and a Supreme Court Decision

The election's outcome hinged on Florida. On election night, TV networks proclaimed each candidate the winner before deciding the outcome was "too close to call." Over the next 36 days, state officials recounted votes in select counties and debated how to resolve ballots that were misprinted, mangled by voting machines, or mailed in after the election. Besides raising the obvious question of who actually won, the Florida debacle shed light on the shoddy practices and procedures of how many states counted votes.

The initial tally had given Bush the state by fewer than 800 votes out of almost 6 million cast. More than 3,000 voters in heavily Democratic Palm Beach County accidentally marked ballots for Pat Buchanan instead of Gore, whom they intended to vote for, because of difficulty in reading a confusing "butterfly" ballot that jumbled names together. Because of faulty instruction in some precincts, many people voted twice or "overvoted," which negated their ballot. In other counties that used punch-card systems, thousands of ballots ended up only partially punched; the result was hanging or dimpled "chads" (quickly a buzzword in the media) and "undervotes" that went unrecorded. Approximately 175,000 votes fell into the category of an overvote or undervote. More than 20,000 African Americans, more likely to vote for Gore, found themselves falsely named on an ex-felon list apparently prepared by Republican officials and were turned away when they attempted to vote.

When some initial recounts appeared to favor Gore, Florida's governor, Jeb Bush, the Republican candidate's brother, and other Republican officials in the state government tried to stop any recount. The Democrats requested manual recounts in four largely Democratic counties whose ballots seemed in question and suggested that Florida law would not allow a statewide recount. Republicans opposed the Democrats' efforts.

On November 21, the Florida Supreme Court ruled in favor of Gore. It allowed the four-county recount to continue until November 26 and told election officials that they should try to determine the intention of voters in deciding how to count ballots with "dimpled" or "hanging chads." In other words, if the voter had attempted to punch the card but the device failed to completely penetrate the card, it could be counted as a vote. Fearful that this procedure would favor Gore, irate Republicans appealed to the U.S. Supreme Court to halt the Florida recount.

Interactive timeline

TIMELINE 1988–2001

AMERICA	YEAR	THE WORLD
Nov Vice President George H. W. Bush defeats Michael Dukakis for the presidency **Dec** Mikhail Gorbachev addresses United Nations in New York, signaling a thaw in the Cold War; meets President Ronald Reagan and President-Elect Bush	**1988**	
Aug Congress begins to tackle mounting savings and loan banking crisis **Dec** United States occupies Panama, a sign of U.S. dominance in international affairs	**1989**	**Jun** Chinese troops crush pro-democracy demonstrators in Tiananmen Square, Beijing **Jun** Mikhail Gorbachev declares eastern European Communist nations are free to choose their own form of government without fear of Soviet intervention; announcement hastens peaceful end of Communist rule **Nov** Fall of Berlin Wall marks symbolic end of Cold War
Jun David Souter confirmed as justice of Supreme Court **Jul** Congress passes Americans with Disabilities Act, recognizing the rights of people previously excluded from full participation in society	**1990**	**Feb** Nelson Mandela freed from South African prison **Aug** Iraq invades Kuwait
Oct Clarence Thomas confirmed as justice of Supreme Court; his confirmation hearings spark anger among many women and their supporters who are convinced he engaged in sexual harassment during the 1980s	**1991**	**Jan–Mar** U.S. leads UN coalition in Gulf War to force Iraq out of Kuwait **Dec** Collapse of Soviet Union
Apr Riots take place in Los Angeles **Nov** Bill Clinton defeats George H. W. Bush and H. Ross Perot to win presidency, a triumph for New Democrats	**1992**	
Feb Al-Qaeda operatives use truck bombs to attack New York's World Trade Center **Jun** Ruth Bader Ginsberg confirmed as justice of Supreme Court **Sep** President Clinton hosts White House signing ceremony of a peace agreement between Israel and the Palestine Liberation Organization **Nov** Congress ratifies the North American Free Trade Agreement	**1993**	

A PROBLEM OF NUMBERS Dueling Democrats and Republicans rally in an effort to influence the counting of disputed ballots in the Florida presidential election in November and December 2000.

AMERICA	YEAR	THE WORLD
Jun Stephen Breyer confirmed as justice of Supreme Court **Sep** U.S. forces out military government in Haiti; President Jean Bertrand Aristide restored to power **Sep** Congress fails to enact health care reform **Nov** Republicans win control of House and Senate, severely constraining Bill Clinton's presidency **Nov** California adopts Proposition 187, denying state benefits to undocumented foreign residents	**1994**	**Apr** Mandela elected president of South Africa **Apr–Jul** Rwandan genocide
Apr Domestic terrorists bomb federal building in Oklahoma City **Jul–Aug** United States, British, and French planes bomb Serb forces **Nov** Dayton Peace Accords for Bosnia are signed **Nov–Dec** Congressional Republicans force shutdown of federal government	**1995**	**Jul** Serb forces massacre 4,000 Muslims in Srebrenica, Bosnia, and provoke a NATO bombing campaign against Serbia
Jul Congress enacts welfare reform **Nov** Bill Clinton reelected president over Bob Dole and H. Ross Perot **Dec** Federal Reserve Chairman Alan Greenspan warns that "irrational exuberance" could lead to unsustainable stock market bubble	**1996**	
Oct Federal government reports surplus	**1997**	
Apr United States mediates peace agreement between Catholics and Protestants in Northern Ireland **Aug** Al-Qaeda bombs U.S. embassies in East Africa; United States launches airstrikes against al-Qaeda in Sudan and Afghanistan **Dec** House of Representatives impeaches President Clinton	**1998**	**Mar–Jun** U.S. and NATO forces bomb Serbia to force it to remove troops from Kosovo
Feb Senate acquits Clinton of impeachment charges **Dec** Showing limits of the appeal of globalization, antiglobalization demonstrators protest meeting of World Trade Organization in Seattle	**1999**	**Dec** Vladimir Putin becomes Russian president
Jul President Clinton hosts Camp David meeting of Israeli and Palestinian leaders in an unsuccessful effort to resolve their conflict **Nov** Close presidential election takes place; results are contested **Dec** Supreme Court declares George W. Bush winner of the presidential election over Al Gore	**2000**	**Oct** Al-Qaeda attacks USS *Cole*
Jan Bush takes office; many Gore voters believe presidency is illegitimate	**2001**	

The high court surprised most observers by intervening in the state process. It first temporarily halted the recount. Then, on December 12, it ruled in *Bush v. Gore* that the recount stop entirely, effectively giving Florida's electoral votes, and hence the election, to Bush. The five more conservative justices formed the majority and the four liberals dissented. The majority opinion stated that a partial recount of Florida's votes—as requested by Gore—violated the rights of voters in counties where no recount took place. How an accurate count deprived anyone of their rights seemed an odd decision. But even if this were true, startled Democrats noted, the problem could be remedied easily by ordering a statewide recount. Instead, the high court simply ordered that all counting cease. Florida's Republican secretary of state promptly certified Bush's victory.

Republicans and some in the middle of the political spectrum applauded the Court for resolving the dispute and deciding the winner. But Justice **John Paul Stevens**, one of the four dissenters, lamented that the real loser of the election was "the Nation's confidence in the judge as an impartial guardian of the rule of law." Embittered Democrats believed the election had been stolen by the Supreme Court. Bush received Florida's votes for a 271 to 266 electoral vote victory (Bush: 50.4 million votes, 47.9 percent, 271 electoral votes; Gore: 51 million votes, 48.4 percent, 266 electoral votes; Nader: 2 million votes, 2.7 percent; Buchanan: 448,895 votes, 0.4 percent). A placard carried by a protester during Bush's inauguration on January 20, 2001, read, "The people have spoken—all five of them."

STUDY QUESTIONS FOR THE DISPUTED ELECTION OF 2000

quiz

1. What were the principal issues in the presidential election of 2000?

2. Why was the election result in doubt?

3. Why were efforts to decide the winner so controversial?

Summary

- The Cold War ended suddenly between 1989 and 1991, as—one by one—the Communist regimes in eastern Europe and ultimately the Soviet Union abandoned communism.
- The administration of President George H. W. Bush sought to create a new world order.
- The United States experienced a technology-driven economic boom in the 1990s.
- The good times of the 1990s generated the largest wave of immigration in more than a century.
- The administration of President Bill Clinton pursued a centrist, New Democratic course.
- Clinton was a popular president, but a sizeable minority fiercely opposed him. He was impeached by the House of Representatives but acquitted by the Senate.
- The United States engaged in a number of international humanitarian interventions in the 1990s, including those in Somalia, Yugoslavia, and Haiti.
- The disputed election of 2000 was decided by a controversial vote of the U.S. Supreme Court in favor of Republican George W. Bush.

Key Terms and People

audio
flashcards

Americans with Disabilities Act
   (ADA) 1046
Arafat, Yasser 1067
bin Laden, Osama 1067
Buchanan, Pat 1053
Bush v. Gore 1071
Bush, George H. W. 1044
Bush, George W. 1068

Clinton, Bill 1052
Contract with America 1062
Defense Advanced Research Projects
   Agency (DARPA) 1055
Dole, Bob 1064
Dukakis, Michael 1045
ethnic cleansing 1066
Gingrich, Newt 1061

Reviewing Chapter 30

1. How did the end of the Cold War affect life in the United States from 1988 to 2000?
2. What changes in the United States and the world economy affected American life in the 1990s?
3. How did scientific and technological advances alter American life in the 1990s?

Further Reading

Atkinson, Rick. *Crusade: The Untold Story of the Gulf War.* Boston: Houghton Mifflin, 1993. An account of the politics and strategy of the successful U.S.-led war that unintentionally set the stage for later regional conflicts.

Beschloss, Michael R., and Strobe Talbott. *At the Highest Levels: The Inside Story of the End of the Cold War.* Boston: Little Brown, 1993. A historian and diplomat collaborate on detailing the events surrounding the Soviet collapse and transition to the post–Cold War era.

Eckes, Alfred E., Jr., and Thomas W. Zeiler. *Globalization and the American Century.* New York: Cambridge University Press, 2003. The authors examine how the emergence of an economically integrated world altered the American economy in positive and negative ways.

Hacker, Jacob S., and Paul Pierson. *Winner-Take-All Politics: How Washington Made the Rich Richer and Turned Its Back on the Middle Class.* New York: Simon & Schuster, 2010. Describes how tax, trade, and spending policies increased inequality.

Johnson, Haynes. *The Best of Times: America in the Clinton Years.* New York: Harcourt, 2001. An entertaining but insightful overview of the 1990s, examining the decade's highs and lows.

Levinson, Marc. *The Box: How the Shipping Container Made the World Smaller and the Economy Bigger.* Princeton, NJ: Princeton University Press, 2008. Explains the key role that this shipping innovation had in expanding global trade and transforming ports and the lives of workers.

Maraniss, David. *First in His Class: A Biography of Bill Clinton.* New York: Simon and Schuster, 2008. A richly textured overview of Clinton's personal background and political career from Arkansas to the presidency.

Ngai, Mae M. *Impossible Subjects: Illegal Aliens and the Making of Modern America.* Princeton, NJ: Princeton University Press, 2004. A thoughtful examination of the many unintended consequences of both "harsh" and "liberal" immigration reforms in the 20th century.

Phillips, Kevin. *American Dynasty: Aristocracy, Fortune and the Politics of Deceit in the House of Bush.* New York: Penguin Books, 2004. Examines four generations of the Bush family and their roles in finance, Congress, and the White House.

Schulzinger, Robert D. *A Time for Peace: The Legacy of the Vietnam War.* New York: Oxford University Press, 2006. As the author shows, the political and cultural legacies of the Vietnam War lasted much longer than the conflict and affected Americans for a generation after the end of combat.

Toobin, Jeffrey. *Too Close to Call: The Thirty-Six-Day Battle to Decide the 2000 Election.* New York: Random House, 2001. A lawyer-journalist examines the legal and political dimensions of the disputed presidential election and how it revealed the politicization of the Supreme Court.

America in the World
GOODS, IDEAS, PEOPLE

CHAPTER 30: After the Cold War, 1988–2001

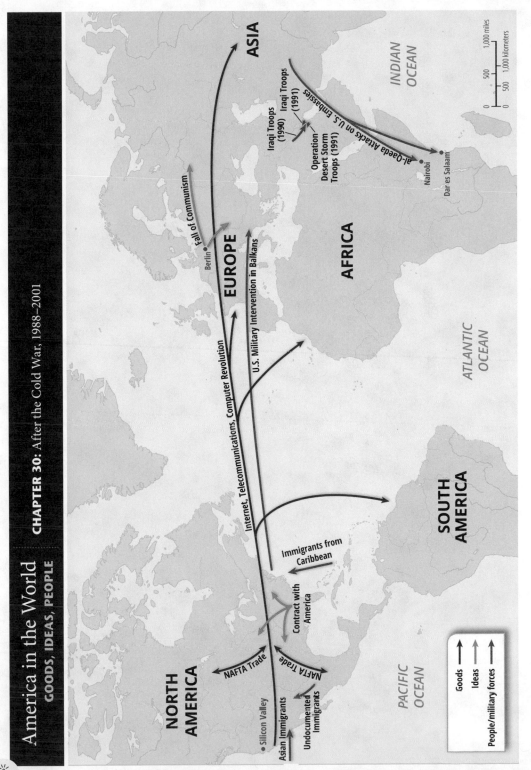

map analysis

ASIA

INDIAN OCEAN

1,000 miles

1,000 kilometers

500

500

Iraqi Troops (1991)

Iraqi Troops (1990)

Operation Desert Storm Troops (1991)

al-Qaeda Attacks on U.S. Embassies

Nairobi

Dar es Salaam

Fall of Communism

Berlin

EUROPE

U.S. Military Intervention in Balkans

AFRICA

ATLANTIC OCEAN

Internet, Telecommunications, Computer Revolution

SOUTH AMERICA

Immigrants from Caribbean

Contract with America

NAFTA Trade

NAFTA Trade

PACIFIC OCEAN

NORTH AMERICA

Silicon Valley

Asian Immigrants

Undocumented Immigrants

Goods

Ideas

People/military forces

Barack Obama at his election night rally in Grant Park, Chicago, Illinois, November 4, 2008.

Twenty-first Century Dangers and Promises

O n February 5, 2003, Secretary of State **Colin Powell** delivered the most antici-
pated speech of his career. As the most respected member of the Bush admin-
istration, Powell had been tasked by the president with laying out before the
UN General Assembly and a world audience the justification for using force to remove
Saddam Hussein from power in Iraq. Since 2002, Bush had called Iraq, along with
North Korea and Iran, part of an "axis of evil," which "no doubt" had produced and
intended to use weapons of mass destruction (WMD).
Speaking from texts supplied by Vice President **Dick
Cheney**'s aides and the CIA, Powell presented what he
called proof of Iraq's drive, despite its denials, to develop and deploy WMD. He showed photographs of
supposed "mobile production facilities used to make
biological agents" and played excerpts from communications intercepts said to confirm that Iraqi laboratories
had produced "500 tons of chemical weapons agents."
Other evidence purported to show Saddam's support
for **al-Qaeda** and his providing terrorists "help in acquiring poisons and gasses." As proof that Saddam intended to "acquire nuclear weapons," Powell described
the dictator's purchase of thousands of specialized aluminum tubes used in centrifuges to produce weapons-
grade uranium.

Despite Powell's plea, the UN refused to act, and
several key allies, including France and Germany, balked
at supporting military action. The Bush administration
then ridiculed UN weapons inspectors in Iraq who had
found none of the alleged WMD. No matter, Bush told a
conservative forum: establishing a "new regime in Iraq"
would not only alleviate a threat to peace but "serve as
a dramatic and inspiring example of freedom for other
nations in the region."

Although Secretary of State Powell did not know it,
virtually every allegation he leveled relied on ambiguous

or false intelligence. Much of what he said had originated with the Iraqi National Congress, a shadowy group of exiles funded by the CIA and Defense Department who hoped to take power after Saddam's removal. The purported links to al-Qaeda and the feared WMD were bait that lured an uncurious president, a cynical coterie of Bush's advisors, a gullible press, and a frightened public into what became one of America's most protracted and divisive wars.

In the new millennium, terrorism became the functional equivalent of what communism had been during the Cold War—an all-encompassing threat that frightened, motivated, united, and sometimes divided Americans. For nearly two decades into the 21st century, it dominated public discourse and diverted attention from the seismic shifts affecting the economy, work, family life, and the natural environment.

⊘ THE AGE OF SACRED TERROR

Aside from specialists in law enforcement and the military, average Americans before 2001 did not consider terrorism to be a major threat. Al-Qaeda catapulted to the top of the international agenda on September 11, 2001, with its assaults on New York's World Trade Center and the Pentagon. President **George W. Bush** responded with a "global war on terror" to destroy al-Qaeda and its supporters. The quick military victories in Afghanistan and Iraq were followed by lingering insurgencies in both those and neighboring countries that defied an American solution.

The United States and Terrorism Before September 11, 2001

Following the August 1998 al-Qaeda attack on the U.S. embassies in the capital cities of Kenya and Tanzania, America launched air strikes against Osama bin Laden's Afghanistan headquarters and other sites linked to the group but failed to kill or capture him. In October 2000, in the midst of the presidential election campaign, al-Qaeda suicide bombers attacked the USS *Cole*, a U.S. Navy destroyer anchored in the port of Aden in Yemen on the southern coast of the Arabian Peninsula, killing 17 navy sailors. The Clinton administration unsuccessfully pressed the government of Afghanistan, ruled by the Taliban, a radical Islamist group, to expel bin Laden into American custody.

Throughout 2001, U.S. intelligence agencies intercepted increasing "chatter" from al-Qaeda operatives around the world hinting at a major strike against the United States. Counterterror official Richard Clarke told Bush's top aides that the nation faced imminent attacks of "spectacular proportions." CIA Director George Tenet warned that "the system was flashing red" by midsummer. In August, the CIA delivered to President Bush a report titled "Bin Laden Determined to Strike in U.S." But Bush and his closest aides dismissed the warnings as deceptions, and the president left Washington for an extended vacation on his Texas ranch.

September 11 and al-Qaeda

Catastrophe struck on the brilliantly clear late summer morning of September 11, 2001, when 19 al-Qaeda hijackers armed with box cutters seized four commercial airliners. They crashed two of them into the two towers of the World Trade Center in New York's lower Manhattan, bringing both buildings down in flames and killing over 2,750 people. A third hijacked plane slammed into the Pentagon, killing 184 people. Hijackers on a fourth jet hoped to crash the plane into the U.S. Capitol building or the White House. But when passengers who realized the plane had been seized stormed the cockpit, the hijackers crashed the airliner into a field southeast of Pittsburgh, killing all on board.

Scenes of the collapsing Twin Towers and damaged Pentagon were seen live on television throughout the world. Nearly all foreign governments and media expressed horror at the attacks and declared their support for the United States and those killed or wounded. Americans of all political persuasions rallied behind the nation's leadership.

Bush and his advisors who had dismissed the pre-9/11 warnings and ridiculed Clinton's interest in nation building now swung around to support a full scale "global war on terror." The president made it clear that beyond destroying terrorist groups linked to the 9/11 attacks, the United States would remove regimes in the Middle East or elsewhere that in some way "enabled" America's enemies.

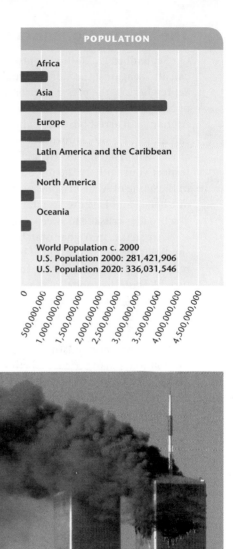

POPULATION

Africa

Asia

Europe

Latin America and the Caribbean

North America

Oceania

World Population c. 2000
U.S. Population 2000: 281,421,906
U.S. Population 2020: 336,031,546

0
500,000,000
1,000,000,000
1,500,000,000
2,000,000,000
2,500,000,000
3,000,000,000
3,500,000,000
4,000,000,000
4,500,000,000

A DAY OF TERROR The New York World Trade Center towers under attack on September 11, 2001

The War in Afghanistan

On September 13, 2001, with just one dissenting vote, Congress authorized an American attack against the Taliban, a policy endorsed by the United States' NATO allies. On September 20, the president promised that "whether we bring our enemies to justice, or bring justice to our enemies, justice will be done." He demanded that the Taliban in Afghanistan arrest bin Laden and turn him over to the United States or face an American attack. He proclaimed war on terrorism, but he denied that the United States was at war with Islam. Directly addressing the world's one billion Muslims, he said, "We respect your faith. . . . Its teachings are good and peaceful, and those who commit evil in the name of Allah blaspheme the name of Allah." Privately, Bush accepted the advice of Cheney and Defense Secretary **Donald Rumsfeld** that the war on terror could serve as a broader crusade to sweep away dictatorial regimes in and around the Middle East.

President George W. Bush, "Address to the Nation," September 20, 2001.

Air strikes in Afghanistan began in early October while the Pentagon dispatched a small number of highly skilled U.S. Special Forces and Army Rangers to bolster Afghan rebels who had been fighting the Taliban for years. In December, these Afghans captured Kabul, the capital of the country, and most other major cities. The Taliban government melted away with few American losses.

The United States installed a new government in Afghanistan led by **Hamid Karzai**, a pro-Western former exile. American emissaries encouraged the Afghans to draft a democratic constitution, promising free elections and equality for women and the country's many tribal and ethnic groups. Karzai won election to the presidency in October 2004, and Washington poured tens of billions of dollars into reconstruction and the building of schools and hospitals. As of 2016, the United States had spent more money on reconstruction in Afghanistan than it did to rebuild western Europe and Japan after World War II. But the Karzai government had little sway over most of the country, was mired in corruption, and squandered much of the aid.

Moreover, the United States failed to capture or kill Osama bin Laden—or the thousands of Taliban fighters who had found a safe haven in Pakistan. They began regrouping after 2005 and soon challenged the Karzai government. By 2008, the resurgent Taliban once again controlled large parts of rural Afghanistan. Initially, 30,000 U.S. troops, assisted by some NATO forces, were spread thin across isolated outposts. With too few troops to control territory, the Americans relied on air attacks to hit suspected Taliban camps. The air strikes often killed Afghan civilians, whose angry relatives turned their anger against

UNDER THE MIDDLE EASTERN SUN U.S. troops fighting Taliban guerrillas in the bleak terrain of Afghanistan in 2010.

the Americans. In 2017, after 16 years of American involvement, the Afghan government remained dysfunctional, the Taliban continued to hold sway in much of the country, and thousands of American troops continued fighting. Like his two predecessors, President Donald Trump committed additional forces in what appeared to be an endless war.

The Iraq War

Within 24 hours after the attacks of September 11, the Bush administration set in motion plans to attack Iraq and drive Saddam Hussein from power. The president instructed his top aides to look for evidence to confirm his gut belief that the Iraqi strongman had been behind the attacks on that day. Administration officials considered it likely that Saddam possessed at least some WMD and might provide them to terrorists even if he did not use them himself. Saddam, however, considered al-Qaeda's goal of imposing Islamic purity throughout the Middle East a threat to his own dictatorship and shunned the group. The Bush administration had not understood that although some Iraqi behavior hinted at possession of WMD, it was a bluff to deter Iran, Saddam's main enemy, which at the time actually was acquiring nuclear technology. Most American print and broadcast news media accepted, without question, the president's case for bringing down Saddam Hussein.

In January 2002, addressing Congress and the nation, Bush labeled Iraq, Iran, and North Korea an "axis of evil arming to threaten the peace of the world." The United States, he declared, "would not permit the world's most dangerous regimes to threaten us with the world's most dangerous weapons." In June, Bush announced, "We must take the battle to the enemy, disrupt his plans, and confront the worst threats before they emerge." Commentators called this justification for preemptive war the **Bush Doctrine** and predicted the president would soon take action against one or more of the nations comprising the axis of evil. In October 2002, Congress voted by two-thirds majorities to authorize the president to attack Iraq to compel its disarmament. Bush told the United Nations on September 12, 2002, that the world body was in danger of sinking into irrelevance if it did not authorize military action to enforce its past resolutions demanding that Saddam Hussein abandon his weapons of mass destruction. In February 2003, as noted, Secretary of State Colin Powell went before the UN Security Council with pictures and transcripts of intercepted telephone calls, which, he claimed, proved that Saddam possessed biological, chemical, and even nuclear weapons. Yet the UN, France, and Germany refused to support military action. The United States organized what it called a "coalition of the willing." This consisted of Great Britain, Italy, and Spain, along with several former Communist states in eastern Europe and some mini-nations like the island of Tonga in the Pacific.

Bush's aides predicted a short, inexpensive war, costing about $50 billion, which could be paid for with Iraq's oil revenue. An Iraq rid of Saddam Hussein, they claimed, would become a beacon of hope in the Middle East, spur a wave of democratic change, and ease tensions between Israel and its Arab neighbors. Ordinary Americans still wanted revenge for 9/11 and were easily persuaded that Saddam was a valid target.

Glib talk of transforming the Middle East reflected ignorance of the diverse region. Although some nations, such as Egypt and Iran, had long national histories, many of the countries stretching from Afghanistan through the Persian Gulf, the Arabian Peninsula, and North Africa were recent creations spun off from the collapse of the Ottoman Empire after World War I and the Anglo-French empires that dissolved after

George W. Bush, graduation address at the U.S. Military Academy (June 2002)

World War II. Afghanistan, Iraq, Syria, Lebanon, Jordan, and Libya, for example, were more geographic expressions than nations. Their populations were riven by tribal and ethnic divisions, as well as bitter sectarian splits between followers of Sunni and Shia Islam. For decades, only the heavy-handed rule of kings or dictators kept them from dissolving. The notion that merely toppling a thug like Saddam Hussein would usher in an age of democracy defied reality.

President George W. Bush declaring "Mission Accomplished" (May 2003)

Nevertheless, on March 17, Bush delivered an ultimatum to Saddam Hussein to leave Iraq or face war. Two days later, on March 19, the United States attacked by air and on land (Maps 31.1 and 31.2). The first Gulf War of 1991 had lasted six weeks, and it appeared that the second war to oust Saddam would end even faster and with fewer American casualties. On April 9, American forces reached Baghdad, occupied the capital, and, as TV cameras rolled, helped a small but jubilant crowd of Iraqis tear down one of the hundreds of statues of the dictator. On May 1, President Bush declared the end of major combat in Iraq when he spoke on the deck of an aircraft carrier under a banner that proclaimed "Mission Accomplished."

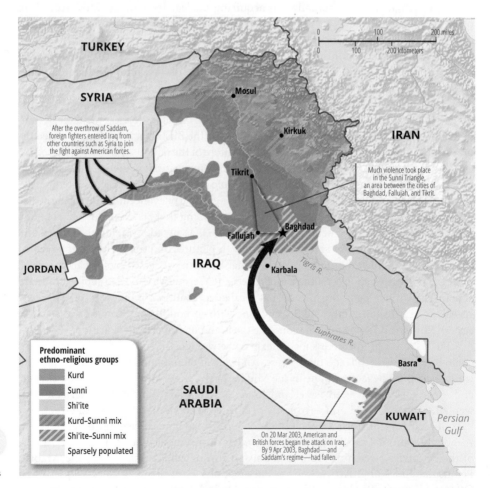

map analysis

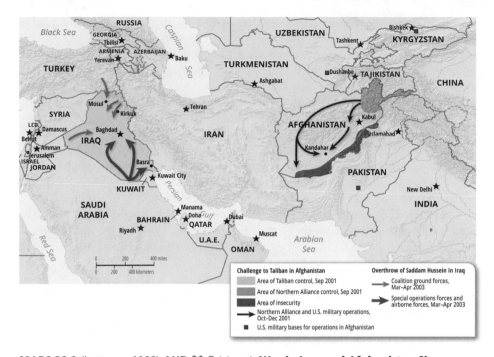

Challenge to Taliban in Afghanistan

- Area of Taliban control, Sep 2001
- Area of Northern Alliance control, Sep 2001
- Area of insecurity
- Northern Alliance and U.S. military operations, Oct–Dec 2001
- U.S. military bases for operations in Afghanistan

Overthrow of Saddam Hussein in Iraq

- Coalition ground forces, Mar–Apr 2003
- Special operations forces and airborne forces, Mar–Apr 2003

MAPS 31.1 (bottom p.1082) **AND 31.2** (above) **War In Iraq and Afghanistan Since 2003** After the devastating 9/11 attacks on the United States, the Bush administration invaded Afghanistan and drove from power the Taliban government, which had backed Osama bin Laden's al-Qaeda movement. President George W. Bush also began planning a war to drive Iraqi tyrant Saddam Hussein from power, even though he had no connection to the attacks of 9/11. U.S. forces invaded Iraq in March 2003.

Disturbing signs appeared even as Baghdad residents fired guns in the air to celebrate Saddam's end. The United States had made few plans to preserve order and restore Iraq's economy. Mobs poured into government offices, electrical power stations, schools, and hospitals, stripping them bare of everything valuable. Looters attacked the Iraqi National Museum, stealing thousands of priceless antiquities. Even more ominously, the weapons of mass destruction that Iraqi exiles assured the United States Saddam had stockpiled were nowhere to be found. Hoping to obscure their mistakes, Bush, Cheney, and Rumsfeld later denied ever saying Saddam had WMD, only that he hoped to acquire them. Saddam, who was captured, tried, and executed, confirmed what UN inspectors had reported before the American invasion: he had ceased WMD programs after his 1991 defeat but had hinted at possessing them to bluff Iran.

Despite claims of victory, Iraq soon descended into chaos and civil war. The Defense Department had not bothered to plan for an occupation, hoped to withdraw U.S. forces quickly, and resisted efforts by the State Department to implement its own more robust blueprint. For two years, the United States directly governed Iraq through a Coalition Provisional Authority (CPA), which had only 34 experienced foreign service officers among its 1,400 employees. The CPA, staffed mostly with personnel chosen for their activism in Republican Party circles, seemed oblivious to the sectarian, tribal, and ethnic rivalries dividing Iraqis. CPA cooperation with the Shia majority quickly alienated the Sunnis, who composed about 20 percent of the population. Eager to rid the country of the influence of Saddam Hussein's Ba'ath Party, the CPA disbanded the 500,000-strong Iraqi army. These armed and resentful ex-soldiers joined the nearly 50 percent of Iraqis who lacked any jobs.

By mid-2003, an insurgency had erupted against the Americans and Iraqis, mostly Shi'ite, who cooperated with them. As the attacks worsened, the Pentagon was compelled to maintain a large occupation force and the American death toll mounted. It passed 1,000 in 2004, climbed beyond 2,750 in 2006, and reached 4,200 in 2008. Approximately 25,000 Americans suffered severe injuries. The death toll among Iraqis was far higher and included a large number of civilians. Estimates ranged from 50,000 to 900,000 in the five years after the war began.

As casualties mounted and Iraqi Sunni and Shi'ite politicians squabbled, the American public's support for the war eroded. As the fighting dragged on, so did the financial burden and the fear that the United States had stumbled into another no-win war like Vietnam.

The idealistic goals of the war were compromised further during 2004 when reports surfaced that U.S. military personnel and CIA operatives had tortured and degraded Iraqi prisoners at the **Abu Ghraib** prison near Baghdad. The story came with pictures of naked Iraqi prisoners, some with bags over their head, being led to mock executions, threatened with snarling dogs, or forced to wear women's underwear over their faces.

Other stories surfaced over the next two years about the mistreatment of more than 500 al-Qaeda prisoners being held at a prison on the navy base at Guantanamo Bay, Cuba. Bush had authorized the CIA to use "enhanced interrogation techniques"—which critics called torture—to obtain information. One common technique, called waterboarding, simulated drowning and had been previously classified by the U.S. military as a war crime. The CIA also flew terror suspects—a practice called rendition—to other countries that tortured prisoners. After dodging the issue for several years, in 2006, the Supreme Court ruled in *Hamdan v. Rumsfeld* that the military tribunals the Bush administration established to try prisoners were unconstitutional and that prisoners retained the right to appeal to federal courts. The law was amended to pass constitutional muster, but it proved exceedingly difficult to conduct trials for prisoners who had been tortured or against whom there was little direct evidence. U.S. officials eventually acknowledged that perhaps a third of those held at Guantanamo were likely

WAR CRIMES In 2004, gruesome pictures surfaced revealing that U.S. guards at Abu Ghraib prison physically and psychologically abused detained Iraqi insurgents. Here, Army Specialist Lynndie England drags a prisoner on a leash. The photographs undermined support for the war at home and abroad.

innocent people seized by bounty hunters in Pakistan and Afghanistan after 9/11 and "sold" to Americans. By 2017, fewer than 50 prisoners remained, but Congress rebuffed then-president Obama's effort to close the prison.

By late 2005, 57 percent of the American public believed that the Iraq War had been a mistake. Public disillusionment with the war contributed to Democratic victories in both houses of Congress in the 2006 elections.

Bush ordered a "surge" of 30,000 additional U.S. troops to Iraq, bringing the total number of Americans to 160,000 by the summer of 2007. U.S. casualties mounted for the first six months of the year as the United States adopted more active tactics to clear and hold territory. Perhaps as important as the surge, the U.S. military paid millions of dollars to Sunni tribal leaders, whose followers made up the bulk of the insurgents, to induce them to stop fighting. By the beginning of 2008, the surge and the new tactics had appeared to bear fruit. Violence against Americans subsided in Iraq, although it remained an extremely dangerous and unstable place.

The frustration with the wars in Iraq and Afghanistan eroded public support for other Bush initiatives. Bush's popularity plummeted from the heights of 90 percent reached after September 11 to the depths of the mid-20s in 2008. Critics said he had himself to blame by refusing to govern from the center. Instead, he sought the support of a conservative base while confronting liberals and ignoring centrists.

Policing Terrorism

The American people rallied around their president after 9/11. With little debate, Congress passed the USA PATRIOT Act, which expanded the power of the Justice Department and other agencies to conduct surveillance on terrorist suspects at home and abroad. The next year, a new Department of Homeland Security was created to coordinate domestic security. The scope of these measures was vast, ranging from enhanced airport screenings to construction of border fences and bolstering emergency preparedness among local first responders in police and fire departments. Hundreds of new private consulting firms, many staffed by retired intelligence and military officers, received lucrative contracts to advise all levels of government on ways to enhance security. These projects cost an estimated $1 trillion. Bush, followed by President Obama, authorized the National Security Agency (NSA) to collect vast databases of phone calls and emails made by Americans and foreigners in efforts to uncover terrorist networks. The scope of this snooping became known to the public in 2013 when Edward Snowden, a disillusioned employee of the NSA, released secret files and fled the country.

STUDY QUESTIONS FOR THE AGE OF SACRED TERROR

1. How did the U.S. government and the American people respond to the terrorist attacks of September 11, 2001?

2. How did the George W. Bush administration justify the decision to go to war against the government of Iraq in 2003?

3. Why did public opinion in the United States and around the world turn against the U.S. presence in Iraq after 2003?

quiz

❂ CONSERVATISM IN THE BUSH YEARS

Conservatives returned to power in 2001 after the interruption in the Clinton years. Bush modeled himself more closely on President Reagan than his own father, President George H. W. Bush. Although he described himself as a pragmatic or "compassion- ate" conservative, Bush and congressional Republicans actually pursued a more stri- dent agenda of cultural and economic conservatism than had Reagan. In Bush's second term, however, growing public uneasiness with the Iraq War and the inept handling of a natural disaster in New Orleans eroded the appeal of cultural conservatism. Increas- ing numbers of Americans became alarmed at the incompetence and cronyism they witnessed in government, and they favored a truce in the culture wars. In 2006, voters returned control of Congress to the Democratic Party.

Culture Wars

In August 1992, former Nixon advisor and sometime Republican presidential candidate **Patrick Buchanan** energized the lackluster GOP convention in Houston by declaring a "cultural war" that was "as critical to the kind of nation we will one day be as was the Cold War itself." Buchanan lambasted "environmental extremists" and "radical feminists" for trashing religion, promoting homosexual rights, and advocating "abortion on demand." He renewed this theme during his unsuccessful 1996 campaign for the Republican presi- dential nomination. If elected, he pledged to use his power to "defend American traditions and the values of faith, family, and country from any and all direction" and to "chase the purveyors of sex and violence back beneath the rocks whence they came." In 2004, as a commentator on cable television, Buchanan declared that liberals and "true Americans" lived in separate moral universes. Along with Hollywood moguls (often code for Jews, who historically played a major role in broadcast entertainment), Buchanan blamed school- teachers, college professors, and judges for subverting traditional culture. Republican pres- idential candidate Donald Trump revived many of these themes during the 2016 election.

Early in his first administration, Bush implemented several policies advocated by culture warriors. These included a ban on using federal funds for most research on stem cell lines derived from human fetuses (a promising area of research into curing diseases such as multiple sclerosis, Alzheimer's, and Parkinson's), reimposing a "gag" rule begun by Ronald Reagan that blocked federal aid to any family planning agencies that even mentioned abortion as an option, and creating a White House Office of Faith- Based and Community Initiatives designed to steer federal money to religious charities. Bush and his appointees also disputed mounting evidence that human activities caused climate change.

Many social service providers complained that the faith-based initiative violated the separation of church and state. Religious groups such as Catholic and Jewish Family Services already received federal and state contracts to provide vital aid to the home- less, the elderly, and substance abusers. However, they could not use public funds to proselytize or to refuse to hire, say, social workers who were not Catholics. The Bush initiative blurred these lines, permitting religious groups, often evangelical Christian congregations, to discriminate in who they hired and to require those receiving services to participate in religious worship.

Nearly all mainstream scientists expressed disdain for Bush's endorsement of in- telligent design, as opposed to evolution, as a scientific theory and for his refusal to

RAINBOW SPECTRUM As gay Americans pressed for the right to marry, the public showed a range of strong beliefs about same-sex marriage. By a substantial margin, younger Americans favored the right of gays to wed.

acknowledge evidence of climate change. To prepare students for the modern world, they considered it vital that schools distinguish between faith, which asked "why" life evolved, and science, which examined "how" it did so. In a series of federal court decisions that mirrored the Scopes Trial of the 1920s, state and federal efforts to mandate the teaching of intelligent design were overturned as religious intrusion into public education.

Marriage in the United States was a troubled institution, and families labored under great stress. Nearly half of all marriages ended in divorce, creating serious problems for children and sometimes for ex-spouses. At least a third of children, and over half among young Latinos and African Americans, were born to unmarried mothers. Women with a high school diploma or less were most likely to become single parents, either from not marrying or from divorce. Lack of affordable child care proved a constant problem for millions of families, especially because women comprised nearly half the total workforce—an all-time high—by 2010.

Early in 2005, the president and congressional Republicans inserted themselves in a "right-to-die" case that they thought might boost their standing among "right-to-life" activists. It involved **Terri Schiavo**, a young Florida woman who suffered cardiac arrest from unknown causes in 1990. After several months in a coma, she partially awoke but sustained profound brain injury. Kept alive by a feeding tube and with no hope of recovery, she lived in a "persistent vegetative state." In 1998, her husband and caregiver, Michael Schiavo, petitioned a Florida court to permit him to disconnect the feeding tube. Terri's parents filed numerous lawsuits opposing his petition. When the suits were dismissed, the Florida legislature intervened. It passed "'Terri's Law," a special act giving Governor

Jeb Bush—the president's brother—power to seize and protect Terri. Early in 2005, however, Florida's Supreme Court invalidated Terri's Law. The involvement of Jeb Bush and several prominent conservative theologians and media pundits transformed the case into a national obsession, with camera crews stationed full time at the facility caring for Terri.

Congress, with President Bush's enthusiastic support, rushed to enact a law on March 21, 2005, that transferred jurisdiction in the Schiavo case from state to federal courts, but to their disappointment, no federal court agreed to intervene. A macabre media deathwatch continued until Terri died on March 31, after the feeding tube was removed. An autopsy confirmed that Terri had been brain-dead for years. Polls revealed that most Americans were offended by political efforts to interfere with a husband's right to decide on end-of-life care for his wife.

In addition to social policy, the Bush administration also pushed through conservative energy and environmental legislation. For example, the Healthy Forest Initiative entailed opening protected federal land to commercial logging. The Clear Skies Initiative permitted higher levels of industrial pollution by rolling back EPA standards. An energy task force convened in 2001 by Dick Cheney included mostly representatives from the petroleum industry who recommended increased federal subsidies and fewer regulations.

Compassionate Conservatism

During the campaign of 2000, George W. Bush expressed concern for the struggles of poor and nonwhite Americans. During Bush's first term as president, his domestic program based on what he called "compassionate conservatism" included tax cuts and a pair of educational and health reforms. The 2001 and 2003 tax reductions, however, tilted heavily in favor of higher-income Americans. Enacted as military spending ballooned, the tax cuts contributed to a growing deficit. Democrats had questioned the size and nature of the tax cuts but were more supportive of the Bush education and health programs, known as the **No Child Left Behind (NCLB) Act** of 2001 and the Medicare Drug Reform Act of 2003.

NCLB was designed to improve educational outcomes, especially for poor and minority children. It renewed federal funding for several existing school programs and provided some additional money for reading and math instruction. In return, all states had to implement "standards-based educational reform," a term that in practice meant standardized testing of students in reading and math and the evaluation of teachers based on student performance. Bush pointed to a similar program he had sponsored while Texas governor that claimed great success. The law required all schools to eventually have 100 percent of students meet or exceed proficiency standards—a near statistical impossibility—or else be classified as failing. Failed schools would have to be reorganized, often as privately run, but publicly funded, charter schools. This idea was especially popular among conservative policy advocates who saw teachers' unions as an impediment to change.

A decade after NCLB enactment, the program had yielded only modest results. Schools in well-to-do neighborhoods continued to perform well, whereas those populated by poorer students lagged behind. As educators had argued, student achievement reflected a complex mix of socioeconomic background, school funding, and teacher quality. In general, charter schools did no better than their public counterparts. Later studies revealed that the celebrated gains in Texas schools under Bush had been wildly overstated.

The Medicare program begun in 1965 had dramatically improved the health and financial condition of the elderly. But its failure to pay for prescription drugs—few of which existed at that time—had become a major burden. By the start of the 21st century, aging patients took a daily regimen of pills for chronic ailments such as high blood pressure, heart disease, depression, diabetes, and sexual dysfunction. The cost of medications sometimes exceeded doctor and hospital bills. In December 2003, Congress, with heavy Democratic support, passed the Bush-designed **Medicare Modernization Act** to take effect in 2006. The program subsidized the cost of some, but not all, medications taken by seniors. The law proved a bonanza to pharmaceutical companies because it helped seniors buy more medication but did nothing to limit prescription costs. Because no additional tax revenues were raised to pay for the program, it further increased the deficit.

The Election of 2004

Democrats had problems confronting Bush effectively in the presidential elections of 2004. Most of the candidates running for the Democratic nomination were senators who had voted in favor of authorizing war against Iraq in 2002. They faced Democratic primary voters who had soured on the war. The eventual Democratic Party nominee was Massachusetts senator **John Kerry**, a decorated Vietnam War veteran who had first come to national prominence at the age of 26 when he spoke out against the Vietnam War. Throughout the campaign, Kerry criticized the Bush administration's poor diplomacy and lack of planning for postwar Iraq. He never disavowed his vote for the war, however, and Bush portrayed him as a waffler on Iraq and the war on terror. Bush defeated Kerry by approximately three million votes. The electoral vote total was tight: Bush 286, Kerry 251, the narrowest victory by an incumbent since 1916.

Following his reelection, Bush declared that he had accumulated "political capital" that he now intended to spend. He spoke of launching a crusade aimed at "ending tyranny in our world." But these large aspirations quickly became mired in an unpopular plan to reform Social Security, a botched federal response to a hurricane, and an increasingly unpopular war in Iraq.

Privatizing Social Security

Conservatives had long condemned Social Security, a pillar of the New Deal, as an emblem of the problems with big government. Equally important, they recognized that many elderly voters—about one-third of whom depended entirely on Social Security for retirement income—felt a special bond of gratitude toward Democrats for creating the program. Social Security faced several funding challenges in the early 21st century because people lived longer after retiring than they had in the 1930s, and the large "baby boom" generation nearing retirement was drawing down reserves. Furthermore, the number of young workers whose contributions helped fund the system had declined. Public policy specialists proposed several solutions, including raising the retirement age, reducing some benefits for those with other income sources, and increasing payroll taxes (by removing the cap on taxed income) that funded the system. A combination of these, imposed gradually, would alleviate most of the funding problems and ensure the program's solvency.

Bush instead proposed privatizing Social Security by converting it to a system in which contributions from workers and employers went into far more risky privately owned and managed stock accounts similar to the 401(k) plans that had replaced many traditional pensions in the private sector. But when most Democrats, some Republicans, and groups representing the elderly condemned privatization as a risky scheme that put retirees in jeopardy, Bush abandoned the plan.

Hurricane Katrina

When Hurricane Katrina smashed ashore in southeast Louisiana early on August 29, 2005, the storm caused one of the deadliest and costliest natural disasters in U.S. history. The botched federal response to the flooding of New Orleans exposed serious flaws in the Bush administration's competence and accelerated the process of disillusionment with compassionate conservatism.

During the last days of August, the National Weather Service predicted the storm would head toward New Orleans, a city that lay below sea level and depended on a massive, but archaic, system of levees and pumps to remain dry. Despite its popularity as a tourist attraction, New Orleans was one of the nation's poorest and most dysfunctional cities. City, state, and federal officials failed to coordinate evacuation orders or to make adequate provisions for tens of thousands of poor urban residents without cars or other means of transportation. As a result, although one million Gulf residents fled inland by car to safety in advance of Katrina's landfall, around 60,000 people from New Orleans were left to fend for themselves when the levees broke and 80 percent of the city flooded. About half of these gathered in public buildings like the Louisiana Superdome, and the rest headed for rooftops.

UNATTENDED CRIES Days after Hurricane Katrina inundated New Orleans in August 2005, survivors clung to rooftops waiting to be rescued.

On September 1, TV news crews aired footage of tens of thousands of refugees clustered in the Superdome without food or water, others clinging to rooftops, and dead bodies floating in flooded streets. Around the world, people watched in disbelief as the rich and powerful United States seemed incapable of providing for the basic needs of its people.

The Federal Emergency Management Agency (FEMA) had responsibility for coordinating emergency relief efforts. Under its director Michael Brown, a college friend of Bush's who lacked qualifications for the job, many experienced career civil servants left FEMA and were replaced by political cronies. By the time Secretary of Homeland Security Michael Chertoff removed Brown from office, the death toll in and around New Orleans had reached nearly 1,600 and that in Mississippi around 238. Property damage surpassed $80 billion. This catastrophic failure haunted the Bush administration for the next three years.

President George W. Bush, radio address on Hurricane Katrina, September 3, 2005

The Election of 2006

As the 2006 congressional elections approached, the public voiced growing frustration with Republican policies and behavior. As noted, the mounting violence in Iraq, along with evidence that the president had relied on and perhaps encouraged faulty prewar intelligence, turned his May 2003 assertion of "Mission Accomplished" into an object of ridicule. Late-night comedians joked that Republicans were the party that believed government did not work, and their performance since 2004 proved them right. A series of sex scandals that erupted after 2005 involving several congressional Republicans further eroded the standing of Bush and the GOP.

Angry voters expressed their disgust by returning control of Congress to the Democrats for the first time in 12 years. On November 7, 2006, Democrats gained 31 seats in the House of Representatives, giving them a majority of 233 to 202. Senate Democrats picked up five new seats. With the votes of two independents, they had an edge over Republicans of 51 to 49.

STUDY QUESTIONS **FOR CONSERVATISM IN THE BUSH YEARS**

1. What were the essential elements of cultural conservatism in the early 21st century?

2. Why did President George W. Bush lose popularity in the years after he won reelection in 2004?

3. What were some examples of compassionate conservatism?

quiz

ECONOMIC TURMOIL

The economy entered the 21st century with unemployment at a historic low of 3.5 percent, worker productivity soaring, and the stock market advancing. In spite of continuing Republican predictions of economic doom unless taxes and regulations were further reduced, Clinton bequeathed a balanced budget to the incoming President Bush, and most economic forecasts predicted a sharp reduction in the national debt over the next decade. Within months, however, the stock market bubble based on the high-tech sector burst and caused a brief worldwide recession. Although the economy bounced back, growth over the next two decades mostly benefited the wealthy. Globalization intensified, with new wealth coexisting with even more crushing deprivation. Many economies in East and South Asia boomed, whereas large areas of Latin America fell behind. By the first decade of the 21st century, many of America's largest corporations earned a third or more of their profits from foreign sales. U.S.-based policymakers and economists continued to promote free markets, limited regulation, and legal protection for private property. At the same time, activists continued to rally against what they perceived as the excessive greed of large corporations and the influence of financial organizations throughout the globe. In 2008, the American and global economy suffered from a crisis in the financial markets that stemmed from overconfidence in risky investments in the housing sector and resulted in massive government intervention to prevent even greater damage. Although growth resumed in the United States after 2010, much of Europe and Japan remained mired in recession.

The International Forum on Globalization, declaration on fundamental flaws in the free market system (1998)

The Dot-Com Bust, Financial Scandals, and the Middle-Class Squeeze

The 1990s had seen major advancements in computing, the Internet, and information technology. These innovations also produced dozens of high-tech start-up companies looking to become the next Microsoft or Intel. Enthusiasm for the high-tech sector soared. Overspeculation in the dot-com market by the new companies caused a stock bubble, which burst in March 2000. Stocks on the whole lost an average of 40 percent of their value between the summers of 2000 and 2002.

Large-scale fraud by several large technology companies exacerbated the financial situation. Borrowing money to expand, company executives at Qwest Communications, WorldCom, Tyco, and Enron paid themselves huge salaries and bonuses and deceived investors about profits. When their schemes unraveled, their stocks plummeted. Thousands of Enron employees lost their jobs, their pensions, and their life's savings.

The Bush tax cuts of 2001 and 2003 primarily rewarded the country's richest citizens and, like those during the Reagan era, increased the gap between the extremely wealthy and the rest of the country. Between 1979 and 2007, the richest 1 percent of Americans saw their incomes soar by 275 percent, whereas the middle 50 percent saw an increase of 40 percent. Low-income households trailed far behind. These trends continued even after the recovery of economic growth in 2010. For much of the 1990s, families faced increasing costs for health care and tuition for higher education for their children, as well as high gasoline prices. Due to these burdens and spending on homes and consumer goods, they also saved less. Household debt grew even faster. Indeed, by the end of the Bush administration, the net worth of the average American household, adjusted for inflation, was lower than when he took office.

Collapse

One sector of the American and world economy surged in the early 21st century. The housing market in the United States and much of Europe soared from the late 1990s until mid-2005. The housing boom in several "hot markets" such as Las Vegas, Phoenix, and south Florida resembled a feeding frenzy as individual purchasers and speculators outbid one another, often for homes still under construction.

At the same time, lenders offered unprecedented numbers of "**subprime mortgages**," offering small down payments and low introductory interest rates but significantly higher rates after an initial period of time had elapsed. Banks provided these loans to borrowers with poor credit or low income. These loans were risky, but during the boom period, banks took this gamble due to low interest rates, faith that housing prices would continue rising, and high capital availability. Borrowers deluded themselves into thinking home prices would rise forever and used their homes as a sort of ATM, borrowing cash on the rising value of property to make monthly payments.

The bubble, however, inevitably burst (Figure 31.1). By early 2007, house prices had dropped 3 percent and fell an additional 15 percent over the next year. During 2007, several subprime mortgage lenders declared bankruptcy or were purchased by larger banks. By the summer of 2007, the collapse in home prices had begun infecting investment banks and other parts of the financial sector at home and around the world.

Washington helped fuel the speculation by its embrace of free markets and its passion for deregulation. In 1999, Congress, with votes from both parties, repealed the Glass–Steagall Act, in place since the New Deal, separating relatively safe and conservative commercial banks from risk-taking investment banks. Under Bush, government agencies that were designed to ensure that markets were transparent and honest were chronically understaffed or led by officials who opposed regulation. Regulatory agencies therefore had neither the resources nor the desire to scrutinize exotic new mortgage-backed securities. Freed of regulation, both investment and commercial banks purchased hundreds of thousands of mortgages during the housing boom and bundled them into high-risk securities to sell off as investments. This new market

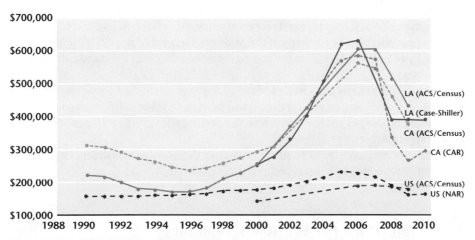

FIGURE 31.1 The housing bubble Home values, along with stock prices, shot upward from the late 1980s through 2008. Banks encouraged marginal borrowers to take out mortgages on homes they could not afford in hope that rising prices would allow them to refinance. They bundled the so-called subprime mortgages and sold them to investors around the world. When housing defaults rose, it triggered a global recession.

spread globally, as banks and governments in Europe and Asia, also proponents of deregulation, purchased securities backed by American home mortgages; banks in Ireland, Iceland, Spain, and the United Kingdom aggressively sold their own versions of subprime mortgages. When mortgage payments slowed or stopped, the economic contraction quickly became global.

For years, stock prices had risen in tandem with the housing bubble, but in the winter of 2008, the subprime crisis hit Wall Street at full speed. By summer, Fannie Mae and Freddie Mac, two huge mortgage lenders, verged on collapse. Treasury Secretary **Henry Paulson** and Fed Chairman **Ben Bernanke** effectively nationalized them in early September to avoid too great a risk to the economy. But then another large Wall Street firm, Lehman Brothers, haunted by its overly aggressive investment in real estate mortgages, went bankrupt on September 15.

Lehman's bankruptcy triggered the international economic collapse of 2008, soon labeled the **Great Recession**. Credit markets around the world froze, and banks stopped lending to one another. Business activity, dependent on lending, went into a downward spiral. In the last quarter of 2008, the U.S. economy contracted at an annual rate of over 6 percent. The meltdown affected financial institutions and governments throughout the world. The world's largest insurance company, AIG, which had also invested hundreds of billions of dollars in housing-related trading, soon faced bankruptcy itself and needed cash. Despite its past claim that government should not intervene in the free market, the Bush administration loaned AIG $85 billion to survive, aid that grew in 2009 to $180 billion.

Amid concerns that the Treasury Department and the Federal Reserve had lost control of the situation, confidence in stocks continued to sink. Bernanke and Paulson turned to Congress with the request to buy toxic mortgage securities from banks in the form of a $700 billion bailout bill. Congress passed the **Emergency Economic Stabilization Act** in late September. It included a provision giving the treasury secretary the power to oversee capital injection into the banks should he see fit.

More bad news emerged in December. The nation's three largest domestic automakers appealed to Congress to receive emergency aid to hold off bankruptcy and prevent a ripple effect in the economy of the Midwest. General Motors (GM) and Chrysler eventually received $13.4 billion in funding, provided they met the standards put forth by Congress.

In March 2008, the Dow Jones Industrial Average reached a 12-year low, dropping below 6,500, a full 50 percent less than it had been in October 2007. With so many private pensions now pegged to stock prices, the decline affected the retirement prospects of millions of Americans.

The economy continued to suffer even after the massive investments by the government. It remained in a recession until early 2010.

STUDY QUESTIONS FOR ECONOMIC TURMOIL

1. Why did the economy expand after 2001?

2. What caused the economic crisis of 2008–2009?

quiz

3. What did the U.S. government do in 2008–2009 to reverse the economic downturn?

THE OBAMA YEARS

The economy, the subprime crisis, and the financial collapse played a large role in the election of 2008, when 47-year-old Illinois Democratic senator **Barack Obama** faced 71-year-old Arizona Republican senator **John McCain**. Obama rode to victory on a wave of new voters who thrilled to his promise of hope and change. He promised to end the incessant partisan bickering of the Clinton and Bush years, end the war in Iraq, restore America's battered international reputation, and pass major economic and social reform laws.

In the first years of Obama's presidency, the country grappled with some of the most severe challenges in nearly a century. The Great Recession proved to be deeper and more prolonged than any since the Great Depression of the 1930s. The war in Iraq wound down, but the one in Afghanistan expanded. Obama promoted a more ambitious agenda of social and economic reform than any Democratic president since Lyndon B. Johnson persuaded Congress to enact the Great Society in the 1960s. The Democratic Congress passed significant legislation, but these successes carried a cost. The angry political divisions of the previous decades erupted, leaving the country bitterly divided over the role and direction of government.

The Election of 2008

Both Obama and McCain were surprising choices for their party's nomination. Obama, the son of a Kenyan father and a white Kansas-born mother, self-identified as African American. He was born in Hawaii and lived for a few years as a child in Indonesia. After graduating from Columbia University and Harvard Law School, he settled in Chicago, where he worked as a community organizer. Elected to the Senate in 2005, he began his quest for the Democratic nomination in February 2007, running a focused campaign that highlighted his steadfast opposition to the war in Iraq. African Americans embraced him with wild enthusiasm after he won an initial victory in the January Iowa caucuses. His eloquence and idealism reminded many of John F. Kennedy nearly half a century before. After a long primary campaign, he secured the nomination over **Hillary Clinton** in June.

McCain was a generation older than Obama. A navy veteran who spent five and a half years in a North Vietnamese prison camp during the Vietnam War, McCain was elected to Congress in 1982. Essentially a business-friendly conservative, McCain portrayed himself as a "maverick." He expected that his national security credentials would help him defeat the less experienced Obama. Iraq faded as an issue in the fall election campaign, as voters' attention turned to the slumping economy. When the financial crisis mounted in mid-September, McCain appeared befuddled and out of touch. Meanwhile, Obama reassured voters by tapping Delaware senator **Joseph Biden**, a respected veteran lawmaker with over three decades of service, as his running mate. McCain, in contrast, tapped the nearly unknown first-term governor of Alaska, **Sarah Palin**, as his running mate. Charismatic but uninformed, her candidacy attracted ridicule after a series of fumbling interviews.

During a swing through Europe in the summer of 2008 and at rallies around the United States, huge crowds turned out to see and hear Obama. His inspirational life story and speaking style energized those who heard him. On November 4, 2008, Obama became the first African American to be elected president (Map 31.3). He received an impressive 52 percent of the popular vote. Democrats emerged with majorities of 257 to 178 in the House of Representatives and 60 to 40 in the Senate.

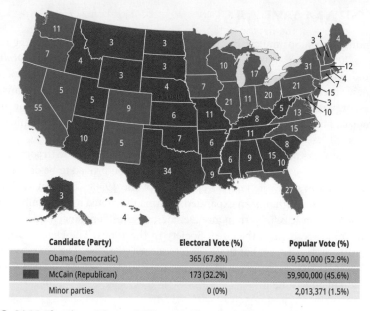

Candidate (Party)	Electoral Vote (%)	Popular Vote (%)
Obama (Democratic)	365 (67.8%)	69,500,000 (52.9%)
McCain (Republican)	173 (32.2%)	59,900,000 (45.6%)
Minor parties	0 (0%)	2,013,371 (1.5%)

MAP 31.3 2008 Election: Obama's Victory After the housing bubble burst in 2008, followed by rising unemployment and falling stock prices, many Americans placed their hope in Democratic presidential candidate Barack Obama. The Illinois senator won majorities in several states—such as North Carolina, Colorado, and Virginia—that had not voted for a Democratic presidential candidate in decades.

Economic Recovery

Obama moved quickly to assemble his top advisors, dubbed a "team of rivals." He asked Bush's defense secretary, Robert Gates, to remain at the Pentagon. He appointed Hillary Clinton as secretary of state. He tried to make good on his promise to overcome partisan bickering in Washington by meeting with McCain shortly after the election and congressional Republicans once he took office.

On Inauguration Day 2009, a crowd of 1.5 million or more heard him take the oath of office. His inauguration speech was sober, as if to acknowledge the enormity of the challenges of the economic slump and the wars in Iraq and Afghanistan. He said, "We are in the midst of crisis" and "the state of the economy calls for action, bold and swift." He implied that Americans had been reckless for the past generation as he called on them to embrace "a new era of responsibility."

In his first months in office, Obama pressed for change. In February, Congress passed the **American Recovery and Reinvestment Act**, a $787 billion economic stimulus bill. The package combined government spending on infrastructure, unemployment benefits, and food stamps with tax cuts. As the unemployment rate surpassed 8 percent, liberal observers thought that the program was insufficient to return the economy to growth, while conservatives complained that it increased the deficit.

The economic stimulus law sent stock prices rebounding after hitting lows in March. But the economy continued to hemorrhage jobs. By the end of 2009, 9.8 percent of the workforce was idle; 16 million were either totally without work or worked fewer hours than they wanted. The economy began to grow again in 2010, but fewer jobs were created than had been lost during the depths of the recession. Surprising skeptics, banks and insurance companies repaid their government loans, and GM and Chrysler quickly emerged from bankruptcy. They closed obsolete plants, won concessions from unionized employees, and stopped producing cars no one wanted to buy. Within a few years, both GM and Chrysler, along with Ford, became profitable again and paid back most of the borrowed public funds. Finally, housing prices began to recover in 2012. By the beginning of 2014, the economy had recovered the nine million jobs lost during the recession, but long-term unemployment and slow growth remained problems. By 2017, the unemployment rate had declined to 5 percent. Even with recovery, however, many better-paying skilled factory jobs continued to be lost to automation and new technology as well as to overseas producers.

In contrast to his predecessor, Obama said that science policy would be based on science, not ideology or religious beliefs. He rescinded the Bush administration's ban on research using stem cells and encouraged scientists to tackle problems such as climate change and alternative energy.

Iraq Withdrawal and the Afghan War

The last U.S. combat forces left Iraq in August 2010, after about 4,500 U.S. service members lost their lives in the war. A year later, 45,000 uniformed Americans remained in Iraq as "trainers." At the end of 2011, a dispute with Iraq over the future status of these trainers prompted the Pentagon to pull out nearly all American troops. By then, nearly 7,000 Americans had been killed in Iraq and Afghanistan, with many thousands more severely injured. The combined military and reconstruction costs of the two wars reached about $4 trillion. Al-Qaeda, in comparison, had spent about $500,000 to carry out the 9/11 attacks.

As Iraqi politicians squabbled over the makeup of their government and as deadly bombings continued, the Bush administration's tarnished dream of Iraq becoming a force for democracy and prosperity in the Arab world appeared dimmer than ever. During 2014–2016, sectarian violence in Iraq reached postwar highs, and the government exercised limited authority outside Baghdad. New insurgent groups, such as the Islamic State, seized large chunks of Iraq and Syria, where they imposed a violent and repressive theocracy.

President Barrack Obama, excerpt from speech at Cairo University (June 2009)

Soon after Obama took office, he surprised his antiwar supporters by dispatching 17,000 additional troops to Afghanistan, but the insurgency only worsened. In the 2010, he committed another 30,000 troops. The aim was to bolster the Afghan government's ability to confront the Taliban. Obama also expanded the use of drone (remotely controlled, pilotless aircraft) attacks against targets in Afghanistan, Pakistan, Yemen, and parts of Africa. U.S. troops continued to fight in Afghanistan after 2014, but disputes with the Karzai government over aid and strategy raised doubts about whether they would remain beyond then. As of mid-2014, about 2,200 Americans had been killed there, along with some 1,000 NATO and coalition forces. Additional U.S. ground forces were sent in 2016. The Afghan leaders who replaced Karzai in 2015 proved no more able to stabilize the country, defeat the Taliban, or survive without continued American money and military support.

The killing of al-Qaeda leader Osama bin Laden by a team of U.S. Navy SEALs in May 2011 brought partial closure to the traumatic events of 9/11. But it had little impact on the fighting in Iraq and Afghanistan. The fact that bin Laden had hidden for years in Pakistan—supposedly America's close ally in the war against terrorists—highlighted the difficulty still faced by the United States in the Middle East and South Asia.

Reefer Madness: Cycles of Repression and Reform in the Long War on Drugs

Long before President Richard Nixon declared a "war on drugs" in 1971, the United States struggled with how to regulate psychoactive substances ranging from opium to alcohol to tobacco. Early in the 20th century, the United States joined a global pact to limit worldwide opium production, and Congress passed the Harrison Act in 1914, effectively criminalizing the use of opium and heroin. The Treasury Department created the Bureau of Narcotics (BON) in 1930 to enforce these laws.

In 1933, the Bureau of Narcotics launched a campaign to nationally criminalize cannabis, or marijuana, then regulated by states. Spurred on by scare stories and pseudo-documentary films like *Reefer Madness*, in 1937 Congress passed the Marijuana Tax Act, criminalizing the use of "pot."

The BON claimed that foreign enemies—first Japan and later the Soviet Union, China, and Latin America—targeted the United States with narcotics as a weapon, but in fact domestic demand, not foreign scheming, drove the market. Congress responded to BON pressure by passing the Boggs Act (1952) and the Narcotic Control Act (1956) that imposed mandatory minimum sentences for many drug crimes, including marijuana possession.

During the 1960s, as both heroin and marijuana use became more common, many reformers questioned the criminal approach. Some favored allowing clinics to administer doses of methadone, a synthetic narcotic taken orally, to heroin addicts. Others urged decriminalizing small amounts of marijuana. Nevertheless, in 1967 the Senate ratified the United Nations Single Convention on Narcotics, a treaty that enforced a prohibition on marijuana.

In the early 1970s, President Nixon created the Office of Drug Abuse Law Enforcement and merged the Bureau of Narcotics and other agencies into a new Drug Enforcement Administration (DEA), which focused on interdiction and arrests. In 1973, Nixon urged Congress to impose mandatory five-year terms for first-time heroin dealers and life sentences for repeat offenders.

After Nixon resigned in 1974, drug penalty reforms gained traction. Probably in response to rising rates of use among middle-class youth, 12 states reduced penalties for marijuana use or possession. But reforms encountered a conservative backlash. Many politicians and citizens linked rising levels of marijuana with cocaine use, sexual promiscuity, and spiking crime rates. President Ronald Reagan stoked these anxieties. He spoke ominously about "narco-terrorism" carried out by left-wing regimes in Nicaragua and Cuba. In 1986, the National Security Council issued a directive calling drug smuggling a major threat to national security. That same year, First Lady Nancy Reagan unveiled her "Just Say No to Drugs" campaign directed at children. In September, President Reagan declared a "national crusade for a drug-free America." Congress passed the Anti-Drug Act of 1986, reimposing stiff mandatory sentences for minor drug violations, requiring drug testing of many federal workers, and mandating far more severe penalties for possession of crack cocaine than for powdered cocaine. Politicians in both parties ignored data showing that arrests and seizures had little impact on the availability, price, or rates of drug use.

President George H. W. Bush escalated the drug war after 1989. He deployed naval and military units to combat drug smuggling in the Caribbean and along the Mexican border. In part, he justified the invasion of Panama as retaliation for strongman Manuel Noriega colluding with Colombian cocaine cartels. Bush also endorsed the Just Say No campaign as well as the school-based Drug Abuse Resistance Education (DARE) program, but these scare-based campaigns fell flat.

The Bush administration and its successors promoted efforts to destroy drug cartels in Latin America through initiatives such as Plan Colombia by providing billions of dollars in military aid to ruling regimes. Although some cartel kingpins like Colombia's Pablo Escobar were brought down, the huge potential profits resulted in a proliferation of smaller production and distribution networks that were more difficult to stop.

THE PRESIDENT MEETS THE KING   President Richard M. Nixon greets singer Elvis Presley on December 21, 1970. In his request for the meeting, Presley expressed interest in becoming a federal agent with the Bureau of Narcotics and Dangerous Drugs in order to help fight drug use in America.

image analysis

When Bill Clinton became president, he expanded military assistance programs in Latin America and echoed calls to jail "super-predators" at home. The 1994 Violent Crime Act mandated longer prison terms for a wide variety of crimes, including nonviolent drug offenses.

The costs of the drug war—whether measured by dollars or by the proliferation of communities scared by both drugs and the large number of young men sent to prison—have been huge. Between 1980 and 2015, an average of 750,000 Americans were charged annually with violating state drug laws, mostly involving marijuana. Although rates of drug use were roughly equal among all racial groups, conviction rates sent a far larger proportion of African Americans and Latinos to prison. Currently, the overall incarceration rate for adult African American males is 6 percent, for Hispanics 2 percent, and for white men 1 percent. A growing prison population enriched private prison operators but did not impede the flow or use of drugs.

Early in the 21st century, change came at the state, not federal, level. As of January 2017, 25 states allowed medical use of marijuana and 8 states allowed recreational use. However, under federal law, marijuana remains a Category 1 drug, bracketed with heroin, cocaine, and methamphetamine.

President Obama, cautious about being seen as "soft on drugs," waited until the end of his presidency to commute federal sentences for a substantial number of nonviolent drug offenders. By then, a new wave of prescription opioid addiction had seized public attention. Policymakers remain as uncertain as ever about what strategies to adopt in fighting America's longest war.

- When did federal authorities begin criminalizing drug use?
- How did politicians use the "war on drugs" for political advantage?

Battles in the Legislature

Despite Republican pledges to block nearly all of his initiatives and make him a "one-term president," Congress enacted significant parts of Obama's ambitious legislative program. For nearly a year, it debated a major overhaul of the nation's health care system designed to increase coverage to more than 95 percent of legal residents and contain the growth of costs. This conflict exemplified the deep partisan divide in American politics.

Until 2010, the United States was the only industrialized country that did not offer some form of comprehensive national health insurance. Since the 1930s, every Democratic president had urged adoption of national health insurance as a basic right and every Republican had opposed it as government overreach and a threat to individual freedom. Americans made do with a patchwork of private and government programs. After 1945, the GI Bill offered veterans health coverage. After 1956, the Indian Health Service supervised care for Native Americans. Beginning in 1965, Medicare covered some medical bills for those over 65 and Medicaid provided limited coverage to the very poor. Most working-age Americans relied on private insurance provided by employers as a job benefit. Until the 1970s, the United States had a relatively young, healthy workforce and only limited foreign competition. This kept insurance premiums in check, and employers easily absorbed the cost. But starting in the 1980s, an aging workforce, increased foreign competition, and costly new medicines and medical procedures drove up the price of health insurance sharply. Many manufacturers and small businesses stopped providing health insurance to their workers. This left a growing number of Americans, especially the working poor and self-employed, on their own. By the time President Obama took office, nearly 50 million Americans lacked health insurance coverage.

Health care spending in the United States, at about 17 percent of GDP, or over $7,000 per person, was by far the highest of any industrialized nation. The uninsured frequented emergency rooms (which by law had to provide services), which passed on the cost to everyone else, and high medical bills became a major cause of personal bankruptcy. Pharmaceutical companies, for-profit insurers, and private hospitals made money on the existing system and had little interest in controlling costs or ensuring quality. Meanwhile, individual doctors became increasingly frustrated with the avalanche of paperwork requirements from private insurers, and many came to favor government regulation as the best way to improve working conditions and patient care.

President Obama asked Congress to develop a plan to contain health spending while expanding the quality and reach of coverage. In hope of winning bipartisan backing, Democrats consulted closely with private health insurers and pharmaceutical companies and incorporated ideas previously broached by Republicans. In fact, the **Patient Protection and Affordable Care Act** closely resembled the 2006 Massachusetts state plan enacted by then governor and later Republican presidential hopeful Mitt Romney. The proposed federal law stipulated that: (1) large employers offer health coverage to their workers through private insurance plans; (2) children be allowed to remain on their parents, plan to age 26; (3) no one could be denied coverage due to a previous medical condition; (4) private insurance plans must adhere to a minimum standard of coverage; (5) individuals not covered by an employer must purchase insurance, with subsidies available to the working poor; (6) the federal government would provide additional funds for states to expand Medicaid coverage for the poor.

The bill was more of a health insurance reform than a national health plan and covered most, but not all, Americans. Despite its modest scope, Republicans derided what they dubbed "Obamacare," complaining that compelling employers to insure workers would kill jobs and that requiring individuals to buy insurance violated personal freedom. Others complained the law would expand access to abortion and birth control. Critics on the left objected to the program's reliance on private insurers rather than a single-payer government system like Medicare. Ultimately, the Affordable Care Act passed the Democratic-controlled Congress early in 2010 without a single Republican vote.

When Republicans gained control of the House of Representatives in November 2010, they insisted on repealing, not correcting, the law. Between 2010 and 2016, the GOP-led House voted over 50 times to repeal the Affordable Care Act. Senate Democrats blocked passage of repeal bills in the upper chamber until the Republicans took control in 2014. During 2015, President Obama vetoed a House-Senate bill to repeal the law. Constitutional challenges to the law also failed in 2015 when the Supreme Court, in a five to four vote, upheld the program. However, the Court permitted states to refuse expansion of the federally funded but state-run Medicaid program, leaving millions of poor people, mostly in Republican-controlled states, without coverage.

In spite of these hurdles, the Affordable Care Act slowed the rise in insurance premiums and the cost of many medical procedures. By 2016, the number of uninsured Americans had fallen from about 50 million to 27 million. Fears that employers would cut jobs rather than offer health coverage proved unfounded.

With less public acrimony, Congress also passed the Financial Regulatory Reform Act, the largest overhaul of the nation's financial system since the New Deal. It imposed tighter regulations on banks' trading practices, which had led to the financial collapse of 2008. It also created a new Bureau of Consumer Financial Protection designed to prevent many of the abuses of borrowers and bank customers that had also contributed to the crash.

Congress failed, however, to pass legislation addressing the potential dangers of climate change. The public initially supported Obama's plans to reduce reliance on energy obtained from the burning of oil, natural gas, and coal and switch to renewable energy sources. But enthusiasm for "green" energy faded as people became more concerned about finding or keeping jobs. The Senate declined to take up a bill passed by the House that would have set limits on the major cause of climate change—the burning of hydrocarbons that emitted gases into the atmosphere. Using his executive authority, in June 2014 Obama had the EPA issue regulations to reduce carbon emissions from coal-fired electrical generating facilities. Industry and Republican leaders fought many of these regulations in federal courts.

Excerpts from report of the Intergovernmental Panel on Climate Change (2013)

Even a major environmental disaster in the Gulf of Mexico did not revive the push to move away from petroleum. In April 2010, a rig owned by BP, one of the world's largest oil companies, exploded in the Gulf. The burst well began spilling oil into the Gulf, fouling beaches and marshes from Louisiana to Florida. By the time BP capped the well in July, nearly five million barrels had leaked into the ocean and impacted lives and jobs along the Gulf Coast.

But this disaster did not translate into a surge of support to move away from reliance on petroleum, a cheap fuel on which many depended for their livelihood and way of life. In fact, new technologies such as "fracking," in which water and chemicals are injected into shale formations deep underground, boosted U.S. petroleum and natural gas production and reduced imports. This method promised more stable energy supplies, but at the possible cost of accelerated environmental damage.

In spite of continued gun violence in America, including several high-profile mass shootings (which accounted for only a fraction of total deaths), Congress enacted no gun safety laws between 1994 and 2016. With almost 300 million guns in circulation, the United States has the highest rate of private gun ownership in the world. Proposals by President Obama to regulate the sale of "military-style assault weapons" were deemed by opponents such as the National Rifle Association (NRA) efforts to undermine the Second Amendment. The NRA and others also noted that handguns, not assault rifles, accounted for most killings. Regardless of how one parses the numbers, the statistics are grim. Since 1970, more Americans have died from gunshots—in both homicides and suicides—than the *total* number of Americans killed in *all* the nation's wars since 1776. In each of the past few years, about 36,000 people have died of gunshots, nearly two-thirds by suicide and the rest by homicide.

Protests on the Right and Left

The partisan battles Obama faced in Congress reflected growing divisions within American public opinion. Two grassroots organizations emerged between 2009 and 2011: the **Tea Party** on the right and **Occupy Wall Street** on the left.

Shortly after Obama assumed office, an upsurge of populist anger against the rescue of the banks, health care reform, and soaring federal budget deficits gave rise to the Tea Party movement. Tea Party activists, who condemned elites and "special interests" but had close links to wealthy business leaders, had a significant impact on the 2010 congressional elections. With many Obama voters sitting out the midterm election, Republicans picked up over 60 House seats, restoring their majority. The Senate added five new Republicans, giving the Democrats only a three-vote edge. Faced with this new reality, President Obama reached a budget compromise in December 2010 with the new Republican congressional majority that kept the Bush tax cuts—which favored the wealthy—in place for two more years. After the Democrats lost their legislative majority in the House, Obama had to rely mostly on executive orders to implement his unfinished agenda on energy, immigration, and climate.

The Great Recession accelerated the growing gap between rich and poor that began during the 1970s. Between 2008 and the end of 2011, the richest 7 percent of American households (about 8 million) grew wealthier, while the net worth of the bottom 93 percent (111 million) declined. The top 20 percent of households earned more than 50 percent of the nation's entire income. Even among the rich, income and wealth flowed mostly to the top 1 percent, and especially to the top one-tenth of 1 percent. A protest movement dubbed "Occupy Wall Street" reacted during the fall of 2011 by staging demonstrations in many cities and condemning tax and other federal policies that they saw as unfairly benefiting the top 1 percent as compared to the remaining 99 percent of Americans. (In fact, the most meaningful economic division separated the top 20 percent of households from the bottom 80 percent.) Camping in parks and in front of banks, Occupy demonstrators received media attention. But unlike the Tea Party activists, the Occupy movement had little cohesion and ignored electoral politics.

Photos of Occupy Wall Street protesters

The 2012 Election

After a bruising primary season, Republicans selected former Massachusetts governor Mitt Romney to run against Obama. Wealthy, handsome, and articulate, he promised to bring his business expertise to government. Unfortunately, Romney's own record worked against him. As a Senate candidate and then as governor of Massachusetts, he had supported abortion rights and had created a state health insurance program that closely resembled "Obamacare." He had difficulty explaining why he now passionately opposed both positions. His opposition to immigration reform alienated many Hispanic voters, a rapidly growing portion of the electorate. Romney also had the misfortune of speaking frankly before a group of wealthy supporters and being caught on tape condemning nearly half of all Americans—including the elderly and veterans—as freeloaders.

In addition to these problems, Romney ran against an improving economy. Even the weather favored the incumbent. A week before the election, Hurricane Sandy devastated the New Jersey coast and parts of New York City. Unlike Bush's lackadaisical response to Hurricane Katrina, Obama made sure that FEMA and other federal agencies were prepared for disaster relief. As soon as the storm surge receded, he flew to New Jersey, where he and then popular Republican governor Chris Christie comforted battered residents. Christie praised Obama's competence and thanked him for the speedy federal assistance.

On Election Day, Obama won handily. In the House, Democrats picked up a net of six seats, reducing the Republican majority. In the Senate, Democrats gained 2 seats, for a 53 to 45 advantage, with two Democratic-leaning independents.

Going Over the Fiscal Cliff

In spite of this impressive showing, Obama faced strong political headwinds. In the Senate, Republicans used the filibuster (which required a 60-vote margin to move legislation) to oppose most presidential initiatives, including measures such as a modest background check on gun purchases introduced after a massacre of schoolchildren in Connecticut in January 2013. The GOP also blocked many presidential appointments to executive agencies and federal courts. In 2014, frustrated Senate Democrats amended the chamber's rules to allow confirmation of some presidential nominees by a simple majority.

But the most polarizing issue proved to be the federal budget (Figure 31.2). By the summer of 2011, Republicans had forced a showdown with President Obama when they balked at raising the debt ceiling (something routinely approved by Congress over 70 times since 1962) unless he agreed to steep spending cuts. Pushed by Tea Party activists among recently elected representatives, GOP House Speaker John Bochner demanded that Obama agree to slash spending on social programs rather than raise taxes if he wanted Congress to raise the debt ceiling and avoid a default on government bonds—something that had never happened before.

Barely averting a default, in August 2011, Obama and congressional Republicans forged a short-term deal that linked a rise in the debt ceiling with vague plans to reduce future spending. Congress reached an impasse at the close of 2011. Republicans balked at tax increases to reduce deficits, insisting on cuts in social programs.

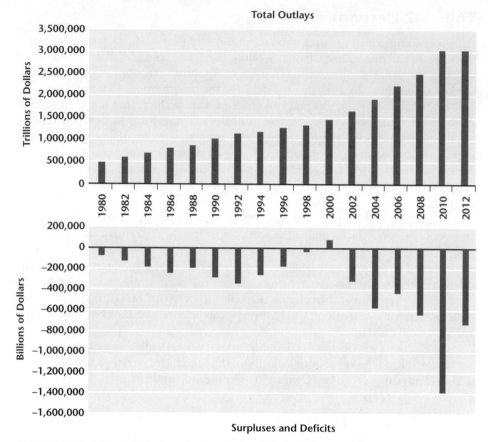

FIGURE 31.2 Worrisome trends: The federal budget Annual deficits and the national debt grew rapidly after 2001. The debt increased by around $5 trillion during the George W. Bush administration due to tax cuts, unfunded wars in Afghanistan and Iraq, and the unfunded expansion of Medicare drug benefits. During the first three years of the Obama presidency, the debt increased by about $4 trillion, largely a product of high unemployment and low tax collections due to slow economic growth. As the economy recovered after 2012, the budget deficit shrank rapidly.

Democrats demanded that in return for reducing social expenditures, the wealthy should pay higher taxes. Each side hoped that its stand would motivate its base and boost the chance for victory in the upcoming 2012 election.

Democrats and Republicans also engaged in skirmishes over the so-called fiscal cliff, a possible default on federal obligations if the debt and borrowing limit were not raised. During 2013, several stopgap measures authorized a small tax hike on high-income Americans in return for some modest spending cuts. When the two parties failed to agree on a budget or rise in the debt limit, across-the-board spending cuts, called sequestration, went into effect.

Rhetoric and reality continued to diverge. Conservatives in and out of government warned that without major spending cuts, the nation would drown in a sea of red ink and suffer runaway inflation, becoming a larger version of bankrupt Greece.

However, with the improving economy, the actual budget deficit shrank substantially after 2013, job creation surged, and inflation virtually disappeared.

Justice in the 21st Century

Bush had great success in making judicial appointments that moved federal courts, especially the Supreme Court, to the right. High court membership had not changed since 1994. For the next decade, the Court often divided between distinctly liberal and conservative blocs. Justice **Sandra Day O'Connor** provided a swing vote, giving one bloc or the other a five-vote majority. The Court's overall conservative tilt showed in its decision in 2000 to give the disputed Florida vote, and hence the presidency, to George W. Bush. In July 2005, O'Connor announced her plan to retire as soon as the president nominated and the Senate confirmed a replacement.

Bush nominated **John Roberts**, a federal appeals court judge, to replace O'Connor. Roberts had begun government service as a young lawyer in the Reagan Justice Department and moved into private practice before Bush appointed him as an appeals court judge. Roberts considered himself a disciple of Chief Justice William Rehnquist and impressed people as affable and well informed.

But on September 3, 2005, before the Senate voted to confirm the nominee, Chief Justice Rehnquist died. Bush then nominated Roberts to fill the chief justice's vacant seat. Bush nominated federal appeals court justice **Samuel Alito**, who had also served in the Reagan Justice Department, to fill O'Connor's place. The Senate approved both appointments.

Roberts and Alito were more congenial than the often abrasive justices Antonin Scalia and Clarence Thomas. Nevertheless, they nearly always voted with the most conservative members of the Court on issues such as business rights versus worker protections. The new justices also took a dim view of abortion rights and the rights of criminal defendants. They were inclined to grant the president wide latitude in pursuing the war on terror. Justice Anthony Kennedy frequently joined the four conservative judges in a five to four majority. On several occasions, Kennedy voted with the liberal bloc in imposing some limits on the president's right to hold foreign nationals indefinitely in military detention. In 2016, Kennedy also joined with four liberal justices in upholding the constitutionality of affirmative action admissions in higher education and in striking down laws in several states designed to close most facilities providing abortions.

However, Kennedy's vote pushed the Court sharply to the right in a pair of 2010 decisions. A majority of justices upheld the notion that the Second Amendment conveyed a broad, though not unlimited, right of individuals to possess guns. In a case known as *Citizens United*, the five-vote conservative bloc struck down as a violation of the First Amendment the 2002 McCain–Feingold Act that limited the amount of money corporations could provide to independent groups campaigning for or against a political candidate or cause. The ruling decreed that corporations had the same free speech rights as individuals and opened a potential floodgate of money from corporations to favorite causes or candidates. It also overturned some campaign finance restrictions passed by progressives over a century before. The decision encouraged the formation of thousands of political advocacy groups, often with secret funders, who influenced campaigns at every level of government. This flood of so-called dark money especially impacted state elections by helping business-friendly conservatives gain control of a majority of legislatures. This enabled them to draw congressional districts that disproportionately aided

Republican candidates. The Court's notion of "corporate citizenship," liberals feared, might be used by conservatives as a justification to unravel many other regulations of business activity.

Chief Justice Roberts, however, surprised many Court observers in 2012 by casting a fifth vote to sustain the signature legislation of President Obama's first term, the Affordable Care Act.

Obama appointed two women to the Supreme Court in his first two years. In 2009, the Senate confirmed Sonia Sotomayor, a federal appellate judge, as the first Hispanic justice. In 2010, he named Solicitor General Elena Kagan to the Court. Both replaced justices who had voted with the liberal minority, so the ideological balance of the Court remained unchanged. Nevertheless, Republicans blocked votes on dozens of lower court judges Obama nominated both before and after his reelection. The death of Justice Scalia in 2016 gave Obama an opportunity to replace him with a more liberal judge—until Senate Republicans opted to block an appointment until after the 2016 election.

Immigration

During the first decade of the 21st century, people from around the world continued to flock to the United States. Some migrants had few job skills but worked hard in the service economy, in construction, and in agriculture. Others had advanced degrees. By 2006, 40 percent of individuals with PhDs in America had been born abroad, and many taught in universities or worked for companies such as Microsoft and Intel. As had been true since the immigration law reform of 1965, nearly 60 percent of those coming to the United States had been born in Latin America and the Caribbean, and almost 25 percent originated in East and South Asia. By 2016, 40 percent of new arrivals came from the Asia/Pacific area, more than from Latin America. Despite popular fears, immigrants did not raise crime rates, and most paid income and Social Security taxes—even though they generally received few benefits.

The question of undocumented immigration (estimated at 11–12 million residing in the United States) and the growth in the Hispanic population emerged as new "wedge" issues between 2000 and 2016. Many, but not all, congressional Republicans, along with several TV and radio personalities such as Lou Dobbs, Pat Buchanan, Glenn Beck, and Rush Limbaugh, warned of a silent invasion across the Mexican border. Anti-immigration crusaders demanded that the undocumented be arrested and deported and that the children born in the United States of undocumented mothers be denied citizenship.

Protesters demonstrating for tougher immigration enforcement, 2016

President Bush, along with two senators, Republican John McCain of Arizona and the late Democrat Edward Kennedy of Massachusetts, proposed a broad compromise that would have combined enhanced border security, a guest worker program, and a path toward citizenship for most of the undocumented. However, conservative Republicans in the House and Senate killed the proposal and pushed through an "enforcement only" plan that Bush signed. Several states, including Arizona, passed laws permitting local police to arrest suspected illegal immigrants. But the Supreme Court invalidated many of the harsh provisions as overstepping state authority.

The Obama administration used executive orders to bar deportation of "dreamers," children brought into the country illegally by their parents years before. But only Congress had the power to effect real change. In 2013, a bipartisan majority of the Senate voted to ease the path to citizenship for the undocumented, but the legislation stalled in the GOP-controlled House. In 2016, Republican presidential candidate Donald Trump made building a "wall" along the border with Mexico his signature issue. Also in 2016,

CROSSING BORDERS   An immigrant family in California rallies in 2006 against efforts by state and federal authorities to restrict immigration and punish the undocumented.

federal courts limited the president's ability to defer deportations of dreamers and other undocumented residents.

The public's perception of immigration was often shaped by media coverage. For example, when an undocumented migrant committed a crime, his or her status often became the focus of news coverage. Between 2014 and 2016, about 75,000 Cubans entered the United States under special provisions dating back to the 1960s. But when about the same number of Central American women and children fleeing violence crossed into Texas, the media labeled it variously as a "crisis" or an "invasion." In fact, most so-called illegals were not border crossers, but legal visitors who overstayed their visas.

Civil Rights for Gay Americans

Gay rights advocates took heart from a U.S. Supreme Court decision in 2003 (*Lawrence v. Texas*) that overturned most state antisodomy laws used to criminalize homosexual behavior and from a ruling by the Massachusetts Supreme Judicial Court that same year that found no legal basis for prohibiting same-sex marriage. In February 2004, the Massachusetts court explicitly ruled that gay men and women had the right to marry in the state. Almost a decade earlier, congressional Republicans had pushed through a national **Defense of Marriage Act (DOMA)**. That 1996 law decreed that no state would be compelled to recognize a same-sex marriage performed in another state, nor would the federal government recognize the existence of such a marriage even if it were performed legally in a state. In 2011, following congressional action, President Obama approved regulations permitting gays to serve openly in the military. Despite predictions of doom, the military quickly adjusted to the new rule.

In 2013, the Supreme Court, by a narrow majority, added to the momentum in favor of marriage equality. It let stand a ruling by a California court that invalidated a state ban on such unions, effectively legalizing same-sex unions in the nation's largest state. The high court also struck down key portions of DOMA, ruling that married same-sex partners were entitled to the same federal benefits as traditional partners. By 2014, 19 states plus the District of Columbia allowed gay marriage, and several more permitted same-sex civil unions. As public opinion polls revealed growing acceptance of same-sex unions, political momentum shifted in favor of marriage equality.

The Supreme Court confirmed this trend in a 2015 landmark ruling in the case of *Obergefell v. Hodges*. By a five to four vote, the justices decided that under the terms of the Fourteenth Amendment's due process and equal protection clauses, same-sex couples had a fundamental right to marry, regardless of where they lived.

A Turbulent World

Beginning in 2011, change came to the Arab world in unexpected ways. That year, a Tunisian street vendor burned himself to death to protest police abuse. His suicide sparked protests that within two years toppled not only the Tunisian government, but ruling regimes in Egypt, Yemen, and Libya and sparked a civil war in Syria. Unfortunately, the ouster of dictators like Egypt's Hosni Mubarak and Libya's Muammar Gaddafi, and the revolt against Bashar al-Assad's regime in Syria, led to chaos rather than democracy. In Syria alone, civil war has caused an estimated half-million deaths. It also created an opening for the rise of radical Islamist groups such as the Islamic State, which seized territory in Iraq, Syria, and Libya. The violence displaced tens of millions of people internally and pushed at least seven million refugees into Turkey, Lebanon, Jordan, and Europe, the largest such crisis since World War II. Although the United States provided financial support to humanitarian agencies, it admitted only token numbers of refugees fleeing this violence.

Monument in Tunisia to Mohamed Bouazizi, whose martyrdom in December 2010 triggered the Arab Spring

In many ways, the political and cultural conflict between liberals and conservatives in the first decades of the 21st century resembles the debates of the Progressive era. Then, as now, Americans questioned the role and scope of government in their daily lives. They debated whether free markets and corporations served the common good or selfish ends and how money influenced politics. As the rich got richer and the middle and working classes treaded water, concern spread over the causes and consequences of growing economic inequality. Partisan divides widened over the questions of how open the country should be to immigrants and how active a role the nation should play in world affairs. Just as the choices made over a century ago continue to influence our lives, the actions taken by this generation will define the contours of the future.

STUDY QUESTIONS FOR THE OBAMA YEARS

quiz

1. To what extent did the Democrats' electoral successes in 2006 and 2008 represent a significant change in U.S. political attitudes?

2. Why did Barack Obama win the presidential election of 2008?

3. Explain the successes and failures of the first years of the Obama presidency.

Addendum: The Unexpected Election of President Donald J. Trump

The 2016 presidential election in the United States defied almost all predictions. On the Republican side, real estate mogul and reality television host Donald Trump vanquished 16 primary opponents with his promise to "Make America Great Again." His campaign slogan "America First" (which echoed the name of the pre–World War II isolationist movement) included calls to build a wall along the border with Mexico, deport millions of undocumented migrants, bar Muslim refugees, and renegotiate trade treaties. Trump's vague foreign policy proposals suggested he would expand the so-called global war on terror, reject international efforts to control climate change, and limit support for America's traditional allies in Europe and Asia. These initiatives, he claimed, would restore prosperity to millions of ordinary working Americans hurt by foreign competition and by the "elites" in both parties who championed what Trump derisively labeled globalization.

Democrats ultimately selected former first lady, senator, and secretary of state Hillary Clinton as their candidate. She faced an unexpectedly strong challenge from Vermont senator and self-proclaimed Socialist Bernie Sanders, who criticized Clinton's ties to Wall Street donors and lack of concern for growing economic inequality. During both the primary and general election, Clinton stressed her past governing experience and competence. Most journalists, pundits, and officials in both parties predicted an easy win by Clinton in the general election, arguing that her appeal among women made her nearly unbeatable.

The campaign played out differently. Trump spent little money on television ads or consultants, communicating instead through tweets or at rallies of exuberant supporters. He attacked Clinton's use of a private email server while she was secretary of state; claimed that she and her husband had broken laws by collecting donations for the charitable Clinton Foundation; and blamed her for endorsing trade policies that drove manufacturing jobs to China, Mexico, and other low-wage countries. Clinton's approval ratings were further undermined by a series of leaked emails—likely derived from hacks by Russian intelligence—that showed discord within Democratic Party ranks.

Clinton struck back by highlighting Trump's insulting behavior toward women, minorities, the handicapped, and others, emphasizing that such behavior made him temperamentally unfit to be president. But Clinton never articulated a clear vision of her presidency and failed to inspire many younger and minority voters who had supported Obama in 2008 and 2012. Her criticism of Trump offered little solace to white, working-class voters worried more about economic and cultural change than about the candidate's temperament.

The election results of November 8, 2016, startled about half the country and most of the world. Although Clinton won the popular vote by nearly three million votes, her margin among women, minorities, and working-class whites fell short. Trump—the first president ever elected without previous government or military service—beat Clinton in the crucial electoral vote, narrowly cracking traditional Democratic strongholds like Wisconsin, Michigan, and Pennsylvania. Republicans retained control of both houses of Congress. Although Trump had only loose ties to the Republican establishment, with the party now in control of Congress and the White House, it seemed likely that the new administration would follow through on promises to appoint more conservative judges

Inaugural address of President Donald J. Trump, January 20, 2017

interactive timeline

TIMELINE 2001–PRESENT

AMERICA	YEAR	THE WORLD
Jun Congress reduces income and estate tax rates **Jul** Congress passes No Child Left Behind Act **Sep** Al-Qaeda terrorists attack World Trade Center and Pentagon **Sep** Congress passes USA PATRIOT Act; Bush declares "global war on terror" **Oct** United States attacks Afghanistan to capture or kill Osama bin Laden **Nov** Enron declares bankruptcy	**2001**	**Dec** U.S. and Afghan allies topple Taliban government
Jun Joseph Stiglitz publishes *Globalization and Its Discontents* **Jun** President George W. Bush announces policy of preemptive war **Oct** Congress authorizes military force against Iraq	**2002**	
Mar United States attacks Iraq **Jun** Supreme Court overturns state antisodomy laws in *Lawrence v. Texas* **Jul** 9/11 Commission publishes its report **Dec** Congress passes Medicare Modernization Act	**2003**	**Feb–Mar** UN weapons inspectors in Iraq find no evidence of WMD despite claims of Bush administration **Mar** Most U.S. allies refuse to join war against Iraq **Apr** Saddam Hussein's government falls **Jun** Iraqi insurgency begins against American forces
Feb Massachusetts Supreme Court rules that gays and lesbians have the right to marry **May** U.S. abuse of prisoners in Iraq revealed **Nov** President Bush wins reelection over John F. Kerry	**2004**	
Jan–Apr Terri Schiavo case dominates news **Apr** Thomas Friedman publishes *The World Is Flat* **Aug** Hurricane Katrina floods New Orleans **Sep** John Roberts named Chief Justice of the U.S. Supreme Court	**2005**	
Jun Supreme Court rules in *Hamdan v. Rumsfeld* that prisoners at Guantanamo Bay have right to hearings in federal courts **Nov** Democrats win majorities in the House and Senate in congressional elections **Dec** Iraq Study Group issues report critical of Bush administration policy	**2006**	**Nov–Dec** Escalating insurgency in Iraq **Dec** Saddam Hussein executed
Jun Congress fails to adopt immigration reform **Oct** Dow Jones and Standard and Poor's stock averages hit peak	**2007**	**Jan** U.S. begins troop surge in Iraq
Mar Investment firm Bear Stearns nearly collapses **Jul** Federal government takes over Fannie Mae and Freddie Mac **Sep** Investment firm Lehman Brothers declares bankruptcy **Oct** U.S. Treasury creates Troubled Assets Relief Program (TARP) **Nov** Democrat Barack Obama elected president over Republican John McCain	**2008**	**Mar–Dec** U.S. economic turmoil spreads to world markets

to federal courts, repeal the Affordable Care Act, dismantle environmental regulations, impose strict immigration limits, and enact tax cuts benefiting wealthier Americans.

During Trump's first six months in office he used his executive power to cancel American participation in the Paris Climate Accord, the Trans-Pacific Trade Partnership,

AMERICA	YEAR	THE WORLD
Jan Barack Obama inaugurated president **Feb** Congress enacts American Recovery and Reinvestment Act to stimulate the economy **Feb** President Obama announces U.S. combat troops will depart Iraq by end of 2010 **Jun** President Obama addresses Muslim world in speech in Cairo **Aug** Sonia Sotomayor joins Supreme Court	**2009**	**Feb** Crowds in Dublin, Ireland, demand resignation of the government for its mishandling of banking crisis **Oct** President Obama awarded Nobel Peace Prize
Jan Supreme Court in its *Citizens United* ruling overturns most limits on corporate political contributions **Mar** Congress overrides Republican opposition and enacts Patient Protection and Affordable Care Act, a sweeping overhaul of the nation's health care system **Jul** Most U.S. combat troops leave Iraq, but over 40,000 American soldiers remain **Aug** Elena Kagan joins Supreme Court **Nov** Republicans regain control of House of Representatives; rise of "Tea Party" activism **Dec** President Obama announces United States will add 30,000 troops to its force in Afghanistan	**2010**	**Dec** Arab Spring begins with uprising in Tunisia, followed by revolts in Egypt, Libya, and Syria
May U.S. Navy SEALs kill Osama bin Laden in Pakistan **Jun–Aug** President Obama and congressional Republicans spar over raising debt ceiling and averting default **Sep** Occupy Wall Street movement	**2011**	**Feb** Egyptian leader Hosni Mubarak forced from office **Oct** Libyan dictator Muammar Gaddafi deposed and killed **Dec** Last U.S. combat troops leave Iraq
Nov President Obama reelected, defeating Mitt Romney	**2012**	**Jan–Feb** Civil war erupts in Syria (continues into 2017)
Jun Supreme Court strikes down federal Defense of Marriage Act (DOMA) **Jun** Supreme Court overturns key provisions of 1965 Voting Rights Act **Jun** Former NSA contractor Edward Snowden reveals vast program of domestic and foreign surveillance **Oct** Republicans in House of Representatives shut down federal government for two weeks **Oct–Dec** Rollout of Affordable Care Act Web site	**2013**	
Nov Republicans expand majorities in Congress Steady but slow economic growth in United States	**2014**	
Jun Supreme Court legalizes same-sex marriage	**2015**	Global refugee crisis worsens as fighting in Middle East persists (continues into 2017)
Jun Supreme Court reaffirms abortion rights **Nov** Donald J. Trump elected president	**2016**	
Jan Donald J. Trump inaugurated president	**2017**	

and several Obama-era initiatives to reduce greenhouse gases and other forms of air pollution. Trump pushed to rescind so-called Obamacare, pledged more federal aid to charter and parochial schools, and began rolling back financial and consumer protection regulations enacted in the wake of the Great Recession.

Summary

- Al-Qaeda, an international terrorist network, attacked the United States in the late 20th and early 21st centuries.
- In 2003, the United States attacked Iraq to overthrow the government of Saddam Hussein and to demonstrate its military power in the Middle East.
- The Bush administration restricted civil liberties in the midst of its war on terror.
- Cultural conservatives enhanced their influence early in the 21st century.
- Lax financial regulation, a housing bubble, and bad bank lending practices led to the Great Recession of 2008–2009.
- Barack Obama was elected as the nation's first African American president in 2008.
- After Republicans regained control of the House of Representatives in 2010, they and President Obama engaged in a series of policy fights that nearly paralyzed the government.
- Obama won reelection in 2012, but Republicans in Congress stymied most of his legislative agenda.
- Donald Trump was elected as the 45th president in 2016.

Key Terms and People

audio
flashcards

Abu Ghraib 1084
al-Qaeda 1077
Alito, Samuel 1105
American Recovery and Reinvestment
  Act 1096
Bernanke, Ben 1094
Biden, Joseph 1095
Buchanan, Patrick 1086
Bush Doctrine 1081
Bush, George W. 1078
Cheney, Dick 1077
Clinton, Hillary 1095
Defense of Marriage Act (DOMA) 1107
Emergency Economic Stabilization
  Act 1094
Great Recession 1094
Hamdan v. Rumsfeld 1084
Hussein, Saddam 1077
Karzai, Hamid 1080
Kerry, John 1089

Lawrence v. Texas 1107
McCain, John 1095
Medicare Modernization Act 1089
No Child Left Behind (NCLB) Act 1088
O'Connor, Sandra Day 1105
Obama, Barack 1095
Obergefell v. Hodges 1108
Occupy Wall Street 1102
Palin, Sarah 1095
Patient Protection and Affordable Care
  Act 1100
Paulson, Henry 1094
Powell, Colin 1077
Roberts, John 1105
Rumsfeld, Donald 1080
Schiavo, Terri 1087
September 11 1085
subprime mortgages 1093
Tea Party 1102
USA PATRIOT Act 1085

Reviewing Chapter 31

1. What were the consequences of the United States' war on terror after September 11, 2001?
2. Who benefited and who fell behind because of 21st-century globalization?
3. How did Americans respond to the Great Recession?

Further Reading

Alter, Jonathan. *The Center Holds: Obama and His Enemies.* New York: Simon & Schuster, 2013. Examines Obama's achievements; the opposition to his policies; and how, despite attacks on his character, leadership, and policies, he won a decisive reelection victory.

Anderson, Terry. *Bush's Wars.* New York: Oxford University Press, 2011. Traces the political maneuvers and manipulation of intelligence that led to the wars in Iraq and Afghanistan.

Bacevich, Andrew J. *War for the Greater Middle East.* New York: Random House, 2016. Examines the causes and consequences of U.S. military involvement in the Middle East since the late 1970s.

Bergen, Peter L. *The Longest War: The Enduring Conflict Between America and Al Qaeda.* New York: Free Press, 2011. An overview of the politics and strategies of the wars on terror and the fighting in Iraq and Afghanistan.

Brinkley, Douglas. *The Great Deluge: Hurricane Katrina, New Orleans, and the Mississippi Gulf Coast.* New York: HarperCollins, 2006. The incompetence of the government response to this act of nature proved terribly hard for its victims and undercut the Bush administration's appeal.

Frank, Thomas. *What's the Matter with Kansas? How Conservatives Won the Heart of America.* New York: Metropolitan Books, 2004. Why, the author asks, do so many Americans apparently vote against their economic interests and support a conservative social agenda?

Heilemann, John, and Mark Halperin. *Game Change: Obama and the Clintons, McCain and Palin, and the Race of a Lifetime.* New York: Harper, 2010. A detailed account of how a skilled political outsider mobilized public support for his candidacy and won the presidency.

Heilemann, John, and Mark Halperin. *Double Down: Game Change 2012.* New York: Penguin Press, 2013. A spirited description of how personalities, politics, issues, and big money shaped the election of 2012.

Henriques, Diana B. *The Wizard of Lies: Bernie Madoff and the Death of Trust.* New York: Times Books, 2011. Explains how a Wall Street scam artist pulled off the biggest Ponzi scheme in history, and examines its consequences.

Issikoff, Michael, and David Corn. *Hubris: The Inside Story of Spin, Scandal and the Selling of the Iraq War.* New York: Random House, 2006. An examination of how the Bush administration "played" the media to win public support for military action.

Lewis, Michael. *The Big Short: Inside the Doomsday Machine.* New York: W. W. Norton, 2010. Highlights the wild excesses of capital markets and government indifference that brought on the Great Recession.

Mayer, Jane. *Dark Money: The Hidden History of the Billionaires Behind the Rise of the Radical Right.* New York: Anchor, 2016. The author explores efforts by "super rich" activists to implement conservative political, social, and economic agendas locally and nationally.

Moore, James, and Wayne Slater. *Bush's Brain: How Karl Rove Made George W. Bush Presidential.* Hoboken, NJ: John Wiley & Sons, 2004. An irreverent but insightful examination of how Republican strategists "packaged" and "sold" George W. Bush.

Morgenson, Gretchen, and Joshua Rosner. *Reckless Endangerment: How Outsized Ambition, Greed, and Corruption Led to Economic Armageddon.* New York: Times Books, 2011. An examination of how private greed and government deregulation contributed to the economic collapse that began in 2008.

Packer, George. *The Unwinding: An Inner History of the New America.* New York: Farrar, Straus and Giroux, 2013. A searing portrait, told through the lives of individuals and communities, of life in America as middle-class jobs and the social safety net disappear.

Taylor, Paul, and Pew Research Center. *The Next America: Boomers, Millennials, and the Looming Generational Showdown.* New York: PublicAffairs, 2014. Analyzes how current and emerging economic trends will shape the fortunes of future generations.

America in the World
GOODS, IDEAS, PEOPLE

CHAPTER 31: Twenty-first Century Dangers and Promises, 2001–Present

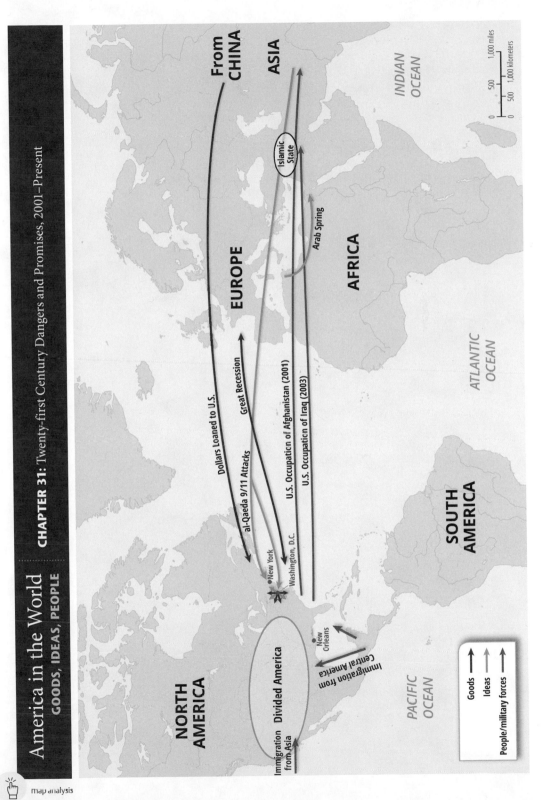

From CHINA

ASIA

EUROPE

AFRICA

INDIAN OCEAN

Islamic State

Arab Spring

Dollars Loaned to U.S.

Great Recession

al-Qaeda 9/11 Attacks

U.S. Occupation of Afghanistan (2001)

U.S. Occupation of Iraq (2003)

New York

Washington, D.C.

ATLANTIC OCEAN

NORTH AMERICA

SOUTH AMERICA

New Orleans

Divided America

Immigration from Central America

Immigration from Asia

PACIFIC OCEAN

0   500   1,000 miles
0   500   1,000 kilometers

Goods

Ideas

People/military forces

map analysis

APPENDIX A

HISTORICAL DOCUMENTS

The Declaration of Independence

When in the course of human events, it becomes necessary for one people to dissolve the political bands which have connected them with another, and to assume, among the powers of the earth, the separate and equal station to which the Laws of Nature and of Nature's God entitle them, a decent respect to the opinions of mankind requires that they should declare the causes which impel them to the separation.

We hold these truths to be self-evident, that all men are created equal, that they are endowed by their Creator with certain unalienable Rights, that among these are life, liberty and the pursuit of happiness. That to secure these rights, governments are instituted among men, deriving their just powers from the consent of the governed; that whenever any form of government becomes destructive of these ends, it is the right of the people to alter or to abolish it, and to institute new Government, laying its foundation on such principles and organizing its powers in such form, as to them shall seem most likely to effect their safety and happiness. Prudence, indeed, will dictate that Governments long established should not be changed for light and transient causes; and, accordingly, all experience hath shown, that mankind are more disposed to suffer, while evils are sufferable, than to right themselves by abolishing the forms to which they are accustomed. But when a long train of abuses and usurpations, pursuing invariably the same object evinces a design to reduce them under absolute despotism, it is their right, it is their duty, to throw off such government, and to provide new guards for their future security. Such has been the patient sufferance of these colonies; and such is now the necessity which constrains them to alter their former systems of government. The history of the present King of Great Britain is a history of repeated injuries and usurpations, all having in direct object the establishment of an absolute tyranny over these States. To prove this, let facts be submitted to a candid world:

He has refused his assent to laws, the most wholesome and necessary for the public good.

He has forbidden his governors to pass laws of immediate and pressing importance, unless suspended in their operation till his assent should be obtained; and, when so suspended, he has utterly neglected to attend to them.

He has refused to pass other laws for the accommodation of large districts of people, unless those people would relinquish the right of representation in the legislature, a right inestimable to them and formidable to tyrants only.

He has called together legislative bodies at places unusual, uncomfortable, and distant from the depository of their public records, for the sole purpose of fatiguing them into compliance with his measures.

He has dissolved representative houses repeatedly, for opposing with manly firmness his invasions on the rights of the people.

He has refused for a long time, after such dissolutions, to cause others to be elected; whereby the legislative powers, incapable of annihilation, have returned to the People at large for their exercise; the State remaining in the mean time exposed to all the dangers of invasion from without, and convulsions within.

He has endeavored to prevent the population of these States; for that purpose obstructing the laws for naturalization of foreigners; refusing to pass others to encourage their migrations hither, and raising the conditions of new appropriations of lands.

He has obstructed the administration of justice, by refusing his assent to laws for establishing judiciary powers.

He has made judges dependent on his will alone, for the tenure of their offices, and the amount and payment of their salaries.

He has erected a multitude of new offices, and sent hither swarms of officers to harass our people, and eat out their substance.

He has kept among us, in times of peace, standing armies without the consent of our legislatures.

He has affected to render the Military independent of, and superior to, the civil power.

He has combined with others to subject us to a jurisdiction foreign to our constitution and unacknowledged by our laws; giving his assent to their acts of pretended legislation:

For quartering large bodies of armed troops among us;

For protecting them, by a mock trial, from punishment for any murders which they should commit on the inhabitants of these States;

For cutting off our trade with all parts of the world;

For imposing taxes on us without our Consent;

For depriving us, in many cases, of the benefits of Trial by Jury;

For transporting us beyond Seas to be tried for pretended offences;

For abolishing the free System of English Laws in a neighbouring Province, establishing therein an Arbitrary government, and enlarging its Boundaries so as to render it at once an example and fit instrument for introducing the same absolute rule into these colonies;

For taking away our charters, abolishing our most valuable laws, and altering fundamentally the forms of our governments;

For suspending our own legislatures, and declaring themselves invested with power to legislate for us in all cases whatsoever.

He has abdicated government here, by declaring us out of his protection and waging war against us.

He has plundered our seas, ravaged our coasts, burnt our towns, and destroyed the lives of our people.

He is at this time transporting large armies of foreign mercenaries to complete the works of death, desolation and tyranny, already begun with circumstances of cruelty and perfidy scarcely paralleled in the most barbarous ages, and totally unworthy the head of a civilized nation.

He has constrained our fellow citizens taken captive on the high seas to bear arms against their country, to become the executioners of their friends and brethren, or to fall themselves by their hands.

He has excited domestic insurrections amongst us, and has endeavored to bring on the inhabitants of our frontiers, the merciless Indian savages, whose known rule of warfare, is an undistinguished destruction of all ages, sexes and conditions.

In every stage of these oppressions we have petitioned for redress in the most humble terms; our repeated petitions have been answered only by repeated injury. A prince whose character is thus marked by every act which may define a tyrant, is unfit to be the ruler of a free people.

Nor have we been wanting in attentions to our British brethren. We have warned them from time to time of attempts by their legislature to extend an unwarrantable jurisdiction over us. We have reminded them of the circumstances of our emigration and settlement here. We have appealed to their native justice and magnanimity, and we have conjured them by the ties of our common kindred to disavow these usurpations, which, would inevitably interrupt our connections and correspondence. They, too, have been deaf to the voice of justice and of consanguinity. We must, therefore, acquiesce in the necessity, which denounces our separation, and hold them, as we hold the rest of mankind, enemies in war, in peace friends.

We, therefore, the representatives of the United States of America, in general Congress, assembled, appealing to the Supreme Judge of the world for the rectitude of our intentions, do, in the name, and by the authority of the good people of these colonies, solemnly publish and declare, that these united colonies are, and of right ought to be free and independent states; that they are absolved from all allegiance to the British Crown, and that all political connection between them and the state of Great Britain, is and ought to be totally dissolved; and that, as free and independent states, they have full power to levy war, conclude peace, contract alliances, establish commerce, and to do all other acts and things which independent states may of right do. And for the support of this declaration, with a firm reliance on the protection of Divine Providence, we mutually pledge to each other our lives, our fortunes and our sacred honor.

The Constitution of the United States of America

We the People of the United States, in Order to form a more perfect Union, establish Justice, insure domestic Tranquility, provide for the common defence, promote the general Welfare, and secure the Blessings of Liberty to ourselves and our Posterity, do ordain and establish this Constitution for the United States of America.

ARTICLE I

Section 1.

All legislative Powers herein granted shall be vested in a Congress of the United States, which shall consist of a Senate and House of Representatives.

Section 2.

The House of Representatives shall be composed of Members chosen every second Year by the People of the several States, and the Electors in each State shall have the Qualifications requisite for Electors of the most numerous Branch of the State Legislature.

No Person shall be a Representative who shall not have attained to the Age of twenty five Years, and been seven Years a Citizen of the United States, and who shall not, when elected, be an Inhabitant of that State in which he shall be chosen.

Representatives and direct Taxes shall be apportioned among the several States which may be included within this Union, according to their respective Numbers, which shall be determined by adding to the whole Number of free Persons, including those bound to Service for a Term of Years, and excluding Indians not taxed, three fifths of all other Persons. The actual Enumeration shall be made within three Years after the first Meeting of the Congress of the United States, and within every subsequent Term of ten Years, in such Manner as they shall by Law direct. The Number of Representatives shall not exceed one for every thirty Thousand, but each State shall have at Least one Representative; and until such enumeration shall be made, the State of New Hampshire shall be entitled to choose three, Massachusetts eight, Rhode-Island and Providence Plantations one, Connecticut five, New York six, New Jersey four, Pennsylvania eight, Delaware one, Maryland six, Virginia ten, North Carolina five, South Carolina five, and Georgia three.

When vacancies happen in the Representation from any State, the Executive Authority thereof shall issue Writs of Election to fill such Vacancies.

The House of Representatives shall choose their Speaker and other Officers; and shall have the sole Power of Impeachment.

Section 3.

The Senate of the United States shall be composed of two Senators from each State, chosen by the Legislature thereof for six Years; and each Senator shall have one Vote.

Immediately after they shall be assembled in Consequence of the first Election, they shall be divided as equally as may be into three Classes. The Seats of the Senators of the first Class shall be vacated at the Expiration of the second Year, of the second Class at the Expiration of the fourth Year, and of the third Class at the Expiration of the sixth Year, so that one third may be chosen every second Year; and if Vacancies happen by Resignation, or otherwise, during the Recess of the Legislature of any State, the Executive thereof may make temporary Appointments until the next Meeting of the Legislature, which shall then fill such Vacancies.

No Person shall be a Senator who shall not have attained to the Age of thirty Years, and been nine Years a Citizen of the United States, and who shall not, when elected, be an Inhabitant of that State for which he shall be chosen.

The Vice President of the United States shall be President of the Senate, but shall have no Vote, unless they be equally divided.

The Senate shall choose their other Officers, and also a President pro tempore, in the Absence of the Vice President, or when he shall exercise the Office of President of the United States.

The Senate shall have the sole Power to try all Impeachments. When sitting for that Purpose, they shall be on Oath or Affirmation. When the President of the United States is tried, the Chief Justice shall preside: And no Person shall be convicted without the Concurrence of two thirds of the Members present.

Judgment in Cases of Impeachment shall not extend further than to removal from Office, and disqualification to hold and enjoy any Office of honor, Trust or Profit under the United States: but the Party convicted shall nevertheless be liable and subject to Indictment, Trial, Judgment and Punishment, according to Law.

Section 4.

The Times, Places and Manner of holding Elections for Senators and Representatives, shall be prescribed in each State by the Legislature thereof; but the Congress may at any time by Law make or alter such Regulations, except as to the Places of chusing Senators.

The Congress shall assemble at least once in every Year, and such Meeting shall be on the first Monday in December, unless they shall by Law appoint a different Day.

Section 5.

Each House shall be the Judge of the Elections, Returns and Qualifications of its own Members, and a Majority of each shall constitute a Quorum to do Business; but a smaller Number may adjourn from day to day, and may be authorized to compel the Attendance of absent Members, in such Manner, and under such Penalties as each House may provide.

Each House may determine the Rules of its Proceedings, punish its Members for disorderly Behaviour, and, with the Concurrence of two thirds, expel a Member.

Each House shall keep a Journal of its Proceedings, and from time to time publish the same, excepting such Parts as may in their Judgment require Secrecy; and the Yeas and Nays of the Members of either House on any question shall, at the Desire of one fifth of those Present, be entered on the Journal.

Neither House, during the Session of Congress, shall, without the Consent of the other, adjourn for more than three days, nor to any other Place than that in which the two Houses shall be sitting.

Section 6.

The Senators and Representatives shall receive a Compensation for their Services, to be ascertained by Law, and paid out of the Treasury of the United States. They shall in all Cases, except Treason, Felony and Breach of the Peace, be privileged from Arrest during their Attendance at the Session of their respective Houses, and in going to and returning from the same; and for any Speech or Debate in either House, they shall not be questioned in any other Place.

No Senator or Representative shall, during the Time for which he was elected, be appointed to any civil Office under the Authority of the United States, which shall have been created, or the Emoluments whereof shall have been increased during such time; and no Person holding any Office under the United States, shall be a Member of either House during his Continuance in Office.

Section 7.

All Bills for raising Revenue shall originate in the House of Representatives; but the Senate may propose or concur with Amendments as on other Bills.

Every Bill which shall have passed the House of Representatives and the Senate, shall, before it become a Law, be presented to the President of the United States: If he approve he shall sign it, but if not he shall return it, with his Objections to that House in which it shall have originated, who shall enter the Objections at large on their Journal, and proceed to reconsider it. If after such Reconsideration two thirds of that House shall agree to pass the Bill, it shall be sent, together with the Objections, to the other House, by which it shall likewise be reconsidered, and if approved by two thirds of that House, it shall become a Law. But in all such Cases the Votes of both Houses shall be determined by yeas and Nays, and the Names of the Persons voting for and against the Bill shall be entered on the Journal of each House respectively. If any Bill shall not be returned by the President within ten Days (Sundays excepted) after it shall have been presented to him, the Same shall be a Law, in like Manner as if he had signed it, unless the Congress by their Adjournment prevent its Return, in which Case it shall not be a Law.

Every Order, Resolution, or Vote to which the Concurrence of the Senate and House of Representatives may be necessary (except on a question of Adjournment) shall be presented to the President of the United States; and before the Same shall take Effect, shall be approved by him, or being disapproved by him, shall be repassed by two thirds of the Senate and House of Representatives, according to the Rules and Limitations prescribed in the Case of a Bill.

Section 8.

The Congress shall have Power

To lay and collect Taxes, Duties, Imposts and Excises, to pay the Debts and provide for the common Defence and general Welfare of the United States; but all Duties, Imposts and Excises shall be uniform throughout the United States;

To borrow Money on the credit of the United States;

To regulate Commerce with foreign Nations, and among the several States, and with the Indian Tribes;

To establish an uniform Rule of Naturalization, and uniform Laws on the subject of Bankruptcies throughout the United States;

To coin Money, regulate the Value thereof, and of foreign Coin, and fix the Standard of Weights and Measures;

To provide for the Punishment of counterfeiting the Securities and current Coin of the United States;

To establish Post Offices and post Roads;

To promote the Progress of Science and useful Arts, by securing for limited Times to Authors and Inventors the exclusive Right to their respective Writings and Discoveries;

To constitute Tribunals inferior to the supreme Court;

To define and punish Piracies and Felonies committed on the high Seas, and Offences against the Law of Nations;

To declare War, grant Letters of Marque and Reprisal, and make Rules concerning Captures on Land and Water;

To raise and support Armies, but no Appropriation of Money to that Use shall be for a longer Term than two Years;

To provide and maintain a Navy;

To make Rules for the Government and Regulation of the land and naval Forces;

To provide for calling forth the Militia to execute the Laws of the Union, suppress Insurrections and repel Invasions;

To provide for organizing, arming, and disciplining the Militia, and for governing such Part of them as may be employed in the Service of the United States, reserving to the States respectively, the Appointment of the Officers, and the Authority of training the Militia according to the discipline prescribed by Congress;

To exercise exclusive Legislation in all Cases whatsoever, over such District (not exceeding ten Miles square) as may, by Cession of particular States, and the Acceptance of Congress, become the Seat of the Government of the United States, and to exercise like Authority over all Places purchased by the Consent of the Legislature of the State in which the Same shall be, for the Erection of Forts, Magazines, Arsenals, dock-Yards, and other needful Buildings;—And

To make all Laws which shall be necessary and proper for carrying into Execution the foregoing Powers, and all other Powers vested by this Constitution in the Government of the United States, or in any Department or Officer thereof.

Section 9.

The Migration or Importation of such Persons as any of the States now existing shall think proper to admit, shall not be prohibited by the Congress prior to the Year one thousand eight hundred and eight, but a Tax or duty may be imposed on such Importation, not exceeding ten dollars for each Person.

The Privilege of the Writ of Habeas Corpus shall not be suspended, unless when in Cases of Rebellion or Invasion the public Safety may require it.

No Bill of Attainder or ex post facto Law shall be passed.

No Capitation, or other direct, Tax shall be laid, unless in Proportion to the Census or enumeration herein before directed to be taken.

No Tax or Duty shall be laid on Articles exported from any State.

No Preference shall be given by any Regulation of Commerce or Revenue to the Ports of one State over those of another; nor shall Vessels bound to, or from, one State, be obliged to enter, clear, or pay Duties in another.

No Money shall be drawn from the Treasury, but in Consequence of Appropriations made by Law; and a regular Statement and Account of the Receipts and Expenditures of all public Money shall be published from time to time.

No Title of Nobility shall be granted by the United States: And no Person holding any Office of Profit or Trust under them, shall, without the Consent of the Congress, accept of any present, Emolument, Office, or Title, of any kind whatever, from any King, Prince, or foreign State.

Section 10.

No State shall enter into any Treaty, Alliance, or Confederation; grant Letters of Marque and Reprisal; coin Money; emit Bills of Credit; make any Thing but gold and silver Coin a Tender in Payment of Debts; pass any Bill of Attainder, ex post facto Law, or Law impairing the Obligation of Contracts, or grant any Title of Nobility.

No State shall, without the Consent of the Congress, lay any Imposts or Duties on Imports or Exports, except what may be absolutely necessary for executing it's inspection Laws: and the net Produce of all Duties and Imposts, laid by any State on Imports or Exports, shall be for the Use of the Treasury of the United States; and all such Laws shall be subject to the Revision and Control of the Congress.

No State shall, without the Consent of Congress, lay any Duty of Tonnage, keep Troops, or Ships of War in time of Peace, enter into any Agreement or Compact with another State, or with a foreign Power, or engage in War, unless actually invaded, or in such imminent Danger as will not admit of delay.

ARTICLE II

Section 1.

The executive Power shall be vested in a President of the United States of America. He shall hold his Office during the Term of four Years, and, together with the Vice President, chosen for the same Term, be elected, as follows:

Each State shall appoint, in such Manner as the Legislature thereof may direct, a Number of Electors, equal to the whole Number of Senators and Representatives to which the State may be entitled in the Congress: but no Senator or Representative, or Person holding an Office of Trust or Profit under the United States, shall be appointed an Elector.

The Electors shall meet in their respective States, and vote by Ballot for two Persons, of whom one at least shall not be an Inhabitant of the same State with themselves. And they shall make a List of all the Persons voted for, and of the Number of Votes for each; which List they shall sign and certify, and transmit sealed to the Seat of the Government of the United States, directed to the President of the Senate. The President of the Senate shall, in the Presence of the Senate and House of Representatives, open all the Certificates, and the Votes shall then be counted. The Person having the greatest Number of Votes shall be the President, if such Number be a Majority of the whole Number of Electors appointed; and if there be more than one who have such Majority, and have an equal Number of Votes, then the House of Representatives shall immediately choose by Ballot one of them for President; and if no Person have a Majority, then from the five highest on the List the said House shall in like Manner choose the President. But in choosing the President, the Votes shall be taken by States, the Representation from each State having one Vote; A quorum for this purpose shall consist of a Member or Members from two thirds of the States, and a Majority of all the States shall be necessary to a Choice. In every Case, after the Choice of the President, the Person having the greatest Number of Votes of the Electors shall be the Vice President. But if there should remain two or more who have equal Votes, the Senate shall choose from them by Ballot the Vice President.

The Congress may determine the Time of choosing the Electors, and the Day on which they shall give their Votes; which Day shall be the same throughout the United States.

No Person except a natural born Citizen, or a Citizen of the United States, at the time of the Adoption of this Constitution, shall be eligible to the Office of President; neither shall any Person be eligible to that Office who shall not have attained to the Age of thirty five Years, and been fourteen Years a Resident within the United States.

In Case of the Removal of the President from Office, or of his Death, Resignation, or Inability to discharge the Powers and Duties of the said Office, the Same shall devolve on the Vice President, and the Congress may by Law provide for the Case of Removal, Death, Resignation or Inability, both of the President and Vice President, declaring what Officer shall then act as President, and such Officer shall act accordingly, until the Disability be removed, or a President shall be elected.

The President shall, at stated Times, receive for his Services, a Compensation, which shall neither be increased nor diminished during the Period for which he shall have been elected, and he shall not receive within that Period any other Emolument from the United States, or any of them.

Before he enter on the Execution of his Office, he shall take the following Oath or Affirmation:—"I do solemnly swear (or affirm) that I will faithfully execute the Office of President of the United States, and will to the best of my Ability, preserve, protect and defend the Constitution of the United States."

Section 2.

The President shall be Commander in Chief of the Army and Navy of the United States, and of the Militia of the several States, when called into the actual Service of the United States; he may require the Opinion, in writing, of the principal Officer in each of the executive Departments, upon any Subject relating to the Duties of their respective Offices, and he shall have Power to grant Reprieves and Pardons for Offences against the United States, except in Cases of Impeachment.

He shall have Power, by and with the Advice and Consent of the Senate, to make Treaties, provided two thirds of the Senators present concur; and he shall nominate, and by and with the Advice and Consent of the Senate, shall appoint Ambassadors, other public Ministers and Consuls, Judges of the supreme Court, and all other Officers of the United States, whose Appointments are not herein otherwise provided for, and which shall be established by Law: but the Congress may by Law vest the Appointment of such inferior Officers, as they think proper, in the President alone, in the Courts of Law, or in the Heads of Departments.

The President shall have Power to fill up all Vacancies that may happen during the Recess of the Senate, by granting Commissions which shall expire at the End of their next Session.

Section 3.

He shall from time to time give to the Congress Information of the State of the Union, and recommend to their Consideration such Measures as he shall judge necessary and expedient; he may, on extraordinary Occasions, convene both Houses, or either of them, and in Case of Disagreement between them, with Respect to the Time of Adjournment, he may adjourn them to such Time as he shall think proper; he shall receive Ambassadors and other public Ministers; he shall take Care that the Laws be faithfully executed, and shall Commission all the Officers of the United States.

Section 4.

The President, Vice President and all civil Officers of the United States, shall be removed from Office on Impeachment for, and Conviction of, Treason, Bribery, or other high Crimes and Misdemeanors.

ARTICLE III

Section 1.

The judicial Power of the United States shall be vested in one supreme Court, and in such inferior Courts as the Congress may from time to time ordain and establish. The Judges, both of the supreme and inferior Courts, shall hold their Offices during good Behaviour, and shall, at stated Times, receive for their Services a Compensation, which shall not be diminished during their Continuance in Office.

Section 2.

The judicial Power shall extend to all Cases, in Law and Equity, arising under this Constitution, the Laws of the United States, and Treaties made, or which shall be made, under their Authority;—to all Cases affecting Ambassadors, other public Ministers and Consuls;—to all Cases of admiralty and maritime Jurisdiction;—to Controversies to which the United States shall be a Party;—to Controversies between two or more States;—between a State and Citizens of another State;—between Citizens of different States;—between Citizens of the same State claiming Lands under Grants of different States, and between a State, or the Citizens thereof, and foreign States, Citizens or Subjects.

In all Cases affecting Ambassadors, other public Ministers and Consuls, and those in which a State shall be Party, the supreme Court shall have original Jurisdiction. In all the other Cases before mentioned, the supreme Court shall have appellate Jurisdiction, both as to Law and Fact, with such Exceptions, and under such Regulations as the Congress shall make.

The Trial of all Crimes, except in Cases of Impeachment, shall be by Jury; and such Trial shall be held in the State where the said Crimes shall have been committed; but when not committed within any State, the Trial shall be at such Place or Places as the Congress may by Law have directed.

Section 3.

Treason against the United States, shall consist only in levying War against them, or in adhering to their Enemies, giving them Aid and Comfort. No Person shall be convicted of Treason unless on the Testimony of two Witnesses to the same overt Act, or on Confession in open Court.

The Congress shall have Power to declare the Punishment of Treason, but no Attainder of Treason shall work Corruption of Blood, or Forfeiture except during the Life of the Person attainted.

ARTICLE IV

Section 1.

Full Faith and Credit shall be given in each State to the public Acts, Records, and judicial Proceedings of every other State. And the Congress may by general Laws prescribe the Manner in which such Acts, Records and Proceedings shall be proved, and the Effect thereof.

Section 2.

The Citizens of each State shall be entitled to all Privileges and Immunities of Citizens in the several States.

A Person charged in any State with Treason, Felony, or other Crime, who shall flee from Justice, and be found in another State, shall on Demand of the executive Authority of the State from which he fled, be delivered up, to be removed to the State having Jurisdiction of the Crime.

No Person held to Service or Labour in one State, under the Laws thereof, escaping into another, shall, in Consequence of any Law or Regulation therein, be discharged from such Service or Labour, but shall be delivered up on Claim of the Party to whom such Service or Labour may be due.

Section 3.

New States may be admitted by the Congress into this Union; but no new State shall be formed or erected within the Jurisdiction of any other State; nor any State be formed by the Junction of two or more States, or Parts of States, without the Consent of the Legislatures of the States concerned as well as of the Congress.

The Congress shall have Power to dispose of and make all needful Rules and Regulations respecting the Territory or other Property belonging to the United States; and nothing in this Constitution shall be so construed as to Prejudice any Claims of the United States, or of any particular State.

Section 4.

The United States shall guarantee to every State in this Union a Republican Form of Government, and shall protect each of them against Invasion; and on Application of the Legislature, or of the Executive (when the Legislature cannot be convened), against domestic Violence.

ARTICLE V

The Congress, whenever two thirds of both Houses shall deem it necessary, shall propose Amendments to this Constitution, or, on the Application of the Legislatures of two thirds of the several States, shall call a Convention for proposing Amendments, which, in either Case, shall be valid to all Intents and Purposes, as Part of this Constitution, when ratified by the Legislatures of three fourths of the several States, or by Conventions in three fourths thereof, as the one or the other Mode of Ratification may be proposed by the Congress; Provided that no Amendment which may be made prior to the Year One thousand eight hundred and eight shall in any Manner affect the first and fourth Clauses in the Ninth Section of the first Article; and that no State, without its Consent, shall be deprived of its equal Suffrage in the Senate.

ARTICLE VI

All Debts contracted and Engagements entered into, before the Adoption of this Constitution, shall be as valid against the United States under this Constitution, as under the Confederation.

This Constitution, and the Laws of the United States which shall be made in Pursuance thereof; and all Treaties made, or which shall be made, under the Authority of the United States, shall be the supreme Law of the Land; and the Judges in every State shall be bound thereby, any Thing in the Constitution or Laws of any State to the Contrary notwithstanding.

The Senators and Representatives before mentioned, and the Members of the several State Legislatures, and all executive and judicial Officers, both of the United States and of the several States, shall be bound by Oath or Affirmation, to support this Constitution; but no religious Test shall ever be required as a Qualification to any Office or public Trust under the United States.

ARTICLE VII

The Ratification of the Conventions of nine States, shall be sufficient for the Establishment of this Constitution between the States so ratifying the Same.

The Word, "the," being interlined between the seventh and eighth Lines of the first Page, the Word "Thirty" being partly written on an Erazure in the fifteenth Line of the first Page, The Words "is tried" being interlined between the thirty second and thirty third Lines of the first Page and the Word "the" being interlined between the forty third and forty fourth Lines of the second Page.

Attest William Jackson Secretary

Done in Convention by the Unanimous Consent of the States present the Seventeenth Day of September in the Year of our Lord one thousand seven hundred and Eighty seven and of the Independence of the United States of America the Twelfth. In witness whereof We have hereunto subscribed our Names,

G°. Washington
Presidt and deputy from Virginia

Delaware
George Read
Gunning Bedford Junior
John Dickinson
Richard Bassett
Jacob Broom

Maryland
James McHenry
Daniel of St Thomas
   Jenifer
Daniel Carroll

Virginia
John Blair
James Madison

North Carolina
William Blount
Richard Dobbs Spaight
Hugh Williamson

South Carolina
John Rutledge
Charles Cotesworth
   Pinckney
Charles Pinckney
Pierce Butler

Georgia
William Few
Abraham Baldwin

New Hampshire
John Langdon
Nicholas Gilman

Massachusetts
Nathaniel Gorham
Rufus King

Connecticut
William Samuel Johnson
Roger Sherman

New York
Alexander Hamilton

New Jersey
William Livingston
David Brearley
William Paterson
Jonathan Dayton

Pennsylvania
Benjamin Franklin
Thomas Mifflin
Robert Morris
George Clymer
Thomas FitzSimons
Jared Ingersoll
James Wilson
Gouverneur Morris

Articles

In addition to, and Amendment of the Constitution of the United States of America, proposed by Congress, and ratified by the Legislatures of the several States, pursuant to the fifth Article of the original Constitution.

   [The first 10 amendments to the U.S. Constitution were ratified December 15, 1791, and form what is known as the "Bill of Rights."]

AMENDMENT I

Congress shall make no law respecting an establishment of religion, or prohibiting the free exercise thereof; or abridging the freedom of speech, or of the press; or the right of the people peaceably to assemble, and to petition the Government for a redress of grievances.

AMENDMENT II

A well regulated Militia, being necessary to the security of a free State, the right of the people to keep and bear Arms, shall not be infringed.

AMENDMENT III

No Soldier shall, in time of peace be quartered in any house, without the consent of the Owner, nor in time of war, but in a manner to be prescribed by law.

AMENDMENT IV

The right of the people to be secure in their persons, houses, papers, and effects, against unreasonable searches and seizures, shall not be violated, and no Warrants shall issue, but upon probable cause, supported by Oath or affirmation, and particularly describing the place to be searched, and the persons or things to be seized.

AMENDMENT V

No person shall be held to answer for a capital, or otherwise infamous crime, unless on a presentment or indictment of a Grand Jury, except in cases arising in the land or naval forces, or in the Militia, when in actual service in time of War or public danger; nor shall any person be subject for the same offence to be twice put in jeopardy of life or limb; nor shall be compelled in any criminal case to be a witness against himself, nor be deprived of life, liberty, or property, without due process of law; nor shall private property be taken for public use, without just compensation.

AMENDMENT VI

In all criminal prosecutions, the accused shall enjoy the right to a speedy and public trial, by an impartial jury of the State and district wherein the crime shall have been committed, which district shall have been previously ascertained by law, and to be informed of the nature and cause of the accusation; to be confronted with the witnesses against him; to have compulsory process for obtaining witnesses in his favor, and to have the Assistance of Counsel for his defence.

AMENDMENT VII

In Suits at common law, where the value in controversy shall exceed twenty dollars, the right of trial by jury shall be preserved, and no fact tried by a jury, shall be otherwise reexamined in any Court of the United States, than according to the rules of the common law.

AMENDMENT VIII

Excessive bail shall not be required, nor excessive fines imposed, nor cruel and unusual punishments inflicted.

AMENDMENT IX

The enumeration in the Constitution, of certain rights, shall not be construed to deny or disparage others retained by the people.

AMENDMENT X

The powers not delegated to the United States by the Constitution, nor prohibited by it to the States, are reserved to the States respectively, or to the people.

AMENDMENT XI

Passed by Congress March 4, 1794. Ratified February 7, 1795.

Note: Article III, Section 2, of the Constitution was modified by Amendment XI.

The Judicial power of the United States shall not be construed to extend to any suit in law or equity, commenced or prosecuted against one of the United States by Citizens of another State, or by Citizens or Subjects of any Foreign State.

AMENDMENT XII

Passed by Congress December 9, 1803. Ratified June 15, 1804.

Note: A portion of Article II, Section 1, of the Constitution was superseded by the Twelfth Amendment.

The Electors shall meet in their respective states and vote by ballot for President and Vice-President, one of whom, at least, shall not be an inhabitant of the same state with themselves; they shall name in their ballots the person voted for as President, and in distinct ballots the person voted for as Vice-President, and they shall make distinct lists of all persons voted for as President, and of all persons voted for as Vice-President, and of the number of votes for each, which lists they shall sign and certify, and transmit sealed to the seat of the government of the United States, directed to the President of the Senate;—the President of the Senate shall, in the presence of the Senate and House of Representatives, open all the certificates and the votes shall then be counted;—The person having the greatest number of votes for President, shall be the President, if such number be a majority of the whole number of Electors appointed; and if no person have such majority, then from the persons having the highest numbers not exceeding three on the list of those voted for as President, the House of Representatives shall choose immediately, by ballot, the President. But in choosing the President, the votes shall be taken by states, the representation from each state having one vote; a quorum for this purpose shall consist of a member or members from two-thirds of the states, and a majority of all the states shall be necessary to a choice. [And if the House of Representatives shall not choose a President whenever the right of choice shall devolve upon them, before the fourth day of March next following, then the Vice-President shall act as President, as in case of the death or other constitutional disability of the President.—]* The person having the greatest number of votes as Vice-President, shall be the Vice-President, if such number be a majority of the whole number of Electors appointed, and if no person have a majority, then from the two highest numbers on the list, the Senate shall choose the Vice-President; a quorum for the purpose shall consist of two-thirds of the whole number of Senators, and a majority of the whole number shall be necessary to a choice. But no person constitutionally ineligible to the office of President shall be eligible to that of Vice-President of the United States.

AMENDMENT XIII

Passed by Congress January 31, 1865. Ratified December 6, 1865.

Note: A portion of Article IV, Section 2, of the Constitution was superseded by the Thirteenth Amendment.

*Superseded by Section 3 of the Twentieth Amendment.

Section 1.

Neither slavery nor involuntary servitude, except as a punishment for crime whereof the party shall have been duly convicted, shall exist within the United States, or any place subject to their jurisdiction.

Section 2.

Congress shall have power to enforce this article by appropriate legislation.

AMENDMENT XIV

Passed by Congress June 13, 1866. Ratified July 9, 1868.

   Note: Article I, Section 2, of the Constitution was modified by Section 2 of the Fourteenth Amendment.

Section 1.

All persons born or naturalized in the United States, and subject to the jurisdiction thereof, are citizens of the United States and of the State wherein they reside. No State shall make or enforce any law which shall abridge the privileges or immunities of citizens of the United States; nor shall any State deprive any person of life, liberty, or property, without due process of law; nor deny to any person within its jurisdiction the equal protection of the laws.

Section 2.

Representatives shall be apportioned among the several States according to their respective numbers, counting the whole number of persons in each State, excluding Indians not taxed. But when the right to vote at any election for the choice of electors for President and Vice-President of the United States, Representatives in Congress, the Executive and Judicial officers of a State, or the members of the Legislature thereof, is denied to any of the male inhabitants of such State, being twenty-one years of age,* and citizens of the United States, or in any way abridged, except for participation in rebellion, or other crime, the basis of representation therein shall be reduced in the proportion which the number of such male citizens shall bear to the whole number of male citizens twenty-one years of age in such State.

Section 3.

No person shall be a Senator or Representative in Congress, or elector of President and Vice-President, or hold any office, civil or military, under the United States, or under any State, who, having previously taken an oath, as a member of Congress, or as an officer of the United States, or as a member of any State legislature, or as an executive or judicial officer of any State, to support the Constitution of the United States, shall have engaged in insurrection or rebellion against the same, or given aid or comfort to the enemies thereof. But Congress may by a vote of two-thirds of each House, remove such disability.

Section 4.

The validity of the public debt of the United States, authorized by law, including debts incurred for payment of pensions and bounties for services in suppressing insurrection

*Changed by Section 1 of the Twenty-sixth Amendment.

or rebellion, shall not be questioned. But neither the United States nor any State shall assume or pay any debt or obligation incurred in aid of insurrection or rebellion against the United States, or any claim for the loss or emancipation of any slave; but all such debts, obligations and claims shall be held illegal and void.

Section 5.

The Congress shall have the power to enforce, by appropriate legislation, the provisions of this article.

AMENDMENT XV

Passed by Congress February 26, 1869. Ratified February 3, 1870.

Section 1.

The right of citizens of the United States to vote shall not be denied or abridged by the United States or by any State on account of race, color, or previous condition of servitude.

Section 2.

The Congress shall have the power to enforce this article by appropriate legislation.

AMENDMENT XVI

Passed by Congress July 2, 1909. Ratified February 3, 1913.

Note: Article I, Section 9, of the Constitution was modified by Amendment XVI.

The Congress shall have power to lay and collect taxes on incomes, from whatever source derived, without apportionment among the several States, and without regard to any census or enumeration.

AMENDMENT XVII

Passed by Congress May 13, 1912. Ratified April 8, 1913.

Note: Article I, Section 3, of the Constitution was modified by the Seventeenth Amendment.

The Senate of the United States shall be composed of two Senators from each State, elected by the people thereof, for six years; and each Senator shall have one vote. The electors in each State shall have the qualifications requisite for electors of the most numerous branch of the State legislatures.

When vacancies happen in the representation of any State in the Senate, the executive authority of such State shall issue writs of election to fill such vacancies: *Provided*, That the legislature of any State may empower the executive thereof to make temporary appointments until the people fill the vacancies by election as the legislature may direct.

This amendment shall not be so construed as to affect the election or term of any Senator chosen before it becomes valid as part of the Constitution.

AMENDMENT XVIII

Passed by Congress December 18, 1917. Ratified January 16, 1919. Repealed by Amendment XXI.

Section 1.

After one year from the ratification of this article the manufacture, sale, or transportation of intoxicating liquors within, the importation thereof into, or the exportation thereof from the United States and all territory subject to the jurisdiction thereof for beverage purposes is hereby prohibited.

Section 2.

The Congress and the several States shall have concurrent power to enforce this article by appropriate legislation.

Section 3.

This article shall be inoperative unless it shall have been ratified as an amendment to the Constitution by the legislatures of the several States, as provided in the Constitution, within seven years from the date of the submission hereof to the States by the Congress.

AMENDMENT XIX

Passed by Congress June 4, 1919. Ratified August 18, 1920.

The right of citizens of the United States to vote shall not be denied or abridged by the United States or by any State on account of sex.

Congress shall have power to enforce this article by appropriate legislation.

AMENDMENT XX

Passed by Congress March 2, 1932. Ratified January 23, 1933.

Note: Article I, Section 4, of the Constitution was modified by Section 2 of this amendment. In addition, a portion of the Twelfth Amendment was superseded by Section 3.

Section 1.

The terms of the President and the Vice President shall end at noon on the 20th day of January, and the terms of Senators and Representatives at noon on the 3d day of January, of the years in which such terms would have ended if this article had not been ratified; and the terms of their successors shall then begin.

Section 2.

The Congress shall assemble at least once in every year, and such meeting shall begin at noon on the 3d day of January, unless they shall by law appoint a different day.

Section 3.

If, at the time fixed for the beginning of the term of the President, the President elect shall have died, the Vice President elect shall become President. If a President shall not have been chosen before the time fixed for the beginning of his term, or if the President elect shall have failed to qualify, then the Vice President elect shall act as President until a President shall have qualified; and the Congress may by law provide for the case wherein neither a President elect nor a Vice President shall have qualified, declaring who shall then act as President, or the manner in which one who is to act shall be selected, and such person shall act accordingly until a President or Vice President shall have qualified.

Section 4.

The Congress may by law provide for the case of the death of any of the persons from whom the House of Representatives may choose a President whenever the right of choice shall have devolved upon them, and for the case of the death of any of the persons from whom the Senate may choose a Vice President whenever the right of choice shall have devolved upon them.

Section 5.

Sections 1 and 2 shall take effect on the 15th day of October following the ratification of this article.

Section 6.

This article shall be inoperative unless it shall have been ratified as an amendment to the Constitution by the legislatures of three-fourths of the several States within seven years from the date of its submission.

AMENDMENT XXI

Passed by Congress February 20, 1933. Ratified December 5, 1933.

Section 1.

The eighteenth article of amendment to the Constitution of the United States is hereby repealed.

Section 2.

The transportation or importation into any State, Territory, or Possession of the United States for delivery or use therein of intoxicating liquors, in violation of the laws thereof, is hereby prohibited.

Section 3.

This article shall be inoperative unless it shall have been ratified as an amendment to the Constitution by conventions in the several States, as provided in the Constitution, within seven years from the date of the submission hereof to the States by the Congress.

AMENDMENT XXII

Passed by Congress March 21, 1947. Ratified February 27, 1951.

Section 1.

No person shall be elected to the office of the President more than twice, and no person who has held the office of President, or acted as President, for more than two years of a term to which some other person was elected President shall be elected to the office of President more than once. But this Article shall not apply to any person holding the office of President when this Article was proposed by Congress, and shall not prevent any person who may be holding the office of President, or acting as President, during the term within which this Article becomes operative from holding the office of President or acting as President during the remainder of such term.

Section 2.

This article shall be inoperative unless it shall have been ratified as an amendment to the Constitution by the legislatures of three-fourths of the several States within seven years from the date of its submission to the States by the Congress.

AMENDMENT XXIII

Passed by Congress June 16, 1960. Ratified March 29, 1961.

Section 1.

The District constituting the seat of Government of the United States shall appoint in such manner as Congress may direct:

A number of electors of President and Vice President equal to the whole number of Senators and Representatives in Congress to which the District would be entitled if it were a State, but in no event more than the least populous State; they shall be in addition to those appointed by the States, but they shall be considered, for the purposes of the election of President and Vice President, to be electors appointed by a State; and they shall meet in the District and perform such duties as provided by the twelfth article of amendment.

Section 2.

The Congress shall have power to enforce this article by appropriate legislation.

AMENDMENT XXIV

Passed by Congress August 27, 1962. Ratified January 23, 1964.

Section 1.

The right of citizens of the United States to vote in any primary or other election for President or Vice President, for electors for President or Vice President, or for Senator or Representative in Congress, shall not be denied or abridged by the United States or any State by reason of failure to pay poll tax or other tax.

Section 2.

The Congress shall have power to enforce this article by appropriate legislation.

AMENDMENT XXV

Passed by Congress July 6, 1965. Ratified February 10, 1967.

Note: Article II, Section 1, of the Constitution was affected by the Twenty-fifth Amendment.

Section 1.

In case of the removal of the President from office or of his death or resignation, the Vice President shall become President.

Section 2.

Whenever there is a vacancy in the office of the Vice President, the President shall nominate a Vice President who shall take office upon confirmation by a majority vote of both Houses of Congress.

Section 3.

Whenever the President transmits to the President pro tempore of the Senate and the Speaker of the House of Representatives his written declaration that he is unable to discharge the powers and duties of his office, and until he transmits to them a written declaration to the contrary, such powers and duties shall be discharged by the Vice President as Acting President.

Section 4.

Whenever the Vice President and a majority of either the principal officers of the executive departments or of such other body as Congress may by law provide, transmit to the President pro tempore of the Senate and the Speaker of the House of Representatives their written declaration that the President is unable to discharge the powers and duties of his office, the Vice President shall immediately assume the powers and duties of the office as Acting President.

Thereafter, when the President transmits to the President pro tempore of the Senate and the Speaker of the House of Representatives his written declaration that no inability exists, he shall resume the powers and duties of his office unless the Vice President and a majority of either the principal officers of the executive department or of such other body as Congress may by law provide, transmit within four days to the President pro tempore of the Senate and the Speaker of the House of Representatives their written declaration that the President is unable to discharge the powers and duties of his office. Thereupon Congress shall decide the issue, assembling within forty-eight hours for that purpose if not in session. If the Congress, within twenty-one days after receipt of the latter written declaration, or, if Congress is not in session, within twenty-one days after Congress is required to assemble, determines by two-thirds vote of both Houses that the President is unable to discharge the powers and duties of his office, the Vice President shall continue to discharge the same as Acting President; otherwise, the President shall resume the powers and duties of his office.

AMENDMENT XXVI

Passed by Congress March 23, 1971. Ratified July 1, 1971.

Note: Amendment XIV, Section 2, of the Constitution was modified by Section 1 of the Twenty-sixth Amendment.

Section 1.

The right of citizens of the United States, who are eighteen years of age or older, to vote shall not be denied or abridged by the United States or by any State on account of age.

Section 2.

The Congress shall have power to enforce this article by appropriate legislation.

AMENDMENT XXVII

Originally proposed September 25, 1789. Ratified May 7, 1992.

No law, varying the compensation for the services of the Senators and Representatives, shall take effect, until an election of representatives shall have intervened.

Lincoln's Gettysburg Address

Four score and seven years ago our fathers brought forth on this continent, a new nation, conceived in Liberty, and dedicated to the proposition that all men are created equal.

Now we are engaged in a great civil war, testing whether that nation, or any nation so conceived and so dedicated, can long endure. We are met on a great battle-field of that war. We have come to dedicate a portion of that field, as a final resting place for those who here gave their lives that that nation might live. It is altogether fitting and proper that we should do this.

But, in a larger sense, we can not dedicate—we can not consecrate—we can not hallow—this ground. The brave men, living and dead, who struggled here, have consecrated it, far above our poor power to add or detract. The world will little note, nor long remember what we say here, but it can never forget what they did here. It is for us the living, rather, to be dedicated here to the unfinished work which they who fought here have thus far so nobly advanced. It is rather for us to be here dedicated to the great task remaining before us—that from these honored dead we take increased devotion to that cause for which they gave the last full measure of devotion—that we here highly resolve that these dead shall not have died in vain—that this nation, under God, shall have a new birth of freedom—and that government of the people, by the people, for the people, shall not perish from the earth.

APPENDIX B

HISTORICAL FACTS AND DATA

U.S. Presidents and Vice Presidents

	PRESIDENT	VICE PRESIDENT	POLITICAL PARTY	TERM
1	George Washington	John Adams	No party designation	1789–1797
2	John Adams	Thomas Jefferson	Federalist	1797–1801
3	Thomas Jefferson	Aaron Burr George Clinton	Democratic-Republican	1801–1809
4	James Madison	George Clinton Elbridge Gerry	Democratic-Republican	1809–1817
5	James Monroe	Daniel D. Tompkins	Democratic-Republican	1817–1825
6	John Quincy Adams	John C. Calhoun	Democratic-Republican	1825–1829
7	Andrew Jackson	John C. Calhoun Martin Van Buren	Democratic	1829–1837
8	Martin Van Buren	Richard M. Johnson	Democratic	1837–1841
9	William Henry Harrison	John Tyler	Whig	1841
10	John Tyler	None	Whig	1841–1845
11	James Knox Polk	George M. Dallas	Democratic	1845–1849
12	Zachary Taylor	Millard Fillmore	Whig	1849–1850
13	Millard Fillmore	None	Whig	1850–1853
14	Franklin Pierce	William R. King	Democratic	1853–1857
15	James Buchanan	John C. Breckinridge	Democratic	1857–1861
16	Abraham Lincoln	Hannibal Hamlin Andrew Johnson	Union	1861–1865
17	Andrew Johnson	None	Union	1865–1869
18	Ulysses Simpson Grant	Schuyler Colfax Henry Wilson	Republican	1869–1877
19	Rutherford Birchard Hayes	William A. Wheeler	Republican	1877–1881
20	James Abram Garfield	Chester Alan Arthur	Republican	1881

	PRESIDENT	VICE PRESIDENT	POLITICAL PARTY	TERM
21	Chester Alan Arthur	None	Republican	1881–1885
22	Stephen Grover Cleveland	Thomas Hendricks	Democratic	1885–1889
23	Benjamin Harrison	Levi P. Morton	Republican	1889–1893
24	Chester Alan Arthur	Adlai E. Stevenson	Democratic	1893–1897
25	William McKinley	Garret A. Hobart Theodore Roosevelt	Republican	1897–1901
26	Theodore Roosevelt	Charles W. Fairbanks	Republican	1901–1909
27	William Howard Taft	James S. Sherman	Republican	1909–1913
28	Woodrow Wilson	Thomas R. Marshall	Democratic	1913–1921
29	Warren Gamaliel Harding	Calvin Coolidge	Republican	1921–1923
30	Calvin Coolidge	Charles G. Dawes	Republican	1923–1929
31	Herbert Clark Hoover	Charles Curtis	Republican	1929–1933
32	Franklin Delano Roosevelt	John Nance Garner Henry A. Wallace Harry S. Truman	Democratic	1933–1945
33	Harry S. Truman	Alben W. Barkley	Democratic	1945–1953
34	Dwight David Eisenhower	Richard M. Nixon	Republican	1953–1961
35	John Fitzgerald Kennedy	Lyndon B. Johnson	Democratic	1961–1963
36	Lyndon Baines Johnson	Hubert H. Humphrey	Democratic	1963–1969
37	Richard Milhous Nixon	Spiro T. Agnew Gerald R. Ford	Republican	1969–1974
38	Gerald Rudolph Ford	Nelson Rockefeller	Republican	1974–1977
39	James Earl Carter, Jr.	Walter Mondale	Democratic	1977–1981
40	Ronald Wilson Reagan	George H.W. Bush	Republican	1981–1989
41	George Herbert Walker Bush	J. Danforth Quayle	Republican	1989–1993
42	William Jefferson Clinton	Albert Gore, Jr.	Democratic	1993–2001
43	George Walker Bush	Richard Cheney	Republican	2001–2009
44	Barack Hussein Obama	Joseph Biden	Democratic	2009 2017
45	Donald J. Trump	Michael R. Pence	Republican	2017–

Admission of States into the Union

	STATE	DATE OF ADMISSION		STATE	DATE OF ADMISSION
1	Delaware	December 7, 1787	28	Texas	December 29, 1845
2	Pennsylvania	December 12, 1787	29	Iowa	December 28, 1846
3	New Jersey	December 18, 1787	30	Wisconsin	May 29, 1848
4	Georgia	January 2, 1788	31	California	September 9, 1850
5	Connecticut	January 9, 1788	32	Minnesota	May 11, 1858
6	Massachusetts	February 6, 1788	33	Oregon	February 14, 1859
7	Maryland	April 28, 1788			
8	South Carolina	May 23, 1788	34	Kansas	January 29, 1861
9	New Hampshire	June 21, 1788	35	West Virginia	June 20, 1863
10	Virginia	June 25, 1788	36	Nevada	October 31, 1864
11	New York	July 26, 1788	37	Nebraska	March 1, 1867
12	North Carolina	November 21, 1789	38	Colorado	August 1, 1876
13	Rhode Island	May 29, 1790	39	North Dakota	November 2, 1889
14	Vermont	March 4, 1791	40	South Dakota	November 2, 1889
15	Kentucky	June 1, 1792			
16	Tennessee	June 1, 1796	41	Montana	November 11, 1889
17	Ohio	March 1, 1803	42	Washington	November 11, 1889
18	Louisiana	April 30, 1812			
19	Indiana	December 11, 1816	43	Idaho	July 3, 1890
20	Mississippi	December 10, 1817	44	Wyoming	July 10, 1890
			45	Utah	January 4, 1896
21	Illinois	December 3, 1818	46	Oklahoma	November 16, 1907
22	Alabama	December 14, 1819	47	New Mexico	January 6, 1912
			48	Arizona	February 14, 1912
23	Maine	March 15, 1820			
24	Missouri	August 10, 1821	49	Alaska	January 3, 1959
25	Arkansas	June 15, 1836	50	Hawaii	August 21, 1959
27	Florida	March 3, 1845			

GLOSSARY

Abolition A pre–Civil War social movement devoted to the emancipation of slaves and their inclusion in American society as citizens with equal rights. (11)

Abu Ghraib Iraqi correctional facility near Baghdad that was widely publicized in 2004 for abuses of Iraqi prisoners of war by the U.S. military and CIA operatives. (31)

Acadians A group of nearly 7,000 French-speaking colonists in Nova Scotia forced to leave Canada by invading British troops during the French and Indian War (also known as the Seven Years' War). Many emigrated to French Louisiana, where they became known as "Cajuns." (5)

Act of Supremacy (1534) English parliamentary act that abolished papal authority over England, making King Henry VIII the head of the Church of England. (1)

Acts of Union (1707) Parliamentary acts that created the United Kingdom by merging the kingdoms and parliaments of England and Scotland. (4)

Adamson Act (1916) Congressional act that granted railroad workers an eight-hour workday and overtime pay. (21)

Affordable Care Act (2010) Health insurance reform legislation designed to cover millions of uninsured Americans. (31)

Agricultural Adjustment Administration (AAA, 1933) U.S. government agency created by the Agricultural Adjustment Act to provide credit, loans, and other subsidies to farmers. (23)

Alamo A mission outpost in San Antonio, Texas, that was defended down to the last man by American and Mexican separatists in the Texas War for Independence of 1836. (11)

Albany Congress (1754) A conference of representatives of seven British North American colonies, held in Albany, New York, to consider strategies for diplomacy with the Indians and dissuade Iroquois from becoming French allies. (5)

***Alianza Federal de Mercedes* (1962)** Organization founded by New Mexico civil rights activist Reies Lopez Tijerina to demand that the government respect land rights granted by the 1848 Treaty of Guadalupe Hidalgo. (27)

Alien and Sedition Acts (1798) Four congressional acts that severely restricted immigration into the United States, gave the president power to deport anyone thought to be dangerous, and restricted speech critical of the federal government. (8)

Alliance for Progress (1961) A multibillion-dollar aid program for Latin America aimed at establishing economic cooperation between the United States and South America. (27)

al-Qaeda A global militant Islamist organization founded by Osama bin Laden around 1989. (31)

American Anti-Slavery Society (AASS) An abolitionist society organized by William Lloyd Garrison in 1833 with immediate abolition as its core objective. (12)

American Colonization Society (ACS) A society of antislavery whites, founded in 1817, which advocated the return of freed slaves to Africa. (9)

American Expeditionary Force (AEF) American armed forces, commanded by General John J. Pershing, sent to Europe during World War I to fight alongside British and French allied units. (21)

American Federation of Labor (AFL) A collective of craft unions, founded in 1886 and headed by Samuel Gompers, that comprised skilled workers and excluded most immigrants and women. (17, 26)

American Indian Movement (AIM) An activist organization devoted formed in Minneapolis in 1968 that was to protecting Indian rights and to upholding established treaties, particularly over land, with federal, state, and local governments. (27)

American Philosophical Society (APS) Scholarly organization founded in Philadelphia in 1743 to promote the dissemination of knowledge in the science and humanities. (5)

American Protective Association (APA) An anti-Catholic nativist organization founded in 1887. The APA advocated strict immigration laws and spread conspiracy theories about Roman Catholics. (18)

American Protective League (APL) Organization of private American citizens who worked with law enforcement agencies during World War I to identify and counteract the activities of German sympathizers and other antiwar advocates. (21)

American Railway Union (ARU) One of the first industrial unions in the United States, founded in 1893 by Eugene V. Debs. The ARU aimed to increase the power of railroad workers by organizing one industry-wide union. (17)

American Recovery and Reinvestment Act (2009) Congressional act allocating $787 billion in economic stimulus funds. The package combined government spending on infrastructure, unemployment benefits, and food stamps with tax cuts. (31)

American System Senator Henry Clay's proposal of 1824 intended to spur domestic economic development as well as tariffs and currency regulation. The System also propounded recognition of Latin American independence movements. (10)

American Temperance Society (ATS) Organization established in 1826 to advocate abstinence from distilled beverages. The movement did not end the consumption of alcohol in America, but it did help convince millions of people to rethink their relationship with drinking. (12)

Americans with Disabilities Act (ADA) Congressional act of 1990 that provided equal rights for people with disabilities. (30)

Anglo-Saxonism As the United States and Great Britain emerged as the world's leading industrial powers in the late 19th century, many began to believe that the English-speaking nations shared common racial characteristics that accounted for their preeminent world standing. Anglo-Saxons, they believed, possessed superior intelligence, were industrious, and had a special talent for spreading freedom and their advanced culture around the world. (19)

Anti-Comintern Pact Agreement signed in 1936 between Nazi Germany and imperial Japan (later joined by Italy) to oppose the Soviet Union and other perceived threats. (24)

Anti-Imperial League American organization formed in 1898 by those who opposed American colonization of the Philippines. (19)

Articles of Capitulation (1664) English policies regarding Dutch residents of New Amsterdam, which granted them religious liberty, freedom from military conscription, property rights, the ability to leave New York within 18 months, and free trade and freedom of movement within the English Empire. (3)

Articles of Confederation The first written framework for a government of the United States, drafted by Congress and in effect from 1781 to 1788. (7)

Astrolabe A navigation instrument used to pinpoint and predict the location of the stars, Sun, Moon, and planets for determining longitude and latitude while sailing at sea. (1)

Atlantic Charter (1941) A joint policy statement issued by the United States and Great Britain that defined the goals and objectives of their alliance at the beginning of World War II. The charter called for disarming defeated aggressors and establishing a permanent system of general security. (24)

Atlantic slave trade The enslavement, trade, and transport of African people to Europe and the Americas, begun by the Portuguese in the early 1440s. (1)

Atlantic world Name given to the area of exploration bordering the Atlantic Ocean and including the five continents of North America, South America, Antarctica, Africa, and Europe. (1)

Baby boom The temporary but noteworthy increase in birth rate in the United States, Great Britain, and Europe in the years immediately following World War II. (26)

Bacon's Rebellion (1676) An uprising of poor white men, free blacks, and some enslaved people led by the English aristocrat Nathaniel Bacon that temporarily drove colonial governor William Berkeley from Jamestown. Participants opposed the government's moderate policy toward local Indians and the concentration of landholding in elite hands. (3)

Balance of powers A model of governance in which authority is distributed to several different branches of government, providing checks and balances against one another. Also known as the separation of powers. (7)

Bank of the United States (BUS) The first federal bank, founded in 1791, that operated until 1811 and provided for the issuance of a national currency and centralization of federal tax collection. (9)

Barbados slave code (1661) English America's first slave code; it prescribed different treatment and contrasting levels of legal protection for enslaved Africans and white servants. (3)

Battle of Bunker Hill The first significant battle of the American Revolution. It actually took place on Breed's Hill, where colonial forces claimed victory and demonstrated that they could resist larger British forces. (6)

Battle of the Bulge The last major offensive by the German army in World War II, fought in Belgium in 1944. (24)

Bay of Pigs invasion Failed operation approved by President Kennedy to invade Cuba with a small CIA-led military force of political Cuban exiles with hopes of liberating the country and removing Fidel Castro from power. (27)

Beaver Wars Seventy-year conflict among Iroquois and their neighbors driven by Iroquois demands for hunting territory and captives. The peak came between 1648 and 1657 with the dispersal of the Huron (also called Wyndat or Wyandotte) Confederacy. (3)

Berlin Airlift A military operation carried out between June 24, 1948, and May 12, 1949, in which U.S. and UK "Candy Bombers" supplied the entire city of West Berlin with 5,000 pounds of food and supplies per day during a critical early Cold War standoff with the Soviets. (25)

Bill of Rights The first 10 amendments to the United States Constitution, ratified by the states in 1791. (8)

Black codes (1865–1866) Laws enacted by southern state legislatures after the Civil War that granted limited rights to former slaves, including the right to marry, own land, and participate in the judicial process, but that also singled out black people under the law and imposed severe restraints on their occupations, mobility, and rights as parents. (15)

Black Legend Politically motivated, factually exploitative conviction that the Spaniards indiscriminately slaughtered Indians, tyrannized them, and imposed Catholicism on them during their 16th-century conquests in the Americas. (2)

Black Panther Party A radical civil rights organization founded in Oakland in 1966 by Huey Newton and Bobby Seale. Members of the Black Panthers advocated black self-determination and armed self-defense against police brutality. (27)

Black Power Ideology that advocated a combination of racial pride and forceful, even violent resistance to anti-black violence during the 1960s and early 1970s. Led by the Student Non-Violent Coordinating Committee (SNCC) and the Black Panther Party, Black Power split the civil rights coalition of the 1960s. It also produced and intensified the white backlash against political, social, and economic gains by African Americans. (27)

Black Tuesday (October 29, 1929) The day that marked the start of the Great Depression, precipitated by a calamitous crash of the stock market. (22)

Blockade Military policy of preventing an enemy from engaging in naval commerce by blocking ports and intercepting ships. (14)

Board of Trade (1696) An advisory council created by King William III of England that was charged with overseeing colonial matters. The act testified to the colonies' growing significance to England's economy. (4)

Boston Massacre (1770) An altercation between occupying British troops and a Boston mob resulting in the death of five colonists. This was a significant incident in the buildup of tensions between Britain and the colonies in the years leading up to the American Revolution. (6)

Boston Tea Party (1773) An act of defiance on the part of Boston colonists to protest the British Tea Act of 1773, a new tax on imported tea, during which 30 to 60 men disguised as Mohawk Indians stormed British tea ships and dumped 90,000 pounds of tea into Boston Harbor. (6)

Bracero Program (1942) Agreement between the governments of Mexico and the United States that granted annual entry to hundreds of thousands of seasonal agricultural workers. Control of the border was generally loosened, and hundreds of thousands of other Mexicans were drawn north by growing opportunities in the greatly expanding U.S. economy. (24)

Bretton Woods agreements (1944) Multinational agreements that established a system for international trade and monetary values to promote economic recovery following World War II. (24)

Brown v. Board of Education of Topeka, Kansas (1954) U.S. Supreme Court decision that outlawed racial segregation in public schools. (26)

Bush Doctrine Foreign policy principles of President George W. Bush, the centerpiece of which was a policy wherein the United States had the right to engage in preemptive war to secure itself against terrorist groups and countries that harbored them. (31)

Bush v. Gore (2000) U.S. Supreme Court decision that determined the winner of the 2000 presidential race between Al Gore and George W. Bush. (30)

Cahokia Once the largest Indian city north of Mexico, located just east of modern-day St. Louis. Peaking around 1100 CE, Cahokia was the capital of a Mississippian chiefdom that extended influence over much of the mid-continent. (1)

Calvinism A Protestant religion that followed the teachings of theologian John Calvin and was practiced by European and American Puritans. (1)

carpetbaggers A person from the northern states who went to the South after the Civil War to profit from Reconstruction. (15)

Central Powers Name given during World War I to the alliance of Germany, Austria-Hungary, and Ottoman Turkey. (21)

Charter of Freedoms and Exemptions (1640) A Dutch West India Company policy that granted 200 acres to whoever brought five adults to New Netherland and promised prospective colonists religious freedom and local self-governance; these offers attracted English Puritans from Massachusetts to eastern Long Island. (2)

Chicano Originally viewed negatively, the term became widely used during the Chicano Movement by Mexican Americans to express pride in a shared cultural, ethnic and community identity.(27)

Chinese Exclusion Act (1882) Congressional act that barred the immigration of Chinese laborers. This law all but ended Chinese immigration and remained in effect until 1943. (16, 18)

Church of England (Anglican Church) English Christian church established by King Henry VIII after his break from papal authority in 1534. (1)

Civil Rights Act of 1964 Congressional act that prohibited discrimination in employment or the use of public places on the basis of race, sex, religion, or national origin. (27)

Civilization Policy First deployed in 1795, Civilization Policy sought to remake Indians in the image of Anglo-Americans, using missions, education, and gifts of livestock and farming equipment to change Native languages, religions, economies, and gender roles. (9)

Code Noir (1685) Slave code mandated by imperial France governing the rights and treatment of African slaves in its colonial territories from the French West Indies to Louisiana. (4)

Coercive Acts/Intolerable Acts (1774) Four British parliamentary decrees enacted in response to unrest and protests in Boston. The acts reorganized the Massachusetts government and placed more authority in the hands of royal appointees. They also imposed royal control over local courts and authorized troops to be forcibly housed in private homes and buildings. (6)

Coinage Act (1873) Congressional act that made gold the nation's monetary standard and halted the making of silver dollars, later referred to by Populists, who wished to expand the nation's money supply with silver, as "the crime of 1873." (18)

Cold War Term given to the political, economic, and military tensions that existed between the United States and its allies and the Soviet Union between 1945 and the dissolution of the Soviet Union in 1991. (25)

Columbian exchange The historic movement of people, plants, animals, culture, and pathogens between the Americas and the rest of the world that began during the time of Columbus. (1)

Committee on Public Information Government agency created during World War I to promote war aims and distribute propaganda. (21)

Committee to Reelect the President (CREEP) Group organized by the Nixon White House to both promote the president's reelection and collect illegal funds to engage in "dirty tricks." (28)

Common law Law based on decisions previously made by judges and courts, as opposed to statutory, or written, laws and statutes; the common law system was rooted in English legal practices. (2)

Commons Lands open to all residents. (2)

Compromise of 1850 Congressional measures created to resolve a series of regional tensions in the United States. The measures admitted California as a free state, organized the remainder of the New Mexico territory, banned the slave trade in the District of Columbia, empowered the U.S. Treasury to assume Texas's debts from its independence struggle with Mexico, and gave the South a much stronger federal Fugitive Slave Law. (13)

Comstock Act Passed by Congress in 1874, this law banned "obscene, lewd, or lascivious material" from the U.S. mail, including anatomy books and information regarding birth control and sex education. (18)

Congress of Industrial Organizations (CIO) Umbrella group of labor unions, formed in 1935, to represent semiskilled workers in major industrial sectors. Unions within the Congress accepted black and other minority workers. (23, 26)

Containment Name given to the foundation of U.S. foreign policy during the Cold War. George F. Kennan argued that Soviet communism was "impervious to the logic of reason," inherently expansionist, and controllable only through "long-term, patient but firm and vigilant containment." (25)

Contraband Legal term denoting war materials that can be seized from an enemy during wartime. During the Civil War, Northern leaders used the term to refer to enslaved people who fled to Union lines seeking freedom. (14)

Contract with America A document conceived by Republican congressman Newt Gingrich in 1993 that promised to make Congress more accountable, balance the federal budget, reverse the tax increases passed in 1993, and reduce the capital gains tax. (30)

Contras Anti-Communist guerrillas funded by the CIA to attack the Sandinista regime in Nicaragua in the 1980s. (29)

Conversion test An exercise developed by Massachusetts Bay Puritans to test prospective church members for membership in their congregation; prospects had to testify to their relationship with God and offer proof that God had saved them. (2)

Copper borderlands Region in southwest United States and northern Mexico where trade and labor networks transcended national borders. (16)

Copperheads Civil War–era nickname for the faction of the Democratic Party that opposed the war. (14)

Counterculture In the 1960s and early 1970s, the name given to the subculture of college-age young Americans who developed distinctively liberal beliefs and practices regarding sexuality, race, gender, politics, and culture; these values stood in contrast to those of the dominant culture of their parents. (27)

Court packing scheme Abortive effort by President Roosevelt in 1937 to increase the number of justices on the Supreme Court. (23)

Covenant As practiced by New England Puritans, an agreement with God that required them to translate their faith into actions that obeyed God's will as revealed in the Bible. (2)

Coverture A principle of British and American law wherein a married woman lost her legal identity as an individual and in which her economic resources would be controlled by her husband. This law prevented married women from owning property. (7, 11)

Crop lien A credit system widely used by southern farmers from the 1860s to the 1920s. This was a way for farmers to get credit before the planting season by borrowing against the value of anticipated harvests. (15)

Cuban missile crisis A tense standoff between the United States and Soviet Union in October 1962 when the United States discovered that the Soviets had begun installing nuclear missiles in Cuba. The incident was the most dramatic nuclear standoff of the Cold War. (27)

Culture war Period of intense secular or religious conflict resulting in political conflict, inability to reach compromise, and polarization of opinion. (25)

Dawes Act (1887) Congressional act that divided two-thirds of Indian tribal lands to be sold off or confiscated. Many Indians who had lived on reservations became essentially landless. (16)

Dawes Plan (1924) A foreign policy that provided a loan from U.S. banks to Germany to stabilize its economy and reduce its reparations burden. (22)

D-Day Code name for the massive Allied invasion of France on June 6, 1944. (24)

Declaration of Independence (1776) American Revolutionary document that declared that the United States was free and independent of the British Empire and sought international recognition for the United States. (6)

Defense Advanced Research Projects Agency (DARPA) U.S. defense agency that created the Internet, originally founded in 1958 to counter Soviet advances in space science. (30)

Defense of Marriage Act (DOMA, 1996) Congressional act that decreed that no state would be compelled to recognize a same-sex marriage conducted in another state, nor would the federal government recognize the existence of such a marriage even if it were performed legally in a state. (31)

Desert Land Act (1877) Congressional act, applicable in 11 western states, that allowed for homesteading on 640-acre parcels of arid land at 25 cents per acre and provided title within three years for a dollar an acre for settled, irrigated land. (16)

Détente Term given to the U.S. relaxation of tension with the Soviets during the 1970s. (28)

Dollar diplomacy Effort by Taft administration to encourage U.S. bankers and businesses to expand into Latin America. (19)

Dominion of New England (1685–1689) A union of English colonies imposed by the English monarchy; it comprised eight contiguous colonies, from New England to New Jersey, under one governor, Edmond

Andros, who dissolved representative assemblies, jailed dissidents, and imposed taxes on lands already owned outright. (3)

Dred Scott decision (1857) U.S. Supreme Court ruling that slaves were not citizens of the United States and were therefore unable to sue in a federal court of law. As a consequence, the federal government had no authority to outlaw slavery in the territories, leaving that choice up to the states. (13)

Dust Bowl Area in the West and Midwest plagued by drought and dust storms in the 1930s. (23)

Dutch West India Company (DWIC) Dutch trading company whose merchants were granted trade monopolies in parts of the New World, and whose activities included the acquisition of territories in the Hudson River valley in New York. (2)

Earthrise First photo of Earth from space captured by *Apollo 8* astronauts on Christmas Eve 1968. (27)

East India Company (EIC) Monopoly trading company of English merchants chartered in 1600 to trade in Asia and India. The company was influential in global British imperial policy into the 19th century. (4)

Edict of Nantes (1598) Proclamation by King Henry IV of France granting rights to Huguenots (French Calvinist Protestants). (2)

Eighteenth Amendment (1919) Constitutional amendment that barred the manufacture and sale of alcohol in the United States. It was repealed in 1933. (20)

Emancipation Proclamation (1863) Proclamation by Abraham Lincoln that freed the slaves living in Confederate states. (14)

Emergency Banking Relief Act (1933) Congressional act that followed the market crash of 1929; it reopened banks and restored bank solvency under Treasury Department supervision. The act also removed U.S. currency from the gold standard. (23)

Emergency Economic Stabilization Act (2008) Congressional act that authorized the U.S. Treasury to budget up to $700 billion to bail out banks and other financial institutions affected by a crisis in subprime mortgage values. (31)

Emergency Immigration Act of 1921 Congressional act that created specific immigration limitations based on national origin. The act banned all immigration from Asia but allowed free immigration from the Western Hemisphere, as the Southwest depended on Mexican and Central American labor. (22)

Encomienda System whereby the Spanish government granted land, villages, and indigenous people to military leaders who conquered land in the Americas. (1)

Equal Rights Amendment (ERA) Proposed amendment to the U.S. Constitution that banned the denial or abridgment of rights on the basis of gender. (29)

Espionage Act (1917) Congressional act passed on the eve of America's entrance into World War I that expanded the definition of treason and defined a variety of acts deemed to comprise espionage. This law was enacted to fight sabotage, spying, and interference with the war effort. (20)

Ethnic cleansing The effort by government or private groups to remove or kill groups of people from land they have traditionally occupied. (30)

Eugenics A popular movement in the first decades of the twentieth century, eugenics aimed to "improve" the human race by genetic engineering, including encouraging the selective breeding of those deemed superior. (22)

Executive Order 9981 (1948) Order by President Truman that established equality in the armed services on the basis of race, color, religion, and national origin. (25)

Exodusters Freed slaves who fled the South in search of better opportunities and treatment in the West after the Civil War. (16)

Factory system The factory system radically changed the ways that workers related to business owners and to one another. It refers to the centralization of manufacturing under the ownership of one person or a corporation. Instead of manufacturing goods in homes or in small family-owned workshops, the factory system brought together many unrelated workers under one roof. (10)

Fair Deal Domestic programs for social reform proposed by the Truman administration. The 21-point program called for an increase in the minimum wage, comprehensive housing legislation for returning veterans, full employment and expanded unemployment benefits, permanent federal farm subsidies, expanded public works projects, and expanded environmental conservation programs. (25)

Fair Labor Standards Act Federal law passed in 1938 that guaranteed workers a minimum wage, overtime pay, and other benefits. (23)

Farmers' Alliance An umbrella movement of agricultural organizations, founded in Texas in 1876, that encouraged men and women to cooperate in running their households and their farms. The Alliance provided the foundation for what would become the Populist Party. (17, 18)

Federalism A system of government that divides powers between a centralized national administration and state governments. (7)

Federalist Papers A series of anonymously authored essays, published in newspapers, supporting ratification of the U.S. Constitution of 1787 by James Madison, Alexander Hamilton, and John Jay. (7)

Feitoria Portuguese name for a fortified trading post, early examples of which were first established in Africa in the 15th century during the early years of the Atlantic slave trade. (1)

Fifteenth Amendment (1870) Constitutional amendment that prohibited the denial of voting rights on the basis of race. (15)

Filibuster A person engaging in unauthorized warfare against a foreign country. (11)

Fireside chats Weekly radio addresses by President Franklin Roosevelt in which he explained his proposals, policies, and actions to the American people. (23)

First Anglo-Dutch War (1652–1654) A naval conflict between England and the United Provinces of the Netherlands that stemmed from trade disputes. England prevailed and secured a trade monopoly with English colonies. Still, English settlers in North America and elsewhere often preferred Dutch goods and continued to trade with the Dutch in defiance of the English monopoly. (3)

First Continental Congress Representatives of the colonies (except Georgia) who met in Philadelphia for the first time in 1774 to articulate their positions and form policies against grievous British laws and regulations. The group charged committees in each colony with vigorously enforcing boycotts; endorsed a declaration of rights and grievances on October 14, 1774; and then adjourned, hoping that the king would change the course of imperial policy. (6)

First Hundred Days President Franklin Roosevelt's first days in office, during which he prevailed on Congress to pass 14 major pieces of legislation including bills to raise agricultural prices, put the unemployed to work, regulate the stock market, reform banking practices, and assist homeowners and farmers in paying mortgages. (23)

Flapper The youthful new woman of the 1920s who, rebelling against her mother's generation, celebrated her freedom by wearing short skirts, bobbing her hair, and smoking and drinking openly. (22)

Four Freedoms Global goals set out by President Franklin D. Roosevelt in January 1941 pledging U.S. support for freedom of speech, freedom of religion, freedom from hunger, and freedom from fear. (24)

Fourteen Points Plan for peace and postwar order proclaimed by President Woodrow Wilson in 1918. (21)

Fourteenth Amendment (1868) Constitutional amendment that guaranteed national citizenship and equality to former slaves and, detailed changes related to the former Confederate states but offered no specific protection of freed people's voting rights. (15)

Fox Wars (1712–1735) A series of wars over slavery and trade in the Great Lakes region that pitted the French and their Indian allies against the Fox (or Meskwaki), Sauk, Mascouten, and Kickapoo nations. (4)

Franciscans A Roman Catholic religious order active in establishing Spanish missions in southwestern North America in the 18th and 19th centuries. (1)

Freedmen's Bureau Shortened name for the Bureau of Refugees, Freedmen, and Abandoned Land, established by the U.S. Army in early 1865 to adjudicate labor disputes in the summer and fall of 1865. (15)

French and Indian War (1756–1763) Also known as the Seven Years' War, a conflict between Britain and France and their respective Indian allies in colonial America. This was largely a conflict between empires for territorial and economic control of the colonies and related trade routes. (5)

Fugitive Slave Act (1850) Congressional act that nationalized the process of slave capture and return by requiring federal judges to appoint "commissioners" to hear cases of accused fugitives and by requiring the active complicity of state officers. (13)

Fundamentalists Christians who interpreted the Bible literally and rejected the notion that traditional faith should enter a dialogue with science and popular culture. (22).

Fur trade The trading of furs, primarily through the St. Lawrence River region, that served as the primary gateway for European goods into North America into the 1600s. (2)

Gag rule Rule adopted by Congress in 1836 to block the discussion of slavery at the national as well as the state level. The rule was repealed in 1844. (11)

Gang system One of two general types of division of labor of plantation slaves, the other being the task system. The gang system involved the work of coordinated groups, supervised by a driver, to maintain an even level of productivity during the workday. (5)

General Allotment Act (1887) Congressional act that divided Indian reservation land into smaller parcels of property. (16)

Gentlemen's agreement (1907) Agreement reached by President Theodore Roosevelt and the Japanese government that stated that the United States would no longer exclude Japanese immigrants if the Japanese promised to voluntarily limit the number of its immigrants to the United States, primarily adult male laborers. (19)

Gilded Age Coined by Mark Twain and Charles Dudley Warner in 1873 to describe how the United States seemed to be gilded, covered with the gold generated for millionaire industrialists. But the gold covering often proved to be a thin veneer, masking a world of greed, exploitation, and poverty. (17)

Ghost Dance Originating among the Paiute Indians around 1870, The Ghost Dance religion was a response to the subjugation of Native Americans by the U.S. government. It was an attempt to revitalize traditional culture in the face of eroding tribal sovereignty. (16)

Glass–Steagall Banking Act (1933) Congressional act that established strict guidelines for banking operations and expanded the power of the Federal Reserve System. The act also founded the Federal Deposit Insurance Corporation. Some regulations associated with the original act were repealed in 1999, leading to mismanagement and scandals in the banking and finance industries and the recession beginning around 2009. (23)

Globalization A term that was popularized in the 1990s to refer to the knitting together of the world's economies through new information technology and the end of the artificial political barrier of the Cold War. (30)

Glorious Revolution (1688) Uprising of the English Parliament against King James II that transformed the English system of government from an absolute monarchy to a constitutional monarchy and the rule of Parliament. (3)

Good Neighbor Policy Policy adopted by the Franklin D. Roosevelt administration after 1933 that pledged the United States would not interfere militarily in Latin America. (24)

Gospel of Wealth A philosophy popularized by Andrew Carnegie that called upon the wealthy few in the Gilded Age to benefit society through philanthropy. (17)

Grand Settlement of 1701 A pair of treaties between Iroquois and the French that stabilized relations between the two in the Great Lakes and northeast parts of North America. (4)

Grandfather clause Allowance created by southern state constitutions in the 1890s permitting any person who had voted before 1867 or had a father or grandfather who had voted to be exempt from the literacy test or other restrictions. The aim of this law was to increase the number of eligible white male voters while eliminating black voters. (20)

Great Depression International economic depression and the United States' worst economic downturn to date. Beginning at the end of 1929 and lasting for 10 years, the catastrophe spread to every corner of the country, wrecking lives and leaving people homeless, hungry, and desperate for work. (22)

Great Migration The large-scale movement of African Americans during and after World War I from the South to the North, where jobs were more plentiful. (21)

Great Railroad Strike of 1877 The first and largest general strike in U.S. history, sparked by wage and hour cuts of railroad workers in the midst of an economic depression. The strike was marked by violence as well as nonviolent sympathetic strikes by workers across the nation. President Rutherford B. Hayes used federal troops to help break the strike after roughly a month. (17)

Great Recession The international economic collapse of 2008 in which credit markets around the world froze and banks stopped lending to one another. Businesses dependent on lending began to downsize and fail. The meltdown affected financial institutions and governments throughout the world. (31)

Great Society President Lyndon Johnson's name for a series of social and economic reforms, begun in 1965, to end racial discrimination, expand educational opportunities, end hunger and poverty, and make health care available for all. (27)

Gulf of Tonkin Resolution Congressional authorization requested by President Lyndon Johnson in 1964 that gave him the power to escalate military action in Vietnam without additional congressional approval. (28)

Guerrillas Irregular combatants who acted locally and outside the laws of war, sometimes attacking soldiers and other times civilians. (14)

Hamdan v. Rumsfeld Supreme Court ruling in 2006 restricting the Bush administration's use of military commissions to try accused terrorist detainees at Guantanamo Bay. (31)

Hard war Union's policy during the American Civil War that targeted the ability of Confederates to fight by destroying infrastructure, transportation networks, and food supplies for the army. (14)

Harlem Renaissance An African American cultural and arts movement of the 1920s centered in the Harlem neighborhood of New York City. (22)

Harpers Ferry (1859) Failed raid led by abolitionist John Brown on the U.S. arsenal in Harpers Ferry, Virginia. Brown's capture and execution led to greater regional tensions leading up to the Civil War. (13)

Haymarket Affair A violent conflict between protesting workers and police in Chicago's Haymarket Square in 1886 that created antiunion hysteria and brought about the demise of the Knights of Labor. (17)

Helsinki Accords A set of principles that accepted the post-1945 division of Europe into East–West spheres. The accords recognized the right of all Europeans to seek peaceful change, and the Soviets agreed in a general way to respect human rights in their sphere. (29)

Holden v. Hardy (1898) U.S. Supreme Court decision that upheld Utah's law limiting the working hours of miners to eight hours per day. (20)

Homestead Act (1862) Congressional act that allowed families to claim 160 acres of land if they improved it over five years of residence. The act opened the western United States to settlement. (15, 16)

Homestead Lockout An 1892 incident in which Carnegie partner Henry Clay Frick locked out workers at the Carnegie steel works in Homestead, Pennsylvania, when they refused a new contract, leading to violence and the destruction of their powerful union. (17)

Horizontal integration An innovation of the modern corporation aimed at eliminating destructive aspects of competition by purchasing competitors or establishing agreements among them to share profits. (17)

House of Burgesses The first representative government assembly and ruling body established in the English settlements in America; founded by the Virginia Company in 1619, this assembly replaced martial law with English common law, setting in motion the development of the county court system. (2)

House Committee on Un-American Activities (HCUA) Congressional committee formed in 1938 to search for Communists and conspiracies within the United States in cluding penetration into the labor movement and federal agencies. Although discredited during the 1950s for its investigations of entertainment and media figures, the committee was not abandoned until 1975. (25)

Hudson's Bay Company English trading company, formed in England in 1670, that competed with the French in North America. (3)

Huguenots Name given to the French followers of Calvinism, a Protestant religion founded by theologian John Calvin. (1)

Immigration Restriction League An anti-immigration organization founded in Boston in 1894 that promoted legislation to restrict the immigration of southern and eastern Europeans. (18)

Indentured servitude An arrangement offered by various English enterprises to attract English people to the colonies, exchanging free passage by ship to America for up to seven years of labor. (2)

Indian Removal Act (1830) Federal law that nullified 50 years' worth of treaties between the United States and many tribes. The law resulted in the relocation of more than 45,000 Indians living east of the Mississippi to points farther west, opening up lands for white settlers. The law committed the federal government to creating an Indian territory west of the Mississippi. (11)

Indian Reorganization Act (1934) Congressional act that slowed the division of reservation land into small plots, encouraged tribal self-government, and established Indian-run corporations to control communal land and resources. (23)

Industrial Workers of the World (IWW) Radical labor union, also known as "Wobblies," founded in 1905. The union embraced all workers in "one big union," called for the overthrow of capitalism, and advocated industrial sabotage. It was especially active in the West up to World War I. (20)

Industrious revolution Preindustrialization period associated with 18th-century British North America during which there was a diversification of labor, development of a market-oriented society, and a labor shift from services to marketable goods. (4)

Initiative, referendum, and recall First proposed by Populists in the 1890s, the initiative and referendum, adopted originally in Oregon, made it possible for voters to place legislation directly before the electorate for a vote in general elections; the referendum allowed voters to repeal state legislation with which they disagreed; the recall gave voters the power to remove any public official who did not, in their view, act for the public good. (20)

Instant cities Urban areas such as San Francisco and Denver that grew rapidly from frontier outposts to major regional cities during the settlement of the West. (16)

Insular Cases (1901–1954) A series of U.S. Supreme Court cases that were applied to all of the new territories added to the United States in which it was ruled that American constitutional rights and liberties did not extend to all lands under U.S. control. (19)

Interstate and Defense Highways Act (1956) The largest public works program in American history, approved by President Dwight Eisenhower, that facilitated the growth of suburban America and the businesses and industries that sustained it. (26)

Iran-Contra scandal Scandalous effort by Reagan administration that involved ransoming hostages in Lebanon, selling arms to Iran, and illegally funding the Contras in Nicaragua. (29)

Jacobite Rebellion (1715) One of a series of attempts to restore James II to the throne of England. England's last Catholic monarch, James II, was deposed by Parliament during the Glorious Revolution of 1688. Thereafter, rebels in England, Ireland, and Scotland launched serial uprisings but were not successful. Many of these rebels—some voluntarily, others by force—resettled in North America. (4)

Jamestown The first permanent English settlement in America, founded in 1607 and located in what is today coastal Virginia. (2)

Jay's Treaty (1794) Treaty with Britain granting the United States trade rights on the Mississippi and in the British East Indies and removing remaining British forts on American territory. (8)

Jesuits (Society of Jesus) A Catholic male religious order, founded in Spain in 1534, that was active in winning converts overseas. (1)

Jim Crow laws State and local laws that originated in the South in the mid-1880s and legally separated people according to race. These laws spread to many public facilities and established a policy of racial segregation that favored white citizens. (20)

Johnson–O'Malley Act of 1934 Congressional act that provided federal aid to improve health care and education for Indian tribes. (23)

Joint-stock companies An early form of shareholding company that was used by the British to finance development of the colonies. (2)

Jubilee In the context of the Civil War, Jubilees were celebrations by black Southerners marking their deliverance from bondage. (15)

Kansas–Nebraska Act (1854) Congressional act that repealed the Missouri Compromise. The bill's new policy of "popular sovereignty," intended to allow settlers in a territory to decide the status of slavery, initiated a strenuous debate about the future of slavery in the western territories. (13)

Katsina Ancestral god spirits of Pueblo peoples. (3)

Keating–Owen Child Labor Act (1916) Law that banned interstate commerce in goods produced by child labor. Struck down by U.S. Supreme Court as unconstitutional in 1918. (20)

Kellogg–Briand Pact (1928) Also known as the "Pact of Paris," an agreement signed by 62 nations that agreed not to use war as an instrument of national policy. The pact was initiated by the United States and France. (22)

Kent State The campus where the Ohio National Guard in the spring of 1970 killed and wounded antiwar demonstrators. (28)

Keynesian economics The idea that the government can boost the economy and counter recessions by increasing deficit spending on public projects. (23)

King Philip's War (1675–1676) Conflict between Indian inhabitants of the New England region, the English colonists, and their Indian allies. Named after the Indian leader Metacom, known to the English as King Philip. (3)

King William's War (1689–1697) The first of several colonial wars between English and French colonists in North America and their Indian allies. (3)

Kiva An underground chamber used by Pueblo Indians for religious ceremonies. (2)

Knights of Labor The first national labor union, founded in Baltimore in 1869. The Knights aimed to organize all laboring people into one large, national union, offering membership regardless of race, gender, or national origin. The organization rejected capitalism and wage labor and demanded a fair share of wealth for workers who produced it. (15, 17)

Know-Nothing Party Antiforeign, anti-Catholic political organization established in 1854 and consisting of a network of secret fraternal associations. The party was largely a nativist reaction against large-scale European immigration. The organization's name stemmed from its secrecy; if asked about the organization, members would essentially deny any knowledge of it, saying that they "knew nothing." (13)

Ku Klux Klan (KKK) An organization associated with the bitterest and most violent opponents of Reconstruction and black freedom. Formed in Pulaski, Tennessee, in late 1865, Klan members devoted themselves to denying African Americans any legitimate role in the public sphere, stressing the superiority of white, Protestant, Anglo-Saxon citizens. The Klan was revived in the 1920s as an anti-immigrant, anti-Catholic, and anti-Jewish organization. (15, 22, 26)

Lady of Cofitachequi A Native American woman who ruled a vast chiefdom in the Carolinas during the 1500s. She was a paramount chief, meaning that she had gained control over other chiefdoms through warfare and diplomacy. (1)

Laissez-faire economics An economic doctrine that insisted that government should not interfere with businesses or the market. The term is from the French, meaning "leave it alone." (17)

Lawrence v. Texas (2003) U.S. Supreme Court decision that overturned most state anti-sodomy laws used to criminalize homosexual behavior. (31)

League of Nations Organization created after World War I to promote global peace and cooperation (21)

Lend-Lease Act (1941) Massive military and economic aid program to assist nations fighting Germany and Japan in World War II. (24)

Levittown First massive planned subdivision, created in the New York suburbs on Long Island, constructed after World War II. (26)

Limited Test Ban Treaty (1963) An agreement between the United States and the Soviet Union that ended aboveground atomic weapon testing but permitted continued testing underground. (27)

Linen Act of 1705 British parliamentary act that encouraged the export of Irish linen to North America. In turn, the act increased the demand in northern Ireland for colonial flaxseed, the source of linen. (4)

Literacy Act (1917) Clause of the U.S. Immigration Act of 1917 that barred the entry of any persons unable to read in their own language on the grounds that this lack demonstrated their ignorance. (21)

Lochner v. New York (1905) U.S. Supreme Court decision that struck down a New York law limiting the hours that male bakers could work. In the Court's opinion, the state had no right to regulate their hours. (20)

Lowell Mill Girls Female workers associated with the textile mills in Lowell, Massachusetts. The mills had a large labor force of young women, who ranged between the ages of 15 and 35 and worked in one of the first large-scale steam-powered industries in the United States. (11)

Ludlow Massacre (1914) An attack by local deputies and state militia on striking United Mine Workers members in Ludlow, Colorado. At the request of mine owners, the militia attacked a camp of striking miners who had been evicted from company-owned housing, killing 14 people, including 11 children. Soon labeled the Ludlow Massacre, the killings sparked violent retaliation by the miners. (20)

Lusitania British passenger liner torpedoed by a German submarine in 1915 while sailing between New York and England. The attack killed 1,200 of the 2,000 passengers and crew, including 128 Americans. (21)

Lynching The murder of African American individuals by a mob, often by hanging, shooting, or burning, that was especially prevalent in the 1890s South. (20)

Malintzín A native Nahua woman from the Gulf Coast of Mexico who figured importantly in the Spanish conquest of Mexico by acting as the translator and advisor to Hernán Cortés, leader of a Spanish expedition. (1)

***Maine* (battleship)** A U.S. battleship that exploded on February 15, 1898, killing 260 American sailors. Americans blamed Spain for the explosion, drawing the United States closer to war with Spain, which was declared two months later. (19)

Manhattan Project Secret U.S. scientific and military program during World War II dedicated to the development of an atomic bomb. The project was led by J. Robert Oppenheimer and employed 150,000 workers at numerous secret sites, including Los Alamos, New Mexico. (24)

Mann Act (1910) Congressional act that outlawed the transport of women across state lines for "immoral purposes." (20)

Manumission The freeing of slaves by their owners. (4)

***Marbury v. Madison* (1803)** U.S. Supreme Court decision that firmly established the principle of "judicial review," the right of the U.S. Supreme Court to rule on the constitutionality of legislation and executive actions. (8)

March on Washington (1963) Civil rights demonstration in which Martin Luther King, Jr., delivered the "I Have a Dream" speech. (27)

Maroons Groups of people who escaped slavery and formed independent communities, usually in inaccessible places. Such communities existed in the Caribbean as well as North and South America. (4, 5)

Marshall Plan (European Recovery Plan, 1948 A massive foreign aid program approved following World War II that called for aid packages to help western Europe, including West Germany, and Japan rapidly rebuild their devastated economies, restore industries and trade, and rejoin the free world. (25)

Massachusetts Bay Company A business enterprise founded by English Puritans and merchants in 1629 that founded the Massachusetts Bay Colony, resulting in a swell of English emigration to the colonies. (2)

Matrilineal A society in which social identity is based on kinship and descendency from the mother. (2)

Maysville Road Bill (1830) A bill authorizing federal investment in a private turnpike company that was vetoed by President Andrew Jackson because he opposed using central power for infrastructure improvement. (10)

McCarran International Security Act (1950) Congressional act requiring the registration of American Communist Party members; the act reinforced perceptions of immigrants as a source of radicalism during the Cold War and set the tone for a contentious debate about immigration in the coming decade. (25)

McCarthyism Term named for Wisconsin senator who engaged in "witch hunts" against real and mostly imagined Communists inside the United States. (26)

McKinley Tariff (1890) Congressional act that ended the practice of allowing Hawaiian sugar to enter the United States duty free, ending Hawaii's favored status and threatening its sugar industry. (19)

McNary–Haugen Acts (1927–1928) Congressional acts that required the government to support crop prices by buying basic farm commodities. (22)

Meat Inspection Act (1906) Congressional act that required federal inspectors from the U.S. Department of Agriculture to inspect livestock in slaughterhouses and to guarantee sanitary standards. (20)

Medicaid A health care plan that originated with President Lyndon Johnson's Great Society programs in which the federal government provided states matching grants to pay for medical costs of poor people of all ages. (27)

Medicare A health plan that originated with President Lyndon Johnson's Great Society programs that provided universal hospital insurance for Americans over 65. (27)

Medicare Modernization Act (2003) Congressional act that subsidized the cost of some, but not all, medication taken by seniors. (31)

Mercantilism An economic philosophy of English and French governments founded on the belief that control of foreign trade—including the acquisition of raw materials from their colonies—was key to securing the kingdom that ruled them. (3)

Methodists A Protestant evangelical sect, rooted in the 18th-century Anglican revival movement, that accepted slaves and freed blacks and opposed government intervention in religion. (5)

Millennialism A belief system organized around an imminent apocalypse, which makes salvation all the more urgent. (12)

Minutemen In Revolutionary War times, local militias in Massachusetts and Connecticut that went on alert in response to pending British military action. (6)

***Miranda v. Arizona* (1966)** Supreme Court decision that required police to tell suspects of their right to remain silent and to have access to legal counsel. (27)

Mississippian societies Name given to Indian societies of the Mississippi valley formed around 700 CE and peaking between 1100 and 1300. (1)

Missouri Compromise Legislation passed by Congress in 1820, admitting Missouri as a slave state and Maine as a free state, in an effort to preserve the balance of power between slave and free states. With the exception of Missouri, the law prohibited slavery in the Louisiana Territory north of the 36° 30' latitude line. The Missouri Compromise was repealed by the Kansas-Nebraska Act of 1854. (9)

Model Cities Federal urban aid program created by President Lyndon Johnson to encourage physical and economic revitalization of the nation's poorest urban areas. (27)

Modern corporation A form of corporation pioneered by railroads before the Civil War and then developed in the last quarter of the 19th century distinguished by its organization, massive scale, and forms of management. (17)

Modernists Religious leaders, influenced by the Social Gospel movement of the late 19th century, as well as Darwin's theory of evolution and archaeological discoveries, who believed Christianity should respond positively to new knowledge and social conditions. (22)

Monetarists Proponents of a conservative economic movement that favored a change to tax and spending policies. Led by Milton Friedman, these economists insisted that prosperity and freedom required reduced government spending along with more stringent control of the money supply. (29)

Monroe Doctrine (1823) Policy introduced by President James Monroe, who declared that the United States shared common interest with other states in the Western Hemisphere and that the political system in Europe was "essentially different" from that of the democratic republics in North and South America. (9)

Montgomery Improvement Association (MIA) An organization of black clergy and community leaders formed in 1955 and led by Martin Luther King, Jr., who refined a philosophy of nonviolent protest for boycotters. (26)

Moral Majority Political lobbying movement organized by religious conservatives in 1979. (29)

Moravians (United Brethren) A Protestant religious sect, revived in Germany in 1727 and brought to Georgia in 1735, that sought to create closed, economically autonomous, sex-segregated communities in which Christian liturgical rituals and piety infused daily life. (5)

Mormons A Protestant religious sect founded by Joseph Smith, who preached a conservative theology of patriarchal authority. (12)

Muckraking An early form of investigative journalism. Believing that exposing facts could rouse the public to demand change, "muck-raking" helped bring about major reforms in the late 19th and early 20th centuries. (17)

Mudsill A sociological theory first proposed in 1858 by South Carolina senator James Henry Hammond, who stated that a division of upper and lower classes was the natural order of society, a view that was interpreted by many as a thinly veiled excuse for exploiting slavery. (11)

Mujahideen Islamic-inspired Afghans and foreign guerrillas who fought the occupying Soviets in Afghanistan during the 1980s. They counted among their ranks Saudi fundamentalist Osama bin Laden. (29)

Mulatto A mixed-race person in the United States. (11)

Muller v. Oregon (1908) U.S. Supreme Court decision that upheld an Oregon law limiting the workday of female laundry workers to 10 hours per day. (20)

My Lai Massacre (1968) Massacre by American troops of 504 unarmed Vietnamese villagers during the Vietnam War. (28)

Natchez War (1729–1731) Rebellion staged by Natchez warriors and African slaves against French colonists in Mississippi, suppressed by the French and their Choctaw allies. (4)

National American Woman Suffrage Association (NAWSA) Organization founded in 1890, headed by Carrie Chapman Catt, that sought a constitutional amendment to give women the right to vote. (20)

National Association for the Advancement of Colored People (NAACP) Civil rights organization founded in 1909 that was innovative in establishing legal action as a powerful basis of the fight for African American rights. (20)

National Association of Colored Women (NACW) A group organized in 1896, and made up largely of black middle-class women, that addressed the needs of black neighborhoods by establishing hospitals, day nurseries, and kindergartens and also attacked segregation and lynching. The organization's motto was "Lifting as We Climb." (20)

National Organization for Women (NOW) An organization founded in 1966 that advocated an end to laws that discriminated against women, opportunity to work at any job, and equal pay for equal work. (27)

National Origins Act of 1924 Congressional act that established strict immigration ceilings and quotas favoring northern European immigrants; it served as the basis of immigration policy until 1965. (22)

National Parks Act of 1916 Congressional act that created the National Park Service and aimed, in part, to preserve national park lands and "leave them unimpaired for the enjoyment of future generations." (20)

National Recovery Administration (NRA) Early and unsuccessful New Deal effort to promote industrial recovery from the Great Depression. The NRA wrote "production codes" for each industry that encouraged cooperation among competing businesses to set stable prices and wages. (23)

National Security Act of 1947 Congressional act that consolidated the U.S. military command. Under the new system, a representative from each military branch would advise a newly created secretary of defense and the president through the Joint Chiefs of Staff Office. (25)

National Security League A private patriotic organization founded in 1916 to promote military preparedness and to push for the "Americanization" of recent immigrants. (21)

National Woman's Party (NWP) A party founded in 1916 by Alice Paul and like-minded suffragists that conducted numerous protests to win women the right to vote, including marches and "silent sentinels" picketing outside of the White House. (20)

Native American Graves Protection and Repatriation Act (1990) Congressional act that encourages ethical research by requiring federally funded institutions to share information about human remains as well as sacred and culturally significant items with descendant communities, which may also arrange for repatriation. (1)

Nativism A rejection of foreigners and foreign influence. This term can be applied to followers of the Delaware prophet Neolin, who in the mid-1700s sought to purge Indian country of British settlers as well as ideas and goods from Britain. Later, it became a name given to a strong anti-immigration, anti-Catholic activist movement that flourished in America from the 1830s to the 1850s and the 1890s to the 1920s. The term "nativists" was given to those who strongly opposed the influx of immigrants into American society. (5, 18)

Nativists Political organizations that formed in the mid 1840s, particularly in New York and other northern cities. Nativists shared general goals: to restrict office holding to native-born Americans, to retain the Bible in schools, and to extend the naturalization process from 5 to 21 years. Although these groups had little electoral success, they established the basis for the network of secret fraternal associations known collectively as the Know Nothings that emerged in the 1850s. (13)

Navigation Acts One of a series of English regulations and taxes on colonial trade dating from 1650 to 1775. (3, 4, 6)

Neoconservatives A small but influential coalition of Democrats and Republicans who rejected many of the tenets of liberalism and détente and called for more limited government at home and a more muscular military stance abroad. (29)

Neutrality Acts Series of congressional laws passed between 1935 and 1939 restricting the power of the president and of private citizens and businesses to aid foreign nations at war. (24)

New Deal Collective name given to President Franklin Roosevelt's programs to fight the Great Depression, first articulated during his 1932 presidential campaign. He pledged to use federal power to ensure a more equitable distribution of income and rebuild the economy from the bottom up. (23)

New England Company The first Protestant missionary organization, founded by Puritans in 1649, that focused on Native peoples of the Northeast. Led by a board of prominent New England colonists, the company appointed missionaries and teachers in an attempt to convert and Anglicize Indians. (3)

New Freedom Name given to Woodrow Wilson's 1912 presidential platform, which promised an attack on "bigness" in government and business, and his advocacy for small business and fair competition enforced by only minimal government interference. (20)

New Frontier Name given to President John F. Kennedy's collection of programs to expand economic and social opportunities in the United States. (27)

New Left Counterculture protest movement of the 1960s whose young activists intentionally distanced themselves from the ideological infighting, Marxist leanings, and labor organizing of the Old Left of the 1930s and 1940s. (27)

New Look President Dwight Eisenhower's military reorganization of 1954 that established the central philosophy of the doctrine of "massive retaliation" linked to expanded espionage as more economically feasible than containment alone. (26)

New Nationalism Name given to President Theodore Roosevelt's platform in 1912 that advocated expansive government activism and regulation for the public interest. (20)

New Woman A term first applied to women in the 1890s who defied traditional middle- and upper-class Victorian feminine ideals by emphasizing education, work outside the home, woman suffrage, and vigorous physical activity. (22)

New world order An idea proclaimed by President George H. W. Bush in 1989 in which the United States, the world's preeminent superpower, would lead multinational coalitions to enforce its standards of international behavior. (30)

Nineteenth Amendment (1920) Constitutional amendment granting women the right to vote. (20)

No Child Left Behind (NCLB) Act Program proposed by President George W. Bush in 2001 to improve educational outcomes for poor and minority children. It renewed federal funding for several existing school programs and provided some additional money for reading and math instruction. In return, all states had to implement "standards based educational reform," a term that in practice meant standardized testing of students in reading and math. (31)

Nongovernmental organizations (NGOs) Independent groups that supported foreign relations and political programs and fostered the growth of global capitalism during the Cold War. (25)

Non-Intercourse Act (1809) Congressional act that reopened trade with countries other than Britain and France. (8)

North American Free Trade Agreement (NAFTA) Trade agreement approved by Democrats and Republicans in 1993 during the administration of President Bill Clinton. This agreement lifted barriers to trade between the United States, Mexico, and Canada; nearly all conventional economists believed that it would lift living standards in these countries. (30)

North Atlantic Treaty Organization (NATO) The organization created in 1949 by Western leaders as an alliance for mutual defense against the Soviet Union. (25)

Obergefell v. Hodges Supreme Court decision in 2015 holding that the Fourteenth Amendment guaranteed same-sex couples the right to marry. (31)

Occupy Wall Street Protest movement active in 2011 that criticized predatory banks and corporations. (31)

Ohio Company of Virginia A group of land speculators composed mainly of well-connected British planters to whom the state of Virginia had granted over 300,000 acres by early 1745. They opened the door to British trade in the South, competing with the already established French traders. (5)

Olive Branch Petition (1775) Petition sent by the Continental Congress to King George III of England seeking his intervention in the conflict with Parliament over taxes. (6)

Open Door Policy Principles drafted in 1899 by Secretary of State John Hay requesting that European powers put an end to the further partitioning of China and open up areas of China claimed by each power to allow them to compete fairly for Chinese trade. These policies asked for unhindered access to markets where they could compete successfully against economic rivals. (19)

Organization of Petroleum Exporting Countries (OPEC) Cartel organized by major oil-producing nations to boost prices for crude oil that became effective in the 1970s. (28)

PAC—see Political action committee. (29)

Palmer Raids Series of actions by federal agents in 1919 and 1920 to arrest and deport radical immigrants. (21)

Pan-Africanism An international movement that aimed to unite peoples of African descent around the world to seek equal rights and cast off white supremacy and colonialism. (22)

Panama Canal A canal opened in 1914 linking the Atlantic and Pacific oceans that enhanced access to U.S. colonies in the Pacific as well as trade with Asia but poisoned U.S. relations with Latin American countries because of the questionable way that the United States gained rights to build the canal. (19)

Parliament Legislative body of the British government. (3)

Patient Protection and Affordable Care Act Also known as "Obamacare," law passed in 2010 that mandated broad health insurance coverage for both employees at larger firms and those without health coverage. (31)

Peace Policy An agreement organized by General Ely Samuel Parker in which the Indian commissioners and leaders of various Christian denominations provided Indians with food and clothing in exchange for promises to abandon cultural traditions and to assimilate into American society. (16)

Pendleton Civil Service Act (1883) Congressional act that established the modern civil service and initiated an examination for a classified list of federal jobs, including most government departments, custom house jobs, and post office positions. (18)

Pentagon Papers Popular name given to a collection of classified government documents that were illegally made public in 1971. The documents outlined decision making by the U.S. Defense Department during the period from World War II to the Vietnam War. (28)

People's (Populist) Party A third party made up largely of rural people frustrated with the unresponsiveness of the Republican and Democratic parties to their pressing needs. The People's Party ran candidates for president in 1892 and 1896 on a platform demanding major reforms, including government ownership of railroads, a graduated income tax, and the free coinage of silver. (18)

Pequot War (1636–1638) Conflict between the Pequot Indians of the Connecticut River valley and British colonists and their Indian allies. (2)

Pietism A Protestant religious movement that linked North America, Britain, the Netherlands, and central Europe. Pietists promoted the personal piety of believers and the evangelization of all, includng American Indians and enslaved Africans. (4)

Pinckney's Treaty (1795) A treaty with Spain that fully opened Mississippi River trade to the United States, provided tax-free markets in New Orleans, settled Florida border issues, and guaranteed Spanish help against Southwest Indians who moved to block U.S. settlers from expanding the West. (8)

Plantation Act of 1740 British parliamentary act that allowed non-Catholic aliens who resided for at least seven years in British North America, received communion in a Protestant church, swore allegiance to George II, and paid two shillings to become citizens. (5)

Platt Amendment (1901) Amendment to the new Cuban constitution that gave the United States broad authority to intervene to preserve Cuban independence and required Cuba to sell or lease land for U.S. naval stations and coaling bases. (19)

Plessy v. Ferguson (1896) U.S. Supreme Court decision that upheld the legality of Jim Crow laws by declaring that segregation based on race was constitutional as long as "separate" facilities were "equal." It soon became clear, however, that facilities for black Americans, such as schools, railroad cars, and waiting rooms, were rarely, if ever, equal to those provided for whites. (20)

Political action committee (PAC) A private group dedicated to the election of a given political candidate or to the influencing of a policy decision in government. (29)

Political machines Political organizations established in most major U.S. cities by the late 19th century that offered a variety of services to constituents, especially immigrants, in exchange for votes and party loyalty. (18)

Polygamy A marriage custom of having more than one partner at the same time, such as a man with more than one wife. (4)

Pope's Day Also known as Guy Fawkes Day, an observance named after the rebel who attempted to blow up both houses of Parliament at Westminster in 1605. Fawkes and his coconspirators opposed Protestantism and wished to restore Catholic rule in England. Caught in the act, Fawkes was executed. Thereafter, British subjects, including North American colonists, celebrated the triumph of Protestantism with raucous festivities, including the burning of the pope in effigy. (4)

Popular sovereignty A policy established in the mid-19th century that permitted settlers in newly established western territories to decide on the policy of slavery for themselves. (7, 13)

Prigg v. Pennsylvania (1842) U.S. Supreme Court decision that established federal protection to southerners seeking to reclaim fugitive slaves who had escaped to the North. (13)

Privateer A government-contracted but privately owned warship used to attack foreign ships and disrupt trade. (1)

Proclamation of 1763 An order issued by King George III of England that prohibited settlements beyond a line west of the Appalachians running from the Hudson River south to Florida. (6)

Pro-slavery defense Based on the idea of racial supremacy espoused by prominent scientists of the day, such as Louis Agassiz and Josiah Nott, pro-slavery defenders joined this modern argument to older endorsements of slavery, reaching back to the ancient Greeks and Romans and to the Bible. (11)

Protestantism A Christian reform movement that arose in Europe during the 1500s and denied the authority of the Catholic Church. (1)

Pueblo War for Independence (1680–1696) A revolt by a diverse coalition of Pueblo Indians that succeeded in forcing Spanish colonists out of New Mexico for over a decade. (3)

Pullman Strike A strike led by Eugene V. Debs and the American Railway Union in 1894 in response to massive wage cuts at the Pullman Palace Car Company. The strike and boycott of trains pulling Pullman cars froze rail service in the Midwest and slowed it elsewhere until federal troops helped crush it. (17)

Pure Food and Drug Act (1906) Congressional act that outlawed adulterated or mislabeled food and drugs and gave the federal government the right to seize illegal products and to fine and jail those who manufactured and sold them. (20)

Puritans Europeans who followed the Christian teachings of theologian John Calvin, defied the Catholic Church, and sought to place the governance of church affairs in the hands of local officials, ministers, and elders. (1)

Queen Anne's War (1702–1713) A war fought between the British and French for control of North American colonies, simultaneous with a war in Europe over the Spanish monarchy. (4)

Quitrent A land tax or rent imposed on colonists by their European governing body. (3)

Reaganomics Informal term for policy of cutting taxes on the well-to-do and reducing government regulation of business to promote growth. (29)

Reconquista Expansion of western European Christian nations during the 1400s into Muslim settlements on the Iberian Peninsula. (1)

Reconstruction Finance Corporation (RFC, 1932) Federal program of President Herbert Hoover to loan money to struggling banks, railroads, manufacturers, and mortgage companies during the Great Depression. (23)

Redemptioners In the 18th century, indentured servants who paid for their passage across the Atlantic by selling their services when they landed. (5)

Requerimiento (1513) A Spanish royal decree read by conquistadors to Native groups in the Americas that encouraged them to either submit to Christianity and Spanish rule or face warfare and slavery. (1)

Rerum novarum A papal encyclical from Pope Leo XIII, issued in 1891, condemning the exploitation of laborers and supporting state intervention to promote social justice. (20)

Revivalists Leaders and advocates of various evangelical Protestant campaigns of the First Great Awakening in the 18th century. Revivalists sought to rekindle widespread religious enthusiasm in the American colonies. (5)

Roe v. Wade (1973) U.S. Supreme Court decision upholding a woman's constitutional right to terminate a pregnancy. (29)

Roosevelt Corollary A corollary to the Monroe Doctrine articulated by President Theodore Roosevelt in 1904 that declared that the United States had the right to intervene in the affairs of Latin American nations to ensure order. (19)

Rough Riders Colonel Theodore Roosevelt and his First Volunteer Cavalry Regiment, who became national heroes for their daring exploits during the Spanish-American War. (19)

Royal African Company A British mercantile firm that received the royal monopoly on trade in Africa. Active in the gold trade, by 1663 the company possessed exclusive rights to buy and transport slaves across the Atlantic for sale in British colonies. (3)

Royal Orders for New Discoveries (1573) Decree by King Philip II of Spain that missionaries should play the principal role in exploring, pacifying, and colonizing new territories; it also mandated that baptized Indians should live on missions, learn to speak Spanish, keep livestock, cultivate European crops, and use European tools to master European crafts. (2)

Royal Society An elite organization founded in London that connected colonists and residents of the capital in the pursuit of scientific evidence and investigation. (3)

Russo-Japanese War A 1904 war between Russia and Japan sparked by rival imperial claims in Asia. President Theodore Roosevelt brokered a peace treaty between the two countries in 1905, earning him the Nobel Peace Prize. (19)

St. Augustine First Spanish settlement in North America, founded in 1565. (1)

Salutary neglect Name given to the practice of colonists to defy or ignore British laws that they found onerous, often with the complicity of those charged with enforcing them. (4)

Science lag Term used to describe the perceived disparity between U.S. and Soviet education programs during the Cold War. (26)

Scopes Trial Highly publicized 1925 trial of Tennessee high school science teacher John Scopes, who was found guilty of teaching the theory of evolution in violation of state law. (22)

Secession The act of withdrawing formally from an existing union with another political state. (14)

Second Anglo-Dutch War (1664-67) Fought between England and the United Provinces for control over the seas and trade routes. (3)

Second Bill of Rights List of "economic bill of rights," proposed by President Franklin D. Roosevelt in 1944, that guaranteed every citizen a job, a living wage, decent housing, adequate medical care, educational opportunity, and protection against unemployment in postwar America. (24)

Second Great Awakening Religious revivalist movement of the early 19th century that echoed the Great Awakening of the 1730s. The movement linked evangelical Christians on both sides of the Atlantic to exchange ideas and strategies that inspired a broad set of social, cultural, and intellectual changes. (9, 12)

Securities Act of 1933 Congressional act that required companies selling stock to the public to register with a federal agency and provide accurate information on what was being sold. (23)

Securities Exchange Act of 1934 Congressional act that created the Securities and Exchange Commission to regulate stock markets and activities by brokers. (23)

Sedition Act (1918) Amendments to the Espionage Act of 1917 that added a variety of offenses to the list of prohibited acts, including the use of "disloyal, profane, scurrilous, or abusive language about the form of government of the United States, or the Constitution of the United States." (20)

Separation of powers Political concept articulated by French Enlightenment philosopher the Baron de Montesquieu that each state should establish a balance between executive, legislative, and judicial powers. (7)

September 11 Shorthand for attacks on the World Trade Center and Pentagon that took place on September 11, 2001. (31)

Settler colonialism A distinctive colonizing strategy (different from trade- or mission-based colonialism) whereby collections of immigrants from foreign places used their numbers to gain control of territory and resources from indigenous peoples. (5)

Seventeenth Amendment (1913) Constitutional amendment that mandated the direct election of U.S. senators. (20)

Sharecroppers Farmers who rented land or farmed on shares, splitting the proceeds from the yearly crop with the landlord. (15)

Shays' Rebellion (1786–1787) An armed insurrection by indebted Massachusetts farmers, led by Daniel Shays, to prevent the state government from seizing their property. (7)

Shelly v. Kraemer (1948) U.S. Supreme Court case outlawing racial housing covenants. (26)

Sherman Antitrust Act (1890) Congressional act aimed at dismantling combinations and trusts that restrained trade. It was the first U.S. law to restrict business monopolies, but loopholes and court decisions rendered it largely ineffective. (17)

Sixteenth Amendment (1913) Constitutional amendment that authorized a federal income tax on both personal and corporate income. (20)

Smoot–Hawley Tariff of 1930 A tariff passed in 1930 at the onset of the Great Depression that made it especially difficult for international manufacturers to sell their products in the United States, resulting in retaliatory tariffs that worsened the international economy. (22)

Social Darwinism A theory, popularized by Herbert Spencer, that purported that Charles Darwin's theory of evolution could be applied to human society as well. This belief that society evolved and improved through competition in which the "fittest" survived justified noninterference by the government in the economy and workplace as well as the massive fortunes amassed by industrialists. (16, 17)

Social Gospel A broad, multidimensional, and international movement among Protestants in the late 19th and early 20th centuries that insisted that Christian principles needed to be applied to social problems. (18)

Social Security Act (1935) Congressional act that established a federally administered retirement system for workers at age 65, funded primarily by contributions—payroll taxes—from workers and employers, not general tax revenues. (23)

Society for the Propagation of the Gospel in Foreign Parts (SPG) Anglican reform organization founded in 1701 for sending missionaries to North America and the West Indies. (4)

Society of Friends ("Quakers") A Christian religious sect that broke from the Church of England and established itself in America during the 17th century. (3)

Soft power The use of marketing and selling of culture products in support of political and military policies. During the Cold War the selling of American culture and ideology through global marketing of everything from Levi's jeans and Coca-Cola to music and movies played a central role in Cold War foreign policy. (25)

Sons of Liberty Groups of colonial protestors, originating with the 1765 Stamp Act, who spread anti-British sentiment between colonies. (6)

Spanish Civil War Successful revolt by the Spanish army, with assistance from Germany and Italy, to overthrow the democratic government of Spain. (24)

Stagflation A slowly growing economy with high rates of unemployment and inflation. (28)

Stamp Act (1765) British parliamentary act that required that many forms of colonial printed materials and products be affixed with revenue stamps, or taxes, paid to the British. (6)

Stono Rebellion (1739) The largest uprising of enslaved Africans in mainland North America during the 18th century in which 80 or more slaves burned South Carolina plantations as they marched toward Spanish Florida. (5)

Subprime mortgages Home loans offered to buyers with poor credit histories. Fees made these profitable to lenders but often resulted in defaults and foreclosures. (31)

Sunbelt Band of warm-climate states of the southern and southwest United States that grew in political, cultural, and economic significance after massive post–World War II migrations. (27)

Tariff A tax on imported goods. (10, 18)

Task system One of two general types of division of labor of plantation slaves, the other being the gang system. The task system assigned individuals specific tasks. Rather than being part of a group that worked continuously to the day's end, the task system allowed individuals to end their workday when their task was done and thus granted them more autonomy. (5)

Tax Act of 1916 A revenue law that substantially raised taxes on high-income Americans and expanded the estate tax on inherited wealth. (21)

Tea Party Grassroots conservative movement active from 2010 that called for limited government. (31)

Teapot Dome Scandal Bribery scandal, uncovered in 1924, implicating Secretary of the Interior Albert Fall, a member of President Warren Harding's cabinet who took bribes in return for lucrative leases to drill for oil on government-owned land. (22)

Teller Amendment (1898) An amendment to Congress's declaration of war in April 1898 that stated that the United States would not colonize Cuba. (19)

Tennessee Valley Authority (TVA) Federal agency created in 1933 to construct a network of dams and hydroelectric projects to control floods, generate power, and promote growth in a chronically poor area of the South. (23)

Third World Term used to classify mostly nonwhite nations considered inferior to "First World" nations such as the United States and its Western allies. (25)

Thirteenth Amendment (1865) Constitutional amendment that outlawed slavery in the United States. (15)

Timucua Revolt (1656) A rebellion that exposed tensions in colonial Florida under Spanish rule. The Timucua, a diverse group of Florida Indians, accepted Catholic missions but rebelled against abusive labor and military policies enforced by Florida's Spanish governor, Diego de Rebolledo. Ultimately, the Timucua lost the conflict and were forced to resettle, but their actions forced Rebolledo to stand trial in Spain. (3)

Townshend Acts (1767) British parliamentary acts that taxed common goods in the colonies such as tea and other commodities.

The acts represented Britain's resolve to control and regulate the colonies. (6)

Trail of Tears Cherokee name for the United States' forced removal of their people from the Southeast to other lands. In early 1838, few Cherokee had prepared for the trip; contaminated water, inadequate food, and disease killed many of those restricted in stockades, and many more perished on the 800-mile journey west. (11)

Transcendentalism An American variant of European Romanticism which turned away from the ratio of the Enlightenment. Transcendentalists desired to know the world through emotion and intuition. (12)

Transportation Act (1718) British parliamentary act that mandated the exile of convicted criminals to North America, mostly those who had committed property crimes such as theft. (4)

Treaty of Guadalupe Hidalgo Treaty between the United States and Mexico that ended the Mexican-American War, signed on February 2nd, 1848. In exchange for $15 million, Mexico ceded to the United States Texas, and all of the land west of Texas stretching up to Oregon, including California. (13)

Treaty of Paris (1763) The treaty ending the French and Indian War. The terms of the treaty transformed eastern North America's political geography. France surrendered North America, swapping Canada for the return of Guadeloupe. France ceded Louisiana to Spain, and Spain traded Florida to the British to regain control of Havana. The British Empire claimed almost all of North America east of the Mississippi. (5)

Treaty of Tordesillas (1494) Treaty signed by Spain and Portugal that divided newly discovered lands between them, specifically those in Africa (to Portugal) and those associated with Columbus (to Spain). (1)

Treaty of Versailles (1919) The treaty that ended World War I and created independent Poland, Czechoslovakia, Yugoslavia, Hungary, Finland, and the Baltic states of Latvia, Lithuania, and Estonia. (20)

Triangle fire A raging fire that in March 1911 swept through the Triangle Shirtwaist Company in New York City, killing 146 workers, mostly young women, and leading to a series of workplace reforms. (20)

Truman Doctrine Policy announced by President Harry Truman in 1947 whereby the United States pledged to defend allies against Communist threats. (25)

Tuscarora War (1711–1715) A revolt by Tuscarora Indians against colonists in North America sparked by grievances over the Indian slave trade and land theft. (4)

U.S. Colored Troops (USCT) Black troops consisting of freed black men and former slaves who enlisted in the Union Army after the Emancipation Proclamation of January 1, 1863. (14)

United Colonies of New England (1643) Union of the Massachusetts Bay, Plymouth, Connecticut, and New Haven colonies to bolster their mutual defenses and negotiations with Indians. (2)

United Fruit Company A Boston-based company originally established for importing bananas to the United States from Latin America. It was known as "the Octopus" for its involvement and influence in the affairs of Honduras, Guatemala, and Costa Rica. (19)

United Mine Workers (UMW) An industry-wide union for mine workers founded in 1890. (17)

United Nations (UN) An organization open to all nations, established in 1945, for maintaining world peace. It is headquartered in New York. (24)

United Nations Security Council A 15-member council tasked under the UN Charter signed on October 24, 1945, with "maintenance of international peace and security." Member nations of the Security Council were obligated under the Charter to comply with Council decisions and resolutions. (25)

United States v. E. C. Knight Co. (1895) U.S. Supreme Court decision that weakened the Sherman Antitrust Act by declaring that the federal government could regulate only monopolies engaged in interstate commerce. (17)

Universal Negro Improvement Association (UNIA) Pan-African organization founded by black nationalist leader Marcus Garvey that emphasized black separatism and "Africa for Africans." (22)

USA PATRIOT Act (2001) Congressional act that expanded the Justice Department's powers to conduct surveillance on terrorist suspects at home abroad. (31)

Vertical integration A hallmark of the modern corporation that cut costs and guaranteed a flow of raw materials by controlling both the production and distribution processes. (17)

Vice-admiralty courts Colonial courts established by the English Board of Trade to enforce the Navigation Act of 1696. (4)

Virginia Company of London English joint-stock company established in 1606 by a royal charter that gave it exclusive rights to colonize from New England south to Virginia. (2)

Voting Rights Act (1965) Congressional act that outlawed literacy tests to vote and gave the Justice Department the power directly to register voters in districts where discrimination existed. (27)

War of Jenkins' Ear (1739–1742) A conflict sparked by an imperial rivalry between Britain and Spain that ensured British primacy in the Southeast and led to the legalization of African slavery in Georgia. (5)

Watergate scandal Composite term for illegal political acts by Nixon administration that culminated in the 1972 burglary of the Democratic Party headquarters and subsequent cover-up. (28)

Whig Party American political party formed in 1834 that supported government investments in infrastructure to stimulate business and, in some parts of the North, endorsed moderate antislavery politics. (6, 11)

Whiskey Rebellion (1794) Violent uprising in western Pennsylvania by farmers who refused to pay a federal tax on liquor. (8)

Williams v. Mississippi (1898) The U.S. Supreme Court decision that upheld Mississippi's disfranchisement amendment aimed at eliminating the black vote. (20)

Women's Christian Temperance Union (WCTU) The nation's largest female reform organization of the 19th century, formed in 1874, specifically dedicated to the banning of intoxicating beverages. The WCTU also sought the vote for women. (18)

Works Progress Administration (WPA) The largest and most ambitious New Deal relief and recovery program. Created in 1935, it employed millions of workers and built much of the nation's public infrastructure. (23)

XYZ Affair (1797–1998) Name given to a scandal caused by French diplomats demanding bribes from American diplomats, leading to a rise in tensions between the United States and France. (8)

Yamasee War (1715–1717) A multinational uprising of Native Americans in the Southeast that challenged colonialism in South Carolina and led to the decline of the Indian slave trade in that region. (4)

Yellow journalism Name given to sensationalist newspaper journalism of the late 19th century. This type of journalism provoked widespread public support for the Cuban rebels. (19)

Yeomen The term applied in the 18th and early 19th centuries to self-sufficient farmers who owned small plots of land, an idealized type. (9)

CREDITS

MAP, FIGURE, AND TABLE SOURCES

Maps by International Mapping.

America in the World (Population) Source(s): United States Population Division; United Nations, Department of Economic and Social Affairs, Population Division (2011). *World Population Prospects: The 2010 Revision*; Massimo Livi Bacci, *A Concise History of World Population* (Wiley-Blackwell, 2001).

CHAPTER 15

Map 15.1   Source(s): Aaron Sheehan-Dean, *Concise Historical Atlas of the U.S. Civil War* (New York: Oxford University Press, 2008).

Map 15.2   Source(s): Aaron Sheehan-Dean, *Concise Historical Atlas of the U.S. Civil War* (New York: Oxford University Press, 2008).

Map 15.3   Source(s): Aaron Sheehan-Dean, *Concise Historical Atlas of the U.S. Civil War* (New York: Oxford University Press, 2008).

Figure 15.1 Source(s): James L. Watkins, *King Cotton: A Historical and Statistical Review, 1790–1908* (New York: James L. Watkins and Sons, 1908).

CHAPTER 16

Map 16.1   Source(s): Steven Dutch, University of Wisconsin–Green Bay.

Map 16.2   Source(s): Samuel Truett, *Fugitive Landscapes: The Forgotten History of the U.S.-Mexico Borderlands* (New Haven: Yale University Press, 2006).

CHAPTER 17

Map 17.2   Source(s): Mona Domosh, *American Commodities in an Age of Empire* (Routledge, 2006), 33.

Figure 17.1 Source(s): O.P. Austin, "The United States: Her Industries," *National Geographic* (August 1903): 313.

CHAPTER 18

Map 18.1   Source(s): *London Times Atlas*.

Map 18.2   Source(s): *Historical Atlas of the United States*, Centennial Edition, ed. Wilbur E. Garrett (National Geographic, 1988).

Table 18.1 Sources(s): Eighth and Twelfth Censuses of the United States.

CHAPTER 20

Map 20.1   Sources(s): Thomas Paterson et al., *American Foreign Relations* (D.C. Health, 1995), vol. 2, 40, 55.

Map 20.2   Source(s): Patrick K. O'Brien, gen. ed., *The Oxford Atlas of World History* (New York: Oxford University Press, 1999, 2007), 270.

CHAPTER 21

Table 21.1   Source(s): Michael Howard, *The First World War: A Very Short Introduction* (New York, Oxford: Oxford University Press, 2007), 122.

CHAPTER 22

Map 22.1   Source(s): *Historical Atlas of the United States*, Centennial Edition, ed. Wilbur E. Garrett (National Geographic, 1988).

Map 22.2   Source(s): James A. Henretta, David Brody, and Lynn Dumenil, *America's History, Sixth Edition* (New York: Bedford/St. Martin's, 2007).

CHAPTER 23

Figure 23.1 Sources(s): United States Department of Commerce, *Historical Statistics of the United States* (1960), 70.

CHAPTER 24

Table 24.1   Source(s): Hans Dollinger, *The Decline and Fall of Nazi Germany and Imperial Japan: A Pictorial History of the Final Days of World War II* (New York: Bonanza Books, 1965, 1967), 422.

CHAPTER 29

Figure 29.2 Source(s): U.S. Bureau of the Census, Current Population Reports, "Money Income in the United States: 2000."

CHAPTER 30

Map 30.2   Source(s): Mark C. Carnes et al., *Mapping America's Past* (New York: Henry Holt and Co., 1996), 267; *Hammond Atlas of the Twentieth Century* (New York: Times Books, 1996), 166.

Figure 30.1 Source(s): $INDU (Dow Jones Industrial Average) INDX, May 1, 2009. Chart courtesy of StockCharts.com.

Figure 30.2 Source(s): Center for Immigration Studies, 1990 Immigration and Naturalization Service Yearbook.

CHAPTER 31

Figure 31.1 Sources(s): U.S. Census Bureau, American Community Survey, California Association of Realtors, Case-Shiller, National Bureau of Economic Research.

Figure 31.3 Source(s): U.S. Census Bureau, American Community Survey, 2009.

PHOTO CREDITS

INDEX

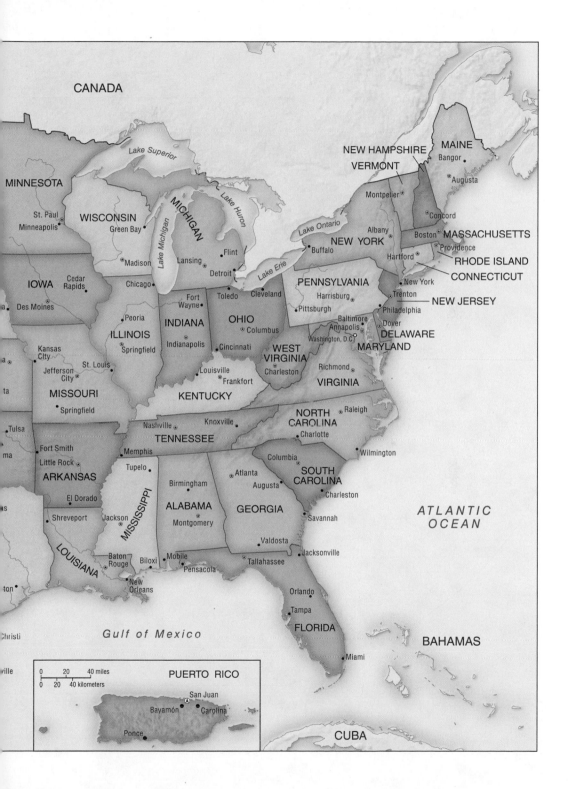

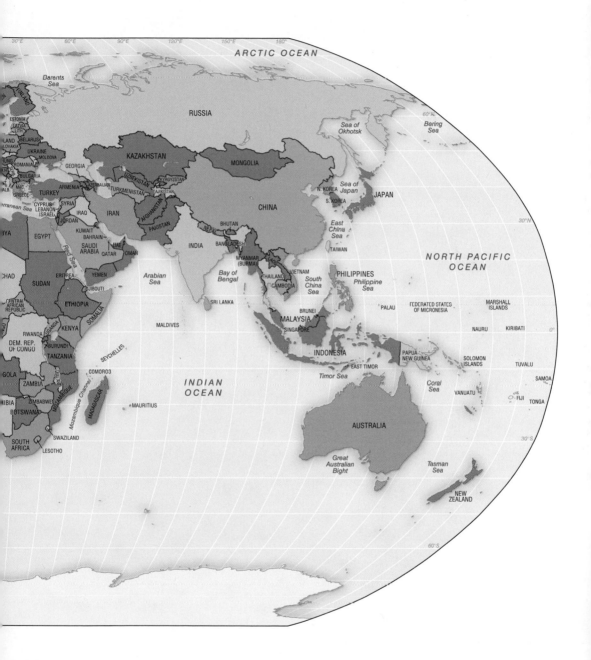